Value Creation for Owners and Directors

Massimo Massa • Kai Taraporevala
Ludo Van der Heyden

Value Creation for Owners and Directors

A Practical Guide on How to Lead your Business

palgrave
macmillan

Massimo Massa
INSEAD
Singapore, Singapore

Ludo Van der Heyden
Flendruz, Switzerland

Kai Taraporevala
Mumbai, India

ISBN 978-3-031-19725-3 ISBN 978-3-031-19726-0 (eBook)
https://doi.org/10.1007/978-3-031-19726-0

This Palgrave Macmillan imprint is published by the registered company Springer Nature Switzerland AG.
The registered company address is: Gewerbestrasse 11, 6330 Cham, Switzerland

To our Families and our Students

Preface

This book discusses key aspects of business, ownership, and governance, and their deep connections to value creation. And to its opposite, value destruction. The interplay between ownership and governance is rarely addressed in the academic and professional literatures, which remain centered on publicly listed firms. Though shareholders of such firms are often referred to as "owners," their number typically reduces their power to that of voting in public elections. Indeed, their interactions with boards of directors and corporate executives are often reduced to listening to presentations at the Annual General Meeting and then voting on the proposals submitted by the board. These are limited, often contentious, and can barely be called conversations.

The situation is completely different when owners are few and identifiable. This is the case for founder and entrepreneurial firms, and for firms owned by private equity, families, or a state. These are cases where ownership manifests its wider dimensions and where ownership truly matters. Yet this subject is rarely addressed from a value creation perspective, governance typically discussing the relationship between corporate boards and executives and, particularly after the 2007–08 financial crisis, between boards and regulatory or government authorities. Yet ownership is critical not just for short-term performance but also for the longer-term sustainability and success of enterprises.

The distinct nature of such identifiable ownership is the focus of this book. We aim to draw a sharp line between the governance of owner-led and owner-governed firms and that of so-called market-led firms, which as we will explain shortly tend to be or become "executive-led" firms. The importance and complexity of the ownership task is largely underestimated. This is the topic our book explores: ownership as an integral and foundational part of governance, with a particular angle on value creation.

The complexity of the ownership task is further amplified by the natural biases that permeate all personal and group interactions. Owners of companies and directors on their boards are particularly prone to these biases. The professional and academic literature rarely details these topics together, nor do they handle them with sufficient clarity. They often indulge in "best practice governance" or in the legal and regulatory aspects of governance. This book aims at starting to fill this gap. Our treatment of these issues characterizes the competencies owners and directors must possess for governance to be effectively exercised in the firms they own and govern, and for value creation to occur in a sustainable way.

The efficient market hypothesis that has prevailed for decades has too often equated value creation with stock price performance. It has left relatively little space for the role of ownership beyond the stock market valuation, engulfing governance in the study of stock market dynamics. Real ownership is typically absent from these debates, as there is no need for it, the market taking care of all matters in an efficient way.

The 2007–08 financial crisis and its global consequences have shown how failures in governance can be disastrous. The roots of the crisis have been well described by Nobel laureate Joseph Stiglitz[1] as a failure of governance at multiple levels (executives, boards, regulators, and governments). Some of its still ongoing effects are being exacerbated in the current COVID-19 crisis: a regime of low-interest rates, large government indebtedness, a growing disconnect between leading value creating businesses, and value appreciation in the financial markets. Again, ownership has hardly been addressed in such discussions, except for the benefits to owners of the appreciation of their shares, or of their challenges in the face of falling equity values.

Following the 2007–08 financial crisis, and again in the COVID-19 pandemic, citizens had to rescue many corporations. They collectively became the ultimate owners of iconic companies like AIG, GM, Royal Bank of Scotland, and UBS. Governments acted on their behalf as proxy owners. The expense was massive and government ownership expanded as a result. Paradoxically, governments, as owners, have often done well in such rescue operations, which is remarkable given the unpreparedness of governments for such ownership.

Another major change in liberal capitalism is the growing size and importance of institutional investors representing end-retail investors (e.g., pension funds, insurance companies, mutual funds). If ownership by the state and ownership by the people—the end-retail investors—are on the rise, surely ownership effectiveness must and will become a subject of greater importance. The impact of state versus private ownership in these funds should also become increasingly clear for all to see, with clear consequences should differences indeed emerge from this comparison.

Changes and crises always have consequences, often unintended. They also have one virtue: they concentrate the mind on the essential factors driving value creation and the key role that effective governance plays in such instances.

The practice of governance has been excessively shaped by what boards of listed firms do, and then particularly in the US, whose firms are the most studied. The US is the biggest economy in the world and has been the Athens of the study of business. US firms have also provided by far the largest amount of high-quality data for academics and governance professionals to examine and research. US listed firms are the most written about in the Anglophone global business media. As beautifully described by Alfred Chandler,[2] they have given a picture of firms as managed and ultimately governed by their executives. And indeed, CEOs often double up as Board Chairs, focusing business scholars on the executive leadership of these firms, or on their stock market performance. We refer to this situation as *executive-led governance*. This is paradoxical as this reality is often referred to as *(stock) market-led governance*. It is far from being solely a US reality; it is equally present in countries such as the UK, France, and Japan.

Our book takes a contrarian view, namely of firms led and governed by their owners, who may or may not be Chairs and/or CEOs of their firms. This starting point is unique and leads to the main contribution of the book: regardless of national and legal aspects, it is crucial, for a thorough knowledge of value creation and governance, to understand that the governance practices of owner-led firms or firms with identifiable owners differ substantially from those Chandlerian firms with many shareholders. Shareholders in listed companies may be labeled as "owners" but de facto enjoy little if any power in the exercise of their ownership beyond a vote at the Annual General Meeting.

Let us add too that stock listed firms are a small minority in the ecology of firms: the World Bank estimates that there are about 43,000 listed companies in the world,[3] approximately 10% of which are listed in the US, while the number of companies in the world is estimated to be above 213 million.[4] Of course, most of these companies are small, if not exceedingly small. But these numbers confirm our point that the world of listed firms is a small and biased sample in the galaxy of companies. The second aim of our book follows from this: to draw what is distinct in the governance of owner-led firms, to detail it, and to guide corporate owners on the trajectory of value creating ownership. The ownership task does not necessarily become more complex as the business grows, for with growth comes the access to greater talent, intelligence, and experience. In comparison, the task of the small business owner appears more herculean.

Ours thus stands at odds with the Chandlerian view of corporate leadership, still shared by many CEOs and Executive Chairmen. This view holds that the crux of business life and value creation rests with executives. Our approach immediately imposes greater precision in the language of governance. In our treatment, a board is a generic term: it is the adjective that precedes it that fully defines and operationalizes the term. We will explain that there are "Owners' Boards," "Corporate Boards," and "Business (Unit or Management) Boards" and we will argue that the roles and responsibilities of each of these boards differ. As each of these three boards impact an organization's purpose and the execution of that purpose, one key question for us will be to examine how to align these boards on value creation. Decisions on growth, risk, and financing are instances of how each board impacts value creation, and how poor alignment may result in the destruction of value. Separate chapters will be devoted to examining these facets of value creation.

Another distinction we draw in this book pertains to executives and directors of a multi-business corporate entity as compared with those of a single business. The board members of a banking group, for example, may consider that they are governing a single business, defined as banking. The reality is much more complex: a banking group typically hosts multiple businesses, such as retail banking, corporate and investment banking, consumer finance, and asset management, to cite only a few. Each of these corporate units, sometimes called "divisions," is a business, with a distinct value proposition and specific competitors, delivering and creating value in its own way, and driven by its own strategy. Ignorance of this multiplicity of businesses inside a banking group might lead the board of such a group to think of formulating a single strategy aiming for specific "business" goals. Value destruction will invariably result as each business in such a banking group requires distinct leadership, goals, and strategies, which cannot be simply "averaged" away or reduced to group statements and decisions uniformly applied to the separate business units. This observation has a second corollary: the roles of corporate (or group) executives are more related to those of board members governing the multi-business corporation than they are to the executives of the group's business units. The latter aim to make a difference in their respective and distinct competitive business contexts. Corporate executives do not run these businesses but rather oversee the group's multiple businesses. These observations invite corporate executives, as well as their board members, to take an interest in this book.

Many owners behave as if they were the Board of Directors, demanding that their boards formally approve what they as "owners" decide. They state that this is their right as the masters and owners of "their corporation." Regretfully for them, and fortunately for the other stakeholders of the business, this is not the way liberal or democratic capitalism functions, which assumes that owners and their corporations are distinct legal "persons" whose interests may align but may also diverge. This is precisely why liberal capitalism puts the responsibility for the corporation with its Board of Directors. When the latter board is "captured" by owners and becomes excessively subservient to them, the board may provide legal protection for the owner (which some devious owners indeed enjoy and need). But such boards will not protect their owners from value destruction. Such situations occur when owners force decisions that lack the necessary operational understanding of the business or when owner decisions are based on erroneous hypotheses regarding the business context or the functioning and capabilities of the owned organization.

An understanding of the differential and complementary roles of owner, corporate, and business boards is fundamental to effective ownership and governance of owner-led firms. This understanding is particularly important for family enterprises which are vital drivers of the economies and societies in which they operate. Detailing the interplay and in particular the value creating roles of owners and owners' boards in such contexts will be the third goal of our book.

Our broadest aim is to underline that governance actors, if they are indeed aiming for value creation and eager to be responsible and effective actors, must possess standard governance competences, as well as basic business and industry knowledge. They must also be able to think through and follow effective board- and group-level deliberative and decision-making processes. They must learn to address the value creation conflicts that invariably characterize interactions between different stakeholder groups. The lessons from the Macondo (BP/Deepwater Horizon) and Fukushima (TepCo) disasters, as well from the many financial and now pandemic crises we have faced, should not be forgotten. These point to major risks and massive costs when governance, ownership drivers, and stakeholder needs are not sufficiently understood, or managed effectively. In sum, there is a mantra that boards ought to take to heart: "*Organizations – just like people - inevitably die; all wish to die well, as healthy and as old as is possible; let foolishness, stupidity or ignorance not detract us from this wish.*" In fact, this mantra is applicable to all of us, including in our personal governance and in that of our families.

Our treatment is divided into three parts, each representing one of the legs of a "tripod" on which ownership effectiveness rests. As is the case for any tripod, all three legs matter: the structural elements (referred to as the owner's **hardware**), the relational elements (the **software**) that allow owners to manage the social and emotional dynamics of ownership, and the fact that owners are people, subject to emotions and egos. Owners have histories, defining experiences, memories, and talents. No owner is perfect. All owners have shortcomings and biases. We will refer to these defining personal and idiosyncratic aspects as the **humanware** of ownership. A single missing or even ill-functioning leg of the tripod risks rendering ownership ineffective. We end this Preface by detailing the main elements of the hardware, software, and humanware of ownership.

Part I describes the **"hardware"** of value creation in owner-led firms. It presents the key structural requirements for value creation. This part deals with the **"WHAT,"** the **"Mission"** of the enterprise, which provides its foundational structure. The literature often refers to this as the purpose of an enterprise, but we will provide a more precise meaning for the notion of Mission and include values and governance arrangements as well. Two frameworks are presented that are key to implementing the Mission inside an enterprise. These frameworks form the backbone of the ideas developed in this first part. One is our **MGSF** framework, which requires the need to align the **G**oals, **S**trategy, and **F**undamentals governing the enterprise, and project it into the future with its **M**ission if value creation is to result. The second is the **Three Boards** framework consisting of the **Owners', Corporate, and Business Boards.** These represent the three governance levels typically encountered in privately owned firms. They provide the main backbone on which governance rests. These three boards are rarely addressed together and distinctly as we will do in this book. This is necessary to avoid the risk of confusion or loss of alignment, and eventually value destruction. No matter how noble one's dreams, no matter how valuable one's insights, our thesis is that businesses require a clear-sighted and disciplined view on what precisely constitutes value creation and how the subject is approached within a corporate and ownership structure. Obtaining clarity and disciplined alignment on these issues is the primary mission of owners. This specification fundamentally distinguishes owner-led firms from publicly listed ones. In the latter this alignment is a rather haphazard outcome of forces applied by shareholders, board members, and other stakeholders, including, of course, executives, but also suppliers and partners, and, increasingly so during the last few years, regulators.

Part II deals with the **"software"** required to sustainably guide and adapt value creation in changing contexts. This part addresses the relational aspects of corporate governance and the omnipresent and dangerous behavioral biases, at individual or group level, that pose serious challenges to effective board work. This part highlights the **"HOW"** of ownership and governance, which concerns the "Process" of decision making that is the heart of board work. The HOW is critically affected by interactions among the members of the three foundational boards. Of concern are the corporate board's interactions with owners on the one hand, and with executives and managers on the other, as well as regulators and other stakeholders. We here follow the path-breaking work of Kahneman and Tversky, who created the subfield of **behavioral economics.**[5] The novelty in their scientific examination of how people make decisions lies in their descriptive viewpoint, which contrasts with the prior normative treatment premised on hyper-rational actors. Their more realistic models allowed substantial progress in our knowledge about human decision making, as we will explain in this second part of the book.

Having convinced our readers of the seminal findings of Tversky and Kahneman and their followers, we present our **FPL** (**F**air **P**rocess **L**eadership) methodology that counters these biases. FPL provides the different governance actors, owners, directors, and managers with a better chance of remaining on the positive side of risk and of traveling the path of effective decision making and implementation for real value creation. FPL also identifies the factors that cause individuals or groups of individuals to enter the path of value destruction. The methodology favors involvement of stakeholders and their commitment to the decisions made. In sum, FPL provides the software to both engage and align owners, boards, executives, and stakeholders in decision making.

Part III presents the **"humanware"** underlying the complex and often surprising human aspects of ownership and corporate governance that Tversky and Kahneman brought to light. They were not the first, as the Greek poet Homer, in both the *Iliad* and the *Odyssey*, beautifully narrated how humans can, tragically, lose their way in matters of ownership, family, and, above all, personal ambition. Anaïs Nin wrote, "*We do not see things as they are, we see them as we are.*" Nin describes how our identity is the principal root of the many biases that cloud individual and collective decision making.[6] Sydney Smith, cleric at the University of Oxford, similarly noted these origins of our biases: "*It is, then, a matter of sovereign necessity, before we decide on great … questions to … review, with an honest severity,* ***those peculiarities of disposition, situation, and education****, which may communicate an unfair bias to the mind, and induce us to decide, not as the truth of things, but as we are ourselves.*"[7] Character, context (parents, family, position in society, the city and country where we came from), and education (by our parents, family members, teachers, and mentors) all shape our biases and, in turn, our contributions to group decision making and dynamics. In short, our third part thus concerns the **"WHOM."** It reviews the different leadership styles and patterns of owners, as well as the critical transitions that they make in their quest and that act as milestones marking their developmental road.

Our treatment of ownership and governance takes distance from the standard treatment in the economic theory on the governance of the firm, where the key model is the *principal-agent model,* generally associated with Jensen and Meckling.[8] The setting of this model concerns the definition of an agreement or contract between the owner (the *principal* in the model) and the business manager (the *agent*). The principal and agent have different attitudes toward risk. The agency problem is cast as defining the contract for the agent that most benefits the principal. The model sits at quite a distance from normal governance contexts: it relies on a single principal (when shareholders are numerous and far from uniform) who owns a company as the sole shareholder. Any application of the agency model to governance immediately hits upon the question as to whether the board should be considered the principal, with management as the agent, or whether the principal is the owner, and the board the agent. The necessary introduction of a Board of Directors sitting between shareholders and management suggests either a doubly layered principal-agent model, or the introduction of three layers of principals and agents (owners, directors, and managers), which is not the model's setting. Viewing the application of the agency model to governance as rather complex and unsettled, our book focuses on the substance and structural complexities of governance, including the dynamic interaction of the three boards (owners, corporate, and business boards) searching for alignment as described by the MGSF framework and supported by a number of other frameworks, where FPL takes a prominent role in supporting positive relationships by the owner with the Board of Directors and the firm's stakeholders.

In developing our ideas, we recognize that much of management and economic teaching and research is still viewed to be "*as clear as mud*."[9] To escape the curse, we have aimed for transparency and clarity in the formulation of our hypotheses, and in the arguments and foundations on which these hypotheses are built. Our aim throughout is to present a practical book for guiding owners, directors, and business leaders, with a particular focus on business families. Entrepreneurial founder-owned firms, as well as state and private equity-owned entities, are in our purview as well.

Corporate governance is the domain of well-written policy and regulatory manuals, of which there are plenty. These writings are usually normative, abounding in the "should" and the "will." They emphasize the responsibilities of board members and the many tensions a professional practice of governance generates. They typically do not present the academic knowledge in a practical manner that helps board members, their owners, and their executives manage these tensions and exercise their responsibilities more effectively. This is what we aim for.

This book is based on the popular INSEAD education course Value Creation for Owners and Directors. The course has its origins in a long and very early morning car ride in 2007 from Fontainebleau to Brussels, where two of the authors debated how to help the owners of a large Belgian family business group become more effective in addressing their challenges. The authors, who had been invited to help this business family, asked the family leaders to first reflect on the mission pursued by their family business, and on the risks entailed in their enterprise, before structuring the leadership succession they faced. They had been asked to present "helpful academic knowledge relevant to the issues at hand." The family did find the authors' presentation insightful and their intervention helpful in addressing their challenges.

This positive engagement encouraged the authors to launch the course for business owners and directors mentioned earlier. Every iteration of the course furthered insights, validating some of the authors' main views while sharpening others. The book that follows presents these insights and views, refined by the now ten iterations of the course. The course and this book are immeasurably better for the many insights and comments gained from our participants. Every group left behind thoughts, histories, experiences, and wisdom. All of them have and deserve our heartfelt thanks. Having tested our ideas on many cohorts, the time had come to write things down for greater diffusion. It generated further reflection. While writing the various chapters, we regularly experienced Oscar Wilde's saying: "*Thought arises between the tip of the pencil and the paper.*"

The third author, and INSEAD MBA, joined the first two after writing a case on governance and succession in the Tata Group. The collaboration was so positive that the original two authors asked him to join in writing this book. His experience in governance as executive, independent director, and investor added a wealth of contextual and conceptual knowledge to the book. The engagement has undoubtedly resulted in a higher-quality book.

Singapore, Singapore	Massimo Massa
Mumbai, India	Kai Taraporevala
Flendruz, Switzerland	Ludo Van der Heyden

Notes

1. Nobel Laureate Joseph Stiglitz has provided one of the best diagnoses of the root causes of the crisis in *Vanity Fair* (January 2009) entitled "Capitalist Fools." One of the authors has also written on the subject in *The European Financial Review* (June–July 2011) under the title "Public and Corporate Governance After the Crisis."
2. *The Visible Hand: The Managerial Revolution in American Business*, by Alfred D. Chandler Jr., Belknap Press (1977).
3. https://data.worldbank.org/indicator/CM.MKT.LDOM.NO?end=2020&start=2000&view=chart.
4. https://www.statista.com/statistics/1260686/global-companies.
5. The seminal book reference for this area of research is *Judgement under Uncertainty: Heuristics and Biases*, by Daniel Khaneman, Paul Slovic and Amos Tversky, Cambridge University Press (1982). Khaneman's latest book, *Thinking, Fast and Slow,* Farrar, Strauss and Giroux (2011), became an all-time bestseller detailing the intricacies of how our brains function and lead to a host of conscious and unconscious biases.
6. Anaïs Nin, *The Seduction of the Minotaur,* The Swallow Press, 1961, p. 124.
7. "On the Predisposing Causes to the Reception of Republican Opinions," in: *Sermons by the Reverend Sydney Smith (Late Fellow of New College, Oxford),* Vol. 1, 1801.
8. Michael C. Jensen, William H. Meckling, "Theory of the firm: Managerial behavior, agency costs and ownership structure," *Journal of Financial Economics* Volume 3, Issue 4, October 1976, pp. 305–360.
9. Title of a review published in *The Economist* of Tourish's 2019 book *Management Studies in Crisis: Fraud, Deception, and Meaningless Research.*

Chapter Outlines

This book discusses the hardware, software, and "humanware" required by effective owners and directors aiming for value creation. Each element of this tripod is exposited in a separate part of the book. Key ideas are presented in a linear, chapter by chapter manner. Our suggestion to readers is to follow the advice to the Rabbit in *Alice's Adventures in Wonderland*: "'*Begin at the beginning,' the King said gravely, 'and go on till you come to the end.*'"

The key concepts developed in the book are presented here, in brief fashion. This should help all readers, particularly those readers that do not wish to follow the advice given to the Rabbit, preferring to read chapters out of order.

Throughout the book, case studies, real-life examples, as well as interviews of owners and directors provide illustrations and context for the arguments presented. Many examples are given, each presenting facets we can learn from. These examples teach us in two ways:

- Positive examples or good practices where owners, boards, and top management got it right. They obey the Anna Karenina Principle, based on Leo Tolstoy's book, where he writes: "*All happy families are alike; each unhappy family is unhappy in its own way*."[1] In these positive instances, success is achieved when a set of principles are all validated. Such examples also demonstrate that success is a systemic property, and not the result of a single "silver bullet," or of a subset of factors. They attest to the systemic complexity of achieving success when all principles must be validated.[2] As we stated earlier, these principles fall into three macro-characteristics, referred to in this book as hardware, software, and humanware.
- Negative examples or bad practices, showing case studies of enterprises that failed. These follow what we might call the Charles Munger Principle, after

the business partner of Warren Buffett. Munger explained this method of learning in his 1986 Harvard School Commencement Speech: "*What [Johnny] Carson said was that he couldn't tell the graduating class how to be happy, but he could tell them from personal experience how to guarantee misery. What Carson did was to approach the study of how to create X by turning the question backwards, that is by studying how to create non-X.*"[3] Case studies here explain why success proved elusive.

An outline of the book, with brief chapter summaries, is presented next.

Chapter 1. Introduction: Corporate Ownership

The introduction illustrates the main characteristics of the exercise of effective ownership. It also presents an ownership typology. We qualify ownership types according to the other roles owners may also assume: founder, Chair, CEO/General Manager, board director, shareholder, or a combination of these. This categorization distinguishes ours from more usual explanations based on ownership structures and looking at ownership mostly as exerting "control" over a business. The typology allows a clearer discussion of the interaction between ownership and governance.

Part I. Hardware: A Value Creation Framework

Value creation is defined by an anteceding requirement: the need to define value by a proper definition of the **mission** of the firm. This underlines that the definition of mission[4] is the essence of the owner's role, from which all else derives. This observation leads us to present our **MGSF** (**M**ission, **G**oals, **S**trategy, and **F**undamentals) framework that we regard as critical for the effective governance of high-performance companies. Our **Three Boards** framework (Owners, Corporate, and Business) provides an integrative governance architecture, which along with the MGSF framework structures the firm's governance for effective value creation.

Chapter 2. The Primacy of an Owner's Mission

The **owner's mission** sets the purpose of a company and gives it a clear direction. Critically, a mission thus determines the value to be created by corporate ownership as progress on this mission.

The ability of owners to determine the mission of the corporation they own is one of the fundamental characteristics distinguishing owner-led firms from publicly listed ones. In the latter, after the mission is set by owning founders, subsequent changes in mission are typically set by the Board of Directors, if not by the management, and then approved at the General Shareholders Meeting. Owners generally know why they own a business and what they seek from it. Well-set out missions provide companies with a clear focus and greatly enhance the chances of longer-term success.

A mission statement thus frames value creation for an owner-led company as making progress on the mission. This cannot be repeated enough. Companies whose missions are not well set out inevitably lead to value destruction, a consequence of wrong and in effect value destroying mission statements. Disagreements or compromises among owners about the mission, or a persistent lack of alignment among owners, boards, and management and continued disagreements on what the mission ought to be, unavoidably follow this state of affairs. They set the firm up for failure.

The first task of an effective **Owners' Board** (OB) is to craft a mission and then anchor this mission in shareholder agreements and in the corporate charter. Missions may be changed when contextual factors force a change, or when owners change.

Owner-led companies consequently benefit from another characteristic relative to their publicly listed counterparts: they are able to change the mission more swiftly. Changing the mission of publicly listed firms invariably leads to shareholder contests about the opportunity or desirability of such a change.

Chapter 3. The Board of Directors: Governing the Mission

The **Board of Directors** (BoD, though throughout the book we will also use the unqualified term board when referring to a BoD) lies in the middle of the transmission chain linking owners with the management. In liberal capitalism, boards are legally responsible for the organization they supervise. Hence, in the legal view of the firm the board is the organization, while the owners are not. This is why it is so important, in owner-led firms, to anchor value creation in the preferences of the owners. It also follows that in such firms it is important for boards to regularly provide feedback to owners and managers regarding value creation, and also to ask for guidance from both.

One of the key tasks of the value creating BoDs is to maintain alignment with the owners. This is done by ensuring that owners indeed see the company to be delivering value, by showing the progress realized by the company in pursuit of the owners' mission. This requires the Board to see to it that its decisions and those made by executives are aligned with the mission. Using an analogy from how a country is governed, the mission acts like a constitution, goals might be considered laws governing the country, and the Board acts like a supreme court ensuring that the laws are aligned with the constitution.

The alignment exercised by the BoD takes many forms: selecting CEOs and other members of the senior leadership team that are aligned with the mission, crafting jointly with these executives the company's goals, in line with the mission, and monitoring their implementation. Indeed, when CEOs and executive teams pursue actions at variance with the mission, they inevitably lead to a clash with owners who will consider value creation to be denied. Boards must then intervene to restore alignment and return harmony to the organization.

One of the outcomes of the BoD's discussion with the executive team may be that it reveals the mission to be impossible or too costly to deliver; in that case it is up to the board to engage the owners in a discussion of a needed modification of the mission, realizing that is not the BoD's purview, but that of the Owners' Board. In crisis times, the BoD often becomes front-line as the crisis typically results from ineffectiveness in the senior leadership team.

Effective boards regularly review progress and check that the goals pursued remain aligned with the mission. In fulfilling their responsibilities, boards of privately owned firms lie at the center of the "duality" between ownership and the management of the owned corporation, ensuring continued alignment so that the business continuously delivers the value expected by the owners, and also the other stakeholders who must be informed of owners' preferences as revealed by the mission.

Chapter 4. The CEO and the Executive Team: Responsible for Executing the Mission

CEOs and their executive team are responsible for turning the mission, defined by the owners, into reality. They operationalize the mission by aligning business activities with the owner's mission by crafting the goals. They also provide feedback to the BoD on progress in value creation, and warn the BoD on challenges in execution. Good governance is defined by the absence of surprises. But surprises do happen; what should not happen is that surprises known to executives are not known by the BoD, or the owners. This is where strategic planning and risk management become essential.

Chapter 5. Goals, Strategies, and Fundamentals

Missions are generally **long term** in nature. **Goals** translate missions into practical, quantifiable **medium-term** objectives that then trigger the search for **short-term action plans**. Goals can be broadly quantified around three main dimensions: **profitability, growth, and sustainability**. It is important that boards and executive teams understand the interactions and especially the trade-offs between these three dimensions. It is impossible to pursue all three goals simultaneously, at least in the short term. Boards need to address this major challenge with executives, as, at least in the short term and possibly also in the medium term, these three goals cannot be pursued simultaneously. Executive teams thus face clear trade-offs which they need to recognize and manage. Boards are there to support executives with necessary clarifications on the goals that need to be pursued.

Strategies are the action plans that executives deploy following the choice of mission by owners and the selection of goals by the board, in collaboration with the executive team. In case growth is chosen as the goal, for example, typical strategic choices are: **build, buy, or ally strategies.**[5] The selection of a strategy does not depend solely on goals, it also depends on company **fundamentals**: the type of industry the firm operates in, the client's ecosystem, suppliers, competitors, regulators, where and how the company generates cash flows, the types of risks the company faces and needs to mitigate against, as well as the company's ability to raise financing. Examples are presented illustrating how strategies are selected by examining cash flow generating opportunities.

Chapter 6. Fundamentals: Financing and Risk

Owners must understand how company fundamentals affect the selection and success of the strategies, and hence of risk, and how they may alter the results expected from good strategy execution. These interactions naturally have a bearing on financing opportunities. This point deserves to be fully recognized, as growth requires financing. Location of a company, for example, has a great influence on cash generation potential, both in supply of investors and demand for investments. These interactions too must not be ignored.

In our discussion of a company's financing needs, we follow the risk-return paradigm of modern finance. This paradigm identifies risk as the fundamental factor in financing. Deviating from the classical Modigliani-Miller treatment, which asserted that financing had no bearing on the value of the firm, equity financing through IPOs enables and influences strategies, as it changes the nature of ownership. The chapter concludes with a discussion of the impact of financing on overall value creation.

This book classifies risk in three types: **volatility, Black Swan, and obsolescence**. Two of these risks, volatility and Black Swan, are investigated in this chapter. The third risk, obsolescence, is dealt with separately in Chap. 7. Obsolescence acts like a cancer, though treatment and recovery are possible. Examples again illustrate the impact of these risks on strategic choices.

Chapter 7. Control and the Corporate Board

Language being central in governance, this chapter begins with a definition of control. Owners, directors, and executives must align on control, and agree on the what, the why, and the how. We illustrate how control is typically achieved through a variety of structural mechanisms. This is our entry point for distinguishing, in a multi-business setting, the responsibilities at the corporate level (Board of Directors) from those at the business level (CEO and executive management of the business units). A clear and complementary differentiation of the role and function of the corporate board as distinct from that of the business unit boards is thus obtained.

Chapter 8. Obsolescence and Counterfactual Thinking

Obsolescence is the silent killer of companies. It often operates insidiously. Through several examples, we illustrate how boards usually do not spend sufficient time appreciating a company's obsolescence risks, understanding when these arise, when they grow, and what they consist of. In this context, we also present **counterfactual thinking** as a key competence for owners and boards to possess. Our recommendation to boards and owners is for these obsolescence risks to be made more visible as a pre-condition for an effective treatment of this corporate cancer, and to apply counterfactual thinking more rigorously as a way of examining what treatments will be more value creating and contribute to greater sustainability. Our formal discussion of obsolescence and counterfactual thinking is another distinguishing feature of our book.

Chapter 9. MGSF and the Three Boards

This chapter closes Part I of the book by reviewing the entire **Mission, Goals, Strategies, Fundamentals** framework (MGSF), underlining again its central importance as a foundational tool for the alignment required for a firm's value creation across the **three boards**: owners' board, corporate board, and business board. The distinction between the three boards is often too foggy, leading to overlap and confusion as to their distinct roles, as opposed to synergy and complementarity. This lack of clarity lies at the root of a great number of governance inadequacies and pathologies and turns a potential synergy into a needless and soon emotional confrontation of power and authority. The resulting deficit of firm performance may ultimately threaten the survival of the enterprise. A good understanding of the proper hardware of governance is vital.

Part II. Software: Effective Collaborative Processes and the Need to Manage Self

This part begins by building proper awareness of the many biases prevailing among governance actors and of the need to understand how these biases affect decision making at individual and group level. Our proposition is that good software is central to decision making in such a context, which is the essence of what boards do.

This chapter shows how good governance software supports and drives proper collaboration between the various actors and organizational units involved in decision making. Board decision making is complex because several groups or individuals (which metaphorically can be regarded as the software modules) must interact synergistically. The use of good protocols and processes (the software macros) is vital to produce good decisions by our three boards, and for the successful implementation of these decisions. Individual and group biases are akin to programming errors in IT software, leading to errors when the corresponding software is invoked. The prevalence of such biases must not be ignored; unfortunately, many of these biases arise unconsciously. Only through an open, collective, and confrontational treatment can these biases be addressed. This is where **F**air **P**rocess **L**eadership (**FPL**) proves invaluable. It is a powerful antidote, if correctly applied, for the ever-prevalent biases that cloud organizational and corporate decision making and action.

The chapter lays out the benefits obtained through the proper application of the FPL framework and explains why its effective use indeed counters the many biases that affect the quality of communications and exchanges between corporate governance actors, and organizational actors more broadly. Effective FPL leads to higher board and corporate performance; conversely, FPL violations reduce board and corporate effectiveness. In one form or the other, be it explicit or implicit, FPL is not just an option, or as we have stated before, a necessary foundational tool for value creation. What is also interesting about FPL is that it introduces fairness in the governance and corporate scene, not as the fair share that is so dear to shareholders and stakeholders, but as fair play among them.

We do believe that the critical role of FPL will increasingly become recognized as a foundation for effective corporate governance. The promise that family-owned and family-controlled enterprises hold in this regard is clear to us. FPL must be rooted at the ownership level to durably impact the enterprise going forward, and become an integral and durable part of it. The absence of the ownership anchor is a risk for listed firms, the market on its own showing no clear proclivity for FPL due to its shorter-term focus. Most conflicts affecting family firms can be seen to result from FPL violations.[6]

Chairs and CEOs may not commit to FPL, possibly out of ignorance. But even when committed, our experience shows that the quality of Fair Process changes as the leader changes. The presence of the "L" in the acronym FPL reminds us of this fact, which may cause a disruption in fair process when chairs and CEOs change.

Chapter 10. Delusions, Confusion, and Biases

Individual and group biases corrupt a rational and fact-based approach to governance. This chapter lays out problems that affect CEOs and their executive teams, as well as owners and their Boards of Directors. A lack of awareness of these biases in companies is akin to flying blind or with only a partial view. Understanding these biases is the first necessary step toward building a more accurate view of reality. The second one is effective treatment of the biases.

This chapter also shows that substantial alignment and durable commitment are required for value creation. At the same time, it is now well accepted that heterogeneity is an essential ingredient for effective decision making, including for correctly framing the challenges facing the enterprise, its governance, and its ownership. Heterogeneity is also fundamental for the effective generation of options and for thoroughly exploring the alternatives available. Yet, heterogeneity may also render board work unmanageable. Heterogeneity thus needs to be managed; left unmanaged it may become destructive.

This makes board composition a crucial decision, often paid insufficient attention to by owners and excessively subjected to owners' biases and preferences. We all know how strategies and tactics in sports teams are highly dependent on the selection of players and coaches. The same holds for owners and their boards. Examples are presented to illustrate this key point, and to highlight the ways boards succeed in conquering this challenge, and go astray when they do not.

Chapter 11. Biases in Action and How High-Performance Teams Address Them

Boards are teams, sharing the common goal of value creation and being collectively responsible for the company they supervise. This chapter explores what it takes for teams to become performing, or, on the contrary, how they lose their performance edge. To make the point vividly and grasp it better, this chapter provides a detailed account of a tragedy that occurred on Everest in 1996 that involved three mountaineering teams led by business owners that were running businesses, albeit small ones. The Everest metaphor works well as boards also are small teams, pursuing a challenging and difficult mission, and regularly submitted to major "storms" and turbulence. Getting out of distress often feels like having to conquer Everest. "Going to the top" is an ambition that fuels any group or board aiming for high performance.

The individual and team biases affecting the performance of the two climbing teams are described in detail. The tragic impact of these biases on the effectiveness of two of the teams is explained, making horrific outcomes easier to understand and appraise. These stories will help the reader spot similar issues on their boards, thus preventing their boards from meeting similarly tragic ends.

Ways to combat these biases are explored, repeating the argument that good processes engender and support effective teamwork, and also why. The translation to effective board work is straightforward. Indeed, we have seen that these Everest stories are very engaging for boards we have presented them to, leading them into a fruitful—and sometimes passionate—discussion of their own effectiveness and their ability to avoid crises and catastrophe.

Chapter 12. Fair Process Leadership: The Path to Positive and Collaborative Dynamics for Owners and Their Directors

Fair Process Leadership (FPL) is an integrative and inclusive approach to leadership that emphasizes high levels of engagement and transparency with stakeholders, as well as objective evaluation of both outcomes and process, driven by an unabating commitment to continuously improving the leadership process. FPL confronts human biases head-on and leads to more effective decision making.

Here we explain FPL as a dynamic framework consisting of a cycle of five stages, identified as Engaging, Exploring, Explaining, Executing, and Evaluating. The disciplined and thorough application of this cycle results in critical voices being heard and addressed, and value creating actions being taken and implemented with strong commitment. Our experience is that the cycle is often not followed in a disciplined way, or when it is followed, it is done so too superficially and with insufficient thoroughness.

A historical example, that of Napoleon Bonaparte and the French Empire that resulted from his forceful actions after the French Revolution, is a strong example of the power of FPL. Details on this period of France history when its power and impact on the world stage were unequaled are provided in Appendix B as not all readers may wish to know the specifics of this mythical leadership figure, who starts out as an executive, then becomes CEO and later Chairman, and eventually owner. The example is interesting for it illustrates the power of FPL in the rise of Bonaparte, the young military officer, who perfectly executes the missions that he is given. But FPL is also useful to pinpoint the enormous destructive power unleashed by the multiple FPL violations that emerged when the general took on his imperial clothes. Having become the nearly sole "owner" of the French Empire, and having transformed it into a family business, Napoleon, the Emperor, destroyed most of what he had contributed to during his ascent to power. Beyond its historical significance, the example attests to the immense destructive powers of ownership when FPL norms are violated.

Chapter 13. Fair Process Leadership Illustrated: Applications to Owners, Board Members, and Executives

This chapter deepens our FPL discourse in the world of owners, board members, and managers. We examine the story of Carlos Ghosn, which in many ways is a modern-day replica of the Napoleonic story. Both Napoleon and Ghosn are uniquely talented leaders, who both had plenty of victories to celebrate in the ascending part of their reign and created empires, Ghosn's consisting of two companies, Nissan and Renault, committing to a formidable alliance challenging large rivals such as Toyota, GM, and VW.

But their ownership was ultimately neither wise nor fair. The ends of these two remarkable leaders are similar: both men end up in prison, on a distant island, Longwood House for Napoleon, a Japanese prison then a Lebanese one for Carlos Ghosn. Both were betrayed by some of their closest associates. Both acted—at least psychologically—as if they were the owners of the organizations they led. Their boards did not stop their destructive behaviors. Their stories illustrate vividly the immensely negative impacts repeated and prolonged violations of FPL have on individuals, leadership teams, boards, organizations, and their multiple stakeholders. As one corollary, these stories also plead for a clear separation of chair and CEO roles.

Part III Humanware: Owners as Leaders and Value Creators

The third leg of our governance tripod is denoted **Humanware.** It connotes the intrinsic and pervasive human dimensions of ownership, governance, and value creation. People come to ownership and boards with their character and personality, shaped by their histories and memories, with their myths and ideologies, anxieties and dreams.

This makes governance an intricate and profoundly human affair. Hardware and software are ultimately activated and deployed by people. We all know from experience that humanware must be compatible with hardware and software for computers and smart phones to be of value to users. When this is the case, value creation results, with a much greater likelihood of sustainability. What is true for computers and smart phones also holds for ownership.

We also know that humanware often interferes with the proper or intended functioning of hardware and software. We close this book by addressing the human facets of ownership and governance. We do this through sharing a set of profiles that show us how, in the end, humanware is critical to driving outcomes. This of course is the case in management and government as well. Good if not great humanware is thus the third part of the governance tripod on which ownership effectiveness rests.

Chapter 14. Profiles in Ownership

Thorough interviews with owners conducted during the writing of this book we present the diversity of ownership types and describe the many challenges founders and owners face when their businesses grow. A principal challenge is the need for founders to manage their own transitions, first becoming effective business leaders, then transitioning again to become effective governors and owners of their businesses.

The profiles show that ownership is a journey, with bright as well as dark days, regularly facing storms of various levels of severity. For all, it consists of repeated journeys, with plenty of learning along the road traveled. Indeed, what we have observed is that successful owners are fantastic learners. They pick up many tools and insights and are not deterred by failure, which often fills them with renewed energies for the next journey. This is one of the lessons of the book: ownership rests both on personal talents and motivations, but also on learning many lessons, including from other owners. There lies one of the advantages of a family business, where ownership examples and experiences—including negative and challenging ones - are at hand for the next generation from an early age.

Chapter 15. Transitioning to Ownership and Developing as Owner

We use the profiles in Chap. 14 to glean key lessons for founders and owners. We illustrate how successful founders are driven by a mission, which they transmit to their enterprise. With time, founders having been CEOs and Chairs return to being "just" owners, where they may continue to support a possibly modified mission of the succeeding generation. This provides them with a final and very meaningful opportunity to continue to provide sense and pride to those involved with the enterprise, even if at that time others carry the torch. At this later stage, ownership effectiveness relies on their ability to inspire and leverage their skills, talents, and energies in others, so that these others can sustain and grow the businesses, like they did in earlier times.

Ownership types are described using a leadership model built around four archetypical leadership types. The profiles from the previous chapter show that it is impossible for one person to have all the talents required for a given venture or enterprise. Missing talents must be compensated by owners acquiring and developing competences, which, however, will not be a complete match for the missing talents. Hence, they must rely on trusted advisors and allies endowed with those talents. Acquiring at least minimal competencies to beneficially interact with these talented advisors then allows a fruitful collaboration. In any case, our view is that business and ownership in the digital age call for greater doses of collaboration, solo players—like solo climbers on Everest—ending up astray, lost on merciless mountains. Value creation is unquestionably a collaborative act.

Chapter 16. Ownership in the Twenty-First Century: Closing Thoughts

The world keeps changing. Businesses are in transition. It is commonly though that the post-COVID world will differ from the world we knew when we entered the global pandemic. Just like the 2007–08 financial crisis forever changed governance, and had major impacts on ownership, it is likely that COVID-19 will leave its trace as well.

Hopefully, the global COVID crisis will help convince boards that they need to prepare for the greatest challenge of this century, which concerns the survival of our planet. Climate change will accentuate the tensions on ownership, including more charged confrontations with the weather and with multiple stakeholders. In this context, we discuss ESG and Sustainability using the models and frameworks presented earlier in the book, further illustrating their relevance.

Looking to the future, we venture to state that companies with clearly defined ownership should be better able to look toward and prepare for the future as compared with publicly listed firms. If they equip themselves with the proper hardware, software, and humanware, as this book argues.

Concretely, and as a final summary, the Appendix defines ten challenges that owners and their boards need to address. We might call them the ten invariants defining effective governance and board work. The list will hopefully be seen as a useful final checklist for owners and board members eager to take specific steps toward achieving greater effectiveness, sustaining their ambition of excellence in meeting the increasing responsibilities with which life on this planet is confronting all of us.

Notes

1. *Anna Karenina* by Leo Tolstoy, Penguin Classics, Penguin; UK ed. edition (30 January 2003).
2. Most of the models in the book have a multiplicative property and are non-compensating: failure to verify one dimension cannot be compensated by the other dimensions.
3. *Poor Charlie's Almanack: The Wit and Wisdom of Charles T. Munger*, by Charles T. Munger, Walsworth Publishing Company; Expanded Third edition (2005).
4. We will use the term mission in this book, which we find more precise and directional than purpose.
5. One now classical treatment is the book *Build, Borrow or Buy*, by L. Capron and W. Mitchell, Harvard Business School Press (2012).
6. Ludo Van der Heyden, Christine Blondel, and Randel S. Carlock, "Striving for Justice in Family Business," *Family Business Review* (March 2005).

Acknowledgments

We gratefully acknowledge our families, for their unwavering support during the endless hours invested in writing this book. We hope they might find some value in reading this book, as many of the ideas are readily applicable to a value-creating family.

We also acknowledge INSEAD. It is a wonderful place to offer educational courses to a multi-national audience. It also allows and encourages the academic entrepreneurship it takes to design and keep offering the course whose content this book summarizes.

The participants of our *Value Creation for Owners and Directors* were invaluable. Their encouragements, contributions, and insights led us on the journey of writing this book.

Finally, we are most grateful to Liz Barlow, the Head of Scholarly Publishing at Palgrave, and her excellent team—Lauren Dooley, Ulrike Stricker-Komba and Antony Sami—for welcoming, guiding, and supporting us throughout the writing.

Contents

List of Figures

1

Introduction: Corporate Ownership

This book is primarily addressed to *corporate owners* and to those interacting with them. The former are also called *equity shareholders*. The latter principally comprise directors and executives. Owners interact with other stakeholders as well, notably employees, partners, suppliers (including of finance), customers, and government authorities, to name a few.

The defining characteristic of a *corporation* is that as a legal entity it is its own person, distinct from its owners. The consideration of a corporation as an entity enjoying rights and responsibilities originated in the Roman Empire. One of the founding principles of the Roman Republic was that the *beneficium* of a position should be proportional to the *officium*, namely, the responsibilities associated with that position or role. Liberal capitalism is acting under a different principle. For several reasons that we will evoke later in this chapter, it is built on a separation of the benefits of ownership from the responsibilities of ownership. Corporate capitalism was built in nineteenth-century Britain on the principle of *limited liability*. Shareholders were given an asymmetric relation with their corporation: they were deemed not to be responsible for any debts and liabilities incurred by the corporation, even though they would enjoy their benefits, coming to them in the form of value appreciation of their shares, or in dividends distributed by the corporation to them.

The corollary principle of corporate ownership is that *responsibility for the corporation* was placed with the *Board of Directors* (BoD), which shareholders would have the right to elect. We will return to this somewhat surprising arrangement shortly in later chapters of the book. For now, it is sufficient to remind the reader that this separation is essential to the functioning of capital

M. Massa et al., *Value Creation for Owners and Directors*,
https://doi.org/10.1007/978-3-031-19726-0_1

markets, which would not function if traded shares also implied a trade in responsibility. Because the responsibility for the corporation is placed with the BoD, owners can trade their shares, which are not associated with any responsibility. Shares can thus be priced for the value of their control and dividend rights and traded as economic products. This provides shareholders and the company with the additional benefit of liquidity, companies being able to issue shares in return for cash. Shareholders in need of liquidity can sell their shares.

Corporations are set up by one or more founding owners for a *purpose*, laid out in their *Articles of Incorporation*. These articles describe the primary purpose of the corporation, the location of incorporation (since a jurisdiction will have to govern the proper execution of these articles), the number of shares issued, possibly distinct classes of shareholding with differentiated rights, and any other rules that the shareholders agree to abide by in the pursuit of their shared purpose.

Stock markets have, with time, overshadowed the notion of corporate purpose, with excessive attention being paid to short-term share price variations, to such an extent that share price for too many has become the main measure of value created by the corporation for its owners. This is deceptive as stock prices are the result of supply and demand conditions, which may lead stock prices to diverge from the underlying economic performance of the firm. The stock market crash of 2007–08 is a reminder of all of this.

Recent business literature has started to correct this, putting purpose back on the front stage.[1] The current debate on environmental, social, and governance (ESG) and sustainability is another instance of this correction. Beyond saving life on planet Earth, the immediate issue that needs to be addressed in this debate is whether sustainability should be an integral part of the purpose of a corporation, and if so, how it then should be realized. Alternate views state this is truly the domain of government and regulatory authorities, which can more effectively address these issues than voluntary and uncoordinated actions by firms that also compete among themselves. Family firms have often embraced the former view, and this book then discusses how they might best do so.

Like humans, corporations are born, grow, and eventually die. It should first be noted that, unlike for humans, corporate death is not necessarily a negative event. When a company is acquired by another company, the acquired company stops its life as a legal entity but also opens a new chapter as a business or organizational unit of the acquiring company. At least in the short run, there are changes in ownership and some changes in leadership, but most employees simply continue their responsibilities, likely with improved leadership and ownership. The continuity, at least in the short run, of the underlying business regardless of the composition of its ownership is regarded as one of the virtues of liberal capitalism. While in the legal sense the acquired company has indeed ceased to exist, the owners that sold typically invest a large part if not their entire proceeds of the sale in other business ventures, initiating a new ownership chapter in the latter.

A different instance of corporate death is when owners indeed decide to disband the corporation, because its original purpose has been achieved or is seen as infeasible or unattractive. Of course, other options are available to owners in such instances, like selling the business to new owners seeing more value in the business they acquire, possibly changing the purpose of the business going forward.

When asked to explain what defines a corporate or business owner, one typically thinks of a *private* individual owning shares of a corporation or business entity. We must immediately add that a corporation could also be state-owned. In such cases the government—through its Council of Ministers, through one of its Ministries or Agencies, or possibly through the country's Sovereign Wealth Fund—is exercising the ownership responsibility on behalf of the ultimate owners, which are the citizens of that nation. Many business entities are owned by other corporations, which legally have the same ownership rights and responsibilities as private individuals.

There is admittedly great diversity in ownership types, as the subsequent section will show. Except for in the third part of the book devoted to ownership profiles, we will not pay great attention to this diversity, namely whether owners are private individuals, owner groups or partners, families, corporations, or states. We mostly focus on the task and responsibilities of owners, regardless of their type. The book then argues for and explains the positive role owners can play in the economy and society, and what is required for them to assume this role in a value creating way. We also wish owners to understand that the ownership task is more demanding and consequential than generally understood.

There is one group of corporations that we will not address in this book, and these are *not-for-profit corporations* (NPOs). These organizations are peculiar precisely because they do not have owners. This is also one of their limitations, as the main point of our book is to point to the positive role and value of ownership, properly exercised. In this aspect, NPOs are closer to listed firms, which, when they have millions of small shareholders, do not de facto have "real" owners, with a voice and decision-making authority. The latter situation, which is regularly described as the "normal" corporation, is neither normal nor ideal, as ownership is emasculated. By numbers, there is no question that the corporation with identifiable ownership is the prevalent case.

1 Ownership Categories

The first categorization of business owners is structural and pertains to *the size of the ownership*: one can be a sole owner, a partner in a joint ownership venture, one may own shares in a family business with a few or many members of the family, or in a private equity firm with investment partners. At the forming venture, owners are either single founders or a few partners. Gradually, the ownership typically becomes more widely held.

Then, the corporation can be *unlisted or listed* on a stock market. When owners decide to list their corporation, they must meet the listing requirements of the stock market authority and submit to various regulatory regimes. For example, in the US, listing automatically implies that a corporation falls under federal jurisdiction, though incorporations are a state matter. The breadth of ownership types that exist in a country like the US and more generally in the world is considerable indeed. It will therefore not be the topic of this book.

Another categorization focuses *on what owners do*: buy and sell shares, found companies, write articles of incorporation, enter into shareholder agreements, appoint members of their Board of Directors, set dividend policy or strategy, and look for executives to run or help run the business, or investment partners to share the risk and help the business. Growth typically involves changes in ownership, which in turn often involves changes in mission, and thus changes in the way the business is conducted. These changes are indeed one of the main motivations for writing this book, as we aim to make owners fully aware of their importance to the business.

The lens that will guide us in this book will be that of governance, which we define as the determination of the future direction of the business entity or organization, either through direct decision making, or indirectly by appointing members of the Board of Directors, who hold the legal responsibility for the corporation regardless of its ownership. This very direct relation between owners and the directors of the owned corporation makes it impossible to fully separate owners from the directors of the corporation they own. There also lies the principal difference between owner-led firms and diffuse ownership, which is the case for publicly listed firms with no dominant and identifiable owner. In the latter, the link between owners and their directors is tiny and distant, shareholders making their presence felt through voting at the

Annual General Meeting or through purchases and sales of shares. In fact, in publicly listed firms loyal shareholders "create no noise" for they do not create any movement in the share price; it is only those losing or gaining interest that create the news.

In owner-led firms, owners often act as directors of the company they own. The first point to realize is that this board role is different from their role as owners. Owners *nominate and approve* the members of their Board of Directors, who all have a fiduciary duty to the corporation, and not to a particular shareholder. These dual roles are hard to fill due to the multiple biases that ownership induces when one is also a director of the corporation one owns. Biases will be the object of the second part of the book, as it is key for owners to understand the many biases, conscious and unconscious, we all can be subjected to.

Owners do not need to be on the boards of their companies, or dominate the board. They approve board members and can remove them at will. Whether they sit on the Board of Directors is one of the defining choices facing owners. Increasingly, we hear voices that claim that having owners on the Board of Directors is, on average, detrimental for value creation because of the conflicts of interest their board presence generates. Following the 2007-08 financial crisis, regulatory authorities have required greater *independence* from board members with the argument that owners and their "representatives" are better at taking care of owner interests than exercising their statutory mandate of *duty of care* for the corporation. Our view here is that the key resides in owners, with the support of their fellow board members, identifying and managing conflicts of interest when they arise. This is a critical board and ownership competence needed for building continued positive dynamics between owners and their boards. We will repeatedly stress how alignment is needed for value creation. Ownership presence at the board can be very useful in building and maintaining this alignment. The transparency that comes with presence maintains the vital trust between owners and their boards.

These considerations provide a first glimpse at the richness and diversity of the human species called "owner." The media is rich with descriptions of tumultuous relations owners have with their boards and with governance itself. These stories often pertain to one category of owners that are largely averse to governance and boards unless these are exercised by themselves: the *entrepreneurs*. Indeed, the word itself connotes "to take in-between" (from the French "*entreprendre*"). Entrepreneurs are doers and creators. They are high on self-determination and low on delegation of authority and trust. They will tend to trust boards only when they run these boards themselves. These traits set the stage for heavy-handed confrontations with their CEOs, another species that is high on self-determination. CEOs have something in common with owners: they have no issue with a Board of Directors run by a Chair if they are the Chair.

These considerations set the stage and present the context for our discussions on ownership and governance across all three parts of our book. Ownership is as varied as it is wide, and even when it concerns a single person, ownership is a dynamic characteristic, consisting of a sequence of stages and varying contexts. The same owner may act differently when the context changes. This is also why we will not even endeavor to list every extant form of ownership.

2 Owner-Founder/Entrepreneur

We start with a particularly rich and complex case of ownership, that of Bill Gates, as it illustrates the dynamic character of ownership and its creative power. On March 13, 2020, Bill Gates stepped down from the Board of Directors of Microsoft Corporation, the company he founded in 1975 with Paul Allen. Since the beginning Gates and Allen were owner-founders. Gates was employed in another computer company. At the urging of Paul Allen, he joined Microsoft, quickly assuming the dual roles of Chairman and CEO. The culture of Silicon Valley entrepreneurs is one of vision, leadership, and genius, not one that pays great attention to formal governance. There is little evidence that Microsoft's board played a great role in the emergence of the company, being dominated, as was the entire company, by the personalities of the Chairman, Bill Gates, and the Vice-Chair, Paul Allen. This seems a defining feature of Silicon Valley boards. Microsoft originated in Seattle but appears to have followed the same pattern, at least in its owner-founder days.[2]

Another owner-founder is Steve Jobs. Contrasting the story of Bill Gates with that of Steve Jobs reveals two similar ownership ventures. Steve Jobs co-founded Apple in 1976 with Steve Wozniak and Ronald Wayne. The three co-founders were working at Atari, where they regularly and intensely discussed the future of the industry and the design of the emerging microcomputers. One day, Wayne invited the two Steves to his house to settle their differences. During this discussion, Steve proposed that they found a company led by Wozniak and him, each being 45% shareholders and Wayne being offered 10% to act as tiebreaker should the two disagree. Wayne wrote the partnership agreement, and Apple was born on April 1, 1976. Wayne also wrote the Apple I manual. However, he was so risk-averse that 12 days after signing Apple Computer's birth agreement, he sold his 10% share of the newly created company to his fellow founders for $800.[3]

It was Wozniak, Jobs's other co-founder, who designed the first successful Apple products, the Apple I and the Apple II.[4] The Apple III, designed according to Wozniak by Apple's marketing department (read the team led by Steve Jobs), was a failure, as was the Lisa. Wozniak thought that product design, under Jobs, had made too many compromises. The Macintosh had benefited from Wozniak's input and leadership until his 1981 plane crash, at which point project leadership was taken over by Jobs. Sales again were disappointing notwithstanding remarkable media reception at launch. The Macintosh was never able to beat the IBM PC, which was the aim when the product was launched. As in the case of Gates with Allen, Jobs's relationship with Wozniak deteriorated until the latter left the company in 1985. He was not shy in stating that the company had been going in the wrong direction for the preceding five years.

Jobs was a true entrepreneur and had genius. He liked to create new worlds, and was not afraid to take risks and make controversial decisions. He was also quite stubborn. In his journey, he lost the support of valuable colleagues and personal partners. His deep motivation lay in creating high-impact digital products, with a look and feel that was seductive and fun, and distinct.

A third type of owner-founder is Warren Buffett, the Founder and Chairman of Berkshire Hathaway. Buffett takes the major investment decisions for Berkshire Hathaway, which he discusses with his small staff, and in particular with long-time partner Charles Munger. Buffett leaves both the governance and the management of investee companies to professional CEOs and their Boards. Buffett is hands-off with regard to these operating companies. His business is ownership in its pure form; it is his only focus. Buffett once was the Chairman of Salomon Brothers, a position he took at the request of his friend John Gutfreund. The company was burning, and Gutfreund had the insight that only Buffet could save Salomon following its attempt to corner the Treasury bond market. Buffett liked to say that it was one of the worst experiences of his life. Having rescued the firm from its potential demise, he vowed never to be Chairman again. He also largely abstained from serving on boards, except for his own.

Founder-owners share a common purpose: *to innovate and create*. The purpose and mission they set for themselves is their principal hardware. They also share similar software: their approach to leadership is hard-fought. When the leadership is a team, it either morphs into a dynamic and complementary duo (like that of Warren Buffet and Charlie Munger), or it becomes antagonistic and falls apart (which happened to Gates and Allen, and to Jobs and Wozniak, even if both pairs eventually made up again). Their humanware shapes them and provides them with their identities, further shaping their hardware and their software. The "characters" of Gates and Jobs made them fall apart with vital partners, while Buffett, whose first teacher and partner was his father, is still with Munger. The identities and characters of these men—and those of their close associates— contributed to their effectiveness as owners and rendered the story and understanding of their success more complex.

This book addresses several questions. Could a better structured owners' board (perhaps with a third founder) and an effective Board of Directors, more independent from the founders, have played more of a coaching role between Gates and Allen? Was the withdrawal from the Apple ownership of Ronald Wayne detrimental to the Jobs–Wozniak relationship, ultimately making the journey harder than it eventually became? Could an effective board not have helped Microsoft deal better with the emergence of the internet? Was Ballmer, Gates's successor at Microsoft, perhaps unintentionally, if this was indeed the case, hampered by the presence of the founding owners? These questions make the point that governance is a topic beneficially addressed at the founding stage, something that Silicon Valley firms are not necessarily great at. The other point we address in this book is that, notwithstanding the departure of Gates, Microsoft has continued to flourish under the new leadership of Satya Nadella. What was the role of governance, of the owners, and of the Board of Directors in this remarkable outcome?

3 Family Ownership

Nicolas Boël is the Chairman of Solvay SA, the Belgian specialty chemicals group. He is also a member of one of its founding families. His father was the "Administrateur Délégué" of the Usines Gustave Boël in La Louvière. His uncle is the CEO of the private equity firm Sofina, which is publicly listed on the Brussels Exchange, but controlled by Solvay family shareholders. Nicolas grew up in an industrial ownership family. He inherited his shareholding from his parents. He succeeded Aloïs Michielsen, the first non-family Chairman of Solvay and its former CEO. At the latter's retirement from the Chair, the family decided it was opportune for the family to resume the chairmanship, in a context where the CEO was not a member of the family. And the family turned to Nicolas Boël.

Like most Solvay family shareholders, Boël's branch also holds shares in the family holding company, Solvac, that owns just over 30% of the Solvay public equity and holds no other shares. Solvac was set up to help the Solvay families control the chemical group. It formally acts as the owners' board of Solvay. Nicolas Boël today is the main carrier of the family reputation and history. One of his responsibilities is to see to it that the wishes in terms of control and expected benefits of its dominant shareholder are met in a way that also meets the interests of Solvay. Of course, as Chair of the Board, his primary fiduciary duty is to Solvay, the corporation.

The Solvay story is remarkable. Two brothers, Alfred and Ernest Solvay, one a businessman and the other a scientist (a common founder combination), in 1863 founded a company in Couillet (Belgium) devoted to the production of soda ash using a process invented by Ernest. The company was financed with the help of Eudore Pirmez, a lawyer and business associate. Three others followed Pirmez as founding investors. Their descendants are now referred to as "the" Solvay families, even though only two trace back to the Solvay brothers. Today the company has become a global chemical empire, with more than 2500 shareholders belonging to one of these Solvay families. They are grouped into six branches, each corresponding to one of the two founding brothers, or one of the founding investors. The structure and identities of these family branches, how they entered the Solvay venture, and how each contributed to the development of the company runs deep into the history of the family business, and remains present today. The challenge of maintaining alignment in an increasingly volatile world is a foundation for the group's continued success, including in its 2011 take-over of Rhodia, the French industrial company that was created in 1999 when Rhône-Poulenc split its chemistry business from its pharma activities.

The story of the Belgian-Brazilian brewer InBev taking over "America's Best-Loved Brewery and Beers" Anheuser-Busch shares this feature of a relatively smaller group ending the corporate life of a former industrial giant. Ownership effectiveness is a big part of the explanation behind these stories. We will detail the story in Chap. 1.

Frank Stangenberg-Haverkamp is Chairman of the Executive Board and of the Family Board of E. Merck KGaA, the German pharmaceutical group. He heads the founding family and chairs the operating company board. Merck's history is 200 years older than that of Solvay, going back to the Engel Pharmacy in Darmstadt, which was purchased by Friedrich Jacob Merck in 1668. Like Solvay, it has a rich history.

In 1887, a long-time employee, Theodore Weicker, went to the US to represent the Darmstadt firm. In 1891, he set up Merck & Co. with a US$ 200,000 capital from Emanuel Merck, the grandson of the founder. The latter was a very successful scientist entrepreneur who invented many drugs and built several factories supplying the chemical and pharmaceutical industries.[5]

Emanuel's son, George Merck, 23 years old at the time, joined Weicker in New York. The expropriation of its US affiliate in 1917 during World War I led Merck & Co. to be established as an independent US firm. It did business outside the US under the name Merck Sharp & Dohme ("MSD"), while the German Merck did business under the name EMD, standing for E. Merck Darmstadt.

All three firms—Solvay, Merck, and MSD—are known for major acquisitions affecting their sectors. These family owners share a common purpose: *to create value for the long run by handing over more value than they inherited from their parents*. This is another example of mission, the hardware cementing strong links between family members and a firm and rendering it more sustainable. These family members also share a similar software pattern: a family approach to leadership, with the capacity to engage non-family members who gradually become part of the family fabric (without necessarily remaining in this fabric forever). The humanware acts both as a strength and as a limit: without the strong personalities and identities of founders and their successors over multiple generations, sustainability would be impossible to achieve. At the same time, these identities shape answers to the usual ownership questions. How much should the family directly manage, and how much should it rely on professional managers? Should it retrench and just supervise and monitor? How important is control for them, as opposed to performance? What trade-off between control and performance are they willing to consider? And if they lose control, will this not affect their mission, which is an essential part of the glue that holds them together?

4 Corporate Owner

As soon as a corporation wishes to do business in another country, it needs to establish a company in that country. One exception to this general rule is the EU Corporation status that companies can obtain in the EU. Such companies can operate throughout the EU's Single Market without having to establish companies in the various EU countries. The EU Corporation status is an administrative innovation in the field of international commerce, as is the organization of the Single Market.

When going abroad, a corporation often seeks local partners to finance the operation, to be better informed about these local markets, or to gain access to new market opportunities. A local company is called a **subsidiary** company when the parent company owns more than 50% of the shares, and an **affiliate** company when the parent owns between 20 and 50% of the equity.

It thus becomes a multi-national company (MNC) and an owner or partial owner of companies in other countries. MNCs are one category of corporate owners. Of course, a corporation can also acquire companies in its own country, thus becoming a multi-company corporation.

The French construction group **Vinci** has the largest number of subsidiaries in the world, 2659 in total. In second place is the US health and pharmaceutical company HCA Healthcare, with 2452 subsidiaries.[6] Construction and financial services are the two sectors that create the largest number of subsidiaries.

German companies are known to have many foreign subsidiaries. **Siemens AG** is a remarkable industrial holding, listing 1031 subsidiaries in its 2017 Annual Report: 129 in Germany; 519 in the EU, the CIS, and the Middle East; 165 in Americas; and 218 in Asia (including Australia).[7] These businesses belong to one of six divisions: Digital Industries (digitization and automation), Smart Infrastructure (energy systems, building, industries), Mobility (transport solutions), Siemens Advanta (unlocking digital futures service company), Siemens Healthineers (medical technology company, managed separately), Portfolio Companies (including the rest).[8]

One of Siemens's main competitors, General Electric (GE), was long organized in a similar manner. However, the leadership at some point started to lose track of the group's mission and its governance. Many consider the growing importance and profitability of its financial division, GE Capital, as creating confusion regarding the mission of GE as a leading technology and industrial group. This change in the previous industrial values and rules governing the industrial group ultimately led the group to increasingly lose business to its rivals, including Siemens. Jack Welch was CEO and Chair for 20 years before he retired in 2001. Despite owning only a tiny percentage of GE's shares, Welch, as CEO and Chair, at some point started running GE as his own company, as its virtual psychological owner. Even more than Jobs, Welch controlled all major decisions, including the appointment of board members. Having built the temple, Jack Welch ended up destroying it, or, at least, seeded and contributed to its demise. How could this happen when the company is being mentioned as exemplary in marketing, operations, strategy, finance, and HR?

Most of the stories about GE have centered around Jack Welch, the iconic CEO and Chair. This is the humanware dimension, which indeed is one of the keys to its demise. But fewer have asked questions regarding the relations between Jack Welch and his board: Where was the board, the guardian of the company's value creation capabilities and its ultimate supervisor? It does appear that the board supervisor did not dispose of the adequate hardware and software. The demise of GE that followed Jack Welch's retirement indeed finds its roots in a combination of hardware, software, and peopleware breakdowns while he was at the helm. This question has been discussed from several viewpoints. The angle we take in this book is indeed the ownership angle and that of the Board of Directors, which was unable to stop the prolonged value destruction that occurred after Welch's exit in early 2001.

5 Private Equity Ownership

Blackstone, Gemini, Apollo, Carlyle. These are all examples of private equity (PE) ownership. They are characterized by direct intervention in the companies they invest in. In developed countries private equity owns and controls, often (though not always) replacing management and imposing its own. In Asia and in less developed countries, private equity firms often take significant minority stakes, usually in partnership with local family-owned businesses. In both cases, private equity owners are driven by a clear purpose: to contribute and unleash long-run value creation. However, while the purpose is long run, the tenure of ownership in the company is more medium term, usually five years, often less, but enough to transform the companies that PE players have invested in. This creates a potential governance tension between longer-term ownership purpose (not really a direct concern for PEs, except for their reputation) and short-term tactical behavior in the owned company, fueled by the PE's impatience with getting the desired transformation started and functioning. That is also why PEs often intervene directly and assume a leading role in the companies they invest in. They know that they require the engagement of the senior leadership of the company and their motivation to succeed in their intended transformation. They also have full interest in having the company continue to operate well following their exit. Humanware is often a hands-on approach, often in a context of cost cutting and downsizing that requires maintaining engagement while taking "tough" decisions. This is tempered by the hope, if not promise, that better times lie ahead and will start soon after the rapid implementation of the tough decisions already made or about to be made.

Finally, looking at their own ownership, PE firms are usually partnerships. Their internal governance challenges are more similar to those of professional service firms than the challenges faced by their investee companies.

6 Government "Stateholder"[9]

The French government owns a 15% stake in automobile maker Renault. The State of Lower Saxony owns a 20% stake in Volkswagen AG (VAG). What is one major purpose of both governments? Ensuring jobs. Where? In the country. Therefore, Renault had no qualms closing their factory in Brussels rather than any of its factories in France. Backlash is much smaller if a foreign plant is closed. This also makes the $5 billion investment in rescuing Nissan so remarkable, for the then Renault Chairman, Louis Schweitzer, must have done a remarkable job convincing the government shareholder, which in another article we coined "stateholder" to underline its special nature. This is also why much of the car production of Volkswagen (belonging to the VAG group) has remained in Germany, when production abroad would have been more economical. The result is that VAG barely made money on the Golfs produced in Germany and Europe, most of its earnings coming from the high-end Audi and Porsche brands, as well as from the MAN truck company. The cost pressures on the Golfs must have been a major driver of the Dieselgate scandal that would cost the group billions in fines.

Temasek Holdings Private Limited ("Temasek"), the government of Singapore-owned investment holding company, owns stakes in many listed and unlisted companies inside and outside Singapore. As a state-owned entity, it is accountable to the Singapore Government who acts as the proxy for the Singaporean people. The degree to which Temasek is autonomously managed is large and surprising. It also is one of the reasons for its success. Temasek's mission statement is very clear: to be an active investor and shareholder aiming for sustainable value delivery over the long term, to act with integrity, to be forward looking, to be committed to excellence, and to strive for the advancement of its Singapore communities over several generations.[10] Its focus is very much on the economic development of the Singaporean nation and communities.

The corporate examples presented here have purposes that transcend pure money making and are, in one way or another, directed at ameliorating their respective local communities. As owner, the government typically appoints directors on the boards of the companies it owns. The extent to which the government becomes involved in the governance of these companies varies greatly, depending on the country, the type of sector (e.g., defense industries are typically governed and even managed very closely), and the issue at hand that may drive the government to suddenly become greatly engaged (e.g., when the French government gave Carlos Ghosn the ultimatum to ensure that Renault would not fall under the influence of Nissan).

Government-owned companies also share a similar software (i.e., relational) pattern in their governance: a potential conflict between policy-oriented decisions geared at their local development missions and more "political" decisions, driven more by party platforms and the ongoing politics inside and across political parties. Development decisions can greatly impact on sectors and particular economic actors.

7 Institutional Owner

GIC is the sovereign wealth fund of the Singapore nation. It was created in 1981 from surplus reserves of the Central Bank that could thus be invested at risk for the longer term to the benefit of the nation. GIC is a global long-term investor having close to US$ 800 billion in assets under management, spread globally across 40 countries. Its conduct is akin to other sovereign wealth funds, making investments internationally, and selling them. It is driven by the goal of increasing its total asset size. Its assets are owned by the Singaporean Government, acting as reserves and thus contributing to the economic stability of Singapore. These assets can be used as a buffer or shock absorber during economic downturns as was the case during the recent COVID pandemic. Second, a strong national balance sheet fosters investor confidence and enhances the monetary stability of the Singapore dollar. Finally, income from these assets can be called upon to supplement government revenues. In fact, in 2021 the annual Net Investment Returns Contribution (an official term in Singapore) contributed 18% of the annual budget of Singapore.[11]

ADIA, the Abu Dhabi Investment Authority, has a mission statement that is very similar to that of GIC, a consequence of the Abu Dhabi government benchmarking on successful sovereign wealth funds (SWFs) and deciding to import into the Gulf several of the key elements of Singapore's success story. Just like GIC, ADIA is asked to sustain the long-term prosperity of Abu Dhabi by growing its capital through a disciplined investment process reflecting ADIA's cultural values: prudent innovation, disciplined execution, and effective collaboration.[12] ADIA does not communicate the value of its portfolio. It is estimated at around one trillion dollars, exceeding that of GIC. This is also the result of the substantial contributions to the fund of ADNOC, the national oil company.

The mission of a sovereign wealth fund (SWF) is to invest abroad and ensure financial stability for the country. How much should the government directly manage, and how much should it delegate to the Board and the CEO, with the government just supervising and monitoring?

Berkshire Hathaway (BH), the PE founded by Warren Buffett, is a "conglomerate holding company" that over the years has created value through strategic long-term investments in a selected number of companies. Berkshire's "hardware" has been defined by Warren Buffett. The approach finds its roots in what is called "value investing." The names associated with the field are Benjamin Graham, Philip Fisher, and David Dodd, both Graham and Dodd being Buffett's teachers when he enrolled at Columbia Business School.

BH is unusual in that it purchases 100% of companies that then become its subsidiaries while also investing in market securities. Buffett generally invests in companies that are undervalued in the stock market relative to their potential, and then waits for the undervaluation to disappear. When successful, these investments provide BH with a premium over the market. Quality of management is another key factor that is a must for BH to invest in a company, and matters much more to Buffett than the quality of governance exercised by the board. BH has owned and owns businesses across a wide array of sectors, ranging from confectionery to retail, railroads, home furnishings, encyclopedias, manufacturers of vacuum cleaners, jewelry sales, manufacturing and distribution of uniforms, as well as several regional electric and gas utilities. It has over the years been remarkably successful. As a result, it has come to be seen as a market maker, if not a transparent market "insider," many investors following BH in its investments. This of course reduces BH's downside investment risk, at least in the short run.

BlackRock, Inc. ("BlackRock") is the world's largest asset management company. Its asset value at the end of 2021 was just under US$ 10 trillion. It was founded in 1988 as a risk management and fixed income institutional asset manager. BlackRock owns shares in a large swath of listed companies around the globe. As an owner, BlackRock is mostly a "passive investor." It is a fiduciary investing clients' money. Most clients are pension funds, allowing the company to take a long-term view. However, it ought to pay attention to a wave of withdrawals at a time when equity prices are low, for it would stand to lose on many investments.

BlackRock does not take or demand board seats in investee companies. It typically "votes" by buying or selling shares without getting involved at board level or influencing the choice of company management in its investments. Its global influence is often regarded as enormous, being referred to as the world's largest shadow bank. However, its business being fiduciary ownership of assets on behalf of investors, its ownership passivity makes its actual influence less than the size of the assets it has under its "management." Many of its clients being pension funds, it can be regarded as a manager of "the people's money."

The common feature of all these players (SWFs, BH, BlackRock, etc.) is that they try not to directly intervene in their investment companies. They mostly reduce their governance risk through diversification. These funds share a common purpose: to create value for the long run by wealth accumulation. They also share the same software pattern: a professional asset management environment and culture that stresses the skills of investment selection and performance, supported by well-honed investment practices, which are part of the hardware of these investment houses. Financial incentives based on objective results are key performance metrics that motivate these finance specialists, so that leadership does not need to pay great attention to human relational aspects—even though these can never be ignored—but more to ensuring that the incentives are correctly computed and fairly implemented.

Institutional ownership of publicly listed companies may lead to no governance intervention by these owners (e.g., BlackRock) or to only occasional monitoring (e.g., Berkshire Hathaway). The latter is closer to family governance with sizable "skin in the game" and long-term horizon. The former is characterized by shorter horizons and regular communications to investors aimed at avoiding substantial withdrawals by investors. The combination of shorter-term horizons and lack of direct involvement at board level creates space for the CEO. The way Larry Fink occupies this space is through his annual letter to CEOs where he shares with them what BlackRock's clients value. If CEOs steer companies in this direction more investments should come their way. Given the many investment funds BlackRock manages, Fink's statements are credible. BlackRock clients might also allocate money across various BlackRock funds, representing no loss to the group. Only withdrawals away from BlackRock to competitor funds would be costly. Interestingly, Fink's letter is addressed to CEOs and not to Boards, reflecting the standing of boards in the US.

8 Conclusion

In this short overview we aimed to begin a process of re-evaluation in the reader's mind of the importance of ownership, its relationship with the corporation, and what responsible and effective ownership consists of and might contribute.

This introduction was also meant to show that ownership is not monolithic and, on the contrary, presents wide diversity. The reader is invited to keep this diversity in mind when we refer to "owners" in the book.

Our examples further attest that owners often hold several corporate roles: founder, CEO, Chairman of the board, director, or executive with general management, divisional, or functional responsibilities. These other corporate roles naturally have a bearing on the exercise of the ownership role. In terms introduced in this introduction, this is where and why good governance hardware and software are essential to induce the governance humanware to function at its best.

As this book progresses, different aspects of ownership and their relation to governance will be addressed. Models and frameworks will be presented in subsequent chapters with the goal of supporting ownership and governance effectiveness, and hopefully moving to excellence in this practice.

In the third and final part of the book, we will return to ownership stories, indicating that corporate ownership is dynamic and that owners typically live through a few ownership experiences, not all positive. Ownership is also about learning from these experiences and turning errors into future success. Steve Jobs is an excellent example of this. He returned to Apple regenerated from his forced exit and could not ignore that his behavior had largely contributed to his ousting by the board.

In the final chapter of the book, we, somewhat daringly, present our views regarding the promise ownership holds for meeting the formidable challenges the world is facing today.

We are now ready to turn to the first chapter of this book, which deals with the most defining act of corporate owners – the framing of a mission.

Notes

1. An example of this literature is *A Culture of Purpose,* written by Christoph Lueneberger and published by Jossey-Bass (2014).
2. https://www.bbc.com/news/technology-58469882.
3. https://en.wikipedia.org/wiki/Ronald_Wayne.
4. https://en.wikipedia.org/wiki/Steve_Wozniak.
5. https://en.wikipedia.org/wiki/Merck_Group.
6. https://www.investmentmonitor.ai/insights/where-are-the-global-hotspots-for-mnc-subsidiaries.

7. https://www.siemens.com/investor/pool/en/investor_relations/faq/Siemens_AR2017_ListSubsidiaries313.pdf.
8. https://new.siemens.com/global/en/company/about/businesses.html.
9. The term was coined by Robert Gogel and one of the authors during the writing of the joint article that appeared in Strategy+Business, https://www.strategy-business.com/article/00005.
10. https://www.temasek.com.sg/en/index.
11. https://www.gic.com.sg.
12. https://www.adia.ae/En/pr/2016/pdf/ADIA_2016_Review_03_Overview.pdf.

Part I

Hardware: A Value Creation Framework

2

The Primacy of an Owner's Mission

1 Primacy of the Mission

From humble beginnings and great poverty, Konosuke Matsushita founded what became **Matsushita Electric Industrial Co., Ltd**. or **Matsushita Electric**, for short. The company went through extremes of success and failure. It came close to bankruptcy and survived World War II. However, it always appeared to emerge stronger from crisis, and more resilient. In 2008, it renamed itself **Panasonic Corporation**

What energized and sustained Matsushita-san, and the company he founded, is an inspiring mission that carried it to the present day. In a 1932 speech to employees, Matsushita announced the guiding principle for the company as follows: "The mission of a manufacturer is to overcome poverty by producing an abundant supply of goods. Our mission as a manufacturer is to create material abundance by providing goods as plentifully and inexpensively as tap water. This is how we can banish poverty, bring happiness to people's lives, and make this world a better place."[1] This mission was expanded on in his 1933 Presidential Message and received two additions in 1937. It remains the company's abiding mission (Fig. 2.1).

Missions such as Matsushita Electric's are important for several reasons:

- They reflect an owner's driving forces and objectives.
- They typically enounce deeply held behavioral principles (values or virtues) that govern how employees and those associated with the company will behave. They often involve a set of moral principles and beliefs or accepted

M. Massa et al., *Value Creation for Owners and Directors*,
https://doi.org/10.1007/978-3-031-19726-0_2

Contribution to Society

We will conduct ourselves at all times in accordance with the Basic Management Objective, faithfully fulfilling our responsibilities as industrialists to the communities in which we operate.

Fairness and Honesty

We will be fair and honest in all our business dealings and personal conduct. No matter how talented and knowledgeable we may be, without personal integrity, we can neither earn the respect of others, nor enhance our own self-respect.

Cooperation and Team Spirit

We will pool our abilities to accomplish our shared goals. No matter how talented we are as individuals, without cooperation and team spirit we will be a company in name only.

Untiring Effort for Improvement

We will strive constantly to improve our ability to contribute to society through our business activities. Only through this untiring effort can we fulfill our Basic Management Objective and help to realize lasting peace and prosperity.

Courtesy and Humility

We will always be cordial and modest, respecting the rights and needs of others in order to strengthen healthy social relationships and improve the quality of life in our communities.

Adaptability

We will continually adapt our thinking and behavior to meet the ever-changing conditions around us, taking care to act in harmony with nature to ensure progress and success in our endeavors.

Gratitude

We will act out of a sense of gratitude for all the benefits we have received, confident that this attitude will be a source of unbounded joy and vitality, enabling us to overcome any obstacles we encounter.

Fig. 2.1 The Mission of Matsushita Electric – The Seven Principles (https://www.panasonic.com/global/corporate/management/code-of-conduct/chapter-1.html). Source: Panasonic

behavioral standards for all those closely associated with the firm. In fact, they are a description of the business philosophy of the firm.
- They include the owner's long-term value and dividend expectations as well as their desires concerning social or local developments.
- They act as a North Star for consistent decision making regarding the governance of the firm.
- They bind people together at an emotional and even spiritual level, providing a motivation beyond the merely economic, and creating a community driven by and committed to a shared purpose – to what French philosopher Rousseau called a "social contract."

A company's mission will affect the actions taken by owners, Boards, CEOs, and employees. Importantly, the mission is a profound statement of the owners' perception of the value to be created by the business and communicates the owners' expectations regarding the actions to be undertaken by the company's members at all levels of the organization to realize this value.

Drucker stated this as well, clearly and succinctly: "*Asked what a business is, the typical businessman is likely to answer, 'An organization to make a profit.' The typical economist is likely to give the same answer. This answer is not only false, it is irrelevant.... To know what a business is, we have to start with its purpose. Its purpose must lie outside of the business itself. In fact, it must lie in society since business enterprise is an organ of society. There is only one valid definition of business purpose: to create a customer.*"[2] All great companies confront the public with their mission statement, from the first contact with their website to the reminders of their owners and the discussions on key strategic topics in boards and management meetings.

When we refer to *mission*, we of the defining statement for what the firm should do and deliver to its stakeholders and, beyond them, to society. Liberal capitalism leaves this great privilege to the owner-founder or founders. It is likely to be their most creative act, and their most important one. Subsequent owners will inherit the privilege. They will alter the mission framed by their predecessors as needed by changing owner preferences and contexts. In later chapters, we will see how other stakeholders (such as CEOs) may—rightly or wrongly—collaborate to trigger a redefinition of a company's mission statement. But, in an owner-led firm, the privilege remains with the owner, not with the stakeholders. A caveat applies concerning government authorities, as they set the context for a business. Through laws and regulations, government may lead owners to alter their mission, or to pursue it in another country.

The mission statement defines which part of society or the world the owners wish to impact and contribute to. As long as the company is owner-led, the mission may be recrafted by owner founders, or by subsequent owners. Identifiable ownership allows companies to change their mission more easily – and with much less friction and contest – than companies with a diffuse ownership. This provides owner-led firms with an agility not shared by "market-led" firms, which becomes a competitive advantage particularly in turbulent conditions.

2 Owner's Mission and the Definition of Value

What is critical to understand is that the *mission statement defines value in an owner-led company*: value creation becomes defined as progress on the mission. We quote Drucker again: *"Defining the purpose and mission of the business is difficult, painful, and risky. But it alone enables a business to set objectives, to develop strategies, to concentrate its resources, and to go to work. It alone enables a business to be managed for performance."*[3] Mission is the owner's privilege, the key entrepreneurial act. It is at the root of what distinguishes publicly listed companies from owner-founded and owner-led ones.

Singaporean Temasek's traditional mission was local economic development. This views value very differently from Singapore's GIC whose mission is to secure Singapore's financial future, and which is thus focused on long-term portfolio value. A philanthropic mission such as the Tata Group results in its owners pursuing value drivers that differ radically from the choices made by a diversified financial institution such as BlackRock. Family owners whose mission is more focused around longer-term societal legacy—like the Hoffmann and Solvay families—will take different decisions from owners whose mission is personal wealth and who will be looking to sell their venture after ensuring its success. Value is the fulfillment of the mission. This point is both critical and defining. It implies that the same set of actions and the same results may be "value creating" for some owners and "value destroying" for others.

In other words, and unlike in public markets, value in owner-led firms is in the eyes of the beholder. Like beauty, it is subjective and means different things to different owners, depending on the mission they have committed themselves to. Corporate finance theory values a firm by discounting a business's future expected cash flows. This provides a number, even a relatively objective one. However, when turning to value generated by an owner-led firm, this number has to be interpreted in light of the mission defined by its owners. Another corollary is that the same business has different values for distinct owners, allowing for arbitrage and trade, after which both owners are better off.

Understanding the connection between an owner's mission, the perception of value, and the evaluation of value creating actions is of fundamental importance. Yet, most treatments of corporate finance or strategy miss the point that different owners will value a corporation differently, depending on the mission they espouse. Put another way, differences in owner objectives lead to different actions, and hence different future expected cash flows. In this chapter, we essentially focus on the owners' mission and leave for later chapters how value creation is pursued and achieved.

Let us examine **Temasek Holdings Private Limited** (Temasek). Temasek's mission is shown in Fig. 2.2. Temasek's major investee companies include Singapore Telecommunications (of which Temasek owns 52%), Singapore

Temasek is an active investor and shareholder

- We deliver sustainable value over the long term.
- Our portfolio companies are guided and managed by their respective boards and management; we do not direct their business decisions or operations.

Temasek is a forward-looking institution

- We act with integrity and are committed to the pursuit of excellence.
- As an institution and as individuals, we act with integrity and are guided by our Temasek values.
- We foster an ownership culture which puts institution above individual, emphasizes long term over short term, and aligns employee and shareholder interests.

Temasek is a trusted steward

- We strive for the advancement of our communities across generations.
- Temasek is a responsible corporate citizen. We engage our communities based on the principles of sustainability and good governance.
- We support community programs that focus on building people, building communities, building capabilities, and rebuilding lives in Singapore and beyond.
- Under the Singapore Constitution, Temasek has a responsibility to safeguard its past reserves.

Fig. 2.2 The mission of Temasek – extract from The Temasek Charter (https://www.temasek.com.sg/en/who-we-are/our-purpose). Source: Temasek

Airlines (56%), and DBS (29%). As a founder and major shareholder in these companies, Temasek's mission directs its portfolio companies. The strategies and actions taken by these companies align with the pursuit of Singapore's long-term economic development. Temasek also pursues another mission, which it states as follows: "*We believe in sharing our successes with our communities. With Temasek Foundation overseeing 19 philanthropic endowments, we have touched 900,000 lives across Asia and Singapore through our community work.*"[4] Temasek's mission is to foster the development of its companies, but also to support the development and well-being of Singapore's citizens.

GIC, like Temasek, is 100% owned by the Singapore Government. Its mission is, however, very different: it is tasked with managing Singapore's foreign reserves (shown in Fig. 2.3). GIC's mission leads it to view value differently from Temasek.

Temasek's nation-building mission results in investments that are geared to the long-term development of Singapore. DBS, a Temasek investee company, was incorporated in 1968. Mirroring Temasek's mission, the bank's initial focus was to provide loans and financial assistance to the manufacturing and processing industries in Singapore. The bank contributed to the general development of the economy by supporting various projects of the Urban Renewal Programme, as well as various tourist schemes. It then aimed to be a different bank, providing financial services that other commercial banks did not offer. It aimed to become a bank for our times.

In 2012 Temasek rescued Olam Commodities, a listed commodities trader, from near bankruptcy by underwriting a US$ 750 million bond issue. This

GIC is a global long-term investor with well over US$ 100 billion in assets in over 40 countries worldwide. We work to secure Singapore's financial future by investing across a range of asset classes in the public and private markets.

We manage most of the government's financial assets and invest for the long term to preserve and enhance the international purchasing power of the funds placed under our management.

The reserves are a critical resource for Singapore's future. First, they are a valuable buffer or shock absorber during downturns. Second, a strong national balance sheet fosters investor confidence and enhances the stability of the Singapore dollar. Third, income from the reserves supplements government revenues.

Fig. 2.3 The mission of Singapore's GIC (https://www.gic.com.sg/about-gic/purpose-of-funds/). Source: GIC

was entirely consistent with Temasek's mission of local development as it helped to fend off market speculation, helping a global food and agricultural group based in Singapore.

GIC, with its mission to preserve the country's reserves, views value through a different lens. It does not prop up companies in distress. GIC is one of the world's largest sovereign wealth funds (SWFs), managing around $390 billion, according to the Sovereign Wealth Fund Institute.[5] It is similar to other SWFs, buying and selling local and international investments frequently in seeking to increase its total asset size and contribute to the financial stability of its country.

Missions are long-term objectives but never cast in stone. Evolving contexts and shifting owner priorities lead to changes in mission. As Singapore developed economically, the government and the country increasingly looked outwards. Temasek and its investee companies followed this expansion. DBS entered Asian markets (ASEAN, China, and India), allowing it in 2019 and 2021 to be recognized by *Euromoney* as the "World's Best Bank." A relentless focus on development was already in its DNA. It proved a distinguishing characteristic when the bank ventured abroad, and it is continuing to serve Singapore's position in today's world.

We note that we are making no judgment here on the choice of mission or on one value perspective being better than another. Citi, Temasek, BlackRock, and GIC all have a purpose. What we did seek to show is how these firms all view value in different ways, corresponding to the distinct framings of their respective missions.

3 Mission and the Family Firm

A key focus of this book is on family-owned or family-controlled businesses. Agreement on a clearly articulated mission is typically the cornerstone of these successes. It also acts as a strong glue among family members and across generations.

Interbrew, now Anheuser-Busch InBev SA/NV (and often referred to in this book by its original name "Interbrew"), was founded in 1366 in Belgium. The incredible transition from having a global beer market share of 1.3% and occupying the 17th position in the 1994 global beer rankings to becoming the world's largest beer company will be presented and analyzed in Chaps. 2 and 3. In this section, we show how Interbrew's three owning families started this transition by agreeing on a shared mission that shaped the families' views on value creation and that united them in their quest over recent decades to the top of their industry.

At the end of the 1980s, a younger generation had taken the leadership of the three owning Interbrew family groups, having in 1987 merged the two major Belgian beer companies and brands, Stella Artois and Piedboeuf/Jupiler, to form Interbrew. They represented hundreds of family shareholders, proud of their traditional brewing heritage. The example of Heineken's worldwide success, achieved with a green bottle (heresy for the Belgians) and a single brand (Heineken), had, however, cast a large shadow on this heritage. As a result of mergers and acquisitions they had gained reasonable scale, but were also clear that they now had to confront a major choice: What was going to be their mission as owning families of Interbrew going forward, and how were they going to meet the global competition coming from such formidable competitors as Heineken and Anheuser-Busch? Was the battle primarily about creating long-term value for the family, extending the legacy and thus competing globally? Or should the family continue to take pride in providing jobs and economic development for their local communities, and reasonable and stable dividends for the family shareholders?

The leaders of the three founding family branches discussed among themselves and also with their family members. They reached a clear conclusion that the primary drivers for their unity were long-term ownership value creation and control over dividends from Interbrew, and that these could be substantial if the firm was well governed. Cohesiveness of the many shareholders in the face of major strategic change was essential, for the family leaders knew that this unity would be tested by their growth plan which promised value, but also greater risk associated with strategic acquisitions and mergers.

It took considerable discussion to bring the families to buy into the transforming plan proposed by the representatives of the three family branches. But in the end, family shareholders agreed to set up a holding company in the form of a Dutch foundation, called Stichting Interbrew. A Stichting is a Dutch legal entity – specific to Dutch law – that allows owners to agree to a joint purpose for a specific time. The Stichting pursues a clear purpose, has no owners, and is governed by a board, called "het Bestuur," which is Dutch for "Management." The Management are given the task to pursue the foundation's purpose. They do so in full autonomy of the owners that set up the Stichting. Interbrew shareholders kept the rights to ultimately receive the dividends that flowed to the holding company, but for 20 years, the Management, composed of members of the three founding families, were given all rights to exercise the ownership, including the voting rights that the Stichting had in Interbrew. This was considered necessary in view of the rocky road they planned to travel, which was also a break from the past. The family shareholders were reassured by the commitment of the Management to always act in unity: each of the three family branches thus held a veto right on all decisions, via their representative in the Management. This would also avoid any blame coming from any branch and would induce considerable discussions in the Management and in the branches, particularly about how the three members of the Management were quite different and complementary.

A Stichting would in other countries be called a financial holding company. It is a perfect instrument with which to implement an ownership mission. A Stichting also provides protection from unwanted take-overs, family shareholders being assured that they will not be robbed of the expected longer-term benefits they are going for. So a mission statement ought to be seen as more than a long-term vision or quest; it also contains or is accompanied by—as the Matsushita Electric example attests—statements on **values** that bind owners and executives, and particular **"rules of the game"**—like the establishment of the Stichting and the unanimity rule for decision making at the board of the Stichting—that will guide all in the pursuit and eventual accomplishment of the mission. In the remainder of the book we will refer to "mission" in this larger sense, including values and rules of the game that bind the framers of the mission.

Having thus framed the mission in a very clear manner, the Stichting gave the board of Interbrew the autonomy to pursue the mission. The Interbrew board soon decided that the operationalization of their mission required them to become a dominant global beer company, which they understood as being in the top 3. This, at the time, meant becoming No 3 after Anheuser-Bush and Heineken. The slogan that was devised to reach this goal was the famous "the world's local brewer," which immediately set Interbrew apart from its rivals Heineken and Anheuser-Busch, who both aimed to conquer the world with a single brand.

The first major acquisitions were Labatt in Canada and Bass and Whitbread in the UK. These provided the Belgian group with excellent international managers. These were tasked with creating and implementing a growth strategy based on the acquisition and integration of new "local" brands, which could then be distributed through Interbrew's existing markets. This would both offer more value to their clients (pubs, restaurants, and retailers) and lower supply costs. Through these acquisitions, Interbrew indeed grew in the global beer rankings. This came along with share and dividend growth. The family shareholders had no need to interfere with decisions made by the Interbrew board and its management, as the mandate given to it by the Stichting was clear and well executed.

The pursuit of this strategy would lead Interbrew to eventually become the largest beer company in the world, under the name AB InBev: an equity partnership with the three owners of the Brazilian investment firm 3G Capital, owner of **AmBev**, the South American beer company with great presence in Argentina and Brazil. The Belgian and the Brazilian owners agreed to consolidate their European and South American beer assets into a single holding company, denoted **InBev** (short for **In**terbrew and Am**Bev**). Ambev then acquired Anheuser-Busch to become **AB InBev**. This exceeded the wildest dreams of the Interbrew founders: they had, with their Brazilian partners, become the worldwide consolidator in the beer industry. The acquisition of **SABMiller** in 2015 was "the cherry on their cake."

It is important to note that full control—an obsession of many family owners—was not part of the Interbrew mission. The Interbrew Stichting, as of December 31, 2019, owned 33.84% of AB InBev shares. Family shareholders were thought to own a further 16.4% through other vehicles. Throughout the journey, the mission has remained focused on long-term value creation and sustained dividends. Control was focused on the mission, which was the key to value creation.

Control of long-term ownership and dividends are common drivers in family firms, as well as the desire to leave a legacy. **Solvay S.A.** (Solvay) is a US$ 10 billion chemicals company, headquartered in Brussels, the birthplace of its two founders, Ernest and Albert Solvay. From the beginning, equity was provided by their father, Alexandre Solvay, and business relatives or in-laws. Their more than 2500 shareholding descendants are grouped into family branches according to the two original founders, and the four original funders: Pirmez, Nelis, Lambert, and Sabatier.[6] Interestingly, only two branches emanate from blood descendants of the founding brothers, which is rarely mentioned. The early equity partnership has led to the practice of speaking about "the Solvay families" as if all were blood descendants. The "shared" ownership seems to have morphed all of them into a single family, which particularly the non-Solvay branches enjoy given the enormous contribution Ernest Solvay and his younger brother made to Belgium. From its inception, control by the founding families was emphasized, including in management. In 1967, 100 years after the opening of the first Solvay plant, all six managers were still family members. Ernest Solvay referred to this as "remaining 'amongst ourselves', a sensible choice."[7]

It was only in 1967 that Solvay listed on the Brussels Stock Exchange. Initially, 80% of the voting share class of shares was in family hands and subject to restrictions. In 1983, the Solvay families created a holding company, Solvac, which was also listed on the Brussels Exchange. For tax reasons, Solvac shares are not open to institutional investors, only to individuals. Those family members who wish to buy Solvay shares can do so directly through purchases of Solvay stock or indirectly through purchases of Solvac. Both Solvay and Solvac contribute to the family retaining control over Solvay. The fact that both Solvay and Solvac are listed provides family shareholders with a transparent valuation of their investments and with liquidity options.

The mission pursued by the Solvay families is stated clearly for all to see: "*Ensure sustained long term ownership value as a world leader in sustainable chemistry, while proposing dividend increases at the Shareholders' Meeting whenever possible, and as far as possible, but without ever reducing it. To ensure the legacy of the founder by having the family retain control over Solvay.*"[8]

Solvay disclosure statements delineate that Solvac owns (at least) 30% of Solvay and that Solvac has approximately 13,000 shareholders. Among them, more than 2000 are related to the founding families of Solvay and Solvac. Together, the latter hold approximately 77% of the shares of Solvac."[9]

The mission has impacted major value-related decisions. For many years Solvay had two divisions: chemicals and pharmaceuticals. By the year 2000, the family was confronting several options: to retain both divisions, sell one off, agree to lose control, or even sell the entire company. A view on value without any concern for the industrial legacy ("sustainable chemistry") might have actively considered a complete sale of Solvay. However, the family mission, focused on maintaining the family legacy as an industrial company, drove the choice in another direction. The company sold its pharmaceutical division in 2009 for euro 4.5 billion to Abbott Labs. The pharma division was in any case considered too small to thrive and hence would be unlikely to contribute to sustainable value creation. Nor was there any real synergy between the two divisions.

Two years later the proceeds from selling the pharma division were used to purchase the French chemicals company Rhodia for euro 3.4 billion. This allowed the family to return to its roots in industrial chemistry, Rhodia being the child of the former French chemical giant Rhône-Poulenc. Through the acquisition Solvay could continue tracing its global legacy in chemicals.

The **Tata Group** is India's largest business conglomerate. It is the owner of over 100 operating companies with combined revenues as well as a market capitalization (for the 28 publicly listed companies that the Group controls) exceeding US$ 110 billion. Its major businesses are software, steel, power generation and distribution, auto, beverages (tea and coffee), watches, and financial services.

Philanthropic trusts, called Tata Trusts, own 65.9% of Tata Sons, the holding company of the Tata Group. The mission of the Trusts is explicitly one of charity and direct philanthropy, which they conduct with the dividends, provided as income to the Trusts. The trusts are focused on "education, health, rural livelihoods and communities, arts, crafts and culture, and civil society and governance."[10] Their mission also shapes how Tata Group companies, and even more so board members and executives of the Group, behave, determining which business ventures the Group embarks on. Although each Tata company or enterprise operates independently under the guidance and supervision of its own Board of Directors, the prevailing governance philosophy for the Group bears a strong imprint from the Trusts, as a former Chairman of the Group observed:

> *The Tata philosophy of management has always been, and is today more than ever, that corporate enterprises must be managed not merely in the interests of their owners, but equally in those of their employees, of the consumers of their products, of the local community and finally of the country as a whole.* JRD Tata, 1973.[11]

This is a generic and remarkably open statement that privileges stakeholder interests. Without providing full clarity as to how these various interests might best be balanced and prioritized, the statement also offers opportunity for misalignment and tensions with both the 65.9% majority shareholder, Tata Trusts, and the 34.1% minority shareholders. Even within the board of the Tata Group there is likely to be disagreement on the mission to be pursued. We will see later how such ambiguity in mission statement allows for frictions and cracks among shareholders and group leaders, which ultimately leads to value destruction.

4 Mission, Values, Value Creation, and Performance Yardsticks

A mission defines value, which in turn yields yardsticks by which owners judge corporate performance. A firm is creating value when it makes progress on its mission. This requires the alignment of the company's goals with the owner's mission and with any objectives that render the mission more concrete. The vocabulary—such as mission—here has a precise meaning that is important and distinct from more casual use of these words. Governance is about words and their meaning should be commonly understood.

We define as goals the way the company aims to progress operationally on its mission and the accomplishment of objectives specified by the owner. This leads us to further define the meaning of "value creation" in an owner-led company as well as the ways to achieve this:

> ***Value creation*** *is defined as making progress on the* ***mission*** *and* ***the specific objectives*** *set by the owner. To enable such progress, the company, as represented by its board and senior management, will formulate a set of* ***goals*** *whose pursuit operationalizes value creation.*
>
> ***A value-creating firm*** *is always an* ***"aligned"*** *firm: it is one where other stakeholder objectives do not impede the mission, and where ideally stakeholders are consistently aligned with the mission, which is then faithfully and flawlessly executed.*
>
> *In contrast, the lack of alignment of stakeholders with the mission invariably leads to* ***value destruction*** *relative to the situation where these stakeholders would be aligned.*

Board members and senior management will thus see to it that this value impairment is recognized and accepted by both owners and stakeholders. To the extent possible, the resulting loss and potential frictions from misalignment will be mitigated and minimized.

Strategies approved by the Board and deployed by the CEO should not result in dilemmas since they must align with the mission statement. Strategies can then be fully committed to and pursued, resulting in effective value creation. Friction with shareholders will be much reduced since boards and managers will remind shareholders of the mission that is driving decision-making at governance and executive level.

An important question that arises is how goals are declined through the organization. The typical tool here is to set **Key Performance Indicators** (KPIs)—or as is more common these days OKRs, **Objectives and Key Results**. The point that we wish to stress here is that these KPIs or OKRs must be set to be aligned with the goals, if they are not the goals themselves. It is typically through their KPIs or OKRs that units and teams link and connect with value creation. KPIs and OKRs that are not aligned with the goals and with the mission statement trigger value destruction.

Alcopa, a family-owned Belgian-based investment company, has roots in the automotive sector, starting with two-wheelers. The family mission and governance agreements are formalized in a 60-page family charter. Dominique Moorkens, former Chairman, comments on such an exercise as follows: "*It was a very enriching reflection exercise, and each member of the family can use the charter as a source of inspiration and a framework for reflection for the future. The process itself turned out to be more important than the final document produced, as it resulted in generating a wider consensus and induced a greater maturity* *about the business within the family. All topics relating to family organization and management were addressed and discussions on these then stopped.*"[12]

5 Evolution of the Mission and Impact on Value Creation

A company's mission is not fixed and evolves with **context**, both internal and external. As Singapore's wealth grew, it began exerting growing influence within ASEAN and, beyond, Asia. Temasek's nation-building mission expanded to include having its investee companies succeed in neighboring countries. As a result, DBS began its successful expansion in ASEAN, China, and India.

In family-controlled firms, as ownership goes through different generations, the mission typically evolves and changes. In such firms, generational succession is often marked by a change in mission. We illustrate this with an episode out of India's iconic industrial group.

The Tata Group was founded in 1868 by Jamsetji Tata. The mission he crafted for the Group was for India to achieve freedom from the British through industrial self-reliance. Jamsetji wrote, "*The strength to defend freedom can itself only come from widespread industrialization and the infusion of modern science and technology into the country's economic life.*" While partly philanthropic, the nation-building objective Jamsetji set for Tata was for him primary. Jamsetji's view on philanthropy was that it was best "*to help on the regeneration of India by helping those elements of Indian life, which displayed symptoms of vitality, and leaving the rest to take care of themselves.*"[13] Jamsetji expanded on this when he further wrote that "*What advances a nation or a community is not so much to prop up its weakest and most helpless members but to lift up the best and the most gifted, so as to make them of the greatest service to the country.*"[14]

Jamsetji thus set the tone for his immediate successors to build India's elite educational, health, research, and cultural institutions. These are numerous and now include the Indian Institute of Science, the Tata Institute of Fundamental Research, the Tata Institute of Social Sciences, and the National Institute of Advanced Studies. Thus, while Jamsetji had a strong philanthropic mindset, he would hardly have imagined that his sons would bequeath the shares they inherited in Tata Sons to philanthropic trusts. Even then, it was only later, with the Chairmanship of Ratan Tata that started in 1990, that the Tata Trusts and hence its holding company, Tata Sons, framed their mission explicitly as one of charity and direct philanthropy. The priorities of institution building and the development of the nation's elites, framed as the mission of the Tata Trusts by Jamsetji, had been largely downgraded. Each succeeding generation seemed to further change the mission.

By 2012, the last year of Ratan Tata's chairmanship, the Tata Group was increasingly dependent on the success of only one company, its software services firm TCS. Through TCS, India had established itself as a leader in software services, successfully implementing the nation-building mission set out by the founders. Many other Tata Group companies were draining its profitability. In July 2014, an analyst pointed this out: "Line up the group in terms of value and net worth, and all you will see is software. If there was no TCS, there may be no Tata Group worth speaking about."[15] The Tata Group had pursued its original mission, but its philanthropic mission seems to have diffused in the Group, resulting in severely unprofitable companies. This, with time, created substantial concern for the Tata Trusts: Would they still be able to fund their philanthropic activities? A change in the original mission pursued by the Group had led to a situation that was no longer sustainable, and a realignment of its activities was urgently needed. Long-term ownership value has become a new mission joined with the traditional philanthropic mission.

Elon Musk is said to contribute forcefully to solutions for climate change. The rise of his companies has been nothing less than spectacular. Tesla had, until 2016, the mission "*to accelerate the world's transition to sustainable transport.*" Indeed, in 2020 Tesla was the company that sold the largest number of electric vehicles in the world. This is a remarkable achievement, coming from an entrepreneur who bought a former underperforming GM plant to produce electric vehicles that are now leading the market.

In 2016 a single word was changed in the Tesla mission statement: it now was devoted "*to accelerate the world's transition to sustainable **energy**.*"[16] This change was presumably made to justify the acquisition of *Solar City*, which was loss making and absorbed into Tesla, which bid $2.6 billion for it. Some shareholders really did not appreciate this move. The members of the Tesla Board of Directors had already settled their lawsuit with the plaintiffs for $60 million.[17] This allowed the plaintiffs to direct their grievances at Elon Musk alone, for breaching his fiduciary duties while on the Tesla board, and for pressuring the Directors to accept the proposed acquisition which they felt was not in Tesla's interest.

This was not the first time Musk became known for difficulties in the governance of his businesses. In 2018, he settled a lawsuit brought by the SEC claiming communications fraud via tweets. The settlement required Musk to step down as Chairman for a period of three years and to agree to governance reform with the appointment of independent directors. It also included financial payments by Tesla and Musk.[18] The lawsuit underlines the difficulty of changing mission statements with public companies, for some shareholders will typically feel slighted. This is why it is important that such changes be done following due process, which demands a vote at the General Shareholder Meeting. The rather light-hearted approach of Musk toward governance is well documented, and the defense at one of his recent legal proceedings confirmed this. One of the elements presented in Musk's defense is that he does not like to be CEO, preferring to spend his time on design and engineering.[19] Then, no one obliges Musk to assume a CEO or board role, particularly after having been obliged to step down as Chair.

The latter example revealed how changing business environments contribute to mission change. The second point to emphasize from these examples is the contrast of changing mission statements in owner-led businesses as compared with publicly listed ones. One area which illustrates this regularly is the domain of state-owned enterprise. Political changes and new governments like to change the mission of large national companies. Such changes may even appear on their electoral platform. This then leads to value destruction, particularly in industrial companies where it takes some time for the organization to align with the mission change. Therefore, state-owned enterprises are best protected through ownership structures like sovereign wealth funds, who act as owners of the enterprises in their portfolio on behalf of their sovereign nations and provide protection to the portfolio companies from sudden political winds or newly elected officials eager to show all their mettle quickly.

Publicly listed firms face difficulties too when the mission needs to change, as the example of Tesla illustrates. Indeed, minority shareholders in disagreement with the mission change will argue with the court that their interests have been harmed. Indeed, as we argued in this chapter, the point has standing.

6 Executing the Wrong Mission: Dirty Business at Volkswagen or How Excellent Execution Can Destroy a Lot of Value

Not being sufficiently clear about the mission or being insufficiently aligned with it creates what we would call **governance risk**. This entails the possibility of disagreements and conflicts about the mission, or implicitly or explicitly pursuing the wrong mission. Governance risk is distinct from business risk in that the issue is not a poor execution of business activities. Being rightly executed and as the management intends, the point is that the overall direction of business activities is wrong or that directions are pursued by different parts of the business but not aligned with the mission. Both cases result in **value destruction.**

In this section we will develop an example of mission divergence that led to a corporate tragedy of human deaths, value destruction, and remarkably cynical business leadership. The episode is now referred to as **Dieselgate** and involves the powerful **Volkswagen AG** group (VAG). We present it to underline how mission disagreements should be considered **pathological** in that a company can only execute a single mission, and not two or more missions that furthermore are at odds with each other. The pathology can take several forms: owners disagreeing leading to a gradual standstill of the company or a condition where goals and strategies of the company are not aligned with the mission. In some pathological cases, there is no written mission, facilitating the emergence of the pathology. Or the mission is pursued without being backed up by goals or strategies, or verified by sound governance processes.

On December 10, 2015, Hans Dieter Pötsch, VAG Chairman, released a statement admitting that the company had placed "defeat devices" in the engines equipping hundreds of thousands of its cars. The devices allowed the cars to meet US emission standards in testing, even though their actual emissions in normal driving substantially exceeded regulatory limits. It was a clear case of cheating by the company, rendered worse by the prolonged and shameless denial by VAG executives and VW's management that cheating had occurred. When finally confronted with evidence, VW management had to admit to the US Department of Justice that over 11 million diesel engines worldwide had been fitted with the cheating devices. Execution had been superb, but the red line had been crossed in each of these 11 million cars.

Top executives were charged with serious fraud, several of them doing time in US jails. The affair cost the company more than €30 billion in fines and compensation in the US alone, where only 500,000 sold cars were equipped with the device. This was certainly a small fraction of total sales. If justice in Europe were to apply the same level of fines, VW would most likely be in bankruptcy. This massive fraud will involve penal charges due to the estimated annual deaths (2500 a year in Europe alone) resulting from the pollution generated by the dirty engines.[20]

The legal and ethical question is to identify who was responsible for this disastrous chain of events. Was the VW board responsible for the maleficence? Was it the top management of VW that was the cause of this fiasco (CEO Martin Winterkorn's lawsuit in Germany has started)? Did middle managers act improperly without the top management being aware of such criminal behavior (several have indeed been indicted and convicted since)? Or could it be that the owners were at the root of this tragedy? From a legal governance viewpoint, the responsibility sits clearly with the board since that is where governance places the responsibility for all the firm's activities, shareholders bearing no responsibility, unless they are members of the board or participate in management.

Ferdinand Piëch, then Chairman of VW, later claimed that members of the VW board knew, at an early stage, about VW's "cheating." His allegation, however, was denied by other board members eager to requalify this as a fraud by management, kept from their knowledge. Hence, they should not be charged for this industrial crime, the neglect being on the management side. As it happens, Piëch was a VAG board member during most of the period.

Whatever the truth behind the allegation, VW owners, the VW supervisory board, and its management board jointly bear a large portion of responsibility in this affair, being at least complicit in the wrongdoing, allowing it, or inducing it. Dieselgate might be described as a near perfect alignment by owners, boards, senior executives, and middle managers with the execution of an indeed toxic mission. Behind this conclusion lies a possibly more fundamental problem: the tensions and disagreements affecting VW's majority shareholders, which gradually diffused within the firm. VW's voting shareholding is shown in Fig. 2.4.

The major shareholder groups indeed did not align on a shared mission and pursued different missions. Most of the Porsche family members wanted dividends and long-term capital appreciation. The first desire of the Lower Saxony Government was to safeguard employment in VW's Wolfsburg manufacturing complex. One consequence of this objective was that labor costs in Lower Saxony were too high, so that the VW brand never made much money, in

Shareholder Group	% Ownership of voting shares
Porsche and Piëch Families	52% (*)
Lower Saxony (Germany) State Government	20%
Qatar Holdings	17%
Other Investors	11%
Total	*100%*

Fig. 2.4 Shareholding in Volkswagen AG. Source: Volkswagen AG

contrast to other brands like Porsche, Audi, and MAN, which were the group's cash cows. Qatar Holdings, playing the long game, is known to seek capital gains. Little has been heard about their contribution to this board.

Importantly, there was deep discord between the two branches of the owners' family. Ferdinand Porsche, the chief engineer behind the original Volkswagen (or "people's car") and the founder of Porsche, had two children: Ferry and Louise. The Porsche family members are descendants of Ferry, while the Piëchs are descendants of Louise. "Rival family" and "non-name bearer"[21] are how some members of the Porsche family referred to the Piëch family members.

Ferdinand Piëch was the leader of the other branch and was the strong man on the board. Interestingly, he always disliked the idea of paying dividends to shareholders, as he felt that these monies would be better spent on new projects that would continue building the VW legacy and uphold the family tradition of major contributions to Germany and the world. That had been his motivation when very successfully rebuilding the Audi brand, and behind the failed and costly Phaeton project, which aimed to turn VW into a competitor with Mercedes and BMW. He was also behind the acquisition of the historic Bugatti brand, which produced one of the fastest and costliest cars in the world, the Veyron.

At some point, Piëch's ultimate dream was to displace Toyota as the world's number one car company, which was selling 10,000,000 cars around the world each year. Piëch committed all his energies to achieving this target and made sure it became VW's mission. This drove the company to aggressively ramp up sales, especially in the US where VW had the greatest sales potential. At some point, the US had fallen in love with the Beetle and the VW van. The time had come to reconquer this lost territory.

Piëch's ambition differed from the mission of the Porsche family branch, which was more set on value creation and dividends. His unabating ambition and aggressive leadership style led to a near-total breakdown in communications with the other branch. Ferdinand Piëch here very much followed in his grandfather's footsteps, being the entrepreneurial force behind VW's engineering and commercial developments. This made him the undisputed leader within the company. "I am a wild boar, you are domestic pigs,"[22] Piëch is said to have told other family members, referring to his drive and hard work which contrasted with their lifestyles of entitlement. Piëch had an abrasive manner and a winner-take-all mentality. One of his famous quotes could leave no one in doubt: "*Either I'm shot dead, or I win.*"[23]

The Porsche and Piëch families held their 52% voting shareholding in VW through a family holding company, Porsche Automobil Holding SE. Ferdinand

Piëch personally owned a 14.7% stake in the family holding. Disagreements in the owning family became known, which led to mixed signals to the supervisory and management boards of VW as to the mission of the firm. Piëch continued to drive key changes in the company. His strong personality seemed to cow the board. Independent voices on the board failed to channel Piëch's fantastic engineering and business drive into a corporate mission and sustainable value creation. It became a typical case of managing "targets" and increasing goals without allowing the necessary debate as to whether they could be achieved.

Piëch acted as an entrepreneurial owner, who was also chairing the board and was CEO. This resulted in internal alignment and in the efficient implementation of the decisions taken at the top. At VW, communication was one-way: from Piëch down. This led to value destruction as the plan being executed was toxic. Indeed, in such a case, the only way to avoid value destruction would be to stop execution, and through people refusing, or at least challenging and stopping, unlawful execution, including through whistleblowing. But the VW culture did not allow such challenge, the energies being directed at full and uncompromised execution.

Piëch appointed Martin Winterkorn as "his CEO." For most of his tenure, Winterkorn, a successor to the previous CEO who had resisted Piëch, only to be finally ousted at the end, was for all intents and purposes Piëch's man. With his appointment, the culture within VW had become fully "top-down," no one daring to refuse orders from above. The modus operandi became execution at all costs. Warning signs were gradually dismissed, and necessary checks and balances were more difficult to set up or hard to put into practice.

This "execution" culture provided the context for the famous meeting in November 2005 at the top of the R&D building in Wolfsburg, attended by 15 engineers concerned with the delays in the development of the new diesel engine. The new engine needed to pass the stringent US emissions standards, known to be more demanding than the European ones. All knew the US was the battleground for achieving Piëch's ambition of selling more cars than Toyota. A proposal was put forward that relied on the use of cheating devices. The senior manager concluded the fateful meeting by stating that there was no other choice but to accept the proposal, low VW margins not allowing more expensive alternatives to meet the engine's performance targets. He concluded the meeting by admonishing his colleagues to keep this information confidential to those in attendance, and certainly not to get caught.

The VAG board, as well as the top management team, knew that alternative power centers existed in the firm and that voices were directing and being heard other than those of the board. Just months before the Dieselgate scandal became public, Piëch and Winterkorn entered a public spat that saw other family members take the opportunity to oust Piëch as Chair of the Board. A few months later it was Winterkorn who had to resign in the face of the Dieselgate scandal, having too quickly stated that he did not know of the decision and that he would have stopped it had he known.

Ferdinand Piëch died in August 2019, a few months after he sold his stake in the family holding company. Before passing away at the age of 82, he confirmed his leadership philosophy: "*It is not possible to take a company to the top by focusing on the highest level of harmony.*"[24] It is not fully certain that he knew about the Dieselgate fraud, though most believe that it is unlikely that a technical and detail-oriented product man like Piëch would not have been confronted with the issue in his "top-down" management style. In any case, the fraud occurred under his watch and driven by his singular mission, unchecked by other family members or the VAG board. The major question surrounding the low profitability of the VW brand loomed large, but did not bother him much, nor did it seem to bother the board. Combined with the enormous pressure on market share, it resulted in providing a context where fraud emerged in the engine design unit of VAG, which several managers knew but all decided to remain silent about. The remaining Porsche and Piëch family members have now reset the mission for the family holding company.

The VW example shows that the definition of a mission, when not properly articulated and not regularly reviewed in changing contexts (e.g., climate change and increasing emission standards), can become so wide that it loses its framing and alignment value. Most if not all owners and directors agreed that it would be nice to beat Toyota in production quantities; they knew that profitability of the VW brand was an issue. But they never addressed the implication of simultaneously pursuing these two contradictory missions.

Some inside the house knew the company was cheating, violating basic rules of how the automotive game is played. Then regulators—especially those in the US—were framed as the enemy of automobile makers and useless green bureaucrats who had no sense of the complexity of building cars, or of competing with Toyota. Regardless, if some of the key engineers who knew had reported the cheating pattern inside the group, it would have saved the company billions, and a loss of public confidence, plus a tragic loss of human life.

Cheating always requires both pressure - here the need to challenge Toyota and succeed in the US market—and a rationalization that there is no other choice, and that the choice is acceptable. The heaters in this case may have convinced themselves that the cheating would last only a short time, that other companies had done it as well, that the California regulators were out to defeat VW's expansion into the US, or that it was up to their bosses to report the misdeed, or to come to agreement with regulators. The governance failure in this case, as in many others, was prolonged over time, and down the chain of command. Governance responsibility involves taking care of the entire organization and its impacts on the surrounding environment. That responsibility also extends down the same chain.

7 Disagreements About Mission: Dirty Business at Renault Nissan After a Historical Turnaround

In 2000, the French Government, as the largest shareholder of **Renault S.A.,** agreed to invest a 36% stake in the struggling, if not bankrupt, **Nissan Motor Co., Ltd.** The Japanese government would retain a substantial shareholding in the company, and a minority, but non-voting, stake in Renault. The cross-shareholding agreement between industrial partners is normal; however, the non-voting nature of the shares held by Nissan in Renault is not, and looks strange and excessive in view of the 42% share of Renault in Nissan. Then Nissan was in virtual bankruptcy, and Renault was the only automotive company that was willing to provide it with its last lease on life. It even managed to fight off an outright acquisition, Renault accepting the equity investment, which provided more of a downside insurance, but also limited its control over Nissan. It was also face-saving for Nissan, which retained its corporate identity, though under substantial foreign ownership. The French must have insisted on not giving Nissan any voting power in the Renault General Assembly. This would, in the end, cost it dearly.

Carlos Ghosn, who had been brought to Renault in 1996 by then Chairman Louis Schweitzer, had himself saved Renault from bankruptcy through massive cost-cutting and a sequence of turnarounds. That was the skill and experience Ghosn brought to the French automotive group, exercised in his previous positions at Goodyear and Michelin. Schweitzer put Ghosn in charge of the Nissan turnaround, a must for Schweitzer to pursue the opportunity offered by Nissan.

Ghosn's views on Nissan were remarkably positive. "Nissan is a great company; it needs [only] a few fixes" was one of Ghosn's regular comments on the Japanese automaker. Renault had failed to increase its sales and remained—like Nissan—sub-scale in the sector, stuck at 2,000,000 cars a year. The synergies of joint procurement would immediately be value creating, ensuring greater power with its suppliers. Synergies in design and manufacturing would

come out on top. Given the drastically different cultures of the two companies, and Renault's failure in its previous attempt to partner with Volvo, keeping two distinct companies would perturb the companies less and allow the partners to concentrate their energies in a more rational way on turning around Nissan.

Ghosn's most significant fix was to alter Nissan's mission, and the values and the rules of the game that would be followed when and after turning around Nissan. This included simplifying the Nissan group into a single Nissan business, geography now being handled by centralized business functions (design, manufacturing, marketing, sales, etc.), and no longer at divisional level. The divisional offices in Asia, the Americas, and Europe were eliminated, as were the divisional management teams led by the barons of the Nissan kingdom. The barons had brought the kingdom down in terms of profitability: of the 43 models, only four were profitable, and factories were running at 50% capacity which in the automobile industry amounts to hemorrhaging. A new king entered the stage— or shall we say a new samurai entered the Nissan village—and the king axed the barons. Ghosn selected a new team at the top of Nissan, fully devoted to his Nissan Revival Plan (NRP). The best and typically younger functional managers in Nissan's three geographical divisions were promoted and given expanded responsibilities. Their commitment to the new mission was key to a successful turnaround of the company. Nissan's virtual bankruptcy was a consequence of prolonged adherence to a mission that was economically loss making. Nissan was an icon in Japan, a showcase of Japanese technology, with a management committed to securing employment for its workers, even in the face of a substandard economic performance. Profitability did not seem to be part of the company's goals. Its organizational structure with strong geographical lines and autonomy made it sub-critical in size, as well as top heavy, with an excess of models. Resources in each of its three geographical areas were diminishing and equipment aging, because of stops on reinvestment.

I0n this context, Hanawa-san, the Group Chair, proved a genius: when Japanese banks and the Japanese government refused further loans and cash infusions to Nissan, he found a company that was willing to inject the needed cash to avoid bankruptcy. He had written to the world's 20 automobile companies, presenting them with the opportunity to invest in favorable conditions in Nissan. After all, Mazda had benefited from joining forces with Ford, and Mitsubishi with the Daimler Group. He was somewhat dismayed that only Renault returned his call and that other Japanese automobile makers also refused to bail out Nissan, even though they had the means to do so. This only serves to underline how dire the situation was for Nissan and how daring

Renault was when it accepted Hanawa's invitation. Schweitzer, the Renault Chair, always stated that he answered because he knew he had a confirmed turnaround champion in Ghosn, but also because he felt Renault needed to be transformed "from the outside," inside efforts failing each time. An alliance with an iconic Japanese brand promised useful benchmarking and learning, and would provide both parties with synergies and a size they sorely missed.

The key in a turnaround – as in surgery – is to focus just on what needs to be done urgently, not to become stalled in unnecessary complexity, and to have the resolve to succeed and the capability to bring people along the journey. Ghosn had developed an unequaled mastery at this game. He had learned that the first vital step was to clearly state the needed change in mission: economic value add had to be paramount on everybody's minds, as profitability had to be restored very quickly. Renault had given Ghosn only two years to turn Nissan around, for which he was given great autonomy and a single cash infusion of five billion euros. As indicated earlier, only four of the 43 models were profitable, and Nissan had too many platforms (eight times more than VW), too many suppliers (ten times more than Ford), too many dealers, and too many factories. Capacity utilization was at 50%, which was far below the industry standard (80% in general, and above 90% at high-tech companies such as Daimler). Of the seven Nissan factories, clearly, three had to be closed, which would immediately bring capacity utilization to 87.5%, a more reasonable number. The math was not complicated. What to do was also clear to most: rationalize, simplify Nissan's organization, and impose a value creating economic logic. What had been missing was the resolve to do so and the leadership capability to turn Nissan around. Nissan had become a giant social security system for the Nissan community and lost its competitiveness in the process. The ride was over, Renault was the only hope for survival, and all wished for the change to happen fast.

A radical change in culture was required. A foreign samurai would appear with the mission to save the Nissan village. The multi-culturality of Ghosn and his deep and broad turnaround experience were key assets here, as was the five billion equity infusion by Renault. Ghosn knew that the time had come to re-orient the company for profitability and value creation. For this to happen, all at Nissan had to understand how they contributed to value add, a radical change from the technical imperatives that had prevailed in the past. Unity was paramount for efficiency and speed, and thoroughness. To avoid resistance, the change also had to be seen as fair. The creation of a single Nissan, with a single functional team at the top, gave the group the leadership that was missing. It allowed rapid decision making in design, manufacturing, supply, capital allocation, and human resource management. The outside and fresh look of the Renault managers also gave the group new impetus and fresh energies.

Ghosn's refreshing of Nissan's behavior and the rapid alignment of the board and top management with the new mission—supported by new values and new rules of the game—allowed Nissan to recover spectacularly fast. Renault Nissan was not a new company; it was an equity alliance that saw Renault make an equity investment in Nissan. Renault did not acquire Nissan, leading Ghosn and his 20 French colleagues to state that they were proud to join the Nissan company, and that they were there only to provide a few needed fixes. This won over the Nissan hearts and minds, many expecting the French to fully take over the company.

Synergies would be fostered by the **Renault-Nissan Alliance** (RNA), a separate operating company based in Amsterdam whose mission was indeed to support and deepen the alliance between the two automotive giants by identifying and exploiting synergies between the partners. Renault and Nissan would immediately benefit from joint purchases with common suppliers, an option greatly facilitated by Ghosn's decision to abandon the Nissan Keiretsu supply system and turn to a competitive supply system practiced commonly elsewhere in the world. This also provided Valeo, Renault's major supplier, a unique chance to enter the Japanese market and supply Nissan through the Alliance.

The turnaround succeeded brilliantly. Just two years after the Renault investment, Nissan was again profitable and growing rapidly into a competitor to again be dealt with. Then something remarkable happened: the two major shareholders of Renault and of Nissan, the French Government and Japanese Pension Funds, appeared to go to sleep regarding their important responsibilities in pursuing the mission of building this very innovative alliance into the world's major automotive group. Perhaps this is predictable for governments that each week must confront new and pressing issues. But that is also the failure of the Nissan and Renault boards, which also appeared to have neglected their fiduciary duties. Furthermore, Nissan dividends were not expected so soon and were suddenly substantial, creating comfort in Paris and reducing the effort to now tackle the needed change in Renault. The urge to keep exploiting the synergies between the two partners waned. In fact, as Renault became increasingly dependent on Nissan and its dividends, Nissan became more focused on itself and increasingly hungered for autonomy. Integration with Renault and collaboration at the level of the Alliance seemed no longer part of Nissan's mission. The difficulty for Renault to benefit from the RNA, and to show growth figures like those of Nissan, also must not have impressed Nissan's managers. The language barrier did not help.

Japanese pension funds that still owned the absolute majority of Nissan shares had as their mission long-term ownership value. The key concern of the French Government was very different: secure jobs in France. Renault plants were now assembling Nissan cars that competed with those of Renault in Europe, and particularly in France, to the dismay of Renault employees and middle managers. While at the time of the birth of the Alliance, Nissan and Renault enjoyed similar production levels (two million vehicles annually), more than a decade later Nissan had tripled its output, while the Renault brand had decreased its output.

These issues came to a head in 2015. Ghosn appeared to single-handedly be on the verge of taking over the role of owner, board, and CEO of both companies. He had built a formidable reputation as a modern captain of industry and amassed considerable wealth doing so. As Président Directeur Général (PDG) of Renault and Chairman and CEO of Nissan, he reigned uncontested over an empire, which most thought of as a single integrated group. But the reality was different: both companies remained self-standing, but less and less integrated. While Ghosn had become the virtual owner, running the two partners, as well as the RNA, he had to single-handedly ensure the alignment between the two partners when in fact the management teams appeared to increasingly pursue diverging missions. Nissan wished to be protected from excessive French interference, and indeed Ghosn appeared to increasingly favor Nissan—and its more formidable size—over Renault, where he was increasingly confronted by the growing annoyance of the French Government owner. This even led to a public dispute with Emmanuel Macron, in late 2014, when Macron was Minister of the Economy and Industry in the Hollande government.

It is likely that Ghosn was preparing for the integration of Renault into Nissan. From an industrial viewpoint, this was logical, Nissan having become by far the larger partner. The acquisition of Mitsubishi by Nissan (and not by both) strengthened Nissan in the alliance and only confirmed Nissan's desire for greater autonomy from Renault. It is equally surprising that Ghosn did not insist on Renault taking an equity stake in Mitsubishi, which it could easily have done, even swapping some of its Nissan stake for Mitsubishi's. Or it could have used the occasion to integrate the equities of all three companies. Alliances are notably unstable arrangements that need to be converted into more stable ownership structures at some point. The failure of a true ownership dialogue is due to both owners, and Ghosn could have played a useful part in bringing the owners together. But it is likely that Ghosn used this absence of mutual ownership engagement to further his own imperial plans. Unfortunately for him, Macron's sudden and strong intentions to strong-arm the much-postponed merger between the two companies must have forced Ghosn to now return to the Japanese executive board with the news that Nissan's biggest shareholder had asked him to deliver on Macron's integration plan. It was a condition put forward by Macron for Ghosn's reappointment as Renault PDG. Macron had cornered him, forcing a mission that would bring him and Renault at odds with their Japanese partner.

What was seen as a needed victory by the French must have been viewed as a possible defeat by the Japanese, who must have also noticed the turnaround in Ghosn's behavior toward them. Ghosn had now made enemies among both major shareholders. His second marriage in a Marie Antoinette-themed party at the Palace of Versailles in 2016 went down poorly in France, particularly in those circles that judged his hubris to be already excessive. Ghosn seemed to have had no friends left when he was arrested in November 2018 at the airport in Tokyo for false accounting and ill-gotten personal gains.

Both Nissan and Renault were now facing unprecedented challenges, their CEO and Chair being in jail, while the two companies had grown apart. All would suffer due to this episode: Ghosn, Saikawa (who had to offer his resignation when it became clear that the coup had been organized with the help of the Japanese management acting against their boss), the boards of Renault and Nissan, and the major shareholders. None had taken any pre-emptive action. The governance failure was total. But the root cause was that two the co-owners, having been close at some point, had started to diverge and pursue different missions that, in difficult economic contexts, became completely incompatible. Both governments had started to view value on their own terms. The global mission of this remarkably innovative alliance had fallen by the wayside because of the gradual divergence in the mission to be pursued.

One major lesson of this story is that the solution was what Macron had suggested to the Japanese pension funds: a direct agreement between owners (owners' board). This was made difficult by the role played by Ghosn, who as executive surely had his own agenda, yet played the role of umpire between the two owners and linchpin of the alliance. The root of the failure lay not so much in executive differences but more in deep ownership divergences that were not addressed at the beginning of the creation of the alliance. These divergences resurfaced with a vengeance once the crisis that had led to the partnership subsided. The critical importance of mission as a directing force and glue is the distinct angle that this book maintains throughout.

8 Mission Capture and Control in Companies with Diffused Ownership

The central role of the mission and the control of a company it provides to owners—as opposed to "the market"—is an important point of this book. Widely held companies have so many shareholders that they have no controlling owners, and thus no owner can have a determining influence on the formulation and management of the mission, and beyond that on the goals and strategies pursued by such companies.

In such contexts, boards and CEOs, sometimes unconsciously and most often eagerly, take on the vacuum left by these anonymous owners and the responsibility of creating both the mission and the company's goals, and formulating and approving its strategies When a powerful CEO then also takes on the role of board chair, with dual powers, those of execution and those of controlling execution, power becomes concentrated in one person who will increasingly identify with the company. Checks and balances are then much diminished and the imperial temptation never far away.

It does not take much for this person to position himself as the owner, while also stating on every occasion that he or she is working for the long-term value of the share. But with so many owners, power is divided into millions of small parts and any countervailing power has ceased to exist. Dissenting directors are soon at risk of being removed, and quickly fall in line or disappear. The situation then is as described in *Alice's Adventures in Wonderland*, where the mouse says, "I'll be judge, I'll be jury…I'll try the whole cause, and condemn you to death." Enlightened dictatorship is not necessarily a bad governance model; the problem is that dictators typically do not remain enlightened. Having been condemned—to use the mouse's words—voices become silent, lights gradually go out, and darkness can start its reign uncontested.

The **General Electric Company** (GE) provides an excellent example of a widely held company where this happened. Boards allowed successive CEOs to take on the role of owner and delegated mission creation to the CEO, who would typically become the Chair and control the board. **Jack Welch** was Chairman and CEO of GE for an entire generation, from 1981 to 2001. While Welch was at the helm GE's share price increased 4000%. There is no doubt that for most of his tenure Welch was an inspirational and excellent leader. He was named Manager of the Century by *Fortune* magazine in 1999 and became an icon of Harvard Business School and its media outlet, the

Harvard Business Review. GE's mission statement projected the company as an industrial giant and innovator (see Fig. 2.5).

Despite the mission being focused on an industrial GE, toward the end of Welch's tenure in charge of the company, GE Capital was contributing a larger and larger share of GE revenues. GE Capital was initially formed to support the sale of GE products to its customers (often governments) who appreciated the total GE package that now included the means to finance their purchases.

As the lucrative yields from financial services flowed in, GE Capital became more of a financial business instead of a support to the industrial side of the company. The mission radically changed, and GE took its eyes and attention away from its industrial business, which was longer term and less lucrative than those earned on. Industrial values became supplanted by financial ones. Timing helped as well, the market environment allowing riskier aspects of GE Capital's business to be masked by healthy profits and an ever-increasing GE share price. The GE stock hit an all-time high in 2000, just one year before Welch handed over control to his handpicked successor, Jeff Immelt.

Close inspection and consideration of the performance of each of GE's businesses relative to their peers together with an examination of GE Capital's risk profile would have made an owner and competent GE board members

GE mission statement 2013

GE doesn't have an official mission statement, but presents it through GE Works Equation. It can be found in the picture below.

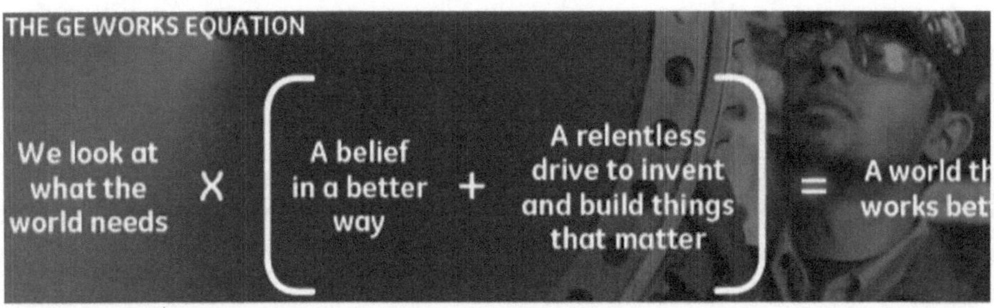

This is how GE explains it:

"We have a relentless drive to invent things that matter: innovations that build, power, move and help cure the world. We make things that very few in the world can, but that everyone needs. This is a source of pride. To our employees and customers, it defines GE."

Fig. 2.5 GE's mission. Source: GE

raise red flags. Welch, however, by then was a larger-than-life Chairman and CEO, the board was "his board," and dissent was not tolerated. There was no longer governance with countervailing power. Even the market became biased in favor of GE, its darling performer.

Another key red flag was that during the latter half of Welch's tenure at least 16 top GE executives left the company and became successful CEOs elsewhere. These star performers included Robert Nardelli of Home Depot, Lawrence Johnston of Albertson's Inc., and James McNerney of 3M. Most people today confirm that Jeff Immelt was not No 1 on the succession list but climbed to the top through a combination of factors: his own competences in traditional manufacturing contexts, perseverance, and the departure of those above him. Appointing a profile like Jeff Immelt when GE needed to tackle the digital revolution also appears strange. It also points to a failure of the CEO nomination and review process. The Board seemed subdued or asleep. GE's fall can ultimately be traced to a long and major governance failure.

Having been Chair and CEO for 20 years, presenting a unique performance record, it is to be expected that the Board had de facto delegated decision making, including on succession, to Master Jack (Welch). In terms of succession planning, it was Welch, not the GE board, who set the agenda and a shortlist of two internal candidates to become the next GE Chairman and CEO. The board should have recognized that Master Jack was a key player, and GE would have been better served if the Board took full responsibility for this process, and regularly repopulated a depleting field of candidates. Jeff Immelt was handpicked by Welch as the next Chairman and CEO. That was his last act to perform, and he failed. But there was neither a Board nor a reference owner to turn things around … until matters worsened. And even then, partly due to market bias, it took considerable time for GE to address the issues confronting it and that would ultimately take it down.

Almost from the beginning of Jeff Immelt's term, a slow but steady deterioration in GE's core businesses began, and GE Capital began to pay the price for its earlier risky businesses. The GE share price went into long-term decline, as shown in Fig. 2.6. When the financial crisis hit in 2008, GE was hit … as a financial company. For 16 years, Immelt was CEO and Chairman of GE, and for 16 years, the GE board, initially perhaps cowed by Welch and then effectively bought in by Immelt, did not forcefully address the decline of the once great company. The value destruction took a further hit in 2016, when Immelt's bet on wind power proved untimely and expensive, as was his decision to venture into the oil business with the acquisition of Baker Hughes.

Interestingly, Immelt's successor and GE insider, John Flannery, inherited the GE governance culture that put all its credence in the CEO. His term

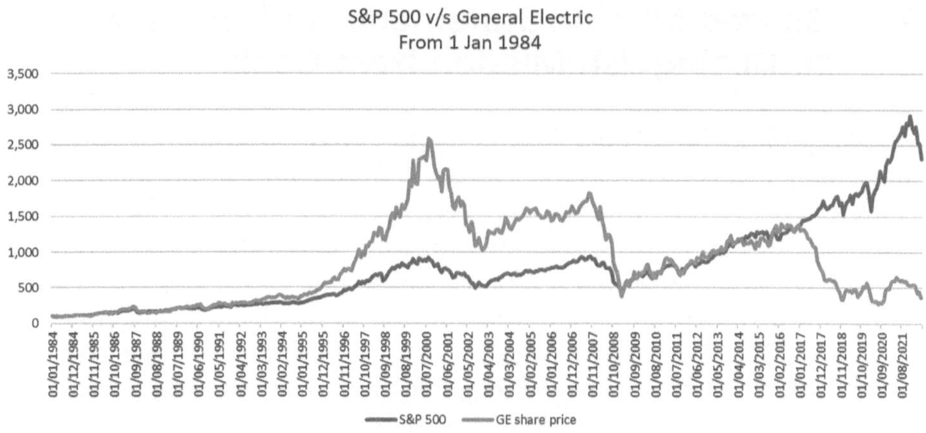

Fig. 2.6 GE share price 1984 to 2018. Source: NYSE

lasted only a year. He was succeeded by an outsider, Lawrence Culp, who decided in July 2020 to fully divest its shareholding in Baker Hughes over the next three years. GE's mission statement then read as follows: "*At GE, we rise to the challenge of building a world that works.*" This was a signal that it was facing serious performance problems, which everyone knew. But it also fell short in terms of redefining GE's mission, which was the key task and the first and necessary step to turn GE's fortunes around.

In November 2021, Culp finally addressed the issue head on. He finally admitted that the old GE mission was now obsolete and stated that GE would now become an aviation company. The health business—one of GE's jewels—would be split in early 2023, and its energy businesses a year later. This was a radical change in GE and its mission. As Scott Davis, CEO of Melius Research stated, "*GE got caught in the past – and now it's the end, it's over.*"[25]

GE is not alone in having faced the challenges of CEOs arrogating themselves extra powers. Examples of all-powerful Chairperson cum CEOs are still easy to spot. In the US, Jamie Dimon has been Chairman and CEO of JP Morgan Chase & Co. (JPM) since December 2006 and is the most famous example. "*JPM is a complex, risk-laden financial institution. Jamie should run the business and someone else should run the board,*" says Michael Garland, Executive Director for corporate governance in New York City's comptroller's office. Garland continues, "*The board needs to take aggressive action to demonstrate to regulators and shareholders that it is exercising strong independent oversight.*"[26] So far Dimon is still firmly in control.

9 Blurred Mission Statements and the Need to Distinguish Mission from Goals

The abrupt firing in October 2016 of Cyrus Mistry, Chairman of **Tata Sons**, the holding that owned the **Tata Group**, was viewed with surprise and even shock in India. Mistry had essentially been selected four years earlier by Ratan Tata, who took the title of Chairman Emeritus upon Mistry's appointment. His sudden and brutal removal was uncharacteristic for the venerable group.

Many stated that the substantial reduction in the dividends paid by Tata Sons to the **Tata Trusts**, who owned 65.9% of Tata Sons, was the main reason. The mission of Tata Sons was unambiguous: to produce steady dividends to the Trusts who would have spent them on charities and local development. But if these were falling short at the beginning of Mistry's chairmanship, this could hardly be his fault. The decline in profitability of nearly all the Tata Group companies, except for the software company TCS, presaged Mistry's reign and began under Ratan Tata himself.

The Tata Group is a large conglomerate whose controlling shareholders are philanthropic trusts. The Group grew and survived both the colonial British Raj and India's campaign of nationalization of many privately owned firms, waged from the 1960s to the early 1980s. The Group lost its insurance, airline, and banking businesses, some of which it later re-entered through JVs. In this campaign it retained its core steel and truck businesses. Its entry into the software services business through **Tata Consulting Services** (TCS) was an early and shrewd move. TCS became the main value contributor in the Group. By then the mission had diverged from the reality.

Ratan Tata reigned as undisputed Chairman from 1991 to 2012, when Mistry succeeded him. He initially pursued clear goals in Tata Sons: he consolidated group companies under him and imposed centralization in decision making. Ratan Tata de facto operated as the owner of the Tata Trusts and of the Group, including its operating units. He pursued several goals without any apparent supervision or challenge. The mission of the Trusts was always clearly articulated, while that of Tata Sons remained nebulous.

However, the goals and objectives pursued by the Trusts, Tata Sons, and Tata Group operating entities were all under Ratan Tata's control and approved, if not set, by him. One of his clear goals was for Tata's main businesses to grow internationally. Confirming the unavoidable trade-offs between profit, growth, and sustainability that we will address later in this book, profitability suffered, as did the sustainability of dividends to the Trusts. The business goal of internationalization was realized, but at the expense of the Group's mission as stated by the Trusts. Mission statements of the operating companies became increasingly vague, and the distinction between business goals and mission evaporated. This allowed Ratan Tata to pursue a series of costly M&A ventures (Tetley, Corus, Jaguar, Land Rover, etc.) which were key to his internationalization strategy.

Desirous to mark the 178th anniversary of Jamsetji's birth in 2017, Ratan Tata wrote the following to all Tata Group employees: "*As one of the largest stakeholder communities for the Trusts, you, the employees, are the inheritors and custodians of the Trusts and of (its) belief in making a sustainable change in society.*" Tata Group operating companies quote the Group's mission on their websites as being "*To improve the quality of life of the communities we serve globally, through long-term stakeholder value creation based on Leadership with Trust.*"

The absence of clear and differentiating mission statements for each of the Group's companies signals a lack of clarity in the direction given to these operating companies by the Group's leadership. Given that Ratan Tata took responsibility for leading these businesses, he had full leeway to do so, and he should be trusted. A more damaging point is that it is far from clear how the large foreign acquisitions Ratan Tata approved would meet the existing and undifferentiated mission statements. In fact, it is precisely the lack of good governance and specific mission statements for each of these businesses that allowed Ratan Tata nearly dictatorial power over the Group. The Group's performance suffered as a result. Indeed, by the end of Ratan Tata's leadership, many of the Group's largest companies—TCS being the notable exception—suffered from financial strain. The absence of governance was revealed to be too costly and only came to the attention of the Trusts once they started worrying about incoming dividends from the Group, which was clearly stated as its mission.

The ease with which mission and business goals are mixed or confused is of course not limited to the Tata Group. One can argue that GE's drive in the energy business was a clear business goal, which it pursued through the acquisition of Alstom and Baker Hughes. It also exposed the GE group to excessive risk, in a way that should never have been the case for a diversified industrial group. Similarly, Renault and Nissan started to pursue different business goals that became overarching for them at the expense of their alliance. The collective commitment to a unifying mission statement for the Alliance was lost in the process but was nevertheless a clear symptom of the increasingly diverging mission statements. Goals are more tangible than mission statements, and there is always the danger that their salience drives out the need to check whether these goals fit the mission and remain consistent with it. This is the first and paramount role of board members: enforcing the alignment of business goals with the mission.

Goals are measurable objectives that are specific and easily evaluated. Doran coined the acronym SMART to characterize effective goal setting: Specific, Measurable, Achievable, Relevant and Time-bound.[27] Missions are qualitative and thus do not readily lend themselves to quantification, particularly when their statement includes behavioral values that owners wish to see implemented in their enterprises. Quantification is easier to come by when specifying basic "Rules of the Game"—as Solvay does when it requires sustainable and growing dividends, and not decreasing ones. Or when owners require a certain level of dividends to be paid to shareholders each year. Figure 2.7 provides a more detailed explanation of the differences between an owner's mission and a company's goals.

We will characterize goals as addressing three criteria: **Profitability, Growth, and Sustainability**. What is important to realize is that these criteria are in general hard, if not impossible, to meet simultaneously, at least at a given point in time. Choices regarding goals thus involve trade-offs. Indeed, growth requires investment, which reduces profitability. By definition, growth is not sustainable. Sustainability limits growth and profitability.

A key question that arose in the Tata Group context—as in any group—concerns the purpose or mission of the operating companies or business units. Do these exist to create lifetime employment, philanthropy, and

<u>Missions</u> are deeply held commitments to certain principles that govern how people ought to behave (over a longer term). Mission statements will typically include the owner's long-term value and dividend expectations, as well as an owner's desires concerning social and local contributions.	<u>Goals</u> are measurable objectives that guide people in a common pursuit for a certain amount of time (short or medium term). Goals do change once objectives are achieved, when goals are shown to be infeasible, or when the context changes. Goals translate a mission into practical, quantifiable objectives and action agendas over limited periods of time.
Missions describe quests: they bind people together at emotional and spiritual levels. They and, although this is not necessary, give them a purpose above and beyond the purely economic and material aspects of a business.	Goals are broadly concerned with statements regarding growth, profitability, and sustainability.

Fig. 2.7 Distinguishing missions from goals

nation-building, even to the detriment of profitability, growth, and sustainability? To a rational observer, it would be better for operating companies to make the highest return on capital to pay high dividends to the Trusts, and for the Trusts then to fund philanthropic pursuits. This would allow the Tata Group to be fully aligned with the mission of the Tata Trusts, which prefer a sustainable and growing dividend stream, which is only possible through profitability over that time span. The mission of the Trusts and the goals of the Group's operating companies became blurred and mixed, and this, in our view, ought to have been addressed by the Board. But Ratan Tata reigned supreme, and the Board did not exercise its fiduciary duties.

The blurring of missions and goals of the operating companies was facilitated by a further structural complication, which is that, with Ratan Tata, the Chairman positions of the boards of the large, listed Tata Group companies were "automatically" filled by the Chairman of Tata Sons. Further compounding the issue, the Chairman had insufficient time to focus on each large company. The Tata Chairman's agenda had usually been that of the Chair of the Trusts, his other roles being subordinated to the main role. But the Chair seemed driven by his intent to internationalize the main Tata companies through international acquisitions. This was a clear goal, but in this context, it hardly constituted a longer-term mission for the Group.

Understanding the difference between mission and goals is essential for value creation. Goals are operational targets that implement a mission, and it is essential for value creation that they are kept distinct. The Tata Group provides an example of how value creation suffers when these concepts are not well understood and become blurred. Immelt seemed to have suffered from the same confusion. Carlos Ghosn too was very clear on goals, but not on mission. His views on mission clearly changed over time. In contrast, the owners, the CEO, and, importantly, the Board of Interbrew did understand the difference between the owner's mission and the goals of the company. This was a main reason for their remarkable success.

10 Mission and Vision

Before concluding this first chapter, we briefly discuss the difference between two related yet distinct topics: the owner's mission and a company's "vision."

The owner's mission is a statement of purpose. It sets out why the company exists and constitutes a set of objectives the owner(s) expect(s) the company to pursue and deliver on. Progress on the mission, as discussed earlier in this chapter, is achieved through goal setting.

Vision statements are more static pictures of where the company might be and what it might look like in the future. Such statements provide a picture of how the company will be expected to interact with its clients and what its offer and supply model might look like in terms of scale, location, and nature. A vision highlights aspects of the company that are deemed relevant to communicate to stakeholders—market, clients, suppliers, employees, public—for clarity of ambition and direction. For example, vision statements might refer to a "50% market share" or a "billion-dollar company."

To distinguish the owner's mission and the company's vision, we show BlackRock's vision statement in Fig. 2.8. It is very different from the mission of BlackRock's owners, which might be described as providing value to customers by capital appreciation obtained through scale. To accomplish this mission, BlackRock sets itself certain goals, which contributed to it becoming the largest and foremost asset manager globally.

Visions can be seen as ways of "branding" the company vis-à-vis employees, customers, suppliers, regulators, and others. The purpose of the vision is often to get employees and customers on board and inform them of certain company goals. The company's aim through visions is to reach those customers

We are a fiduciary to our clients

Put simply, your goals are our goals. We represent your voice, your needs and your investment goals in every decision we make.

We are passionate about performance

We take emotional ownership of every aspect of the work we do, prizing strong subject matter expertise and an insatiable appetite to learn.

We are One BlackRock

We know that working in silos is not conducive to our best work. We pride ourselves on our solutions that result from the constant collaboration between our diverse teams.

We are innovators

We are proud of our long history of innovation, driving continuous change to help investors achieve their goals. This culture of innovation has been and continues to be, the foundation of our success.

Fig. 2.8 Vision of BlackRock (https://www.blackrock.com/corporate/about-us/mission-and-principles). Source: BlackRock

who seek these aspects of the value proposition, while informing others that the company is unlikely to deliver value for them.

To conclude this section, consider "a green vision" or a social responsibility statement by a corporation. Such statements often qualify more as providing a vision than as a fundamental mission statement. They may also qualify as components of the mission statement when describing the values adhered to in the pursuit of the mission or when communicating some basic rules of the game guiding the delivery of the mission.

One way to distinguish between mission and vision is to query owners as to whether they are willing to sacrifice profitability or economic value creation to, for example, become "greener" or more "socially responsible." If the answer is negative, the vision statement amounts to a goal. If, however, the answer is positive, or if a trade-off is at least acceptable, then the vision statement can be qualified as forming an integral part of the company's mission.

11 Conclusion

The **mission** sets the objectives and the direction the company will pursue and engage in. It is the primary and most fundamental decision for any owner. Critically, it determines how the owner perceives business value. Operationally, it frames value creation as making progress on the stated mission. Its importance cannot be overstated. Great mission statements provide direction clarity, defining the area where the company and the owners will engage and commit. They also provide a great platform for engaging stakeholders, directly or indirectly, in value creation.

Clearly set out missions substantially enhance a company's chances of success. Companies whose missions are not well set lead to value destruction, as a consequence of wrong mission statements, or through disagreements among owners, or among owners, boards, and management about what the mission ought to be. Lack of alignment among these three groups increases the risk of value destruction, and ultimately failure. Many difficulties among stakeholders are the result of a lack of mission clarity. Conversely, a clear mission provides direction and clarity of expectations that invites relevant stakeholders to partner with the company and keeps away those that are not relevant.

Mission crafting is one of the fundamental characteristics distinguishing owner-led firms from publicly listed ones. It should be the first task and main focus of owners. A mission originally set by founders will of course be reset by founders or subsequent owners as a function of changing contexts or preferences. Proper alignment requires this to be done in collaboration with the

Board of Directors and the management, and approved at a General Shareholder Meeting. Owner-led companies are able to change mission more easily and swiftly than publicly listed ones, precisely because they control the company.

This chapter reviewed a number of major corporate failures at Tata, Renault-Nissan, Volkswagen, and GE. We showed how in each case, wrong mission statements or mission disagreements became the root cause for their remarkable value destruction episodes. The discussion of mission and of mission changes in the face of changing environmental conditions is one of the primary responsibilities of boards of directors. The major difference in owner-led firms is that owners themselves bear this ultimate responsibility, which then calls for owners to exercise leadership in this domain. In publicly listed firms this responsibility becomes diffused among a large number of shareholders, the board, and the executives, invariably raising issues of leadership and often generating value-destroying misalignments and confrontations.

Notes

1. https://www.panasonic.com/global/corporate/history/konosuke-matsushita/story2-06.html.
2. The Essential Drucker, Chapter 3. The Purpose and Objective of a Business, HarperCollins, 2001.
3. The Essential Drucker, Chapter 3. The Purpose and Objective of a Business, HarperCollins, 2001.
4. https://www.temasek.com.sg/en/our-community/temasek-foundations.
5. https://www.bloomberg.com/news/articles/2019-07-03/gic-s-extra-33-billion-is-more-hard-work-in-tough-environment.
6. https://www.economist.com/news/leaders/21591174-25-years-blackrock-has-become-worlds-biggest-investor-its-dominance-problem.
7. https://www.economist.com/news/leaders/21591174-25-years-blackrock-has-become-worlds-biggest-investor-its-dominance-problem.
8. https://www.solvay.com/sites/g/files/srpend221/files/2018-11/Assembl%C3%A9e%20G%C3%A9n%C3%A9rale%20des%20Actionnaires%20documentation_1.pdf.
9. https://www.solvay.com/en/investors/share-information/major-shareholders.
10. http://www.tatatrusts.org/article/inside/about-sir-ratan-tata-Trust.
11. https://www.tata.com/business/tata-sons.
12. https://trends.levif.be/economie/trends-information-services/une-bonne-gouvernance-est-synonyme-d-entreprise-familiale-performante/article-publishingpartner-813367.html?cookie_check=1592212490.

13. Famous Parsis, Biographical & Critical Sketches, Published by B.T. Dastur The Bombay Parsi Punchayet Funds & Properties, 2004.
14. http://www.tata.com/aboutus/articlesinside/The-quotable-Jamsetji-Tata.
15. https://www.firstpost.com/business/money/if-there-was-no-tcs-there-may-be-no-tata-group-worth-speaking-about-1981083.html.
16. http://panmore.com/tesla-motors-inc-vision-statement-mission-statement-analysis.
17. https://www.reuters.com/article/us-tesla-solarcity-lawsuit-idUSKBN1ZT2HF.
18. https://www.sec.gov/news/press-release/2018-226.
19. https://www.postandcourier.com/testifying-in-lawsuit-musk-decides-best-defense-is-offense/article_7527afea-e352-11eb-b2fe-db303c9257b3.html.
20. Sources for this estimate are:
    (i) Anenberg SC, Miller J, Minjares R, Du L, Henze DK, Lacey F, Malley CS, Emberson L, Franco V, Klimont Z, Heyes C. Impacts and mitigation of excess diesel-related NOx emissions in 11 major vehicle markets. *Nature*, 2017 May 25; 545(7655): 467–471. https://doi.org/10.1038/nature22086. Epub 2017 May 15. PMID: 28505629.
    (ii) Impacts and mitigation of excess diesel-related NOx emissions in 11 major vehicle markets. *Nature*, 2017; 545 (7655): 467. https://doi.org/10.1038/nature22086.
    (iii) Estimate of VW's market share of diesel cars in Europe, https://theicct.org/blog/staff/diesel-revival-german-economy-20190801.
21. Battle between Piech, Porsche families highlighted in German documentary by Stefan Wimmelbuecker, *Automotive News Europe*, October 20, 2017.
22. Battle between Piech, Porsche families highlighted in German documentary by Stefan Wimmelbuecker, *Automotive News Europe*, October 20, 2017.
23. The Porsche Story, A Fierce Family Feud by Dietmar Hawranek, *Der Spiegel* July 21, 2009.
24. Auto. Biographie by Ferdinand Piech, Hoffmann & Campe, Jan. 2002.
25. https://www.nytimes.com/2021/11/09/business/general-electric-break-up.html.
26. https://www.reuters.com/article/uk-jpmorgan-idUKBRE93C02720130413.
27. Doran, G. T., "There is a S.M.A.R.T. way to write management's goals and objectives," Management Review 70(11), 35–36, 1981.

3

The Board of Directors: Governing the Mission

1 Origins of Corporate Governance

Governance is a much used noun in both business and society. The word governance has its etymological roots in ancient Greek, where the verb *kubernáō* means to steer. The EU is said to suffer from a governance crisis, and US democracy is living through one. The global financial crisis was described by Nobel laureate Joseph Stiglitz as having its roots in governance failure at multiple levels.[1] COVID-19 and global warming are other examples that point to the massive costs when governance fails or is absent.

Andrew Hacker, the well-known American political scientist, sums it up beautifully: "*The condition we take for granted, that men will rule and obey in a civilized manner, is our legacy from the ancient [Greeks]. Government and politics may seem necessary prerequisites for the realization of the good life, but nowhere is it decreed or ordained that men will be guaranteed these arrangements.*"[2]

The practice of governance via thought and reasoning brings us back to the Athenians who, through much "trial and error, by reason and intuition," and plenty of *philosophia* (love of wisdom), developed an innovative system of democratic governance. In 507 B.C. Cleisthenes, the highest magistrate in Athens, introduced a political system that he called *demokratia*, which denotes power (*kratos*) by the people (*demos*). He thus shifted power from the aristocracy to the people, even though citizenship was restricted to men above the age of 20 with the right birth criteria and having completed their military training. Citizenship could be granted for extraordinary service to Athens and could also be removed. Only 10–20% of the city's population were citizens;

M. Massa et al., *Value Creation for Owners and Directors*,
https://doi.org/10.1007/978-3-031-19726-0_3

women, foreigners, slaves, and freed slaves could not participate in debates about the *polis*.

Athenian demokratia was built on an institutional tripod. One leg of this tripod was the Ekklesia, the assembly of citizens, which debated about the city's affairs. It was a direct democracy, not a representative or parliamentary democracy as we know it today. The Ekklesia would vote on war, on those who would manage the city, and on the laws. The second leg of the democratic tripod was the Boule, the administrative body of the city, comprising 50 elected officials from each of the city's ten districts. It had responsibility for maintaining the cavalry, the soldiers, and the fleet, oversaw the city's finances, and drafted *proboulemata* for the Ekklesia to approve. The third institution was the judicial system. Judges appointed by the Boule decided on cases brought to it by citizens whose rights were protected by the laws approved in the Ekklesia.

The three institutions of Athenian democracy have given rise to the legislative, executive, and judicial branches of government in modern democracies. Corporate governance similarly rests on such an institutional tripod, the three legs being the general assembly of shareholders (its Ekklesia); the Board of Directors (its Boule); and the shareholder agreements, the corporate charter, and the courts and regulatory bodies who see to it that laws (including shareholder agreements and corporate charter) are applied and the rights of the corporation are upheld.

Corporate governance is governance applied to a "corporation." The word "corporation" derives from the Latin *corpus*, meaning body. The great invention of Roman corporate law was to consider a corporation as having rights (of commerce) and responsibilities (duty of care) like those enjoyed by any Roman citizen. This allowed corporations to benefit from a license to engage in commerce across the Roman Empire. This arrangement contributed greatly to the Pax Romana: when nations joined the Empire, their citizens and corporations could do business across the Empire, protected by Rome's legislation.

There are numerous different types of corporate entities. Regardless of this diversity, however, all "corporates" have legal lives and are born (or constituted) with a charter, which requires approval by a government. Figure 3.1 shows the charter of what is thought to be the first industrial company in the western world. The company was incorporated in 1347, much before the town of Falun, which developed around the mine, was chartered in 1624.[3] It was granted by the then King of Sweden. Governance is always an affair involving the State.

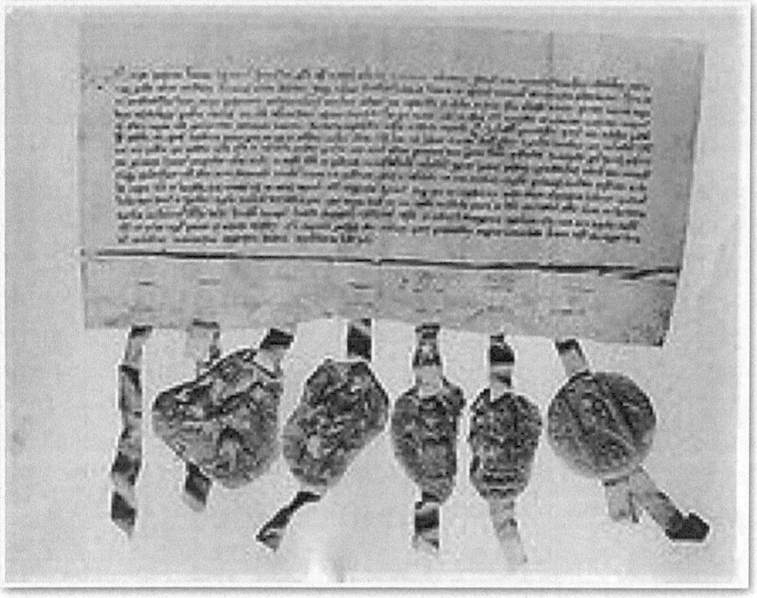

Fig. 3.1 The Stora Kopparberg Mining Company charter obtained in 1347 from King Magnus Eriksson. Source: Storaenso

Corporations, like humans, have eventful lives. A cave-in at the Falun mine in 1687 was a major setback for the town. The company survived by investing downstream into manufacturing. It became the Stora Kopparberg Bergslag in 1862, encompassing mining, iron, and wood activities.[4] Wood was needed for the furnaces required to extract metal. In the 1970s, Stora changed its mission and sold its mining and metal operations to concentrate on forestry, pulp, and paper.

In due course, corporations die, through dissolution, when their mission has been achieved or has been ended, or when they no longer have the means to carry it out (bankruptcy or insolvency). This occurred in 1998 for Stora, when it merged with a Finnish company, Enso Oyj, to form Stora Enso, and to become, as it proudly attests, "The Renewable Materials Company." The new merged company focuses on all the possibilities of renewable materials, with trees and forests as the foundation for its endeavors. The merger ended Stora's life as an independent company. But its operations continued in a modified legal form. Similarly, when BP bought the American oil producer Amoco, the latter was incorporated into BP and became the center of gravity of BP's North American operations. But this also ended Amoco as a self-standing business entity, as it was integrated into the "corpus" of BP.

Corporate governance is thus the exercise of governance in the affairs of a business entity (or corpus). This amounts to addressing many questions whose answers shape and influence the future of the corporate entity. It typically involves decision-making authority and the exercise of business, legal, and moral responsibilities. The key questions surrounding corporate governance are: Who governs? What decisions are necessary to sustain the entity and on what grounds? How do we debate? What constitutes "good corporate governance"? Who is responsible for the corporation, for what part, and how do we delegate authority to the management? What does "responsible governance" entail? And, importantly, what is the relation between governance and the performance of a corporation? We address these questions in the next section.

2 The Duality of Corporate Benefits and Corporate Responsibilities

The "legal" view of corporate governance is built on a duality: the Board of Directors is collegially responsible for the corporation, but directors are voted in by shareholders and accountable to them. This means that if someone wishes to attack a corporation in court, that person will attack and face the Board of Directors. Shareholders are typically liable for the equity they invested in the company, which they lose once the share price falls to zero, as in the case of bankruptcy. If shareholders were responsible for the corporation, stock markets would have great difficulties since trades would not only be about future dividends and cash flows, but would also involve unknown future responsibilities. This would limit trading of shares, since buyers would not know what they were buying.

Too many shareholders and businesspeople still have the mistaken impression that board members have to abide by the desires of the shareholders. The G20/OECD Principles of Corporate Governance, which are considered the gold standard on the topic, now endorsed by the G20, are very clear on the topic:

> *As a practical matter, however, the corporation cannot be managed by shareholder referendum. The shareholding body is made up of individuals and institutions whose interests, goals, investment horizons and capabilities vary. Moreover, the corporation's management must be able to take business decisions rapidly. In light of these realities and the complexity of managing the corporation's affairs in fast moving and ever changing markets, shareholders are not expected to assume responsibility for managing corporate activities. The responsibility for corporate strategy and operations*

is typically placed in the hands of the board and a management team that is selected, motivated and, when necessary, replaced by the board.[5]

Liberal or democratic capitalism is thus built on a separation of the benefits of ownership (which the Romans called *beneficium*) from the corporate responsibilities that fall on the shoulders of the Board of Directors (which the Romans referred to as *officium*). The members of the Corporate Board are typically nominated by the owners and approved, as is usual, by all shareholders at their Annual General Meeting. Owners thus exercise control over their corporation in three ways: first, by the framing of the mission; second, by the nomination of members of the corporate board that bears responsibility for the corporation; and third, by the revocation of the board members should owners perceive that the nominated board members are not acting consistently with the owners' mission.

Corporate board members are regularly called shareholder "representatives," which suggests actions on behalf of the shareholders—similar to how one expects labor representatives to act in union negotiations. Legally, this is not the case: though shareholders are privileged stakeholders by virtue of being able to nominate and approve the members of the corporate board—as well as having the right to terminate their appointments – the latter have a fiduciary duty toward the corporation for whom they are the legal representatives. This implies that in the exercise of their duties they ought to be driven by and pursue what is best for the corporation, and not necessarily what is in the best interests of the shareholders. This is one of the subtle foundations of liberal capitalism, which places the interests of the corporation squarely on the shoulders of the members of the corporate board, recognizing that shareholders would be foremost driven by personal interests.

The arrangement is needed for another reason: most shareholders do not agree on matters, and might even severely disagree. Such debates ought to take place within the owners' board, whose role is precisely to ensure that owners, though possibly disagreeing among themselves, end the debate speaking with a single voice, so that alignment can result. Hence, the word "representative" is confusing, if not abusive. It applies mostly when members of the Board of Directors are asked, as a matter of courtesy, to represent absent shareholders when voting at the Annual General Meeting (AGM). The correct word is "nominee" since they still must be approved by a Nomination Committee for their credentials, and sometimes by regulatory authorities, as is the case now in the banking sector. When they are approved, their board behavior ought to be guided, like all directors, by the best interests of the corporation, regardless of who nominated them.

In certain legislations, a legal entity may be entitled to name a board member. That individual then may truly hold the legal title of "representative" of the legal entity she or he represents on the board. However, even then this board member, like her or his colleagues, must pursue the interests of the company as a member of the corporate board. Should she or he be conflicted between the interests of the company and those of the legal entity they represent, they will abstain from voting on the corporate board, due to their conflict of interest. These are subtle issues, and board members are advised to be conservative and disciplined when facing potential conflicts of interest. Current practice holds that even perceptions of conflict of interest are to be managed, for their presence diminishes the credibility of the board and its decisions.

Other forces have added to the separation between owner responsibilities and corporate responsibilities. Ever since the Global Financial Crisis of 2007–08, society has asked for business to be conducted in a more responsible way. Climate change has added force to this movement. Shareholders are numerous and come and go. They can sell or donate their shares at any time they wish, leaving it impossible to know who exactly the shareholder will be in the future. Shareholders do not agree on many issues, and even if they agree today, they may not tomorrow. An exchange of shares allows easy exits for shareholders who do not agree with the direction taken by a firm in which they own equity. The other side is that the firm cannot be submitted to the whims of shareholders and need continuous governance to deliver continued performance. One of the remarkable features of liberal capitalism is that it has found the intelligent solution to decouple the benefits of ownership from the governance responsibility of the firm, placed with the board, as a collective body. Economists regularly make a massive and erroneous simplification of liberal capitalism when they refer to "the" shareholder as the one overseeing and controlling the management. Indeed, in the famous principal-agent model by Jensen and Meckling,[6] the shareholder is often thought of as the principal and the manager as the agent. This completely projects away the central role of the board, which, acting collectively, is the representative voice for the corporation and the corporate decision maker.

The separation of corporate benefits from corporate responsibilities has several implications for shareholders, board members, and executives that we will detail in this book. Most importantly, the separation provides clarity on the benefits and responsibilities of corporate ownership. Even though the 2015 G20/OECD Principles still refer to a duty of loyalty to "both the company and its shareholders," we will assume this standard for the rest of our discourse, which mandates as the first loyalty of directors a loyalty toward the corporation. It is the fact that the voice of a company lies with its board and not with its shareholders that allows that company to speak with a clear voice, which shareholders typically cannot.

Of course, shareholders have rights. Their first right is to decide on the mission of the business enterprise, which binds them and guides their relations with stakeholders. It is the ability to be clearly guided by a mission that distinguishes owner-led firms from all others, including executive or board-led firms. In the latter, the mission is either unclearly defined or imposed by the Chair, the Board, or the CEO and the management team. Alignment on a mission is far from automatic. Indeed, the mission often becomes the object of continued debate and eventually a power struggle, between the board that needs to approve it and the management that needs to execute it, or between subgroups fighting for their views. Everyone is biased in favor of the mission they develop and formulate. When not anchored by owners, the mission becomes the outcome of a political negotiation, with consequences that can change with prevailing political winds. Economists refer to this value destruction using the term "agency losses." Changes in board and executive leadership typically re-initiate discussions of mission change.

The owner-led firms we are concerned with in this book should not have to face this problem, as this is a principal ownership task. The first way to manage this task is for shareholders to clearly discuss and lay out a mission statement, as we argued in Chap. 2. There we underlined that the mission statement ought to be understood in a broad sense, including longer-term objectives and a commitment to certain values and basic rules of the game in how the enterprise will be governed while aiming to fulfill these objectives. The mission and the process to modify it will typically be written down in a shareholder agreement or ownership policy and will serve as a glue between shareholders. This will guide the firm's relations with stakeholders, who will thus become clearly informed of the objectives and principles guiding the owners in the governance of their enterprise. This point is fundamental. When effectively executed, owner-led firms thus obtain alignment with stakeholders based on a mission, and not on partial statements that can change regardless. In contrast, publicly listed firms are often subjected to a debate between shareholder primacy (the fiction that the firm ought to be governed exclusively for shareholder value) and the interests of particularly powerful stakeholders.

The second right of shareholders is the ability to select and appoint board members, who are then held accountable by the shareholders for the governance of the enterprise during their mandate. These shareholders also reappoint board members when they feel that they have accomplished their role effectively. One of the main complexities of the board role thus lies in the simultaneous management of their accountability to shareholders and their fiduciary responsibilities on behalf of the company. The G20/OECD Principles qualify this accountability as follows: "*The Board should be able to exercise objective independent judgement on corporate affairs.*"[7] Though governance is filled with dualities, this is certainly the most fundamental one, and owners should be fully cognizant of this requirement when appointing board members. In practice, though, owners regularly nominate and appoint board members whom they instruct with a duty of loyalty to them, which goes against corporate governance law. Board members too often do not realize that they are legally obliged to assume as their first duty a fiduciary obligation to the corporation.

The dual commitments and complementary competences exercised when appointing and fulfilling board memberships cannot be repeated enough, as they are far from natural or obvious. The competence of owners is to clearly frame a corporate mission that provides an enticing value creating platform for both board members and executives, and to select and invite effective directors to exercise this mission with full independence as to how best to so. The complementary competence of board members that accept the invitation is to commit to this mission and exercise it with the duty of care[8] and the independence the task demands.

The common understanding behind the notion of independence is the integrity to behave and share one's viewpoint regardless of consequences, including the possibility that the shared views might jeopardize one's board appointment. Independence also requires that board members should not depend on board fees, or on the status their board appointment connotes, and that they should not be told how to exercise their board mandate. Beyond the notion of independence, board members are expected to have broad business and industry knowledge to be able to exercise proper judgment on the matters presented to the board. When they cannot, they are supposed to tool up, abstain, or exit. When they abstain too often, they should exit.

Beyond the right to frame the mission and the authority to select and appoint board members, owners may hold several other rights that vary depending on the country in which the company has been incorporated. The G20/OECD Principles of Corporate Governance capture this well:

> *Additional rights such as the approval or election of auditors, direct nomination of board members, the ability to pledge shares, the approval of distributions of profits, shareholder ability to vote on board member and/or key executive compensation, approval of material related party transactions and others have also been established in various jurisdictions.*[9]

3 The Board of Directors as the Nexus of the Governance Scene

With the Board of Directors serving at the invitation of the owning shareholders, and also serving the corporation as fiduciaries, the board can be considered to lie at the center of a circle on which the company's various stakeholders are positioned, as shown in Fig. 3.2. The main groups of stakeholders are shareholders, executive management, employees, government regulators and the courts, the communities the company interacts with, and, finally, the company's clients who are the ones whose contributions pay for the company's payouts, including dividends to shareholders. Shareholders are privileged stakeholders as they own the right to appoint board members, and to dismiss them.

In his *Markets and Hierarchies*, Williamson observed that interactions inside the company are governed in hierarchical fashion, by delegation of the board, whereas relationships with most external stakeholders are governed

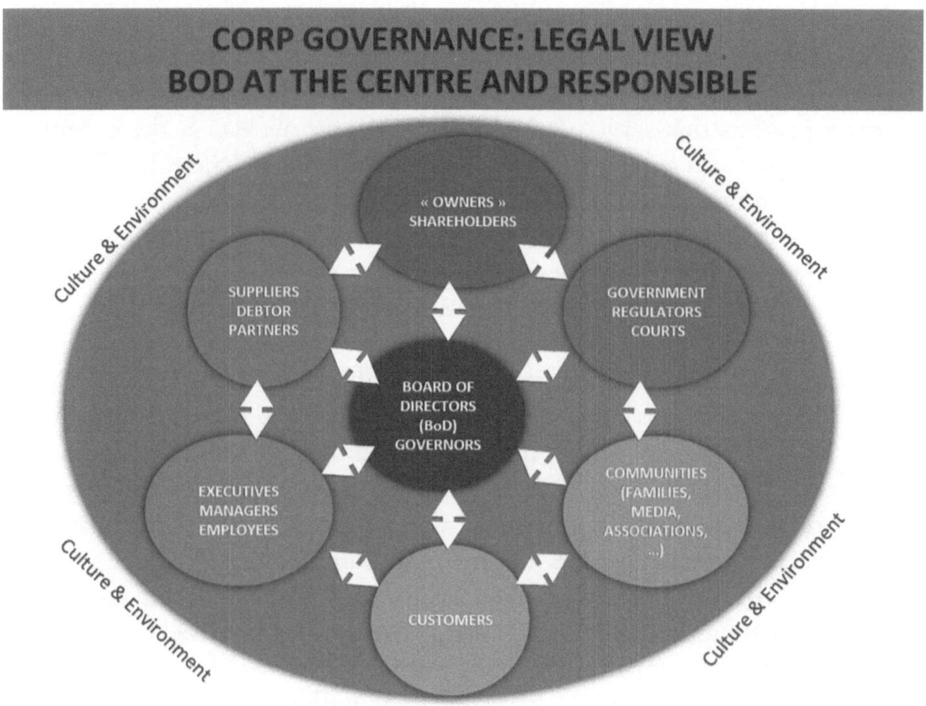

Fig. 3.2 The legal view of the corporation: Board of Directors at the center balancing the interests of various stakeholders

through market exchanges.[10] The latter take the form of market transactions governed by the laws of supply and demand. This is the case for labor markets, supply markets, and even equity markets. A company also has non-market interactions in the form of legal and regulatory constraints, governmental obligations such as taxes, as well as actions by motivated members of communities such as customer associations, unions, or local groups where the company is active. These non-market interactions can be quite complex to manage. Market interactions are more standard, and on regulatory and legal requirements it is a matter of compliance.

The simplest form of governance arises when, apart from shareholders, the board is not formally connected to other stakeholders, other than through the laws and regulations prevailing in the corporation's place of business. Complexities arise in the form of interdependencies and conflicts of interest due to relations between various stakeholders. Examples of such complex interactions are when shareholders, executives, suppliers, or clients are on the board, using their board seat to force viewpoints and decisions that are in their interest, but not in the interest of the corporation. These could also be shareholders wishing to take advantage of corporate resources (cars, airplanes, cash, real estate, etc.), executives arguing for unwarranted pay, suppliers forcing excessive prices, and customers driving prices down. State-owned enterprises (SOEs) face these issues regularly when governments force companies to enter projects that serve particular government interests at the expense of the company's interest and financial viability. This is where the Board of Directors demonstrates its full value by safeguarding the company in the pursuit of its mission, unperturbed by side winds coming from parties with private interests and pursuing their own agenda at the expense of the company. All these lead to various groups exercising various pressures on the board to see the company serve their interests. This is another requirement for the independence criterion applied to board members.

There are numerous challenges faced by corporate boards aiming to be effective. They typically consist in the board addressing a number of dualities such as the pursuit of long-term versus short-term objectives, the respective attention paid to various claimants on the company, or whether to hand out dividends to the shareholders or invest in valuable growth opportunities. Finding an effective balance between competing tensions is the board's main task. The most significant tensions are due to pressures exercised by stakeholders who wish the company to pursue a direction that is favorable to them. When all stakeholders have interests that align with the company, board work is much easier. This is, of course, rarely the case. When tensions increase, the risk is great that the board becomes indecisive or, worse, begins to pull apart when addressing these tensions, leaving the corporate ship rudderless.

Let us briefly describe some major dualities involving stakeholders:

1. *Owners vs the Company:* This is the duality between loyalty to the owner and loyalty toward the company. What might benefit the company may not benefit the owner, and vice versa. The owner sets the mission for the entire enterprise, but there is nothing that prohibits an owner from setting a mission that is negative for a corporation or some stakeholders, since an owner bears no responsibility for the corporation. It is only when board members and managers agree to implement that serious damage results. Only board members who are independent enough to uphold their fiduciary duty to the company can prohibit an owner from imposing his private interests when they are contrary to the company's interest. Therefore corporate legislation placed the responsibility for the company with directors, and not with the owner. This is also why owners eager to abuse a company will place obedient directors on the company's board, or directors that "bought into" the value destroying scheme, and which, like the owners, derive personal benefit from agreeing to execute such a destructive mission, typically in the form of "facilitation payments" from the owners or agents working on behalf of the owners.
2. *Owners vs Stakeholders:* A company may also have owners excessively eager for profits and dividends. In pursuing this objective, stakeholders' interests risk being downplayed. Employees may be insufficiently paid, leading to motivational problems and an exit of talent from the company. Suppliers might be squeezed, as might be product or service offers. Customers will then be presented with excessive prices for the service rendered, leading the company to develop a poor reputation in its user community. Thus, while the corporate board needs to align its actions with the owner's mission, it also needs to understand how it becomes affected by the actions of particular stakeholders. A great example of this is the Brent Spar incident, where Greenpeace through a boycott of German Shell customers was able to block Shell's plans to dispose a buoy into deep Atlantic waters.[11] Unable to sway the company, activists often go directly to customers who provide the needed oxygen to the company. This tactic was very well executed in the Brent Spar case: Shell in the end agreed to reutilize the controversial buoy in the building of new harbor facilities in Norway. But the incident resulted in Shell losing its considerable reputation.

Board vs Executives: When should boards monitor and advise? When should boards step up the pressure and take control? In a normal course of events, boards should not be involved in day-to-day operations, as this is the domain of management. Finding the right balance between two extremes—full trust in the executives and complete control over them—is a common challenge for boards. As always in the case of complementary dualities, the answer lies in finding an effective balance between the two extremes. Board members, frustrated with repeated poor managerial decision making, tend to tell executives what to do. When then confronted with insufficient zeal at following up on their orders, board members may double down on management, with the consequence of a further reduction in management's commitment. This is particularly the case when the board's decision is viewed as wrong, too risky, or insufficiently promising. At the same time, executives, as their name indicates, prefer to run their own show than follow a script provided by the board. Hence, they may not even give much space to board members to advise and challenge them. Key questions here center around the extent to which boards can engage executives in framing the company's challenges and then inviting these executives to find answers to the challenges collaboratively determined. We return to this in Chaps. 11 and 12 when discussing the implementation of fair board processes.

4 Value Creation Gone Wrong in Owner-Led and Public Firms: VAG and BP

Value creation requires, as stated earlier, boards and stakeholders to agree on the course ahead and then to act in such a way that the intended progress materializes. The warning that this section issues is about the danger of aligning on the wrong mission and then forcing execution along that path. VAG's Dieselgate, presented in Chap. 2, is in that sense an interesting case: it shows how Ferdinand Piëch, whom most viewed as the principal owner (which he was not), convinced all to align on a mission that ultimately led them and the company down a very dark and indeed toxic road. The story of BP's Macondo disaster is similar but concerns a publicly listed firm: it shows how long-term shareholder value creation cannot in any way be equated with short-term optimization of the share price and, furthermore, how headquarters' obsessions with the share price can lead a company astray by paying insufficient attention to operational issues in its operations abroad. Both the BP and VAG stories share another silver lining: the ultimately beneficial and disciplining roles played by regulatory overseers and independent investigators when internal audit and compliance units fail, themselves a consequence of a failing board.

The purposeful fitting of illegal "cheating" devices to show lower than actual emissions in over 11 million diesel vehicles resulted in VAG having to pay US fines and penalties totaling US$ 25 billion,[12] with further fines to be expected from criminal and civil cases in Europe and Asia. Hans Dieter Pötsch, who became VAG Chairman after Dieselgate was uncovered, admitted that "*we are talking here not about a one-off mistake but a chain of errors.*" There was, according to Pötsch, "*a mindset in areas of the company that tolerated breaches of the rules.*" The dictatorial tendencies of the lead owner, Ferdinand Piëch, had permeated the entire company, and the board let this happen until ultimately a stakeholder, the US regulator, stopped the imperial tendencies of the one who had either directly instigated the collusion or created the conditions so that the wrong decisions were taken at the middle levels of the company due to a toxic "tone at the top of the company." The board surrendered too quickly to Piëch's ambitions and was blinded to the fact that Piëch's nearly dictatorial leadership had installed a corrosive culture within VAG where any means would eventually be applied to reach the mission so clearly stated by the owner and Chair. The board found itself in left field on the wrong end of the governance equation. It had abdicated its supervisory duties and failed in its fiduciary obligations to the company.

To fulfill this mission, the board must have the capacity to look more widely than the owner does. It must thoroughly examine and validate that the direction proposed by an all-powerful owner is truly in the interest of the company and does not put the company at risk by a delusional project pursued too long and too far. When owners go off the rails, boards typically do not sufficiently rein them in, either because they do not have the courage to confront the owner, because they are "fogged in" by a very talented seducer, or because they are precisely installed to approve and implement the owner's diktats. All-powerful owners, or Chairs and CEOs that act as psychological owners, broker little if any dissent. When times are good such Chairs may be effective, as in the first half of Ferdinand Piëch's career, when he revitalized Porsche and re-energized VAG through the development of the Audi brand into a worthy competitor of BMW and Mercedes.

When the board no longer has a group of directors with the will and power to stand up to an autocratic CEO, the company becomes vulnerable to the whims and fancies of its imperial owner. Dieselgate can be seen in such a light, as can Jack Welch and Carlos Ghosn at the end of their eras. Christopher Cox, former Chairman of the US Securities and Exchange Commission, paints a more positive vision, relying on the vital role of the board in this regard:

> *Happy companies have robust growth in revenues, strong balance sheets, and healthy profits that reflect genuine business success, not phony book-keeping. And they share other important traits as well. They abide by high ethical standards, which is key to their solid success. They don't obstruct the flow of information to shareholders, but rather view the shareholder as the ultimate owner and the ultimate boss. They choose directors on the strength of their abilities, character, and capacity for independent judgment. And their internal controls work well so that the company's executives can take immediate corrective action when something goes wrong.*[13]

Another example of board ineffectiveness was clearly in evidence during the 2010 Gulf of Mexico disaster, which pitted BP against the main contractor of its Macondo platform, Transocean. BP, which was the operator and the principal developer of the Macondo Prospect, had a 65% stake, while Anadarko and Mitsui owned 25 and 10% as co-investors. BP immediately blamed Transocean and Halliburton for the accident involving the Deepwater Horizon rig which Transocean owned and BP had chartered. In such cases, the responsibility for the rig is with the operator. The court indeed apportioned 67% of the responsibility for the tragedy to BP, 30% to Transocean, and 3% to Halliburton.

The impact on stakeholders of what is now known as the largest ecological disaster in US history is enormous. The explosion cost the lives of 11 workers and major damage to human and animal life in the Gulf of Mexico. The total cost to BP increased to US$ 65 billion by January 2018, more than three times the US$ 20 billion settlement fund originally agreed to by BP at the urging of former US President Obama.[14]

Boards are often said to have a primary supervisory role, leaving execution to hired management. This statement completely leaves out the responsibilities held by the board for the company and its relations with stakeholders. There is no responsibility without authority. Boards need to display proper **"duty of care"** when delegating their authority to executives. It is their fiduciary responsibility that allows board members and, in certain cases, even obliges them to overrule the executives when the latter appear not to exercise their delegated authority wisely. Proper governance requires that this delegation be knowingly assumed on both sides, with proper information on mutual and respective commitments, and not as an option or as time and conditions permit. This makes governance a collaborative play, akin to defense and offense in soccer. Neither side can effectively operate without the other, and errors can be made on both sides. This requires both sides to keep an open dialogue regarding the quality of the governance exercised, and their respective contributions to it.

Board members rarely end up in jail, short of outright and manifest fraud. Corporate justice still has a long way to go, the "normal business judgment" rule being typically invoked to defend wrong decision making, and absolving the guilty parties. Negligence is rarely punished. Even in the BP case only middle-level executives were sentenced, when it was clear that BP's US safety record was the worst in the industry, including an explosion in its Texas refinery killing 15 workers in 2005 and a major spill in Alaska at its Prudhoe Bay oil field the following year. These incidents should have triggered more active investigations by board members into BP's safety practices. National cultures and jurisdictions are not uniform in giving power to boards and to shareholders for challenging boards. The US is known for a culture of shareholder primacy and one where majority takes all. In addition, it is known for a culture of execution, and not governance. A meeting is successful in the US when it ends with a clear decision, so execution can proceed under the right conditions. The typical US comment here is that one does not know whether the decision was the right one unless execution has been excellent. Governance is about ensuring not just that the decision was clear, but foremost that it also was the right one in that context. We comment on why the role of boards has been minimized in the US.

Alfred Rappaport has clearly argued that one main fact that has been ignored in classical finance—including agency theory—is that shareholders are far from uniform. This is one of the principal reasons why boards are there to make choices. These choices will implicitly favor certain shareholders and stakeholders over others and certain strategies over others.[15] Boards have power, and are needed, precisely because there are many shareholders and many ways to deliver value to them. This makes shareholder primacy an attractive concept, but a virtual and false one nevertheless. Moreover, even in the US, stakeholder concerns have recently become recognized. For example, the Business Roundtable (BRT) declared outright that the purpose of a corporation is not just to serve shareholders (which was their position), but "to create value for all stakeholders."[16] This statement reminded all involved of the social role business plays through delivering value to customers, being good partners of suppliers, investing in employees, and supporting communities in which companies operate, including by embracing sustainable business practices. The BRT statement ended with a commitment to generate long-term value for shareholders.

The other reason shareholders often have little power is that US boards are challenged by shareholders only when more than 50% of them unite. US boards with a large and diffused shareholding are thus able to exercise nearly unlimited power, which then flows to the CEO. The UK built its stock market for smaller investors in the seventeenth century, buying shares of ships going off to India and other merchant locations. These investors were rightly concerned that they might be abused by the majority owners. Hence, UK corporate legislation vested substantial rights into minority owners: 5% of the owners can call for a General Meeting where their resolutions will be debated and voted upon; 10% of the shareholders may request a full audit of the company even when a company is otherwise exempt. Minority rights, when violated, invariably trigger a beneficial dialogue between shareholders and boards. Continuing execution without recognizing these minority shareholders only adds fuel to a growing fire. Board decisions affect more than controlling owners and shareholders. They impact a wide array of stakeholders, including the public and the environment, as the BRT statement reminds us.

The lack of true sanctions for board members is one of the reasons, in our view, for the poor state of governance in the world. The root cause of corporate failure is typically found not in poor management, but in poor governance by the board. Poor appointments, excessive tolerance for sub-performance, and an ability or will to forcefully address these issues are some of the underlying symptoms and also causes, with stakeholders ultimately paying the highest price, not shareholders or board members.

This was evident in the aftermath of the Global Financial Crisis (GFC) where not a single board member—or senior executive for that matter—ended up in jail. "Talk is still cheap" when one thinks of societies taking governance seriously. This points to yet another major advantage of owner-led firms, where directing owners or owners' boards see one of their main roles as ensuring and enabling proper governance. The BP incident and the GFC have shown that publicly held companies too often treat governance as a legal obligation, and not as a virtue or a foundation of their approach to business. A committed and continued interest in stakeholders and the impact of corporate and board decisions on them is often an indicator of an engaged ownership.

Turning to its internal supervisory role, the first priority of any board is to develop and nurture a vital link with the CEO. The CEO is the key actor in execution, but also governance when it pertains to the organization. Poor relations with the CEO render governance very difficult, if not impossible. Her or his importance cannot be understated. One tension in this relation is that the CEO is also key to performance. Most boards realize too late the costs of an average CEO. The point becomes clear only once they encounter a good or great CEO. At the same time, trust is a mutual currency, and a great CEO will understand that building a strong relationship with the board is also their responsibility, and not just that of the board.

Trust is an essential currency to develop with the CEO. An effective way to do so will be presented in much detail in Part 2 of this book. At this point, it will suffice to state that in this domain too the role of boards of owner-led companies differs from their counterparts in publicly listed ones: in these boards an underestimated part of the task is for boards to help the owners gain trust in the CEO, and vice versa. Boards in such companies are truly transmission engines between the owner and the owner's mission, and the CEO's goals and strategies. Pushing this point to its limit, one can say that especially in owner-led firms, boards are not "it"; they are a means to an end, which is alignment with and accomplishment of the mission. In firms with diffused ownership, debate often turns on the power of the executive relative to that of the board. A clearly stated and enforced mission reduces the politics, as does the presence of effective owners who will mediate such power struggles.

The ability for boards to create effective communications with owners and the CEO is thus a critical capability of owner-led boards. To discharge this, boards will regularly provide feedback to owners on progress in the accomplishment of the mission and on the ultimate achievement of the mission within acceptable bounds given the company's and the world's current context. Part of that feedback consists in the board communicating with owners on the CEO's performance and how the goals and strategies proposed and being pursued by the CEO align with the owner's mission. The Board will also, jointly with the CEO, address the management and communicate to them the continued central importance of the owner's mission, and the spirit and purpose behind the mission statement. Boards partner with the CEO and the executive management in setting goals and strategies for the company and ensuring that these remain in alignment with the owner's mission. The tasks of the board, in relation to owners and the CEO, are summarized in Fig. 3.3.

Reciprocity is key here for good collaboration and alignment, from owners to board to managers, and ultimately all employees. The board needs to trust both owners and the CEO, and the converse is true as well. Trust is created through communication and actions aligned with what has been said. In this conversation, all parties—owners, board members, and the CEO—need to possess enough self-confidence and humility to accept, based on facts, feedback that the parties provide to each other. A company can be stated to possess a governance culture when all in the company join in this responsibility,

The Board and Owners

- Feedback to owners on mission and progress
- Approve the company's goals in alignment with the mission
- Goals and tradeoffs concerning growth, profitability, and sustainability
- See to it that the owner's mission is translated into practical, quantifiable action points
- Monitor risks, especially of obsolescence
- Highlight the impact of financing on company health and sustainability, and its implications for ownership and control

The Board and the CEO

- Select and hire the CEO best able to ensure progress on the mission
- Partner with CEO in setting goals and strategy
- Partner with the CEO in navigating risks, especially obsolescence and financing
- Monitor and review CEO performance
- Mentor and guide the CEO
- CEO succession planning
- Top management development
- Exiting the CEO, ensuring the relay with the successor and ultimate handover

Fig. 3.3 The dual responsibilities of the Board toward owners and the CEO in owner-led firms

and when all recognize that the formal responsibility is placed on the board, but that the support and contributions of all to the board is expected and a key to that company's success.

The next section in this chapter provides a contrast between two family-controlled businesses that followed opposite paths. They illustrate the successes of companies when their boards and their owners handle their governance tasks well, and the difficulties faced when they do not. The two examples also demonstrate that owners have a wide array of choices available when deciding about the governance of their project, and that choices here have performance implications.

5 A Tale of Two Contrasting Family Businesses: Interbrew and Merck

Interbrew's success in growing through acquisitions and building its leadership position among major beer brands owes much to its owners. The mission to create long-term ownership value by choosing growth was the result of a conscious decision adhered to by the family shareholders at the time who agreed that growth was vital to avoid the continued erosion of its market position and relevance.

While during the first part of their history they pursued such objectives alone, merger with the Brazilian Ambev and the creation of InBev further consolidated the mission set by the Belgian owners, now joined by three remarkable Brazilian business leaders, and above all provided them with the right CEO to continue to pursue growth and at the same time concentrate on an urgently required strategy of cost cutting. Carlos Brito proved superb at this. The acquisition of Anheuser-Busch to form AB InBev was likely the master act.

It is not usual to find such value creation led by owners and such a clear case of alignment between owners, board members, and executives. Successful division of complementary tasks, adherence to the respective and agreed upon roles, and filling all with great talent will remain an example of owners set to reconquer a world of beer where they had found themselves in danger of becoming irrelevant. The Interbrew boards, both before and after the acquisition of Anheuser-Busch, have been relatively large, with a substantial number made up from the Stichting InBev, the key structure of the Belgian family holding. The 2008 InBev board consisted of 13 members, all of whom were non-executive (not the culture in either Belgium or Brazil), eight of which were nominees of Stichting InBev. The annual report included the following important insights into the functioning of the board:

- "In 2008, the Board held 9 regular meetings and 13 extraordinary telephonic meetings."[17] The final decision on making the winning bid (for Anheuser-Busch) was approved in a short board meeting conducted by telephone. This was a board aligned with the owner's mission and one that partnered the CEO in setting clear goals and strategies to be pursued. It showed decisive leadership in making the final decision to acquire a formidable competitor.
- This is a board that understood the mission of the owners (as described in Chap. 1 as long-term value accretion and dividends) and was clear about

the risks to this mission resulting from obsolescence. Remaining a relatively small, local beer company was considered riskier in terms of achieving the mission set by the owners.

- The Annual Report further comments on board process: "Several of the (board's) regular meetings, by design, were held in the various zones in which the company operated. On these occasions, the Board was provided with a comprehensive briefing of the relevant market. These briefings included an overview of performance, key challenges facing the market, and the steps being taken to address the challenges. Several of these visits also provided the Board with the opportunity to meet with employees and customers." The InBev Board is an example of an engaged board that stays extremely well informed on company performance, both in the aggregate and at the level of the business in each of the zones. This is an essential prerequisite for understanding allowing motivated and fact-based feedback to the owners and CEO and for allowing rich communications between owners, boards, and local and corporate executives.
- "Major Board agenda items in 2008 included the acquisition of Anheuser-Busch Companies Inc.; the 9.8 billion USD Rights Issue of the company; the long-range plan; achievement of targets; sales figures and brand health; reporting and budget; consolidated results; strategic direction; culture and people, including succession planning; new and ongoing investment; as well as discussions and analysis of acquisitions, divestitures and governance." The board agenda shows a mix of goal setting, strategies, and targets, monitoring of performance, and key decision making. All these are essential board tasks. Acquisitions as a necessary strategy against obsolescence and appropriate financing for executing this strategy were regular board agenda items as well.
- "The Chief Executive Officer (CEO) is entrusted by the Board with responsibility for the day-to-day management of the company. The CEO has direct operational responsibility for the entire company. The CEO leads an Executive Board of Management that comprises six global functional heads and six Zone presidents, including the two Co-Chief Executive Officers of AmBev." The board stays out of the CEO's operational responsibilities but has direct knowledge of and influences them through active engagement with the CEO, his functional team, and the executive management in each of the zones.

InBev's streamlined structure ensures that there is a clear demarcation between owners who set the mission, the CEO who has full responsibility for operationalizing the mission, and the board that links the owners and the

CEO, in setting company and business unit goals, while also mentoring and monitoring the CEO and senior management team. However, companies rarely attain this level of clarity and alignment in the understanding of the difference between corporate mission and specific business goals, and about the respective roles of owners, boards, and executives.

Our next example provides a contrast. It points to the problems that emerge when these notions may not be properly grasped. **Merck KGaA**, "Merck," traces its origins to 1668 when it was founded by Friedrich Jacob Merck. Very few companies have such a long ancestry, even if Interbrew, founded in 1366, can boast greater longevity. The North American Merck now belongs to a separate company, even though they were once part of Merck KGaA. But it was nationalized by the US government during World War I. Entering the twentieth century, Merck was one of the most international companies, present in nearly every country and continent. Merck shares many features with Interbrew in terms of family ownership (family holding on top and strong direction-setting from the family). There is a major difference, however, in their businesses, which renders the governance of Merck far more complex: Merck is an industrial holding active in several business sectors, whereas Interbrew operates in one industrial sector (beer). Brewing, in addition, has seen little technological progress over the last 2000 years.

Today Merck is a large pharmaceutical, life science, and performance materials company with sales of over 16.2 billion euros (2019) and a presence in 62 countries. The company was privately held by descendants of the founder until 1995 when it offered 30% of its shares on the Frankfurt Stock Exchange. This represented one of Germany's largest IPOs at the time. The family, now with members of its 13th generation, continues to hold 70% of the capital of the company through a family holding company, E. Merck KG. Frank Stangenberg-Haverkamp, Chairman of the Executive Board and of the Family Board, commented in a press interview[18] on the commitment of the family to the company as follows: "*I am from the 11th generation of my family, and we have 239 bloodline family members; 153 are owners with voting rights. All of them are descendants of the three sons of my ancestor Emanuel Merck who transformed Merck into an industrial company in 1827.*"[19]

Though there are similarities in its ownership with Interbrew, Merck appears to also have structured the interaction between the supervisory board and the executives in a more complex manner. These governance complexities are often paid insufficient attention as they impact performance. Chairman Frank Stangenberg-Haverkamp explained the structure in his 2015 press interview[20] as follows: "*E. Merck KG is the holding company of all Merck companies, and it does not have any operating businesses. In 1995, we decided to bring*

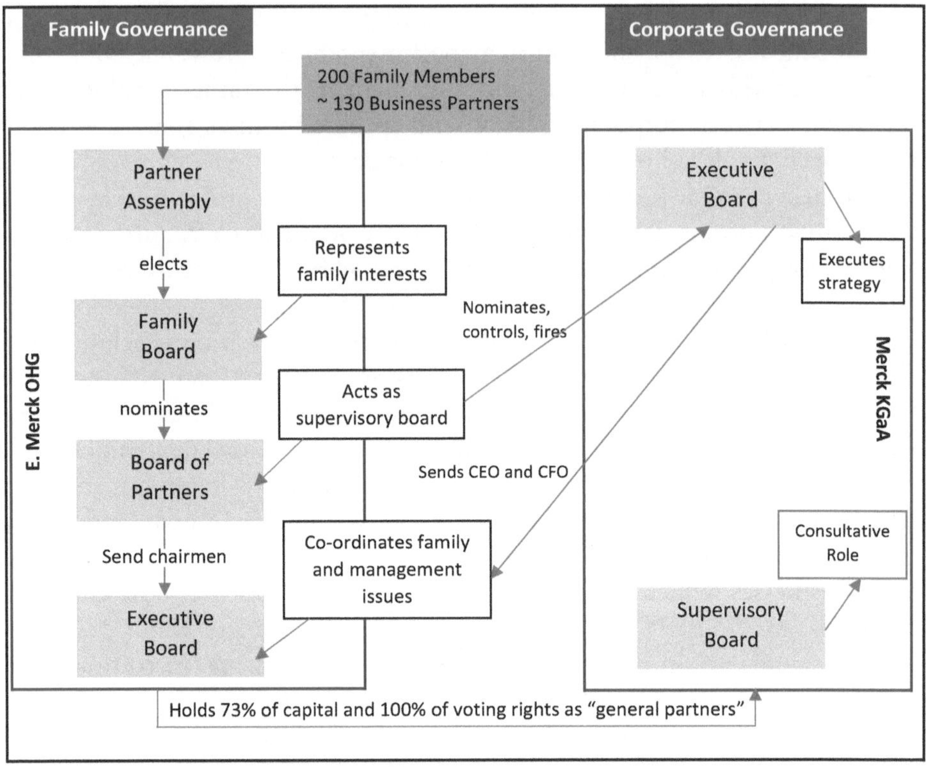

Fig. 3.4 Merck governance structures. Source: Merck KGaA

external shareholders [in Merck KGaA] and diluted nearly 30 percent of the total share capital while the rest (70 percent) is with the family via the 'general partner' E. Merck KG. The interests and control of the family in running Merck are executed through a Family Board, Board of Partners, and an Executive Board." Thus, in total there were five boards at the time, as shown in Fig. 3.4.

Further explanation of these many boards is provided below. It is largely taken from the company's website[21] and appears in italics:

Partner Assembly

The Partners' Meeting is a gathering of all partners of E. Merck KG and comparable to the Annual General Meeting of a German stock corporation (Aktiengesellschaft). It receives the reports of the other corporate bodies, elects the members of the Family Board, decides on changes to the participation relationships in Merck KGaA, on capital increases and contract amendments. It takes place at least once a year.

Family Board

The Family Board defines the strategic direction of all the Merck companies and represents the entrepreneurial interests of the Merck family of owners. Its members are elected by the Partners' Meeting and are members of the Merck family.

Board of Partners of E. Merck KG

The Board of Partners is elected by the Family Board and corresponds to the Supervisory Board of a German stock corporation. It decides upon the appointment and dismissal of Executive Board members of Merck KGaA. The board supervises the management of Merck KGaA, grants approval of extraordinary business transactions, especially major investments, and approves the annual financial statements of E. Merck KG. Apart from five members of the Family Board, four external members of the business community belong to the Board of Partners.

Executive Board of E. Merck KG

The Executive Board is the management body and the face of E. Merck KG. It conducts the businesses of E. Merck KG, represents the company externally and coordinates the work of the corporate bodies of E. Merck KG. Furthermore, it implements the resolutions passed by the Partners' Meeting and the Family Board and fulfills their duties to Merck KGaA. The Executive Board consists of the chairmen of the Family Board and the Board of Partners, the Chairman of the Executive Board, and the Chief Financial Officer of Merck KGaA, as well as elected members.

Because Merck KGaA is a listed company, it also has a **Supervisory Board.** Following German co-determination rules, half of this board is made up of nominees selected by Merck employees and the other half by the shareholders, essentially the Merck family. German governance rules indeed do not foresee the presence of so-called independent members as would be expected in Anglo-Saxon capitalism. For consistency and coordination needs, family members on this board are also members of the Family Board of Partners. The Supervisory Board hires and monitors the performance of the Executive Board of Merck KGaA. However, its role is more advisory to the Partners Board of E. Merck KG since that is the board which in practice holds real responsibility for overseeing the Executive Board of Merck KGaA.

This Merck governance structure has resulted in a clear voice for the "239 bloodline family members," of which "153 are owners with voting rights." We would argue that the structure does more than that. Indeed, the website attests that "*the family through E Merck KG does not participate in the management of the company, but it makes the fundamental entrepreneurial decisions of the Merck*

Group." Governance is thus clearly in the hands of the family, through the elected members of the Family Board. The question is whether the structure which provides voice and input for family members effectively ensures corporate performance.

Such a structure, however, raises several concerns. First, it is rather complex, with overlapping responsibilities between several boards and multiplication of roles held by the Family Partners. The lack of clarity in responsibilities transpires from the picture, with too many distinct structures having a hand in "strategic" decisions. The additional qualification of the Family Board as representing "the entrepreneurial interests" of family owners is worrisome. The sentence is very open ended. Furthermore, entrepreneurs like to intervene directly and make decisions themselves, while having, like Steve Jobs, little patience with structures, and even less with governance structures, which they regard as excessively bureaucratic. Our general view is that because governance issues are complex by their nature, simplicity and clarity in the governance structure is preferable.

The CEO has to eventually deal with all these owners with entrepreneurial interests, and is tasked with implementing their decisions, without, it seems, being able to address them formally. Indeed, his formal Supervisory Board is advisory to the Board of Partners of E Merck KG, which is a corporation other than the company that employs him. Equally concerning is a dangerous overlap and possible confusion between mission setting and the creation of goals and strategies for each of the multiple businesses held by the group. Having the Family Partners, helped by a few non-family members, discuss and confirm the mission of the Merck Group is where matters are similar with Interbrew. But having these same individuals decide on entrepreneurial actions and strategies of a group involved in multiple and distinct business sectors and geographies, each with their own competitive contexts and fundamentals, seems a herculean task.

Finally, the power of independent supervisory boards balancing the interests of each of the businesses with those of the owning family and pursuing alignment exists only in the Board of Partners and Executive Boards. The Merck board structures appear to suffer from excessive reliance on family members and their close associates, and in our view represent an example of **governance risk**, due to the lack of clarity and complexity of the governance structures of the family and the business.

Let us now turn to performance of Merck. The industrial challenges Merck faced were:

- Maturing market and the need to re-focus and reenergize its product portfolio;
- Increased global competition: consolidation in the pharmaceutical industry was occurring rapidly and there was the increased importance of brand differentiation;
- Increasing purchasing power with buyers: there was a shift from build to stock to build to order, product life cycles were becoming shorter, and distribution requirements were increasing on a global scale, when Merck appeared to be sub-scale.

Merck's complex collection of boards appears to have been unable to take appropriate action to combat the obsolescence risks the company was facing in a very competitive and changing context. Despite being one of the oldest surviving pharmaceutical companies (and perhaps the oldest), Merck today is neither a top 20 pharmaceutical company (based on 2019 revenues) nor does it have a large R&D pipeline of new drugs or treatments that could help propel it into being a larger and more profitable company.

By 2005, Merck was, remarkably, no longer a top pharmaceutical company (Fig. 3.4). In 2006 it had the opportunity to address some of these challenges by acquiring rival Schering. Schering was the world's market leader in contraceptives and had a strong focus on oncology and the central nervous system. These were areas where Merck wished to grow. Through the acquisition of Schering, Merck could address main weaknesses: it would double overall sales to €11.2bn and it would greatly enhance the attractiveness of its product pipeline (Fig. 3.5). Finally, Schering owned a strong distribution network in the US and Japan, where Merck was weak. The overlaps between Merck and Schering were minimal, facilitating integration. To top the list of benefits expected from the acquisition, Merck would substantially diversify its relatively limited pharmaceutical offering (Fig. 3.6).

The problem was that, due to the family dominance in their governance, the decision had to be taken by the Partners Assembly. This created inertia and bias. The risk family members immediately apprehended was the downside of the business risks taken, and the distress the decision might create, financially and in the family. Comforted by a family history that had spanned centuries, the risk of obsolescence must have been far from their minds. This is something that Heineken's superb marketing and growth made very visible to Interbrew shareholders. In contrast, the Merck owners must have minimized the risk associated with foregoing the Schering deal. The Supervisory

Company	Pharma Sales ($bn)
Pfizer	46.1
Sanofi-Aventis	31.8
GlaxoSmithKline	31.4
Johnson & Johnson	22.1
Merck & Co	21.5
Astra Zeneca	21.4
Novartis	18.5
Roche	17.3
...	
Bayer	11.8
...	
Schering	6.3
...	
Merck KGaA	4.9

Fig. 3.5 Merck's global position among pharmaceutical companies (2005). Source: Company filings

Company	Phase I	Phase II	Phase II	Filed	Total
Merck	4	8	1	1	14
Schering	N/A	11	12	2	25
Bayer	12	11	3	1	27
Novartis	26	20	17	13	76

Fig. 3.6 Merck pharmaceutical product line compared with key competitors (2005). Source: Company filings and West LB broker report

Board was largely dominated by family members. The lack of independent directors at the Partners Assembly did not allow useful and countervailing sources of information and hypotheses to be discussed. This would have been most helpful when brainstorming on how best to manage disruption and obsolescence.

Given all this, the Merck board and family balked at the high price to be paid for Schering. They also would not consider greatly diluting the family stake, something Interbrew owners accepted to fulfill their agreed upon mission. The Interbrew board members were indeed blamed by investors and by some family members for overpaying their early acquisitions, and for diluting the family's stake. But they in unison repeated that this was the price to pay for substantial performance increases and particularly for avoiding increasing obsolescence.

The eventual regret at having missed the Schering acquisition must have convinced the "entrepreneurial" Merck owners that they had to move. Merck purchased Serono, a biopharmaceutical company, in 2007 for 10.3 billion euros, followed in 2010 by the purchase of Millipore Corporation, a life sciences company, for US$ 7.2 billion. Neither acquisition was transformative, nor did it make a meaningful, significant impact on Merck's market position. Serono owners are generally considered to have been the great beneficiaries of the sale to Merck, particularly because the two company cultures proved difficult to combine, making some doubt that Merck got the true value out of the acquisition. To make matters worse, Merck had to finance these acquisitions and reduce its leverage. To do so, it sold its generics business for 4.9 billion euros to Mylan Laboratories Inc. While generics represented a high-volume, lower-margin business than research-driven specialty drug development, the sale closed off Merck's options in a rapidly growing market segment without successfully enhancing its options in drug R&D.

In 2018 the company sold its Consumer Health business for 3.4 billion euros to Procter & Gamble (P&G), closing another large market option. On the organic growth side, Merck continued to face difficulties. High-profile challenges included Merck stopping clinical development, in September 2014, of two drugs the company had invested considerably in and returning the rights of the Kuvan drug (a treatment for a rare disease) in October 2015, to Bio-Marin, "in order to focus on its core businesses."[22]

Merck's failure to remain a leading pharma company can, in our analysis, be traced to a failure of the family ownership, particularly that the latter openly assumed responsibility for all "major entrepreneurial decisions" of the Merck Group. The Merck family effectively decided upon the appointment and dismissal of Executive Board members of Merck KGaA, including its CEO, and "approved extraordinary business transactions, especially major investments."

The future of Merck, for the 13th generation of the family, is now uncertain. It finds itself back in the position of the Interbrew generation when they took over from its predecessors and decided to resolutely embark on a growth journey to avoid obsolescence. Unlike the case of Interbrew, there appeared to be no clear division of labor between owners, boards, and executives, different family members weighing in excessively on various strategic decisions and goal setting. The absence of strong challenges from independents and executives appears to us to be at the root of the Merck mishaps over recent decades. The problem of insufficiently appreciating the critical difference between mission set by the owners, on one side, and goals and strategies on the other, the latter set by executives supervised by independent supervisors, appears to loom large.

Like any owner, Merck family members longed for sustainable ownership and long-term value creation, but they proved unsuccessful in meeting the challenges of obsolescence and growth. Without scale and size, long-term ownership may eventually become unprofitable, even if for the time being Merck remains a reasonably sized company, albeit a largely German one.

The lesson again is that owners should foremost focus on mission, on core values and governance principles, and let executives craft and come forward with goals and strategies. The latter will be the subject of the next chapter. Before we turn to that topic, we examine the difficulties owners face in obtaining value from boards and identify the characteristics of great board members.

6 Getting Value from Boards: A Step Change in Diversity Perspective[23]

Diversity and competence are two keys to the board's value creating role. But which diversity and which competences? In practical board terms, diversity and competence represent a trade-off between a narrowness of deep expertise and viewpoint and a breadth of expertise necessary to achieve strategic and business oversight, which one can only fall short of with a limited number of board members.

Historically, the emphasis has been on financial expertise, the board's first language. This was duly reinforced by the financial crisis, which indeed required boards to "more carefully check the numbers." This view rests on the assumption that the financial crisis was a failure of financial understanding. The reality—as identified in numerous reports and books, from the Davies Report onwards—has actually not been there, but rather to "blame" board conduct, and more specifically, to point to behavioral deficiencies of boards in lacking debate, discussion, and challenge of the gaps separating the operational performance of companies and their strategic intent. Psychologically, the skills of detailed financial analysis are indeed rarely combined with those yielding a good strategic perspective. Indeed, a number of the most widely used psychological recruitment tools regard these as contra indicators. Diversity again is the answer here. The essential role of the Board is to bring a "balance" of multiple interests and viewpoints. This role is more effectively played by individuals capable of multiple viewpoints and insights. Board dynamics are substantially helped by board members reaching out to others and challenging colleagues with skill and competence on the other side of the argument. This reduces the chances of particular directors exercising their power by virtue of their monopoly on a particular attribute or of the board functioning as a group of silos, board members exercising their views in their silos without contributing or taking much interest outside their silo. Fundamentally, diversity helps in brainstorming and better framing of problems, as we will see in later sections, as long as diversity is well managed. Diversity is both a value and a risk. The best way to manage this risk is to have a healthy dose of diversity in each board member, and to keep specialist language outside the boardroom. Finally, a key to diversity is the degree of "skin in the game." Independent directors typically have no skin in the game, while owners do. This implies that political/social/reputational/legal implications will tend to make independent directors act in an excessively conservative way. In the case of Merck, for example, a financial decision that involved a drastic increase in leverage would have been discarded as "too risky" by independent directors that are legally liable in case the firm gets in distress, while facing no liability in the case the corporation becomes obsolete. Therefore, a key source of diversity is not having a board just made up of independent directors, which was the case for Carlsberg, a firm that did not move forward as positively as InBev did. Then InBev governance was led by family members with skin in the game, but who were also acutely aware of the duty of care toward family shareholders.

Building on these ideas, and on the work that has characterized effective collaboration among managers, there is a benefit from seeking directors "benchmarked" on multiple perspectives. These perspectives are now detailed:

- **A FUNCTIONAL "Perspective"** reduces the bias that comes from being grounded and shaped in one function, valuing directors having at least one other functional strength (e.g., CFO with strong marketing experience). Such a director more easily provides perspectives not just emanating from a bias rooted in one functional background or expertise. A second functional perspective gets people out of their silo perspective, while possessing three functional perspectives further grows one's understanding of functions, their values, and their diversity.
- **A BUSINESS-INDUSTRY "Perspective"** offers a perspective from across differing business sectors and industries, for example mobile phone to banking or music business to mass engagement businesses. It avoids directors being locked into the thinking dominating one sector or industry. Again, three industry perspectives will generate greater perspective and wisdom regarding the validity of industry practices and rules of the game.
- **A CULTURAL-NATIONAL "Perspective"** understands that perspectives differ across cultures and nationalities. People with such perspectives are invaluable "bridges" linking distinct cultural and national perspectives in a multi-cultural board. Such members allow boards to avoid being trapped in contexts or stereotypes. Culture is indeed best understood with distance and contrast. An appreciation of two perspectives risks becoming trapped in these two distinct perspectives. Three perspectives typically provide a jump in cultural relativity.
- **AN OWNER "Perspective"** is obtained by having close experience with ownership, either through birth and family, or through prolonged exposure, as well as from having "skin in the game." Given that one of the main points of this book is that owner-led corporations differ from publicly listed ones, having such perspectives allow boards not to be trapped in a single ownership perspective. Again, family members having been exposed to a single ownership culture but having other family perspectives on the Board of Directors is particularly useful and is another value provided by non-family directors. The same holds for state-owned or entrepreneurial enterprises, which are often too rigidly anchored in "their ways" of governing. Innovation often consists in importing outside practices into a family or an industry.

This approach provides owners with a language and framework that allows boards to be formed with a rich set of desirable characteristics:

- Members would make different and multiple contributions in the skills/experience/competence matrix used to tabulate the characteristics needed and already present in the board.
- There would be more overlap among board members than would appear from a traditional skills matrix built on a one- or two-dimensional characteristic and this would give an edge to people who can contribute meaningfully to diverse discussions and through a multiplicity of viewpoints.

The main point of our argument is to underline that owners need to seek diversity in board members in more dimensions than is the case for functional executives and even general managers. Superb but one-dimensional executives do not necessarily make for great board members, even if they are highly valuable as expert advisors or functional managers. The benchmarking and discussion among board members is simply of a different nature than that practiced by managers.

As the global economic sands shift, the need for both a wider and deeper vision from the "collective" board becomes stronger. The need to build diverse boards that see beyond the myopic short termism and create profitable, socially aware and people-focused businesses has never been greater. We will return to this key issue in later chapters.

Notes

1. https://www.vanityfair.com/news/2009/01/stiglitz200901-2.
2. https://cluelesspoliticalscientist.wordpress.com/2017/05/17/what-is-political-theory-by-andrew-hacker-a-summary/.
3. https://www.britannica.com/place/Falun#ref154668.
4. https://www.storaenso.com/en/about-stora-enso/our-history.
5. G20/OECD Principles of Corporate Governance, p.18, http://www.oecd.org/corporate/principles-corporate-governance/.
6. Theory of the Firm: Managerial behavior, agency costs, and ownership structure, by M.C. Jensen and W.H. Meckling, Journal of Financial Economics, Vol. 3 (4), 1976.
7. G20/OECD Principles of Corporate Governance, p. 50, http://www.oecd.org/corporate/principles-corporate-governance/.
8. G20/OECD Principles of Corporate Governance, p. 48, http://www.oecd.org/corporate/principles-corporate-governance/.

9. G20/OECD Principles of Corporate Governance, pp. 18–19, http://www.oecd.org/corporate/principles-corporate-governance/.
10. Markets and Hierarchies: Analysis and Antitrust Implications, by Oliver E. Williamson, Macmillan Publishers, 1975.
11. https://www.reutersevents.com/sustainability/business-strategy/brent-spar-battle-launched-modern-activism.
12. "How VW Paid $25 Billion for 'Dieselgate' — and Got Off Easy," *Fortune* magazine, February 6, 2018.
13. https://www.sec.gov/news/speech/spch111105cc.htm.
14. https://www.reuters.com/article/us-bp-deepwaterhorizon-idUSKBN1F50NL.
15. Alfred Rappaport and John C. Bogle, *Saving Capitalism From Short-Termism: How to Build Lon-Term Value and Take Back Our Financial Future,* McGraw Hill Professional (2011).
16. https://www.businessroundtable.org/business-roundtable-redefines-the-purpose-of-a-corporation-to-promote-an-economy-that-serves-all-americans.
17. AB InBev 2008 Annual Report.
18. https://www.businesstoday.in/magazine/features/frank-stangenberg-haverkamp-e-merck-kg-on-company-plans/story/222095.html.
19. https://www.businesstoday.in/magazine/features/frank-stangenberg-haverkamp-e-merck-kg-on-company-plans/story/222095.html.
20. https://www.businesstoday.in/magazine/features/frank-stangenberg-haverkamp-e-merck-kg-on-company-plans/story/222095.html.
21. https://www.merckgroup.com/en/company/who-we-are/management/e-merck-kg.html.
22. https://www.merckgroup.com/press-releases/2015/oct/en/Return-Kuvan-Rights-EN.pdf.
23. This section is based on an article by Helen Pitcher, Chairman of Advanced Boardroom Excellence Ltd., and one of the authors. It is available at https://blogs.insead.edu/idpn-globalclub/a-step-change-in-diversity-perspective-the-shifting-sands-of-diversity/.

4

The CEO and the Executive Team: Responsible for Executing the Mission

1 The Captain of the Ship

Henry David Thoreau wrote, "*If you have built castles in the air, your work need not be lost; that is where they should be. Now put the foundations under them.*"[1] Missions are like Thoreau's castles in the air. Missions are intent; they need to become reality. This is the role and responsibility of CEOs. Without a CEO, the most inspiring of missions remain pieces of paper. The value and critical role of a great CEO is often underestimated. This is the case, for example, when a board views their current CEO to be not that bad. Such a conclusion confirms that the board does not understand the opportunity cost imposed on the company of not having a great CEO. Only when the latter arrives does a board often grasp what they have been missing.

Beyond the value of the leadership brought to a company by a great CEO, what often receives insufficient attention is the requirement that the CEO needs to ensure that goals and strategies are implemented in a manner that is aligned with the owner's mission. Indeed, the latter is the condition for value creating goals and strategies.

At the inception of a business, there is a simple and direct connection between the founder's beliefs and expectations, the enterprise's goals and strategies, and the execution of these strategies. The entrepreneur insures all of this. A strong feature of start-up enterprises is this alignment. Being present as the only or most dominant voice in multiple roles, the owner-founder-CEO ensures that there is close to perfect consistency between all levels of the organization and the mission originally set out by her or him. Masayoshi Son famously described his start at Softbank as follows: "*I only had two part-time*

M. Massa et al., *Value Creation for Owners and Directors*,
https://doi.org/10.1007/978-3-031-19726-0_4

workers and a small office. I got two apple boxes, and I stood upon them in the morning as if I was giving a speech. In a loud voice, I said to my two workers, 'You guys have to listen to me because I am the president of this company.' I said, 'In five years, I'm going to have $75 million in sales. In five years, I will be supplying 1,000 dealer outlets, and we'll be number one in PC software distribution.' And I said it very loudly."[2] Alignment is not the prominent issue at the birth of an enterprise. The main complexities are rather of another kind: growth, financing, and risk are usually greater challenges confronting the founder entrepreneur.

Alignment emerges as a complex and thorny issue when enterprises grow. When it is no longer enough r even feasible to stand on an apple box and direct employees as a master chef does in her or his kitchen, the need for founding owners' driving forces and beliefs to continue to be integrated and adhered to at all levels of the organization now emerges as a much greater challenge.

The need for CEOs to lead the business is well accepted among professionals and academics. However, continued alignment with the owner's mission as a key condition for value creation must be regularly thought through and revisited. Central in this constantly evolving drama is that, just like the founder, there are two other key stakeholders, the board and the CEO, and we include in the latter the senior leadership team—that also have visions about the best direction to be followed by the corporation. These centrifugal forces invariably create a fair amount of entropy in most firms, particularly when the strategic stakes are high and complex. This is what makes a regular if not continued discussion on mission alignment by the "team at the top" so valuable. This team consists of the owner(s), the Chairman of the board, and the CEO, and his senior management team, if he is a team player.

Divergence from the mission will manifest itself when translating the latter into goals and strategy for the business and finally into the company's daily operations. Theodore Roosevelt noted in his famous "Man in the Arena" speech: "*It is not the critic who counts; not the man who points out how the strong man stumbles, or where the doer of deeds could have done them better. The credit belongs to the man who is actually in the arena, whose face is marred by dust and sweat and blood; who strives valiantly; who errs, who comes short again and again because there is no effort without error and shortcoming; but who does actually strive to do the deeds.*"[3]

Roosevelt's most important "man in the arena" is the CEO. The mission is only a dream unless it is turned into a reality, and that is the task of the CEO. When a company is created, the founder is both owner and CEO, and is the "one man in the arena" operationalizing driving forces and dreams. As the enterprise becomes larger and older, the CEO is no longer part of the founders' group yet remains the one who must give reality to and drive the mission, by setting medium-term goals, checking action agendas, and leading strategy formulation and implementation.

A vivid illustration of growing divergence between a leader's quest and a corporate mission is the story described in Chap. 1 concerning Carlos Ghosn. As long as Ghosn was supervised by Schweitzer, the Renault Chair, value creation was proceeding well. The discontinuity came when Ghosn succeeded Schweitzer as Chair and CEO of Renault. Nissan had by then become by far the stronger partner of the alliance, while Renault seemed to stagnate. Even though they had been writing a remarkable and most innovative alliance chapter in the history of the global automotive industry, the two companies started to drift apart, pursuing different missions. Ghosn seemed to increasingly distance himself from its largest shareholder, the French state. Remarkably, the French state owns 15% of shares of Renault—as much as Nissan does, but with non-voting power—and is by far the largest shareholder of Nissan (44%). Nevertheless, alignment was lost, which suggests ownership failure in setting and managing mission. All three parties eventually lost out: Ghosn, Renault and the French state, and Nissan, which again became one of the lesser performing automotive manufacturers.

The unfolding Dieselgate at VAG similarly shows how a family CEO and Chair can usurp all power and twist missions and company activities into risky terrain, and eventually onto the rails, to the detriment of himself, the other owners, the company, as well as its stakeholders.

CEOs must have a helicopter perspective to oversee progress toward a future vision, a medium-distance operational view to check alignment of the many different parts of a company, as well as the ability to occasionally dive into the nuts and bolts of a company's operations to spot major issues and unblock managerial and organizational bottlenecks that impede progress. Ram Charan first developed a framework for helping CEOs gain the capacity to operate at different altitudes, which Woodward coins as operating at 50,000 feet, at 50, and at 5.[4] Operationalizing the mission requires the CEO to have these capabilities. DBS CEO Piyush Gupta is an example of a leader who looks keenly at goals and strategy, yet equally guides his team at the "coal face." He famously "monitored the queues himself at ATMs in his early days to assess the [then] underperforming retail unit."[5] At InBev, Carlos Brito complements his deal-making with a ceaseless focus and even involvement in costs. The *Financial Times* reported that Brito immediately took his executive team to Anheuser-Busch's St Louis headquarters the day after the acquisition was announced.[6]

Alfred Sloan was the CEO behind the many decades of success enjoyed by General Motors. He accumulated several roles: President (1923 to 1937), CEO (1923 to 1946), and Chairman (1937 to 1956). In 1923, when Sloan became General Motors' President, the Ford Motor Company was the dominant car company in the US. General Motors claimed a mere 12% of the market. Sloan's mission to provide "a car for every purse and purpose" eventually resulted 4 years later in General Motors selling double the number of cars Ford did.

The approaches pursued by both companies could not be further apart. When Ford focused on just the Model T, and then in black only, Sloan diversified the product portfolio through a "federal decentralization" of the corporate structure. He focused corporate board decision making on oversight of the mission and allowed business divisions to make their decisions with due autonomy. This resulted in the business divisions – Chevrolet, Pontiac, Oldsmobile, Buick, and Cadillac—providing reliable cars to their customers in well-defined customer segments. Annual strategic and marketing planning exercises expanded the nascent car market and shaped how Americans lived and worked. The objective was to neatly move the American worker and manager across the different GM brands while he was progressing through the ranks and through life. This system was later copied by companies worldwide. One could argue that VW still mimics this system with its SEAT, SKODA, VW, Audi, Porsche, Bentley, and Bugatti brands. What is equally remarkable is how Sloan's successors were unable to sustain the mission at GM, which ultimately had to be bailed out by the US Government, after many years of market share losses. Misalignment at CEO succession looms large.

The importance of appointing CEOs cannot be understated. Neither can the mission framed by the owner. The overarching obsession of a CEO should be to turn the mission into reality.

2 Operationalizing the Mission and Facing Trade-Offs: The Interbrew Case Continued

In this section, we focus on how CEOs operationalize a mission, given the ownership context they face. We illustrate the question by returning to **Interbrew**.

Interbrew had always pursued a mission of long-term value creation and dividends. However, the goals defined to achieve this changed radically over time. For a long time Interbrew had, like most beer companies in Europe, a strong position in its home market, where its beer brands enjoyed great notoriety. But, except perhaps for neighboring countries, the notoriety abroad was much less. It could have kept milking its nearly monopolistic local position in a fragmented European beer market. - That would demand the selection of a CEO who understood and agreed with the strategy and would maintain Interbrew's Belgian company culture and management. The CEO would likely be an internal promotion.

However, changes in beer consumption patterns and the emergence of the European single market changed industry fundamentals. Beer was no longer drunk in a pub but increasingly at home. The bargaining power of beer producers in the distribution channel deteriorated when facing giant retailers like Carrefour and Tesco rather than pubs they either owned or could easily control. Competition intensifying, differentiation and hence loyalty were less than commonly thought. A large integrated European single market also attracted large international players, such as Heineken and Anheuser-Busch, whose German roots made a return of the St Louis-based US brewer to Europe likely. Under those conditions power with distributors became a premium. One way to achieve this was to acquire more brands that would increase "space on the shelf.. Interbrew risked ending up like one of the smaller or mid-sized sharks in Fig. 4.1, as prey to larger competitors. Short- and medium-term profitability could be focused upon but would likely make the firm irrelevant ("obsolete") in the long run.

Given these considerations, the option that owners, board, and management finally aligned upon was to focus on quick growth, with the aim of becoming number one ("the bigger sharks" depicted in Fig. 4.1). This implies focusing on size and scale, becoming a more dominant beer company regionally, and possibly reaching global scale over time. Interbrew could use the steady cash flow position that came with its strong position in the home market to start distributing its high-quality products internationally, something Stella Artois had tried in the past, unsuccessfully.

Fig. 4.1 Interbrew's choice regarding how to operationalize its mission

Interbrew would have to move aggressively in foreign markets. It also would need to acquire companies and therefore significantly leverage up, taking more distress risk and potentially reducing dividends. The consequence of the choice for growth was that Interbrew, for several years, would be unprofitable, likely overspend in acquisitions, and leverage up to finance its acquisitions. Interbrew had chosen growth over profitability and sustainability.

An important point to retain from our discussion is that to achieve its mission Interbrew had to focus on a short-term goal of growth. The path Interbrew followed for several years was to be non-profitable—and thus not sustainable—precisely to continue to deliver on its mission of longer-term value creation. Acquisitions was the thrust chosen to meet the goal of rapid growth, speed being important in a concentrated global market.

The other point to stress is that the choice of a specific strategy necessarily implies the choice of a particular CEO profile. CEOs are not highly versatile. They must have a number of basic **competences**, covering strategy (both market and supply strategies), team leadership, and finance, to cite the most important (and what typically is covered in MBA programs). But what distinguishes them—just like sports athletes—are their **talents**. Competences are needed for talented people to leverage their talent. Invariably both competences and talents are needed. But while competences can be learned, talent is innate. One can acquire competences through learning and practice, but talents cannot be learned. Talents are natural, sustainable, fun, and easy to display. Competences are acquired, require effort, and erode when not regularly practiced. When competences are easily acquired, the talent source is never far away.

These points are vital for CEO selection. Some CEOs are talented at acquisitions, others at growing companies organically, and finally others, like Carlos Ghosn, are superb at turning companies around. So Interbrew owners realized that they had to have new competences and talents on the board. Before even starting the growth task, the company had to be restructured both in terms of ownership structure and integration of processes. Therefore an "integration" team was selected. A new Chairman and a new "restructuring" CEO had to be appointed: Jacques Thierry, Chair of BBL, one of Belgium's leading banks, became the first Chair, while José Dedeurwaarder, head of Renault in the US, was named CEO. The complementary financial and industrial experiences of the new Chair and the new CEO would prove most valuable. Dedeurwaarder's task would be to integrate the two merged companies, Piedboeuf and Artois, into a more efficient Interbrew organization. The CEO's automotive experience would prove very valuable here as 1000 people had to be laid off, five production sites had to be closed, and the company had to be completely reorganized into a more efficient beer manufacturer. Overall productivity indeed more than doubled, from 2.5 hectoliters per man-hour in 1990 to 6.5 hectoliters in 1995. The company soon achieved full ownership of the Belgian Belle-Vue brewery, the Hungarian Borsodi Világos in 1991, and Romania's Bergenbier and Croatia's Ozujsko in 1994. All these sites had to be integrated into Interbrew's growing manufacturing and distribution network.

However, Dedeurwaarder made a cultural mistake that was the result of the world he came from: he put too many automotive managers at the heads of the new organizational units. They did not effectively represent the desired brewing culture.[7] Dedeurwaarder was abruptly terminated in 1993, "having accomplished great work." The main sticking point was the fall in profitability by 28%, which may indeed have been the result of insufficient knowledge about newly acquired local market realities. Perhaps having to merge two strong cultures, representing two former competitors, Artois and Piedboeuf, very different and both conservative, proved harder than expected. They were not ready for the considerable restructuring imposed by the CE0 with force. This may have proven to be too much of a challenge for Dedeurwaarder and his team and had a cost in terms of profitability. Whatever the reason, the board replaced him with Jean-Marie Descarpenteries, who immediately provided the needed restructuring change impetus. Descarpenteries accomplished his mission and left Interbrew to become Chair and CEO of French IT company Bull.

The time was now ripe for starting the growth phase, full steam ahead. A new CEO was chosen for this task: Hans Meerloo. Under him, in 1995 Interbrew launched itself in the acquisition of Labatt, one of Canada's two main brewers and distributor of Interbrew's Stella Artois brand there. This opened a new chapter for the formerly sleepy beer company. The job of Meerloo was pursued by Hugo Powell with a massive expansion in the British market (acquisition of Whitbred and Bass). However, this led to a spiraling of leverage to 440%, with profitability again being badly affected by the acquisition costs. This led to the call for a new "restructuring CEO." He was found in Carlos Brito ("Brito"), the former CEO of Ambev with which Interbrew merged in 2004 to create InBev.

Soon appointed CEO of InBev, the new combined entity, Carlos Brito immediately engaged in serious cost cutting and restructuring. Brito and the AmBev owners knew two things about the beer industry: first, that the industry would keep consolidating; second, that the industry was great for steady cash flows and dividends if one could remain on top. This for them meant continued acquisitions of competitors, successful integration of the acquired units, and cost-based restructuring. Brito's big strategic issues were limited: the major part of the strategy had already been written by the owners and validated with the board. Acquisition targets were known; the key was how to win, in both the acquisition and the restructuring games. That is where Brito's talent lay. It led him to remain CEO of the group until his retirement in 2021. Like Buffett, Brito stuck to the game he excelled at. He was the master of two talents: acquisition wars and restructuring.

Brito's largest deal was the all-cash acquisition of Anheuser-Busch (AB), the largest US beer company and owner of the largest American beer brand, Budweiser. AB was itself controlled by two families (the Anheuser and Busch families). After the rejection of a series of Interbrew bids, AB finally agreed, on July 13, 2008, in the midst of a global financial crisis, to be bought by Interbrew for $52 billion. The InBev Board, intent on carrying out the acquisition and having thoroughly prepared for it, famously gave its formal approval via a brief telephone board meeting. They had been well briefed by their CEO and family owners and the board were in full alignment with Brito. They were confident that they had a CEO who could integrate this giant company into the newly formed AB InBev, while also delivering on the desired cost-based restructuring.

The Interbrew owners had truly met their dream CEO. Brito lifted the profitability of AmBev from 20% in 2000 to 36% in 2003. He then lifted InBev's profitability from 21% in 2003 to 37% in 2007. AB's EBITDA was 23% in 2007; by 2010 it had risen to 38%.[8] The match and alignment between Brito and the InBev owners (now owners of AB InBev) was superb. The complementary role distributions between owners, board members, and the CEO had reached near perfection.

Once Brito had accomplished his cost-based restructuring, the company had to re-focus on quality and marketing. This led to Brito's retirement and the hiring of a new CEO, Michel Doukeris.[9] Brito had increased market capitalization from $26 billion to 141 billion. The EBITDA margin over that period increased from 28.6 to 36.9%, annual revenue increasing from $14.5 billion to 46.9 billion.

Carlos Brito is credited with having created the world's largest beer company. The personalization of this achievement does not, however, give sufficient credit for the crafting of a strong mission by the owners, their commitment to the execution of this mission, as well as their responsibility, with independent board members, for the company's remarkable and very risky journey. However, there is no doubt that Brito has faithfully "operationalized" the owners' mission for long-term value creation and steady dividends. Most recognize that without Brito and his team, the owners' mission would not have become the reality it is today. Few could even imagine the current reality at the time of the first acquisitions. Brito's successor has a formidable challenge, not unlike that faced by Immelt, Jack Welch's successor at GE.

3 Operationalizing the Mission and Facing Trade-Offs

Ayala Corporation ("Ayala") is the diversified Filipino holding company belonging to the Zóbel de Ayala family. The family traces its origins to Spanish and German ancestors having come to the Philippines in the 1800s. Seven generations have been at the helm. The mission of Ayala is stated as follows:

> *Anchored on values of integrity, long-term vision, empowering leadership, and with a strong commitment to national development, Ayala fulfills its mission to ensure long-term profitability and value creation. Ayala creates synergies as it builds mutually beneficial partnerships and alliances with those who share its philosophies and values.*[10]

Their values are *Integrity, Long-Term Vision, Empowering Leadership, and Commitment to National Development.* They could have added *Innovation* and *Professionalism.* Ayala brings the professionalism and rigor of private capitalism to projects that ensure the development of the Philippines. The Ayala view is a stakeholder one, with a focus on the Filipino people. This is clearly stated in the Ayala vision statement: "*We will be the most relevant, innovative, and enduring Philippine-based business group, enabling shared value and prosperity for the many stakeholders we serve.*"

The mission given to the Ayala Corporation by the family is to be an industrial holding, very much like GE, Siemens, or Samsung, to the benefit of the country's development. What the family brings is integrity and professionalism, and stable and trustworthy governance ensuring that stakeholders, including entrepreneurs, employees, suppliers, investors, and partners, indeed benefit from their association with Ayala. This provides Ayala with a capital of trust that has become its hallmark. Efficiency is greater than what would have been the case if these initiatives had been government funded and managed. Diversification spreads the risk and further reduces the group's cost of capital. The risk premium required by investors and partners is also reduced, relative to public market funding. The company in this way increases value creation opportunities in the Philippines. Sticking to a known geography, its powerful network of connections and broad knowledge of the market and the institutions are key strategic weapons the company deploys across several sectors. When it does so, the key competence for owners to display and develop is the ability to make the appropriate trade-offs among stakeholders in ways that continue the building of trust that Ayala partners can legitimately hold about them.

The holding company, Ayala Corporation, as well as the major group-controlled companies are all listed. This allows outside capital to be made available to both the corporation and its operating companies. It also reduces the family's exposure in what remain risky ventures yet retains the ability to deliver dividends to the Ayala Corporation and from there to the family holding company. Splitting the holding among several companies also mitigates the risks of social tensions and political pressures that could appear in a developing country if there is one huge and dominating business.

For the publicly traded businesses it holds, Ayala plays the ownership role, deciding what businesses to invest in or divest from, and how to allocate capital across them. It manages them at arm's length and with limited involvement of the Ayala board. In the unlisted businesses, Ayala plays more the role of an incubator, nurturing them and participating more actively in their management, possibly bringing them to the market. In both cases, it is the business CEOs who operationalize the Ayala corporate mission, each in their respective sector.

The core activity of the group was real estate, but from there the family has branched out to banking, utilities, telecommunications, and other sectors. Why? To reduce risk and for synergy. Indeed, in a developing economy, real estate development needs good infrastructure and utilities. The government not being able to provide the needed infrastructure efficiently, Ayala then enters the sector and goes into the utility business. To sell property you need clients with a mortgage. If the banking system is not sufficiently developed, Ayala's "do it yourself" approach leads it into banking. The development context is fundamental in the approach, as is a stable stakeholder-oriented ownership.

The CEO of Ayala, **Jaime Augusto Miranda Zóbel de Ayala II**, has continued the group's already considerable diversification. Ayala is now a dominant or major player in Philippine real estate, banking, retail, telecommunications, information technology, power generation, water infrastructure, education, renewable energy, and electronics. The holding company, Ayala Corporation, as well as the companies it controls are listed in Fig. 4.2.

One point worth noting is that, while this risk management growth strategy creates value for the geographically undiversified controlling family, it

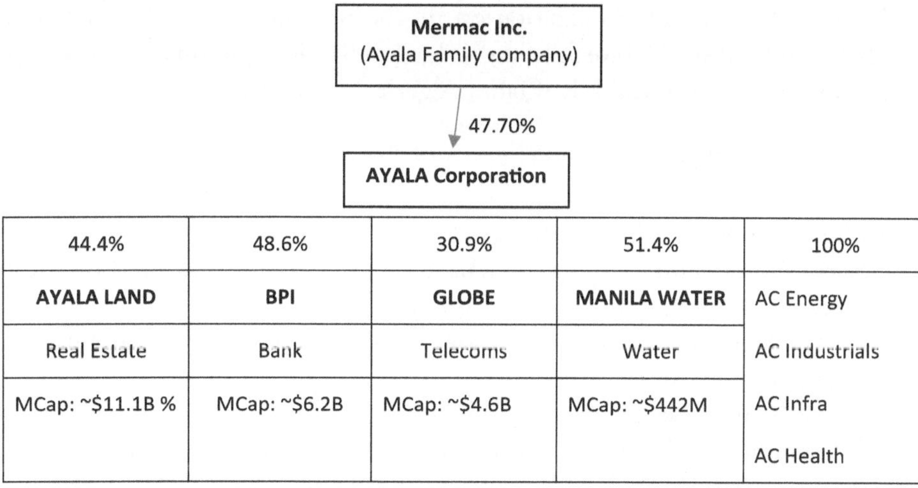

Fig. 4.2 Ayala Corporation: major ownership of listed companies. Source: Company filings

destroys value for shareholders that invest in Ayala and are already diversified. This shows up in the fact that Ayala Corporation is undervalued in the stock market and worth less than the sum of the values of the held companies. It also might indicate that too much value is shared with stakeholders.

It is also interesting to note that the Ayala Corporation in the Philippines bears similarities to **A.P. Møller – Mærsk A/S,** an integrated Danish shipping company that has taken a similarly central role in their country, not based on real estate but on shipping. It was founded in 1904 by two Danes, Peter Mærsk Møller and his son Arnold Peter Møller. Arnold Peter Møller's son Arnold Mærsk Mc-Kinney Møller ("Møller") became CEO in 1965. Møller set up the A.P. Møller Foundation, which is controlled by the family. The foundation owns stakes in the various family businesses through a holding company, **A.P. Møller Holding**. Most of the dividends received by the holding company flow to the foundation, which funds philanthropic ventures in the Scandinavian countries. The foundation pursues the goal of sustainable long-term profitability so that it can continue its philanthropic work forever.

The need to retain control and reduce risk led to industrial diversification:

- Møller first diversified within shipping: it built the largest fleet of ships under a single ownership by entering nearly every segment of the shipping market: container ships, VLCCs (Very Large Crude Carriers), product tankers, rigs, car carriers, Ro-Ros, and offshore supply vessels.[11]

- It went into oil and gas exploration in a joint venture with Royal Dutch Shell and Gulf in the North Sea: this later expanded into oil and gas exploration businesses in the UK, Qatar, Algeria, and Kazakhstan.

Further diversifications included:

- A shipbuilding yard in Denmark
- Maersk Air-operated cargo and chartered passenger services (sold in 2005)
- A supermarket company, Dansk Supermarked A/S
- Maersk Data, initially set up to provide software to the shipping business (sold to IBM in 2004)
- Danske Bank, a Nordic bank
- KK Group providing power electronic solutions to wind turbines

Of course, the diversification done by the family would not have been required if the owner were a well-diversified equity fund, but for the family owners, it was essential and a key part of the mission.

4 A Contrasting View: CEO Operationalization of Mission in Widely Held Companies

In widely held companies with a mix of retail and institutional shareholders, one of the key questions the Board and their CEOs must decide on is whose mission to operationalize. This is a question that does not arise in owner-led companies. Inevitably, CEOs of widely held companies end up operationalizing the mission of their institutions, especially when, like Jack Welsh and Jeff Immelt at GE, or Jamie Dimon at JP Morgan, they hold the dual positions of Chair and CEO. Until recently, the latter was the norm for widely held firms in the US, but also in France, where the PDG used to reign supreme. Let us review some of the recent history of Citibank, an iconic US institution.

Citi traces its history back to The City Bank of New York, founded in 1812. Citi's present structure is very different today, the result of numerous mergers and acquisitions. Well-known CEOs include Walter B. Wriston (CEO from 1967 to 1984) and Walter Reed (CEO from 1984 to 1998). Reed pursued growth by acquisitions that saw Citi become the largest bank in the US and the largest charge card servicer in the world. It grew to 275,000 employees and 200 million customer accounts in over 100 countries worldwide.[12]

As a result of a merger with the Travelers Group, Sanford I. "Sandy" Weill became Citi's CEO in 1998. In a boardroom fight, he ousted Reed and became sole CEO. Weill, like Reed, had built up the Travelers Group through acquisitions. His sustained and clever lobbying, using both senior Republican and Democratic Party officials, resulted in the repeal of the Glass-Steagall Act that separated investment and commercial banks after the Great Depression.

In 2007, Charles Owen "Chuck" Prince III was the CEO, having taken over from Weill in 2003. Due to the sub-prime crises, the US government spent upwards of $45 billion to bail out Citi. The government felt Citi was one of those firms that was "too big to fail." The US people would pay the bill. The true (psychological) owners of Citi were not really the many shareholders, but the Chair and CEO, and then the Chair. However, the capital that they played with was not theirs, but belonged to many dispersed shareholders, often pension funds that did not sufficiently act as concerned and prudent owners. Though one often hears about "market discipline," the market typically reacts late and only gradually. It bears little similarity to identifiable owners. It is the presence of the latter that makes owner-led capitalism so distinct from so-called Wall Street capitalism.

The diversification pursued by institutions such as BlackRock, whose mission is an aggregate increase in the value of their large portfolios, allows if not encourages individual company CEOs to take outsized risks. Indeed, from the perspective of BlackRock that has stakes in many banks, investing in each bank is like buying a lottery ticket. What do you want from each lottery ticket? A high pay-off, that is, a lot of risk taking. One of the authors was explained the intuition behind investments in a diversified fund: "*You own 100 companies: in 50% you lose everything, in 30% you break even, in 20% you make so much money that at the aggregate level you generate very high performance for your investors.*" This indeed explains the success of Softbank (being lucky with the investment in Alibaba) and the success of Naspers (being lucky with the investment in Tencent).

CEOs of firms such as Citi have, in this sense, faithfully operationalized the mission that their largest shareholders—such as BlackRock—wish them to implement. But the retail shareholders bear the brunt of these high-risk actions. CEOs in these firms aim for high-risk growth at the expense of sustainability. As in a lottery, some of these firms succeed, but many fail. For BlackRock, the aggregate performance is satisfactory, while the CEOs, even of bankrupt companies, are rewarded by leadership positions in other companies, their experience having contributed to making them better CEOs.

In such contexts, governance takes the form of stock picking, diversification, and selling ("Walking the Wall Street Way"). Voting rights are never exercised. In fact, they are not appreciated as they involve fiduciary duties on the side of investors who then have to exercise them. If BlackRock does not vote well, this exposes it to fiduciary lawsuits from its own investors. However, if the stocks confer no voting rights, this problem disappears.

The social media company **Snap Inc**. allows shareholders to invest only in a class of shares that has no voting rights. The founders, Bobby Murphy and Evan Spiegel, have 88% of the voting rights. Spiegel, as the owner-CEO, can operationalize the owner's mission as if Snap were a private company, while still enjoying the benefits of outside capital sharing in his economic risk taking. When Snap was IPOed their shares were oversubscribed by well-diversified investors who did not care about voting rights.

The latest trend is using cryptocurrencies to raise capital through Initial Coin Offerings (ICOs) and Security Token Offerings (STOs). These are discussed later in the book. At this stage, we mention them as another structure through which investors are asked to invest in businesses, but without necessarily obtaining voting or control rights. Founders can then operationalize their missions in whatever manner they wish to, without any checks and balances from those providing high-risk capital. The excesses this leads to have been noted, particularly among Silicon Valley firms. A salient example is Theranos, where Elizabeth Holmes, founder, allocated herself the great majority of voting rights, only to lead the company into major fraud and ultimate bankruptcy.

Notes

1. *Walden* by Henry David Thoreau.
2. Japanese-Style Entrepreneurship: An Interview with Softbank'S CEO, Masayoshi Son by Alan M. Webber *Harvard Business Review*, January–February 1992 Issue.
3. http://www.worldfuturefund.org/Documents/maninarena.htm.
4. https://knowledge.insead.edu/blog/insead-blog/the-three-altitudes-of-leadership-7541.
5. https://www.dbs.com/media/features/putting-the-customer-first.page.
6. h ttps://www.ft.com/content/d6029592-0eb9-11e5-8aca-00144feabdc0.
7. https://www.lesoir.be/art/interbrew-dedeur-s-en-va-descarpentries-un-profil-de-de_t-19930225-Z06FFU.html.
8. https://hbr.org/2012/04/the-beliefs-that-built-a-global-brewer.

9. https://www.ab-inbev.com/content/dam/abinbev/news-media/press-releases/2021/04/ABI_CEO_050621_EN.pdf.
10. https://www.ayala.com.ph/about-ayala.
11. https://www.independent.co.uk/news/obituaries/maersk-mckinney-moller-owner-of-the-worlds-largestcontainer-shipping-company-7648152.html.
12. Bailout Nation: How Greed and Easy Money Corrupted Wall Street and Shook the World Economy by Barry Ritholtz.

5

Goals, Strategies, and Fundamentals

Chapter 1 introduced the primacy of the owner's mission, the first and main differentiating element with publicly listed firms. Chapter 2 illustrated how the corporate board is truly "in the middle" between owners and executives, acting essentially like a transmission chain linking both. Chapter 3 described the vital and often underestimated role of CEOs in executing the owner's mission, and the implications for boards charged to select and supervise them.

These chapters taken jointly underline the major differences between owner-led and so-called market-led boards, which often become executive-led boards. They also stress that the governance structure in owner-led boards relies on a tripod of boards: the owners' board defining the mission and its governance, the Board of Directors responsible for the proper execution of this mission, and finally the executive board, tasked with turning the mission into reality under the supervision of the board.

This chapter deepens our exploration of value creation and the contributions owners, corporate boards, and CEOs and their executives make to value creation. The areas that we deal with here are the responsibility for generating and managing cash flows, for capital allocation, for financing decisions, and for managing the risks these decisions entail.

1 Goals, Sub-Goals, and Fundamentals

In operationalizing the owner's mission, the first decision the CEO will make—possibly the most important one—is setting out the path that will be followed in the fulfillment of the mission he has been tasked to realize. Great

M. Massa et al., *Value Creation for Owners and Directors*,
https://doi.org/10.1007/978-3-031-19726-0_5

CEOs excel at this exercise, not only in terms of setting targets, but also in building entire scenarios of short- and intermediate-term tasks that motivate the teams and can be feasibly achieved, ensuring that the plans become reality. This is both a competence and a talent, making the task of the corporate board so much easier when the CEO has those capacities. It also provides the right context for an active and mutually motivating dialogue of the board with the CEO and his team. A great CEO engages the Board to craft the major (risk-related) goals and engages the executives and lower ranks to craft the short-term sub-goals and their strategic operationalization.

This exercise is sometimes referred to as the "unpacking of time." It amounts to studying a "map of possible scenarios," selecting one, implementing it, and adapting it as required along the way. This contingent approach, known as scenario planning and advocated very convincingly by Arie De Geus at Shell, supports the search for greater clarity on the road ahead. It applies T.S. Eliot's statement "the end is where we start from."[1]

Great CEOs indeed proceed in three steps. They start at the end, with a longer-term goal that is visionary and engaging. They then present the intermediate sub-goals that are key milestones to realize the envisioned future. They end with action-oriented agendas and goals for the short-term priorities. Alignment results when this sequence of sub-goals makes sense, each sub-goal naturally leading to the next one. In the end, people are clear on where to go, why, and how, ready and motivated to get on with their agendas and understanding key priorities.

Goal setting, including sub-goal setting, is as delicate as it is important to value creation, and subtle. A historical example illustrates this point vividly. It concerns the Battle of Vimy Ridge, a pivotal episode from World War I, fought from April 9 to 12, 1917.[2] It represented a breakthrough in the war, tilting the balance in favor of the Allied side. The mission was simple: take Vimy Ridge, a strategic point occupied by the Germans in front of Lens in northern France. A Canadian observer at the time described it as a place where "more of the war could be seen than from any other." More than 100,000 mostly UK soldiers had sacrificed their lives in vain trying to take the hill in prior months. The attack on Vimy Ridge had another goal: it was meant to divert the Germans from a major "breakthrough" assault by French General Nivelle in the Champagne region, south of Vimy. Vimy succeeded as brilliantly as the French attack failed.

The Canadian leaders, for the first time in command of their own troops (and not under English command), did not wish to see their comrades die at the rate of their French and English counterparts. Their first goal, therefore, was to learn how not to replicate prior military disasters. The first insight generated by their thorough planning exercise was to completely change British attack tactics: British generals tended to bring more troops where offensives stalled, only leading to more deaths and further stalling. Canadians determine that the same method would only produce similar outcomes. The Canadians finally adopted a contrarian strategy: pour in troops where there is advance and allow decentralized decision making by lower-ranked officers to take advantage where success arises in battle.

The second observation made by the Canadians when they studied the British command was that the latter set targets ranging from 500 to 700 m for a day's progress, which was typically revealed as too ambitious. One of the reasons was that the artillery needed to prepare a follow-up attack once ground was gained but would generally not follow the initial progress fast enough. Muddy terrain was often the culprit. The result was that further attacks would proceed without the artillery being set up close enough to effectively support the second wave. Preparatory artillery rounds would rapidly become too imprecise. Subsequent attacks would unavoidably grind to a halt, particularly with the "three lines of defense" typical of German trench warfare. The Canadians thus shortened their sub-goals: the targets for an assault were now set at 200 or 300 m, after which the troops would halt and consolidate gains. Artillery could then move up, particularly when artillery and troop transport was secured by engineers who were trained to quickly set up defenses and secure reinforcements and supplies. In modern parlance, the Canadian army units became much more agile than the British units on which they benchmarked.

The final insight of the Canadians in this masterful exercise of scenario planning was to confront the fact that long runs in open terrain were too risky and especially too costly in terms of human life. To protect their troops, the engineers started to build tunnels and subways, bringing troops safely in front of German lines without having to cross the deadly "no man's land" which had taken such an enormous toll among British and French soldiers. Attackers would completely surprise German defenses when coming out of their tunnels. They additionally were instructed to use German equipment captured in the assaults, greatly accelerating the speed with which submachine guns and artillery could be set up for the next attack.

In sum, the first sub-goal was to learn about the **fundamentals** of the battle (terrain, opposition, tactics of the opponent, or one's own failures). The second sub-goal was to develop **one or more scenarios** that had a reasonable chance at success. The third sub-goal was to prepare the logistics and support required to sustain the plan. When all this was completed and thoroughly understood, achievable milestones (or further sub-goals) could be set for the targeted progress in the attack.

The result of all this Canadian planning was a remarkable success. "Only" 3600 Canadians died in the three-day battle, all sub-goals being attained. Vimy remains to this day Canada's most celebrated military victory. It marked a turnaround in the Allied misfortunes against the Germans and changed their battle tactics. Some describe Vimy "as the birth of a nation," as this was the first time that Canadians from all provinces had fought together as a single Canadian force. Byng, the British General commanding the Corps, would be succeeded by the Canadian Arthur Currie, who had led one of the four divisions in the attack. Canadians would increasingly come out from the shadow of British command and earn a separate representation in the Paris peace talks after the war. Vimy Ridge became a defining moment for the Canadian nation.

What our Canadian military example further shows is that sub-goals – and more generally management and governance - must fully consider the context in which they are set. The sub-goal can be to gain 700 m of enemy territory, or 300 m; whether this sub-goal is good or bad depends on contextual fundamentals that involve the quality of the terrain, the weather, the resources one disposes of, or the obstacles one faces. Sub-goals are not absolute. Sub-goals always need to account for fundamental contextual conditions or parameters, which are invariably context specific, and can be favorable or not.

Sub-goals involve targets and choices, depending on clear measures. Returning to business and finance, we review the financial mathematics that govern choices regarding corporate goals.

2 The Simple Financial Math of Goal Setting

We can generically divide goals into one of three buckets: **profitability, growth, and sustainability**. As seen earlier, Interbrew opted for growth while Ayala, the Philippine holding company, focused on profitability and risk management through diversification.

While setting goals, it is important to realize that all three factors are, at a given point in time, incompatible. It is thus important that boards understand the impact on the other goals of pursuing one. Goal choices unavoidably imply trade-offs. These trade-offs constitute the essence of the governance choice, as illustrated in Fig. 5.1.

We now explain the lenses that are typically used to evaluate goals. Our purpose here is to provide sufficient understanding of the language used when setting company goals, and when risks of strategies are evaluated. Understanding this language is fundamental for good governance.

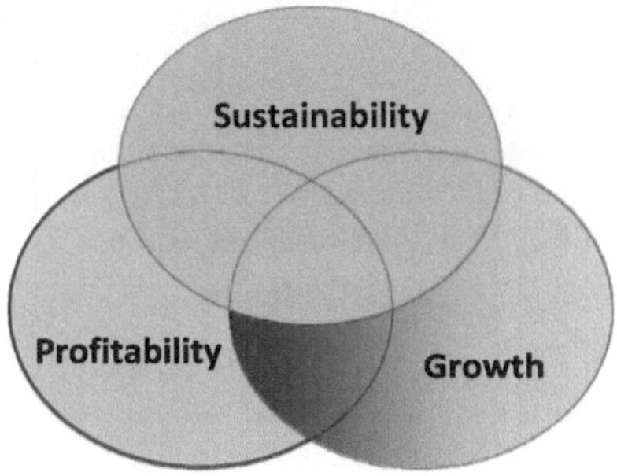

Fig. 5.1 Fundamental trade-offs when choosing company goals

Profitability

Profitability is a function of two overriding parameters:

- **Business profitability**: this is the extent to which a business can generate a healthy return on the capital that has been invested in it. The measure is called **Return on Invested Capital**, or **ROIC** for short.
- **The cost of sourcing the invested capital**: this is the called the **Cost of Invested Capital**, or **COIC** —and also "COC" —for short. It measures the sourcing cost, which is the other defining element of business profitability.

The firm is profitable when its ROIC is greater than its COIC. In the simplest of terms, if the company cannot make a return greater than its cost of capital, then it is destroying **Economic Value**, or **EV** for short.

The Cost of Invested Capital is critically affected by the risk incurred in the investment to which the capital is allocated. Investors are risk averse, leading to the fundamental risk–return relationship in finance: the riskier the investment, the higher the return requested by the investor who commits to the investment. This fundamental law has an automatic corollary: the more diversified the investment, the less the Cost of Invested Capital. Diversification of investments thus reduces the cost of capital and increases profitability (given a return profile).

Figure 5.2 shows how diversification of an investment portfolio reduces risk, and hence lowers COIC. This occurs because idiosyncratic risk, the particular risk associated with each company or investment, becomes smaller as the portfolio is more diversified. Each investment's idiosyncratic risk is assumed to be unconnected (the financial or statistical term is "uncorrelated"

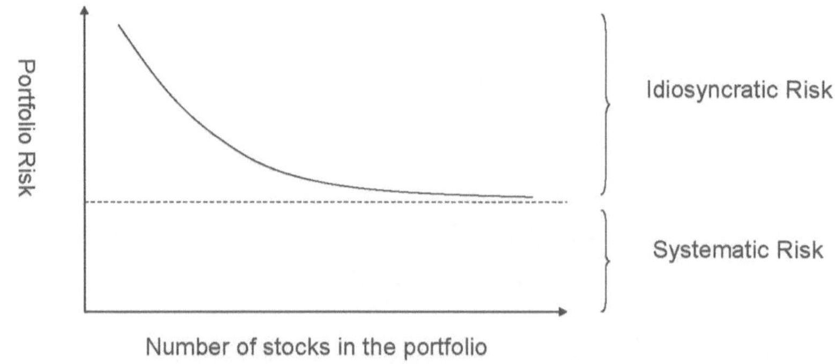

Fig. 5.2 Diversification reduces portfolio risk

or "independent") to other investments' **idiosyncratic risks**. This allows the risks to cancel each other out when computing averages, just like successive wins and losses cumulate at the roulette wheel in a casino. What remains is the average or **Expected Value** of the return on the portfolio**.** When an investment portfolio is sufficiently diversified, and each investment represents a small value of the total investment, all the investor sees is the portfolio or average return, individual returns being averaged away. This of course is the principle of investing in funds, sought for their overall returns and not for the returns of their individual components.

The only risk that cannot be diversified away is the **systematic risk**, the risk that applies to the entire market or economy. This risk is inherent in and borne by the overall market. It depends on **the economy's fundamentals** at a given point in time. An ideal diversified portfolio is one where the idiosyncratic risk has been diversified away through compensating corrections, leaving the investor facing the systematic risk only.

An understanding of ROIC and COIC provides a perspective on how different owners might approach their investments in the same company (with a given ROIC) differently. In Chap. 1 we saw, for example, how BlackRock, the world's largest fund, aims to be a fully diversified investor and how it treats its investments accordingly. This is the context for a state or especially a family owning a single company (such as the Interbrew owners) and thus invested in a single sector. Institutional owners such as BlackRock are highly diversified and thus face a lower cost of capital, also allowing for a wider range of profitable investment strategies. While BlackRock will diversify its portfolio, families, not being able to diversify their portfolio due to the need to retain control of the company they own, try to diversify the company instead. Examples of the latter were covered in earlier chapters and are the Zobel Ayala and the Mærsk Mc-Kinney Møller families.

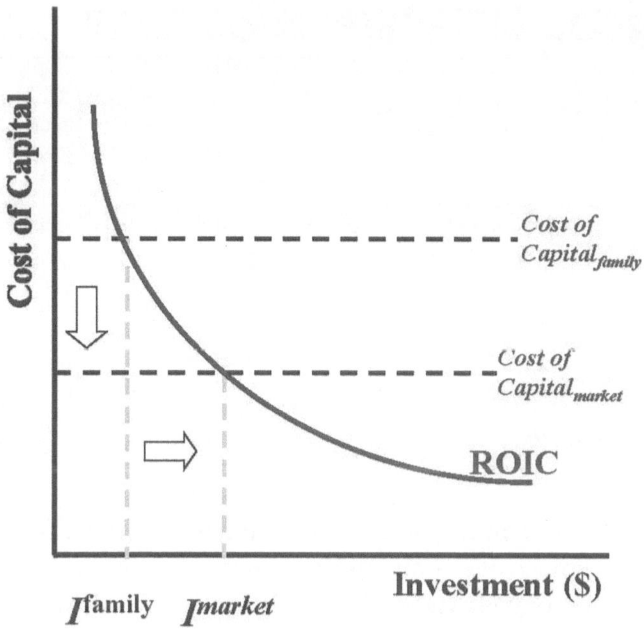

Fig. 5.3 ROIC and cost of capital for family owners and institutional shareholders

Figure 5.3 illustrates ROIC and COIC for two types of owners: a diversified owner such as BlackRock, and a focused company such as Stichting Interbrew. It also explains why focused companies are characterized by higher rates of return, another fundamental in finance.

A common measure of describing profitability is **Economic Profit**, also referred to as **Economic Value Add (EVA)**. EVA is **value accretive** or **value accruing** when the ROIC exceeds COIC. Figure 5.4 provides an explanation of ROIC and its connection to EVA. EVA captures in a single number the economic value a company generates over and above its cost of capital.

These considerations suggest that a company is profitable only if its ROIC is greater than its COIC. High ROIC may not imply profitability for a very risky business. This would be the case mostly for a non-diversified owner.

Another fundamental law of finance is that Growth creates Economic Value only if investments are profitable. It does so **sustainably** if such investments can be sustained along with their yield.

Growth must be sustainable, that is, compatible with the financing requirements. Let us consider a non-listed company. It can finance itself using debt or internal reinvested earnings. Without additional finance (equity or debt) the maximum rate at which a company can sustainably grow is equal to the

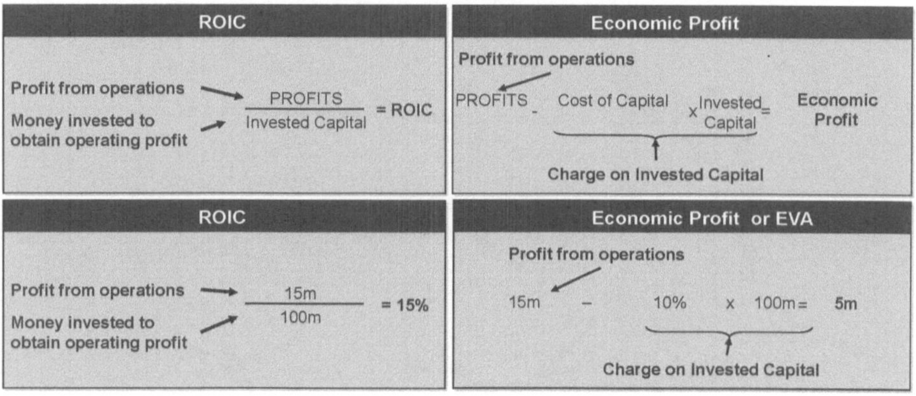

Fig. 5.4 ROIC and EVA

Profitability (ROIC) multiplied by the Investment Rate. The **Investment Rate** is the percentage of a company's earnings not paid out as dividends, that is, one minus the **Payout Ratio**. In this "Limits to Growth" scenario, a self-funded company can increase its growth only under two conditions: (i) it becomes more profitable or (ii) it pays out fewer dividends to its owners. This is summarized in the following formula:

$$\text{Growth} = \text{Profitability} \times \text{Investment Rate}$$

The second way in which a company can grow is through **Leverage**. Growth can be higher than the company's self-funded limits if the company is able to raise capital through outside means. The more straightforward means are to use earnings (effectively "ploughing back money" and restricting dividends) or to raise more **debt** from creditors. These considerations suggest that, to be sustainable, growth has to be consistent with the company's **Payout Ratio** and ability to **Leverage.**

Market analysts are often obsessed with quarterly growth figures disclosed at regular intervals by companies. We have already noted that growth creates firm value only when the company is also profitable. But this has a red line as its converse is also true: value destruction results, often on an even larger scale, when the company grows without being profitable. This constitutes a vicious capital-raising cycle, where continuous growth makes a firm less and less profitable. The case of Amazon is remarkable and rare. The company was unprofitable for years, building up dominance in its sector. In that period, Amazon followed the normal scenario for companies building up positions in their industries: companies buy their way to a position where they become profitable only then. Good ownership and board practice is to raise red flags when growth, especially high growth, occurs when a company is not profitable, as such a course of action is not sustainable, and must be pursued with clear time limits unless owners "have deep pockets."

At any time, companies thus need to choose their goals carefully: they must decide whether goals focus on profitability, growth, or sustainability, or whether their goal is to pursue a mix of these. It is not feasible to pursue all three simultaneously. Even pursuing two goals implies trade-offs between them. Simply put, growth needs to be "bought" and this generally comes at the expense of profitability. The case of Apple illustrates this fact clearly: the company suffered from prolonged profitability issues, which eventually led to the demotion of Jobs and his eventual departure. Some companies, such as Microsoft and Alphabet, have grown rapidly while still displaying high profitability. These are exceptions rather than the rule; second, their owners and boards were not focusing on both. In both cases, growth was their goal for a certain period, and high profitability was largely a consequence of a particular combination of industry structures and business fundamentals.

Conversely, focusing too long on just profitability or growth is typically detrimental to sustainability. First, profitability alone can be temporary due to the company facing a variety of risks (volatility, Black Swan, and obsolescence), as we will discuss in Chap. 6. Growth without profitability destroys value. The correct balancing over time of these three goals is one of the major tasks faced by boards of directors. Boards thus ought to be lucid on which combination of these three goals should be pursued during a particular time, as they are contradictory and pose great risk if pursued without any regard for the other two goals. The next section further illustrates this conclusion.

The oldest continuously operating business, according to the *Guinness Book of World Records*, is the Keiunkan Inn.[3] It opened in 705 AD offering hot springs and accommodation with a view of Mount Fuji to travelers, soldiers, and wealthy people in search of harmony and well-being. The second longest operating business is the Hoshi Ryokan, a business very similar to the first one (though likely the owners would dispute this statement) and founded in 718.[4] It is not an accident that both companies have remained single-entity businesses, centered on inns created in the eighth century. Sustainability has been their principal goal, which has been achieved by sacrificing both growth and profitability. Their owners remained focused on a single location, pursuing the mission to sustain the property and successfully transfer it to the next generation. Very creative ownership transmission strategies had to be devised to succeed in this mission.

Running a company for profitability is very different from running a company for sustainability or growth. It changes incentives, the type of managers one has, and the strategies one pursues. Our three "pure" goals are thus fundamentally contradictory. One of the major questions that boards must decide upon is the appropriate goal profile and sequence over time. In particular, it must be appreciated that goals drive strategy and that strategies can only be discussed once goals are set. Proper goal setting requires joint collaboration between the board and the CEO. At the same time the choice of the CEO is linked to the choice of the goal as a good growth CEO may not be, and likely will not be, a good profit-enhancing CEO or sustainability-driven one. This creates both a need for collaboration to craft proper goals and a tension that results from the question whether the CEO is the right person to implement the goals commonly set. The board has to lead this discussion, and needs information from the CEO and the executives, without becoming involved in micro-management and actual implementation. It cannot be stated enough that good governance requires good allocation of tasks and division of labor between the two, and plenty of collaboration. Effective board work is team play.

3 Value Creation Metrics and the Evaluation of Strategies

Having selected goals, the next question to be addressed by directors and executives concerns the strategy to be followed to reach these goals. Strategies involve choices and trade-offs in the pursuit of goals. The key strategic choices facing companies concern the determination of the battlefield, namely the company's place and arena of engagement with clients, which is also the place of confrontation with competitors, employees, and other stakeholders.[5]

Three key value creation metrics assist boards in evaluating a strategy (Fig. 5.5):

- *Cash Flows*: Where will the company generate cash flows when implementing the strategy, how much cash flow will be generated, and for how long?
- *Risks*: What risks will be faced when implementing the strategy, and how might these risks be mitigated?
- *Financing*: What financing can the business rely on to deploy its strategy given the owners' control requirements?

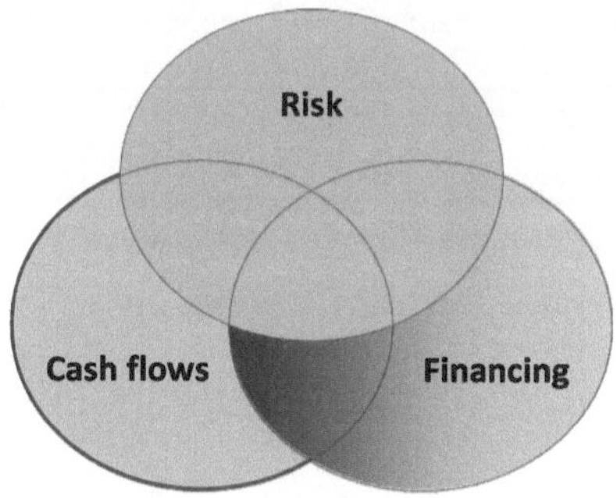

Fig. 5.5 Key value creation metrics

An understanding of these three value creation metrics is critical for a company to sustainably create value. We explain each in turn.

Cash flows directly determine profitability, which is of course critical. A disaggregation of the factors behind cash flow generation shows that cash flows are affected both by operational decisions and by decisions pertaining to the financing of a company. Figure 5.6 summarizes, without introducing the additional complexity of taxes, how these two types of decisions are the main components of value creation.

The **Operations Management** side of value creation depends on two factors:

- **Earning Margins**: The ratio of profits (excess of revenues over costs) divided by revenues. The higher the margin, the higher the economic performance of the company. Margins also depend on the market side, which tests the pricing power of the company. On the supply side, costs depend on procurement prices, the company's ability to influence purchase prices, and, more generally, the business model and technology choices of the company. These combine to determine the operational efficiency of the company in transforming its inputs into outputs (products and services).
- **Capital Turnover**: The ratio of a company's total revenues to its shareholders' equity. This ratio indicates the speed with which a business "turns over" its equity into revenue. The higher the speed for a given level of shareholders' equity, the more efficient the company from a financial viewpoint. Businesses presenting economies of scale will boast a turnover that grows with the scale of that company's operations.

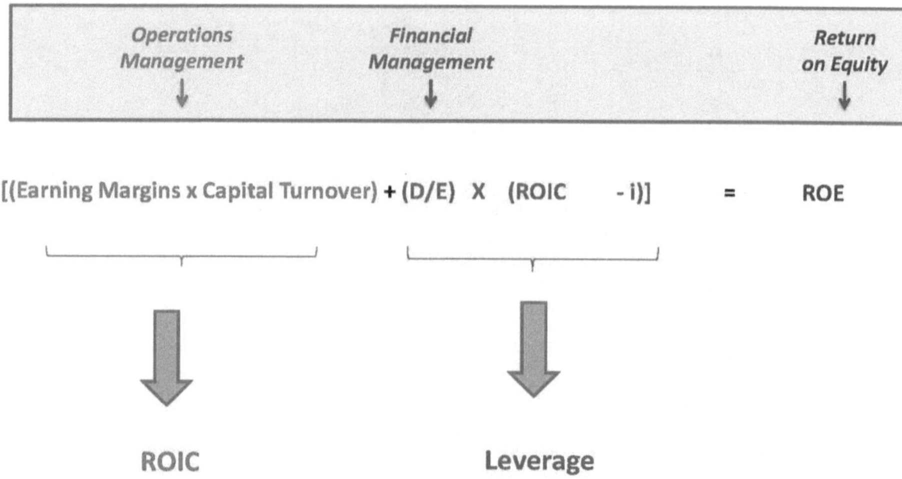

Fig. 5.6 Components of profitability

High earning margins and asset turnovers translate into high **Free Cash Flows** (FCF). These are the cash flows available to the firm for investment or dividend, once all cash outflows required by the company's operations have been taken care of.

The advantage of deriving and closely monitoring cash flows is that shareholders invest cash and demand payments back in cash. Accounting profits are financial numbers. By themselves, these numbers do not provide a currency with which a shareholder can be satisfied. Accounting profits can be more easily manipulated, while cash flows are more easily measured and verified. Contrasting cash flows with accounting profits, investors make a clear choice: investors invest cash and demand payment in cash.

The other side of the business concerns the **Financial Management** of the company. The key decision here involves the choice of debt versus equity to finance the company:

- **Debt to Equity ratio** (D/E): This ratio describes the extent to which the company relies on debt relative to equity to finance its operations.

A truism is that the more a company relies on Debt, the less the company needs to rely on Equity financing. The danger with debt, however, is the increased risk of bankruptcy that results from debt financing. This has an implication of limiting debt financing: greater debt increases the cost of debt and the interest rate the company has to pay to service this debt.

ROIC is the result of the operational decisions of the company. We indicated in the previous section that the company is value creating when ROIC is higher than COIC. Financial Management concerns the determination of the **Leverage** of Equity, defined as the amount of Debt a company can raise for a given size of Equity.

These operating and financing ratios result, as shown in a simplified (with no tax considerations) definition in Fig. 5.6, a company's **Return on Equity** (ROE). ROE is the company's annual profits divided by the average shareholder's equity. It is a key metric that drives owners to finance a business.

We now turn to examples that show how ROIC was in each case determined by earnings margins and capital turnover ratios. These examples also illustrate that there are trade-offs to be made between earnings margins and capital turnover. **Southwest Airlines**, which is our first example, focuses on scale and a high capital turnover to achieve a high ROIC. The second example, the high-end fashion company **Hermès International S.A.**, achieves high profitability because of its high margins. Both are examples of companies that grew tremendously because of superb operational choices and selection of strategies that generated high cash flows enabling formidable companies to be built.

4 Building a Company from the Inside through Superb Operational Strategies: Southwest Airlines and Hermès

Southwest

There was a time when flying by airplane was reserved for the very wealthy. Many airlines were either state-owned or required government licenses to operate. There were few airports, and these were generally situated in major cities.

The US then started to deregulate its airline sector in 1978. Europe and Asia soon followed. Low-cost airlines gradually took over market share from established national carriers, many of which disappeared. Figure 5.7 shows the difference in how low-cost carriers—such as Southwest and Ryanair—choose to operate and compete.

The secret of their success derives from deep insights into current market gaps, and hence opportunities. Figure 5.7 shows that these companies refused the traditional **low-cost** vs **value differentiation** trade-off advocated for so long by Porter.[6] Southwest focused on customer attributes that legacy carriers did not effectively provide for and thus identified a market opportunity. It

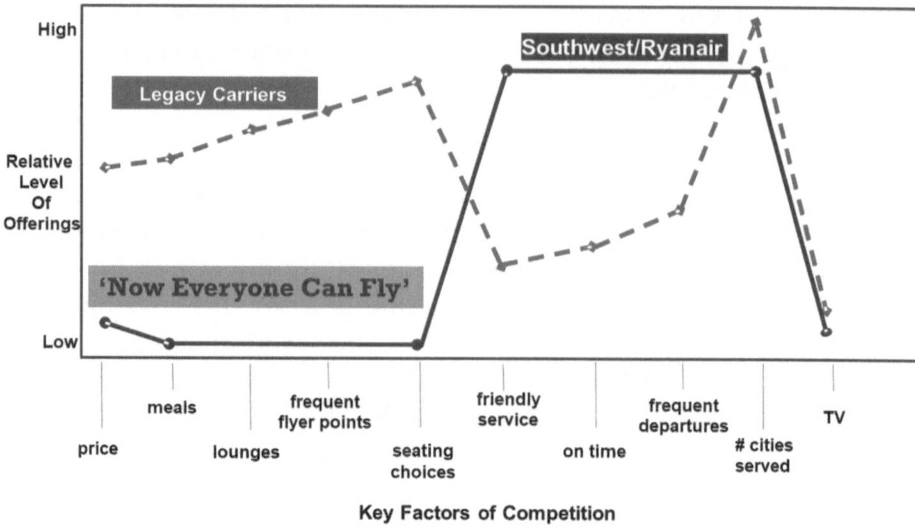

Fig. 5.7 Low-cost vs established airlines: services offered

purposefully avoided directly "contesting" legacy carriers on dimensions where they were strong and attacked them instead where they were vulnerable. This approach was studied by Kim and Mauborgne, who named it **value innovation.**[7] It is fundamentally at odds with Porter's competitive strategy dichotomy. Ryanair and Southwest focused on market segments and made this their battlefield. They conquered these through superb operations. The implications for FCFs and ROIC were remarkable: high margins coupled with high volumes.

The operational strategy of low-cost airlines consisted of using only one or two aircraft types, reducing maintenance requirements. Low-cost airlines fly many more flights to smaller, regional airports with a much smaller cost basis. They also utilize their aircrafts more than established companies do. Figure 5.8 contrasts the resulting operational performance of Southwest with two legacy airline companies, Continental and United.

In effect, Southwest was using its assets much more effectively than legacy carriers such as Continental and United. This provided Southwest with a higher capital turnover, resulting in a more profitable business and one that generated much higher cash flows. A key intuition of the low-cost airlines was to focus on Capital Turnover as opposed to Margins. Indeed, the main source of costs being the stock of airplanes, the goal was not to keep them too long on the runway. The legacy airlines did not understand this. They made the classic mistake of trying to become more profitable by cutting costs, for

B737-500 Productivity (Q2/2002)	Southwest	Continental	United
Flights per day	8.2	3.9	4.3
Average trip length	400	719	564
Seats per aircraft	122	104	109
ASMs per day per B737-500	400,160	291,626	264,347
Aircraft utilization (hours)	10.2	8.3	7.5

Fig. 5.8 Aircraft operations: comparing Southwest with Continental and United. Source: Peter Belobaba, company filings

example by de-unionizing employees and paying them less. Such actions do not address the cost issue well, as it is better addressed by incentivizing staff to fly more often.

A Capital Turnover strategy is driven by the amount of **fixed costs**. In the presence of high fixed costs, increasing revenues should always be the focus as it provides operating leverage, that is, the increased sales help to spread fixed costs over more units. This of course does not work in the case of high variable costs. Then, a margin strategy is required. This is the case of Hermès, the iconic fashion business.

Hermès

Hermès International S.A. ("Hermès") is an example of value creation through operating with sustainable high margins. Hermès is a high-end fashion company, designing and manufacturing all its products in special workshops, which all carry the Hermès brand. The company does not aim at selling high volumes at low cost, such as Amazon or low-cost airlines. They instead rely on limited-edition branded products offered and sold at extremely high prices.

What is the intuition here? In the presence of high variables costs (i.e., the high cost of manufacturing a luxury bag) increasing sales does not help as it increases costs as well and stretches limited manufacturing capacities where talent and craftsmanship are the currency. The best strategy then is brand building based on uniqueness, reducing quantities, and increasing margins by increasing prices. This is the strategy followed by luxury brands and famously pursued by Ferrari and others.

The consistency of the Hermès offer is the result of a long culture and tradition of high craftsmanship typical of Parisian and French fashion. It is rare to find and nearly impossible to replicate (the only one able to do so, and only partially, are other French companies, LVMH and Kering). New designs consist of relatively small deviations of existing designs that maintain yet refresh the brand, prohibiting it from becoming dusty and old.

5 Building a Company Through M&As and Superb Operational Integration Strategies: Interbrew (Again)

The next two sections examine the cash flows that resulted from Interbrew's remarkable growth into becoming the largest beer company in the world. We already evoked in Chap. 2 how Interbrew's goals and strategies were a logical conclusion of its owners' mission and its industry structure. Interbrew's acquisitions and mergers from 1988 onwards are summarized in Fig. 5.9.

We have already explained how, facing increasing irrelevance in its core markets, Interbrew's owners switched to a strategy of growth aimed at building scale, and through this gain ultimately accessed the high cash flows that

<table>
<tr><td>Brouwerij Artois
(Belgium)</td><td>Piedboeuf
(Belgium)</td><td></td><td>Brahma
(Brazil)</td><td>Companhia Antarctica Paulista
(Brazil)</td></tr>
<tr><td colspan="2">Merger (1988)
• Interbrew</td><td></td><td colspan="2" rowspan="2">Merger (1999)
• AmBev</td></tr>
<tr><td colspan="2">Acquisition (1995)
• Labatt Brewing Company (Canada)</td><td></td></tr>
<tr><td colspan="5">Merger (2004)
• InBev</td></tr>
<tr><td colspan="5">Acquisitions:
o Cerveza Quilmes (2006, Argentina)
o CND (2012 - Dominican Republic)
o Lakeport Brewing Company (2007, Canada)
o Anheuser-Busch (2008 – the USA)
o (Included Harbin Brewery acquired by Anheuser-Busch 2004, China)
Renamed AB InBev

Acquisitions:
o Grupo Modelo (2012 - Mexico)
o SABMiller (2016, UK)
o Includes Miller (USA), South African Breweries (South Africa), Bavaria Breweries (Columbia), Fosters (Australia), Meantime Brewery (U.K.)</td></tr>
</table>

Fig. 5.9 Mergers and acquisitions of Interbrew resulting in AB InBev

were eluding them. The problem that Interbrew had to solve was where and how to generate these high cash flows.

AB InBev's last major acquisition, that of SABMiller, required, due to the increasing domination of the beer markets, a long drawn-out anti-trust investigation. Regulatory authorities ruled that some of the SABMiller brands had to be disposed by AB InBev. These disposals did not prohibit the company from consolidating its position as the world's largest beer company, with annual sales over $55 billion and a 28% share of the global beer market.

After the SABMiller acquisition, CEO Carlos Brito commented that "As a truly global brewer, we will be able to achieve more together than each of us could separately."[8] What Brito meant, and this was again the key driver for this acquisition, was that the combined entity was going to benefit from a substantial cost reduction. This had been Interbrew's and then AB InBev's strategy all along: reciprocal synergies and elimination of redundant resources was the primary rationale for their acquisitions. The secondary rationale was the reduction of competitive pressures due to the integration of a formidable competitor, as well as a more enticing offer to B2B clients (pubs, restaurants, retailers, wholesalers). The latter could only contribute to generating higher revenues as well.

The advantages of scale in bringing about higher cash flows were apparent even before the SABMiller acquisition. A Morningstar analyst report said[9]:

> Anheuser-Busch InBev has one of the widest moats and is among the most efficient operators in our consumer defensive coverage universe. Vast global scale and near-monopoly dominance in several Latin American markets give AB InBev a significant cost advantage… This plays out in the firm's excess returns on invested capital and best-in-class profitability. AB InBev generates mid-30 s EBIT margins, well above the next profitable firm…
>
> AB InBev leads the industry in its operational performance as well as financial performance. It boasts best-in-class operating and cash cycles, asset turnover ratios, and working capital management. It delays payments to trade creditors 17% longer than its closest rival, and it converts around 30% of its revenue to free cash flow, more than 3 times that of the number-two player.
>
> [Through acquisitions] AB InBev can enhance profitability by removing duplicate costs, expanding volume (it has tripled Budweiser's volume in China in less than three years and has doubled its share in the United Kingdom), and bringing distribution in-house, thereby capturing the downstream margin opportunity.
>
> We believe AB InBev has a wide economic moat derived from two sources: a material cost advantage over its peers and its intangible assets. The strongest source of AB InBev's moat, in our opinion, is its cost advantage. AB InBev's

procurement advantage is significant. For example, the firm buys 15% of the U.S. rice crop every year. Furthermore, AB InBev's scale is concentrated in local markets, which allows it to generate meaningful cost economies from its size. This concentration of scale in its key markets reduces manufacturing complexity, leverages the firm's high-fixed-cost base, and lowers the average cost of production, which is apparent in AB InBev's best-in-class profitability. The firm generated $40 in EBITDA per hectoliter in 2013, well above the $26 per hectoliter generated by second-place Heineken, and it boasts industry-leading operating margins in the low 30 s.

This is all the more remarkable considering that the firm's two leading brands, Budweiser and Bud Light, are mainstream rather than premium brands.

Of course, success brews enemies. Furthermore, the rise of craft beers has changed the fundamentals of the beer sector, forcing a rethinking of the business model and the company's strategies. Cost cutting has met its limits in the rise of craft beer. This may have contributed to the sudden departure of Carlos Brito, even though age limits and long tenure likely contributed to this decision as well. But in doing so, AB InBev, and Interbrew before it, returned to its previous principle: a change in strategy is best accompanied by a change in CEO. Again, all was properly managed by the AB InBev board, which once more proved its effectiveness.

6 Building a Company Through Partnerships and Alliances: Interbrew's Joint Venture with the Sun Group

In 1999, Interbrew entered the Russian beer market through a joint venture with the SUN Group. The SUN Group was owned by an Indian business family, the Khemkas. The family had been trading and doing business in the erstwhile USSR since 1958. The Khemkas built up excellent local connections and developed the know-how to operate in Russia. When the USSR broke up into 15 different countries, the Khemkas bought five breweries, turned them around, and consolidated them. The owners were fully integrated into the Russian economy and its politics. They knew how to operate there.

For Interbrew, entering the Russian market appeared most promising at the time. It would drive up revenues and increase its dominance—albeit in joint venture mode—in major and promising beer markets. The joint venture with the Khemkas allowed Interbrew to enter an arena with high uncertainty as they did not know much about the Russian market. Their partner knew how to navigate the local political and business systems there. In a press interview Shiv Khemka, the family patriarch, said, "I have found it a great privilege and very fulfilling to work with my Russian partners and develop strong bonds of friendship and trust with them that have lasted many years. Speaking Russian, however, is very important to be able to communicate openly."[10]

In 2004 Russia had become the second-fastest-growing beer company worldwide. Interbrew believed it had learned enough about the local market and had gained the confidence to manage the business without its partner. Also, it needed full control to exercise top-down centralized application of best business operating procedures. Interbrew bought out the Khemka family in a 9.2 billion euro cash and shares deal, giving the Khemkas a 3.4% stake in Interbrew and a seat on the Interbrew supervisory board, but without voting rights.[11] The Khemkas had such a small ownership that control was no longer an issue for them. They were guaranteed to dispose of a small percentage of Interbrew's growing cash flows.

What had changed? The switch to integration, restructuring, and cost cutting had shifted gears towards a top-down approach focused on consolidation. This tilted the balance against JVs and in favor of full-fledged M&As. In particular, it led to the collapse of InBev's JVs with Anheuser-Busch, which subsequently led to the acquisition of the latter company by InBev. In summary, the Interbrew growth story illustrates the simple yet key strategic criteria for choosing between growth through M&As and through JVs. Cash flow criteria favor M&As when cost reduction is of paramount importance. JVs are favored when revenue enhancements are the main drivers, and when one is uncertain about one's ability to secure these revenues through acquisition. When cost reduction becomes paramount, JVs are typically replaced with M&As. This further suggests that a CEO with talents and skills in cost cutting and restructuring will not necessarily be compatible with a switch to JVs, and vice versa.

This chapter has proposed a sequence for the board's discussion: owners set a mission for the company, directors then set the goal profile that will be pursued over time, and executives devise strategies that will reach these goals. These are the three vital tasks to unlock the company on a value creation path. The time profile of goals and strategies is a consequence of the fact that at any given time, the three possible goals pursued—profitability, growth, sustainability—are contradictory and hence impossible to pursue simultaneously. Changes in goals invariably lead to changes in strategies.

The goal profile over time considers the fundamentals governing the company, like market, regulatory, and government contexts. In such a scenario, executives are tasked with having to propose strategies on how to best reach the goals set by the board when fundamentals and goals change. This discussion may of course involve multiple cycles.

We reviewed the three main growth strategies—**Build, Buy, or Ally**—along with a review of different cash flow criteria under which one or the other strategic priority is best applied. Examples were provided for each strategic option. We also highlighted the contingencies that drive strategic options.

We are now ready for the next chapter, which examines risk and financing challenges and how these two aspects enter strategic decision making, along with growth.

Notes

1. Arie de Geus, *The Living Company,* Nicholas Brealey (1997).
2. https://thecanadianencyclopedia.ca/en/article/vimy-ridge.
3. Visit their website at www.keiunkan.co.jp.
4. Visit their website at www.ho-shi.co.jp/en.
5. Richard Rumelt, The perils of bad strategy, *McKinsey Quarterly*, June 2011.
6. Michael Porter, *Competitive Strategy,* Free Press (1980).
7. W. Chan Kim and Renée Mauborgne, *Blue Ocean Strategy,* Harvard Business Review Press (2004).
8. https://www.chicagotribune.com/business/ct-megabrew-ab-inbev-sabmiller-merger-20161010-story.html.
9. http://analysisreport.morningstar.com/stock/archive/c-archive?&t=XNYS:BUD&region=usa&culture=zh-TW&productcode=QS&cur=&urlCookie=8997523520&e=eyJhbGciOiJSU0EtT0FFUCIsImVuYyI6IkExMjhHQ00ifQ.eY-s57E4rNn2aO0mdtQy4usd4MgSf5udSvrSfPlx1CR8UvQL-J2fAl-VM8li_sYc2QXO6QycfEv8yVzZ2N7bvNHC1yYrw-7azD4-Pf7enaNTK3hrGGLRpuQvnb2fsYaVrl-rfNY9qF3MT8zv4yY_C5NnYALL7i3LU5WCtOqboUw.iwvYb9QzHz9tiTU6.b1EtzaNCVJLT-wN7nrWWU9ZQn7_OGtfjIvpEdxG7NfHa1yz5DACf2DqQpY81QZyqOxd0tKNnorEdis7OdtDYff3cciQOYIv1UMV7KsWI5niMGxHHw1nh4ozFv3nYYdqLDS71TH6mxu-rpQGcH18aD8HBBdTvFussfYiSI7U88YebdZhlGyZVxBAiYvgZteGXZN1xQKJTWc1Z2pQPdzn9-KaIDqVz2XsG87r6LOGk.SkvwYrJFtA4f2pft6D_Jxg&docId=682451.
10. https://www.rbth.com/articles/2009/02/09/090209_khemka.html.
11. https://www.theguardian.com/business/2004/aug/13/russia.

6

Fundamentals: Financing and Risk

1 Risk: Definition, Typologies, and Valuation

While the owner's mission dictates ultimate objectives, the choice of the goals and the strategies to deploy depends on the fundamentals affecting the company's business. A significant part of these fundamentals is contributed by the firm's environment, like the markets and industries it is competing in, and the country or countries it is operating in, different countries presenting distinct competitive conditions. Performance is the result of the interactions between the company's environment, its strategy, and the capability of the organization to execute the strategic choices and deliver the expected results.[1] Risk can then be defined as any possibility that does not allow the desired results to be realized.

This definition immediately provides us with a first typology of risks:

- **Business**: This is related to the factor of production (suppliers, assets, commodity), customers, competitors, and so on.
- **Financial**: This is related to the financing of the firm (e.g., interest rate and distress) and to external factors (e.g., currency, market).
- **Environmental**: This is when factors in the environment disrupt the effectiveness of the strategy or its execution. Changes in a sector in which the company is active or in a country one is operating in would fall into this category. A typical example is government-related risk (sovereign risk, expropriation, political risk, taxation changes, inflation, inconvertibility, repatriation risk). More recently global warming and climate change are examples of environmental risks.

M. Massa et al., *Value Creation for Owners and Directors*,
https://doi.org/10.1007/978-3-031-19726-0_6

- **Organizational**: This risk concerns dysfunctions within the organization, such as when a lack of compliance is not identified or when errors—perhaps fraudulent—are committed. These risks also occur when appointing individuals to positions they are not capable of fulfilling, either at management, operational, or governance level. For example, when Tesla started to manufacture cars, an area where its CEO had no prior experience, its organizational risk was very high.
- **Strategic**: Every strategy—including doing nothing—has an inherent risk profile associated with it, distinct from environmental or organizational factors. M&A is inherently risky, JVs are difficult to operate, organic innovation strategies are not guaranteed to succeed. A historical example is the risk created by Napoleon when he started the Russian Campaign of 1812 to sanction Alexander's Russia for not complying with his Continental Blockade strategy. The decision exposed the French Army and his own Empire to considerably greater risk.

One of the major complexities is that these types of risks are interdependent: entering a new strategy or a new environment typically increases organizational risk, if only because the management has not changed. This also changes political risk and directly impacts business and financial risk. A case in point is when **BP** acquired US rival **Amoco** in 1998. BP was led by Lord Browne, for turning BP around through an ambitious set of acquisitions that included, beyond Amoco, Arco and five other companies. He then also proved to be an aggressive cost-cutter. These actions triggered a further series of mergers in the industry, of which the largest was Exxon-Mobil. Browne was also the first CEO in the sector that foresaw the negative impact of hydrocarbons on the climate. He rebranded BP in the early 2000s already as "Beyond Petroleum."

Climate change is a clear environmental risk, likely to trigger regulatory responses in the oil and gas and automotive sectors. Operating in Alaska's Prudhoe Bay represents environmental risk as well. Investigations into the 2002 Prudhoe Bay accident—which involved the explosion of a well—revealed that workers had expressed safety concerns to the management and lacked trust in the safety of the facility. Further incidents in 2005 (the toppling over of BP's showcase rig, *Thunder Horse*, during Hurricane Dennis due to poorly installed valves), 2006 (oil leak causing the largest spill ever on Alaska's North Slope), 2009 (explosion in its Texas City refinery), and 2010 (intentional release of 500,000 pounds of poisonous emissions over 40 days) all confirm a flagrant lack of an effective safety culture and poor safety management in BP's North American operations.[2] The report by the Chemical

Safety Board (CSB) identifies the complexity of multi-party risk management between an operator and a drilling contractor as a major risk and recommends improved and more explicit safety roles and responsibilities, including in oversight.[3] The joint venture strategy created organizational risks. More broadly, BP was vulnerable to strategic risk: focusing on economic and financial indicators without adequate attention to non-safety indicators, such as accidents and near-accidents, shows that safety was not a strategic priority. This is a case of "one governs what one measures."

When discussing financing, it is wise to start by reminding oneself of the fundamental law governing finance which relates risk to return. This relationship states that risk has a price, as investors need to be compensated for the risk incurred by their investment. Typically, the return expected by investors grows more than proportionally with the risk incurred. Conversely, this law states that lower-risk companies will be able to attract capital at lower cost than higher-risk companies.

Our second observation is that owners must understand that not all risks are equally critical for a company's strategic decision making. In other words, one might say that there is risk and risk. Depending on a company's industry and specific business approach, different risks will be more or less critical. So, from an owner's perspective, it is useful to classify risk into one of three types according to its criticality for the company.

Volatility risks are those based on typically shorter-term fluctuations. These include variations of input, output, and transformation prices such as transportation costs. They are exemplified by interest rate, currency, commodity, and business risk. Airlines, for example, face volatility risk in the changes in the price of oil, one of its major cost items. Branded food companies, such as Kraft Heinz, and Nestlé, are greatly affected by the price volatility of certain of their agricultural inputs. This naturally leads retailers to also be exposed to price fluctuations. Most companies—whether they sell abroad or just domestically—are affected by exchange rate risk.

Volatility concerns the second moment of the distribution and is "symmetric" around the first moment. This volatility fluctuates around the mean, with the result that sometimes we lose, sometimes we gain. But we can relax here: if we hold out for the long run, we should be safe; negative fluctuations will be compensated by positive fluctuations, "things simply canceling themselves out over the medium to longer term." Volatility risks are symmetric in the sense that periods of negative effects (e.g., currency devaluation) are followed by periods of positive effects (e.g., currency revaluation)—their average effect for a *long-run investor or a well-diversified investor is limited.*

With some abuse of notation, though following a practice in the literature, we define **Black Swan risk** as the opposite of volatility risk. This risk consists of unidirectional shocks that are just negative with no positive counterparts (leading to skewness or kurtosis). At the firm level, these correspond to, for example, expropriation risks, political risks, reputational risks, organization and environmental risks, and bankruptcy. At the macro level, these concern global shocks to the financial or economic system, such as the emergence of COVID-19. The 2007–08 financial crisis, whose consequences are still affecting EU countries, and the Fukushima disaster, which is still affecting Japan today, are other telling examples of Black Swan risks. Black Swan risks typically impact a company's performance in major ways. The sustainability of a business demands that the company be able to withstand Black Swan events.

Some Black Swans are so-called **Dirty Swans**, as they are predictable, but with a possibly very nuanced and insightful analysis (and hence with low probability). The forest fires that raged in Australia and California in 2021–22 were unprecedented. And yet, they result from changing climate conditions that we know are getting worse every year. This would make these fires closer to Dirty Swans, as they represent a risk that should have been expected and predicted. The same holds for the BP and Transocean Macondo disaster in the Gulf of Mexico. BP's safety record in North America could objectively be described as very poor at the time of the accident, with oil spills, illegal discharges, air pollution violations, and, finally, an explosion at its Texas City refinery, killing 15 workers and injuring another 180.[4] The Board ought to learn to spot Dirty Swans.

Obsolescence risk is the third risk we wish to identify. It often goes unrecognized until it is too late. We saw in Chap. 2 how the German Merck gradually lost its leadership position in the pharmaceutical sector. It took several risky decisions that did not produce the intended results and contributed to rendering the company undersized compared with its competitors. We also saw how Interbrew, on the other hand, embraced obsolescence risk as a challenge and motivated it to transform itself. Interbrew owners had identified and understood the risk that was rendering them. They also masterfully governed its response and, in doing so, became the largest beer company worldwide. Obsolescence risk is, in our view, largely ignored by companies. Paradoxically, the ignorance of obsolescence risk is potentially the most significant risk these companies face. We devote a separate chapter (Chap. 7) to a detailed discussion of obsolescence.

Given the turbulent dynamics experienced by the world economy in the first two decades of the twenty-first century, CEOs and corporate boards are now spending considerable time examining these risks with great care. Risk oversight is one of the more complex governance tasks facing boards. It truly calls for excellent collaboration between the board, management, experts, and owners. It is often mixed or understood as risk management, which is an executive function in the enterprise.

Risk oversight is the evaluation and control of the risk exposure of the company. Understanding the difference in the type of risks being faced will help to ensure that the right strategy is selected, and that deployment is as effective as possible. A minimal 3×3 matrix, with environmental, organizational, and strategic risk as rows and the nature of risk (Operational, Black Swan, Obsolescence) as columns is a good beginning for owners, their boards, and their managers) to understand and master the multiple risks they face.

2 Risks in Strategy Choice, Strategy Execution, and Governance

Our first example that concretely illustrated how risk affects both governance and execution was the story we told earlier of **BP**'s acquisition spree in the US, including of its American rival, **Amoco**. The example showed how strategic choices focusing on the economic aspects of its M&A strategy led to a disastrous breakdown in safety management that was not identified and mitigated at governance level.

Our second example concerns **British American Tobacco plc** (BAT), a tobacco company listed on the London Stock Exchange, which resulted from a joint venture agreed in 1902 between the UK's Imperial Tobacco Company and the American Tobacco Company. One of BAT's major investments is the Indian tobacco company ITC Limited, erstwhile Imperial Tobacco Company of India Limited, which was its name when it was formed in 1910. It changed to Indian Tobacco Company in 1970 and, finally, ITC Limited in 1974. With independence, ITC's environment changed, Indian regulations favored protectionism, and many companies were being nationalized. This led BAT to reduce its stake in ITC, falling to 29.3% in 1995. When the environment changed again, India starting to liberalize, regulations relaxed, and foreign direct investment now encouraged, BAT believed the time was right to increase its stake in ITC to 51% and retake control of a company that had substantially diversified into the hospitality sector. BAT appreciated the more favorable market conditions and happily entertained the prospect of improved results in the Indian market.

However, BAT miscalculated the type of risk it was facing and needed to manage. The risk it faced on the transaction was not foremost one of economic valuation or pricing, where it felt it could persuade shareholders to sell shares with the right offer. The risk was rather one of having to deal with the Indian Government, which through state-owned banks and financial institutions owned close to 30% of ITC Limited, a stake like that of BAT (i.e., political risk). The backlash against BAT was so strong that as recently as 2018, renewed press reports appeared describing political moves to block BAT from increasing royalties or imposing any control over the company.[5] BAT's risk now became one of expropriation: BAT was facing a Black Swan type of event that blocked it from being an actual owner of Indian assets. If this risk had been properly recognized, BAT would likely have navigated the situation differently than it did. BAT's risk miscalculation had a high cost: some have stated that it set BAT back over 25 years.

Chapter 4 illustrated how a company's strategic choices are critically affected by whether the company is looking for cost reductions (favoring mergers and acquisitions) or revenue enhancements (favoring joint ventures). Risks similarly affect strategic choices, as we now will demonstrate by returning to the choices Interbrew faced, as described in Chap. 4.

Interbrew, like almost all companies, faces considerable volatility risks. These include variations in packaging costs, raw materials (cereal grains, usually malted barley and hops), transportation costs, or labor costs. As Interbrew grew larger, a greater scale provided Interbrew with increased bargaining power with packaging and raw material providers, as well as with employees. Scale reduced volatility risk. For example, Interbrew faces significant changes in the price of hops (a key ingredient in many types of beer). Between 2010 and 2020, Interbrew had to navigate price variations for hops ranging from a low of US$ 3.14 per pound to a high of US$ 7.72 per pound. The difference between the high and the low price over this decade was 145%. Interbrew grew larger via mergers and acquisitions. Its size allowed it to exert pressure on hop producers, reducing the volatility affecting hop prices.

Through its acquisition of SABMiller, the monopolistic power of Interbrew grew further. It now was able to purchase hops in large quantities from SAB Hop Farms. This led to regulatory issues, as in 2017, Interbrew's hop requirements led the company to purchase the entire production of SAB Hop Farms, causing a shortage of hops for other beer manufacturers. Interbrew's decision to pursue a strategy of M&As allowed it to corner the market for hops and reduce volatility risk, but this also increased its regulatory risk.

A different risk associated with Black Swans led to a different strategy for Interbrew in Russia. Chapter 4 described how Interbrew pursued a JV strategy there. In 1999, with the fall of the USSR, the market presented several Black Swan risks. A major one pertained to businesses being expropriated, a major risk still in too many countries.

In 2004 Interbrew was able to take full control over its JV with its partner, the Khemkas. JV typically do not last, one partner being more interested in the JV, and more able to govern it and benefit from it. In 2017 Interbrew again formed a joint venture, now with Anadolu Efes, belonging to the Turkish Anadolu Group. The latter has extensive relationships and contacts in Russia. The JV strategy in Russia has allowed Interbrew to participate in an important and growing market while minimizing the risk of losing its business entirely to appropriation.

In summary, Interbrew's strategic choices between M&As and JVs were influenced by risk and led to the following strategic thrusts:

- M&A helped reduce volatility risks, especially with respect to input costs;
- JVs minimized Black Swan risks, such as expropriations, in attractive, complex, and uncertain markets.

A key insight is that there is no "free lunch." An organizational structure that reduces volatility risks (M&A, full control) increases Black Swan risks (expropriation, bankruptcy). An organizational structure that reduces Black Swan risks (JV, alliance) increases volatility risks by not allowing the centralization of cash flows and central cash, liquidity, and interest rate management, as well as sourcing and invoicing critical to reduce volatility risks. A very high leverage may be required to reduce obsolescence risks, but this will increase bankruptcy risk.

In the next section, we discuss how financing and ownership structures have a significant effect on the choice of strategy.

These considerations define some principles on how cash flow and risk affect the growth strategy, summarized in Fig. 6.1.

Drivers	Acquisitions & Mergers	Joint Ventures
Cash Flows	Decrease Cost	Enhance Revenue
Risk	Decrease Volatility Risk	Decrease Black Swan Risk

Fig. 6.1 Value driver metrics applied to growth strategy decision

3 Financing

Microsoft was founded in 1975 by Bill Gates and Paul Allen. The company famously raised capital through an IPO 11 years after it was founded. Its primary motivation was to have a hand on a liquid "currency" it needed to attract and retain valuable employees. Venture capital needs was thus not the reason why Gates was driven to IPO. Neither did Gates aim to monetize his or Paul Allen's shareholding. In fact, during the IPO, Gates insisted on selling part of his shares at the minimum price of the IPO range.[6] Of course, Microsoft is an exception in that most companies raise capital either in the start-up phase (to survive, or to be able to present a "credible" business, thanks to a tested prototype or a demonstrated business idea), or, later on, to cover capital expenditures, fuel growth (inorganic or organic), or because one or more shareholders wants out to "cash in," partially or wholly. However, in the case of Microsoft, as in many other cases of owner-led firms, the owners decided on the financing choices.

Once the need for additional capital is identified and acknowledged, the key decision is to consider where the best source of capital may lie. The dichotomy here is based on **internal financing** (via retained earnings) versus **external sources** (debt, equity, hybrid instruments). Internal financing typically funds ongoing maintenance expenditures. It can also be used to grow, but, as we indicated in Chap. 4, this limits growth at the early stage, since Growth = Profitability × Investment Rate. Thus, higher-growth companies often need to secure additional capital.

Debt financing provides the attraction of a tax shelter because interest expense is typically tax-deductible. Dividends paid to equity holders usually are not. There is a limit, however, to the amount of debt that can be raised. Larger borrowing increases the risk of financial distress.

The three financing decisions described in Fig. 6.2 interact among each other. Different firms select different options depending on the owner's mission, the company's goals and strategies, and the circumstances the company

At what <u>Level</u> of the enterprise will the capital be raised?	From <u>Whom</u> is the capital raised?	What <u>Terms</u> should be agreed to which sources of capital?
○ Holding company ○ Business units	○ Private placements (institutions / individuals) ○ Public markets	○ Return guidance or guarantees ○ Control rights

Fig. 6.2 Financing decisions

		Subsidiaries	
		Private	Public
Parent	Private	Kohler	TATA
	Public	GE	Ayala

Fig. 6.3 Public listing strategies for conglomerates/groups

is in. Figure 6.3 illustrates how the factors governing equity financing are typically dealt with by large companies and conglomerates alike. Each instance will be exemplified by mentioning one specific corporation that illustrates the situation.

Private Parent – Private Subsidiaries: Kohler Co.

Kohler Co. is a US-based conglomerate whose companies are involved in many manufacturing and service businesses, including plumbing products, furniture, tiles, engines, hospitality, real estate, power plant services, and private equity. The CEO of the holding company is David Kohler, a fourth generation descendent of John Michael Kohler, who founded the company in 1873.

The Kohler family is clear that it does not wish to share control over its companies, including its subsidiaries, with any third parties. In 1998, a subset of the Kohler family bought back shares owned outside the family. All family members now have shares with restricted rights but enjoy full dividends. For example, shares cannot be sold outside of the family. Kohler raises finance through internal accruals and debt. The family stays away from public equity markets due to its aversion to dilution.

Public Parent – Private Subsidiaries: GE

General Electric Company (GE), whose corporate board and CEOs we discussed in Chap. 3, is a listed US conglomerate with divisions and subsidiaries in aviation, healthcare, power, renewable energy, lighting, and venture capital/finance.

While the holding company is listed, each division or subsidiary is unlisted. The advantage of having unlisted subsidiaries is that GE controls them fully. Like Berkshire Hathaway, GE appoints CEOs for each business, approves their strategies, and then collects dividends and cash flows from these businesses. Unencumbered by outside shareholders, GE, as owner, decides the allocation of capital within these businesses as well as the payment of dividends to the shareholders of this listed holding company. For a long time, GE was a standout among US corporates demonstrating consistent value add at the group level. When buying GE stock one was truly betting on GE's corporate leadership, its ability to sustain dividends and accrue value through group governance, regardless of the businesses held at any given time.

GE did stray from this strategy in 2016 when, under the leadership of Jeff Immelt, it merged its oil and gas business with Baker Hughes, a listed company. GE ended up owning more than 50% of the merged company, in line with GE's desire to control the companies it owns. However, in September 2019, GE announced that it would sell its stake to raise capital for its other businesses. Many stated that Immelt's bet had turned sour, that the risk taken had not panned out due to a rapidly deteriorating oil and gas sector. But GE must also have found the constraints of managing a listed entity it did not fully own—and the transparency it had to give to these shareholders of its accounts—quite onerous and cumbersome.

Private Parent – Public Subsidiaries: The Tata Group

Tata Sons, the Tata Group holding company, is unlisted. It is 68% owned by philanthropic trusts. Most of the Tata Group's major businesses are held through one of 28 listed companies. Tata Sons owns less than 40% in all but one of the major listed companies, TCS, its consultancy services business where it enjoys full control. The major Tata Group listed companies and the group's level of control of each of these companies are shown in Fig. 6.4.

As each company requires further equity capital to grow, the Tata Group decided it would be best to publicly list its companies, all operating in very different sectors, and grow these companies with market financing.

Company	Shareholding of Tata Sons in TATA Group companies (%, as of Sept 30, 2016)
TATA Consultancy Services Limited (TCS)	73
Indian Hotels Company Limited (IHCL)	39
TATA Global Beverages (TATA Tea in 1990)	36
TATA Power	33
TATA Motors Limited (erstwhile TELCO)	32
TATA Steel Limited (erstwhile TISCO)	31
TATA Chemicals Limited	31
Titan	25

Fig. 6.4 Shareholding of Tata Sons in major listed Tata Group companies. Source: Bombay Stock Exchange (BSE)

This strategy is preferred by most investors, as they favor investing in sectors and companies they select. However, there is another reading: TCS is the major profitable company in the Group, allowing the Group to remain profitable itself. Many of the other Tata companies have been loss-making, even though they are controlled by the group, who as the major shareholder has the power of governance on these companies, including decisions about inter-company flows and transfers. One should note that losses of group companies are conveniently shared with the market, while profits are syphoned off. This is a standard in business groups around the world when the same owner has control over many listed (and unlisted) entities having more "control rights" (often coming from a web of cross-ownerships) than "cash flow rights" (often concentrated in a few companies within the group).

The Tata Group has occasionally relied on the sale of shares in its large and thriving software company, TCS, to fund the activities of the other businesses. Without TCS, the Tata Group might have had to consider listing its holding company, Tata Sons, to finance the group's businesses. The synergy among the various businesses is largely one-sided and financial: TCS is the group's flagship that fuels all other entities of the Group and is the major provider of dividends to the trusts.

Public Parent – Public Subsidiaries: The Ayala Corporation

Ayala Corporation is a Philippine listed company (already discussed in Chap. 2) 47.7% owned by the Zóbel de Ayala family. As illustrated in Chap. 2, Ayala Corporation founded, scaled, and then listed many companies in a range of businesses in telecoms, real estate, banking, and water infrastructure.

By listing the holding company, the Zóbel de Ayala family obtained outside capital to help it continue its diversification strategy while at the same time retaining control over the holding company and its subsidiaries. In each of the listed operating companies, Ayala attracts strategic investors who share in the financing of growth, knowing that they do so with a well-connected local partner, regarded as the core of the value add. In return, Ayala benefits from resources from abroad that are leveraged by the corporate owner in the Philippines. Investors who want a proxy investment for investing in the entire country invest in the holding company. In this way, Ayala caters to investors interested in partnering with the family and the Philippines, while other investors find Ayala companies useful instruments to conquer local markets guided by partners who know these markets inside out. Furthermore, the listing of Ayala Corporation allows the group to enter new businesses without diluting its stake in the businesses in its portfolio. However, as mentioned, the fact that this is still a business group in which the diversification desire of the family clashes with the "single player" desire of the market undervalues the holding company when compared with the sum of the market value of the listed subsidiaries.

4 Interbrew: The Relations Between Financing and Strategy Choice

We recounted in Chap. 1 how the owning families of Interbrew took the strategic decision to IPO. As the then Interbrew CEO, Hugo Powell, said in a *Financial Times* interview, "The listing will be the start of a new era. Access to external funds is a major advantage which will optimize Interbrew's acquisition opportunities." Chairman Paul De Keersmaeker told the *New York Times* that a rationale for the IPO was that "expansion on the international level is vital for our company." The IPO closed on December 1, 2000. The company was valued at US$ 2.5 billion.

The IPO financing provided the financing that allowed Interbrew to complete the acquisitions of Bass and Whitbread, and also of Beck's, one of Germany's largest beer companies,. Soon after, in 2008, Interbrew completed its acquisition of Anheuser-Busch and subscribed a rights issue for 6.4 billion euros. This helped pay down some of the debt it raised for the acquisitions.

Interbrew's IPO in 2000 and its rights issue in 2008 show how there are mutual feedback loops between company financing and the businesses' strategy. Interbrew's acquisition strategy drove it toward an IPO and rights issues, and equally, the IPO and rights issues allowed Interbrew to pursue its aggressive M&A strategy.

Financing has wider implications, going beyond strategy. One such implication concerns the control over key business decisions. The next chapter explores this important consideration.

Notes

1. José Santos (2013), M.EOS: How General Management Matters, *INSEAD Working Paper* 2013/75/ST.
2. https://www.pbs.org/wgbh/pages/frontline/the-spill/bp-troubled-past/.
3. https://www.csb.gov/macondo-blowout-and-explosion/.
4. https://www.nytimes.com/2010/05/09/business/09bp.html.
5. https://economictimes.indiatimes.com/industry/cons-products/tobacco/govt-should-raise-stake-in-itc-to-prevent-hostile-takeover-by-bat-sjm/articleshow/66256643.cms?from=mdr.
6. https://techcrunch.com/2017/08/08/a-look-back-in-ipo-microsoft-the-software-success/.

7

Control and the Corporate Board

1 Definition of Control

Chapter 1 defined "value creation" in an owner-led company as progress on the company's mission as crafted by the owners. We then confirmed that the first task for the board and the company's executive leadership is to agree on the pursuit of company goals that, when reached, attest tangible progress in the achievement of the company's mission. Company goals themselves will then be declined through a series of sub-goals, which are objectives pursued by lower levels in the organization. The alignment of these goals and sub-goals with the mission is a necessary and critical condition for actual value creation. The importance of an "aligned" firm cannot be overemphasized, with the caveat that alignment on wrongly formulated goals and sub-goals will lead to value destruction.

These considerations lead us to formulate "control" over a company as the ability to:

- Define the Mission
- Formulate Goals that connote progress on the realization of the Mission
- Set and execute Strategies that achieve the company's Goals

Control further means that the owner(s), the Board of Directors, and the executives understand the risk assumed by the adopted strategies and that financing strategies have been put in place that meet the financial requirements of a proper execution of these strategies.

M. Massa et al., *Value Creation for Owners and Directors*,
https://doi.org/10.1007/978-3-031-19726-0_7

Control is an interesting word, as it is often misunderstood and typically triggers emotions on all sides, from owners to board members and managers. Owners too often feel they "own" the company, when they own the right to define the mission, set some values and certain governance principles important to them, appoint board members, and collect the benefits of a successful realization of the defined mission. As we saw in Chap. 2, the responsibility for the company in its relations to stakeholders, including shareholders, lies with the Board of Directors. This subtle and possibly surprising institutional arrangement in liberal capitalism obliges owners to meet the "filter" of the corporate board. Owners, therefore, cannot force a board to accept something that the board does not view to be in the interests of the company (including in its relations with stakeholders). Owners dissatisfied with the board they appointed must call for an extraordinary meeting of the shareholding and present a motion of distrust of the current board. The vote of the shareholders will decide on the dismissal of the corporate board. This is their countervailing power with regard to the board they have appointed.

What owners cannot do, however, is literally dominate the corporate board, tell them what to do and approve, take over the CEO reins, force execution, and de facto dominate the entire chain of command. Liberal capitalism limits the power of owners to formulate the company's mission and appoint corporate officers that have the responsibility for the execution of that mission. The wisdom of "liberal capitalism" is that it follows the principles of democratic governance arrangement by forcing checks and balances so that the emergence of dictatorship— where a corporate dictator abuses her or his power at the expense of the "people" (shareholders, employees, other stakeholders) —is minimized. In that sense, one can say that Jack Welch and Carlos Ghosn exercised dictatorial powers at the end of their reign, with very negative consequences for GE and Renault-Nissan, respectively.

Astute observers will mention a "loophole" to the governance system when owners appoint "obedient" board members that act as transmission chords for their orders, regardless of the implications for the company's sustainability and interests. Indeed, as we saw in earlier chapters, corporate law has provided a corporation with its own legal status. We should admit that this practice has existed for a long time and, unfortunately, too often remains true. The professionalization of boards that has been triggered by the 2007–2008 financial crisis—and the Enron, Tyco, and Worldcom scandals that preceded it (all in 2002) —has provided a major impetus in reviewing and improving governance practices following the massive value destruction that the crisis and these scandals occasioned. Many of these concern publicly listed firms, where executives yielded too much power, the CEO often doubling up as the

Chairman. The latter was the case for Enron, Tyco, and WorldCom, the Chairman and CEO acting as if they were, psychologically, owners of their firms.

The latest scandal concerning Theranos founder Elizabeth Holmes shows that this practice has continued.[1] It has become a symbol of poor governance practices in Silicon Valley and was liquidated in 2018, after a Wall Street journalist uncovered the fraud that was rampant in the company.[2] Elizabeth Holmes left Stanford College at the age of 19 to found Theranos, a name that refers to therapy and diagnosis. The company promised low-cost and painless blood tests (avoiding syringes). It was supposed to be based on its Edison technology and it was valued at US$ 9 billion in 2015. The Theranos Board was a typical US all-star board, including two former US Secretaries of Defense and State (Henry Kissinger, George Schulz, and William Perry), admirals and generals (including Jim Mattis), the former CEO and Chairman of Bechtel and Wells Fargo, as well as a former Vice-President of Amgen. It seemed to have submitted to a much younger and less experienced Chair and founder. In 2016, the company announced its medical advisory board, consisting of former presidents and board members of the American Association for Clinical Chemistry. That no one on this all-star board understood the hype and outright lies the company was generating is mind-boggling. It should not have been that difficult for Board members to get a clearer view and at least entertain some skepticism regarding the abilities of their Edison technology, communicated with great hype and plenty of lies by CEO Holmes. Particularly when Ian Gibbons, the Chief Scientist, was fired in 2010, to be rehired in a low-rank position due to the lobbying of former employees, and when Stanford Professor Ioannides in 2015 points out that not a single peer-reviewed paper had been published in the scientific literature about the Theranos technology. Professor Diamandis from the University of Toronto went further that same year when he concluded, following his analysis of the technology, that "most of the company's claims are exaggerated."[3] The signals were there for board members to see if they cared and wished to.

The case shows the value of having independence at board level (including from the owner-founder) and the danger of filling one's board with "stars." A former employee quotes Holmes as stating that "the Board is just a placeholder … I make all the decisions here."[4] This essentially sums it up but appears not that uncommon among Silicon Valley boards. In 2013, Holmes forced a resolution that assigned 100 votes to every share she owned. This gave her 99.7% of the voting rights. That this did not raise further suspicion with Board members is one of the many surprises in this corporate governance debacle spurred on by the owner and her partner Sunny Balwani. The company claimed that shareholders approved this arrangement. Some shareholders have contested this, confirming that they did receive the information from the company, but never signed off their agreement with the proposal that the company circulated. Holmes was finally convicted of fraudulent behavior in 2022, as was Balwani.

The regulatory intervention was very timid when considering that Holmes defrauded investors of US$ 700 million and destroyed US$ 10 billion of capitalization (recognizing that the latter value was built largely on lies and hype). The SEC authorities fined Holmes US$ 500,000 and told her to return stock to the company. She was also barred for ten years from board positions. That the Theranos story is real may be the biggest surprise. It also attests to the relatively weak governance culture that prevails in Silicon Valley. US culture favors entrepreneurship and execution over governance. Mishaps like Theranos are the result.

Control is in no way about limiting information or about appointing board members that have false or too limited information about the company. Nor is it about keeping a lid on employees' ability to communicate the true state of the company to Board members. Control is about ensuring that announcements are accurate and not manipulative, and that stakeholders, whether shareholders or regulatory authorities, not be presented with sudden and major surprises. The first element of control concerns alignment with the mission imposed by the owners, and that this mission is honestly and consistently pursued.

The counter sometimes heard to this notion of control is that its enforcement by the regulator might require the regulator to act like a cop and demands putting too many cops on the street. But that argument is wrong: the law has power because it can and will sanction; seeing many cops is an indication that the threat of sanction is insufficient. A better method is likely to have greater deterrence, not to put more cops on the street. A good place to start is for regulatory authorities to better screen the individuals that can serve as board members. This is the approach followed by the European Central Bank, which, ever since the 2007–08 financial crisis, has paid much greater attention to the profiles of individuals selected to be board members of major banks inside the EU. This is a radical change from past practice, which was more eager to regulate and set specific goals and targets for boards, such as Capital Adequacy Ratios (CARs). These have direct and uniform implications for bank management, precisely punishing those banks that are able to function well with lower CARs. Reviewing the governance of the banks, including how capital is allocated and the bank governed, would seem a better approach.

Another poor practice of control was provided in Chap. 2, where we saw how the Merck family board imposed its strategy, or at least its strategic views, at multiple levels of the enterprise, to their detriment. Interbrew provides a healthy contrast, with a family exercising control over matters that it regarded as essential to the accomplishment of its mission. The first and determining aspect regarding control is thus the ability for owners to frame and commit to a mission. The second and more classical aspect of control is to see to it that this mission is pursued until the owners understand that the mission ought to be changed. The nomination of directors, immediately presented by effective owners with the mission that is the first and deep purpose of the enterprise, is the third step in exercising control.

Achieving control in this sense immediately has several consequences:

- owners who share the same mission can more easily join forces;
- owners who do not share the same mission will be in a position where they will need to agree on a new mission, which unavoidably destroys value for at least one if not both of the parties;
- financing an enterprise through a holding company that sets the missions of its subsidiaries in line with the mission set for the holding company by its owners preserves and leverages the value creating abilities of owners.

In both Solvay and Interbrew, the owning families shared a mission which they then controlled by forming family holding companies, Solvac and Stitching AK Netherlands, respectively. The principal raison d'être of the latter companies is to control the two-family companies, Solvay and Interbrew, that are tasked with pursuing and operationalizing the missions crafted by the respective family holding companies. This is one of the main differentiators between owner-led firms and publicly listed firms, where the mission is left to the discretion of the board, if not the executives when the latter control the board.

2 Ensuring Control: AGM Tactics, Pyramids, and Cross-Ownership Structures

Credit Suisse (2018)[5] defines family-controlled listed firms as those where a family group has at least a 20% ownership of the voting shares. In Asia, for example, except for Japan, such listed family-controlled companies dominate the business landscape (Fig. 7.1). Cheng (2014) studied the emergence of

Country	% Of all listed companies controlled by	
	Business families	The State
Indonesia	71.5%	8.2%
Malaysia	67.7%	13.4%
Hong Kong	66.7%	1.4%
Singapore	55.4%	23.5%
South Korea	48.4%	1.6%
Philippines	44.6%	2.1%
Japan	9.7%	0.8%

Fig. 7.1 Family ownership of listed companies. Source: Credit Suisse

family firm ownership in China and found that their family firms are becoming the dominant force.[6] While family firms on the Shenzhen and Shanghai exchanges amounted then (2014) to only 13.6% of the firms listed on these exchanges, by 2012 the total number of firms listed had doubled to 2460 and the percentage had grown to 55.8%. Interestingly, Cheng noted that the founding owners were by far Mainland Chinese and that family firms also had a significant presence in capital-intensive industries, which are the sectors least likely to be family-controlled. Even in more developed economies, the presence of family-controlled firms on stock markets is important, even if this is the environment where one does not naturally expect them. Most family firms indeed prefer to remain private precisely for reasons of control.

Family firms are prevalent in the S&P500 as well. Anderson and Reeb (2003) showed that 35% of the stock listed on that exchange belonged to family owners.[7] Corstjens, Peyer, and Van der Heyden (2006) confirmed a similar prevalence of family firms in European exchanges as well: 48.5% in France, 38.8% in Germany, and 32.9% in the UK.[8]

A widely accepted definition is that family-controlled firms are the ones where the largest shareholder is a single person, like the founder, or a family, or a set of families. However, in many cases, the largest shareholder block has less than 50% of the shares. In fact, companies tend to be controlled by identifiable ownership groups who own much less than a simple majority of the shares.

Most shareholder decisions are decided via majority votes of those shareholders present (including via proxy) and voting at a shareholders meeting. Many shareholders realize that they do not own enough shares—and often only an infinitesimal amount – leading to shareholder apathy and absence from the shareholders meetings. In other cases, a focus primarily on economic returns (share price and dividends) rather than on exerting control has the consequence that many shareholders are absent from these meetings, and do not even bother to give proxies to express their views and preferences in the votes held at the meetings.

If we now take the viewpoint of the controlling shareholder, this apathy implies that a smaller absolute shareholding expands into a larger shareholding when considering those voting. This then allows the former to effectively control the company. Figure 7.2 shows the effect apathy has on control. It illustrates that when only 25% among the non-controlling shareholders vote, a controlling shareholder owning 20% of the shares effectively controls the company, without having to ask for proxies from other shareholders. This is the typical case for firms listed in US stock market firms. As a specific illustration, it is how the Wendel family, through their family investment firm, Wendel Investissements, took control of Crown-Cork and Seal, the Philadelphia-based listed firm, owning only 20% of the shares.[9]

In Canada, Germany, and Italy, control is regularly exercised via cross-shareholdings and pyramid structures. In these countries a family can retain control over a large company through a cascade of companies while effectively owning only a small economic interest. Figures 7.3 and 7.4 illustrate these mechanisms. Figure 7.3 shows a chain of corporate owners possessing sufficient ownership for effective control at each level. For example, after three levels of 51% ownership, the "Owner" at the top of the pyramid controls Firm C while possessing only 13.3% of Firm C's equity. Figure 7.4 is a case of cross-ownership, which occurs when two firms own shares in each other. As

	% Of non-controlling shareholders who attend or participate via proxies in shareholder meetings						
% Ownership by "Controlling" Shareholder	**10%**	**15%**	**20%**	**25%**	**30%**	**35%**	**40%**
20%	71%	63%	56%	50%	45%	42%	38%
30%	81%	74%	68%	63%	59%	55%	52%
40%	87%	82%	77%	73%	69%	66%	63%
49%	91%	86%	83%	79%	76%	73%	71%

Fig. 7.2 Effective shareholding of a controlling shareholder in shareholder meeting votes

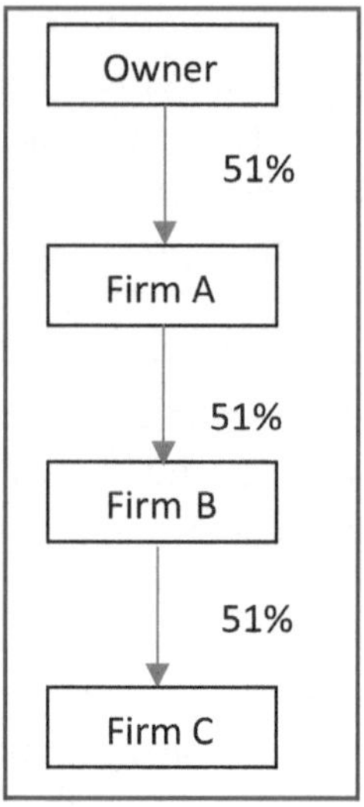

Fig. 7.3 Pyramid structures

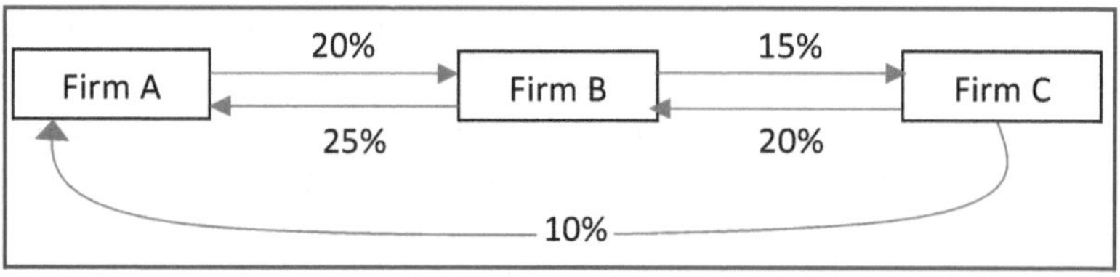

Fig. 7.4 Cross-shareholdings

shown in the figure, firm C has a 10% share in firm A. Through its cascade of ownership (via firm B), C controls 35% of firm A.

3 Example: From Fiat to Exor

The Agnelli family is an example of how cross-shareholdings and pyramid structures have allowed a family to maintain and exert control over an industrial empire. Giovanni Agnelli was an early investor in the Fabbrica Italiana di Automobili Torino, which later became Fiat.[10] The company produced horseless carriages and was a project of Count Emanuele Cacherano. The latter was looking for capital, and Giovanni in 1900 put about 400 euros into the venture (worth approximately 11,000 euros today). One year later, Agnelli was appointed Managing Director. He became Chairman of Fiat in 1920. Agnelli was an active investor and industrialist. His ambition was to indeed take greater control over Fiat. To this end, he set up a holding company in 1927, Industrial Financial Institute (IFI), that would eventually realize his ambition and own a majority of Fiat's shares. IFI then became an investment vehicle for Giovanni Agnelli to control other businesses, including beverages, concrete, coal, an airline, hydroelectric power, publishing, construction, and a football club.

Agnelli had a clear view on how IFI should be run:

- "One leader at a time": Giovanni Agnelli instituted the practice that, after him, one family member would lead the company and be appointed as its head. Others could share in the economic fortunes of the family, but there should be no dispute as to who was governing and running the company.
- Setting up a pyramid structure whereby IFI appointed CEOs of each of the businesses it controlled and then ensured that each CEO was provided with a clear mission that became the CEO's guiding objective.

Figure 7.5 shows the main components of the Agnelli holding structure in 2003 when Giovanni's grandson, "Gianni" Agnelli, who headed the family business passed away.

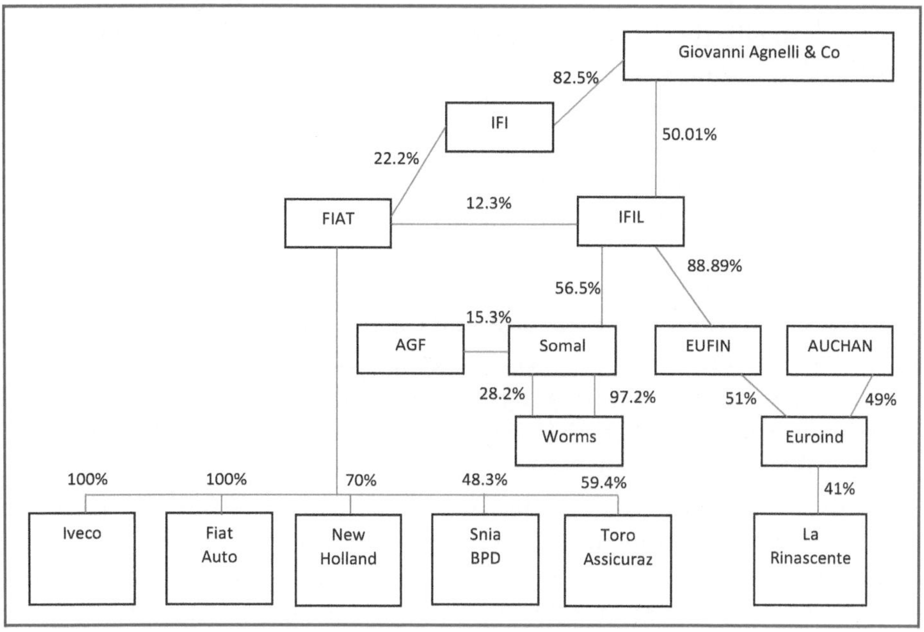

Fig. 7.5 Agnelli ownership of business structure 2004. Source: Company filings

Company	% Of Share Capital	Voting Rights
PartnerRe	100%	99.72%
Economist Group	43.40%	20%
Juventus F.C.	63.77%	63.77%
GEDI	5.99%[6]	6.26%
Fiat Chrysler Automobiles	28.98%	42.44%
CNH Industrial	26.89%	42.22%
Ferrari	22.91%	35.80%

Fig. 7.6 Exor shareholding and voting rights in major businesses (2019). Source: Company filings, press releases

In 2008, John Elkan, Gianni Agnelli's grandson, was leading the family holding. Simplifying the ownership structure, Elkan merged IFI and IFIL to create Exor. Exor is listed with the Agnelli family owning 56.89% of the share capital. Exor, in turn, owns shares in many major businesses (Fig. 7.6).

Pyramid structures, cross-shareholdings, and other ownership structures have proven effective in allowing owners to exercise a level of control exceeding their economic rights. But they also have a cost: operating efficiencies often suffer due to the complexity of governance arrangements and processes. One major consequence is the dilution of clear mission statements, in turn triggering value destruction. Exor offers diversification to its shareholders, which private owners, who are wealthy and wish to remain so, appreciate from a risk perspective.

For many business families, control is a necessity and a right they are willing to pay for. The ability to impose and oversee the company's operations to align with the mission is seen as a necessity for these owners. They see the benefits of control as outweighing the cost of operating the complex cross-shareholding arrangements that may be required to obtain their desired level of control. Choice of equity partners then becomes fundamental, as partners allow the owning family to maintain control as their shareholding is gradually diluted. This is something founder Giovanni Agnelli knew: the creation of IFI owed much to his close relationship with Riccardo Gualino, himself an early Italian business magnate and business partner of the founder of the Agnelli business dynasty.

4 Raising Capital While Keeping Control: Different Classes of Shares, Non-Voting Shares, ICOs, and STOs

Earlier chapters showed how growth required financing, challenging owners to raise capital without parting with control. This chapter discusses ways in which owners ensure this.

Different Voting Rights and Shareholding Classes

The easiest way to raise capital without losing control is to separate control rights from economic rights when issuing shares. This typically leads to the issuance of different classes of shares, where the voting rights associated with certain share classes are diminished if not removed altogether. Such ownership structures started with entrepreneurial founders and families eager for control. A telling example is Google.

When Google went public in 2004, it offered Class A stock to the public, while co-founders Larry Page and Sergey Brin, along with other Google executive managers and directors, attributed themselves Class B stock which held ten times the voting rights of Class A shares.[11] It then went further in 2014 when the company went for a two-for-one split of its A shares: each such share was issued a new class C stock that had no voting rights. In 2015, Google changed its name to Alphabet, but that did not impact the shareholding, only the company name. As of January 2021, Alphabet's shareholding was composed of about 301 million A shares and about 31 million B shares. The latter amount to 310 million votes at the General Shareholders Meeting. This thus allows the original founders to control the firm. It also allows Class C stock to be issued to current executives and other shareholders without any loss of control by the Class B shareholders. There is typically a minimal difference in the share prices between Class A and Class C shares, except when there might be a challenge for the control of Alphabet, which would then see the prices of Class A shares rise relative to the non-voting Class C shares. The difference amounts to a **control premium.**

Brian Roberts, who is Chairman and CEO of Comcast, a firm founded by his father, has an unusual arrangement. Comcast's Class A shares trade publicly on Nasdaq. But its Class B shares are controlled by Roberts and provide him with an undilutable 33.3% voting power, regardless of how many shares the company issues.[12] Shareholder agreements play an essential part in guaranteeing control.

Companies such as Buffett's Berkshire Hathaway have similar arrangements. The original shares of Berkshire Hathaway are Class A shares, which Buffett always stated would never be split. They are typically offered to long-term investors. Each Class A share traded, as on June 20, 2020, for US$ 271,000 per share. Class B shares were issued by Berkshire Hathaway due to stock splits, the first in 1996 where the stock was split 30–1, followed by a second 50–1 split in 2010. Combining these two splits amounts to a ratio of 1500–1. Each Class B share has one 10,000th of the voting rights of a Class A share. Class B shares traded, as on June 20, 2020, for US$ 180 per share, which equates to US$ 270,000 after correcting for the split. Clearly, the distinct control rights make no difference to the share prices of the two classes at that time. This is to be expected as shareholders of Berkshire Hathaway buy the stock for economic reasons, hoping to gain from Warren Buffett's market insights and investment strategies. In no way would they wish to control him, nor would he tolerate any control. The absence of any difference in the share price confirms this. Berkshire Hathaway is an example where the market exercises investor control, and not the boards of directors. If one disagrees with Buffett, one sells. No need to talk. General Assemblies of Berkshire Hathaway are notorious for being great barbecues, with Buffet serving products of companies he profoundly appreciates (e.g., Coca-Cola and Heinz). Buffett's original logic was that he wanted like-minded longer-term shareholders to buy and keep Class A shares, whereas smaller retail and other shorter-term investors could buy and sell the class B shares, which are more easily traded. Owners of Class A shares can convert their shares into Class B shares, but Class B shares cannot be aggregated and converted into Class A shares.

A different arrangement is to issue **preferred stock**. This class of stock has a higher claim on dividends than **common stock,** and receives a better treatment in cases of liquidation, though less good than creditors. It typically has few if any voting rights and offers less capital appreciation than common stock. Like bonds, preferred stock is issued at nominal value and associated with a fixed dividend schedule, though without an end date. Preferred stock offers an investment vehicle that sits somewhere between common stock and bonds.

Silicon Valley is notorious for dual class shareholdings, which have increased substantially, as Jerry Davis shows in his article that appeared in *The Conversation*.[13] Davis calls the justification the Ayn Rand myth of the founder, according to the author of the book *Atlas Shrugged*.[14] The book glorifies the founder, who like Atlas, must oppose forces aimed at bringing him down and prohibiting him from doing his wonderful work. In Greek mythology, Atlas sides with the Titans and fights the "Olympian" gods. He loses and Zeus punishes him by making him forever have to hold up the Earth and the skies on his shoulders.

Research has shown that divergence between insider voting and cash flow rights affects managerial extraction of private benefits of control.[15] As this divergence widens, corporate cash holdings are increasingly worth less to outside shareholders, CEOs receive higher compensation, managers make shareholder value-destroying acquisitions more often, and capital expenditures contribute less to shareholder value. Theranos founder Elizabeth Holmes, discussed earlier, illustrates the point in the extreme.[16]

Non-Voting Shares at Snap Inc.

Snap Inc., a social media company, headquartered in Santa Monica (California), completed its IPO on March 2, 2017. Its IPO document presents its three classes of shares with a rather cynical "innovation." A class shares normally have greater power than B or C class shares. This is reversed at Snap Inc., as their IPO document explains:

> *We have three classes of common stock: Class A common stock, Class B common stock, and Class C common stock. The rights of the holders of Class A common stock, Class B common stock, and Class C common stock are identical, except concerning voting, conversion, and transfer rights. Class A common stock is non-voting. Anyone purchasing Class A common stock in this offering will therefore not be entitled to vote. Each share of Class B common stock is entitled to one vote and is convertible into one share of Class A common stock. Each share of Class C common stock is entitled to ten votes and is convertible into one share of Class B common stock. The holders of our outstanding Class C common stock, each of whom is a founder, an executive officer, and a director of the company.*

Through such a structure, the Snap founders, like Elizabeth Holmes, sought to retain full control while raising capital. And indeed, they raised close to US$ 30 billion. These shareholders received very limited if any voting rights. Other companies such as Domo, Dropbox, and GreenSky all followed in Snap's footsteps and issued non-voting shares.

The phenomenon is relatively recent, traceable back to 2015, as Jerry Davis points out. It shows a remarkable aspect of modern stock markets in the technology and financial sectors: one can raise money from investors interested in financial returns without giving up much if any control. The rationale of investors appears similar to that of investors in Berkshire Hathaway: just follow the master, as there is little value to be gained from boards supervising founder executives through independent directors. The entire game is one where investors smell an opportunity by betting on founders and taking a share in the opportunity, without having any interest in the governance of the company.

ICOs and STOs

The latest trend in raising capital is via cryptocurrencies. Two instances are Initial Coin Offerings (ICOs) and Security Token Offerings (STOs). These go even further than non-voting shares. We start our discussion with a brief explanation of cryptocurrencies.

Cryptocurrencies are a form of digital currency that uses blockchain technology. Under a blockchain, when a participant legitimately transfers a cryptocurrency to another participant, a record of this transaction is made separately in millions of computers that form part of this cryptocurrency's network. The record for this transaction is locked into and joined with whatever transaction occurred just before it, as well as into the transaction that is made after it. In this manner, the transaction and new owner of the cryptocurrency are securely and safely recorded. There is no requirement for a bank or any central authority to confirm that a participant owns the cryptocurrency or to facilitate the transaction. Blockchain ensures and records the transaction in a very public manner. Should additional security be needed, a transaction can be "legitimated" online. This is when a significant number of the millions of participants in the network verify the credentials of a participant engaged in a transaction. This reduces the risk of one or a few participants "stealing" cryptocurrency.

ICOs have begun to be used, mostly in startups, as a method to raise capital. Investors invest via usual currencies or cryptocurrencies and receive a token that provides them with certain rights. These rights include benefits such as access to the digital business being created. Owners of these tokens are, however, not owners of the company. They act more like stakeholders, possibly like partners. The ICO tokens are liquid in that investors can trade their tokens among each other and with new investors. Companies do not have to pay dividends, and there is little in the way of corporate governance required for this "rights" market to function. In fact, the security is provided through the network and the programming of transactions in the network.

As is the case with any innovation, ICOs have been misused. Celebrities such as rapper T.I. and boxer Floyd Mayweather have advocated ICOs, only to be sued by the SEC for fraud.[17] A new form of ICOs, called Security Token Offerings (STOs), was created consequently. STOs usually have a non-digital business for which capital is being raised. STOs are also classified as securities under existing SEC regulations, in contrast to ICOs that are regulated as utilities. Like ICOs, STOs usually give investors limited rights and allow the owners to govern the company as they wish. Critically, STOs often replace voting rights with "usage rights," that is, the rights for investors to use the service of the company for free or at a prespecified (discounted) price. This resembles a century-old model well diffused in Europe: cooperatives. Figure 7.7 summarizes the difference between an STO, ICO, and an IPO.

	STO	ICO	IPO
Regulatory framework	Specific regulatory framework (securities regulation), with options for light-touch regulation or exemptions	Unregulated	Specific and well-defined regulatory framework
Maturity of the company	Early-stage or mature	Early-stage or mature	Needs minimum track record
Purpose of funds	Specific or long-term development	Specific or long-term development	Long-term development
Rights	High level of flexibility, limited rights may be given to token holders	High level of flexibility, limited rights may be given to token holders	Shareholders have well-defined rights
Target investors	High net worth or institutional investors	Retail market	Often institutional investors
Economic exposure	Direct economic exposure to issuer possible	No direct economic exposure to the company. Financial returns from token only through speculation on the secondary market (token exchanges).	Direct exposure to the company
Transparency	Varied and flexible levels	Low	Transparency levels and levels of reporting prescribed by listing rules
Disclosure	Flexible (formal prospectus or private information memorandum depending on the regulatory status of the token	No prescribed market standard for offering information	Complies with the market standard for offering information

Fig. 7.7 Comparing STO, ICO, and IPO. Source: "How to do an STO in Singapore," Ressos Legal Memorandum, January 2018

5 Structuring the Governance Inside Holding Companies: Corporate Layer, Business Units, and the Separation of Governance and Executive Roles

We now focus on the governance responsibilities in a corporate multi-business setting. These settings are typical for multinational enterprises, where each country or product line can be run as a distinct business (unless a matrix structure is chosen). The main point of this book is that owners have the key responsibility to set a company's mission and to control its execution, possibly adapting the mission when conditions change, and the chosen mission becomes less desirable. Corporate CEOs and executives in what is commonly called a **holding company** exercise similar ownership responsibilities by delegation from the board. The important point to stress is that they do not run the businesses held—this is done by the business managers—but govern these businesses.

What is important to observe at the outset is that holding companies are financial—and thus virtual—companies. The real business is done in the businesses being held. The only exception to this is when such holdings operate in a matrix structure, which invariably involves corporate executives in business decisions.[18] With that proviso, holding companies are thus "owners" of the businesses held by the corporation. The immediate and vital consequence is the point already mentioned above: corporate executives in such holdings are not running businesses but are supervisors of the businesses held. One of the principal responsibilities of corporate executives is thus to define the mission of the various businesses inside the holding. When such corporate executives think they run a "single, large business," they are mistaken about their role, and this confusion will typically result in value destruction, sometimes in considerable amounts. As members of the corporate executive board, they are corporate governors and not the executives of the businesses held by the holding. These governance responsibilities accrue to them through delegation by the corporate Board of Directors. One of the recurrent errors made by leading corporate executives, such as Jeff Immelt at GE and Carly Fiorina at HP, is to assume a disproportionate role in leading and managing the businesses inside the company, to the detriment of the executives of these businesses, and ultimately at the expense of the performance of these businesses and their corporations.

More specifically, in large corporations, there is a corporate layer that oversees the many "business units" held by the corporation. Each such "business unit" is managed by a CEO and a management team. The terminology underlines that the unit is a "business" by itself. Whether the unit and its management have the autonomy to run the business effectively is one of the core governance questions that the board of any corporate holding must reflect upon and decide. We call this the question of designing the "governance architecture" inside the holding. A recurring question, for example, is whether countries are seen as businesses, or more as organizational units (e.g., local sales units). Examples of both exist, but the governance point is that one should be clear about the choice made and act consistently with it.

Corporate executives thus exercise ownership responsibilities, by delegation of their Board of Directors. They are thus well advised to act more like owners and directors than business managers. Indeed, cash flows are generated by the businesses and not by the corporate center. Corporate executives are typically less knowledgeable about each business than would be the case in a single business corporation. The management teams running these businesses typically know much more than the corporate executives, except possibly for the business area these corporate executives emanated from.

The knowledge and information gaps separating corporate and business executives only grow with the number and variety of businesses held. This issue faces multi-business corporations much more severely than single businesses. To protect themselves from such information gaps, corporations make use of several practices. For example, they will rotate their managers across distinct businesses to make them aware of these knowledge gaps and to reduce them. More importantly, these rotations reduce the anchoring by future corporate executives on successful experiences they may have enjoyed when leading these businesses. Indeed, we will show in later chapters how such biases, if left unrecognized, may greatly diminish their effectiveness in their corporate governance duties. Rotation across businesses, sectors, functions, and geographies contributes to preparing executives for successful transitions as governance actors.

It is thus paramount to value creation inside a multi-business corporation that executives understand and recognize the difference between governance and executive roles, a fact that is all too often glossed over. For example, when corporate executives seek increased profitability, they tend to look at cost reduction initiatives; when business executives seek greater profitability, they look for increased revenue initiatives. Revenues and market knowledge in a corporation are decentralized; costs, on the contrary, are centralized (through procurement, investment, or HR functions). Figure 7.8 reminds us of the differences between corporate strategy and business strategy. The strategy of a multi-business corporation firstly concerns the choice of investments to be

For a Multi-Business Corporation strategy answers the following questions:

- Which sectors are we in?
- Within each sector, which assets do we invest in?
- Which synergies (finance, soft, hard, ...) do we seek?

For a Single Business Corporation strategy answers the following questions:

- What is our Target Segment?
- What is our Product-Service Offer?
- What is our Business Model (or Set of Activities and the Managerial Relations amongst those supervising these activities)?
- What are our Performance Measures?

Fig. 7.8 Distinguishing multi-business corporate strategy from business strategy

made and the synergies that can be obtained from these investments. These questions differ substantially from the strategic questions that arise in a single business. The implication in terms of governance is also interesting and rarely mentioned: one should speak of **business governance** and **corporate governance** as two distinct even if related topics.

GE is an interesting instance of a corporation, regarded as one of the most successful US businesses, known for the quality of its leaders, its strategies, and its technologies. Too many looked at GE as a business. In fact, GE was organized along **divisions** which each could be seen as a holding corporation. It cannot be stressed enough that if GE did so well for so long, and across so many sectors, it is because of the quality of its internal governance. It had sustainability in terms of its performance. All GE CEOs were named CEO of the Year at some point. In true US style, its governance was exercised much more by the corporate center than by the actual board of GE, which would have had too many businesses to oversee and was consequently too far from any one of them. One of the "rules of the GE governance game" was that businesses had to be either No 1 or No 2 in their respective sectors; if a business was not, its leader would be changed, or the business would eventually be sold. It is this kind of governance that turned every business into a top business.

The corporate center also reviewed each CEO at the beginning of the annual corporate planning cycle. Between 150 and 250 CEOs would thus be reviewed each year by the corporate center, which thus developed an unequaled capability for attracting, evaluating, developing, and motivating business leadership talent. It is this capability that earned GE its nickname as the US's #1 Leadership School for business executives. It also became one of the pillars of its performance.

The corporate and divisional centers would also review the business strategies of the 150 to 250 businesses it held. Hence, the GE governance practice would acquire that capability too. Competition for GE was, as for every corporation, at the business level. Competitors of GE's businesses would therefore not just compete with the GE business teams, but the competition would also extend to the governance level. This was where a major difference would lie with many of its competitors, save for a few, Siemens being one. It followed a logic like that of GE when it came to distinguishing corporate and business responsibilities, but never grew a financial unit like GE Capital.

If we turn to the oversight of Jack Welch and his corporate team by the GE Board (furthermore chaired by him), the general view today is that the governance was very passive. It continued to indeed remain passive following Welch's departure as it took far too much time to address the declining performance of GE in the new century. Jeff Immelt remained too long at the helm of GE, his term becoming identified with largely destroying much of the value that GE had built under predecessor Welch. The passivity of the GE Board likely owes much to the fact that Welch was both its chairman and powerful CEO for too long. One of the startling paradoxes of GE is that while it was the #1 business leadership school in the US, it completely missed the succession of its iconic leader, and then failed to correct it in a sufficiently speedy manner. GE certainly does not come out of this episode as #1 in governance. Jack Welch, being the Chair for a long time, must bear responsibility for this as well.

One of the key questions that Jack Welch did not effectively address was the gradual drift of GE from an industrial corporation to a financial one, the profits generated by GE Capital becoming ever greater, changing the outlook on the businesses, which became a way for GE Capital to generate massive value. This gradual drift ultimately became a question of mission that neither the executive team nor the board appeared to adequately confront. As a result, GE was badly hit by the financial crisis as a financial company, and not as an industrial company. It had to be bailed out by the Federal Government at the staggering amount of US$ 134 billion.[19] As part of the settlement, the government forced GE to return to its previous mission, that of being an industrial business. The financial result for the government was far from brilliant; the government never got its bailout investment back, while GE Capital gradually disappeared. When Larry Culp Jr. arrived at the helm, he declared the old GE dead, and refocused GE on a single business, aviation.

Returning to the linkage between cash flows, risk, and financing, the examples we refer to below illustrate how this tripod plays out in the governance of corporations:

- The corporate level (holding company) looks at all three aspects: where to invest for the future, managing risks, and making financing decisions affecting the businesses;
- The business units are responsible solely for generating cash flows since financing decisions belong to the corporate level and because the risks associated with the business units, when uncorrelated, will to a substantial degree cancel each other out.

In this manner, business units in well-governed corporations focus, laser-like, on formulating the (business) strategies that will deliver the cash flows. The corporate level approves business leadership, their strategies, the execution of these strategies, and business performance. Corporate also oversees the generation of cash flows; however, its fundamental value add lies in utilizing the cash generated by the business units efficiently, either for investing in the most interesting new projects proposed by the business units, or in the form of approving capital expenditures across the existing business units. When corporations start sitting on increasing amounts of cash due to the great performance of its businesses, the management of that cash would require an internal unit at corporate level that manages the cash (Cash Center or In-house Bank). This was likely the genesis of the creation of GE Capital within GE. It is the poor governance of this unit and of its impact which lay at the root of GE's demise.

The need to formalize the separate roles of the corporate and business unit levels was the impetus for the creation of a corporation, **Alphabet,** of which **Google** is a subsidiary. In 2015 Alphabet's then executive chairman, Eric Schmidt, explained to his shareholders that the holding company's creation from its beginnings in Google was inspired by discussions with Warren Buffett. Google's founders were impressed by "the scale of the success of [Buffett's] model." After visiting Buffett, the founders decided they should copy Buffett's principles, including "the independence of the CEO" and "a strong brand" for the parent company.[20] Eric Schmidt said, "*Alphabet is an attempt to build a holding company like Berkshire Hathaway out of an existing operating company. We're trying to push the Alphabet companies to be separate companies, not divisions.*"

The holding company, Alphabet, takes capital allocation decisions and effectively uses the cash generated by Google where it sells digital advertising in its data-gathering business ("organizing all the world's information") and invests this into more experimental long-term businesses that are run by CEOs and independent business unit boards making their cash flow impacting strategic decisions. Alphabet is also concerned with managing risks and ensuring that their capital allocation decisions provide the various businesses with sufficient financing to grow.

In 2015, when Alphabet was formed, Schmidt was asked in an interview, "How do you think about capital allocation for Alphabet?" His reply was as follows: "*We have about $70 billion in cash. Currently, it sits in Google, which is controlled by the parent, and at some point, we'll move it around. The process for funding is the same as always. There's a competition for the best ideas. Take Google Fiber. It's an incredibly good business, once it's established. I've argued that we should be as aggressive as possible.*"[21]

In addition to Google, the other major companies Alphabet presently holds include:

- Waymo – self-driving cars
- Calico – health-focused research and development company
- Sidewalk Labs – focused on smart cities exploring how data-gathering sensors can be used to manage crowds and traffic
- DeepMind – acquired by Google in 2014, which is a UK-based company researching artificial intelligence and machine learning
- Wing – drone delivery service
- Loon – brings internet access to areas with poor connectivity, by floating solar-powered hotspots over regions where building phone masts would be too expensive

The Berkshire Hathaway and Alphabet structures are of course not new. In 1924, Alfred Sloan, whose leadership of General Motors we briefly examined in Chap. 2, set up a "federal decentralization" structure for the company. Most analysts look at Sloan's GM primarily as a marketing project. Indeed, Sloan set up five separate brands and five price ranges for five different types of consumers. At each price point, buyers would find the appropriate GM car. As buyers became wealthier, they could upgrade to the next higher model and thus become a "GM-for-life" customer. This was, however, more than just marketing genius. Each of the five car brands— Chevrolet (the cheapest car for first-time buyers), Pontiac, Oldsmobile, Buick, and Cadillac—was run as a separate business unit. Sloan effectively decentralized decision making within the group. Each business had integrity thanks to the alignment with the mission of each of the five business units. To stress that the center did not run the businesses, he purposely named the Executive Committee the Policy Committee, concerned with group-level decision making.[22]

Sloan's successors, in search of operational efficiencies, started to make business decisions, focused on cost synergies. This led the corporate center to interfere with the businesses, resulting in the gradual convergence of the GM businesses with each other. They lost their original integrity and drifted away from their respective missions, which were not checked for distinction, but for similarity. Without realizing it, the corporate executives had crossed the line from corporate into business territory, with regrettable consequences in terms of both business and group performance. We have witnessed this over the last 30 years, and it ultimately contributed to the need to bail out the US automotive industry. Some have noted that the bailout led to governance changes that seemed infeasible before the bailout.[23] Free market scholars argue that US customers were not short of automobile choices and hence that bailouts were not truly necessary.

6 Corporate and Business Unit Boards – The Cases of Berkshire Hathaway, Ayala Corporation, and Tata and Sons

The previous section showed the advantages of placing distinct and complementary responsibilities at the corporate level and the business unit level. In conglomerates with many businesses, such as is the case in Alphabet or Berkshire Hathaway, a logical consequence of this separation of duties is the need to have distinct boards, one at the corporate level—the corporate board—and a second type at the business unit level—the business unit boards.

The advantage of this is best seen in **Berkshire Hathaway**. Much has been written about Buffett's investment philosophy and impressive investment track record. Much less is said about his equally remarkable and insightful focus on the mission by Berkshire Hathaway, while leaving the investee company CEOs plenty of autonomy in decision making as long as the mission was being pursued.

Buffett, together with his business partner of many years, Charlie Munger, controls Berkshire Hathaway, a listed holding company. As of August 3, 2019, Berkshire Hathaway owned 72 operating companies (in most of which it owned 100% of the shares). It also made an additional 49 significant investments in other large, listed companies. How does Buffett manage to generate superior returns with such a large portfolio of operating companies?

Buffett's governance system is simple. Berkshire Hathaway acts as the corporate board, setting the broad objectives and the mission for each of the businesses held, focusing on capital allocation, and carefully selecting the leadership of the operating companies. In a CNBC interview Buffett said about Berkshire Hathaway's subsidiaries[24]:

We have [excellent] managers for our businesses but we [the corporate board] determine the dividend policy of our subsidiaries. We control their capital allocation. Just take See's Candies. We bought that in 1972. We've moved several billion dollars from the candy business to other types of businesses. We'd love it if we can use it all in the candy business, but it just isn't that sort of business, and in addition to that we free up our managers from less productive use of their time.

The management teams, led by strong CEOs, have few operating constraints. The performances of the CEOs are measured by profitability after the cost of capital for the business is subtracted. The CEO and the business unit board govern each of the businesses. Alignment between Buffett, the Berkshire Hathaway corporate board, and the business unit boards is of paramount concern to Buffett.

A common mistake when looking at Buffett, whether reviewing his financial business operations or his investment strategies, is to try to blindly copy aspects of his business. As Charles Munger, Buffett's business partner, says, *"Our model's not right for everybody. We've decentralized power in our operating businesses to a point just short of total abdication."* The key lesson, in our view, is not Buffett's operating structure per se, but that at each key level of the enterprise, starting from himself and his business partner Charles Munger as the controlling owners, to the business boards and CEOs, there is a clear understanding of the role of each stakeholder, as well as clarity about the commitment to the owner's mission. Each stakeholder has its place and adheres faithfully to its responsibilities. Expertise in one role is not necessarily transferred or transferable to another. There is a clear demarcation between the owner, the boards of directors, and the company CEOs. Thus, Berkshire Hathaway provides a level of ownership and governance uncommon in the US, with spectacular long-term results. Berkshire Hathaway and Alphabet impose the decisions of the corporate board on capital allocation and risk assessments on the 100% owned or controlled subsidiaries. In family-owned conglomerates, a similar complementarity can be seen between corporate and business unit boards, even when some of these subsidiaries are publicly listed.

In Chap. 2, we examined how Ayala Corporation, the holding company of the Philippine Zóbel de Ayala family, controls four large, listed companies:

- Ayala Land – a real estate company (Ayala Corporation owns 44.4%)
- BPI – a bank (48.6%)
- E Globe – a telecommunications company (30.9%)
- Manila Water – a public utility (51.4%)

These companies are separately listed and have their own boards, as well as their CEOs and top management teams. The various business unit boards take key decisions relating to strategies, including growth. However, the corporate board of Ayala Corporation, as the founder and largest shareholder, decides on capital allocation decisions and dividend policy of the four companies. Outside shareholders create an additional level of complexity, but dividends are paid pro rata to shareholders. Ayala Corporation, as the ultimate owner, decides where to invest the dividends it receives from the four companies and entertains additional investments in newer projects and companies that may be unlisted at the start, but are likely to be listed once these businesses achieve the appropriate scale and profitability.

In Chap. 5, we illustrated how Tata Sons, the Tata Group holding company, owned stakes in many listed companies. Each of these, mostly large, listed companies had their own boards. However, while there was formal governance, there was also a lack of substance in terms of separate corporate-level and business unit boards. In 2012 when Cyrus Mistry was appointed Chairman of Tata Sons, he was, like Ratan Tata before him, also appointed Chairman of the boards of seven large, listed Tata Group companies. In 2017, in the aftermath of Mistry's firing as Chairman of Tata Sons, N. Chandrasekaran, the new Tata Sons Chairman was similarly anointed Chairman of these large, listed companies. In this manner, the insufficient separation between the corporate ownership level and the business unit level endures.

Capital allocation decisions, operating cash flow considerations, adequate perspectives on risks, and financing all risk becoming the preserve of one person who invariably will start merging the various and distinct responsibilities in his single persona. Unlike in Berkshire Hathaway or Alphabet, where the holding company exerts its powers on key non-operating cash flow decisions, in Tata Group this overlap between the corporate and business unit boards makes it structurally more difficult to take tough decisions or to question the Group Chairman. It is quite difficult to hold oneself to account; most of us indeed would benefit from having a proper board to which we are accountable. It would also provide us with greater support, in terms of emotional and decision-making support.

Notes

1. John Carreyrou, *Bad Blood: Secrets and Lies in a Silicon Valley Startup,* New York, NY: Alfred A. Knopf, 2018.
2. https://www.nbcnews.com/business/business-news/theranos-trial-verdict-sunny-balwani-elizabeth-holmes-rcna33701.
3. https://en.wikipedia.org/wiki/Theranos.
4. John Carreyrou, *Bad Blood: Secrets and Lies in a Silicon Valley Startup,* New York, NY: Alfred A. Knopf, 2018.
5. The CS Family 1000 in 2018, Credit Suisse - Research Institute, September 2018.
6. Q. Cheng (2014), Family firm research – A review, *China Journal of Accounting Research* 7:3, 149–163. https://doi.org/10.1016/j.cjar.2014.03.002.
7. Ronald C. Anderson and David M. Reeb (2003), Founding-Family Ownership and Firm Performance: Evidence from the S&P 500, *Journal of Finance* 58:3, 1301–1328.
8. Marcel Corstjens, Urs Peyer, Ludo Van der Heyden (2006), Performance of Family Firms: Evidence from US and European Firms and Investors, INSEAD Working Paper 2006–53.
9. Christine Blondel and Ludo Van der Heyden, *The Wendel Family: "Affectio Societatis" (B) – CGIP: The family as "Shareholder Entrepreneur" (1977–1996),* INSEAD Case 4784, 1999.
10. https://en.wikipedia.org/wiki/Giovanni_Agnelli.
11. https://money.usnews.com/investing/articles/goog-vs-googl-stock-difference.
12. https://money.usnews.com/investing/articles/goog-vs-googl-stock-difference.
13. https://theconversation.com/ayn-rand-inspired-myth-of-the-founder-puts-tremendous-power-in-hands-of-big-tech-ceos-like-zuckerberg-posing-real-risks-to-democracy-150830.
14. Ayn Rand, *Atlas Shrugged,* New York, NY: Random House, 1957.
15. Ronald W. Masulis Cong Wang, and Fei Xei, "Agency Problems at Dual Class Companies," *Journal of Finance* 64(4): 1697–1727, 2009.
16. https://www.forbes.com/sites/petercohan/2015/11/03/theranos-letter-shows-elizabeth-holmes-tried-to-take-control-from-shareholders/?sh=2c7d4b2c2c53.
17. https://fortune.com/2020/09/11/rapper-t-i-fine-fraudulent-initial-coin-offering/.
18. https://papers.ssrn.com/sol3/papers.cfm?abstract_id=1362515.
19. https://theweek.com/articles/761357/fall-ge.
20. https://www.cnbc.com/2017/06/07/alphabet-shareholders-meeting-eric-schmidt-says-warren-buffettt-inspired-alphabet.html.
21. https://medium.com/cs183c-blitzscaling-class-collection/cs183c-session-8-eric-schmidt-56c29b247998.

22. https://papers.ssrn.com/sol3/papers.cfm?abstract_id=1362515.
23. https://knowledge.wharton.upenn.edu/article/auto-bailout-ten-years-later-right-call/.
24. https://www.youtube.com/watch?v=JvEas_zZ4fM.

8

Obsolescence and Counterfactual Thinking

1 Obsolescence: The Unrecognized Corporate Killer

Bankruptcy risk, country risk, currency risk, and operational risk are examples of risks that are at hand, and which we discussed extensively in Chap. 5. However, there is one risk that both managers and owners are less cognitively aware of and that we like to focus on in this chapter. It is one that often acts like a "silent corporate killer": **obsolescence risk** is what we like to discuss further.

Many corporate boards seem to find it easier to try to keep a company in status quo and to let their CEOs to play a competitive and value destructive "red ocean" game, rather than to govern the company against the risk of obsolescence. Yet, obsolescence is one of the principal reasons why businesses decline.

Recognition of such risks unfortunately often occurs very late if not too late when companies already are in terminal decline. Obsolescence risks pretty much act like cancers, doing much of their destructive work unrecognized and being detected too late when suddenly owners, corporate boards, and CEOs wake up to the realization that their service or product is no longer relevant in the market. Furthermore, the forces of inertia are doing their work without interruption, contributing to boards not even scanning for the possibility of obsolescence. Obsolescence is unavoidable in competitive markets. Monitoring and mitigating such risks are capabilities all firms ought to acquire and refine. And because this risk threatens the company's survival, it should be of prime concern to the board. One of the great classics of obsolescence is

M. Massa et al., *Value Creation for Owners and Directors*,
https://doi.org/10.1007/978-3-031-19726-0_8

Kodak. We will detail the story in a later chapter on corporate biases, as biases is one of the main reasons why companies and their boards do not see the gradual erosion of the firm in its markets. Indeed, it is amazing how Kodak, having been a first mover and true innovator in digital photography, mismanaged the risks of obsolescence it was subject to. In this chapter we pay particular attention to the acquisition decisions that companies consider once they realize they are subject to obsolescence risk. We will show that companies regularly fail to do the acquisition math correctly, mainly because they are mistaken on the benchmark used for computing expected value generated from an acquisition or a merger.

This chapter proceeds as follows. In the next section we contrast two major deals that competitors made in the steel industry. The first deal we examine is the creation of ArcelorMittal, which created the No. 1 steel company in the world. Tata Steel's acquisition of Corus is presented as a contrast. It led to severe financial stress for Tata and did not create the dominant position Tata aimed for in what all knew was an increasingly competitive global industry.

The chapter then analyzes the acquisition of Conrail, a major railway company in the US, eyed by two US railway companies, CSX and NS. US railways had already gone through two waves of bankruptcies. This acquisition was driven by an explicit desire to avert a third wave of obsolescence.

We also present the delicate mathematics of value-creating acquisitions. These are often misunderstood and misapplied, leading people to erroneously conclude that high prices are associated with value destruction, just when such high prices are required for threatened companies to keep creating value.

We conclude this chapter by looking at a more recent case. It concerns the sale by Rupert Murdoch of 21st Century Fox to the Walt Disney Company. We show that both Murdoch and Disney benefited from this transaction as they navigated a media sector subjected to major disruption in online streaming by companies such as Netflix.

2 Survival in the 2000s: A Tale of Two Steel Companies: Mittal and Tata

In 2006 and 2007 two mega steel acquisitions shook the steel world: **Mittal Steel** completed a US$ 32 billion acquisition of European giant **Arcelor**, while **Tata Steel** acquired the Anglo-Dutch **Corus,** for US$ 12.1 billion.

Steel-producing companies had faced several challenges over the preceding decade:

- *Increased competition* from large Russian producers who launched aggressive exports after the fall of the Soviet empire, and from Chinese producers who increased their capacity at an annual rate exceeding 30%. Russia and China, from almost nowhere, became the second and third largest steel exporting countries in the world (just behind Japan). As a result, the rest of the steel industry entered a phase of rapid consolidation and started seeing many M&A deals.
- *Huge increases in raw material prices.* Russian and Chinese producers had access to "in-house" and less expensive raw materials (coal and iron ore). European and Indian producers, on the other hand, continued to face an oligopoly of the three iron main ore producers—CVRD, Rio Tinto, and BHP Billiton—who controlled 70% of the international market. In 2005, these companies increased iron ore prices by 72% and by another 19% in 2006. The coal market, being dominated by a few producers, was cooking as well, the top five controlling 58% of global supply in 2004.
- *Customer buying power.* The auto and packaging manufacturers were the major steel customers. They were sophisticated buyers, increasingly consolidated, and fewer in number. They bought in large quantities, earning them buying power that pressed steel producers on price and features. Figure 8.1 shows the rapid consolidation in the global automotive market, one of the largest buyers of finished steel.

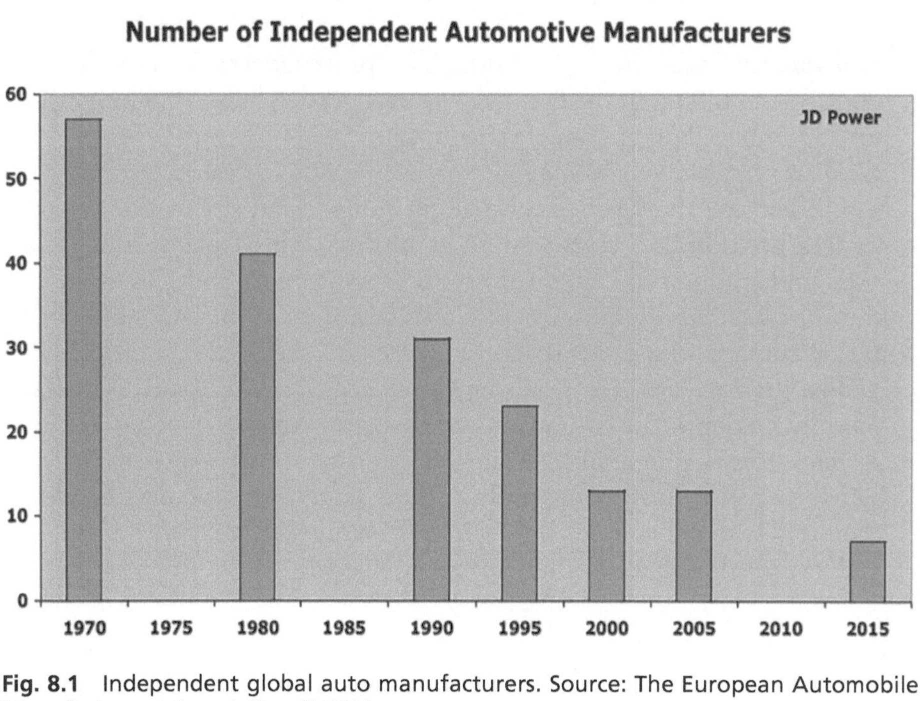

Fig. 8.1 Independent global auto manufacturers. Source: The European Automobile Manufacturers' Association (ACEA)

- *Substitutes.* Aluminum, ceramics, and composite materials were increasingly being used as substitutes for steel. Combined with greater efficiencies, steel demand was now clearly under pressure.
- *Changing technologies and loosening regulations.* Historically, each country had its domestic steel producers. Steel making traditionally employed a large workforce. This contributed to steel making being increasingly seen as "strategic" by governments, when initially this aspect was a remnant of two World Wars. Moves to reduce employment were resisted. However, between the 1970s and 1990s, technological changes substantially reduced the number of employees required to make steel. At the same time, end-use industries, who also were large employers, demanded lower prices and more efficient producers. In the late 1990s, governments thus gradually loosened their resistance to closing steel plants or to seeing them acquired by overseas companies.

The multiplicity of severe changes to the steel industry proved too much for many steel producers. Between the late 1990s and 2003, more than 50 independent US steel producers fell into bankruptcy.[1] Plant closures are always more difficult to achieve in Europe. European governments thus started to welcome the acquisitions by foreign competitors of previously protected companies, such as Arcelor and Corus.

A similar rationale was given by both acquirers:

- *Economies of Scale—Synergies.* Mittal Steel projected synergy benefits totaling US$ 3.4 billion in the first three years. Tata Steel saw US$ 300 million to US$ 350 million of annual synergies.[2]
- *Gain market share and thus bargaining power with customers.* ArcelorMittal would become the No. 1 steel making company in the world, assume a leading position in 5 large western countries, own 61 plants in 21 countries, and still have the opportunity to grow in India and China. In contrast, the Tata Steel acquisition of Corus gave Tata a No. 1 spot only in the UK, a country whose manufacturing base had been in long-term decline. Unlike the ArcelorMittal deal, the Corus acquisition did not propel Tata Steel into a dominant position in any new geography.
- *Acquire technology.* Mittal Steel and Tata Steel were both seen as technologically inferior to Arcelor and Corus. Their acquisitions would provide the acquirers with valuable technological know-how that could be deployed and leveraged in their own less advanced plants.

If we turn to prices, we see that Tata Steel's winning bid was 68% over the pre-bid price of Corus shares. Mittal Steel almost doubled its bid price and loosened control conditions to win the Arcelor bid. According to some statistics, it paid almost 100% premium over the synergies. In both cases the buyer paid *more than the value of the target company inclusive of all the synergies*. Rival offers and a momentum to do the deal drove both acquirers to substantially increase their offer prices. Therefore, both buyers had to take a large amount of high-cost debt to finance their respective deals.

Why did they do it? Because, in the face of the major disruptions affecting steel producers, acquisitions were seen as means to survive. The deals were thus immediately considered "strategic." Tata Group Finance Director, Ishaat Hussain, saw the Corus deal as a must-do. Soon after winning the Corus bid, he said, *"Consolidation [in the steel industry] will take place going forward. It [Corus] was perhaps the only significant player which we could see as a possible acquisition in this consolidating phase. That's why Corus was so important to Tata Steel."*

Both acquisitions, unfortunately, proved immediately challenging for the buyers. Both Mittal and Tata were pressured to provide commitments to national governments not to shut plants and not to lay off workers, at least for a reasonable period. The 2007/8 subprime crises came too soon after the acquisitions were completed and substantially dampened demand. The crisis also disrupted the government support national steel companies had historically enjoyed.

The lessons from these two major acquisitions are that disruption and obsolescence risks need to be very carefully analyzed and managed. Both Mittal and Arcelor engaged in risky and very expensive acquisitions to survive in a consolidating steel industry. The alternative they envisaged was to become irrelevant or disappear altogether. The fact that each of them was looking at the other player and was eager to strategically react and anticipate moves by the other player created pressures to engage in these acquisitions. Their biggest concern was that they would lose the chance to build greater sustainability in the future. What would have been feasible and realistic if another path had been taken going forward. That question is rarely asked and is difficult to answer. But these thoughts should be first on the mind of board members: what is the opportunity cost of doing the acquisition? What are the alternative paths that could have been pursued? And would they have led to better outcomes?

These acquisition moves should, from a board perspective, thus be evaluated from two different lenses? The first is the execution of the acquisition decision: was it carried out effectively, how efficiently was the firm acquired and integrated for value creation? What was the contribution to value creation in the end? Were the difficulties in managing the integration and the needed compromises with governments considered in the acquisition mathematics, or were they ignored and not anticipated? These questions concern the calculation of the expected value creation of the acquisition.

A different set of questions—possibly more important as it determines the outcome eventually chosen for the first are: what are the alternative paths that were considered prior to focusing on one acquisition, and what would have been the value creation expectation of each should it have been chosen? It is this duality of questions that renders the acquisition math so complex.

3 Survival in the 2010s: The CSX-NS Acquisition of Conrail

Railways are often seen as strategic national assets. China and India, for example, run their railways as divisions of their central governments. Switzerland runs one of the best railways in the world, as a government institution until 1999, and as a fully special stock company owned jointly by the Federal Government and the Swiss Cantons. The value of the 1993 deregulation of British Railways is still hotly debated today. The collapse of Railtrack led to its assets being transferred to Network Rail, which is state-owned and is now fully in charge of track maintenance.[3]

In the US, railways have largely been in private hands from the beginning. US railways expanded rapidly over the 1790–1930 period, gradually covering most of the vast American territory. US railway companies flourished as they each enjoyed a monopoly over long-range transportation in a vast country. It took 140 years from the birth of US railways to witness the first wave—14 in total—of railway bankruptcies in the 1930s. Passenger traffic had by then seriously declined due to the use of private cars and the emergence of commercial airlines. The second wave of bankruptcies (22 in number) occurred 40 years after the first wave, in the 1970s, when trucking took over commercial transportation from the railroads. Trucking now accounts for 70% of all freight transported in the US.

These two big waves of bankruptcies provided the background for the acquisition of **Conrail** in 1997, nearly 30 years after the second wave of rail bankruptcies. The deal, consumed in 1998, saw the two initial bidders, **CSX Transportation** (a subsidiary of CSX Corporation) and **The Norfolk Southern Railway**, jointly purchase Conrail and split up its assets between them. **Conrail** (erstwhile Consolidated Rail Corporation) was formed by the Federal Government in 1976 with what potentially were the profitable lines of several bankrupt railway companies, including the Penn Central Transportation Company and the Erie Lackawanna Railway.[4] Conrail provided rail connections between the northeastern region and the major midwestern hubs of Chicago, Detroit, and Milwaukee. Conrail indeed became profitable in 1980.

The Norfolk Southern Railway (NS) operated rail services in the eastern part of US and Canada. In 1984 it won a bid for Conrail. This would give NS a dominant and contiguous railway covering the northern and midwestern states of the US, and their neighboring Canadian provinces. Facing regulatory delays, NS withdrew its bid in 1986 and Conrail was then privatized the next year and listed in the stock market. NS remained the most logical buyer for Conrail, which would provide it with network efficiencies and a higher quality offer. A purchase by NS remained a possibility.

CSX Corporation (CSX) is a diversified and intermodal freight transportation company that includes shipping and railways, the latter through its subsidiary CSX Transportation, which operates rail services in southeastern and midwestern states. In 2013 CSX made an unsolicited bid for Conrail. After a drawn-out bidding war, CSX and NS jointly purchased most of Conrail and split its assets approximately in half. The tactics used by each side is most interesting but best kept for an M&A audience. Our focus here is the strategic intent of CSX and NS and the rationale behind their bids.

Conrail had a great position in its industry, enjoying the highest revenue per mile of track operated and per ton among all major US railway companies. Unfortunately, it had operating cost ratios that were worse than those of its competitors. NS, in contrast, boasted the highest efficiencies and the highest returns on sales. Yet, the deal's strategic rationale was not one driven by these financial parameters. The major driver was to avoid a third wave of obsolescence-driven bankruptcies. The argument goes as follows:

- *Competition in the transportation sector* was again becoming acutely intense. Trucking and air freight provided tough competition to railways, requiring renewed efficiency gains for survival.
- *Intermodal connectivity was vital.* A key challenge for railways is the need to efficiently onload and offload goods. Without contiguous miles of track, railways must interconnect and coordinate with other modes of transportation (essentially ships, trucks, and air cargo) to deliver their client's goods at their intended destinations.

- *Long-haul, contiguous, routes* connecting southern, northeastern, and midwestern states is the game in the US. There were very few large railways left to consolidate with. Conrail was the only major railway company in the eastern and midwestern states left to be acquired.

For NS, the Conrail-NS combination would give it a dominant railway position in the eastern US and neighboring Canada. For CSX, Conrail gave it an avenue to expand further north and into the midwestern states. The benefits accruing to both companies of an acquisition of CSX were about the same, amounting to approximately to US$ 33.50 a share.[5] These would result largely from cost savings generated by greater network efficiencies and revenue benefits due to these companies no longer having to compete with CSX.

However, a careful analysis identifies another factor shaping this competitive situation: the losing bidder, among NS or CSX, would face significant downside due to now having to face a much stronger competitor, able to harm it by attracting passengers due to better network economies and service offer. The loss to CSX from NS winning the deal was estimated at around US$ 8.50 a share. In contrast, the loss to NS from CSX winning the deal was estimated at about US$ 17 a share.

The final economic computation is surprising. To simplify matters a bit, let us, in this argument take the share price as the estimated value of the company. Starting with a Conrail share price of US$ 71 per share the induced benefit to NS from the Conrail acquisition, considering opportunity costs avoided, would amount to US$ 71 + 33.50 + 17 = US$ 121.50. CSX's benefits, on the other hand, would amount to only US$ 71 + 33.50 + 8.50 = US$ 113 per share. The main point of this computation is that the "Do Nothing" option, which would amount to letting the other side win, was for neither side a costless option, as it would result in a deteriorated market position, corresponding to a negative NPV loss due to the consolidation of Conrail in the competitor's network. Facing both options, both actors should be willing to pay a premium up to the downside they would incur if they lost the bid. These considerations change the value mathematics considerably.

CSX, the one with less to lose in this situation, made the first bid, but NS, who had more to lose, bid more. The final price at US$ 115 per share put the deal out of CSX's value-creating range and priced the Conrail stock 62% higher than its pre-acquisition level. This was not the end of it, however. On March 3, 1997, CSX and NS then announced an agreement where CSX would buy Conrail at US$ 115 per share and would split the company approximately 50:50 with NS at that price. The value implications are remarkable. Both CSX and NS overpaid for Conrail, way more than the market value inclusive of the full loaded value of the synergies but avoided the scenario in which the other player had become a monopolist. The big winner was Conrail's shareholders who ran away, thanks to the competitive bidding, with most of the value generated by the deal, over and above the pure synergies generated.

Two conclusions then. First, stock markets allow selling shareholders to capture a big part of the future value to be created, including the opportunity costs that the winner avoided. Second, in this context, the real value-creating action of the board of Conrail would have been to start the bidding war, engaging the bidder with less to lose (CSX) in the contest, and attracting it with favorable conditions (i.e., no-talk clauses, exclusivity agreements, breakup fees) that would induce it to make the first bid. Once that bid was made, the war was started and competitive dynamics would take over. That would unleash value by other competitors raising their bid. And, indeed, that is what Conrail did!

4 Survival in the 2020s: Disney and Fox

In April 2020 Netflix released its latest quarterly results, showing its online streaming service had 182 million subscribers. Online streaming services offer on-demand entertainment (music, sitcoms, film, and other streaming media) through the Internet or other telecom data connections. Netflix is not alone in disrupting the entertainment industry. Hulu, Amazon Prime Video, HBO, Google's YouTube and Apple all provide such online services.

Cinemas were first disrupted by cable and satellite on-demand services. That disruption has now been accelerated by online streaming services that subject cable and satellite on-demand services to the same treatment they applied a few years ago to cinemas.

The disruption is occurring in three ways:

- Delivery of entertainment via online streaming provides millions of additional viewers access to content in the comfort of their preferred location.
- Pricing is usually a flat fee for unlimited usage/viewing per month/quarter/year, thus effectively charging a fraction of the cost of a movie ticket (the pricing benefit growing due to economies of scale with the number of viewers).
- Content is increasingly being produced by the distributors themselves, decreasing their reliance on traditional content producers such as Disney and 21st Century Fox.

The Walt Disney Company (Disney) was founded in 1923 by Walt and Roy Disney. They started making animation films. Thanks to their market success, they then diversified via organic growth and acquisitions. In 2017 it had become a film production, television broadcasting, and theme parks company. While it is most publicly known for its theme parks and films, it is noteworthy that more than 50% of Disney's profits used to come from ESPN, a cable sports channel. These revenues and margins came under threat from the online streaming services. In addition, Disney movies, traditionally aired in cinemas, also faced headwinds from online streaming, while its theme parks were expensive to manage, providing thin margins.

21st Century Fox had been acquired by Rupert Murdoch, the media mogul, and was part of his media empire, **News Corporation**. It was like Disney, except that it did not have theme parks. 21st Century Fox had production, international television broadcasting businesses, as well as a 30% stake in Hulu, an online streaming service that competed with Netflix.

In 2017, Disney announced a US$ 71 billion "mega-acquisition," of Fox. This came after a very expensive bidding war with Comcast for the Fox assets. Disney had waited too long in a sort of prolonged status quo, indulging its success which it thought would continue for considerable time. Its overconfidence led it to miss entering the online streaming business earlier. Like Sleeping Beauty, it woke up to find its world changed.

Disney's beliefs were that its 21st Century Fox deal would further boost its already large library of content, produce annual cost savings of around US$ 2 billion (Disney's 2017 operating expenses were US$ 41.3 billion),[6] and generate greater exposure outside the US (principally in the UK, Europe, and India). Perhaps more importantly for Disney was that it ended with a 60% ownership of Hulu which it hoped would complement its streaming service Disney+. All these considerations raised the amount Disney was willing to put on the table to avoid Fox's assets being snatched by Comcast.

Whether the large amount of content thus acquired will help Disney compete with Netflix and with the many other competitors in the online streaming services remains to be seen. However, one point is unequivocal: the risk of obsolescence by remaining in its previous status quo position was very big, and Disney had started to realize that the cost of such position had become too high. Disney seemed to have had no better choice to buy itself a great position in a changed world. It enthusiastically entered this deal. CEO Bob Iger explained the deal to the press in August 2019 as:

> *We analyze the 21st Century Fox opportunity entirely through the lens of our future business. We're also focused on leveraging Fox's vast library of great titles to further*

enrich the content mix on our DTC platforms. Our play ... is to have general entertainment, we'll call it Hulu, more family-like entertainment, which is Disney+, and sports.

Iger also went to say that customers would get bundles of content at a flat "good price" like how Netflix and Amazon Prime Video price their services.[7] The deal allowed Disney to catch up with Netflix and avoid its growing obsolescence in a transforming industry. As in the case of the railways, the big winner was Rupert Murdoch, the seller of Fox, who had started the war between Disney and Comcast using the same set of enticements that Conrail used (such as no-talk clauses, exclusivity agreements, and breakup fees).

The insights gained from these cases and their principal lessons are that firms contemplating obsolescence can create value for themselves even if they pay more than the value of the firm they acquire. The common (folk) wisdom that M&As generally destroy value for the buyer firms while targeted firms gain, as do their financial advisors, is thus wrong. The gain in value for the targeted firm is thought to be adequately reflected by its share price gain at the announcement of the bid (which is wrong), while the drop in share price of the buying firm is considered to confirm a value loss for the latter (which is wrong too). This reasoning has fueled a widely held view that companies engaged in M&As typically destroy value (for themselves) and that bidder prices of target companies are excessive.

However, this logic is faulty as it pays no attention to the counterfactual scenario where the bidder does not proceed with the acquisition. Avoiding the losses incurred in the latter scenario should be fully credited as value captured when completing the acquisition. This insight leads to a different value creation logic, which we denote as **counterfactual value creation,** and which is to be distinguished from value creation seen solely as the result of synergy gains (net of the costs of completing the acquisition). This approach sees value destruction not only as excessively high bids, but also as the result of missed opportunities to avoid value destruction due to obsolescence. In a context of major technological and economic disruption (such as the digital revolution), one should thus accept higher value bids and a greater number of them to be economically rational, all motivated by the rationale of avoiding obsolescence related losses, the size of the bids reflecting the degree of the obsolescence faced.

The second insight from this analysis is the value of the stock market for owners that sell their company. Not only does the market allow them to extract the value of the assets they put up for sale, but competitive bidding for these assets will allow them to capture a part of the value of future synergies to be created by the acquirer, as well as the value of opportunity losses the acquirer avoids through the purchase. This also explains the attraction of the market for private equity players. This also suggests that a key source of value creation for the board is to sell as opposed to buy. Indeed, a common indicator of bad governance is the reluctance of CEOs to sell and a key source of value creation is for companies and private equity activists to engage and trigger hostile M&As in which the bought company is forced to sell what the CEO did not want to sell. In the example of Arcelor, the main reason the company was undervalued was that the French CEO, Guy Dollé, used the cash of the company to engage in job-saving M&As. Of course, while this can be considered good for employment, it was clearly value destroying for the shareholder of Acrelor.

5 The Power of Counterfactual Thinking

Counterfactual thinking is central to effective owners and boards. When applied to M&A contexts, the logic alters the upper limit on the amount of value-creating bids, and more considerably so as industries are subjected to obsolescence and concentration. Counterfactual thinking, however, is not limited to M&A value computations. It also drives board decision making in such settings as CEO appointments and succession planning or the setting of CEO incentives, areas that are recognized as responsible for considerable value destruction due to board misunderstanding or misapplication of the concept.

A thorough understanding of counterfactual value creation is critical for a Board of Directors to be effective. Such a board will accept a drop in the share price in order to create long-term shareholder value and will collect the returns for doing so as the market proves able to differentiate between boards that are competent in counterfactual value creation and those that are not. The former boards will be ready to pay an acquisition premium that is greater than the value of the synergies expected from the deal, particularly if the firm they govern faces the risk of rapid obsolescence.

The capability of proper counterfactual thinking is thus an essential capability of effective owners and boards. Counterfactual thinking extends to CEO remuneration and incentives. The first implication is that assessing value as a function of the stock market's reaction—short or long term—is not only wrong, it also is dangerous as it will change the incentives for the CEO to act in a true value-creating way. Any compensation or incentive set on short-term market price variations actually incentivizes a rational CEO to take the wrong course of action, for short-term gain, and not for longer-term value creation. In the case of Corus Steel, counterfactual thinking would have led the boards and owners not to bid too high for Corus Steel, or not to bid at all, having reflected on its limited abilities and experiences in owning and operating steel mills away from India.

Our second consideration is that current standard corporate governance thinking is not well suited to overcome the problem we outlined. Standard behavioral decision-making biases (e.g., cognitive inertia, anchoring, representativeness) will make it difficult for an average board, camping on its past experience and the erroneous knowledge it may have accrued in the process, to correctly evaluate how to handle the disruptive forces of obsolescence. Extrapolating from the past, the board will expect—like the market—that that the status quo will continue, at least for a while. This poses the risk that the board will not ask the key counterfactual question as to "what will happen if we do not do the deal? what happens if we do not sell now?" At the same time, however, loss aversion and disposition effect may induce the CEO to magnify the peril of not doing the deal as we will see in the Kodak case. This suggests how critical it is for the board to draw on the right benchmarks, recognize the biases inherent in being CEO, and be more cognizant that prospects may have been gradually shifting without the board realizing it.[8]

Moreover, common incentives may work in opposite to the direction suggested by counterfactual thinking. For example, independent directors face issues in terms of reputation and liabilities. Indeed, in order to avoid obsolescence risk, the company often has to lever up, by a considerable amount. Such strategies increase the risk of distress, sometimes substantially. However, while distress has serious legal and reputational implications for the board members, obsolescence, given its very gradual nature, is less cared for. Indeed, no board member has been subject to a lawsuit for making the company gradually obsolete! This consideration will mostly impact the independent board member who, by the virtue of being independent, has no skin in the game! In contrast, obsolescence risk is more effectively dealt with by family board members who have a lot (if not all) at stake! As an example, it led the Auchan family to divest early from its textile assets and invest in downstream retail, before the textile sector entered its crisis. This provides a very different view on the role and usefulness of the independent board members and puts a shadow on the common definition of independence.

The board thus faces natural difficulty to challenge the CEO to come up with counterfactual scenarios which are by essence more hypothetical and also more virtual, and which the CEO will not appreciate, being biased on his or her own scenario. Boards and executives excessively eager for certainty and anchored in a wish to see a deal go through will not be really motivated, or properly incentivized to take the time to examine the counterfactual scenarios in thorough detail, particularly if they are seen to be part of a really virtual exercise.

One further implication of this argumentation is interesting: not properly aware of counterfactual opportunity losses, boards and their executives will likely underbid in the face of a value-creating deal, leading to fewer deals actually materializing than would be consistent with true value creation. Complaints about bids being regularly excessive are thus erroneous under this reasoning. Facing digital disruption and growing emerging acquisition power from China, a greater number of larger bids should be expected.

Conversely, a short-term horizon CEO will not act consistently with the above conclusion. He or she will not engage in a complex counterfactual analysis that provides benefits only in the long run, and even then, possibly only in the form of lower losses. Executive compensation can render matters even worse. No equity-based CEO will have any incentive to discuss counterfactual losses. The CEO may prefer to suggest being acquired than arguing for a deal that will result in a decline of the share price (at least in the short and medium run). Counterfactual value creation argues for considering longer horizons when evaluating CEOs. It is at odds with simple market and share price driven logic. CEOs in family firms and long-term owner-led firms will find their boards and owners more receptive to this thinking.

Competences in counterfactual thinking at owner, board, and executive levels are fundamental to correct decision making in our turbulent environment. Such competence provides further benefits, including in improved CEO evaluation. Comments that the CEO was not replaced yet, for being viewed as "not that bad," raise the question of limited counterfactual thinking once one realizes that the CEO provides huge leverage in the quest for value creation. Here too opportunity losses loom large: having a CEO that is only average carries a high opportunity cost, namely foregoing the opportunity of appointing a really great one. So, in this domain too counterfactual thinking is fundamental for boards.

Notes

1. https://www.ukessays.com/essays/economics/competitive-advantage-of-arcelor-mittal-economics-essay.php.
2. https://www.marketwatch.com/story/tata-group-executive-says-price-for-corus-is-strategic.
3. https://en.wikipedia.org/wiki/Privatisation_of_British_Rail.

4. https://en.wikipedia.org/wiki/Conrail.
5. Computations by one of the authors.
6. https://marketrealist.com/2018/03/how-will-disney-benefit-from-its-21st-century-fox-acquisition/.
7. https://www.cnbc.com/2019/08/06/fox-deal-will-continue-to-drag-on-disney-earnings.html.
8. The traditional reference here is that of the "gradually boiling frog" who does not jump out of the pot in which the water is gradually heating up, but which would escape if confronted with hot water at the outset.

9

MGSF and the Three Boards

1 The MGSF Ramework, the Three Boards, and the Question of Alignment

Having spent a good number of pages over different aspects of what we call the *hardware or structural requirements* of value creation, this chapter summarizes our exposition to date of the first challenge that many companies face, namely the challenge of *alignment*, which is the first pre-condition for value creation.

Alignment is greatly fostered by a multi-dimensional framework called *Mission-Goals-Strategy-Fundamentals*, or *MGSF* in short, that defines the major objectives and constraints encompassing governance. We have alluded to this framework and its elements in earlier chapters. We would like to address here in a more formal way, also as way of summarizing the main points made so far in this book. Its major components are:

- *Mission*: Sets *the long-term objectives pursued by owners of the corporation*. A mission statement makes explicit the owners' wishes regarding long-term value delivery. This, of course involves expectations regarding dividends but also includes describing the owners' desires concerning non-financial aspects of corporate performance and contributions. Too often, these, though real, are insufficiently stated in an explicit manner, possibly because being taught to be *homo economicus* only, they are insecure of the legitimacy of such non-financial objectives. Value creators like Bill Gates and Steve Jobs were more driven by a mission than by financial objectives. Most value creators are as serial New York Times best-selling author Daniel Pink clearly

M. Massa et al., *Value Creation for Owners and Directors*,
https://doi.org/10.1007/978-3-031-19726-0_9

demonstrates in his book *Drive: The Surprising Truth About What Motivates US.*[1] Pink characterizes the drivers of these value creators not primarily as money or the accumulation of wealth, but much more as an internal impetus where purpose and impact on society reign big, as well as the desire for mastery over one's craft or subject matter and the ability to enjoy a large degree of autonomy (of means, including time and support) to pursue one's purpose as well as further develop one's mastery.

- *Goals*: These are the *objectives pursued by the corporation*, translating the owner's wishes into goals to be aimed for and realized by the corporation. This is the core task of the corporate leadership and needs to be approved by the board, regardless of who came up with these goals or how they were obtained. What is of paramount importance is that these goals should be the right ones for the corporation, given its current state and context, and given the owner's mission. Goals normally should result from or at least involve extensive discussions among both board members and executives, as well as jointly, even if this is only for alignment. These objectives identify the nature of the steering of the company, indicating where the company's main efforts should be directed so as to be aligned with the owner's mission. Goals typically fall within three main criteria that are distinct: *Profitability, Growth, or Sustainability*. The board's work consists in deciding the relative weights to be given to each of these criteria over periods of time, as these criteria correspond to different ways of managing the corporation. It also calls for different talents as well, particularly at the helm.
- *Strategies*: Having determined the goals, the discussion turns to the *key strategic decisions* that allow these goals to be reached, considering the company's fundamentals, including its context. Strategies define the key areas of engagement for the company, also called *its main battlefield areas*, central to the achievement of the goals. It is important to recognize that strategies are dependent on the chosen goals. For example, if growth is chosen, the corporate strategies for growth can be described as *buy, build, or ally with partners*. When the company is a single business, the strategic choices evolve around the following choices: *target market segment, product-service offer, and business model for going to market*. All these are domains where the key work is done by the executives, with inputs and challenges from the board, eager to contribute to ensuring progress on the mission, and being appraised of it.
- *Fundamentals*: An awareness of the *fundamentals affecting a company's competitive position and moves* is key to a fruitful discussion on goals and strategies and the mission. Fundamentals pertain to *constraints* the company is subjected to. These typically come from customers, suppliers, competitors,

partners, regulators, or technology. Risk appetite, location, a company's financing abilities, or the fact that is being listed are other examples of fundamentals that influence a company's specification of mission, goals, or strategies. We have observed that successful companies have owners that set the mission with a full understanding of the fundamentals of the company, its industry, and the ecosystem in which the enterprise operates. For example, Amancio Ortega Gaona, the founder, and owner of the successful ZARA brand (part of the INDITEX Group), frustrated with repeated cost-cutting of the retail clients he was supplying, decided to become a retailer himself. Ortega focused on offering fashion to young 16–18 people since these were the potential customers he had available in the coastal town of La Coruna. Indeed, people above 18 years old would have left the area for university or employment in larger Spanish towns. Few would ever dare to recognize La Coruna as a fashion hub. The fundamentals of location (small coastal town), the challenge regarding his own supply company that risked being squeezed out by its own retail clients, coupled with the opportunity to supply new younger market segment, provided Ortega with a unique opportunity for his company: be a provider of fast fashion for the 16–18-year-olds. This is a great example of how an owner-founder shapes an enterprise through the formulation of a unique mission that builds and takes account of the fundamental constraints and opportunities associated with the company's context. Further examples of entrepreneurial leadership are Steve Jobs at Apple, Bernard Arnault at LVMH, and Jack Ma at Alibaba. The crafting and final commitment to their missions did not occur at the board level but at the owner level. Of course, in such cases, the center of gravity of the governance system then lies close to the owners.

When approving measurable goals, the corporate board will ensure that goals are aligned with the mission and consistent with existing regulations as well as the reality of its position in the industry and prevailing practices. All this under the oversight of the owner, who may or may not be a member of the corporate board, but who will remain informed of the decisions made by the board and progress on the mission realized by the corporation.

Given the mission and goals, the board's most important task will be to search and select the profile that can best navigate these goals across turbulent waters and attain them. The corporate board then invites the CEO and senior management to formulate good sub-goals and strategies that will allow the most effective way to achieve these goals. To allow proper monitoring by the corporate board, the corporate board will ask the executive team to present a set of shorter-term milestones and objectives that will provide the corporate board with reasonable assurance that the medium-term goals will be met. The enterprise's "fundamentals" will be discussed as well, both for leverage of the strategies and for a mitigation of the constraints on execution.

In summary, owners impose the *Mission*. Corporate boards help to select and approve *Goals*. Boards select the executive team members that will formulate and execute Sub-Goals and *Strategies*. All this within a context defining the *Fundamentals* that owners, board members, and executives need to recognize. This is the framework that is key to ensuring progress and alignment around value creation.

In owner-led firms the Goals and Strategy discussion is initiated and framed by the definition of the Mission. That is the defining difference with market-led firms where mission might be partly stated in the articles of incorporation (at the time of founding the corporation) or defined by the Board of Directors. In reality, the Mission over time becomes set by the CEO, either formally when she or he doubles up as Chairman, or informally through greater understanding of the organization, and due to the authority and influence that come with the CEO title. The respective roles of each of these stakeholders in owner-led firms are summarized in Fig. 9.1.

It might be of interest to decline the implications of Fig. 9.1 in terms of cash flows and risk:

- The Owners' Board sets constraints and expectations defined in terms of Mission;

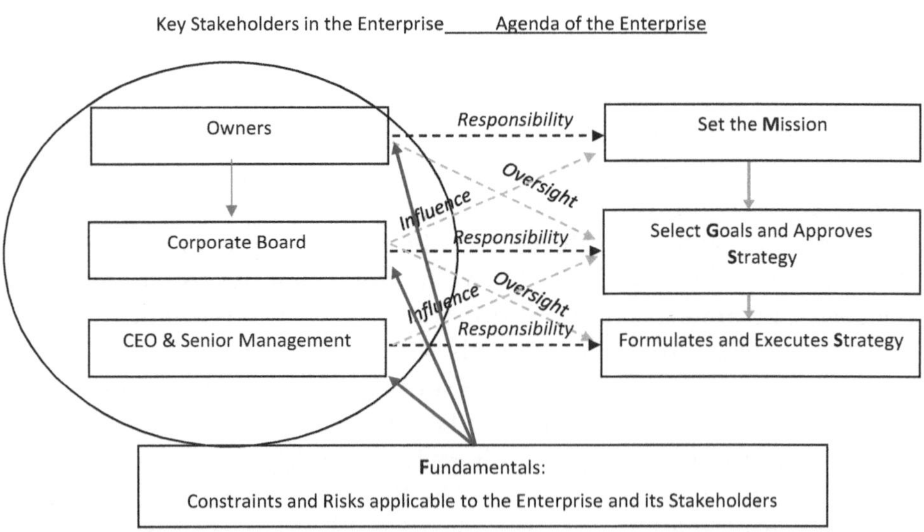

Fig. 9.1 The MGSF framework for ensuring alignment on value creation

- The Corporate board decides on capital allocation, financing, and risks, appraises itself of the cash flows;
- The Business Unit board determines how cash flows (in terms of cost and revenue strategies) are generated and lead to value creation.

Figure 9.1 also tries to provide clarity as to which of the three boards (owner, corporate, and business) does what and how these boards align their work. If we define Fig. 9.1 at the level of individuals, the picture might become more blurred as one individual (as owner, board member, or executive) may be a member of two or all three of the stakeholder groups described. Indeed, an owner often insists on sitting on the corporate board, or on chairing it. An owner-founder is its first CEO, and often its first Chair as well. That, in most cases, reduces the degree of independence among and in these boards, and thus checks and balances. Hence, these overlaps in membership favor alignment of these boards, but also the possibility of unchecked power and authority.

The hope then is that the owner-chairman-CEO, as our corporate "dictator," is and remains enlightened. This hope of course flies against the lessons of history: dictators, even when they start with plenty of lights on, typically do not remain enlightened, and gradually see their lights phase out. This is a situation of *governance risk*, by which we mean the risk that proper governance fails, while execution is still good. In the case discussed here it occurs due to the insufficient possibility of challenging the decisions made by one powerful actor. If this actor remains enlightened, little harm will be done. However, with time and changing contexts, entrenchment typically sets in, particularly if the once powerful actor becomes less successful and stubbornly refuses to recognize his mistakes and learn from them, and eventually refuses to let go.

One way to mitigate this governance risk is to regularly remind individuals "wearing multiple hats" that they ought to wear different hats depending on the role assumed in a particular meeting. A wise Chair and CEO might provide space for a Senior Independent Director to lead the challenge to his or her proposed courses of action. A good rule is for the person leading a discussion to not have a conflict of interest (including emotional) on the issue being debated and to then ask to be excused from leading that part of the board discussion. Exemplarity by board or committee chairs is educational for all. Another wise statement came from a CEO having attended our classes. He stated that he left class resolved to only wear his governance hat when attending board meetings, and to focus only on what was in the best interest of the corporation. He even surprised fellow board members when he would make comments on the CEO at such meetings, wondering whether he realized he was speaking about himself. He aptly replied that he was indeed commenting as Board member on his other self, the CEO, surprising Board members with a tough critique on his own actions as CEO.

One way "the lights go out" is when stakeholders are regularly rebuffed and put "back in their place" when challenging proposals. They will tire from these rebuffs and restrain their conversations with dominant CEOs or Chairs. In such situations, board members will be tempted to take the safer option, which is to agree and align, even when this is likely to result in suboptimal decision making. This also happens when Chairs are excessively obsessed with efficiency at board level, which goes against engaging in a deeper discussion, particularly in board matters that are rarely "open and shut." Chapter 6 provided an illustration of this in the Tata Group, when the multiple roles became mixed up to the detriment of the enterprise.

The first duty of care and loyalty of board members is toward the corporation, as we explained in Chap. 2. The requirement of liberal capitalism is that board members exercise their fiduciary duties in full independence, to the best of their abilities. The dependence on shareholders is through the Mission, as we explained in Chap. 1, and not a submission to the shareholder. This distinction is fundamental and subtle. So subtle in fact that many tend to forget it, preferring to accept a subservient relation to a dominant or specific shareholder, at the expense of the corporation and the other shareholders, "since no dog can serve two masters." So, board independence is not something to strive for but rather something to uphold. In that sense, it is usefully reminded in the Articles of Association and at the time of appointment. Discussions in the context of board evaluations are also good practice. It is important to realize that the owners are the only stakeholders that benefit from the increase in firm value. All the other stakeholders—lenders, suppliers, clients, employees—they have a "contractual" relationship that is fulfilled by the board due thanks to its duty of care to the corporation. However, the owners put their equity at stake so they are entitled to the "excess"—that is, the profits. This implies that by creating value the board fulfills its fiduciary duty vis-à-vis the owners.

The MGSF and the three boards framework are the two main hardware structures within which value creation is discussed and achieved. In these structures, the voice and direction set by the owners loom large. Different owners perceive value differently depending on their views of the mission statement or its interpretation. This is precisely the object of discussion on the Owners' Board, which to be effective must result in owners approving and agreeing with a single mission statement. We saw how Temasek focused on nation-building, how the Interbrew families aimed for value creation through long-term dividends and share appreciation, and how the Zóbel de Ayala family aimed for profitability. These mission statements are broad and provide the corporate boards with sufficient space and autonomy to also do their share in the quest for value creation. In each case, value creation occurs when a company achieves its owner's objectives: DBS in continuing Singapore's strategic nation-building tasks, Interbrew in becoming a dominant beer company, and Ayala Corporation through successful diversification. That, in addition to the values dear to owners and their requirements in terms of governance is all owners should focus on when discussing at the owners' level.

As a final comment, we must stress the importance of understanding and identifying the fundamentals applicable to a company. These need to be carefully analyzed, for they constrain the appropriate actions to be taken. These also can result in different financing structures: the Interbrew families and their holding companies experienced the need to go to the financial markets with the Interbrew IPO to allow growth; for the Ayala Corporation, its many subsidiaries provided means to grow, and to diversify market risk (though not geographical risk).

The MGSF framework and the three boards lay out a simple structure within which owners, the corporate board, and executives can focus and work toward value creation. Alignment of all parties with these structures and the decisions made is a key and final constraint here for value creation to indeed occur.

2 Three Boards Aligned in Value Creation

Excellent examples of the three successful boards in action are found in Interbrew, Solvay, Ayala Group, Berkshire Hathaway, and DBS, the Singapore bank controlled by Temasek Holdings. Each of these cases is characterized by a clear and unique mission statement, controlled by an Owners' Board, supervised by a corporate board, and executed through multiple business unit boards. Finally, and equally importantly, all have a particular grip and mastery over the fundamentals governing their industry.

One Mission

In the case of Interbrew and Solvay, despite having a great number of family members, all have their shares in a small number of family holding companies who are able to control their main company, and provide it with a mission which they can enforce. In Warren Buffett's Berkshire Hathaway, there is one voice, even if Charlie Munger has regularly contributed to Buffett's decision making and helped Buffett balance his outlook. The clarity and persistent pursuit of a mission by a company often is the consequence and hallmark of an effectively owner governed company. In contrast, market-led companies go through regular contests on what the mission might be, initiated by some shareholders who by definition are too numerous to agree, by members of the corporate board, or by the executive.

The Owners' Board

In Interbrew, there is a Dutch foundation at the top—Stichting AK Netherlands—which provides direction and steering. In Solvay, there is Solvac, the holding company of the Solvay families.

The holding companies consolidate the ownership of the founding families. The family holding companies have their own governance and rules. Their "raison d'être" is the preservation of the long-term family mission. Temasek plays a similar role, albeit with one ultimate owner, the Singapore People acting through their elected government.

In addition to upholding the mission and verifying its progress, these Owners' Board also pay attention to the financing requirements of the operating companies. They also nominate the corporate board members, whom they trust to oversee progress on their stated mission. They are typically careful in separating the duties and responsibilities of the Owners' Board with that of the corporate board, providing protection to excessive dependencies on particularly dominating personalities in their midst. They often benefit from the legal counsel in ensuring both the complementarity and the separation of the Owners' Board from the corporate one.

The Corporate Board

In all these cases, the operating companies have their corporate board, who decide on the goals of the company, approve strategies, appoint the executive leadership, and evaluate key risks. Corporate boards are the key link between the Owners' Boards and executive management. They ensure proper progress on the company goals and continued alignment with the owners' mission.

The Business Unit (BU) Boards (in Case of a Multi-business Enterprise)

These boards are tasked with operationalizing a specific mission and attaining the goals given to them. They are led by the CEO of the operating companies or subsidiaries of the parent company. They develop strategy, obtain approval by the board, then implement until goals and milestones are reached or proven impossible to reach. In both cases, the Board of Directors decide upon the next set of goals to aim in consultation with the executive team. Opportune or necessary changes to the mission are discussed with the owners, who prevail in this matter.

While there are overlaps between memberships of the Owners' Board, corporate board, and business unit board, all three boards must carefully stick to their respective roles for value creation to result: owners on the mission and on the values and basic rules of the governance game in pursuit of the mission; Board of Directors on goal setting and approval of executive team appointments, capital allocation and strategies; executive or management board on development and implementation of the strategies that should lead to the attainment of the goals set by the Board of Directors. These respective responsibilities do not imply the existence of clear and unrelated silos; quite on the contrary, what is required is that each has its responsibilities and tasks clarified, including the relationships with the other boards, whom they need to support and engage with, if only to maintain alignment. Alignment then starts resembling a "matryoshka" or Russian doll, where the major one (the owner's one) holds all others and where all subsequent dolls must fit within the major one. Value destruction will occur when one of the subsidiary dolls does not fit with its larger antecedent sisters—and sticks out. When there is too much space between two successive dolls, opportunities for additional contributions are insufficiently recognized or addressed. It could also be that mission and goals are too loosely specified, providing too much autonomy to some boards, at the risk of a loss in alignment on a well-specified mission.

3 The Perspective of an Engaged Owner on the Three Boards

Daniel Janssen is the Honorary Chairman of the Solvay Group, was Chairman of its Board of Directors (1998–2006), and CEO or Chairman of its Executive Committee before that (1986–1998). During that period, he also was

Vice-Chairman of the Board of UCB (1984–2006), the Belgian chemical company, which he joined in 1962 and where he rose to become Chairman of the Executive Committee (1975–1984). He assumed that position until he was invited to lead Solvay.

UCB was born in 1928 as a Belgian "spin-off" of Solvay by CEO founder Emmanuel Janssen, the grandfather of Daniel Janssen. It contained new innovative chemicals and pharmaceuticals whose development was viewed not to fit the mission of the Solvay Group.[2] The spinoff occurred in the context of a booming global chemical sector, which had seen the emergence of ICI in the UK, IG Farben in Germany, and Allied Chemicals in the US. Emmanuel Janssen thought that Belgium should have its national champion as well. He was joined in this entrepreneurial venture by other shareholders of the Solvay Group.

In his foreword to the ninetieth-anniversary book that describes the developments of UCB, Daniel Janssen stresses that over its life, the Janssen family always was the reference shareholder of UCB, ensuring its solvency with repeated cash infusions when needed. Without these financial injections, the group would have disappeared, particularly after a most challenging wartime period.

Emmanuel's three sons, Charles-Emmanuel, Roger, and André, took over from their father in 1948 and saved UCB, which had of course suffered tremendously from the war. This first commitment initiated a set of increasing further commitments to UCB, leading it to repurchase the shareholding of Solvay (25.2%) in 1959. Looking for scale, UCB merged in 1961 with three other Belgian chemical companies (Fabelta, Sidac, and Pegamoïd). Rhône-Poulenc, the French chemical giant, was a shareholder of these three companies. The merger led to become a second reference shareholder with 20% of the shareholding. The 1981 French election selected Frédéric Mittérand as President. The implementation of his socialist program included the nationalization of Rhône-Poulenc. Government owners typically have little interest in owning assets abroad. So, the family, with the help of Belgian insurance company La Royale Belge acting as a white knight, was able to repurchase Rhône-Poulenc's shareholding. The family now controlled UCB, control being exercised through a family holding, Tubize.

Daniel Janssen joined the family company in 1962 as a young industrial engineer, already convinced of its promise. He is part of three family members who were UCB Chairs or Vice-Chairs, and is one of the three family members who assumed the CEO role. Daniel is keen to repeat how the family's actions were always guided on one hand by solid scientific and industrial values, but that three other values also steered the family and its group: a commitment to

Belgium, integrity, and societal responsibility. Integrity in the Janssen family is understood in a broad sense including honesty, legality, fairness, respect for people and for the word given. Daniel Janssen proudly evokes the family's logo "Rectitudo" as perfectly summarizing its values. Societal responsibility is centered on a desire to serve patients and ultimately mankind. Human as well as professional competences and talents are vital here. Daniel Janssen's views, as owner, Chair, and Vice-Chair of the UCB and Solvay boards, and former CEO of both companies, provide us with unique and important perspectives on the three boards and on the conditions to be met for these boards to align on value creation. They echo and validate in his words many of the themes evoked in our book.

A Fundamental: Understanding the Different Requirements of the Three Boards

Janssen underlines the fundamental need to understand that the requirements of serving on one or more of the three boards differ greatly and demand distinct competencies, as well as ethics. "I always found it important to understand the huge differences between these roles—and the corresponding competencies required for each role. Not understanding this unavoidably creates conflicts and loss of alignment, if not outright value destruction," is Daniel Janssen's comment when we interviewed him for his views on ownership.

Owners' Board

> I always take the hypothesis of a minimum 5-year horizon as owner, and I often stretch it all the way to my children who will succeed me as owner. The owner requires a great dose of trust in the Board of Directors and in the Management. The first obligation of owners then is to check whether their trust is legitimated. I know many owners who are in this position, and they all look first at the alignment of the Board and the Management with their mission. Profit generated comes second as it is a consequence of this alignment when board members and executives are well chosen. Very important to owners is, of course, the receipt of dividends, as owners need to 'eat.' Beyond this, dividends are one way to validate the trust of the owner-investor and closes the loop so to speak. Social status associated with ownership is not to be neglected: one is 'in society' by virtue of one's shareholding. That becomes part of one's identity and changes one's outlook.

Owning 1.5% to 7% of the equity in a family firm brings a different perspective to the discussion, as compared with a single family member who owns 51%. For the former, their weapons too often are complain and nag, or, eventually, sell. However, such owners can indeed become effective and active members of the Owners Board, if, through their views and contributions, they can muster the support of the other owners and convince them. An Owners Board is a key mechanism where family firms build and keep unity. Active debates are its 'raison d'être.' An effective Owners Board makes a huge difference in terms of effective information sharing and exchange. This in turn builds trust and strengthens resolve and commitment. It is a must for durable success.

Owners on the Corporate Board

Owners on the corporate board exercise a very different role when compared with the independent non-executive directors. An owner on a corporate board has a dual responsibility: managing his or her wealth, while also bearing fiduciary responsibility for the firm. Whether the family company is listed or not is not the most important feature. What is more important is ownership. As a member of the [corporate] board, an owner must pay attention to strategy, values of the firm (sustainability, loyalty to country or region), the leadership of the firm, and the danger of obsolescence. That requires competencies that are not common, and that not all owners possess. It includes the need to subordinate one's personal private interests to those of the company, as perceived by most board members, who are its deciding voice. It requires understanding of the role, and the discipline to execute it well.

Another key character trait that is necessary for owners who sit on a corporate board is collegiality with the other board members. This is particularly easy when colleagues think like you but becomes a greater human challenge with those that do not share one's opinion, particularly when one is an owner. However, while acting on the corporate board, an owner must understand that she or he, as a board member, has an overarching responsibility towards ensuring that the firm functions effectively and durably. This responsibility may at times conflict with personal views and ownership preferences and wishes. When the conflict is too big to bear, the owner ought to volunteer to leave the corporate board, possibly leave the firm and sell his or her shareholding if indeed convinced the lack of trust in the board and a misalignment with personal views are not convincingly remedied.

Most Wall Street people only think about their interests first, leaving firms bought or sold in poor shape. The disaster in London and on Wall Street is to have promoted to corporate leadership individuals who think of themselves first. That makes no sense as the firm is a social enterprise where mishaps have disastrous collective and social consequences. Capitalism fails in this regard when it allows people to lead firms excessively driven by their sole interests and their ego. The firm becomes an instrument, if not a toy at the pleasure of its leader. When such a person is also a representative for a family, this carries huge risk for the family. It is likely in time to lead to serious conflicts if not outright value destruction.

Daniel Janssen thus harbors strong views about why family members ought to join the corporate board: "A Board needs to have owners, for two reasons: i) such owners can make the family's values and views understood by the board and the management; conversely, their presence facilitates the owners' understanding of board and management viewpoints; ii) these owners on the corporate board link the board with the controlling shareholders—and avoid that the board or the management take over from the shareholders, which is always a risk."

Owners on the Business Unit Boards

Daniel Janssen views owners' participation in the management of companies very positively: "For alignment can then be perfect! Owners in management can take quick decisions that are very favorable, if not necessary for value creation. In the life of a (medium-sized) enterprise, there are daily little events that come to the attention of the top manager and are key to fathoming the reality of the company. These little events are important to appraise well and early. An owner-manager will typically take the right decision faster, and alignment with the decision will typically be greater. When this is the case, opportunities too can be identified faster. Decisions taken would have been more difficult and certainly slower in the absence of such alignment. On the contrary, when the leader does not think of the enterprise first and reacts or is driven first by her or his interests as shareholder and owner, the owner and the corporation suffer."

However, warns Daniel Janssen, "the Owner-Manager can propose any course of action, but must remain obedient to the Board which will check whether the proposals do not submit the firm to excessive risk. She or he must be very attentive to stakeholder interests while keeping the interest of the enterprise first. When I was appointed CEO [of Solvay], I always said that if the alignment was missing, I would leave. This, I say humbly, seems a rare viewpoint today. Today's CEOs rarely have this fuller sense of the enterprise

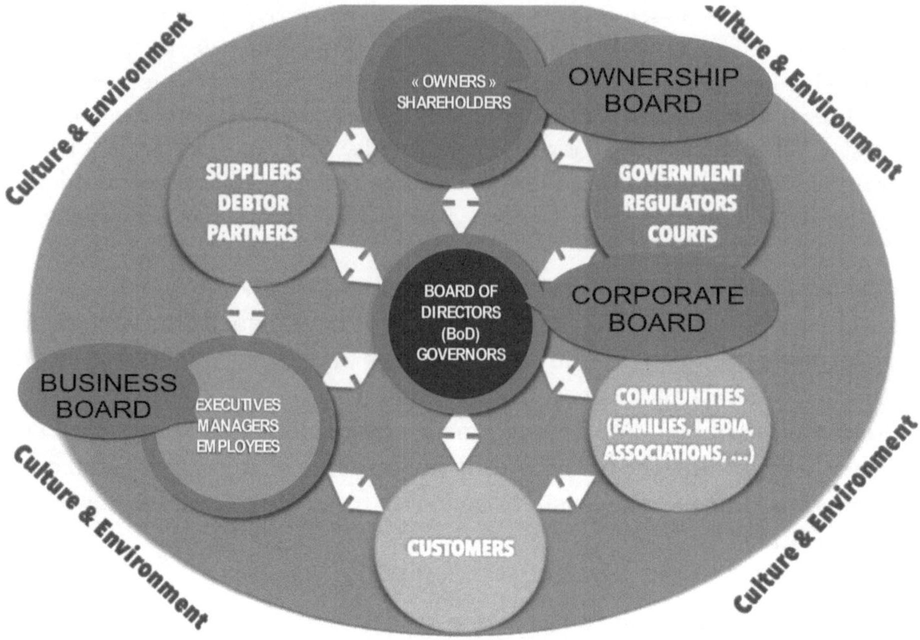

Fig. 9.2 The three boards and the question of alignment

they lead. Perhaps it is because they are named for 3–5 years and that knowing this, they are induced to care mostly about themselves, or their record over this period, since it is difficult to change the corporation fundamentally and durably over such a short period" (Fig. 9.2).

4 Pathologies

In his masterly novel *Anna Karenina* Tolstoy stated that "happy families are all alike, but every unhappy family is unhappy in its own way." We concurred already with Tolstoy in the Preface and mentioned that hardware, software, or peopleware failures, alone or in combination, might destroy this happiness. There are plenty of failures that could occur in hardware and software. Even more might surface in humanware, as all of us are unique in our own distinct ways.

Most cases of corporate failure evidence either a lack of effectiveness in one or more of the three boards, or a lack of alignment between these boards. The roots of such misfunctioning may lie in owners disagreeing on the exact mission to be pursued, in their interpretation of this mission, or in a lack of fundamental commitment in the three boards to the effective governance of the company, in line with the owners' mission. A lack of alignment with a sufficiently clearly defined mission often provides one individual with the opportunity to take control over one of the three boards and from there to force alignment around a restated mission, unavoidably leading to value destruction when considering the prior mission. The following instances attest to such destructive dynamics:

- In VW Ferdinand Piëch ended up controlling all three boards, having directed all three. It then became exceedingly difficult to keep the roles of the three boards separate, as he dominated all of them. He would not tolerate much challenge to his mission, either at board level or within the company, of "Das Auto," which would make VAG the biggest automaker in the world, surpassing TOYOTA. This would ultimately lead executives to cheat regulators and customers with cars that used the so-called "cheating devices" and were truly toxic. Serious death resulted from the toxic exhausts. The Board, which was numerous and acted more like a parliamentary approval board, did not exercise much real control over VAG, or if it did, it controlled its progress on a toxic path.
- In the case of RENAULT and NISSAN, Carlos Ghosn took on the role of owner, corporate board, and business unit CEO for each of the three BUs, namely RENAULT, NISSAN, and the ALLIANCE, with the task to ensure alignment and synergies among these three entities. Yet, Ghosn was conflicted in the exercise of his multiple roles as he did not prevent the two businesses under his command (RENAULT and NISSAN) from increasingly diverging. Here too, it looks like the corporate boards did not exercise any effective control beyond the control wished for by the almighty Ghosn. The governance picture shown here is a perversion of good corporate governance.
- In the Tata Group, Ratan Tata controlled the Tata Trusts, Tata Sons (the holding company), and was Chairman of all the major Tata Group companies (many of them listed). This looks remarkably like dictatorial control. When his successor, Cyrus Mistry, seemed to protest and resist, a coup was organized to replace him. It is unclear, due to the control of the Tata Trusts on the group, why this coup had to happen at all, given that he was the chosen successor, and why so suddenly, and in such a ruthless way. Furthermore, differences between Ratan Tata and Cyrus Mistry could have been handled at the Owners' Board, since both were owners, or proxies of the owners (Ratan). Events showed that the latter did not function, leading

to the absence of mediation at the Owners' Board and a lack of engagement by the two owner groups on what the mission actually ought to be.

- A fourth remarkable example of this pathology is the Theranos affair, already described earlier. Though founder Elizabeth Holmes assembled a stellar board. Investigative journalism from the Wall Street Journal exposed the scam, with Holmes listening to her partner and Theranos President Balwani much more than to her Board of Directors. She clearly also did not have a functioning Board of Directors, which she, as founder and leader, could have presented her challenges in developing the company and make true on her promises to investors. As in many such cases, pressures from biased expectations set by the company's leaders eventually led to conscious fraudulent efforts to hide the inconvenient truth from the board and shareholders.

In all these cases, checks and balances, and controls were missing or fell seriously short. What was at issue as well is what we call the peopleware aspect of governance, namely that one talented individual came to dominate all three boards, leading the boards to find it difficult and then outright impossible to carry out their duties. The mission gradually went out the window as the key instrument for driving behaviors, goals eventually being set to suit an increasingly imperial leader, and then ensure the survival of the person who has become the owner-founder of the firm, even if this ownership is largely or fully psychological. In the Tata Group, the philanthropic mission of the trusts morphed with the goals pursued by the operating companies. This contributed to the gradual emergence of a culture of benign tolerance for non-performance. Philanthropy now extended to employees, irrespective of whether value was being created. Apart from one company, the remarkably profitable software giant TCS, other Tata Group businesses showed little if any profitability. The company had drifted far from what the original Tata founder had in mind.

The case of the German Merck showed the other extreme. Its drift toward a middle-of-the-road pharmaceutical company is the result of what we might call "aristocracy governing poorly in the absence of a good king or queen": Merck had five boards making up its governance structure. While this gave a voice to the "239 bloodline family members," of which "153 are the owners and have voting rights," the structure grew far too complex. It gradually became unclear which board set and safeguarded the mission, which set the goals, and which board was tasked with operationalizing the mission. The family "barons" seem to be in all the major discussions, each pushing their own views and interests. The result was that the Owners' Board effectively morphed with the corporate and business unit boards. The corporate board was the particularly weak link in the governance structure, as it proved unable to evaluate and approve the goals and strategies appropriate for each of the major Merck business lines. CEOs succeeded each other, failing to leverage Merck's superb head starts and developments, and the remarkable record they built in earlier times.

5 Applying the Three Boards Structure to a Wider Range of Companies

The above pathologies are the consequence of three board structures that become ineffective when the three boards do not operate independently and with sufficient force. This leads some of the legs of the tripod to not function, causing failure of the governance structure.

The benefits of using the three boards framework are illustrated here in larger conglomerates. If we return to GE under Jack Welch, we observed that it was a holding structure containing a great number of businesses, divided in divisional structures. This can be seen to replicate the three-board structure with the ExCom operating as an ownership board, with the divisional committees (health, energy, aviation, …) being subcommittees of this ownership board supervising in greater detail the governance of the operating companies in each of the GE divisions. If GE's ExCom, together with its divisional committees, had only continued to focus on the governance of the mission inside GE and its divisions, the chances that GE would collapse as it did would have greatly diminished. Indeed, and as argued earlier, one of the central confusions that led GE astray was confusion between following its mission as an industrial company or indeed gradually pursuing the road to becoming a more financially driven group, as GE Capital was increasingly generating most of the profits for the company.

The "3 Boards" structure is also a useful concept in smaller holding companies, including founder and family-owned companies. To this, we expose the story of Alcopa, a family-owned investment firm headquartered in Belgium.

Alcopa

Alcopa's origin dates back to 1937, when Albert Moorkens set up a company to produce and distribute motorcycles. Over the years, it grew from its automotive roots importing cars and motorbikes into Belgium to becoming a diversified holding that invested in automotive and motorbike distribution companies in Western Europe, as an operating partner, strategic advisor, or more simply as a provider of long-term capital. Dominique Moorkens was the youngest son of founder Albert Moorkens, whom he eventually succeeded. Today, third to fifth generations of the family are active in the holding group or in its operating companies. Dominique Moorkens, whose journey to ownership will, together with other profiles, be described in Chap. 13, shared with us how ownership in this privately held family group is exercised:

- *Family Holding and Owners' Board.* There is a holding company, AGM, named after the founder and his wife. It is supervised at the top by a *Family Owners Board or Committee* (*Comité d'Actionnaires Familiaux*, or "*CAF*" in short). The six members of the CAF are elected by the family shareholders, in a democratic election where people have as many votes as they have shares. Given that the second generation (G2) had six members, it was felt beneficial to break the representation of the family shareholders by their branch representative, and to unify the ownership structure into a single board, the CAF. Members on the CAF were no longer representing their branch but represented and were elected by all branches and were also accountable to all. Diversity was also ensured by having people elected from different generations. "CAF membership," says Dominique Moorkens, "has nothing to do with their number of shares: members are elected for their competence and the trust they can generate amongst family shareholders." The focus of the CAF is to agree on the mission of the family holding and to ensure that the family group is well supervised. It is at the CAF where shareholder risk is evaluated and adjusted if needed. And the CAF indeed made the decision a few years ago to diversify away from the automotive industry. Finally, the CAF also discusses capital rewards, as well as succession planning, and reviews progress on the mission and corporate strategy. But the key role of the CAF is to frame a vision of family shareholding that is shared by the family and then appropriately governed by the corporate board, which it appoints.
- *Corporate Board.* The six elected CAF members nominate and appoint the members of Alcopa's Board of Directors, who are accountable directly to the CAF. The appointed board members govern the group on behalf of the family, with whom they interact largely through the CAF. The Alcopa Board is presently chaired by a non-family member because the current co-CEOs are both from the family. When the CEO is non-family, the Chairperson should ideally be from the family, for reasons of trust and commitment. The Chair of the CAF is a member of the Alcopa Board, also

for trust and communication reasons between the CAF and the Board, but not its Chair, as the role is distinct (and would then contribute to appointing him or herself). It is the Chair of the CAF who presents and comments on Alcopa's performance over the last year to the annual meeting of AGM shareholders.

- *Business Unit Boards*. The two co-CEOs, both from the family, uniquely complement each other: one is more strategic, while the other is more operational. In this period of transformation of the group, the dual structure is seen as richer and more secure. Interestingly, they used to be Board Co-Chairs, but the inversion with the introduction of a non-family and independent Chair has proved most beneficial. The two co-CEOs now jointly lead the executive team in overseeing the various businesses that are held by the group and in transforming the investment portfolio away from the automotive sector.

When asked what role he as former CEO and Chair still plays in Alcopa, Dominique Moorkens's answer was immediate: "I now occupy the role of major shareholder. I no longer have any other function in the group and do not interfere in decisions. I sniff and probe around. My role is a sort of caring ('bienveillant') and engaged shareholder when all is difficult, demanding when all is easy, and never ceasing to ask questions. I prepare my questions a lot, with due care and thought. My contribution today is for the family to have an active shareholding that is at the opposite of an inert mass of shareholders coming to an AGM solely for dividend information and distribution."

Alcopa is a medium-sized firm, yet its use of the three boards framework has allowed it the flexibility to thrive and transform itself, with little if any destructive debate, from a small auto and motorbike distribution activity into a successful investment firm focused on growth opportunities and sectors.

We do not claim that the three boards structure fits all types of organizations. However, even in partnership firms, some parallels are useful to keep in mind, as Nicolas Pictet, the former Senior Partner of the Pictet Group, explains.

The Pictet Partnership

Pictet began as a "financial partnership in a very large sense (more like investment banking, brokerage). Little of this is left except for the spirit, the organizational model (a partnership), and the partners' succession (partners do not buy goodwill, come in at a nominal price, and leave at a nominal price). You own part of the equity while partner and typically start with a small percentage. The other partners loan you the money to buy your share of the equity. The senior partner will inform you on the speed with which you are allowed to increase your shareholding." The partners are the only shareholders, and they must redeem their shares when leaving the partnership.

Regarding the important aspect to sustain the ownership of the group, Nicolas Pictet comments as follows: "Meritocracy is key, and from a longer-term perspective, being governed by owner-manager has proven best for the bank. The partners indeed are united in their commitment to private ownership of the bank. This certainly has contributed to its conservative nature, but it is balanced by the fact that all partners are and behave like first-generation owners. All partners, when appointed, know that they start with 0 shares, and that they will end up with 0. In addition, they are initially heavily indebted to their more senior partners who loaned them the money to buy their shareholding. That provides healthy entrepreneurial energy to the bank, as profitable growth will allow them to repay their shares more easily and faster. Children of successful partners will follow the same rules and processes that their elders followed. Merit will allow them to be invited to join the partnership, not lineage." Together, the partners form what we have called the Owners' Board in this book. The Owners' Board meets three times a week. This is much more often than in a traditional corporate structure. It has the virtue of maintaining closeness among the partners. In these meetings, partners deal with and review both mission, goals, and strategies. Nicolas Pictet says, "In our meetings, we go down into the businesses, which enables us to know what our businesses are and how they operate. We have been there and come from there. That is also why we meet so often: we like to know what goes on in all our three businesses (private wealth management, asset management, asset services). Typically, two partners are assigned to manage each business on behalf of the other partners. Indeed, our governance rule is that all partners share all main business issues amongst ourselves. There is no big decision that is taken individually; ours is a truly collegial governance structure." Partners also share directorships in Pictet's corporate boards:

- Four banks around the world,
- PAM (the asset management business),
- PWM (the wealth management business),
- PAS (the asset services business),
- An alternative investments business.

Nicolas Pictet says that governance is an ongoing topic among the partners. Over time, they have moved toward greater empowerment of the two partners in charge of the three businesses, with greater delegation of authority. "As partners, we needed to move towards larger topics and delegate daily operational issues more, allowing greater autonomy in the running of the businesses. We feel that as partners we are a great value-added to the group. Compared to boards that must believe what they are being told, we delve into the problems and struggle with them until a satisfactory solution is found. Hard to fool the partners!"

* * *

This chapter ends Part I of this book. Part I presented the "hardware" that owners must master and struggle with. The chapters presented the key structural questions that occupy owners and their directors: missions, goals, strategies—and the governance structures that approve and contribute to their formulation and oversight. The focus was on rational and logical knowledge, and skills for value creation.

We now are ready to begin Part II, devoted to "software." In this part, we examine the challenges in implementing MGSF based value-creating ideals in a world with people that interact, each with their own voices and views, and their biases. Fair Process Leadership will be one of the major frameworks presented in Part II. It is a fundamental key to support owners, directors, and the key executives to experience value-creating dynamics, preserving, and enhancing both relations and value creation.

Notes

1. Daniel H. Pink, *Drive: The Surprising Truth About What Motivates Us*, Riverhead Hardcover (2009).
2. Kenneth Bertrams, *The First Ninety Years: 1928-2018*, Lannoo Publishers (2018).

Part II

Software: Effective Collaborative Processes and the Need to Manage Self

10

Delusions, Confusion, and Biases

1 Biases: Why Does Effective Decision Making Remain So Elusive?

Part I of our book dealt with the science of value creation, which was conceptual and might be described as "how things ought to work." Part I did not address the human and practical aspects of the task, described as "how things actually work." Part II of this book deals with the behavioral issues faced by owners and board members as they interact, among themselves, with executives, and, beyond, with a wide variety of stakeholders. In short, it may be referred to as addressing the "knowing-doing gap."

As soon as we enter the "messy" governance world and the people who inhabit it, we immediately face interests, emotions, and egos. For governance is power—over people, appointments, strategies, partnerships, employees, investment budgets, remuneration, and dividends, to name the most evident elements of power. Power is the ability to make people do that they would not do on their own. Boards have power, and that immediately attracts a lot of interest, from nearly all shareholders. Boards are responsible to owners for "getting things done." Boards may also constrain owners as the fiduciary duty of board members is to the organization, not to the owners. One indeed can only hold one fiduciary duty at any time.

The triangle that is of interest to us therefore is power-governance-outcomes, which mirrors the owner-board-executive tripod. To this, one should add that stakeholders have egos too and will exercise the power they have to move the board closer to in their direction. These considerations explain why governance has both a "hard science" aspect, and a possibly even harder human

M. Massa et al., *Value Creation for Owners and Directors*,
https://doi.org/10.1007/978-3-031-19726-0_10

side. A treatise on governance is therefore obliged to examine the so-called soft or human aspects guiding the interactions among diverse stakeholders, each moved by their interests, power, and ego. The challenges of facing and resolving competing demands from stakeholders require a good understanding of individual and group decision making. Thanks to the pioneering work of Kahneman and Tversky, among others, we now know this field to be rife with biases, illusions, and delusions.[1]

The following (urban legend) story illustrates our point.

> Two battleships assigned to the training squadron had been at sea on maneuvers in heavy weather for several days. I was serving on the lead battleship and was on watch on the bridge as night fell. The visibility was poor with patchy fog, so the captain remained on the bridge keeping an eye on all activities.
>
> Shortly after dark, the lookout on the wing of the bridge reported, "Light, bearing on the starboard bow."
>
> "Is it steady or moving astern?" the captain called out.
>
> Lookout replied, "Steady, captain," which meant we were on a dangerous collision course with that ship.
>
> The captain then called to the signalman, "Signal that ship: We are on a collision course, advise you change course 20 degrees."
>
> Back came a signal, "Advisable for you to change course 20 degrees."
>
> The captain said, "Send, I'm a captain, change course 20 degrees."
>
> "I'm a seaman second class," came the reply. "You had better change course 20 degrees."
>
> By that time, the captain was furious. He spat out, "Send, I'm a battleship. Change course 20 degrees."
>
> Back came the flashing light, "I'm a lighthouse."
>
> We changed course.

The lessons from the story above are multiple. The most obvious ones are:

1. It is hard to be aware of one's biases. Most of our biases are unknown to us. They impose themselves upon us, most of the time subconsciously.
2. Biases are not "out there," affecting only others. They are first and foremost within each of us. They lead us to blame others before turning to ourselves. Our biases also are more easily observable by those interacting with us or observing us. Others have a capability we do not have by observing us, they help reveal our biases.
3. Because biases are so ingrained in our human fabric, it takes a lot of time and effort to break free of our habits, which also are our shackles.

4. When approaching biases, the reader is urged to look within, and observe others. Being aware of one's and other people's biases is the key to helping oneself and others address and overcome them.

Robyn Dawes in his book *Everyday Irrationality* explains how prevailing our irrationality is.[2] All of us suffer, to some degree, from the two most common psychological afflictions: neurosis and psychosis. Mental illness arises when, due to these afflictions, individuals are no longer able to live normal lives and face everyday situations.

Neurotic thoughts and behaviors are automatic, subconscious efforts to manage deep anxiety.[3] We all, to a certain degree, are neurotic: we tend to whine, to feel unappreciated, feel unloved, or even disrespected, if not hated. In contrast, psychotics are upfront about their views and beliefs, which include delusions (false beliefs) and hallucinations (beliefs not shared by others). They have difficulty understanding what is real and what is not. Sometimes psychotics believe they are other people.

While most of us are neither psychotic nor neurotic, we nevertheless often use faulty, irrational thoughts, and reason in a manner that is misplaced. These irrational habits are the root of our human biases. They have been widely studied, particularly over the last few decades.[4] Our purpose here to highlight the most egregious and recurring biases that affect owners, boards, and executives. Awareness is the first step toward wiser and more effective leadership. We start with a story illustrating how a lack of awareness of these biases led to a downfall of a once remarkable company.

2 Biases at Work in the Demise of a Corporate Leader: The Kodak Story

Let us look at Kodak. By 1976, Kodak had a 90% market share of the US film market and produced 85% of the cameras sold.[5] While cameras did change considerably since the day George Eastman made his first camera, the company followed the same basic economic model as in 1888. This is described as the "*razor and blades strategy*," successfully copied by Gillette. The company sold cameras cheaply and made plenty of money off film processing, and the chemicals and paper (the "consumables") required to print the photographs. Kodak's R&D engineers were great inventors and cornered the mechanical camera business. But as disruption came in the form of digital cameras, the reaction was complex and faulty. It caused the demise of Kodak (Fig. 10.1).

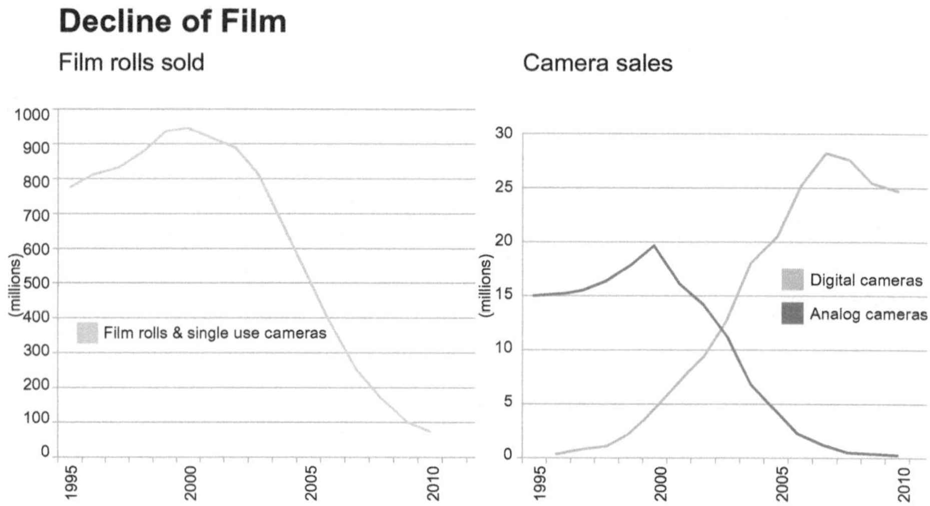

Fig. 10.1 The decline of film and the rise of digital cameras. Source: Jake Nielson via Twitter

Why did Kodak succumb to obsolescence? A big part of the answer lies in the individual and especially group biases that took hold of Kodak managers first and then were transmitted to their boards. This phenomenon is sometimes described by the statement, "there are no mature technologies, products, or markets; there are only mature minds." Kodak was ideologically stuck in its leadership mindset of making money from consumables. At the same time, it was very concerned by the rise of digital camera, investing too much money too early and still leaving its cash cow (mechanical photography) exposed to the attack of its competition (Fuji). The huge investment in digital was wasted by the mentality governing Kodak in its previously dominant technology: essentially, its "Photo CD" was a blank CD on which photographs could be digitally stored and displayed on TV sets and computer monitors. However, the device sold as a "special CD" player costing US$500 per device, while a CD was sold for US$50. In comparison, the fully digital business model had low margins, plenty of storage, and costless dissemination over email and through new social media apps. The Kodak product posed no threat to their digital contenders.

A key moment in this story is the appointment in 1993 of a new CEO to help Kodak face the disruption caused by digital photography. George Fisher joined Kodak from digital Motorola. He knew the future lay with digital photography. However, Fisher made one fundamental transition management error: he swung the pendulum too far and too quickly to the other extreme, killing most of Kodak's still profitable though diminishing core business. One of Fischer's first decisions was to divest all businesses unrelated to digital photography. Kodak spun off Eastman Chemicals, a firm originally set up for the manufacturing of raw materials used in traditional photography. By 1993 Eastman Chemicals had grown into a successful, stand-alone business. It could have provided the cash flows needed for managing the technological transition on which Kodak embarked. It could not only have provided a financial cushion, but also relayed while Kodak learned how to manage and eventually grow its digital photography business. Multiple errors in framing led to these poor decisions. One was to believe that there is no money to be made in a declining business.

Fuji, Kodak's longstanding rival, chose a very different course and avoided its eventual obsolescence. Fuji neither invented the digital camera nor did it have the market intelligence that Kodak disposed of quite early and that warned the latter about the impending disruption of its highly profitable film business. Fuji destroyed Kodak by cannibalizing its cash cow: mechanical cameras and the film the cameras used. To buy itself time, Fuji bought a majority equity stake in its copy machine joint venture with Xerox. Profits from this diversification sustained Fuji while it developed its digital expertise without, like Kodak did, investing all its resources in this technology. Fuji thus relied on a mix of revenues to navigate the uncertainties created by the disruption of its main business. Its corporate strategy allowed the digital business to emerge without destroying its cash cow. On the contrary, Fuji expanded its traditional business due to Fisher's decision to immediately withdraw from that business.

3 Biases Exposed and Compounded: Analyzing the Kodak Story

The first step in obtaining greater awareness into biases is to gain a better understanding of how these biases arise. The standard treatment of biases is not to directly address intuitive and biased responses that are deeply ingrained in us, but rather to work on becoming more aware of our biases, how they operate, and particularly how they are triggered. Increased awareness of the triggers at play allows us to reprogram our natural reactions and develop better habits.[6]

Kodak is remarkable for it thoroughly illustrates the biases that affected the leadership of the company, and that contributed to its demise. Even if the organization had all the resources needed for managing this technological challenge, save for an effective Board of Directors. Neither did it have an identifiable owners' group, or an effective owners' board, which could have contributed to a more favorable outcome for the company. Indeed, good owners—such as those of Interbrew—experience obsolescence more vividly, more emotionally, and more intelligently. That leads them to also react differently, including through acquisitions aimed at countering the perceived obsolescence of their firm. We illustrated this in our chapter on obsolescence and counterfactual thinking. Shareholders, sharing such intuition, will simply sell their shares, leaving "the market" to manage the obsolescence. This is also why owner-led family firms have more longevity than market-listed firms, whose woes are often addressed by the management of the firm that acquires them.

Looking at Kodak's corporate actions and examining the internal debates and managerial actions from publicly available sources, we can see broad patterns in the processing of the competitive context by Kodak's managers and Board of Directors. These demonstrate that Kodak was unable to properly reach the right risk-return trade-off, proved incapable of dealing with the flood of data that was staring at them, and that emotions and egos affected information processing and decision making to such an extent that they rendered these ineffective. The story also indicates what can happen when several biases combine and reinforce each other, as opposed to mitigate each other for a more balanced outcome.

Reference Points in the Mental Processing of Contexts

When developing prospect theory, Kahneman and Tversky stressed the importance in decision making of awareness about the starting point of reference.[7] They stated that the starting point is the origin from which we consider changes, which we then evaluate for improving or worsening our condition. The second aspect of their theory is that we are greatly more sensitive to losses away from our initial position than we are to gains. Initial position thus matters greatly too when it comes to the risk assessment of a new prospect.

In 1975, Kodak had invented the digital camera and had become the dominant company in this sector. Its success was based on selling analog cameras which is where it drew its prestige from. Yet, it was making most of its money from consumables (film rolls, chemicals, paper) and from processing the pictures. This naturally became its reference point when framing the different prospects it came to consider.

The key decision Kodak had to make in the mid-1970s was whether and how to push forward on its invention of digital photography and start commercialization. The positives of doing so were real, even if uncertain: the opportunity to create a new market space and gain a head start over rivals in a technology Kodak's internal teams already knew would be the future. Yet should it follow this path, the expected and uncertain advantages would also be accompanied by sure losses: the first and principal loss would be the cannibalization of its highly successful "razor and blades strategy." This loss was not only an economic loss as this technological change would change the power inside the Kodak organization, with digital folks taking over from the "silver" chemistry people. The latter, sitting on top of plenty of cash flow earned over many years and having the power—initially won the internal confrontation, when they should have passed the baton to younger colleagues aware of the emerging technology. Kodak's senior leadership for a while rejected entering the new digital photography market which they understood much less than their traditional "pictures and film rolls" market and which they considered as much riskier (particularly that they did not know it). Their decision was based not on a yet unknown upside, but much more on consideration of the real and huge potential losses Kodak would incur if it were to displace its lucrative silver photography business.

When digital camera sales then started to pick up in the mid-90s, Kodak was again faced with the decision it had faced 20 years earlier. This time however its reference point had changed. Digital cameras were being adopted, consumer behaviors were changing, digital computers becoming the law of the land. Electronics was taking over from mechanics and chemistry. This new reference point altered Kodak's loss aversion calculation. Losses again loomed larger than gains, but this time expected losses if Kodak did not enter the digital camera business were huge. Kodak thus logically entered the digital space, now putting all its resources into this technology. Loss aversion drove Kodak's strategy again. But this time, Kodak also succumbed to another bias, the mental accounting bias.

Conservatism and Representativeness

Representativeness is a bias where one gives higher credence to events one is familiar with or can easily recall, than to events one is less familiar with. It renders people conservative when facing phenomena that are distant from their experience.

Let us consider Kodak one more time. The company maintained its view on what consumers appreciated in photography, despite new information about the impact of digital photography with which they had much less familiarity (conservatism). Consumer needs shifted from carefully taking a few good pictures and then printing out to taking a much greater number of pictures, then sharing these digitally, and storing them, all for free and easy to do. This change left Kodak completely flat-footed. Admittedly, the practice of taking pictures at any moment through a mobile phone may have been difficult to imagine in the 1970s. Yet, Kodak remained wedded to its ideas of how a camera should work, despite mastering the digital technology as a result of its huge investment in it (and which left its cash cow unprotected).

So, Kodak remained wedded to the hybrid model of the photo-cd for storage, pictures being printed from there for viewing. Kodak analyzed the business situation through the lens of what had worked so well in the past and what was most easily available to them. Kodak did not think about the new consumer trends that digital would allow and foster. Kodak made money through the sale of consumables. Thus, even when Kodak managers finally accepted that digital photography was key to their company's success, they could not imagine that clients would care about storing memories first, and that printing photos would become a much less common habit. The razor and blade had changed from selling the blade to selling the razor. How Kodak failed to grasp this fundamental change in their market can only be explained by enduring collective biases having taken ahold of the Kodak management in charge with the development of digital technology.

Mental Accounting

Mental accounting is the process by which people categorize and evaluate outcomes by grouping them according to some "characteristics." For example, individuals place "buckets" of wealth and finance into separate "accounts" without realizing that these are fungible. The mental accounting bias occurs, for example, when cash is treated differently due to a person's perception as to where the cash comes from. Such mental accounting violates the core reality that "cash is cash." Another common example of the mental accounting bias occurs when the domestic market counts more than the foreign markets. This occurs when losses in the home market are considered acceptable at least for a while, and then triggering excessive investments to redress the situations as such losses are evaluated as unacceptable. In contrast, similar losses in foreign markets would lead to immediate drastic action, including withdrawal. The name was first coined by Richard Thaler, the 2017 Nobel Prize in Economic Sciences.

This bias was present in the Kodak story too, compounding the bias that took hold of the firm. We explained earlier that in 1993, George M.C. Fisher, as the new Kodak CEO, decided to divest from all businesses unrelated to digital cameras. The company consequently lost all its non-digital camera, cash flow generating businesses. They acted like entrepreneurs, obsessively focused on growing the revenues associated with the digital camera business. The Kodak leadership seemed to have mentally accounted for the non-digital cash flows as of a different nature and associated with a different business. All the businesses Kodak sold could have been sources of financing while Kodak experimented, learned, and grew its digital photography business. But having agreed that the business was doomed, all cash flows from that part of the business seem to have been mentally discounted, which contributed, together with the "core business" notion, to focus excessively on the digital camera market.

As if suffering from the first two was not sufficient, Kodak suffered additionally from another major bias when bringing its first digital camera product to market. We explain next how this occurred.

Narrow Framing

This bias is triggered by a narrow framing of the problem that omits the real and broader picture or context facing a decision maker, who then is led down the suboptimization path, which in the case of Kodak was huge and happened several times during Kodak's demise. In the first instance, it led Kodak to invent digital photography only to shelve plans to develop this market as it was fully focused on defending its existing chemical photographic technology and business model. Clients no longer wanted to have their pictures printed when they were able to see them much more easily and cheaply in their digital recording. Yet, when Kodak finally turned to develop its digital products and offer, it again suffered from narrow framing. It created an expensive digital camera that would print the output. "Silver" executives must have found the digitally printing camera a great and natural idea to leverage the new digital technology. They locked the firm into a narrow framing of the product. They were unable to see or grasp the big shifts that occurred in the market and that would allow very different customer experiences and demands using the new digital technology. Kodak executives kept framing their business in terms of selling "physical" cameras and did not grasp that its products were fulfilling a fundamental consumer need of selling instances of life, memories, and not cameras. Consumers wished to share and store these memories and recall them at their convenience. Which they now could.

Even when Kodak finally entered the digital photography market, it did so via a hybrid film-based digital product. Its narrow framing of customer needs again handicapped its ability to succeed in the new era. Another instance of narrow framing was when the new CEO, George Fisher, decided to withdraw Kodak from all its non-digital business.

Another example of narrow framing is the end of IBM's big computer machines. It came in the 1980s at the hand of the smaller PDP-11s, produced by DEC. These were much less performing when considering their computational speed, which was IBM's key metric. but the PDP-11s proved, however, greatly more convenient for laboratories and smaller organizational departments, which could now dispose and have full access to their own computers rather than the much bigger time or user sharing machines.

IBM missed the threat posed by the PDP11 as they considered these machines as "inferior" to theirs. They were biased by their own metric and not by the metrics that drove PDP11 customers to order such machines. Most remarkably, and proving the prevalence of the narrow framing bias, having disrupted IBM, DEC fell into the same trap. The company was unable to update its mental framing when desktop computers emerged, which DEC engineers—just as their IBM predecessors—considered inferior compared to their better-performing PDP-11s.

The phenomenon of narrow framing is common when so-called *disruptive technologies* emerge. Leading technologies often miss seeing the disruption emanating from technologies that are emerging and eventually will make them obsolete. One of the main reasons is narrow framing and biased thinking in favor of the existing technology, and against the emerging technology. For example, sailboats kept being praised for "being driven by the wind," contrary to the early steamships that suffered the drawback of carrying their own coal.[8] So arguments favoring sailboats led people to dismiss the potential of steamboats. Finally, being a much younger and unproven technology, the potential progress of steamboats once they were put in use was naturally discounted. We will return to this in the final section of this chapter.

Overconfidence and Self-attribution

The inability to properly process information, number fallacy and problems with reference points leads to decision taking not substantiated by hard and reliable data. However, if the outcome is a success, the decision maker will tend to attribute the credit to himself. The more he will get lucky and successful, the more he will grow overconfident.

One telling example, is the Challenger tragedy, where the space shuttle exploded shortly after take-off. Columbia University Professor Diane Vaughan has written extensively about the disaster demonstrating that NASA managers did not properly account for the weather forecast data.[9] Professor Vaughan writes about "a long incubation period with early warning signs that were either misinterpreted, ignored, or missed completely." The fact that early launches were successful generated confidence. In the case of the Challenger, NASA observed leaks from special seals on the shuttle's booster rockets. A group studying these leaks determined that there should be no safety concerns if they were limited to small leaks. "They redefined evidence that deviated from an acceptable standard so that it became the standard," writes Vaughan. As leaks kept occurring, these occurrences, unfortunately, became "normalized." On the day the Challenger exploded, the weather was so cold that the leak was larger than anticipated, triggering the disastrous explosion we all came to know.

The NASA Challenger disaster also demonstrates the self-attribution bias. Self-attribution leads people to excessively attribute successes to their expertise and contribution. Failures are told to result from factors that are force majeure and are beyond one's control. During the Challenger disaster investigation, NASA seemed to imply that the tragedy was due to conditions beyond their control. It took the iconoclastic and independent-minded physicist Richard Feynman to identify the leak from the seal as causing the explosion.

The official investigative commission, of which Feynman was a member, initially refused to incorporate his findings in their report. So, Feynman wrote a 13-page memo entitled "Personal Observations on the Reliability of the Shuttle."[10] This report is a must-read for all senior managers in any business sector. Feynman writes that "NASA managers had 'exaggerated the reliability of the space shuttle to the point of fantasy' and had 'fooled themselves' into believing the shuttle was safe. Commenting on NASA's estimate of the probability of such a disaster as one in 100,000… I saw considerable flaws in their logic. I found they were making up numbers not based on experience. NASA's engineering judgment was not the judgment of its engineers." The fact that the shuttle flew many times without failure was accepted as an argument that it would fly safely again, a clear example of representativeness. "Because of this reasoning," he said, "weaknesses that should have been obvious triggers for concern were accepted again and again."

Kodak, after its phenomenal success in photography, had a lot to be proud about. But the success also bred its overconfidence, which greatly contributed to its demise. Several decisions attest to this. Probably the most important is that the leadership was way too confident in managing the digital challenge it faced. First, its narrow framing led it to invest excessively in digital technology, only to apply what was learned to design products and offer that resembled the mechanical and chemical technologies way too much. It lacked the humility to understand that digital would completely revolutionize the way customers would take pictures, store them, and use them. It seemed to lead Kodak to never ask the fundamental counterfactual question: is it possible that the solution we came up with is wrong or inferior to the one our market competitors will come up with? That question should at least have been asked at a board level if it was not seriously considered at an executive level.

The humility that Kodak's leadership was missing is explained by the self-attribution bias. With the phenomenal success Kodak had enjoyed for so long, it is easy to imagine that its leadership felt more powerful and capable than it was, particularly in a new technological context. This is where having on the board independent thinkers, joined with enthusiasts of the new digital technology, is critical for a balanced discussion of the transition that Kodak had to govern and manage. Kodak suffered from this bias again with the arrival of George Fisher from Motorola in 1993. Fisher steered Kodak full steam into digital, which was a very risky 180° turn. He must have been fully convinced, coming from a very successful Motorola, that he could easily turn around Kodak's fortunes. Indeed, Motorola at that time had just demonstrated the world's first working digital cellular system and phone.[11] In 1994, it introduced the first commercial digital radio, combining paging, data and cellular communications, and voice dispatch. Motorola would become a pioneer in wireless telephone handsets, yet prove unable to turn its technological and early market success in dominating this market segment. Its communications division would eventually be absorbed by Google, which would provide it with a more favorable context and governance.

Loss Aversion

Loss aversion makes people to react differently to gains and losses. If one is in the area of loss, he will act more irrationally, taking more risk just for the purpose of making it up for the loss.

A frightening illustration of the damage caused by loss aversion is BP's Deepwater Horizon disaster, where one of BP's wells, located in the Gulf of

Mexico, blew up in April 2010. The incident ranks as one of the world's worst environmental disasters. The well was one of the deepest ever drilled. Deepwater Horizon was the name of the ultra-modern oil rig that belonged to Transocean, which operated it. The operator is required to check major decisions regarding exploration with the client, in this case, BP, who then assumes responsibility for their decisions. Following the disaster, BP sued Transocean. Investigations as to the cause of the explosion identified BP's drive for cost-cutting and its poor safety systems (inherited from its acquisition of Amoco and insufficiently addressed) as two of the systemic problems plaguing the company. Deep-sea rigs such as Deepwater Horizon were pushing the limits of drilling technology in exploring ever deeper oil wells. The first commercially prospected oil wells were an average of 3635 feet deep. The Deepwater Horizon well was a total of 35,000 feet below the sea surface. Drilling so deep under the ocean floor adds substantial complexity to the operation. The "Deepwater Horizon Accident Investigation Report," issued on September 8, 2010, states that "key negative-pressure test results were accepted although well integrity had not been established."[12] This test would ensure that the pressure difference between the oil and gas in the reservoir and the pressure building up in the oil well (casing and cement) could be contained without the appearance of leaks. Unfortunately, the test showed that the pressure difference was not being sufficiently contained. The Accident Report states that, driven by their bias to produce, amplified by the substantial delays that had been incurred, "the Transocean rig crew and BP well site leaders reached the incorrect view that the test was successful, and that well integrity had been established." The negative-pressure test having been erroneously accepted, BP decided that digging could proceed. This resulted in an explosion that the various safety systems on the platform would prove unable to contain. It has been argued that loss aversion may have been a bigger culprit.

Indeed, BP was coming out of two major disasters (the fire in its Texas refinery in 2005 and the largest Alaskan oil spill in 2006). After each disaster, BP was sitting even more in the domain of losses. It therefore was willing to take even more risk to return the situation to a normal one, focusing excessively at erasing prior losses, rather than objectively contemplating the possibility of increasing losses further.

In the case of Kodak the loss was just the potential loss of market share due to digital. One of the key mistakes made by Kodak, as we pointed out earlier, was spending too much money too early in digital. Colby Chandler, Kodak's Chairman and CEO from 1983 to 1990, returning to Rochester after attending a presentation of Sony's Mavica digital camera, was so scared by what he saw that he ordered that a substantial amount of money be devoted to digital, taking it away from its cash cow (mechanical camera). Fuji did not make the same mistake and gradually ate away the now undefended market share of Kodak in mechanical cameras. Effectively, Kodak, the market leader saw digital as a major threat that would have destroyed its leading position, so it was acting in the area of loss: digital was a mortal threat from which it would have very little to gain. Hence, it overspent, and ignored the impact of this decision on its classical business. In contrast, Fuji started with a tiny market share, so it saw digital as a major opportunity from which it had to gain! Fuji's framing was completely different: it saw digital as an additional opportunity. Kodak was effectively operating in the area of loss, and therefore overspending due to loss aversion. In contrast, Fuji, operated in the domain of gains, and acted more rationally. Loss aversion suggests that market leaders may be dangerously close to acting irrationally because they have more to lose.

Inertia

Individuals can become paralyzed and not take actions, even if these would provide clear benefits in terms of risk and return. This may be due to being afraid of feeling responsible for the negative outcome coming from their action (which is a form of loss aversion). People playing the game of Blackjack may become afraid of asking for another card, even if they know that this action could help them. The fear is that, even if asking another card might on average make them win, they are afraid that asking another card will make them lose. This leads to "cognitive inertia." Inertia is a key problem in decision making and prevents boards from asking the right question. A good chairman can overcome inertia by exploiting loss aversion! That is, he can simply frame the status quo as the reference point in the "area of loss." That way the Chair effectively uses the loss aversion bias to counteract the inertia bias. The other one is to thoroughly investigate the inertia scenario by asking questions such as "what happens if we do not do anything?"

Anchoring, Attention Grabbing, and Social Norms

Our framing can also come from the way information is provided. A simple experiment revealed the depth of the anchoring effect. Participants in a US experiment were shown an average bottle of wine and then asked if they would be willing to pay an amount equal to the last two digits of their Social

Security Number (SSN). The result was startling: those with the highest SSN would pay three times more than those with the lowest SSN! Whereas those with SSNs ending in 00–19 were willing to pay $8.64 for the bottle, whereas those with SSNs ending with numbers 80–99 were willing to pay an average of $27.91 for the same bottle.

Anchoring is also the reason why people pick the less expensive option between two similar-looking cameras costing $250 and $300 each, while selecting the middle option when a more expensive third option, priced at $400, is shown to them.

Anchoring affects many board decisions. Many boards are excessively anchored in thinking by the CEO's presentations of how she or he sees the issues affecting the company. And indeed, CEOs like to anchor their boards in their own thinking, which is poor governance practice. IPOs are examples where company valuations are anchored in specific references or hypotheses. For example, companies more easily make people believe that they are high growth because they have been engaged in M&As before, even when their prospects are poor.

Similarly, the power of the Chairman flows, among others, from her or his ability to set the agenda. Presenting and choosing the set of options for discussions already narrow the ensuing discussion and the board's choice. Indeed, if the Chairman wishes to induce the board to select a riskier choice (B over A) he can simply add another even riskier third choice (C). The third option, just like in the example of the cameras, will push the board—that in the comparison of choices A and B would have chosen the safer A—to select the middle-of-the road riskier choice B, just because the very risky choice C has been added to the set of options!

Social norms can also bias board discussions. This is particularly the case in relational cultures, where feedback is too often immediately personalized, stopping the discussion. One consequence is that it leads the CEO to often not receive negative feedback, until, suddenly, he hears that his CEO term has been terminated.

This concludes our discussions of the multiple biases, conscious and unconscious, that characterize our thinking and drive our behavior, and those of the executive and board teams governing us. As we indicated, awareness of these biases, is the first step. To build this awareness, we have classified the biases according to the different ways they are triggered. We have thus identified biases that flow from the way we examine our context and environment, or that are generated by others who may anchor us wrongly, or that flow from our own attitude toward uncertainty and ambiguity which does not allow us to properly evaluate our options and their associated risk-return trade-offs.

Awareness is the necessary ingredient that allows us to then reflect on their presence and counteract them before they pervert the decisions we make or the conclusions we reach.

The next chapter goes into detail into the story of three teams that were climbing Everest, meeting very different outcomes. These teams were not mere sports teams, but teams assembled in the context of guiding people up the mountain or filming this majestic mountain. Their stories illustrate how small teams can be led astray by biases that develop inside these teams. They also are presented here as metaphors for the owners' board and Board of Directors, who typically are teams of similar size, meeting unforeseen events and often having to operate in conditions that while not being Everest-like, are nevertheless experienced similarly in terms of the turbulence and challenge generated. What happened to the Kodak leadership is one such story: its biases led it to go astray in the storm generated by the emergence of digital photography.

Notes

1. Daniel Kahneman, Paul Slovic & Amos Tversky (Eds.), *Judgment under uncertainty: Heuristics and biases.* New York: Cambridge University Press, 1982.
2. Robyn M. Dawes, *Everyday Irrationality: How Pseudo-Scientists, Lunatics, and the Rest of Us Systematically Fail to Think Rationally*, Routledge, 2001.
3. https://www.webmd.com/mental-health/neurotic-behavior-overview#1
4. Daniel Kahneman, Thinking Fast and Slow, Farrar, Straus and Giroux, 2011.
5. Henry C. Lucas, "The Search for Survival: Lessons from Disruptive Technologies".
6. The classical source for habits and for changing them is *The Power of Habit: Why we Do What we Do in Life and Business*, by Charles Duhigg, Random House Books, 2013. In it, the author convincingly argues that people should understand the triggers of particular habits they like to change, identify them, notice when they arise, and program better responses to these triggers than their natural responses. Triggers are not under our control, but responses are, once we learn to look for triggers.
7. Daniel Kahneman and Amos Tversky, "Prospect Theory: An Analysis of Decision under Risk," *Econometrica 47(2): 263–291*, 1979.
8. Richard N. Foster, *Innovation: The Attacker's Advantage*, Summit Books, 1986.
9. Diane Vaughn, *The Challenger Launch Decision: Risky Technology, Culture, and Deviance at NASA*, University of Chicago Press, 2016.

10. https://science.ksc.nasa.gov/shuttle/missions/51-l/docs/rogers-commission/Appendix-F.txt
11. https://en.wikipedia.org/wiki/Motorola
12. https://www.sec.gov/Archives/edgar/data/313807/000119312510216268/dex993.htm

11

Biases in Action and How High-Performance Teams Address Them

1 Four Teams Climbing Everest: The Story

This chapter considers how biases play out in groups and what might be remedies to their prevalence and their indeed "deadly" impacts, as the example of this chapter shows. Ownership boards, supervisory boards, executive teams, project teams are all groups of small size that can be affected by the same biases that affected the climbing and filming teams described in this chapter.

The stories that we tell here involve small businesses (in the leisure industry), and our focus will be on the small teams that are at the core of these micro-enterprises. We immediately add credence to our story by indicating that also, in bigger companies, leadership dynamics at the top involve smaller size teams (management boards or boards of directors). The dynamics described in this chapter involve stakeholders—owners, managers, clients, partners—that also contribute to team operations (as in a supermarket, where clients do the shopping). As is common in start-ups, these firms barely have boards of directors, and the supervision typically occurs within the team (through internal or self-governance). Board members in smaller firms and start-ups often contribute to operations as the board is one way for these firms to gain access to resources they otherwise would not have access to or be able to pay for. Strategic, marketing, legal, and technological advice are examples of such support that board members may be able to provide. Investment advice and access to investors is another domain of activity for board members. So, we present this example as an integral part of our treatise, and not as an interesting diversion. These leaders were all running businesses which they founded.

M. Massa et al., *Value Creation for Owners and Directors*,
https://doi.org/10.1007/978-3-031-19726-0_11

Failure in this example is unambiguous: owners die, managers die (the assistant guides), as well as customers. We like this case, as performance evaluation is relatively straightforward and unambiguous. The lessons these cases provide are numerous and easily remembered. This tragedy also illustrates the horrendous implications of the human biases of the participants, which are easy to understand which we all share and can understand and empathize with. When discussing these biases in terms of corporate decisions, it is easy to paper over particular irrationalities that may be hard to understand with the benefit of hindsight and distance. However, that is the case as well for the disasters already discussed in this book (BP's Macondo, the NASA Challenger, VAG's Dieselgate). This example provides a clear and stark picture of the most pernicious biases, the dynamics of how they arise, and the challenges faced in countering them.

Everest is the tallest mountain on earth, rising 8848 m on the border between Nepal and China. It is the highest prize in mountain climbing, as one is literally at the top of the world. Climbing Everest is technically not that difficult compared to other summits like Annapurna (also in Nepal) or K2 (on the border between China and Pakistan). The difficulties on Everest have to do with height and remote location, which create several difficulties and risks:

- High altitude sickness leads to the possibility of deadly edemas in the brains and lungs (due to reverse water flows). This is the first major risk all mountaineers must manage. Long acclimatization of the body in "rare oxygen" conditions is the first protocol to be followed. When it hits climbers on the mountain, the protocol is to move them down as soon as possible (but helicopters cannot function that high).
- Sleeping at high altitudes is difficult; combined with physical exertion, this contributes to great tiredness, and, hence, reduced lucidity and greater risk.
- The weather is another major risk: at 8000 m, one is in the jet stream. Winds and snow conditions can be horrific. The surprise is not the fact that there could be a storm; it is about when the storm will appear, how severe it will be, and whether mountaineering teams will be able to face them.
- There is only a small window between the end of the winter season and the beginning of the monsoon season (typically two weeks early May) that provides climbers with a decent chance at an ascent.
- The lack of oxygen is the third major risk. Lack of oxygen adds to fatigue and renders brain functioning and decision making hazardous and problematic.

- Then there is the long route up the mountain. Climbers go from the base camp through the now melting and often changing Khumbu Icefall, which requires the crossing with ladders of deadly crevasses. There are incessant "ups and downs" across four base camps (from 5300 m to 7900 m).
- The challenge is not limited to going up. Most accidents occur on the way down, when bodies and minds have reached a state of exhaustion which greatly reduces attention span and focus. There is an "iron rule" among Everest mountaineers: climbers must start descending Everest at the latest by 2 pm. Any later and a combination of fatigue and darkness render the descent too risky. Winds also pick up at the end of the day.

Climbing Everest used to be the exclusive domain of mountain enthusiasts and experts. Despite its multitude of risks, Everest has become a tourist attraction. This has added another hurdle: long waits that result when teams must wait for other teams to pass bottlenecks, like the Hillary Step. Every minute of waiting is energy lost, as the body consumes energy without progress. It also increases the danger of returning in darkness, and facing strong winds and bad weather on the descent.

On May 10 and 11, 1996 (at least) three teams were attempting to reach the summit of Everest:

- An Indo-Tibetan Border Police expedition, climbing from the North face (Tibet side), with Tsewang Samanla, a highly accomplished climber part of the six-member summit team that was the first to climb the north route that year.
- The Adventure Consultants (AC) team, led by Rob Hall, the firm's co-founder, that for a $65,000 fee, was guiding eight clients up Everest. Hall was assisted by two guides, Michael Groom and Andy Harris, as well as eight climbing Sherpas, who carried most of the team's load and supported clients as well.
- The Mountain Madness (MM) team, a firm similar to AC, led by owner Scott Fischer. On his first commercial expedition Scott was assisted by Anatoli Boukreev and Neal Beidleman and eight climbing Sherpas and, like the AC team, eight clients.

Together the above teams lost eight lives, not due to avalanches or natural disasters, but principally due to "human errors."

- There was also the so-called IMAX team, led by mountaineer film-maker David Breashears, who was filming an IMAX documentary of Everest growing by an average of 6 cm each year—amounting to 1 mile over the last 26,000 years! The film also meant to illustrate the challenges of climbing Everest by featuring climbers who had never been on Everest before. One of them was the son of Norgay, who was the Sherpa who went up with Hillary and conquered Everest for the first time. These novice climbers provided a "human" dimension to the film.

- The IMAX team was not directly involved in the tragedy but was indirectly affected as it was on the mountain when it occurred. Uncertain about weather conditions and seeing other teams come up after them, they had decided to go down and wait for the other climbing teams to return from their ascent. They would then resume filming a less populated mountain (recall that the mountain was supposed to be the hero of their film, not the climbers). The IMAX team provided invaluable help to a few of the stricken climbers, first sharing their supply of oxygen bottles, then helping stricken climbers down the mountain. The behavior and conduct of this IMAX team provide a stark contrast to the three teams that each lost team members. As a result of the unfolding tragedy the focus of their film became the tragedies, and not the continuous and slow growth of Everest, which was their original goal. As we show below, the superb conduct of the IMAX team also allows the illustration of key learning points about team decision making and leadership in crisis conditions.

The Indo-Tibetan Border Police, Mountain Madness, and Adventure Consultants teams all had highly experienced leaders: Rob Hall had climbed Everest four times before this expedition; Scott Fischer had climbed Everest once before and was well known for his ascent of many of the world's highest peaks; Tsewang Samanla was an accomplished mountaineer who had climbed Everest 12 years earlier. In technical mountaineering skills, they were among the best in the world. Yet, all three leaders violated the "iron rule" of starting their descent no later than 2 pm. All three also violated another rule, that of not separating team members (often "roped" together). This separation prevented team members from helping each other when the ascent turned problematic.

Three climbers of the Indo-Tibetan Border Police expedition radioed their base camp at 15:45 Nepal time to say they had reached the summit (the other three had turned around with frostbite). There is some dispute about whether the three climbers were on the summit, as Jon Krakauer, a journalist with the AC team, stated he had seen them 150 m below the summit. In any case, the Indo-Tibetan team was near the summit well after the 2 pm deadline. Tsewang Samanla, the team's leader, nevertheless decided to spend more time on the summit performing religious rituals and told the other two climbers to start their descent. Remarkably, he broke up his three-person team at the most critical time. No further communication was heard from any of the three climbers. It is alleged that the next day a Japanese expedition did meet at least two of the missing Indian climbers but did not provide any assistance. The Japanese team, which did admit passing other climbers on their ascent, denied this, citing communication difficulties.

The AC and MM teams encountered multiple delays during the climb, including a major one due to fixed ropes not being in place for the final climb as expected. Precious time was thus lost while the ropes were being fixed. To this date it is not clear why the ropes had not been laid. The prevailing hypothesis is a lack of coordination, let alone of collaboration between the Sherpas of both teams. These delays caused the groups to become entangled. The guides then decided to create a single group of 33 people aiming for the summit. Due to these delays and the formation of a new team during the ascent, discipline was lost in the approach to the top. Many climbers did not reach the summit by the 2 pm deadline for starting the return.

Doug Hansen, a postal worker for whom reaching Everest was a life-long dream, was a member of the AC team. A year ago, Rob Hall turned Hansen back 300 m from the summit. Empathizing with Hansen's great disappointment, Rob promised him to "push him to the top if needed" in a future year. He would literally do this the next year, but this would prove fatal to both.

At 3 pm, AC Sherpas found Hansen near the Hillary Step and ordered him to descend. Hansen refused. When Rob reached them, the Sherpas offered to take Hansen to the summit. Now Rob Hall refused, informing the Sherpas he would do so and telling the Sherpas to go down. Rob Hall must have felt that he owed one to Hansen, due to his promise the previous year. Being so close to the summit, the moment seemed right to settle the debt.

Four of the clients did not appreciate Rob breaking the 2 o'clock turn-around rule to push Hansen to the top and refused to follow him going down. They would all be safe.

Beck Weathers, another member of the AC team, joined Rob and Doug, aiming for the summit. Unfortunately, Beck had recently undergone eye surgery and became nearly blind due to a combination of high altitude and ultra-violet radiation. Not aware that Beck could no longer see, Rob told him to wait for his return from the summit with Doug. Beck agreed, even adding prophetically, "cross my heart, hope to die."

On May 11, at 04:43, 28 hours after starting for the summit from camp IV, Hall radioed his base camp manager and informed of the terrible news. He had reached the summit, but Hansen was "gone." He had collapsed at the worst location and moment. Hall further mentioned that Harris, who climbed Everest for the first time, had been with him earlier, but that he too was now missing. The ascent of what Scott called "a yellow brick road" had turned into a tragedy.

What occurred from the late afternoon of May 10 to the end is not precisely known. Only that Rob, Andy, and Doug died, and that Beck survived, though no one exactly understands how. All that is known from these final tragic moments is that Hall's body was found behind a rock where he had sought relief from the gusting and deadly winds.

Andy Harris, the other AC guide, had reached the summit of Everest at 1:12. On the way down, he made a fatal mistake. Instead of reducing the use of oxygen from his canister, he turned it fully on, depleting his oxygen canister early. Team members on the descent never appreciated the difficulties Harris was having. They lost contact with him. His body was never found. He had no experience on Everest and should never have been an assistant guide to Rob, nor should the latter have asked him. The role that he could have played well was to be an apprentice, experiencing what it takes to guide clients safely on a mountain he did not know.

The other climbers, being late and exhausted from their long climb, encountered a wild and sudden storm coming up from the valley, not far from camp IV. A storm had been mentioned as a possibility, but no one expected the suddenness and force of the storm, particularly after a really good day, even if a bit windy. All suddenly became dark and windy. The ten-person group coming down could no longer see the camp nor find their way to reach it. The team became disoriented and stopped, hoping the bad weather might subside and normal conditions return. Fortunately for a group that was freezing to death, Neil Beidleman, one of the MM guides, miraculously spotted the camp during a sudden lull in the weather. He got up, returned to camp, and looked for help. Anatoli Boukreev, the second MM guide, was already sleeping in his tent and readily answered the call. Neil soon reached exhaustion, leaving Anatoli alone to rescue the stranded climbers.

Yasuko Namba, a Japanese lady, was the fourth fatality on the AC team. She reached the top of Everest around 2:10 pm. This was a great accomplishment, as it was the last of her Seven Summits (climbing the highest mountain tops on each of the seven continents). A lot of attention was on her, as she was the second Japanese woman to do so after Junko Tabei. On her descent, her oxygen ran out just above the South Col. She refused to move, exhausted. Guides, particularly Beidleman, dragged her further down the mountain with them. They eventually could no longer carry her. Neither could they rescue her in the night as by then she was not moving any longer, and no one had the strength to pull her. When they returned for her early the next day, she had died as well. She was the second client of the AC team to die on that ascent.

On the third team, Scott Fischer, the leader of the MM team, had a few days earlier descended from Camp II to help a friend and team member get down to base camp. The latter suffered from altitude sickness, which was known when Scott accepted him to join his team. This indeed was madness: due to his condition, this friend posed a risk for himself and for the team, and Scott should never have accepted the risk of taking him into the team. Being the team leader, he should not have spent his energies bringing him down, and instead saved these for the team. But, like many mountain people, Scott's motto was autonomy. Indeed, people who are not autonomous are not a liability for their teammates, so autonomy is one of the key values among mountaineers. After bringing his friend down to base camp, Scott climbed back up to Camp II. But he continuously trailed the team as it continued its ascent up the mountain.

And so it came that the MM team, having reached the summit and celebrating its ascent, waited for their leader to arrive, burning energies they needed for a safe descent. They finally took the decision to go down. They met Scott, their leader, still going up. Several noted that he looked very tired and they tried to persuade him to turn around and come down with them. After all, they were a team and had summited. Fischer proved stubborn and indicated that he wished to continue his ascent, and possibly summit too. They wished each other luck and went their opposite ways.

Scott finally reached the summit at 3:45 pm, aided by one of his Sherpas. He crashed through the 2 pm rule. He was by then suffering from life-threatening high-altitude edema. On the descent, Fischer realized that he had gone beyond his limits and told his climbing Sherpa partner to descend without him and get help. This breaking up of their two-person team compounded Scott's problems. Help eventually reached him on the following day: when Boukreev found Scott, he had died from hypothermia. By now, both leaders had met their fate. Once the MM team members learned of the news, they immediately reminded themselves of how awful he looked when they met him on their way down. They also felt awful about not having forced him to go down with them.

2 Analysis of Our Leaders: Individual Biases of Those "on Top"

Narrow Framing

The first key lesson from the Everest tragedy is that both teams anchored on a wrong framing of their project. All just focused on getting to the top when all know the dangers generally lurk on the descent. This is a clear example of having a wrong starting reference point (*narrow framing*). This caused climbers not to pursue alternative strategies when certain milestones were not reached or when conditions fell "outside of the band of safety" (a play on words, as on Everest, this band is quite narrow).

Loss Aversion

It is easy to understand that team leaders are averse to letting clients "down," by taking their money and then not succeeding in hauling them up the mountain. Reputation and ego effects would play for sure, and the pressure would even be greater when making pledges, as the one Rob made to poor Hansen. Such promises then become psychologically binding, no matter the conditions and the context.

Rob seemed to suffer from a general aversion to failure to take up his team to the summit. That aversion seemed to have spread like a virus and taken hold of every member of both teams (leaders, assistants, and clients). They had invested so much in terms of time, money, and hardship to reach Camp IV that they could not conceive of abandoning the ascent, even though that is exactly what Rob had ordered Doug to do 300 m from the summit the previous year. Not going up would have felt like losing everything that they had done. Such thinking becomes psychologically damning, as each step pushes climbers deeper into the loss. Indeed, one of Everest's biggest traps is that every step toward the top brings each climber closer to one's goal and makes it harder to abandon before reaching the summit. But team leaders are aware of this trap; guides should be reminded of this and should be asked to remind the leader not to fall into this psychological crevasse. The application of simple turnaround rules or contributions of team members is key to avoiding falling into the "attraction" trap of the summit.

A major problem of the two ventures is that they never seemed to apply any counterfactual thinking. Neither seemed to have an *exit strategy* or consider *contingencies* for continuing their climb. *Modular* strategies succumb less easily to a growing loss aversion: a succession of intermediate targets with clear milestones to clear helps avoid being trapped in the escalating commitments that took ahold of the climbers and leaders of both teams.

Overconfidence and Self-attribution Biases

The leaders of both the AC and the MM teams—as well as the Indo-Tibetan Border Police team—were overly confident in their abilities to lead their members up and down the mountain. They also underestimated their teams' capabilities to ultimately manage risks on their own. Having conducted previous expeditions, without loss of life, the leaders were prone to the *self-attribution bias* and were convinced, at least for Robert Hall (as already mentioned, Scott Fischer's mantra was autonomy, a point we will return to), that their abilities in bringing clients back down were primarily due to their abilities, regardless of mountain conditions. They discounted the good luck that allowed previous outcomes, including weather and other team conditions, including the difficult decision that Rob made regarding stopping Hansen's ascent. These biases contributed to render the leaders careless. Tsewang Samanla, from the Indo-Tibetan team, was so confident of his abilities that he even performed rituals on the summit and told his teammates to descend without him. With tragic consequences he and his two Indian teammates all became trapped in the storm and died.

When Rob Hall caught up with his client, Hansen, below the summit at 3 pm, he should have clearly and immediately ordered Hansen to go down. The emotional weight of the past failure to take Hansen up the mountain and his pledge should have been irrelevant in such a situation. Emotional and perhaps also physical sunk costs played havoc here. It takes particular guts—and plenty of good mentoring, coaching, and training—to admit temporary setbacks, to retreat when required, to live to fight another day, and foremost to guide others on these dangerous trails.

Fisher, Hall, and Samanla demonstrate how unconsciousness turns into arrogance, and finally into reckless stupidity. Was it the thin air he was breathing—a potential condition he was fully aware of—that led him to continue his climb up the mountain with Hansen, and that led him to nearly condemn a blind Beck Weathers by ordering him to wait for his return? Beck's prophetic reply, "Cross my heart, hope to die," stands as an ominous summary description of the entire journey.

MM's Scott Fischer demonstrated overconfidence turning into folly when he descended from Camp II to help a friend get down. He climbed straight back up to the summit of Everest, all this in the space of 24 hours. He crashed through the 2 pm rule. And should not have accepted a friend on the team known to suffer from high altitude sickness. It is the compounding of errors that led to his death. The team was lucky in the end, when Beidleman suddenly saw the camp nearby, which saved the group coming down, except for Namba. Then Beidleman was lucid enough to be awake and look, and strong enough to reach Boukreev in Camp IV.

Fischer also showed a callous disregard for organization, believing that all could be sorted out by his tremendous climbing capabilities and energies, and by the autonomy granted to team members who thus would find their own solutions. All guides were to have radio communication apparatus so that if problems arose, they could communicate with each other. Yet, the two senior MM guides, Beidleman and Boukreev, did not have such radios, severely impeding communications among team members. Good communications could have saved several team members, including through tough and pointed conversations among the leaders and their assistants, and possibly involving team members. We are thinking here also of the four AC members that decided to split from the team, no longer trusting the leader to pay sufficient attention to team members' conditions.

3 The Enron Board

Another Everest-like story is Enron Corporation, which ends with an entire organization hitting the crevasse. Such failures invariably are the result of major governance failures, involving a small number of players, namely the Enron Board and its C-Suite. It is another unfortunate example where biases adversely affect a company's board and C-Suite.

The company is known for major fraud. However, the fraud was itself the consequence of unchecked biases that pushed the leadership of a remarkable company to take risks that were underestimated. When the risks taken backfired, major corporate officers—in particular the Chair & CEO, in collaboration with the CFO—tried to cover up the excessive risks that the company had engaged in. The pressure on these leaders to cover up these negative outcomes—and the opportunity also provided by their external auditors at Arthur Andersen, who took their firm down with them—led these leaders to imagine that they could get away with what they should have realized was a fraudulent cover-up of bets that had turned sour.

Enron was a US energy company founded in 1985 as a merger of two small regional companies, Houston Natural Gas and Nebraska's InterNorth.[1] In

August 2000, its shares reached a peak value: its market capitalization topped US$70 billion, making it, at the time, the seventh largest publicly traded company. Fortune magazine had named Enron "America's Most Innovative Company" for six consecutive years, which must have further convinced their leaders that their corporate jewel had to be saved.

In December 2001, only 16 months later, Enron filed for bankruptcy because of financial fraud. The opportunity for fraud was the result of Enron's special-purpose entities (SPV). These were partnerships used to obscure the failure of its investment through off-balance sheet items. Enron's CFO Andrew Fastow set up these SPVs with the knowledge of Enron's board. He even named one of them LJM2, initials corresponding to the first names of his wife and two sons. These SPVs were essentially used to hide the losses and continue to enrich management at the expense of shareholders. These were also the principal motivations for the fraud that took the auditors, Arthur Andersen, down with them.

How could the Enron board approve these vehicles and transactions? The dominant hypothesis is that there was insufficient transparency regarding the real functioning and purpose of the SPVs. Information about the actual functioning of these companies having been concealed, Enron's board, probably *anchored in* all the positive hype about the company, without ever sniffing foul play. One can argue that the board was a willing conspirator in the cover-up, having insufficiently explored the downsides of the SPVs that were multiplying. Particularly it was clear that Enron increasingly was more like a hedge fund than an energy company. And that Enron's board—like was the case for the Tata & Sons board—was considered of high quality, consisting of many well-known "experts."

The way in which the board became or was set up largely contributed to the biases, which came to more than offset the quality of the board members. One was the highly regarded (former) dean of Stanford Graduate School of Business, Robert Jaedicke. Jaedicke was a star accounting teacher before becoming dean of one of the world's leading business schools. At Enron, he chaired the audit committee. That for many acted like a stamp of high quality, just what was needed for such an innovative and complex company.

So one needs to understand how group biases came to prevail the intrinsic quality represented on the Enron board. The SPV partnerships were created to increase Enron's ROA and reduce its debt-to-assets ratio, making the company more attractive to investors and credit ratings than it was truly worth. Indeed, considerable risks taken by the company were hidden in the SPVs, allowing greater leverage and higher ROA, while hiding the true debt assumed by the company. The SPVs were presented to the board as a tool for improving Enron's earnings. Management kept reporting gains from its transactions involving these partnerships, causing a continued growth in share price and market capitalization, and executive rewards which were possibly the strongest bias to keep the schemes going. New heights were reached across the board. Jaedicke was a perfect front, and his chairing of the audit committee provided further ground for an Illusion of transparency.

The board completely overestimated its ability to know what was truly going on inside the company and its accounts. Overconfidence was omnipresent, while challenges and dissent—sometimes referred in board talk as "positive friction"—were absent. Directors seemed to ask few questions to management and, when they did,too readily accepted the answers provided. There rarely were dissenting votes throughout this episode. Virtually every board decision was unanimous. The single exception concerned a decision to acquire a water business.

Board members appeared to be ignorant of their inability to handle new data professionally or to frame the hard questions in a proper way. At the same time, CFO Andy Fastow was taking the use of SPVs to new heights of complexity and sophistication, capitalizing them not only with hard assets and liabilities, but also with increasingly complex financial instruments, including derivatives, Enron's own restricted stock, and rights to acquire stock and liabilities. The slow down of the economy in 2001 would prove fatal to Enron. It should have been the ideal moment to announce to the market and regulators what gambles had been engineered and taken. But that would have required integrity, knowledge and competence, and courage, ingredients that were missing when taken jointly.

In 2001 when the Enron scandal was first revealed, there were 15 directors on the board and five committees. Key board features that contributed to this corporate tragedy were:

- *Length of tenure*: Several of the directors had been on the board of Enron or its predecessor companies for 20 or more years. Kenneth Lay was Chairman of the Board from 1986 until he resigned in 2002 (a total of 16 years). Being together for so long, and with the company increased the risks of homogeneity, anchoring on the successful emergence of ingroup biases. As a group, the board lacked independence from the company's management as it was too close to it, and led by it.
- *Experts*: John Duncan, in hearings before the US Congress Committee investigating the Enron collapse, described his fellow Board members as "well educated, experienced, successful businessmen" as well as "experts in areas of finance and accounting." The "expertise" was so pervasive that the

directors collectively overestimated each other's abilities and comforted each other in the ongoing success. They seemed to anchor on each other's competence, leading to a bias of collective ignorance. Not a single board member seemed to fathom the reality unfolding in front of their eyes.

- *Consensus*: Enron Board members uniformly described internal Board relations as harmonious. They confirmed that Board votes were generally unanimous. They could recall only two instances over many years involving dissenting votes (both pertaining to the acquisition of a water company). Directors also described a very good working relationship with Enron management. The board succumbed to the fundamental attribution error, overemphasizing personality-based explanations, which they then all agreed upon.
- *Personal Relationships*: Several had close personal relationships with Kenneth Lay, Founder, Board Chairman, and Chief Executive Officer (CEO), until he named Skilling CEO of Enron in 2001, the year of its bankruptcy. Skilling was also slated to succeed Lay as Chair in 2002. All board members, including Lay, indicated they had great respect for Enron's senior officers, Jeffrey Skilling (COO) and Andrew Fastow (CFO), trusting their integrity and competence. No one bothered to check whether the trust and integrity remained warranted.
- *Meeting frequency and lengths*: The Board normally met five times during the year, with additional special meetings as needed. Committee meetings generally lasted between one and two hours, as generally did full Board meetings. It was impossible to do anything else than examine the aggregate corporate figures presented to the board by the CFO. These macro-figures provided no insight into the huge and novel micro-complexities contained in Enron's business and revenue models.

A special investigation committee of Enron concluded that the "Enron Board of Directors failed … in its oversight duties," with "serious consequences for Enron, its employees, and its shareholders." Despite the auditor telling the board that Enron was using accounting practices that "pushed limits" and "were 'at the edge'" of acceptable practice,[2] no detailed follow-up investigative action was taken. This, from a governance viewpoint, is negligence. The board brushed aside warnings of a whistleblower describing him as "ill-informed" two months before Enron filed for bankruptcy. At this point, the board had become not just ineffective, but grossly negligent. Defensive routines anchored in previous success and mistaken self-evaluation must have prompted board members to deny the evidence unfolding in front of their eyes.

This amicable board set itself up to succumb too easily to herding and framing biases. Members had been on the board for so long that it became more akin to a London or New York private club than a challenging board overseeing a very innovative energy company. One-hour meetings only allowed the board to approve the motions presented by the executives. The extreme of harmonious discussions and lack of dissent comforted groupthink. One analyst described the board as follows: "There are several law degrees and one person who served as the dean of a law school. There are two physicians. One current University President sits next to one who is now emeritus. Multiple Harvard MBAs can discuss their alma mater with one of its current professors in government. One director has written multiple articles for the Journal of Law and Economics."[3]

This plethora of "experts" all came from similar if not identical backgrounds and universities. They collectively may have assumed that each director or the executives individually and collectively were taking care of risky matters. They simply could not, given time spent, have a full and real insight on Enron's affairs. Enron's governance became a ritual, beautifully choreographed five times a year. It was fully at odds with the extremely complex and demanding contractions underlying the company's financial dealings.

Arthur Andersen, with operations all over the globe, was Enron's auditor. In June 2002 Enron was found guilty of obstructing justice. While the conviction was later overturned due to the trial judge's erroneous instructions to the jury that convicted the firm, Arthur Andersen lost the trust of its worldwide clients and never returned to its former glory.[4] It continues to operate in a much smaller manner under the banner of Andersen Global, its consulting arm, now operating under the name Accenture, split off from the auditing practice before the scandal broke.

As stated, the Enron episode prompted changes to board governance worldwide, and particularly to audit practices at board level. In our view, the key risk was too much homogeneity and collegiality, insufficient independence and thoroughness in the exercise of the board's fiduciary responsibilities, and a surrounding governance culture and ecosystem that fell too easily in line with a poor failing governance practice. This seemed to make it difficult and at some point, impossible for individual board members to take meaningful and responsible supervisory decisions and actions. It is as unfathomable as the Everest story we presented in the first section of this chapter.

More effective board selection and greater attention to the simple, yet key counterfactual question as to whether something was not possibly amiss would have contributed to investigating the risks facing the firm, with possible mitigation when this was still feasible. Executive incentives loom large in this story. More radical leadership should have emerged from one of the existing characters. The long term of the Chairman, with a rapidly complexifying business, is also another "red line" that was easily crossed by all, including regulators. The root cause of this debacle again finds its roots in a failing governance practice.

In the end, the company disappeared not because it was not innovative, but because it was too innovative, and the board did not adjust its decisions in the face of the increased corporate complexity. The innovation spilled into the way accounts were presented to a board that seemed solidly asleep to the realities unfolding under their supervisory watch. The fact that Enron was presented as an energy company rather than the financial company it really was may have contributed to put regulatory authorities to sleep as well.

Finally, the example illustrates the lack of a responsible and competent owner, or owner group. Though the Chairman and some executives may have felt like owners, they also failed in that dimension. Skilling, who Lay appointed early 2001 as Enron CEO, unexpectedly resigned his position on August 14, 2001, citing personal reasons and soon sold large amounts of his Enron shares. He was found guilty of 19 counts, ranging from conspiracy, insider trading, making false statements to auditors, and securities fraud, and sentenced to 24 years in prison. Lay was found guilty of ten counts of securities fraud and died three months before his scheduled sentencing. Fastow, who was fired shortly before Enron filed for bankruptcy, made a final trade with federal authorities. He entered into a plea agreement and cooperated with investigators. This allowed him to be sentenced to only six years in prison, followed by two years of probation. He has since engaged in public speaking on the topics of business and ethics, admitting having been an unethical and unprincipled CFO at Enron.[5]

The board members, short of Lay and Skilling, walked out free, save for reputational damage of having supervised the biggest US bankruptcy at the time, only to be surpassed by Worldcom the following year.

4 Group Diversity as the Technology to Counter Individual Biases

Groups are a powerful mechanism for transforming data into information and insight, prerequisites for effective decision making. The advantages of groups in facing complex tasks are numerous and relatively well understood.[6] People tend to perform better when competing with others than when working alone, even though, as we will see, the oppositive might be the case too. Collectively groups possess more information—and have greater memory—than individuals. Effective groups also are better at correcting each other's mistakes. Groups are less likely to get stuck and pick up on each other's ideas in the way rugby players score a try as a team. Tries in rugby are very rarely scored alone.

The second point about groups is that they are beneficial if they are diverse and relatively uncorrelated: 1000 people with the same opinion are as wrong as one. Our unique histories (both genetic origins and determining live events) bring variety in our lives and make us different from others. A confrontation of diverse and independent opinions results in a forecast that is better than any single opinion. In statistics this is called *the law of large numbers.* Contrary to its name, it kicks in even if numbers are small. In group dynamics we refer to it as *the wisdom of small teams.*

It is precisely because of the prevalence of individual biases that organizational responsibility is vested in groups, and not on a single individual. It is the primary reason why Boards are composed of multiple individuals, and why CEOs are advised to listen to their executive teams, or why in certain countries like in Germany, executive committees share their responsibilities collectively, with the "CEO" being their speaker.

Groups come together to explore data and then, after due evaluation, they transform data into information that can be used for subsequent exploration of paths of success, followed by decision making. Group decisions are of course dependent on the inputs they seek, obtain, or are provided with. This transformation of data into decisions and then action can be described as taking up to five steps[7]:

1. *Data acquisition*: Data is not just brought to the group but typically sought after and searched after by the group or provided by another group.
2. *Data processing*: The data is then evaluated, analyzed, and transformed into ideas and alternative options formulated. A number of decisions that could be taken based on the analysis are formulated.
3. *Decision*: Data analysis having concluded, it is time for the group to "take" a decision from among the alternative decisions prepared by the group.[8] A narrative explaining the choice is typically arrived at as well, for communication to all concerned stakeholders, including of course, those individuals that are essential to execution. *Execution*: The time for executing the decision has now come, no more time for argumentation about what the best decision might be, or for exploring options further. Results should indeed now "result," on the condition of course that decisions are well executed,

and that exploration of the challenges and their agreed resolution was flawless. *Evaluation*: At some point, execution has been completed, a has been reached, or further execution is viewed as undesirable. At that time, it is necessary to evaluate both the outcomes generated and the way these outcomes have been obtained. This step is often skipped, or done too superficially or hastily. Yet, the step is key to benefiting from the lessons that defeat or victory leaves us with—and which may be their greatest gift. The effects of the decision process, the decision itself, and its communication are reviewed for accuracy and effectiveness, and for errors. Outcomes generated are compared to expectations and objectives, and lessons learned for improvement should the issue have to be faced again.

The first requirement for a group to function well and to creatively come to solutions is a good process. This truism cannot be emphasized enough. The dish is only good as each step of the cooking. That requires all steps to be well executed, all members focusing on the same step at any time, working thoroughly rather than superficially or hastily, and ultimately sloppily. Therein lies one of the main tasks of the Chair or group leader: ensure that the group goes through all steps thoroughly, together, all members contributing positively, and with the group following the process in the right sequence. This is what is called *process leadership*, a fundamental requirement for a group to produce positive results in its exchanges.

Individuals are biased, no question about this, and every day there is more research on how deep biases run. These are hard to change. A good process counters one bias with another one in the oppositive direction. So, the answer to effective group decision making is not to ensure or pretend that members are unbiased—none are on all issues—but rather to focus on a good process that recognizes the prevalence and multiplicity of biases and that addresses them up front, and integrates them in an unbiased way, for the "wisdom of small teams" to prevail. A good process integrates the diverse views in a final decision, with the aim that the final decision reflects the knowledge of each of the members, biases being substantially reduced if not cancelled in a dialectic that converges to a good enough "true" answer.

Teams and groups can thus be seen as a "technology" that transforms data into information and then decisions and implementation, with feedback and evaluation at the end. One should be aware, however, that groups are not necessarily better than individuals in collaborative processes, as Nemeth and Nemeth-Brown convincingly argue.[9] At each stage of the above decision process, biases may emerge. For example, successful conclusion of a process may be hijacked by "influencers" who turn the decision their way. These can be formal authorities or informal ones:

- A powerful President or Chairman of a board has formal authority. The Chairman can allow or disallow agenda items to be discussed, can close meetings, or not hold them at all, rendering his board ineffective. Equally, a President might have the power to summarily dismiss or fire dissenting voices or simply not call upon them.
- An "expert" in a group may be considered to have deeper knowledge that makes others hesitant to question options being recommended and tempted to follow the expert rather blindly. This behavior is especially common among non-executive directors impressed by data-rich expert explanations of executives or experts.
- Anchoring through strategic sequencing—that is, the order in which group members voice their views can affect how individuals react. If the first three members vehemently support one option, it becomes very difficult for the fourth member to suggest a contrary path.

Having recognized that some conditions need to be validated for a team to work effectively, we present a framework that is useful in validating whether conditions for effective group work are met. This will be the object of the next section.

5 An Alignment Framework for Effective Teamwork: The OVRxRPxI Model

Effective team leadership requires a structured and aligned approach to managing the various dimensions that define and affect team collaboration. Such an approach is provided by a framework, called *OVRxRPxI*, corresponding to the first letters of the six dimensions fundamental to structuring teams for performance (see Fig. 11.3). The framework prescribes a well-defined order in which the six dimensions need to be defined. These six basic dimensions are[10]:

- *Objectives*: The first necessity for effective collaboration in a team, whether board, management, or any team, is agreement and commitment to a common objective, or set of objectives, which the team aims to accomplish. This immediately sets a direction for the team and a yardstick to measure progress and success. The objective refers explicitly to an objective pursued by the team collectively (e.g., reach the top as a team, or ensure one team member reaches the top), and not to the individual objectives that motivate team members. Indeed, some members may truly wish to go to the top, whereas others may desire to go up as long as the climb is not too hard, and that they feel like doing it on the day of the climb. Others may climb the mountain as long as the walk is interesting, while Sherpas do it largely for the money. The common qualifier for objectives is that they be SMART, namely Specific, Measurable, Attainable, Realistic, and Time-bounded.[11]

- *Values*: Values are the first glue for building trust among team members. These values are assumed to drive the behaviors expected from team members. Ex-post they might be regarded as obvious: they consist, for example, of values such as honesty, integrity, excellence, or support of team members. What is challenging here is not only for a team to be explicit about these values, or to be complete, but rather for all team members to truly and consistently abide by these values. Honesty, for example, is clear but requires courage: how else will a team member admit to the leader that the latter is no longer trusted? So, the issue is not just knowing the values, but foremost, practicing them.
- *Rules of the Game*: Every team needs discipline. Discipline is obtained through the application of rules that guide the team. Rules are the easiest way to impose discipline. The 2 pm return time for teams climbing Everest is a clear example of this. Every functional team has rules that exist not because team members can cite them, but because they all abide by them.
- *Roles*: Teams have several tasks to accomplish, such as carrying food and equipment, laying fixed ropes, watching time, or guiding individuals across multiple challenges (climbing rocks, passing crevasses, …). People are given responsibility for tasks, and for ensuring that the tasks are correctly executed. In the Everest climb, a big miss was that the fixed ropes were not laid as they were supposed to. To this day, no one knows why they were not there. One reason is that it is, to this day, not clear who had been given the responsibility for ensuring that the ropes were in place.
- *Processes*: Assigning team members to laying ropes, bringing the ropes up, ensuring that the ropes have the desired length, and that they have been laid correctly are the steps (or atoms) of a process. Exploration of options, counterfactual thinking, and decision making are steps defining a decision process. Processes are the way team members collaborate to produce outcomes. Each process involves several operations, typically performed in a sequence. If the process is incorrectly described or executed, it will result in

errors in outcomes that are unavoidable. A person involved in the operation may not be qualified, not really motivated, or maybe insufficiently trained or attentive. Motivation is thus key for output performance, which leads us to the last generic tool, which is also fundamental to team success.
- *Individual Commitment*: As suggested above all the above descriptions remain virtual precepts unless the individuals concerned are fully motivated and committed to these prescriptions. Therein lies the final and, regularly, the most challenging task of the leader, and also of each of the team members, to dedicate one's full energies to carry out what is expected and agreed upon in prior planning meetings. Without individual action and thus commitment, all team prescriptions will amount to nothing, and no new reality or realization will occur.

The Solidarity Platform: Forming the Team by Defining What Members Share

The most important task when structuring a team is its *objective(s)*. It also defines that the performance will be measured. It is the first glue among team members. It thus ought to be set carefully, as it is the key leverage for everything else team members do. Once people no longer commit to the objective, they pursue private agendas at the expense of the team's performance. Energies are wasted pursuing personal objectives at odds with team performance.

Values come next and have to be subordinated to the objective. Not all values are useful, nor even helpful; some may be counterproductive. For example, if the objective is innovation, compliance is not a great value for the team; diving with sharks is inconsistent with a "safety first" approach. So, values are the second glue for a team. They facilitate delegation, trust, and collaboration, and are the first way to support the realization of the team's objective. In mountaineering, key values are self-reliance (or autonomy), consideration for others, integrity, character, and a respect for the rugged environment that a mountain presents climbers with.[12]

Rules of the game are key for linking team members with each other. Every team has them, and they complement through their prescriptive nature the aspirational values the team members have subscribed to. They are meaningful only if people can be trusted (which is a value); hence values, in the rank ordering, come after rules of the game as they give greater credence to the rules of the game.

All these three elements (objectives, value, and rules) are to be adhered to by all members in the team and form the team's *basic platform or approach*.

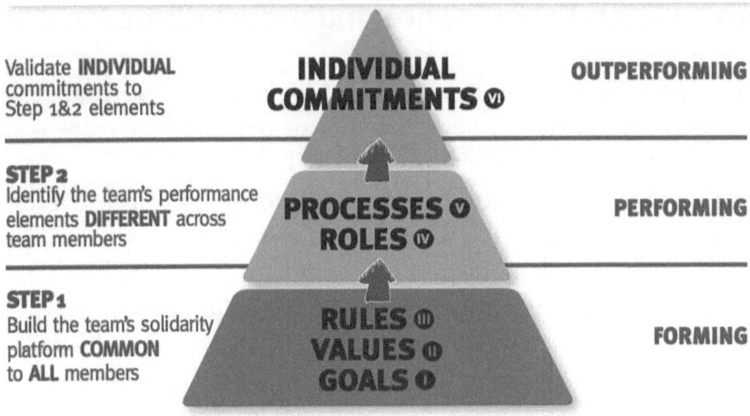

Fig. 11.1 OVRxRPxI: a hierarchical model for high-performance teams. Source: Goudsmet and Van der Heyden (2023)

The OVR tripod is the basis for forming the team and ensuring solidarity (rather than performance, which comes next). It acts like a contract that cements the team members to each other, building trust and commitment. This platform is *common* to all team members, is definitely not optional, and is managed by all team members collectively, not solely by the team manager or by one member (Fig. 11.1).

The Distinct Elements of Performance

Having framed the team's objectives, the leader will then turn to the tasks to be performed, allocating them to team members. Allocations will be made based on talents and capabilities. Team members' commitments to these roles will fuel all team members.

The next step is to invite those responsible for the tasks to define the process(es) that will be followed to accomplish the task. In our hierarchical model, it is the member responsible for the task who also is responsible for defining the process that will be followed to accomplish the task. Should the process be given to him or her, then that process becomes a rule of the game for the team. This is where motivation comes in, as members, like all of us, are more motivated by decisions they make themselves than by decisions that are imposed upon them. Hence, in this hierarchical model, those given roles also receive the autonomy to define the process for ensuring the accomplishment of the task.

The Key to High Performance: Individual Commitments

The final element underlines the duality of high team performance: teams do not perform, individuals do, hence the performance of the team is the result of individual actions. Yet, they are the final dimension of the hierarchical model for all the intermediate dimensions need to align to provide the optimal context for the actions to lead to the achievement of the team's goals. That is why motivation is such an important ingredient for individual actions to be forcefully executed and as intended for optimal team performance.

Alignment is necessary and requires all the attention of the team's members. This leads us to consider another duality, that of private agendas and preferences possibly not aligned with team goals. If that were to be the case, these would likely act against the team's success. However, it is important to note that this does not need to be the case. Objectives being SMART, they are time-bound (T), so commitment to a team is necessarily of limited duration. The central idea of the high performance OVRxRPxI model is to underline that commitment is to the solidarity platform (OVR), and to people assuming roles (R) and leading processes (P) that ensure that objectives will be met. Commitment is thus not to individuals, as often understood or practiced in relational cultures, but to individuals fulfilling roles in the accomplishment of the team's objective. As an example, this model is fully consistent with a team leader promising full support for a member's future career if the latter performs well during a project, even if the member is eager to leave the organization following the project's conclusion. In this scenario, the leader, concerned with his team member's welfare engages the member on her or his preferences, and using the latter's private agenda to commit that member even more strongly to the team's success. That is the sense in which private agendas can be used to further align team members with the projects' objectives. That then is the final task of the team leader, ensuring that all team members are personally committed to the team's success, and to the way the team has been constituted.

To ensure this outcome, it is useful for individual agendas to be shared among team members, as this provides the opportunity for members, and especially their leaders, to align their teammates with the team. The principle is simple: alignment with team objectives is the overriding priority, and that pertains to private agendas as well which need to be considered only as the final element. If individual commitments prove infeasible with the team's objectives and constitution, exit from the team, or refusal to join the team is the likely outcome.

A clear statement of values and rules of the game will greatly induce personal behaviors in line with objectives. It will also provide leaders with the authority and means required to deal with private preferences of team members, which remains one of the key challenges in managing teams, as the Everest example illustrates so clearly. Only after objectives, values, and rules of the game have been specified, as well as roles allocated and processes defined, the question of each team member's full commitment to the team can be validated, and only then. The reader will note that the OVRxRPxI framework demands commitment to the solidarity platform, or to individuals filling certain roles, and not to individuals per se.

6 The Imax Team Illustrating the OVRxRPxI High-Performance Model

To illustrate our high-performance model, we tested it on David Breashears, who led his IMAX team on the mountain. Because conditions were too crowded for filming, he decided to bring the team down, waiting for the other teams to return to base camp after their ascent. The mountain would then belong to them and would provide better filming conditions. With the other teams running into trouble, the project changed. They became a rescue team before resuming their ascent on their second trial.

We summarize how the model is validated by the approach chosen by Breashears's team. We review each of the six dimensions of the framework in turn.

- *Objective*: Their objective was to make an IMAX movie about Everest growing a couple of inches each year and how their team, including well-known Everest novices like Norgay's son, apprehended the mountain. Reaching the top was never the main objective for the team. IT was considered an option if things went well. The principal objective was to film Everest with an IMAX camera, which had never been done before, and represented a first on the mountain. IMAX would provide fantastic shots showing the majesty of the mountain like never before. The climb would provide further opportunities for great views and interesting stories about apprehending climbing the earth's tallest mountain. Consistent with his philosophy of mountaineering, Breashears considers it important to avoid the trap of experience and routine. His method for doing this was to bring novelty to each of his climbs. This year the novelty was assured by the IMAX camera:

no one had ever been able to bring such a heavy camera, and the thousand meters of film, up the mountain. The other novelty was to bring novices on the mountain, who were encouraged to express their concerns and fears to the more experienced climbers. This would contribute to keeping the latter prudent. As soon as they reached base camp, the film already was a success, as they already had made film history at that point. The only question then was how high they might go to film. And indeed, they did reach the top, but missed having film to shoot there. But the *optionality and modularity* that was designed into their project would withstand this miss.

- *Values*: Breashears paid particular attention to values when selecting team members. He wants team members that are selfless, have respect for Everest, are great explorers (prudent and daring), and have standards of excellence in all they do. Consequently, they are a real team, willing to drive themselves hard and not afraid of being driven hard.
- *Rules of the Game*: David's key rule on Everest is "going up is optional, coming down is mandatory." The key to face uncertainty, according to Breashears, is to have slack, dispose of well-rehearsed options, and being able to call off the ascent. These are repeated like mantras to the members of the team, so that even the leader cannot change these by himself when guiding the team on the mountain. The other rule concerns his producer: just as one respects the mountain, one respects the contract signed with the producer, but without allowing the producer to become the leader and issue dictates from California, unaware of the real conditions facing the team.
- *Roles*: Self-aware and driven, Breashears likes assistants that are better than him. That provides forced governance inside the team: no major decisions are made without the input of assistants. This collective leadership provides self-governance to the team. The consistent involvement of David's assistants makes him a better leader and contributes to securing the project and the team. He also chooses his assistants to be complementary, Ed Viesturs taking care of the logistics and guiding, whereas Schauer could take over the filming. The project thus has contingencies and alternate leaders should Breashears be out of action due to an accident. Like the assistants, each member on the team has his specific role. The "beginners" are the main actors in the film and provide freshness to the team. Cleverly, Breashears engages them to manage risk, encouraging them to ask questions on concerns they may have on their way up, even if these concerns derive from their lack of experience, and the fear this lack may generate. Their questions help the "old hands" remain careful during the climb.

- *Processes*: Breashears is aware that high performance is reached through processes, continuously refined and improved toward excellence. The filming equipment was tested in Utah, where the camera was slimmed down to half its final weight, greatly reducing the risk of the entire project. Team selection is paramount and well-honed, as is the planning of 150 scenarios. On Everest, there is not enough time or oxygen to think, so David relies substantially on pre-planned and tested routines communicated to the participants ahead of the climb. Participants are engaged in the exercises by being challenged to identify scenarios they might change and improve. When they do, the proposed changes are discussed and validated. Feedback and communication are key, with the possibility of a series of adaptations each hour of the day when climbing conditions change.
- *Individual Commitment*: Once the above dimensions are specified, the final question to each member, who by then knows the team's climbing objectives, principles, strategies, and tactics, becomes straightforward: now that you know the project, and its various components, are you ready to commit? Are there missing elements that might need to be provided? Would this allow us to gain your commitment? This final question is fundamental to make the whole approach to climbing an inclusive and co-created one. Each member thus contributes some elements under the guiding principle: if you have a better idea, let us know, let us discuss, and if the idea is good, we adopt! This way, commitment from the team members is gained by removing barriers to gaining this commitment while the team is reinforced as a result of managing this last dimension of the model.

The IMAX team's climb finally might be described as hitting high performance. The film earned Hollywood fame and other filming awards. A great story, well filmed, beautiful scenes, but also a team both very well prepared, able to assist the other teams during the tragedy that were failing, and concluding with a climb of the majestic mountain. The failure of the other teams, paradoxically, helped the IMAX team, changing the scenario and subject of the film. The poor luck of the other teams became their break. What had started as a film about Everest and novices discovering the mountain on their first climb became a film about tragedy, humanity, leadership, and loss … in the most beautiful and most cruel of settings. The Breashears team validated Pasteur's statement: "Luck favors the prepared mind."

7 Group Biases and How to Counter Them: Wisdom of the Crowd, Devil's Advocacy, and Dialectical Inquiry

The very need to have a common objective, common values, as well as rules of the game *creates new biases*. Indeed, people instinctively perceive that, with team members very similar to them, they should reach the same conclusion. This implies that any difference will be first perceived as "antagonism" and may then be taken to a more personal level. Moreover, group homogeneity increases the tendency to take consensus for granted, to give preferential treatment to teammates and unfavorable treatment to member of other teams, and to create silo mentalities.

More specifically the biases that groups forming teams and members of teams might suffer from are the following:

- *Ingroup homogeneity bias*: individuals see members of their own group as being more homogeneous than members of other groups.
- *Projection bias*: the tendency to unconsciously assume that others share one's thoughts and values.
- *Ingroup preferential treatment*: the tendency for people to give preferential treatment to others they perceive to be members of their own groups.
- *False consensus effect*: the tendency to overestimate the degree to which others agree with them.
- *Fundamental attribution error*: the tendency to overemphasize personality-based explanations for behaviors observed in others.
- *Halo effect*: the tendency for impressions (positive or negative) of a person, product, company, … to "spill over" into similar feelings or opinions in other areas of that person, product, company or related people or areas.
- *Illusion of transparency*: people overestimate others' ability to know them, and they also overestimate their ability to know others.
- *Illusion of asymmetric insight*: people perceive their knowledge of their peers to surpass their peers' knowledge about them.
- *Egocentric bias*: people claim greater importance to themselves and their opinions than reality warrants.

These multiple biases may be summarized by stating that people tend to be kinder to themselves than to others and that the same applies to the groups they belong to. People also are naturally closer to who they are with and how those close to them behave than to the groups they decided not to join or do not even know. Furthermore, people tend to underestimate the role of context and luck, while overestimate the effectiveness and importance of their own actions and thoughts.

Moreover, homogeneity within the group will impede brainstorming and renders deviations more difficult to accept. Group decision making—as a "technology" or process—continuously has to manage a constant tension between two opposite needs for any group:

- *Homogeneity*: This tendency allows the group to more readily agree on matters. It facilitates the efficient and smooth functioning of the group. The danger is that homogeneity reinforces and amplifies group think and group biases.
- *Heterogeneity*: This characteristic permits different viewpoints to be considered, substantially mitigates risks of group think in framing and herding, which are the two most pernicious biases affecting groups.

To avoid herding and erroneous framing, it is necessary to continuously stimulate brainstorming, exchange, and discussion. This is what heterogeneity promotes and provides. A good "middle" solution is simply to ask individual contributors—individually or in sub-groups—to come to the group event with their estimates or solutions discussed prior to the meeting. If the individuals or sub-groups are sufficiently diverse, heterogeneity results and convergence can be tested. Another technique is to ask certain groups to assume the role of promoter while others are assigned to be devil's advocates. We return to this later in this chapter.

When heterogeneity is insufficiently managed, the risk is that chaos may arise. One should never forget that diversity operates exponentially: another member adds a large number of interactions with the group he joins. Smaller groups thus have an easier time managing diversity. Multiple research results confirm that smaller teams have higher satisfaction among members, communicate and support each other better, and tend to be more productive.[13] One of the factors killing bigger teams is the Ringelmann effect, which is that individuals refer less effort to achieve an objective when they work in a group than when they work alone. The phenomenon is also referred to as "social loafing."

Larger groups tend to polarize in an in-group and an out-group. This quickly stops exchange from being constructive and cumulative. Divisiveness increasingly kills any hope of progress. A degree of homogeneity is thus required to allow any team to function and to counter the tendency for a team to break up. That is the sense of the solidarity platform consisting of the first three dimensions of the OVRxRPxI model: shared agreements on objectives, values, and rules of the game create a degree of homogeneity necessary for a team to operate effectively, including when it grows. It recedes the team size constraint on effectiveness.

Our third and final remark pertains to the multiplicative nature of the OVRxRPxI model: a team can fail because of a failure in only one of the six basic dimensions. This is the non-compensating characteristic of the model: failure in one of the dimensions can only marginally be compensated by increased performance in the other dimensions. Each dimension thus has its own specificities. The first three dimensions are collective (Objectives, Values, and Rules), the next two pertain to particular individuals or sub-groups, and the last one is strictly individual, albeit in a team context.

The non-compensating characteristic of the model, in addition to its hierarchical nature, is what makes the model demanding: for a team to perform, it must do well in all six dimensions, as failure in one of the dimensions opens the team to failure, and it must address the various dimensions in a strict order to truly be cumulative. Few teams in our experience, when diagnosed according to the model, score well on all dimensions. That makes the diagnosis useful in the identification of risk factors which may cause a team to be inefficient, and require more effort than would be necessary, or to be ineffective and fail altogether.

In conclusion, groups, notwithstanding their diversity, are subject to biases as well.

Having argued the prevalence and pervasiveness of individual and group biases, it is time to turn to address how leaders and groups might structure their decision-making processes to mitigate the main risks posed by these biases. We broadly provide three types of answers in this book.

The first alternative to a linear, top-down process of decision making by an enlightened leader is radically at odds with top-down leadership: it consists of not relying on a single expert individual but on a large number of individuals, giving them equal weights and simply averaging out their answers. The original reference dates back to Aristotle in his essay on *Politics*, where he writes that "it is possible that the many, though individually good men, yet when they come together may be better, not individually, but collectively." The classic reference goes back to Francis Galton, who observed in 1906 that the median answer among 800 people who were asked to guess (independently of each other) the weight of an ox in a fair in Plymouth lies within 1% of the true weight.[14] This result has been replicated many times and is best known as the *wisdom of the crowd*.

Remarking that not all crowds are wise, Surowiecki identified conditions that render a crowd wise: *diversity and independence of opinion*, *decentralization* by which he means that individuals can draw on *local knowledge*, *aggregation of individual judgments* into a collective forecast, and *trust in the collective group regarded as fair-minded* (as opposed to being driven by emotional purposes or other pressures that would lead it to lose its fairness). Surowiecki presents bubbles as resulting from judgments that are insufficiently independent and diverse. Unfortunately, the final outcomes of a crowd are subject to the way people in the group interact. What is a better average of independent views may degenerate when people influence each other and interact.

Moreover, Surowiecki's result is limited to the estimation of continuous quantities (like sizes, e.g., of individuals or returns). The key choices boards face typically concern choices among a limited number of options (e.g., acquisition of another firm, hiring of a CEO, going to another country). The wisdom of crowds result is less useful there and more useful when estimating parameter values that might influence these choices. Certainly, the conditions under which crowds are wise are to be retained.

To support the choice among a finite number of alternatives, the *Devil's Advocacy* and *Dialectical Inquiry* processes are the two best known methods (see Fig. 11.2). In their most basic form, both methods consist of a practice of constantly asking and exploring what might be wrong with a given alternative before deciding to implement it, if it survives this brutal testing. What favors one alternative often does not favor another, so both practices end up clarifying the pros and cons of both alternatives. Devil's Advocacy counters the risk

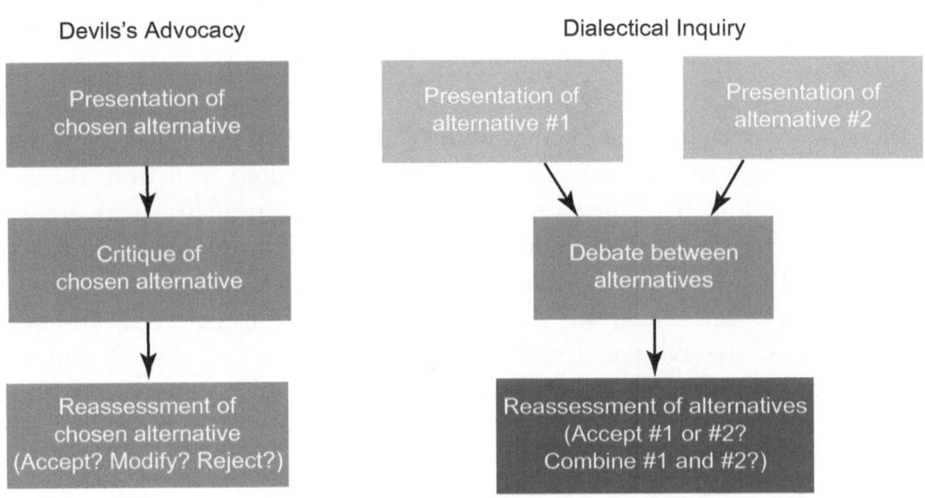

Fig. 11.2 Devil's Advocacy or Dialectical Inquiry processes and structures

of overconfidence by leaders who are thus forced to look at the downside of any decision, reducing the ignorance of risk. It also prompts the generation of mitigating actions.

Devil's Advocacy would have forced the AC and MM teams to address questions such as:

- Could it be that we might reach the summit, but late? What implications might this have?
- Could someone in the group collapse? If this happens, what do we do?
- Weather conditions might make an ascent impossible. Are we ready for that?
- What if (one of) our leaders or members start suffering from altitude sickness or delusion?
- Under what conditions might it be better to turn down rather than to keep climbing?

The practice of *Dialectical Inquiry*, where the leader explicitly asks his advisors or group members for alternative scenarios and options. These are then analyzed, improving the team's understanding of arguments for and against the various alternatives. It typically leads to the generation of new alternatives that combine the advantages of distinct options.

In Dialectical Inquiry, it is useful to ask two or more distinct groups to find solutions and to generate alternate scenarios. Each group is responsible for evaluating alternatives and selecting one or a few of them. The whole group is then tasked with commenting and eventually selecting (e.g., by voting) the best alternative among the various solutions presented by the various sub-groups.

There was little Dialectical Inquiry or Devil's Advocacy in the AC group because of the commanding style of its leader. Both the group and the leader paid a heavy price for this. There was one counterfactual sub-group, however, which consisted of the four members that split on their own from the AC group. These four had started to discuss the leadership of Rob Hall among them, whom they found did not pay sufficient attention to vulnerabilities in the team. They were clearly right. They decided to leave the team as a subgroup. That is where they left the team to its own deficiencies. They missed the courage to share this analysis in a more open fashion with the entire group and its leader. Having done so would have required confronting the authoritarian leader but might have saved the leader and several team members from their fatal run at the summit. Then this is an ex-post comment, and we were not there with them.

As for the MM group, the practice of autonomy certainly attracted stronger members. Those feeling more insecure would have chosen the *apparently* safer commanding leadership of Rob Hall. Stronger members are also better at generating alternative options and at executing them. It was in the absence of their leader that the MM group became a team, working collectively and debating the better alternatives at saving themselves on their way back to Camp IV. Their lives depended on it. The absence of Rob Hall proved fatal to the AC team, while a similar absence of their leader allowed the MM group to become a team, sharing a common objective, survival. What the story—including the account of David Breashears's team—indicates is that the teams and sub-teams that followed the precepts of the OVRxRPxI model appear to do better than those that did not.

8 Simple Scoring of Team Performance

Before concluding this chapter on high-performance teams, we provide a simple scale for measuring performance. Many scoring rules are too complex, creating unnecessary complexity and fog. In our applications, we have appreciated working with a simple scoring rule which more effectively supported feedback that then proved useful when working with owners, boards of directors, or executive groups. It has been our experience that the virtue of simplicity of a rating scale is that it fosters effective feedback and quality follow-up. For example, it is easily applied to score the quality of a board meeting, the CEO's performance, or a product's quality.

Figure 11.3 shows our rating scale. It consists of a double pyramid, each consisting of three elements: (1) a "bar" which defines the acceptable result that the group needs to achieve and that sharply separates the two domains of performance; (2) three ratings above this bar which connote a positive performance, and (3) three ratings below this bar, corresponding to a negative performance. This defines 3 × 2 = 6 possible ratings, *above or below "the bar."*

The first point to notice is that the presence of the bar indicates the existence of a "must deliver" outcome, and that the scale is relative to this bar. Some leaders are biased when setting the bar, which is regrettable. If set too low, the team is likely to underperform relatively to what it can do; if set too high, it leads to discouragement and a sentiment of unfairness, "the dice being stacked against the team." We should also say that, as is very often the case in governance issues, there is no perfectly correct position of the bar; what is to be avoided is indeed one of the two above outcomes: a bar set too low, or too high. The key parameter though is the existence of a bar. What is below, is

Fig. 11.3 A simple and effective performance management system (Alain Goudsmet, *Attitude Coach*, Kluwer, 2003)

"nonacceptable" and defines the area of loss of the actor or player. It also incentivizes the actor to take risk to exit this area.

The three positive outcomes "above the bar" are the following:

- *Satisfactory*: This is when the team—with its individual and group biases—delivers the results that were expected from it, that it aimed for, and that were achieved. One can then say that the team has been *effective* and *delivered the results expected from it.*
- *Performing*: This is when the team delivers more than what is expected from it. This can be in one or more attributes (cost, time, effort, …) and results in a team being not only effective but also *efficient*. Such a level is often defined as a motivator for a team to develop its capabilities by being coached "to go the extra mile." This practice becomes the basis for *continuous improvement*, where improved performance is gradually understood and then mastered. This practice is called *Kaizen* in manufacturing and has been core to Toyota's leadership in the automobile industry. Efficiency also is key when pursuing innovation, as innovation is terribly demanding of additional resources, time in particular. Hence, innovative teams that are efficient in meeting its requirements leave them enough time to explore improvements, and to aim for high performance.
- *Highly Performing or Outperforming*: This is when the team achieves a performance level that defines a new standard of excellence—for itself, for the

company, or for the industry. This level then literally defines "best practice"—at this time AND consistent with this scoring rule, to be improved in the future. Continuously improving teams reject the notion of best practice, as today's best practice is superseded by tomorrow's "better practice." Hence, they continuously search for such "better practice."

When presenting teams, executive groups, or boards with this scale, we have found ready adoption. We believe that one reason of its ready use is that this scoring rule is as much psychological as it is numerical. It is also the scale that is commonly used by athletes and sport teams.[15]

The bottom part of the scale is a mirror of the top part. It rates outcomes "below the bar:"

- *Unsatisfactory*: This is when the team—with its individual and group biases—does NOT deliver the results that were expected from it and that it aimed for. One can then say that the team was *ineffective*.
- *Disappointing*: This is when the team delivers MUCH LESS than what was expected from it. This can be in one or several attributes (such as cost, time, effort, …), or in failing in a less dramatic way on several dimensions. Such a performance rating is a dire warning to the team that it needs to improve its performance level radically and quickly. Teams that procrastinate in explaining the many reasons why they did not achieve better, and why their failure is to be accepted and understood, signal in doing so that they do not have a performance culture. They cannot be trusted to do better or to constructively address their challenges, demonstrating the opposite of a Kaizen culture, one sometimes refers to such culture as a "BlaBla" culture.
- *Failing*: This is when the team achieves at such poor level that the only word that aptly summarizes their performance is "failure." Shame must be the prevailing emotion at such level. The greater the self-awareness and rapid acceptance of this poor rating, the more hope is allowed for a turnaround in the future. Then the team may not be around, having found to be completely ineffective.

This rating scale presents two great advantages. The first is to allow rapid and clear feedback on achieved results, allowing a rapid and honest result-based discussion. Such a rapid feedback loop is essential to continued commitment and improvement, particularly when things do not go well. The leader who regularly asks and provides feedback based on this scale will trigger the discussions that are vital for sustaining performance on the team and will see her or his effectiveness confirmed, if not grow.

The second advantage is that it allows a deeper preparation of scenarios and strategies at the planning stage. The performance pyramid leads the team in looking for options that might deliver the sought-for Performance and even High Performance, using the terms of Fig. 11.3. The bottom part of the scale corresponds to probing for things that might go wrong and produce ineffective and possibly failing outcomes. This is the domain of ex-ante *risk assessment*, a key practice of performing teams. This avoids teams experiencing these uncomfortable situations by devising strategies that avoid such negative outcomes.

9 Lessons for Owners, Boards, and Management

Having gone to excessive length over this tragic 1996 Everest story, we conclude by making explicit the lessons of the story of these teams for owners, supervisory boards, and managers.

- Everest in this story is a metaphor for the quest that is being followed by owners, boards, or executives. The first lesson that the story holds is that most people that die on the mountain do so after reaching the summit. It is important to go up, but the most important is to live another day, where other "Everests" can be attempted. In modern parlance, sustainability of the firm is more important than being named once "firm of the year." Many CEOs earning that honor—like Carlos Ghosn or Jack Welch—indeed do not end well. This is why in this book we have given so much attention to the story in this book.
- Pursuing this metaphor, owners might be thought of as project leaders, board members as guides and supervisors, and executives as the main operators of the project.
- Biases, conscious and unconscious, are at the root of most errors and failures, not because people know they do things wrong, but because they do the wrong thing with purpose, thinking they are right.
- "We see the world not as it is, but as we are or as we wish it was." (Anaïs Nin)
- The most dangerous is in not recognizing that we are biased or susceptible to bias. As is stated, problems come not so much from people who know they don't know but rather from people who think they know when they don't. Humility and continued self-questioning are a virtue among board members.

- Owners, board members, and senior executives are particularly susceptible to biases, which at board level, just as in the Everest case, can have huge consequences. In fact, every board meeting, and every project can be conceived of as an Everest.
- Leaders' biases often are reinforced through group think by the entire team. Leaders' biases are countered through greater independence and diversity of inputs, as illustrated by the wisdom of team principles, Devil Advocacy, and Dialectical Inquiry practices.
- One of the principal roots of biases is the wrong framing of the issues: issues are often framed too narrowly, or much bigger and threatening than they really are.
- One way to counter biases is by submitting decisions prior to their execution to the team for feedback. Another is by the discipline of searching for counterfactual evidence: could it be that we are wrong here, that other solutions are better, and that the decisions we envisage have consequences that are unintended and possibly quite negative?
- Biases occur at the macro-level through the adoption of a biased approach, or at the micro-level when executing steps of the approach in a biased manner.
- One particularly useful approach for ownership, supervisory, or executive boards is the OVRxRPxI high-performance model. It is a non-compensating model: errors at one level cannot be compensated by errors at a subsequent level. This framework for high-performance team dynamics is particularly applicable for owners of corporations as their first responsibility lies in the formulation of the Mission of the firm they own. Succinctly put, a firm's Mission has three dimensions: Objectives to be aimed for, Values guiding the pursuit of these objectives, and Rules that ensure consistency and provide boundaries in the pursuit of team objectives and in the applications of the Values that guide this pursuit.

Notes

1. https://www.journalofaccountancy.com/issues/2002/apr/theriseandfallofenron.html
2. https://www.govinfo.gov/content/pkg/CPRT-107SPRT80393/pdf/CPRT-107SPRT80393.pdf
3. https://www.acton.org/node/6296
4. https://en.wikipedia.org/wiki/Arthur_Andersen
5. https://en.wikipedia.org/wiki/Andrew_Fastow

6. For a good discussion of group performance we refer the reader to Chap. 10. Working Groups: Performance and Decision Making, in: *Principles of Social Psychology—1st International Edition*, by Charles Stangor et al., B.C. Open Textbook Collection, 2011.
7. This is a brief description to the fundamental decision process that will be presented and further explored in Chap. 12.
8. The words are very revealing here. The French, describing kingly tradition, "take" a decision (among those presented by the king's advisors), whereas the Americans rather "make" a decision, the leader being all powerful and enlightened, leaving the followers "to just execute"—unless the verb actually connotes the fact that the followers literally "make" the decision issued by their leader (we do not think so).
9. Charlan J Nemeth and Brendan Nemeth-Brown, Better than Individuals? The Potential Benefits of Dissent and Diversity for Group Creativity, Chapter 4 in: *Group Creativity: Innovation through Collaboration*, Paul B. Paulus and Beranrd Nijstad, Eds., Oxford University Press, 2003.
10. This model, referred to as the OVRxRPxI model, is a refinement by Alain Goudsmet and Ludo Van der Heyden of the GRPI model first presented by Richard Beckhard, in his article "Optimizing Team Building Effort" that appeared in *The Journal of Contemporary Business 1(3)*, 23–32, 1972, and further applied and popularized by Noel Tichy, for example in his book *The Leadership Engine: Building Leaders at Every Level*, by P. Pritchett, N.M. TIchy, and E. Cohen, Pritchett & Hull Associates, Inc, 1998. See Alain Goudsmet and Ludo Van der Heyden, "The 6 Dimensions of Winning Teams," *INSEAD Working Paper*, 2023.
11. George T. Doran, "There's a S.M.A.R.T way to write management's goals and objectives," *Management Review 70(11): 35–36*, 1981.
12. https://www.vanityfair.com/culture/2015/09/sandy-hill-pittman-mount-everest
13. https://georgfasching.com/team-size-dynamics-where-is-the-science-on-this/
14. James Surowiecki, *The Wisdom of Crowds*, Doubleday, 2004.
15. We learned about this scale from Alain Goudsmet, founder of the Mentally Fit Institute in Brussels, former sports coach of the Belgian Tennis and Hockey Federations, and now applying sports techniques to executives and board members (https://mentallyfit.global/en/about-mentally-fit/).

12

Fair Process Leadership: The Path to Positive and Collaborative Dynamics for Owners and Their Directors

1 Motivation

Great owners and great directors energize those they engage with. The quality of these interactions defines their leadership. Some have a talent at transmitting energies of purpose and vision and of team spirit on the journey toward that vision. Others generate emotional energies of trust, commitment, and pride. Certain owners and directors inspire with their superior intelligence and insights in their business, while others are impressing us with their entrepreneurial skills and initiatives. Finally, there are some who possess a superior sense of timing, understand momentum, and understand nearly instinctively where one is heading towards.

It is worth pausing a bit to understand the five distinct and fundamental distinct energies we, leaders and followers, all possess, albeit in various degrees and quantities. The energies that fuel our actions and behaviors are of five kinds: spiritual energies and purpose, intellectual energies in the form of understanding and insights, emotional energies in terms of motivation, support, and caring, so-called physical energies connoting decisions and actions, and, finally, energies of time, as without time nothing happens nor is transformed. As a colleague stated, without energy a body is just a corpse, and an organization is just a building. These energies fuel individuals, teams, organizations, as well as countries, put them in movement. They are shown in Fig. 12.1[1] and explained in greater detail in Appendix A.

This conceptual model of five energy batteries might appear a bit conceptual, but is intuitively clear, except perhaps for the presence of the time dimension. The latter might deserve a bit of an explanation. There is the explanation

M. Massa et al., *Value Creation for Owners and Directors*,
https://doi.org/10.1007/978-3-031-19726-0_12

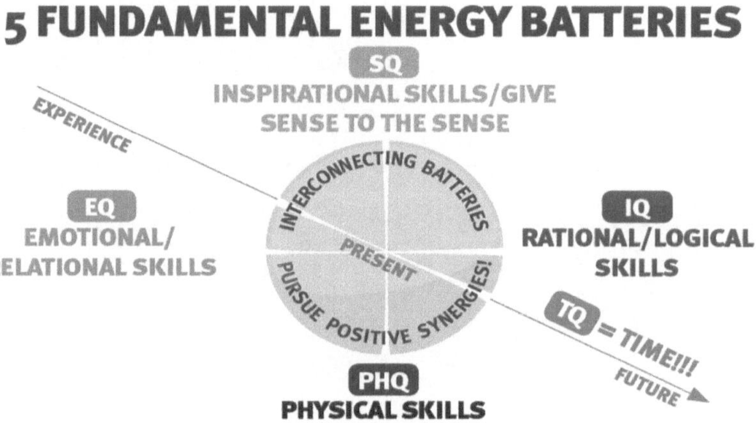

Fig. 12.1 The five energy batteries of great board members. Source: Goudsmet and Van der Heyden (2023)

in physics with Einstein's formula that relates time with matter (the physical) and speed (movement). This is also the case in life and in business: everything we do takes time, every transformation demands time, what we know comes from the past, and a big part of our motivations are generated by our visions of a better future. We often say that we are short of time, and a truism heard everywhere these days is that time is accelerating. When we stress for time, we become anxious, and our purpose quickly shifts to reducing this mounting stress and anxiety. We switch into coping or survival mode, and our energies turn to that purpose. Conversely, when we have too much time, we slacken, start loafing, lose focus, enjoy ourselves, and get diverted by things we like to do, away from the things we need to do. Entropy sets in and we start wasting time relative to the goals we pursue. So, time interacts with spirit, emotion, intellect, and action, these four batteries changing all the time. One major distinction between time and the four other energies is that time is linear, always going forward, while the other energies go up and down, in non-linear ways.

Peter Senge, the well-known leadership thinker, identified winning companies as those that learn faster and better than its competitors.[2] He also identified the five disciplines required for such organizations and their leaders. In our language of energies, the first four refer to an ability to continuously develop and deepen the energies inside the organization, be it of purpose and vision, or of the mental models that frame how people inside the organization see and understand the world around them, communicate with others, and learn with them. These mental models are rife with biases. The learning organization indeed is one that tackles and reduces these biases. Senge's Fifth

Discipline is *Systems Thinking* which he viewed as fundamental to as integrating the other disciplines characterizing the learning organization. The concept is even of higher relevance to the owners and directors of these organizations, as without their learning attitudes, it is hard to envisage the organizations possessing these capabilities.

Fair Process Leadership (or *FPL* in short) is a discipline that is remarkable in many ways. It generates positive energies (even though the exact way in which it does so is hard to know). It also can be seen as operationalizing Senge's precepts clearly and more simply, which renders it so powerful. It can also be seen as removing the fog surrounding the abstract *Level 5 Leadership* defined by Jim Collins in his classic on companies to make the jump from good to great.[3] FPL is largely unknown that addresses many issues generated by the pervasiveness of bias. The framework is particularly beneficial in the multi-layered context where owners, board members, and executives must collaborate with each other to align, and where they need to interact with other stakeholders eager to protect their interests as well.

The defining elements of *FPL* are threefold:

- *F*: a set of *Values* that are those typically associated with *Fair Play*;
- *P*: a well-defined *Process* to be followed leading to Value Creation;
- *L*: the *Leadership* that is required for the proper and continued application of fair process.

We now present these elements in greater detail.

2 Fairness at the Top

The straightforward, yet surprisingly performing FPL framework relies on a most important human feeling when it comes to sustained collaboration: fairness. However, most people immediately think of fairness as *fair share*, reflecting on whether the outcome they obtained is fair. FPL focuses on the antecedent of the outcome, which is the *process* that produced the outcome. If we take the analogy of cooking, there is a recipe (a process) to be followed, the cooks need to be fair play in terms of following the recipe and not play tricks with it, and finally a master chef ensures that the right cooks are selected and that the cooks execute well. Conversely, bad recipes, not following the recipe, playing tricks by not putting the ingredients as specified, or the absence of control by the master chef all lead to cooking disasters, like Gordon Ramsey, the famous British chef, restaurateur, and blunt TV personality, shows us in his vivid TV show where he troubleshoots failing restaurants.[4] In this chapter and the next one, we aim to illustrate how conflicts among owners, boards, executives, as well as stakeholders generally result from violations of the FPL framework and, conversely, how a disciplined application of the FPL framework reduces the probability of conflicts and mediates them, and how FPL contributes to creating the alignment between these groups, and then enables sustainable value creation, or shows that alignment is not possible, and also avoids value destruction. FPL thus is a great key to inducing positive dynamics between the firm's various stakeholders.

After elaborating on the three defining elements of FPL—fairness, process, and leadership—we illustrate the power of the framework by analyzing the rise and fall of one of the world's great leaders, who rose to the leadership of his nation and to assume its ownership in a very real sense, only to end up destroying it all: Napoleon Bonaparte.

Bonaparte's journey is a prototypical owner-manager-chair story. It is one that the owners and directors in our classes embrace, stating voluntarily that they experienced similar figures and patterns in their contexts. Indeed, FPL provides a very useful metaphorical lens through which one can quickly benchmark contemporary owners and leaders. So, the story is not so much provided for historical interest, but for demonstrating that the patterns that brought Napoleon to supreme power only to largely destroy what he had achieved to create is still occurring regularly today. Enron is one such story, and we are still waiting to see how Elon Musk will fare going forward.

Another such example, developed in Chap. 12, is the story of Carlos Ghosn. It replicates to a remarkable extent—albeit at a smaller scale and in a different context—the life of Bonaparte. Their rise is similar, both are military in their leadership approaches, and both become leaders of an empire (France and Renault-Nissan, respectively). Both end up in jail, betrayed by their team members, Longwood House on Saint Helena surely qualifying as superior to Ghosn's prison cell in Japan. The analogy supports the allegorical power of Napoleon's story, particularly when seen through the FPL angle. It leads to a key question we have regularly addressed to leaders: "Are you not in danger of becoming too Napoleonic in your leadership?" Or more pointed, "Have you ever considered you might end up like the Emperor, having lost all of what you conquered so brilliantly?"

Our main point—and one that cannot be overemphasized—is that FPL is a much greater contributor to sustainable leadership and ownership than fair share. Owners especially should also be aware that the converse also holds: the quest for greater shares that one would be entitled to often comes through

FPL violations, which will generate negative energies and impede the quest, or render it unsustainable.

In conclusion, fair play is much more central to sustainability than fair share. Indeed, one of the strong ways family firms obtain a high commitment from their employees and partners is by their willingness to sacrifice part of what could be their "fair share" for the benefit of the community because of their fair play engagements. The immediate return will be commitment in difficult situations, and sustainability of that commitment over the longer term. That makes FPL a must know for owners. For directors, it greatly contributes to effective and high-performance relations with board members, executives, and also other stakeholders.

3 Fairness Matters More so than Commonly Thought

Fairness is one of the most important human drivers. This fact has been strongly illustrated again during the pandemic with the *Black Lives Matter!* Movement. Black people denounced that they still do not enjoy the same opportunities and treatment like that of white people. The BLM call was one for social justice, equal treatment, and opportunity. This right was cemented in the 15th Amendment to the US Constitution, voted in 1870, which guaranteed equal rights regardless of "race, color or previous condition of servitude." The #MeToo movement was of a similar vein. It confronted societies with a radical question, remarkably asked in the beginning of this twenty-first century: hasn't time come to provide equal and fair treatment to women and black people? That the question could be so strongly asked in the US and gain such strong echo—the land of Liberty and Opportunity—is not the smallest paradox. Then again, like in Boston's Tea Party in 1773, the cry originated there, and that is to America's credit and the world became better as a result.

With wealth comes a greater abundance of choices and better options, like exiting crowded cities, enjoying better health and superior medical treatment, and legal protection when needed. Such realities immediately raise the issue of fairness as equality of opportunity. To avoid confusion, we all must be aware of the distinction between inequality in outcomes—instances of unfair shares—and inequality in opportunities—indicating unfair play. The notion of Fair Process Leadership underlines an insufficiently known fact: fair process deserves greater attention than fair share. Indeed, communist regimes intent on the pursuit of equal shares have largely failed precisely because of excessive

unfair process leadership, a notion we still need to define more precisely. Democracies face substantial inequalities which are endemic to them. These inequalities need to be addressed in a fair process manner for these differences to be societally acceptable and avoid revolutions or uprisings. FPL can be described as the intelligent management of inequalities in shares and endowment. This is one of the key argumentations for the practice of FPL by owners and directors, who precisely are people who have earned and likely received substantial shares. Rather than to pursue our sociological reasoning, which risks leading us far from our subject, we illustrate the difference between fair share and fair process through two well-known games, the so-called Ultimatum and Dictator games, which refer to experiments that have been carried out on many people.

The Ultimatum game was first described by Nobel laureate John Harsanyi.[5] One person (the "proposer") is given a certain sum of money. The proposer is then asked to share the money with the second person (the "responder"). The proposer can only make one offer to the responder on how the money might be split. If the responder accepts, the money is divided among both, according to the proposer's offer. If the responder rejects the offer, they both get nothing. Both the proposer and the responder know the rules governing the game, and its possible outcomes. The *Dictator game* is a variant of the Ultimatum game, where the proposer becomes a dictator who decides unilaterally how the money is to be split. In this variant, the responder has no active role, all power resting with the dictator. In the Ultimatum game, the responder has the power to block the disbursement of the money. We summarize a few of the key findings, as motivation of what is to follow in this and the subsequent chapter.

In the Ultimatum game, the proposer often offers close to a 50:50 split of the sum. This is a clear instance of fairness as Fair Share, amounting to equality of shares. Experiments have confirmed that when the proposer offers to share less than 30% with the responder, the latter often rejects the offer. Doing this, the responder makes an *ethical* choice: the responder prefers to lose himself in the process of upholding fairness.[6] But by rejecting an "unfair" proposal the responder thus harms her or himself, teaching the proposer that the responder is ready to punish unfair ethics, signaling the latter to avoid such unfair behavior. If the responder was a pure *homo economicus* he would never refuse any offer made to him. This is a clear proof that process fairness matters to people, as they are willing, and in some cases even eager, to refuse a benefit if it comes to them because of what they perceive an unjust process.

Experiments with the Dictator game produce the surprising finding that even when the dictator has full control over the outcome, fairness will influence the sharing of the pie. Pure economic rationality would lead the dictator to keep all the money and share none. Yet, most prefer to share a "fair" portion with responders, enjoying less money, but feeling more at ease leading a process that is fairer. This conclusion lies at the heart of Fair Process Leadership, which generates benefits over time that are typically greater for both proposer and responder, though not necessarily in equal or proportional amounts.

Fairness is a forceful and fundamental motivator. Fair societies grow, feed their people, and attract immigrants; unfair societies shrink, have famines, lead to emigration, and end up destroying themselves.[7] Fairness is fundamental to create the alliances between owners, boards of directors, executives, and other stakeholders that are so necessary for sustainable value creation. Fairness works in the small—deal making—just like it works at the larger societal level—alliances for building coalitions for social change. Owners perceived as fair will attract investors, board members, and managers. The converse is also true: owners perceived as unfair will either not attract investors or will have to pay a higher price for attracting them and will likely attract them for shorter periods of time; same for board members and managers. We might call it the *unfairness risk premium.*[8] Sarah Brosnan and Frans de Waal's experiments on capuchin monkeys[9] confirm the innateness of a sense of fairness including in primates. These researchers saw that a monkey who receives a cucumber instead of a preferred grape from her partner monkey quickly becomes enraged. The monkeys have been known to hurl their cucumber back at the researchers in protest of the unfairness of the offering; de Waal concludes that primates "dislike inequity." So do all of us, from an early age.

Fairness is not simply a matter of nurturing or of socialization, educating children into keeping to certain social norms or customs. Neuroscientists have shown that fairness is "*hardwired*" into our brains. For example, there is an area of the brain called the *striatum* that is activated when we get a monetary reward. It is also activated when we punish (or execute) somebody for a previous transgression. When somebody shows trust in us (e.g., through a gift), our levels of *oxytocin*—a pleasure-inducing polypeptide that's active in mammalian brains—rise. When we repay others, thereby proving ourselves trustworthy, these oxytocin levels rise even higher. Trusting and proving trustworthy literally makes (most of) us feel good. Sociopaths cannot trust other people and are not trustworthy, including to themselves. They have abnormally low levels of oxytocin in their brains. When experimental subjects are given extra oxytocin, their propensity to trust doubles.

The seminal experiments of Paul Bloom, Professor of Psychology at Yale University, show that a sense of fairness is in-built into human beings. He concluded that the earliest signs are "the glimmerings of empathy and compassion—pain at the pain of others—which one can see pretty soon after birth. Once they're capable of coordinated movement, babies will often try to soothe others who are suffering, by patting and stroking. We have found that even 3-month-olds respond differently to a character who helps another than to a character who hinders another person."[10]

This childhood appreciation of fairness changes and gets nuanced as we mature. Bloom says that for young children, fairness pretty much reduces to equality—everyone gets the same. It's only with development that we come to an appreciation of the complex ways in which fairness might diverge from equality, such as when one person deserves more (e.g., by working harder) or faces greater need, or has been short-changed in the past. Bloom thus points out that we do not just have "hard-wired moral universals," but that, as we grow, we add to these innate views by imagination, our capacity to reason, and be influenced by our environment.

To summarize, we have "basic" or intuitive responses to fair and unfair settings that have been hard-wired in us. Individuals, in their interactions with others, rely on talents they inherit at birth and on competencies they acquire through training. That is thus also the case for owners, board members, managers, and employees.

When turning then to an examination of the fairness topic, the first fundamental point, beyond the role of fairness in human relations, is to thoroughly understand the distinction between the two principal notions of fairness: fair play—or fairness in the way "the game" is played—and fair share—or fairness in the outcomes and results obtained by those concerned. It has been our experience that all too often owners, directors, and executives are remarkably ignorant about this fundamental distinction, thinking of fairness mostly and instinctively in terms of "fair share" and reacting quickly, as young children, to receiving an unfair "share of the pie."

To conclude our discussion on fair share, a topic that has been amply discussed by philosophers and scholars, there are only three distinct principles that can be applied when aiming a fair division of the pie:

- *merit* where one's share of the pie is proportional to that individual's contribution to the production of "the pie" (or common objective);
- *equality* when all are given the same share;
- *needs*, where shares of the pie are proportional to that individual's needs, the neediest people being allocated the largest shares.[11]

It is important to realize that these principles are *substitutes* and not complements. They cannot be applied together: the application of each principle generates different outcomes. A distribution based on merit, for example, leads to unequal shares, those without merit receiving little or nothing, while those with merit receive benefits that may be way beyond what they need, nor provide them with their more fundamental needs. Workers and labor unions typically argue against executive salaries citing them as excessively unequal, not properly accounting for merit and not covering the basic needs of the poorest workers in the firm. These discussions are filled with biases as we are less aware of other people's efforts than our own, and we tend to overestimate what we deserve while we underestimate what we owe to others and what they deserve.

One major argument on behalf of the FPL framework is that there typically are different views in a group on what principle should determine a fair division. FPL indeed must start by engaging members on how different options will be evaluated. Owners, employees, suppliers, and other stakeholders (like partners, communities) will likely invoke the three distinct principles for such allocation, which are merit (for employees), equality (inside the firm and with shareholders), and needs (unions, owners). Hence, a fair division of corporate results and outcomes necessitates a decision on the principle for governing the division of the corporate pie among the various stakeholders particularly when these stakeholders are governed by distinct fair share logics. This is where fair process provides an effective answer. Fair play among these parties demands a disciplined discussion first on the relative weightings of the three fundamental principles that will be applied to dividing the pie (merit, equality, needs). This "frames" the division by obtaining agreement from the stakeholders on the criterion that will be applied for judging the fairness of the division they need to agree upon. That discussion needs to happen and conclude before possible options for this division can be thoroughly explored. No final division of the pie can result and be agreed upon unless there is agreement on the criterion for deciding fairness of any division. That is the simple logic of FPL, which is regularly violated, or brushed over too hastily.

This is also why the leader who oversees the fair process also should demonstrate fair play himself or herself, so that the leader's biases and preferences do not pre-determine or unduly influence the discussions. When power prevails the process will be biased by the unfair leader who will skew the process to his or her preferences. Negotiations, for example, are typically not fair play since outcomes are greatly determined by the relative power of those negotiating. Suppliers to the big automotive companies have long complained about this. Fair play enters the negotiation discussion when the diverging parties agree to arbitration, which must be perceived to be fair process for the parties to accept it. For this, the mediator or arbitrator must be fair play.

The leadership dimension is crucial: a fair leader will be swayed by the need to maintain process to be perceived as fair; an unfair leader will not. The roles of business owners thus are critical: owners "set the tone at the top" through their mission, their statement of values, the way they incarnate the mission and their values in their behavior, and the rules of the game regarding the governance of the corporation. It is in the latter that owners can durably frame the role of fair process in their enterprise.

Character, identity, preferences, and priorities play a crucial role here, something that we will address in the third part of the book, concerned with the "people" part of the ownership equation. Owners' education matters too, as it fosters awareness and trains people about appropriate behavioral changes, for example when hardware and software need to be reset, or more directly when they transition from management to board directorship, or to ownership. Marwell and Ames established a startling result in their experiments in behavioral economics: they demonstrated that economics undergraduates act differently and more selfishly than those pursuing other undergraduate majors.[12] It does confirm that education matters and shapes us. Then, our first school is the education received, explicitly or implicitly, in the family we were born in.

The major benefit of FPL is that FPL generated outcomes will be perceived as fair by the parties involved in the process and pose few issues, if any, at the implementation stage. That argument is major indeed: FPL leads to an intelligent management of differences in views, priors, and outcomes, rationally, emotionally, spiritually, physically, and temporally. This in turn leads to more sustainably performing groups, organizations, and nations.

4 Trust, Performance, and Fair Play[13]

Fair play is thus a formidable key to sustainable performance in collective action. Conversely, unfair play organizations do not sustain themselves, as social harmony suffers, and energies are used destructively.

Our next task then is to operationalize fair play for owners and managers. And introduce a language that is not self-referencing and does not refer to such things as fair, equity, justice. This is where one of the great figures in modern sociology, Gerald Leventhal (1980), has done the work for us.[14] Leventhal identified fair play through five characteristics that all can be observed and probed for through questionnaires:

- *Consistency:* when persons and issues are treated in the same uniform way, without bias against some, when all parties are given an equal opportunity to contribute, and when this treatment perdures over time and across issues;
- *Clarity*: when decisions are transparent, understood, and full explanations are provided;
- *Communication without fear of retaliation*: when ~~these~~ parties are given a voice that is heard and which they can express freely, without holding back out of fear of retaliation for speaking up or for what they say;
- *Changeability:* the possibility of correction because of new and convincing information and evidence (and not just opinion);
- *Culture of ethicality:* when individuals share an authentic commitment to doing the right thing for the group or community (in the given context).

What is important to realize is that fair play requires all five characteristics to be fulfilled. Failure on one dimension leads to unfair play. This non-compensating feature was already noted in an earlier model for high-performance teams. This renders fair play very challenging as we easily admit that, because of our biases and natural behaviors, we are rarely very good in all five dimensions, and consistently so with time. Some of our basic instincts do not serve us well here: for example, respect for elders and for authorities inhibits honest feedback and promotes silence over voice, or compliance over protest. We also have preferences in this regard. We "eat at lunch what we killed yesterday or in the early morning" and are survivors. These "natural" reactions regularly can lead us astray and are then perceived by others as unfair play. Such natural "grabbing" behaviors generate reduced commitment, trust, and motivation of others to go forward with us.

These natural reactions are reinforced by ethnic cultures. For example, one Asian student in our program for directors returned in the second module, quite displeased at having "protested" to his chairman only to be dismissed from the board. By the third module he informed us that he had lost all his board seats (the country being small and village-like). This is an important point: the above characteristics should of course be interpreted according to the prevailing culture. Protests should be expressed in a way that they can be heard without leading to retaliation. Even in western countries feedback questionnaires often are anonymous. In Asia, where the desire for harmony is strong and where face saving is important, feedback is best initiated off-line and in a more collective way. This is the Kaizen practice in Japan, where workers are invited to provide collective feedback to the plant manager.

Our advice here is always the same, regardless of culture: first, engage one or a few people you trust and can be open with; in a second stage and when you have validated your views with the first group, engage people who might hold contrary opinions and see whether you can convince them, or whether this leads you to, perhaps marginally, change your views for greater acceptance in the larger group; only then, go formal in meetings. One of the motivations of this way of engaging, which may appear cumbersome to some, is that one-on-one meetings by themselves often do not amount to much. Any authority "protested against" will instinctively react negatively, if only to maintain its authority, regardless of the merit of the protest. Therefore, testing one's ideas off-line and finding allies, who correct you, join you, or amend you, is a good practice particularly in complex matters, across all cultures.

Another comment on cultural differences is that when one asks for the characteristics of a desirable leader, people typically mention, without necessarily referring to fairness, fair play characteristics. These indeed characterize the leaders who create positive energies around them, by engaging team members, provide a large degree of autonomy, communicate well and often, seek feedback, and are willing to admit mistakes and learn from them. This answer is quite at variance with leadership theories that advocate personality traits such as charisma or physical traits like being large and attractive (which work in the short run but fail in the long run when not supported by fair play behaviors).

Fair play teams led by fair play leaders tend to be more performing, fair play companies tend to attract and retain better talents, fair play countries attract immigrants while unfair play countries are associated with emigration. Fair play behavior, sometimes taken too easily for granted, is best appreciated when shown in contrast to a dictatorial, unfair, behavioral style. Figure 12.2

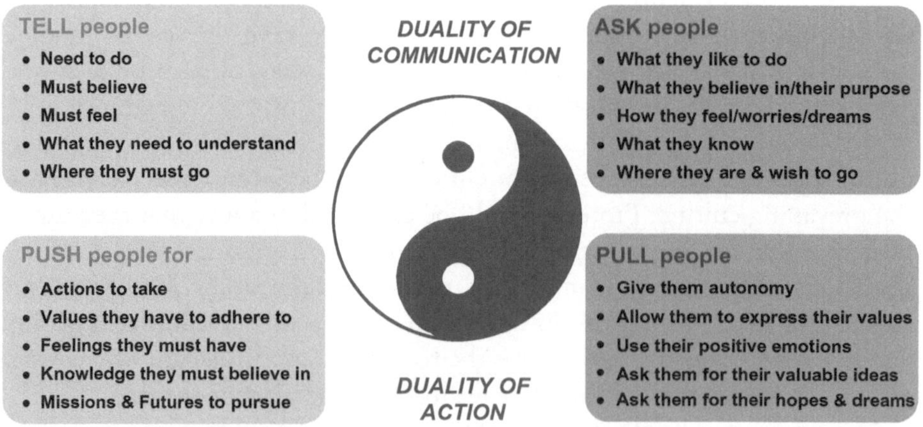

Fig. 12.2 Duality of communication and action styles—push vs. pull

shows this duality in communication styles and behaviors. Fair play leaders spend considerable time in ASK mode, when dictators typically push their decisions on those that report to them, mainly operating in TELL mode (Fig. 12.2). The astute reader will observe that the behaviors are described in reference to the five fundamental energies evoked at the beginning of this chapter and evidenced in Fig. 12.1.

Formalizing effective board work through fair play is a first requirement on the "How" of board work. To have a good normative prescription of this work, we still need to further define the "What?" of board work, namely its process and the steps that boards need to go through to create value. This is what the next section is about.

5 From Fair Play to Fair Process Leadership

The issue of fairness has sparked a great deal of interest among organizational researchers, whose writings have defined the subfield of procedural justice.[15] This field has identified the main fairness violations in the procedures and processes being followed by decision makers. However, what was missing for a long time is a prescription to be followed by decision makers wishing to be fair in their decision making and leadership behaviors. This is the gap filled by the *Fair Process Leadership* framework, which is motivated by the question: how should an owner, board member, or manager behave to be perceived as fair by the people (s)he manages or governs?

An operational framework that supports and generalizes fair process behavior within a board or an entire organization is based on the extension of the industrial Kaizen practice, visible in all factories around the world these days and associated with Toyota, which is its originator. The practice is also known as PDCA: *Plan* for an improvement, *Do* an experiment that validates the planned improvement, *Check* whether the experiment indeed produces the desired improvement, and, if so, *Act*, namely, generalizes the idea throughout the factory. The framework exhibits a process consisting of a clear number of steps that guide the fair process leader. The adaptation of this framework to a governance and management setting is provided in Fig. 12.3.

The reader will immediately see that the model substantially differs from PDCA in its first dimension, named *Engaging, Seeing, Framing.* This underlines that a key dimension for a successful governance or management is a proper framing of the question that is dealt with. Factory workers, following the Kaizen or lean management practice introduced by Toyota, do not need this step. The framing for them is evident: Kaizen seeks productivity

Fig. 12.3 The Fair Process Leadership framework

improvements through cost reductions, or quality and speed improvements. Being obvious to all, it does not appear in their model. But in management beyond factory work, especially for owners and board members, framing is of the essence: get this wrong, and you are executing on the wrong frame and are likely to be pursuing a path of value destruction. The Everest example, discussed in Chap. 10, made this point very clear by pointing to a common framing error of the mountaineers aiming for the top of the mountain: they should have framed the journey as one guided by a spirit of safety, and the need to return safely to base camp. Instead, most climbers who got in trouble was due to framing the task as "going to the top." This is a fatal framing error as most accidents occur when people come down.

When things are poorly framed at the outset, little good can result. The initial response in the US and the UK to Covid attests to this. When the framing of the issue is wrong, planning misses the mark, as does decision making. And in the end, as happened during the Covid pandemic, the medical equipment and support, as well as the vaccines, that should be there are not. Enron's failure is the result of its board being unable to correctly frame the predicament the company was under. Similarly, Carlos Ghosn, at the end of his term as NISSAN's Chairman, attributed the non-performance of the company on members of the executive team, while not taking responsibility. He literally—to make a play on the US interpretation of the word *framing*—and unfairly "framed these executives" leading the latter to take their revenge by framing him in return. Finally, the board of BP viewed the series of accidents affecting its North American operations as a failure of the implementation of BP's safety culture in its US units, many of which had been acquired from Amoco whose safety culture was not up to BP's standards. In sum, framing is a key step in governance and management, a lot of value destruction results from framing errors, particularly if this mistaken framing is followed by forceful and effective execution. Value destruction then results, and its amount is proportional to the quality of execution.

This first step in the FPL process consists of *engaging* stakeholders in *framing* the question that needs to be addressed. What do people *see* to be the issues at hand? What opportunities? And what challenges? What about the risks in this context? What about the ethical and sustainability dimensions? What is the scope of stakeholder impacts? What are the facts? In legal processes, this is where the prosecutor, the defense, and the judge spend much time engaging people who have information (witnesses) and are involved in the matter, including their motivations. It cannot be stated enough how crucial this first stage of FPL is. It results and ends with a particular "framing" of the challenges and opportunities that need to be addressed.

A recurring question from people first presented with the framework concerns who needs to be engaged. A bit of reflection and our energy framework provides the answer. First, all those physically involved in the matter, and, in particular in its execution, should be engaged. Their engagement will result in their commitment to the issue at hand, as they will then perceive it as their issue and not just that of the leader. Another category of individuals consists of those opposed to the project and who can block it. Understanding their rationale and their tactics can only help leaders reach the right decision. This is where stakeholder analysis and engagement are most beneficial, allowing the leaders to gain a full picture of the opportunity or challenge. A third category is composed of the experts, people who have expertise or have experienced similar issues earlier. Their lessons are invaluable allowing the project to gain from their knowledge and experience.

The second FPL step is devoted to *exploring* the issue. This step consists of *creatively generating* options or "solutions" to the question that has been framed at the first step. Then follows the examination of each option, involving a useful confrontational and counterfactual debate of the "pros" and the "cons" of each of the options. Board competence and diversity are of the essence here, enabling a plurality of options and as well as a thorough examination of contrarian views. This is the time for questions such as: what could go wrong if this decision is implemented, what are its risk factors, are we missing alternatives? This is not a time yet for decision making, or agreeing on a common course, as indeed the cons against one option often become the pros of another option. The emphasis here is thus not on decision making, though clearly inferior options will be *eliminated* at this stage. The focus is on building shared understanding through the creative generation and exploration of potential options.

Having framed the issue, having examined the options available, time has come to decide and develop the right rationale for choosing one of the options examined in detail at the previous step. This is the third step of the FPL process. This is the time for the judge to conclude the deliberations and announce his or her decision, its rationale, and its consequences for the various stakeholders of the issue at hand. Boards in many respects hold roles that are like those held by judges. Transparency and clarity of decision, unambiguous explanations communicated to all concerned are the keys to generate perceptions of fairness and confidence in the leadership, as well as commitment to the implementation of the rewards or sanctions contained in the decisions.

The fourth FPL step then proceeds with the *execution* of the decisions announced at the previous step, *realizing* the results expected from those decisions. The expectations will be met if the preparatory analysis was well done, and if indeed the decisions correctly executed, a question that will also have been discussed at the planning stage. The step will conclude with *rewarding* the actors in charge of this execution, in line with the expectations formulated at the decision step. Returning to judicial practice, prisoners having completed their sentence earn their freedom. Rewards that are commensurate with expectations generate trust; rewards that are inconsistent with expectations cause distrust. Some ask whether these rewards should not be the result of an evaluation. And the answer is indeed yes, but in this model, the answer is given by the fair play requirements of clarity, consistency, and communication. Integrity and changeability may lead certain people to refuse their rewards; that is an issue that is dealt with through the last FPL devoted to adaptation. If results, contributions, and expectations are clear, little discussion should be expected at this stage. What might be discussed are whether these rewards and sanctions will be maintained in the future; that, again, is the subject of the next step. Trust is built by holding one's word, particularly in difficult contexts. Finally, one needs to underline that this execution step moves the framework from a decision-making one to a managerial and governance one.

The last step is another major key element is FPL. It is devoted to the *evaluation* of the outcomes reached, and what was *learned* as a result of this examination. The absence of a thorough review of experience is often at the root of future mistakes. BP had a poor safety record containing many near misses and several major accidents in North America. Yet, they were insufficiently analyzed for root cause: the pressure to produce, an insufficient safety culture which came from Amoco, which had sold its North American operations to

BP, which was known for a good safety culture, and the bias of ignoring low probability events. The result was the explosion of the Macondo platform in the Gulf of Mexico. Beyond preventing mistakes, there also is the need for all of us to recognize our mistakes, in front of our teammates. This allows the team to recommit emotionally, spiritually, and intellectually to the leader and the team members, particularly after mistakes have occurred. But learning from mistakes is not sufficient: the final step of FPL is to *adapt* the individual, team, and organization so that mistakes will not repeat. That will bring the security and confidence needed for team members and stakeholders to continue to commit to the leader, the team, and the organization for another FPL round.

Till now, we have defined a process consisting of five steps, visibly shown in Fig. 12.3. However, processes do not live on their own, they have *leaders* who are responsible and accountable for them, as Fig. 10.1 indicates. Another way to underline this dependence is that a change in leadership typically affects the quality of the process. A new CEO typically changes the strategy process, or the process of growth of the company. A change in CFO normally changes the financial processes of the company. If nothing changes, that leader simply follows what was initiated by his or her predecessor. Though Mandela was a fair process leader, his successors certainly were not. The failed succession of Mandela, first with Mbeki and especially with Zuma, created huge difficulties for South Africa. This is the meaning of the addition of the word "leadership" and the coinage of the term *Fair Process Leadershi*p (or FPL), as FPL is like a tripod, where the three legs—fair play, process, and leadership—matter and are interrelated. In other words, FPL is an example of systemic thinking advocated by Peter Senge.

Fair play allows a process to be effective and leadership allows the process to run smoothly. Process is the core engine. Just as factories make products, fair processes generate fair outcomes, as well as trust and individual commitment. FPL thus lies at the heart of effective collaboration. Fair processes require leaders that govern these processes and adapt and improve them over time, forbidding them from slipping into unfair process territory. That was missing in South Africa following Mandela's succession.

6 An Iconic Example: Napoleon Bonaparte Examined Through the FPL Lens

To illustrate both how important FPL is for emerging leaders and also for leadership to be sustainable, we have included a detailed discussion of an iconic historical figure known the world over, Napoleon Bonaparte. Appendix A provides the detailed analysis of his leadership from an FPL perspective. We here focus on its conclusions.

The historical distance from the facts—more than two centuries—allows an easier comment, even though this analysis, when presented to a French audience, regularly evokes quick and occasionally violent emotional outbursts. The reader will hopefully conclude that Napoleon Bonaparte is quite common in business and politics. The story is to be read as relating to a company (in this case France) that went into bankruptcy and failed (due to incompetent Bourbon kings unable to adapt to changing contexts and expectations). The company thus had to be restructured (the French Revolution), leading it to survive (from Habsburg attempts to restore Louis XVI to the throne). It emerged from these early years thanks to the efforts of many, including the generals and soldiers who met the Habsburg forces in the north of France and Belgium. In the south of the country, heroic action occurred at the direction of one of its most able executives, leading to the conquest of Northern Italy (General Bonaparte). Notwithstanding a return from a disastrous campaign in Egypt, Bonaparte saves the Republic from a coup by the royalist troops in Paris, and has a second masterful campaign to recover the Italian Republic that was lost while he was in Egypt. That would earn him to become Chairman for life and found a new aristocracy and a new Empire. Having assumed ownership of France (and returning into an aristocratic imperial state), Napoleon is unable to secure peace with his enemies, and particularly with the UK which successfully leads an alliance against the Emperor. He will ultimately be stopped after two disastrous defeats at Leipzig and Waterloo. The Brits ensured that the upstart owner would not escape again by assigning him to Longwood House on the island of Saint Helena.

The importance of Napoleon, executive, chair, and owner cannot be understated: creator of the French Empire, of modern French institutions and a Civil Code that will bear his name (a terrible idea), of the first European Union (under French law and leadership), father of modern Germany, Italy, Austria, and Switzerland, a contributor to the modern US through the Louisiana Purchase by the young Republic, and indirectly, following the French invasion of Spain, of modern Latin America. Napoleon started as a low-level military in the French Army of the Revolution, became General in

Chief, then CEO (as First Consul), and finally Founding Chairman and owner (as Emperor). He returned France to an aristocratic regime and governed France and his Empire as a family business.

The story is a must-know for owners, as well as directors (which were sorely missing in this saga) and executives (which were most talented, but ultimately too complying to a leader going of the rails). It illustrates how talent and power, unconstrained by effective governance, can lead to massive value destruction. Its lessons remain, and regularly ignored. The story of a powerful leader turning dictatorial, then destroying what he co-created is timeless. The story of Alexander the Great is a more ancient version. Mao, who installed Communist regime in China and initiated a terribly destructive Cultural Revolution to remain in power, offers remarkable parallels with the Napoleonic saga. Turning to the business scene, the story of Carlos Ghosn, which we will examine in the next chapter, is a near repeat of Napoleon's rise and fall, and ends in similar ways (with Longwood House now in Lebanon).

The lesson behind these stories is the following pattern. These leaders evidenced Fair Process Leadership—or many aspects of it—on their way to reach the pinnacle of their respective arenas. They then abandoned the FPL practice that had helped them reach the top, not being aware of the extent their leadership style had contributed to this outcome. They became increasingly dictatorial, and this shift was tolerated by their associates who thus contributed to a self-fulfilling vicious cycle to dictatorships. Oppositions were rationalized as evidencing envy, jealousy, unfairness, or stupidity. Their dictatorial ends also marked them ultimately as Gods fallen from the Pantheon.

It is not too hard to imagine that a more sustainable FPL practice would have rendered their leadership and success more durable. Then FPL requires a humility that surely escaped these dictatorial leaders. FPL, when fully and consistently applied, forces leaders to continuously engage their teams and their stakeholders, to confront their failures, and to continue to adapt. It is the FPL practice which greatly sustains effective leadership. The lesson applies to all owners and board members aiming for sustainable value creation.

Notes

1. A. Goudsmet and L. Van der Heyden, *The Six Dimensions of Managing High Performance Teams*, INSEAD Working Paper, 2023.
2. Peter Senge, *The Fifth Discipline: The art and practice of the learning organization*, Doubleday, New York, 1990.

3. Jim C. Collins, *Good to Great: Why Some Companies Make the Leap … and Others Don't*, HarperCollins, New York, 2001.
4. The series is named *Ramsay's Kitchen Nightmares* and was first broadcast on Channel 4 in 2004.
5. John C. Harsanyi, "On the Rationality Postulates underlying the Theory of Cooperative Games," *The Journal of Conflict Resolution 5(2): 179–196*, 1961.
6. Anatol Rapoport and Albert M. Chammah, *Prisonner's Dilemma*, University of Michigan Press, 1970.
7. Amartya Sen, *The Idea of Justice*, Penguin Books, 2010.
8. Some might object citing the mafia as a counterexample, where loyalty is regarded as a key value. The counter to this is that most men die because of violent "settlements," with the exception perhaps of the very senior people that indeed survive, safe and hidden. Another counter is that one sees few women engaged in the mafia: wives typically become widows.
9. Megan van Wolkenten, Sarah F. Brosnan, and Frans B. M. de Waal, Inequity responses of monkeys modified by effort, Biological Sciences, November 20, 2007|104 (47) 18854–18859. https://doi.org/10.1073/pnas.0707182104
10. https://www.scientificamerican.com/article/the-moral-life-of-babies/
11. There are of course an infinite number of hybrid variants.
12. Gerald Marwell and Ruth E. Ames, "Economists Free Ride, Does Anyone Else?", *Journal of Public Economics 15:295–310*, 1981.
13. The reader eager for more detail will find these in "Setting a Tone of Fairness at the Top," *Business Compliance* 05/2013 and in "Fair Play Leadership," *Generali Bolletino*, June 2017, both articles by Ludo Van der Heyden.
14. Gerald S. Leventhal, "What should be done with equity theory? New approaches to the study of fairness in social relationship," in: K. Gergen, M. Greenberg, & R. Willis (Eds.), *Social exchange: Advances in theory and research*, pp. 27–55, Plenum Press, New York, 1980.
15. John Thibaut and Laurens Walker, *Procedural Justice: A Psychological Analysis*, Lawrence Erlbaum Associates, 1975, and W. Chan Kim and Renée Maurborgne, "Implementing global strategies: The role of procedural justice," *Strategic Management Journal* 12(S1), 1991.

13

Fair Process Leadership Illustrated: Applications to Owners, Board Members, and Executives

Having in the preceding chapter and in Appendix B provided the theory of FPL and illustrated an example using a historical figure, Napoleon Bonaparte, we turn in this chapter to applications of the theory. We provide examples of the essential role played by FPL in providing the right "software" for owners, board members, and executives. Our first example concerns Carlos Ghosn, the fallen Renault-NISSAN leader. It is quite literally a modern version of the Napoleonic saga. The scripts are remarkably similar, which points to the fact that the lessons from the earlier story should be learned by modern leaders, so as not to repeat them. The Spanish philosopher George Santayana said as much: "Those who cannot remember the past are condemned to repeat it." What FPL offers is a tool to see the mechanics at play in their rise, as well as in their demise as well. The violations of FPL generated very negative consequences to their organizations, their close associates, and themselves.

1 The Rise and Fall of Carlos Ghosn[1]

The Context

In 1999, Renault and NISSAN, led by Louis Schweitzer and Yoshikazu Hanawa, the Chairmen of these two companies, formed a strategic alliance to save NISSAN from bankruptcy and allow Renault to learn from NISSAN's manufacturing prowess, gain access to the US and to substantial scale.

Hanawa, without further help from other Japanese automobile companies or financial institutions, in a last nearly desperate gesture turned abroad in its

M. Massa et al., *Value Creation for Owners and Directors*,
https://doi.org/10.1007/978-3-031-19726-0_13

search for the financial support required to avoid bankruptcy. Ford and Daimler had been approached first, as well as German automotive giants, but none showed any interest. So, Hanawa turned to other European automobile makers. Renault was the only firm that was ready to engage with NISSAN.

Intense negotiations forced NISSAN and Renault corporate executives to demonstrate the benefits of a deal and the possibility of a serious return to Renault. Renault shareholders included the French Government, who initially would be skeptical as it had to defend the huge and risky commitment it was taking to French citizens. The deal was thus explored in detail by the management of the two companies, and the argument on the Renault side had to be solid. At the time the Renault-NISSAN Alliance was discussed, NISSAN had shown losses in six out of the seven previous years. The company had spent US$1 billion in interest payments in 1998 alone. Much-needed investments into new product development had to wait, even though only 4 out of 43 Nissan models were profitable. Its seven Japanese plants were running at an overall 50% capacity level. A general rule in the automobile industry is that plant utilization ought to exceed a minimum of 80% for a company to break even. For highly automated companies like Mercedes, the number is even higher. Below this figure, the financial numbers turn heavily and rapidly red. This was the predicament NISSAN found itself in over the last years. In addition, NISSAN employees enjoyed lifetime employment, which had led the management to abstain from any layoffs. Due to the impending bankruptcy, all jobs now were at risk of being lost.

Like other Japanese automakers, NISSAN had a tradition of "keiretsu," an interlocking set of relationships with dedicated suppliers which demanded considerable investments by NISSAN into its supply network. Funds for such investments were now limited and dragged suppliers down with NISSAN. None of the other Japanese and global car makers wished to help NISSAN out of a largely self-inflicted crisis. Hanawa's call on Renault was its last chance to save NISSAN.

Schweitzer, the Renault Chairman, should be credited for recognizing the opportunity for his company to make a remarkable leap forward. Indeed, the envisaged Renault-NISSAN Alliance, if it could be made to work, would create the fourth largest automotive group in the world. The two companies had many complementary features in markets served, product ranges, and expertise. Furthermore, Schweitzer believed that in Carlos Ghosn, he had the leader who could make this complex and most risky project happen.

Renault and NISSAN ended up agreeing on an equity and strategic partnership deal, Renault investing more than 5 billion euros into NISSAN and receiving a 36.4% stake in the company for it. It was further agreed that

NISSAN, when out of financial distress, would buy 15% of Renault shareholding. Surprisingly, these shares would come with no voting power, something that the Japanese had to swallow, and took badly from the outset. It would remain a major point of friction between the partners which Renault has refused to ever address.

Samurai Ghosn Sent to Save NISSAN Village

Most industry experts were skeptical about the chances of success of the alliance, primarily because of profound cultural incompatibility between the two companies. Many believed that the deal risked bringing Renault down as well. According to these views, both companies were non-performing. In these matters, unlike in mathematics, combining two negatives does not create corporate strength. Both companies had strong nationalistic cultures that were considered fundamentally incompatible. Furthermore, thinking that a government-owned firm could save a Japanese automobile giant seemed implausible. Rival PSA described the project as way too risky for any private entity, claiming that only a government-owned entity could take such a gamble. Without great surprise rating agencies downgraded Renault upon the announcement of a deal.

Schweitzer put Carlos Ghosn in charge of the NISSAN turnaround. A Franco-Lebanese engineer, Ghosn had gained prominence in the Michelin group restructuring its North American operations. It included, among others, the acquisition and integration of Uniroyal Goodrich. Ghosn left the group when it became clear that the family-owned group would appoint a Michelin heir to the CEO position he aimed for.

The NISSAN turnaround was not only surprisingly successful, it also was remarkably swift. It made the Renault-NISSAN Alliance (RNA) an iconic example of successful cross-cultural management. What is less recognized is that Ghosn's leadership of the turnaround nearly perfectly demonstrates Fair Process Leadership in action. We here illustrate some of its most salient aspects, faithfully displaying the five FPL steps presented in the previous chapter.

Engaging

Ghosn indeed engaged to lead the turnaround by Renault Chairman Schweitzer. Given its considerable size and risk, a great number of discussions took place at corporate headquarters to analyze the opportunity and forecast the ROI that the investment could yield. Challenges to the realization of the expected benefits were also identified and studied. Many of these discussions were held between the two men, and with Renault's corporate staff.

NISSAN was desperate for Renault's investment. It provided its hoped-for partner great transparency on its current situation. No other suitor had come forward which eliminated any concern about unfair treatment of other potential investors. In sum, this allowed an unusual and deep engagement of the two corporate staffs and allowed Renault to see what NISSAN amounted to. It increased Renault's interest in the deal and must have contributed to better assess the risk.

One of Ghosn's conditions for leading the turnaround was that Schweitzer allow him to hand-pick 20 Renault executives whom he would take with him to help achieve the turnaround of NISSAN. Schweitzer also agreed to provide Ghosn with considerable autonomy from Renault corporate headquarters, on the condition that NISSAN would break-even after two years and that a single cash infusion of more than 5 billion euros would be sufficient. Both men by then were highly committed to the deal and trusted each other. The same was true for the senior staffs in both companies.

Within NISSAN, Ghosn also demonstrated considerable FPL engagement. This was appreciated since FPL shares roots with Japanese Kaizen management techniques:

- Ghosn clearly framed his mission when taking the NISSAN assignment: he was no longer a Renault employee and proud to join NISSAN, which he explicitly described as a great Japanese company in need of a few changes. His "I am very confident that, given your enthusiasm and pride, we can bring Nissan back to recovery and growth" resonated strongly with NISSAN employees, as was his promise to resign if NISSAN was not turned around after two years.
- He visited many NISSAN plants, interacting for three months with many employees and suppliers. Only then did he formally start his appointment at NISSAN. During these visits, he kept asking very simple questions to the employees he met: "What are your problems? What do you think needs to be done? What do you contribute to NISSAN?" This allowed him to "see" with his own eyes what the issues were that affected NISSAN. His turnaround experience in Michelin and then Renault proved priceless during these rounds.
- Ghosn perfectly engaged NISSAN Chairman Hanawa. He asked him to select the Japanese members of the new and reduced NISSAN Executive

Board, trusting Hanawa to select individuals compatible with him. After all, Ghosn had selected the French members of the new NISSAN team, so it was only fair to reciprocate by asking Hanawa to choose the Japanese members of the leadership team. Furthermore, Hanawa knew these managers much better than Ghosn and could appraise them better. Having learned to appreciate Ghosn, he trusted Hanawa would choose the right people, as their interests were aligned.

- A new language, English, was chosen as the language of top management. This ensured that the French and top Japanese executives could communicate with each other. Ghosn insisted on a dictionary to be certain that all understood the meanings of the new words in the NISSAN vocabulary (commitment, authority, objectives, targets, budgets, ...). Management and governance require clear communications. Ghosn did not leave anything to chance.

Exploring

The 20 young people who Ghosn selected in Renault to be part of his team at NISSAN were great experts, all in their 40s, and obviously risk-takers and open-minded. They also were chosen for their collaborative skills. Solo players were not invited to join this special assignment.

Ghosn first assembled the team in France to explore and further refine the project with them. He wished to ensure that they would function as a team and be accepted by their Japanese counterparts. It was critical that they were aware that the project was not to create a new Renault-NISSAN company, but that they indeed were there to support NISSAN and its managers with capabilities that were missing or weak in NISSAN, and not behave as if they were in conquered territory. This first training contributed to the project becoming viewed by them as theirs and not solely as one owned by Ghosn and the top brass of both companies.

In NISSAN, Ghosn continued his engagement and exploration activities:

- Nine Cross-Functional Teams ("CFTs") were set up, composed of middle managers selected by the NISSAN Executive Team and approved by Ghosn himself. The total number of people involved across these CFTs would eventually number 500, ensuring that the turnaround plan had truly been devised by the middle management of NISSAN, with great attention to operational details. Most remarkably, the plan was written by those that would implement it, as we will confirm later. Its implementation would be flawless.

- Within NISSAN, Ghosn engaged the unions in the formulation of a capacity reduction plan. In true FPL fashion, Ghosn shared the dreadful context NISSAN was in and convinced union leadership that only drastic action and cooperation could save a fraction of the jobs, short of which all jobs would be lost. The math was simple: at 50% utilization of seven factories, only four factories were needed, three had to be closed. He invited the unions to present him with a layoff plan that would shut down three factories. Given the unprecedented nature of the plant closings, the union's plan was expensive. The plan had to sway the workers. In a sort of winner's curse, more workers accepted to be laid off than the management had expected. Ghosn accepted the union's plan to gain the workers' commitment to the plant closures, and speed.

The NISSAN Revival Plan (NRP) was formulated containing 400 action proposals coming largely from the CFTs and approved by the leadership. The latter subsequently realized that it would be a good idea to task the CFTs with the supervision of the implementation, since they would be the best "owners" of plans they had conceived. This succeeded brilliantly.

Ghosn communicated objectives clearly, with a positive if not admiring attitude toward NISSAN employees. He did this regularly and consistently. Some of his remarkable statements were:

- "We are going to turn around the company, not waste time on merger issues (like Daimler Chrysler did)."
- "NISSAN is a great company."
- "NISSAN just needs a few fixes."

Ghosn instilled a new leadership style in the company. He accepted open debate and disagreement. Ideas were rejected when judged insufficiently aggressive by the leadership. He also was careful to set clear expectations. Ghosn stated that "What we think, what we say, and what we do must be the same. We have to be impeccable in ensuring that our words correspond to our actions. If there are discrepancies between what we profess and how we behave, that will spell disaster." Ghosn was not afraid to call the shots as needed and live with his decisions.

And indeed, three plants were closed in Japan, while new factories would soon open in the US. These were critical as the US was the geography where new revenues were expected to be earned relatively rapidly.

Executing

Having set clear expectations, having put NISSAN CFTs in charge of supervising and supporting execution, the scene was set for success. All knew their own jobs depended on the successful execution of well-prepared plans, which fueled commitment. Ghosn's insistence, if not obsession, with full clarity once execution started contributed greatly to matters being indeed fully detailed at the latest at the time of decision making. "If people don't know the priority, don't understand the strategy, don't know where they're going, don't know what the critical objective is, you're heading for trouble. Confusion is the first sign of trouble. It's the leader's duty to clarify the environment, to make sure there is the maximum light in the company." Ghosn's obsession reassured people and spurred all to do their best. The NISSAN turnaround will remain one of the more remarkable corporate turnarounds in history. It is a stellar example of FPL practice.

Evaluating

As time and process evolved, Ghosn was prepared to adapt as a function of the results that were flowing in. He soon would be preparing the Nissan 180 Plan, which would be the second phase of the growth strategy the company would embark upon.

NISSAN's turnaround is widely considered a tremendous success. Figure 13.1 shows Nissan's profits before the Renault investment and through the end of 2019. In 2007, just before the subprime crisis, NISSAN's Net Income was US$4.8 billion. The Renault-NISSAN Alliance was then considered one of the leading automobile makers in the world, contesting rival TOYOTA for global domination.

In 2017, Mitsubishi was added as a third partner in the alliance. Somehow surprisingly, Mitsubishi was placed under full ownership of NISSAN, furthering the growing imbalance between the two partners. Another point that the graph identifies is that the profitability gained because the turnaround was not sustainable. This foreshadows the difficulties the two allies would encounter going forward. It does not take away from the great achievement the turnaround represents.

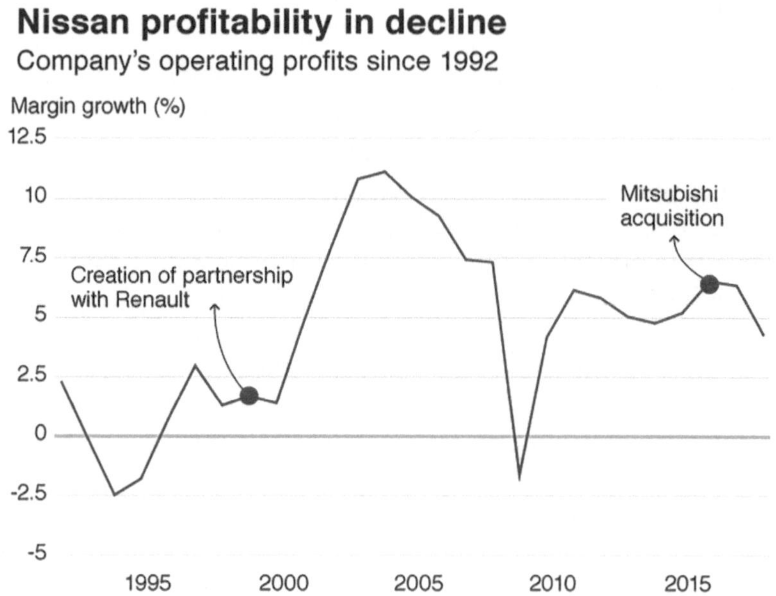

Fig. 13.1 Nissan operating profits from 1992 to 2019. Source: Company filings, BBC

Establishing an Imperial Reign and Ending in Demise

With Carlos Ghosn as Chair of Renault and NISSAN, and of the R-N Alliance, Ghosn dominated all three organizational units. Akin an Emperor, Ghosn had the final say in all three entities, including in the top pay from all three entities. The boards at all three companies were filled with Ghosn acolytes, providing few checks and balances. The voice of the owners, including of the French Government (the Japanese were never given a voice in Renault from the start), was greatly diminished as a result. The fact that it was only Ghosn personally who was holding together the three companies with their distinct cultures added to his power but created increasing tensions with the ultimate owners and the ministries, and increasingly represented a risk at the top of the companies.

Carlos Tavarez, No. 2 of Renault and former head of American operations for NISSAN, announced in late August 2013 that there was no room for two people at the top of the R-N empire and left the group for arch-rival PSA (where he has done extremely well). Alarm bells should have gone off. Ghosn at the time, was being evaluated by the Renault board for his renewal, and Tavares was signaling that he was ready to take over. But the board preferred to renew Ghosn, which led Tavarez to join PSA. All three companies now lacked clear succession plans.

Tensions appeared not only inside the group but also with the owners. The French government became increasingly concerned with NISSAN's increasing power within the alliance, and its increasing disinterest if not frustration with the alliance. Being out of financial distress and growing much more rapidly than Renault, the alliance increasingly mattered less for NISSAN. For Renault, which lacked sales progress, the alliance and NISSAN were increasingly vital for its continued competitiveness. NISSAN's limited voice had always been a point of discord, but Renault always considered that the alliance was an industrial and equity partnership, and not a takeover by Renault. Renault's lack of growth changed that view: it increasingly saw NISSAN as an investment that needed to be secured for its own survival.

Two successive French ministers, Arnaud Montebourg and Emmanuel Macron, now exerted pressure on Ghosn to force a full merger. The government passed the Loi Florange in March 2014 doubled the voting power of longer-term shareholders (holding shares for longer than two years). This suited the government perfectly as it increased its control on the company and its Executive Chairman (or *Président Directeur Général,* abbreviated in French to the acronym *PDG*). The move was seen by NISSAN as a breach of their partnership. The secret purchase on the stock market of additional Renault shares by the French Government finalized the breakdown of trust with the Japanese partner.[2] Ghosn appeared to have chosen sides with the Japanese, strongly arguing against the wishes of the French Government owner. By then Macron had become President of France and was happy to apply some French "dirigisme," a practice where the state exerts a determining influence in business affairs.

When the French Government made a merger with NISSAN a condition for his renewal in 2019, Ghosn was forced to submit if he wished to remain the Renault PDG. It is very likely that this forced a switch in his position toward NISSAN and may have greatly diminished any remaining trust of his Japanese colleagues. The sacking of his Japanese colleagues in the NISSAN executive team as a sanction of NISSAN's low profitability seemed to seal the break with his executive colleagues, led by Hiroto Saikawa, the CEO Ghosn as Chair of NISSAN approved in April 2017. NISSAN's 2018 operating profits declined 45% compared with the previous year. Things at NISSAN were not on track, and the pressure on Ghosn was only increasing.

One of the key issues to understand is that one of the main problems of the entire issue was that the deal between Renault and NISSAN had never been structured as a proper M&A, but as a joint venture with Carlos Ghosn as the unifying linchpin. But the root of their differences is that the two major owners pursued very different Missions: the Mission of the French Government was to create jobs in France and sustain Renault's profitability, while the Japanese Funds and the government there aimed for long-term ownership value. The clash of Missions between owners that doomed Volkswagen was at play here again. The major difference is that the clash of Missions allowed the CEO (Ghosn) to become the virtual "owner," agreeing with each owner to secure his position and his power, but never truly getting the owners to agree explicitly on the Mission of the JV, and how the JV would add value to each of its members. He seemed more adept at playing off one owner against the other.

The final episode in this remarkable saga was the falling out between Ghosn and NISSAN that occurred at the end of 2018.[3] Ghosn, and long-time senior NISSAN colleague Greg Kelly, who was Ghosn's Chief Administrative Officer, were suddenly accused by the Japanese Minister of Justice of fraudulent transactions that personally enriched both without the approval or knowledge of NISSAN's Board or shareholders. They were both arrested in Japan in December 2018, while Ghosn was Chairman of Renault, NISSAN, and Mitsubishi, as well as CEO of Renault. The charges concerned hidden retirement benefits organized by Kelly, as well as expenses and real estate deals paid by the company for the personal benefit of Ghosn. Ghosn spent several months in Japanese jail, was released on bail only to return to jail again on other changes. On December 30, 2019, media outlets reported that Ghosn had escaped in Bond-like fashion to Lebanon, via Istanbul. He had first been arrested by Tokyo District prosecutors on November 19, 2018, upon a return flight from Europe. Ghosn settled with the U.S. Securities and Exchange Commission over claims of failing to disclose more than $140 million in payment to him from Nissan.[4] He was fined $1 million while Nissan was fined $15 million and Kelly $100,000. Ghosn neither admitted nor denied the SEC's charges, but accepted a ten-year ban from serving as an officer or director of a public company. France eventually issued an international arrest warrant against Ghosn in connection with channeling more than 15 million euros of payments by the R-N Alliance to Ghosn via an Omani distributor.[5] Lebanon does not recognize extradition requests for its nationals, so Ghosn is safe there but cannot afford to travel.

The parallel in the rise and fall of Ghosn and Napoleon, two imperial leaders, is striking. They both rise as extremely talented turnaround experts, corporate for Ghosn and military and government for Napoleon. Their most impressive and successful campaigns are fought abroad, they display boundless administrative and centralizing energies, and both embrace imperial privileges. In the end, their respective organizations and leadership fail, correcting governance is absent, and close team members do not provide the feedback, and when they do, they are punished (Talleyrand, the Foreign Minister, is fired when suggesting Napoleon better pursue peace in Europe) or threatened (Bernadotte takes refuge in Sweden, fearing for his future). Some then outright betray them (Marmont, with the help of Talleyrand, surrenders to the enemy in front of Paris rather than defending the capital; Saikawa, the Ghosn appointed heir at NISSAN organizes the fall of Ghosn in Japan, with his colleagues on the Executive Committee). Their imprisonment and escape from Elba and Japan respectively are further points of similarity. These underline that these are not only idiosyncratic stories—even though every story is unique—but stories that illustrate value destroying leadership patterns and dynamics.

The FPL Angle

There is no question Ghosn did an excellent job reviving NISSAN and creating value for Renault through the R-N Alliance. Mitsubishi CEO Osamu Masuko said, “I don’t think there is anyone else on earth like Ghosn who could run Renault, Nissan, and Mitsubishi.” A NISSAN spokesperson added, “Mr. Ghosn was the lead architect of the Nissan Revival Plan, which transformed the company from near bankruptcy to profitability within two years. [Under Ghosn, NISSAN had] higher profit margins than many rivals and expanded geographically.”

However, Ghosn, as Napoleon before him, gradually gave up on a practice of Fair Process Leadership, that they had required at the beginning, when they realized they depended on the contributions of many others and less certain about their engagement and their understanding of the contexts they were in. Engaging Ghosn became increasingly hard with time, his leadership style moving from the FPL “ask” mode in his early NISSAN days to a dictatorial “tell,” substituting the “pull” of engaging and energizing to the “push” of commanding. Energies and collaboration decreased, as did performance. Probably the biggest mistake of Ghosn was to increasingly receive credit in public interviews for his turnaround of NISSAN, when this had very much been a common endeavor of many, including his team of “French samurais” and the NISSAN managers and employees.

This is the same as Napoleon getting credit in his *Bulletins de la Grande Armée* for victories were assured by others, but who would not get that recognition in the Army’s Bulletins. One picture is worth a thousand words, and it concerns the painting by David celebrating the great victory at Marengo, shown in Fig. 13.2.

Several features allow us to categorize this picture as "fake news of the gravest kind." Marengo is a French victory over the Austrians, fought in 1800, which ended the Second Italian Campaign against the Habsburgs who had reconquered Italy while Napoleon and his best generals were in Egypt. Remarkably, Marengo is a Napoleonic defeat. Few French know this, as the point is subtle and also a bit lucky, if not miraculous.

Indeed, the battle plan devised by First Consul Bonaparte goes awfully wrong: a surprise attack by General Michael von Melas on the main French troops led by Bonaparte's close and loyal associate, General Berthier, appears to announce a decisive defeat. The French center is broken around 2:30 pm. The French's only move is to hope for an orderly retreat, which they do. Their luck is also that Melas returns to his camp early, eager to write a note to his

Fig. 13.2 Napoleon crossing the Saint Bernard (Painted by Jean-Louis David, 1801)

Emperor announcing the great victory just obtained. In his absence, the Austrians appear to slow down their pursuit and further elimination of the French retreating troops.

Having heard the canons firing on the Marengo battlefield and also suspicious that Napoleon's order to send him away from the battlefield may not be the best decision, General Desaix decides on his own to return to the battlefield, which he reaches around 17:00.[6] By that time Napoleon is desperate, conscious that a major defeat will be sufficient to remove him from power and convinced that his heroic journey is coming to an end.

Desaix is said to have told a very despondent First Consul, "Sir, this battle is lost, but there is time to win another!" One of Napoleon's many strengths was to fully transfer authority, without further control or micro-management, when the situation was becoming critical, when one of his associates saw or offered a better solution. Desaix at this point took over the French command and ordered his troops immediately into action. The Austrians, who were maneuvering too slowly by then, were completely surprised by the charge and failed to convert their win into a decisive victory that was there for the taking. The tide turned fully in favor of the French with a superb cavalry charge in support of the movement initiated by Desaix and led by Murat and the young Kellermann. The Austrian army is now completely taken by surprise. The sudden combined counterattack stops the Austrians, completely disorganizes them, and allows the rest of the French infantry to return to the battlefield and cement a late French win. The victory is as complete and decisive as the defeat that was looming a few hours earlier.

Unfortunately, Desaix, the hero of the Marengo battle, is shot during the charge and dies on the battlefield. Napoleon unceremoniously takes the limelight and credit for the victory, as the painting in Fig. 13.2 suggests (and where Desaix is completely absent). An informed eye will notice that the painting does not show Napoleon on the battlefield, for that would have been a sorry scene indeed. It depicts Napoleon crossing the Grand Saint Bernard to take attention away from the annoying fact that his strategy for the battle was a failure, which, according to historians, could have allowed Austrian forces to invade France already in 1800. Entirely exuding non-FPL, the painting shows a God-like figure, pointing to the sky, reminding the viewer of the Creation of Adam by Michelangelo. It celebrates Napoleon, the Adam of the new French order in Europe. The painting is one more illustration of Napoleon's superb propaganda machine, started during the first Italian campaign, directed to bring Napoleon to the heights of French society.

Napoleon would go on to assume the leadership of France, and create an Empire. However, unable to secure peace and unabating in his tireless effort to submit Europe to his will, the European nations will ally against him and have the better end. His fall and that of France will be stark and spectacular. That the generals, who knew events on the Marengo battlefield, never insisted at least on a Requiem at Notre-Dame in Paris in honor of Desaix, their fallen comrade, is another remarkable aspect of this story. Yielding to their pleas, Napoleon accepts that his body is brough back from Milan cathedral to France, but at the last minute, the order comes to leave him at the Saint-Bernard pass, where his body rests to this day.

Napoleon, having been defeated at Marengo, may have needed the illusion of immortality more than his generals. He may have tasted defeat and bitterly so. Again, like Muiron at the Pont d'Arcole and later Murat at Eylau, comrades saved him from failure. Napoleon must have enjoyed, if not be reassured, at this beautiful depiction of strength and glory by David. But it was a grave misrepresentation of the facts and done at the expense of one of Napoleon's most talented generals, who had sacrificed his life for the cause.[7] The glorification based on "fake news" is quite cynical and should have been countered by the marshals and generals. They failed to muster the courage to confront Napoleon collectively and early. They must have become accustomed to these grandiose misrepresentations and lost their nerve to do so, nor did they probably understand the need to do so. Those who did were framed as enemies of the Empire, and joined the opposing ranks, like Moreau or Bernadotte. This was perhaps wise for them, but regrettable for France as it allowed the increasing power grab. The gradual decline of FPL at the top foreshadowed a decline in force and performance of imperial leadership, and, subsequently, of the armies.

The lesson is clear: Napoleon benefited from a remarkable team of marshals, engaged, and motivated by good FPL practice when he was on the rise. Remarkable and unprecedented success was achieved on the European scene. But with this success, FPL practice was gradually abandoned, and relatively early so. Napoleon, the Emperor, did not have the humility nor the intelligence to consider the merits of a more durable exercise of FPL. One trusts that modern leaders may learn the lessons associated with his downfall. One can only judge a leader's true and permanent understanding and commitment to FPL when the latter is at the top and has the power. Washington and his "band of brothers" fared much better and are a stark contemporary contrast to Napoleon and his group of Marshals (Appendix B).

Both stories lead us to a remarkable conclusion: Fair Process Leadership by itself is not a stable competence, and certainly not a talent (for it would then not erode). FPL often arises when solutions are far from obvious to leaders and when unprecedented levels of cooperation are required (as in crisis and war). When things return to normal, and when leaders think they have the solution, they return to a “decide and announce” leadership style, skipping the first two steps of FPL.

FPL truly is a discipline that leaders must work at with their teams to ensure that success, and the power and occasional arrogance that come with it, do not take the place of the more engaging and collaborative fair leadership that brought these leaders to their top.

Owner-led businesses greatly benefit from strong leadership like the one displayed by Bonaparte and Ghosn, but in their early days. They can also suffer from the strong and increasingly erratic leadership displayed by these leaders in their more mature and later days. If only the leaders had fallen, that would have been only fair. But they brought their organizations and countries down with them. That was definitely unfair share for the people in these organizations and countries, which only a fair process practice and culture could have prohibited.

2 Benefits and Implications of Fair Process Leadership for Owners and Boards

The stories of Napoleon Bonaparte and Carlos Ghosn thus vividly demonstrate the powerful effects of both fair process and unfair process for owners, boards, and the organizations these boards govern. Given that FPL cannot be considered to be natural, a formalized approach to ownership and board is beneficial to ensure its continued practice. When fair process prevails, owners, their board members, and those that interact with the board—the executive leadership team and also other stakeholders—commitment and individual satisfaction will be high, resulting in collective performance; when the opposite is true, commitment will wane, engagement and implementation will be haphazard, and performance will suffer.

As further argumentation for the above proposition, let us consider the situation when owners, board members, or executives come to their discussions with entrenched attitudes and closed positions. The board will submit to unflinching executives or owners—which will certainly not release the greatest energies and deny the board any chance of value-add—or turn into a negotiation session between sub-groups, where power will prevail. Alignment will be illusory, the engagement will turn into a power play, which ultimately owners may win, but at a cost in terms of commitment and value creation.

The powerful will enforce their wrong positions, others will comply, and the saner ones will resign.

This is the antithesis of what a good board meeting should be: a fair hearing about what is best for the organization, with desired levels of openness and integrity, and a willingness, after thorough debate, to align with what is better for the organization, or, if the board is undecided, submitting the question to the owners for their consideration and final decision. True board work demands members committed in a collegial manner to debate about the better future for the organization, fully conscious that such decisions may go against interests or private agendas that may have motivated initial positions to start with.

Secondly, just as in the court of law, FPL allows owners and board members to fully appraise themselves of context, facts, and issues, and to individually contribute to the outcome. A good owner co-creates the future with her or his board, and with executives. This co-creation is the key success factor for implementation. All of us—when psychologically sane and endowed with sufficient self-preservation instincts—will always be more committed to a decision that we contributed to than to a decision that is imposed on us. We tend to reject the latter soon or even instantly, precisely because it is not ours and we look for reasons not to adhere to it. It is the opportunity to defend our ideas in a fair discussion process that leads us to recognize that our ideas might indeed be sub-optimal. Not only does a good debate highlight where our initial views may have been wrong or biased, and thus allows those ending up on the losing side of the debate to adhere to the outcome. What is needed for such acceptance is that the debate be a fair one, and that no individual or even sub-group did force a decision on a collective body where they are only a minority and where the majority believes that the decision is wrong. That the authority ultimately makes the decision is not the issue acceptable, as closure needs to be enforced. What is necessary is that this authority is perceived as fair by those engaged in the debate or affected by it.

The Fair Process model also provides a good description of the dual roles of non-executive and executive directors. Executives have specific, operational responsibilities, know the organization better, and do most of the analysis and the execution of the decisions. Executives typically are strong willed, having gained and merited their way to the top. Like Bonaparte and Ghosn, their rise will be greatly enhanced by engaging the right people. Because their role is to change the future, these leaders will be endowed with good doses of self-confidence and be positively biased toward their own decisions and capabilities. As they rise, their leadership is validated. The risk then is that which risks become increasingly wedded to their viewpoints and biased in favor of the decisions they reach. To reduce this bias, boards and their owners will do well to request that executives present several options and comment on the opportunities they present, and the risks that are inherent in each. That provides contrast and more sharply describes opportunities. Non-executives bring different perspectives and add objectivity to corporate decisions such as C-level appointments, strategy, policies, corporate architecture, and organizational moves.

Thorough exploration of options is necessary to capture the framed opportunities and challenges. Discipline, talent, and thoroughness in this exercise are required for the effective exercise of the board's fiduciary duty on behalf of the organization. At this stage disagreements do not yet need to be resolved: people's concerns against an option are qualified as a risk (or minus) of that option; people's preferences in favor are registered under the plus of that option. Differences of intensities might be listed as A (high benefit or risk), B (good benefit or real risk), or C (benefit or risk), and the distribution of intensities of views noted. At this stage one records differences of views and captures nuances. What should be eliminated at this stage are not feasible options, but wrong descriptions and biases in favor of or against options—without accepting reasonable counters.

The FPL framework also provides a clear template for the Chair in his or her management of the Board. The Chair will see to it that different board members do not address different steps at the same time in the discussion, but that the different steps are addressed in the right sequence, and with sufficient thoroughness. FPL usefully decomposes the system of formulation, decision making, and execution, so that board members are "on the same step" at any point in the discussion. No process survives a bad leader—only policies and procedures do, as they do not depend on a leader and are to be applied regardless of the leaders. It is essential not to confound process with procedure, a confusion often encountered when presenting fair process. The distinction pertains to the L in FPL: a process is only as good as its leader, whereas procedures do not need leaders, they need collective enforcement by all.

Fair Process Leadership theory states that the quality of the outcome generated by the board will be largely the consequence of the quality of the board process, itself largely influenced by the leadership of the board process and the quality of engagement of the stakeholders on the issue being addressed. This has two direct consequences. First, all board members ought to take responsibility for the board process and for its leadership, contribute to it in a positive way, and not just delegate these matters to the Chair. Second, the Chair better have a good degree of detachment regarding the outcome, to remain open to input from board colleagues. Like a good judge, she or he ought not to commit too rapidly to a particular outcome, nor be too easily influenced by positions taken early by board members. Anchoring one's leadership in the board process sits fully at odds with applying one's authority to influence a particular outcome. It is often the rigid pursuit of outcomes that often introduces unfair process in the board and lies at the root of many dysfunctions. Effective leadership by the Chair to enforce fair process at the board necessitates *engaged detachment* by the Chair: very engaged in maintaining the process but with a good detachment from the actual outcome, considered fair as a result. As a final comment, we can only mention a truism: there is no fair process without a fair leader. The practice of fair process imposes behavioral requirements on the leader, which nomination committees and owners best keep in mind. The requirement also pleads for the separation of the roles of Chair and CEO: it is hard for a Chair to be unbiased with respect to one's own proposal, or attacks on it.

We will shortly turn to the horrible governance saga of HP during the 2000–2010 era. It is largely a failure of governance and ownership, with many psychological undertones. It cost the organization and those responsible for it dearly. The organization failed to assure its renaissance while several protagonists suffering and dying from cancer certainly were not helped by the huge pressures surrounding the board room. Unfair processes at play will be identified. They include repeated leaks to the press of board discussions, a lack of openness and transparency in the meetings themselves, unclear expectations, a culture of deceit, inconsistency in CEO treatments, biases turning into stubbornness and ultimately stupidity. Over this period three Chairs and as many CEOs were sacked, and in sequence. This attests to the destructive consequences of the widely prevailing FPL violations. The unwinding of the US financial sector can be explained in a similar fashion,[8] as does the disastrous management of the COVID pandemic in many countries, including the US and Brazil.[9]

One caveat remains, often misunderstood: a fair process demands a certain time and information commitment upfront, to allow an adequate framing and exploration of the issues. This investment of time can be shortened with good FPL competence and a good dose of talent in recognizing the issues and formulating the challenges. Yet, effective engaging and exploration of the issues unavoidably takes time. So, decision making might appear slow as a result, particularly when contrasted with the speed of a more dictatorial style of decision making. The argument in defense of FPL is that rapid dictatorial decision making often results in unprepared or insufficiently planned execution, with value destruction as the consequence. The Russian Campaign by Napoleon is one telling example. Effectiveness in governance and management trumps efficiency; or, in slightly different words, coming quickly to the wrong decision and then rushing to execution only speeds up value destruction. The effects of investments in engagement and exploration are rewarded by dual improvements in decision making and ~~improved~~ execution, ultimately leading to greater and more speedy value delivery and capture once execution starts. Returning to the Napoleonic example, the engagement of a few or even a single Russian general—or a thoughtful engagement of former associate and then Prince of Sweden Bernadotte—would have greatly improved their preparation for their "special military operation" intended to return Russia as a reliable, even if forced ally of the French Empire. It could have avoided the impending disaster altogether. Such engagement should not have taken much time, but it would have required greater openness to advice that was counterfactual to the planned operation. Both Bernadotte and the Russian General Kutuzov had predicted that the French would not succeed and likely not survive the harsh Russian winter, even if both might have underestimated the scale of the disaster that befell courageous French troops, set up by their leader for failure.

Engagement and commitment rise quickly among boards introduced to FPL and unused to function in this manner. One should never forget that the criterion for judging decision making at board level is first effectiveness in contributing to value creation, and not efficiency in decision making. FPL competence by the Chair is exactly what is required for effectively leading board discussions at adequate speed. Fair process will not fall upon a board through the air conditioning system, but rather through enforcement of fair process by the board's leader, the Chair. That ideally will be a consequence of commitment by the owners to FPL and their insistence on selecting fair process leaders as Chairs and board members.

This leads to the question as to the existence of any limits to the benefits of the exercise of Fair Process Leadership. A Chair not willing to listen to the arguments of others—because, for example, of private agenda issues not revealed to fellow board members—would find the model's prescriptions futile and would not have the integrity required for the role. Then he would not apply FPL. The robustness of the Fair Leadership Process, however, is that it makes the concealment of private agendas more difficult and induces their revelation. For example, engagement of different opinions invariably reveals some options that are good. By refuting options that appear good to fair and independent members, these members will protest and conclude that the Chair is indeed driven by a private agenda as he consistently refuses discussion of certain options that appear good. So, displaying a certain naivety, disciplined by FPL thinking and a good degree of independence and FPL among board members, is a powerful technique for revealing private agendas among certain members, including the Chair.

FPL also is a mutual commitment by owners and board members, starting with the Chair, trickling down to the CEO and the executive team, and finally infusing the entire organization in its relationship with internal stakeholders as well as outside ones. The application of good process and fair play, widely communicated and explained to those impacted by the decisions reached, invariably leads to improved decisions and, from there to improved acceptance of the decisions reached, and ultimately to more engaged execution as a result of a deep sense of fairness and trust in the decision-making process and those that lead it. Fair Process Leadership is the concept that ensures that justice and collective interest prevail over private interests in board and ownership discussions.

The rest of the chapter will be devoted to narratives of known major governance failures, analyzed through the FPL lens. Board stories typically remain confidential and take some time to become public. We like to assure the reader that the examples are timeless and continue to plague many boards to this day, as the Elizabeth Holmes saga and her Theranos venture attest.[10] The main goal of these narratives is not to be current in our storytelling, but to convince our readers of the extraordinary power and promise of FPL at ownership and board levels. Conversely, these stories are intended to convince the reader that a denial of FPL can trigger extra-ordinarily negative and destructive consequences, which a good application of FPL would have stopped.

3 Unfair Process at the Deutsche Börse Board[11]

The Deutsche Börse was established in January 1993 as a holding company for all of Frankfurt's exchanges and securities depositories. In April 1993 Werner Seifert was appointed as its CEO. Over the next ten years, Seifert successfully united Germany's local exchanges and transformed the Deutsche Börse (DB) into a leading exchange services business, introducing a new electronic trading system, consolidating share trading from the various regional exchanges to Frankfurt, setting up pan-European alliances, and creating a world-leading clearing, settlement, and custody company, under the name of Clearstream.

In 2000, having completed the integration of Germany's exchanges, Seifert began discussions with the London Stock Exchange (LSE) on a merger that would produce Europe's dominant player and one that could be reckoned with globally and compete with the dominant US exchanges. He did so with the full knowledge and consent of the Deutsche Börse board.

Complementarity between the two exchanges was excellent: London was strong in equity, Frankfurt excelled in bonds. One was on the continent, the other was in the world's most global financial place. Talks between the two exchanges were on and off. Tired by this, Seifert in December 2004 submitted an all-cash offer for the LSE which the LSE board rejected. He clearly signaled that the door remained open for further discussions and improved conditions. Seifert, eager for what was a great deal, decided the company would make a new public offer. After again obtaining approval from the Supervisory Board, Deutsche Börse went public with an offer that valued the LSE at US$2.6 billion. It was an all-cash bid that was 23% above the previous day's closing share price. It had the support of the LSE Chair, but not of the CEO, who likely was more defensive about keeping her position and power.

One of London's financial jewels being under attack, Seifert soon faced strong opposition from UK hedge funds. These were not well known in Germany, which was more familiar with fixed income and private equity. The funds had managed to own around 27% of Deutsche Börse's shares. Led by TCI and the Rothschilds in London, they launched a coordinated and aggressive campaign to stop the LSE acquisition. One of their priorities was to remove Seifert as CEO of Deutsche Börse. The hedge funds claimed that the Deutsche Börse would do better to return the monies set aside for the LSE acquisition to shareholders rather than blow it on an acquisition that they stated was motivated to serve the greater glory of Seifert and the other executives and board members of the Deutsche Börse. The campaign waged against Seifert was at best unfair, at worst built on lies.[12] In the meantime, DB employee unions feared for their jobs and a possible reverse take-over by the LSE management, should the acquisition play out.

On March 6, 2005, the Deutsche Börse board finally decided to bow down to the forceful and deceitful campaign of the hedge funds. The company withdrew its offer for LSE and did so despite a majority of Deutsche Börse shareholders being in support of the deal. While the board did not accede to the hedge funds' demands to remove the CEO, Seifert by then felt that the board had insufficiently supported him. He resigned being also very bitter for the unfair way in which his amazingly successful reign had ended and decided to leave the business scene altogether. That by itself was very sad: there was no reason for Seifert not to be honored for his extra-ordinary achievements on the German and European exchange scenes.

It should be observed that the German corporate scene is unusual when it comes to governance: corporate law specifies that for companies of a certain size half of the board members ought to be shareholder nominees, while the other half should be employee nominees. This was a result of the famous "German compromise" reached after World War II between unions and the shareholders, many of whom were blamed by the unions for cooperating with the Nazis during the war. There is no mention in this arrangement for the independents so dear to Anglo-Saxons.

The Chair is a shareholder nominee, with a vote that counts double in case of a tie. Labor representatives elect a Vice-Chair. In the German two-tier board governance system, the CEO is not a member of the board, nor necessarily the powerful CEO in the US sense. The board is supervisory and contains only non-executives. He often is the speaker of the Management Board, which is the second collective body in German Governance. The CEO and executives are members of the Executive Board (the "Vorstand") the CEO being typically invited to attend supervisory board proceedings, with colleagues as appropriate and needed by the board's agenda. When the CEO has a conflict of interest with an issue, the CEO is asked to leave the board room, possibly asking her or him for views on the issue. The board then proceeds to discuss matters without her or him.

It is quite hard to obtain factual insight into board dynamics and discussions. Most of the time these remain confidential. We often must infer what happened from the decisions made and outcomes that resulted. We will do so here. Our main aim is to illustrate the multiple ways in which fair process was or could have been denied, by the Deutsche Börse supervisory board and possibly also, most likely unconsciously by Seifert, the CEO. Our purpose here is not to award blame or guilt but rather to use the story to illustrate how fair process violations indeed lead to negative outcomes and value destruction. It also is to illustrate how easily FPL mistakes or omissions can or could be made. It is interesting to note that Brexit has led the LSE to again be more open to commercial links with continental exchanges, be it Deutsche Börse or EuroNext.

The board had to address several key issues which we examine in turn. We focus on three specific areas: organization and leadership, strategy, and interactions with shareholders and stakeholders.

Organization and Leadership

The board's decision not to sufficiently back and defend Seifert during the unfair attack was surprising and ungrateful to him in view of his achievement of building Deutsche Börse into the single German exchange as we know it today, and one that became a global player. Several observations can be made.

The first concerns framing the leadership required to successfully acquire the LSE. The person who unified the German exchanges may not have been the best person to lead a similar effort at the European level—particularly in the context of a hostile attack on the London Exchange. For sure, a British person would have more easily interacted with LSE and engaged with the leaders of the City.[13] Hedge funds are well known in London, but were largely unknown in Germany then, which did not have the rich and boisterous UK shareholder tradition.

The board up to that point had fully backed Seifert in his ambitious plans to unify the German exchanges. The move on LSE was seen as a logical continuation of this strategy at the European level. But it was not a pure extension, in fact it was a disruption, geographically and corporate wise. Herein lies the power of the FPL framework, which demands good engagement of concerned parties at the process start to underline this point. Having integrated Germany's local stock exchanges, there were several paths forward for DB. One was indeed to take on LSE, the European #1. This move would undoubtedly lead to a contest. Most would agree that the City and the London financial community would unlikely lay the red carpet. Engaging the latter community in an effective discussion was a must. So the issue not only was the management of LSE, but all the stakeholders that the LSE was serving and who might find the project of greater interest than the LSE Board and management whose initial reaction was likely to be defensive.

Other strategic options imposed themselves on DB's forward path. One consisted of uniting smaller European exchanges, or even exchanges outside of Europe, to favor access to emerging countries for DB investors and to allow corporates to find equity inside Germany, and from there inside continental Europe. So, DB should at least explore the idea of buying second-tier exchanges. That was the strategy that LSE would eventually pursue, after it had been woken up by DB's hostile attack. Another option was to approach American exchanges, which Euronext did. So, a host of choices faced DB, of which LSE was certainly a prominent one, but not necessarily the best one, nor the easier one to implement.

For sure, the leadership issue would need to be raised once an option had been decided as it was the first implementation choice for the option. Having been a great German unifier, the battle would shift to foreign soil, and Seifert was not likely the most suited for the task. Seifert himself could have raised this question, inviting each board member and executive ought to creatively contribute to board discussions by thinking what is best for the organization.

Too often boards remain captive to successful CEOs, who like to anchor the board in their thinking and into options that fit them, prohibiting more radical changes.

The Board could also have done a better job engaging their CEO on his letter of resignation, the letter itself proving a level of disengagement that caused the letter to be written. Prolonged frustration, and probably tiredness, must have led Seifert to write the letter. This was not only because of the activists' aggressive attacks, possibly also with himself, finding the journey to LSE quite different from what he was used to. It is likely that he may have viewed as having provided him with insufficient support during what would be his last battle, and in the face of the vicious attacks by the hedge funds. It is in these times that the Board makes a great difference, there was no reason for the Board not to support Seifert, without giving him a blank check on the targets, on the strategy, or even on his continuation in the post. He certainly appeared lonely in the fight. It was revealing that he apparently took the plane to London to meet with TCI but was unable to locate their office. He had been looking for a big building, not realizing that these raiders were just a couple of individuals in an office. German investment bankers were not foreigners in London, yet no board member presumably joined him on that trip or arranged appointments for him, not just with TCI but also with the City's other stakeholders. If that indeed is the case, that would be a failure on both sides, Seifert and the board for the entire board should have been engaged in approaches to British and also German stakeholders.

Regardless of the motivation for his resignation, the Board might have immediately stated that the CEO and the Board are united, and that in any case they would not easily accept the hedge funds' demands to sack the CEO, and that under no condition they would abandon him. They could, for example, have confirmed, regardless of the outcome, an honorary position on the board for the contribution he made to the company. In succession, the first task of the board is to take good care of the outgoing CEO. Seifert had done a fantastic job building the company to its strong current position, and the board should have more strongly and more publicly recognized this great contribution. Instead, the board seemed to have thrown Seifert "to the lions" which must have been very hard on him and was unfair. If the board had supported Seifert, even while withdrawing the LSE bid, this would have ensured Seifert's cooperation in dealing with the ensuing crisis. Seifert might still have been able to perform well for the company, including perhaps as an advisor or ambassador, a future board member, or with an honorary title, connoting recognition and respect for his huge record.

In sum, having completed the unification of the German exchanges, it was necessary for the company to take a deep breath and start discussing the direction it would pursue next. That would correspond to starting a new FPL cycle and engaging each other and new individuals (experts, candidate board members, and the CEO and the executives). That was not the sole responsibility of the Chair; it was the responsibility of every board member and, ultimately, of the CEO himself.

Strategic Review Following the Setback

The question that concerns us here is what Deutsche Börse could look like going forward, after its setback in its hostile move on LSE, and what its strategy might be to get there? Should Deutsche Börse regroup before resuming its attack? Should it give up fully, retreat temporarily, or change tacks and set its sights on other exchanges? Consistent with the logic presented in the earlier section, it would appear logical for the Board to examine these questions before turning to Seifert's continuation as CEO.

Given the turmoil that took hold of the company as soon as the attack on LSE was launched, a key question on the agenda of the board would be to realistically frame the current situation: did Deutsche Börse reach a crisis point during the execution of its strategy (involving possibly regrouping or retreating to relaunch later) or did the company reach the definite end of its envisaged scenario? A positive answer to the latter question suggests that it is time to turn to the next phase of the company's life; a negative answer suggests that the retreat might be temporary and that the company might return to LSE later. These are two very different conclusions and states of the world. An effective application of FPL would have been to explore these scenarios, with Seifert and the executives, but not only with them. The question of Seifert's future and that of the executive team could only be settled once a clear position had been taken on which fork of the road they would decide to embark on next.

There is no question that acquiring LSE was a true disruption for Deutsche Börse. The move would radically alter the nature of its relations with competitors, shareholders, and stakeholders, from employees in Germany to the City's actors and beyond. One of the consequences that the board ought to have explored is the impact of the acquisition inside the group, and here one thinks first on DB's technology business. That is the corporate strategy discussion, which pertains to the portfolio of businesses to be held by the group, and the discussion of synergies inside the group. So, the question of the exchange does not limit itself to the exchange business but has to consider the synergies, positive and negative, inside the group. Expanding the exchange business has immediate consequences on the technology business, positive or negative. Also, there is the further point that the monies for the LSE acquisition were largely contributed by the technology business. This is the financial strategy issue, but not an operational one. The question whether these two related but distinct businesses ought to continue to live together in one group thus imposes itself as a key strategic question at group level and can be summarized as to the growth opportunities for DB's other business that would be reduced or enhanced by the LSE acquisition. Group boards ought to keep in mind that corporate and business strategy questions are distinct and interrelated.

In sum, the move to acquire LSE raised a number of fundamental and complex organizational, strategic, and leadership questions which the board seemed to have insufficiently addressed, despite supporting Seifert's strategy up to that point. Relying on Seifert was natural given his track record. Given the path forward it no longer was. Hence, the first disruption to discuss the possible change of course lay with the board itself. It had to put itself in gear for what would be very different discussions. In other words, starting with a board self-evaluation looked like a more promising path than starting with an evaluation of the CEO. A Board conscious of its failures and vulnerabilities can more easily exercise effective leadership. Such awareness immediately changes the nature and tone of the discussion on Seifert's proposed resignation and increases the likelihood of a good outcome.

The attack by hedge funds, naturally attracted by the cash Deutsche Börse had set aside in support of its acquisition plan, should have been anticipated. This and other issues suggest that the Board itself was insufficiently prepared for this new phase. Before taking on major strategic and potentially disruptive decisions, a thorough self-evaluation of the board for composition and competence on the issue under examination is needed. Instead, inertia largely prevailed as often the case with boards which must be built for the future, and not anchored in the past.

Activist Shareholders and the Upcoming General Assembly Meeting

The Board was hard pressed by activist shareholders (such as TCI and Atticus) to return to shareholders some of the monies set aside for the LSE acquisition, possibly in share buy-backs. The Board had to decide its response to this challenge, and what possible actions it might commit to. It clearly was puzzled.

Seifert wrote to TCI after the board's decision: "The most difficult task before the company is the melding of a very broad range of shareholders' opinions into a cohesive strategy. Only a handful of our 28,000 shareholders shared your concern that the LSE should not be acquired at any premium." Yet the board appeared to have backed down in the face of the hedge funds' aggressive PR campaign.

Seifert and the top management team were inexperienced in dealing with hedge funds, particularly active in the UK because of the power held by minority shareholders there, able to challenge the board on some of its decisions even with minimal voting power. In such a context, the board's reluctance to take the question for a vote at a shareholder meeting was surprising, given that such meetings are the occasion to settle differences with shareholders. Seen from London, the decision adds fuel to the camp that was against the intrusion of a foreign and especially German player, who obviously did not understand the City and its governance. The board and the company eventually succumbed to shameless attacks by hedge funds, which confirmed that they seemed unprepared for events that should have been expected once hostile takeover moves were decided. Instead, being insufficiently prepared, the board got cold feet at a crucial moment, leaving its CEO to hang out in the cold which contributed to his resignation.

The principle of shareholder democracy states that it is only proper to allow shareholders to decide on courses of action that drastically alter the company's risk profile, and hence financial return given the fundamental risk-return relationship. Even though a shareholder vote was not required under German corporate law, many would argue that a shareholder discussion and vote would have been the proper thing to do. General Assemblies are the place for shareholders supporting a strategy to come forward, possibly confirming that if the share price were to drop further, they would happily acquire even more shares. The existing institutional shareholders could have provided greater credibility to the strategy at a General Shareholders Meeting than defensive executives.

The conclusion from an FPL angle is that the story appears to be a sequence of missed engagements by the Deutsche Börse board, leaving executives to lead the charge. Mispricing in the stock market is not something one simply complains or whines about, but something one actively takes advantage of, correcting the mispricing as a result. Engagement in and of the stock market seems to have been weak and contributed to the outcome. The board severely underestimated the challenge, a consequence of insufficient engagement and exploration of knowledgeable individuals before strategic decisions were taken. A closer examination of the Deutsche Börse board reveals that it had these experts, and that it certainly had on the board individuals who could contact such experts.

To conclude, we argued that several FPL failures likely contributed, if not caused what was a very negative outcome for Deutsche Börse's leadership. Governance is not first about the Board finding the right answers, but rather to engage people with the expertise and experience in the matter at hand, and who may have the right answer. The Deutsche Börse Board's main failure was an overall failure in engagement strategy and tactics, ranging from shareholders to board members, executives, and, more broadly, valuable stakeholders.

4 Prolonged Unfair Process in the HP Board[14]

The *Hewlett-Packard Company* ("HP") was born in 1939 in Palo Alto, California, which also houses Stanford University, where both founders met while undergraduates and which they then greatly contributed to. HP grandfathered Silicon Valley. HP was for years held up as a paragon of innovation and one of the best companies to work for. It was one of the companies that Steve Jobs admired, together with Disney and Intel. Jobs and co-founder Steve Wozniak tried to sell Apple five times to HP, failing each time.

From 1999 onward the HP Board began a dubious record of hiring and firing three CEOs in a row (Fiorina, Hurd, Apotheker) and seeing its three Chairs (Fiorina, Dunn, Lane) resign in succession. These individuals being quite different, the problem cannot be attributed to them, but reflects a governance gone bad.

The fall in HP's share price—especially relatively to the performance of Silicon Valley sister companies Apple, Sun Microsystems, and Cisco—has been equally spectacular to that of its leaders, as has been the number of lawsuits involving directors, executives, and shareholders. Good governance preserves and delivers value creation; the events at board level over the 1999–2009 decade proved that bad governance can cause considerable destruction. The HP governance system appears to have been the subject of a more than a decade long viral attack. The episode was only terminated with a full reset of the governance of HP following the split of HP into two distinct companies, HP, devoted to hardware, notably printers and PCs, and HPE, dedicated to services.

Our motivation here is to illustrate how the board's missteps were mostly the consequence of unfair processes at board level.

Enter Carly Fiorina

The 1999 appointment of Carly Fiorina as HP's CEO resulted from the Board's conclusion that the culture of HP had to change in a major way. The Board asked Fiorina "to revolutionize HP, the HP way." This itself is a contradiction, and a possible setup to fail for an incoming CEO who cannot do both: people know how to start a revolution, but then do not know how to control and eventually terminate it. HP itself had been a revolution and Silicon Valley was its major legacy.

Departing CEO and Chair Lewis E. Platt largely directed the search for his successor, with help from Richard Hackborn, HP's former No 2 who had turned down the offer to take the post. Platt had initiated a thorough introspection of the company seeing it bypassed in its own backyard by such companies as Apple, CISCO, and Sun Microsystems. One of its conclusions was that HP needed big cultural shifts, and that implied finding an outside CEO with the right features. Consistent with this realization, Platt spun off HP's original diagnostic, test, and measurement equipment business under the name *Agilent Technologies, Inc.* The IPO at $2.1 billion set a record. It included a health care and medical products business, subsequently sold in 2001 to Philips Medical Systems, and a manufacturer of integrated circuits, sold in 2005 to two PE entities, KKR and Silver Lake.

Platt had successfully grown HP sales by 187% during his seven years as CEO, reaching $47.1 billion in his last year. He was fully a product of the collaborative and autonomous management philosophy of the HP founders, referred to as "managing by walking around." He regularly had luncheon with HP employees at the cafeteria. He was very instrumental, with Richard Hackborn, in bringing Fiorina to HP. Fiorina never engaged Platt for advice on HP matters. This would prove to be a mistake.

We already mentioned that the HP Board's invitation to Fiorina lacked clarity in its framing. It is likely that Fiorina heard the first part of the invite, dealing with HP's need for a revolution, and less the second part, which invited her to manage "the HP way." Revolutions are rarely paragons of effective and innovative collaboration, the hallmark of the old HP.

Realizing she was an outsider, Fiorina asked Dick Hackborn, Board member, Acting Chair, and HP old timer, to serve as her mentor, particularly regarding HP matters and culture. In HP's Hall of Fame Hackborn appeared soon after the founders. He was a close associate of Platt in the introspection exercise and in the succession process. He chaired both HP and Agilent when the latter was spun off.

Another element of unfair process at the beginning of Fiorina's term was that Hackborn soon stopped mentoring her. He commented later, after her exit from HP, that he quickly became concerned about her leadership of the company. What Hackborn failed to admit in the article is that as mentor, he should have engaged Fiorina on his growing view "that she did not have what it takes." Direct and pointed feedback from her mentor could have led to usefully self-assess her leadership and modify her leadership behavior accordingly. Then, Hackborn may have concluded that trying to convince her was pointless anyway.

Regardless, Hackborn stepped down from the HP chairmanship six months into Carly's term. Carly must have been overjoyed to assume the Chair of HP, joining a formidable list of powerful CEOs of US listed companies that double up as Chairs of their boards.

Early Revolutionary Moves: PwC and Compaq

Carly's arrival into HP indeed was a revolution. As Lucent CEO she put commercial sense into AT&T Bell Laboratories, host of many leading scientists and Nobel laureates. Her background was marketing and not engineering. She was a woman and not afraid to take the front stage. Intent on revolution, she soon proposed to buy the consulting arm of PwC for $16 billion, an offer the Board refused.[15] It seems that Carly did not quite learn the main lesson for CEOs: never break your engagement with the Board. IBM eventually ran away with the PwC business, for less than $4 billion. The bursting of the dot.com bubble had changed the scene, and valuations. Her lack of sense making of the board's turndown of her offer for PwC was a miss in terms of building greater understanding and complicity with the board.

Resolute on her revolutionary assignment, Carly met Capellas, the CEO and Chair of Compaq, in summer 2001. Both rapidly concluded that their firms would benefit from a merger. Many industry observers were skeptical, judging the cultures of the two companies to be too far apart. HP was technologically more advanced, while Compaq was built for mass production and customer orientation. This description belied the fact that HP was also in mass production, making printers and computers and having sold many of the advanced technology in the Agilent spin-off, while Compaq had some technologically advanced product lines (like network servers) that would complement HP's product line. The product lines of the two companies were largely complementary, which would facilitate the integration of both companies and not necessarily cause major difficulties. The new company had five major business units, none greatly affected by the merger, and each largely emanating from one of the two companies. The strong offerings of both companies could thus continue their journey in this "merger of equals." In truth, this was a misnomer as HP had acquired Compaq to become HPC. The statement turned HP loyalists against the merger.

Growing Frictions with the Board and with the Larger Shareholders

Fiorina was seen by the Board as insufficiently engaging the VPs and their staffs who were leading the business lines. The VPs were essentially CEOs of HP's five business units. Following the merger announcement, too many senior executives were left uncertain too long about their prospects in the merged company, leading some of the best ones to leave HPC and be poached by competitors or Silicon Valley neighbors. This suggested that the acquisition had been insufficiently prepared. Realizing this, the board asked Carly to consider hiring a COO to support her in her engagement of her business unit heads. "The board has no business telling me how to run the group" was Fiorina's unfortunate reply to what was an insightful suggestion from the Board. Thus, Carly missed another opportunity to seriously engage with her board. Eventually the board hired Mark Hurd, who very much was the COO type Carly refused to consider. Mark Hurd would constantly confirm that he was implementing and following Carly's strategy.

The numbers would confirm the board's advice and its leadership decisions: the sequential CEO tenures of Carly Fiorina and Mark Hurd led HP to exceed $100 billion in revenues as of 2007. The revolution had occurred, but the HP way, a collaborative FPL-like spirit that characterized HP's internal culture under Bill Hewlett and David Packard, had disappeared. Carly had largely contributed to this, and the board had allowed it to happen.

Carly's relations with the Board were not helped by her increasing conflict with Walter Hewlett, son of founder Bill Hewlett and President of the Hewlett Foundation, a 10% shareholder. The HP founder's son eventually issued a public letter against the acquisition, after having signed the deal as board member. As a concerned shareholder—this was his statement—he had to attack the company in court for disseminating false information to the public. This was hardly fair process on the part of a board member, who outside the board room enjoyed playing the role of activist investor (against the company he owned and was on the board on). Hewlett remarkably initiated a crusade for better governance in US board rooms.

Hewlett lost his suit against the company. However, his lawyer exposed unfair process by the company, revealing at the hearings that HP had exerted undue pressure on its banker, Deutsche Bank, to "bring in votes in favor of merger." The banker was told by HP's CFO in no uncertain terms that DB was to vote the proxies it controlled in favor of the deal if Deutsche wished to remain HP's banker. This was illegal.

Shareholders approved the merger with the smallest of majorities. This confirmed that the company had not convincingly made its case, and employees noted the fact. As a result of Hewlett's public letter against the deal, internal approval ratings fell from 84% approval to 55%.

A better course of action would have been to take a "pit stop" and to hear the various objections from internal stakeholders and shareholders. The company could then return to both with a more convincing case. Instead, Carly took the majority vote as a win and that was good enough for her. Hewlett was pushed to resign his directorship. It left him a loud critic of HP's leadership, extending his unfair process as a former board member.

Employees and senior management took little solace from the general assembly vote, worsening existing divisions within the company. At the board level, these divisions in the company and outside furthered maneuvering to build a coalition against HP's increasingly imperial leader.

The Unraveling of Fiorina's Leadership

Hackborn convinced the board to bring back Perkins, HP's first general manager of its computer division and later co-founder of Silicon Valley's prime venture capture firm Kleiner, Perkins, Caufield & Byers. The firm had bankrolled Google, Amazon, and other legends. Though Fiorina was against the appointment, she had to allow Perkins to join the board.

The entry of Perkins would have wide ramifications. Together with Keyworth, the representative of the Packard Foundation, Perkins and Hackborn created the Technology Committee of the Board, officially to oversee and recommend HP's technology strategies. They invited HP's CTO to the committee and kept the CEO away from joining it. This was another mistake made by Carly as her presence would have allowed her to gain greater exposure and knowledge of HP's technology issues and would have eliminated the possibility of this committee becoming an instrument to plot Carly's demise. The Committee started to lecture both board members and executives, rapidly crossing the line separating governance from executive roles.

These engagements also helped the Committee obtain standing with the board and with the Executive Committee.

Strengthened in their resolve to counter Fiorina, the boys on the Technology Committee called a secret board meeting at the beginning of 2005 in Fiorina's absence. The topic on the agenda was HP's fate going forward. But it would seal Carly's fate. The meeting was leaked to the press. In Davos, an ocean away, Fiorina denied that she was in trouble.

On a stopover in Chicago, Carly met Patricia Dunn who informed her that the Board indeed had met to ask for her resignation, with a $20 million check and a thank you note for services rendered. While HP denied the press report, Fiorina walked away with the check in February 2005 and was replaced by Mark Hurd, the COO-like figure the Board had recommended Carly hire. Patricia Dunn took the Chair from Carly Fiorina (as a reward from the boys?), who was so upset by Dunn's betrayal that she vowed to leave business altogether.

There is an interesting conundrum to this story, typical of unfair process contexts: both the Board and Fiorina agreed on the unfairness of the other side but were much less conscious of the unfairness they imposed on the other side. This is not uncommon. Harmony, unity, and performance were lost as a result.

Life Continues at HP Without Fiorina, but Unfair Process As Well

In September 2006, Newsweek reported that HP Chair Patricia Dunn had hired investigators to find out who among the board members leaked strategic information to the press. Dunn had authorized pre-texting by investigators who were spying on her fellow board members. The person eventually identified himself: it was George Keyworth, representative of the Packard Foundation on the HP Board and co-conspirator, with Hackborn and Perkins, of Carly's fall. As a result of this scandal, several board members, including Tom Perkins, a Silicon Valley veteran, and Chairperson Dunn were forced to resign. The scene was indicative of board power plays.

With Mark Hurd as CEO, HP continued the recovery initiated by Carly Fiorina. Revenues passed the $100 billion mark. No one would have placed a bet on this outcome at the beginning of Carly's tenure. Fiorina and Hurd, working in sequence, had succeeded in turning HP around and returning it to prominence among US IT firms.

Hurd, in turn, was forced to resign due to an alleged sexual harassment complaint and a lack of transparency in (relatively small) payments for corporate services (including to the female advisor he allegedly harassed). These events broke the board's trust in Hurd. There was also a view that Hurd was very operational and not the person to conceive the next chapter in HP's remarkable saga as a leading technology company. The board awarded Hurd a US$40–50 million severance payment. Larry Ellison, founder and Executive Chairman of Oracle Corporation, immediately hired Hurd, and publicly thanked HP for the opportunity.

Subsequent events confirmed that Hurd was also not a Fair Process Leader. He became the subject of an investigation by the US Congress for insider trading due to the "timely" sale of HP stock that occurred just before announcements that were likely to reduce HP's stock price. Research on repeated cases of market abuse by CEOs and Directors of major US and global companies confirms that Enron, Parmalat, and other WorldComs were the Olympic medals of a much less visible hive of unfair activity and wrong "tone at the corporate top."[16]

Following Hurd's departure, the HP Board finally decided that it was time for a reset. Ray Lane, former Managing Partner of Kleiner, Perkins, Caufield & Byers, was elected to become the new Chair. He was an HP veteran, having served as Division VP at HP Enterprise Services. It returned some "HP way" to the Board, yet the Board's first move was another corporate governance disaster and further evidence of a lack of FPL at board level. The PE members of the Board, led by Lane, pushed for the appointment of Leo Apotheker from SAP, apparently without many board members even meeting or interviewing him. Apotheker's term would be marked by a series of muddled strategic announcements, the biggest of which was his initial comment that he would make HP as cool as Apple!

The lack of FPL continued with the purchase of UK's Autonomy, valued at over US$11 billion and nearly fully written off a year later. Several people had warned about the possibility that Autonomy was highly overvalued. Their warnings were ignored. The review at board level of the transaction was at best superficial. Apotheker's claim concerning HP and Apple was an early signal that something was wrong with his appointment too. His tenure would last just under one year.

The Board Finally Reflects Upon Its Previous Failures and Splits HP into Two Distinct Companies

The PE members on the Board, realizing that things had not gone well, finally took a pit stop and did some introspection. This likely contributed to the board being more successful with their pick in September 2011 of Apotheker's successor, Meg Whitman. Whitman had led the emergence of eBay from 1998 to 2008, after stints at Bain & Company, Walt Disney, and Florists' Transworld Delivery. Whitman had joined the HP Board the preceding January.

The combined arrivals of Meg Whitman and Ray Lane at the top of HP finally returned better collaboration (read HP way/FPL) at the top of HP and restored a more harmonious board-CEO relationship. The discussion with regards to HP's mission continued and yielded a remarkable decision in 2015, similar to the one that ended GE's ordeal: the Board, with Meg Whitman now as Chair, brought to a close the bloody chapter in HP's history by splitting HP into two companies, HP Inc (the computer and printing businesses) and HP Enterprise (the infrastructure and enterprise services business). The HP Board finally returned to more normal and simpler business discussions, away from the scandals that rocked it over the 2000–2010 decade. To confirm the split of the two companies, HP Enterprise decided to relocate its headquarters to Houston from San Jose, California. Meg Whitman stepped down from the HP Chair in 2017 and remained as CEO of HPE until February 2018.

Summing Up

The point we argued for in this final section—and throughout the chapter—is the value, if not imperative, of FPL practices at the top of organizations, and particularly at ownership and board levels. Kaizen, a hallmark of Toyota's manufacturing practices, has imposed itself in factories across the world. Kaizen practice represents FPL on the shop floor of factories. FPL is a framework that extends this practice to the middle and top management floors, and all the way to the board and its owners.

Organizations that adopt FPL will, over time, be less influenced by biases and will be associated with both greater value creation for the corporate stakeholders and increased trust of these stakeholders and of society in their business practices. HP having been founded on FPL principles, finally returned to these healthy collaborative ways with Lane and Whitman, recovering normalcy in performance in line with what the theory predicts.

The lesson for the reader then is the following. Fairness, sometimes invoked as a wish list or even a commitment, is in fact not an option at the top of companies; it is a must, intimately linked with business continuity and performance. It leads owners, boards, and executives to collaborate more effectively. It improves relationships with external stakeholders. FPL is the "secret sauce" to the alignment that is so fundamental for the successful pursuit of a clear and purposeful mission.

Notes

1. See, e.g., *Nissan's U-Turn: 1999–2001*, INSEAD Case No. 5095, by K Hughes, J-L Barsoux, and J-F Manzoni, 2003 & 2007 (Awarded the 2007 European Case Clearing House Award in the category "Strategy & General Management"), as well as the considerable number of articles written on the topic in the media.
2. https://www.latribune.fr/entreprises-finance/industrie/automobile/affaire-ghosn-et-si-tout-avait-commence-avec-la-loi-florange-799083.html
3. https://www.nytimes.com/2018/12/30/business/carlos-ghosn-nissan.html and https://www.ft.com/content/02891aff-d9cd-40a0-9beb-764c1fc2f48f
4. https://www.sec.gov/news/press-release/2019-183
5. https://www.nytimes.com/2022/04/22/business/france-arrest-warrant-carlos-ghosn.html
6. There is controversy about whether, as he wrote in his *Bulletins*, it was indeed Napoleon's order that made Desaix return to the battlefield. More likely is the account by which Desaix on his own, hearing the canons firing at Marengo, took the decision to return to the battlefield.
7. Desaix also conquered Upper Egypt with 1500 grenadiers. He was remarkable and Napoleon intended to name him Minister of War. This also attests that the French victors were never a one-man show, and that in fact Napoleon got to endure only because of the sacrifice of some of his close associates.
8. https://www.vanityfair.com/news/2009/01/stiglitz200901-2
9. https://papers.ssrn.com/sol3/papers.cfm?abstract_id=3560259
10. https://medium.com/swlh/the-theranos-saga-55ddccdde490
11. This section builds on the INSEAD case relating the event https://publishing.insead.edu/case/deutsche-borses-strategy-derailed-hedge-funds and also on press accounts.
12. In the modern age, regulators ought to intervene faster and more strongly on market actors spreading false information.
13. A similar issue concerns the appointment of French EU Commissioner Barnier to lead Brexit negotiations with Britain: surely, if the EU were intent on succeeding, the choice of a Scandinavian or Portuguese negotiator might have been wiser.

14. This section is largely built on the INSEAD case https://publishing.insead.edu/case/board-leadership-successions-hewlett-packard-1999-2014-roller-coaster-a-carly-fiorina-1999-2005
15. PWC Consulting was eventually bought by IBM after the IT bubble burst, for less than $4 billion.
16. Bebchuck, Grinstein, and Peyer have confirmed this in their 2006 paper (revised 2010), identifying the phenomenon as "lucky CEOs" receiving "lucky grants" from their boards. https://papers.ssrn.com/sol3/papers.cfm?abstract_id=945392

Part III

Humanware: Owners as Leaders and Value Creators

14

Profiles in Ownership

The literature on leadership is voluminous. Beyond military and historical figures, it mostly addresses CEOs and managers. This book shifts the emphasis to the leadership exercised by owners and directors. In this chapter we present five distinct ownership profiles to illustrate the wide diversity of owners, as well as the events that trigger individuals to enter and fully commit to active ownership.

The contexts of these owners vary greatly. Warren Buffett requires little introduction, only to underline that he represents the true owner-investor profile, who does not meddle much with boards or management. His ownership principles are deep and wise, and ought to be known by anyone aiming to do well at this craft. At the opposite is the profile of Priscilla de Moustier, who heads and directs the owners' board of her more than 300-year-old family firm, Wendel. Then there is the second-generation owner, Dominique Moorkens, who received his first training into owner-management by his father, and then set out to firm up the governance structure of the Moorkens family firm. Anu Aga is a very different example of second generation Indian owner, who governs the firm with her husband first, and then with her daughter. Finally, there is the story of the "orphan" owner, Bart Huisken, who was never taught about ownership, and discovered ownership "on the way." His story underlines how important it is to ensure that the ownership journey is traveled with the right partnership and colleagues, including in shareholding.

Together these stories are intended to convey both the uniqueness and the diversity of these ownership histories, and the many transitions they entail. Underlying questions that may be of interest to readers pertain to how one leads as owner as distinct from leading as manager, or as a passive owner.

M. Massa et al., *Value Creation for Owners and Directors*,
https://doi.org/10.1007/978-3-031-19726-0_14

Family contexts, mentors, and circumstances—which the Romans would evoke as occasionally the work of the goddess "Fortuna"—loom large in these stories. So do purpose, drive, persistence, and talent. These stories also address both the issue of falling into ownership and exiting from it. They all underline that ownership is not a straightforward road to travel. It is one fueled by particular transitions, and not necessarily a successful one in terms of bringing the intended venture to its hoped for destination.

The profiles presented in this chapter largely show a more positive side of ownership than the dramas of the stories presented in earlier chapters. They also show how one prepares for ownership, or falls into it. Successful owners are like athletes, endowed with talents, very much developing and refining their game over time, using setbacks as learning moments to reflect upon, while also being guided and inspired by mentors whose images, advice, and principles played a fundamental role in developing their ownership craft. Apart from that of Warren Buffett, the profiles are based on interviews we conducted. We hope these stories may inspire our readers, as well as allowing lessons, some being about what to avoid going forward.

These profiles provide the material and context for the commentary we offer in the following chapter, where we will elaborate whether ownership is a talent or a competence, or both.

1 Warren Buffett: A Relentless Drive for Mastery and an Unabated Focus on Pure Ownership[1]

Warren Buffett is the owner of Berkshire Hathaway (BH), his publicly listed investment firm. Its main ownership lesson is that it provides us with a portrait of pure ownership, focused only on decisions regarding investments, which lie at the heart of ownership.

The Determining Influence of Home and the Early Years

Buffett's early years had a defining influence on him. He was born in 1930 in Omaha, Nebraska, the second of three children and only son of US Representative Howard Buffett. He never felt as comfortable as in Omaha. He did not like the hustle and bustle of New York and Washington, as his nickname "the Oracle of Omaha" connotes. His father was a fierce critic of the interventionist New Deal policies, both domestic and foreign, and many of Warren's choices would be conservative as well. Buffett's family was relatively wealthy. His father was a stockbroker. In 1942, his father was elected to the first of four terms in the United States Congress.

Even as a child, Buffett displayed an interest in making and saving money. He was very impressed by a book he had read at age seven, *One Thousand Ways to Make $ 1000.* He went door to door selling chewing gum, Coca-Cola, or weekly magazines. Coca-Cola would become one of his most successful investments. For a while, he worked in his grandfather's grocery store, experiencing customer preferences. While still in high school he was successful at making money delivering newspapers, selling golf balls and stamps, detailing cars, and other means. Filing his first income tax return in 1944, Buffett took a $35 deduction for the use of his bicycle and watch. Buffett's interest in the stock market and investing also dates back to his childhood.

He regularly visited his father's stock brokerage where he chalked stock prices on the office blackboard. Friends and acquaintances found him to be a mathematical prodigy who impressed them by adding columns of numbers in his head. He spent days in the customer lounge of a regional stock brokerage near the office of his father's own brokerage company. On a trip to New York City at the age of 10, he made a point to visit the New York Stock Exchange. At the age of 11, he made his first purchase: three shares of Cities Service Preferred for himself, at the share price of US$ 38. Not long after the purchase the stock fell to US$ 27. Warren was relieved to quickly sell the shares when they hit US$ 40. However, when the share price later climbed to US$ 200, Warren had learned his lesson in the value of patience and longer-term investing.

In 1945, in his sophomore year of high school, Buffett and a friend spent US$ 25 to purchase a used pinball machine. They placed it in the local barber shop. Within months, they owned several machines, each in different barber shops. He sold the business for more than US$ 1000 $ before graduating from high school. With the proceeds, he invested in a business owned by his father. He also bought a farm and put a tenant farmer in charge. It was clear that he was an early prodigy in ownership.

Having made more than US$ 5000 Buffett felt he was ready to enter business, but his father convinced him to go to college. He attended the Wharton Business School, left after 2 years, and finished his undergraduate studies in business administration at the University of Nebraska aged 19. He was turned down by Harvard Business School for being too young. This proved fortunate as Buffett then enrolled at Columbia Business School after learning that Benjamin Graham—author of *The Intelligent Investor,* one of Buffett's favorite books on investing—and David Dodd, another well-known securities analyst, taught there. He earned a Master of Science in economics from Columbia in 1951, also attending the New York Institute of Finance.

Shaping the Mind of a Master at Investing

Buffett started to buy stock in Berkshire Hathaway as of 1962 after noticing that the share price would rise every time a mill was closed. Seabury Stanton, the owner, offered to buy back Buffett's shares at US$ 11.50 per share. The offer came in at 11 3/8, which made Buffett furious. He decided to buy the firm instead, kicking out Stanton in the process. He eventually closed Hathaway Mills in 1985.

By 1967, he started to expand into insurance, buying GEICO (Government Employees Insurance Company) shares. GEICO grew to become Berkshire Hathaway's core investment in the insurance sector, and a major provider of its capital. Buffett in 2010 admitted that buying into the textile industry was his biggest mistake ever, costing him compounded opportunity losses of about US$ 200 billion over the subsequent years relative to having invested these sums directly in the insurance sector. Berkshire Hathaway's share price on January 11, 1991, was US$ 6800. On January 15, 2021, it was US$ 350,320. The multiplier over 30 years exceeds 51 representing an annual compounded interest rate over a 30-year period of 14%. Over the same period the Dow Jones Index grew at an annual rate of 8.5%, half of Berkshire Hathaway's rate. Buffett made close to 95% of his formidable wealth after reaching the age of 60. In 2008, Buffett was ranked by *Forbes* as the richest person in the world with a net worth of US$ 62 billion. Buffett personifies the pursuit of single-minded mastery of investing and capital allocation. He is considered the most gifted follower of Benjamin Graham (1894–1976), the British-born American professional investor and father of value investing. Graham began teaching this approach at Columbia Business School and subsequently refined it with co-author David Dodd through various editions of their famous book *Security Analysis*. Graham's followers make up a long list, of whom the most famous, beyond Buffett, are William J. Ruane, Irving Kahn, and Walter Schloss.

Buffett's second mentor was Philip Arthur Fisher (1907–2004), an American investor best known as the author of *Common Stocks and Uncommon Profits*, a guide to investing that has remained in print ever since it was first published in 1958. His "scuttlebutt" technique, which involves searching all out for information about a company, was praised by Buffett at the 2018 Berkshire Hathaway Annual Shareholders Meeting. Buffett was once described as being influenced 85% by Graham and 15% by Fisher.

WB#1: Never lose money.

WB#2: Analyse the company well enough so that you understand the facts and the story – that leads you to largely reduced investment risk.

WB#3: Invest for the long run – in the end, the market catches up WB#4: There are lots of undervalued companies out there.

WB#5: Invest in sufficiently undervalued companies that there is little or no risk.

WB#6: The basic ideas of investing are to look at stocks as a business, use the market's fluctuations to your advantage, and seek a margin of safety. That's what Ben Graham taught us. A hundred years from now they will still be the cornerstones of investing.

WB#7: Be an "owner" – hold onto stocks for the long term (until market corrects undervaluation, but even beyond).

WB#8: Do not manage the companies you invest in – appoint trusted advisors and collaborators on the board and let them oversee the managers.

WB#9: Let the managers manage the company.

Fig. 14.1 Warren Buffett's ownership principles

These were the great masters that inspired and shaped Warren Buffett. They led him to develop a clear set of guiding principles for his ownership decisions (see Fig. 14.1.). What is particularly startling, given the focus of our book, is Buffett's single-minded purpose on ownership and investment. Buffett abstained from running any company and even shied away from being on boards of companies other than his own. This also came about because of his stint as Chairman of Salomon Brothers, which we explain next.

A Stint as Chairman of Salomon Brothers at a Time of Crisis

Berkshire Hathaway was the biggest shareholder in Salomon Brothers (US$ 700 M) when the latter firm got caught in 1990 trying to corner the Treasury Bills market. Mozer, the mastermind of his devious plot, put in fake orders by client asset management companies to control the market. When identified, Mozer compounded his actions by stating that he had done so only once, which was a lie. Gutfreund, who ran Salomon Brothers at the time, ought to have gone to the US Treasury to acknowledge the issue; inexplicably, he did not. The unlawful practice continued until one of Salomon's clients realized in

1991 that Salomon was using their name with the authorities and blew the whistle. Gutfreund, the "King of Wall Street," was forced to resign, together with other senior executives. Gutfreund then called Buffett to save Salomon.

Buffett had invested more than US$ 700 million of Berkshire Hathaway money and accepted to replace Gutfreund as Chairman and CEO. Buffett immediately appointed a CEO after asking ten or so potential candidates' a single question: Who should be the new CEO of Salomon? An Englishman, Maughan, was named at the conclusion of the interviews. Buffett addressed Solomon's directors warning them that funny business was over and that if they even strayed close to the line, they would be fired. Contracts with Washington lobbyists were terminated. Buffett was running a clean Salomon and impressed supervisory authorities that authorized Salomon to resume trading operations. It had been a very close call. Buffett as Chairman had saved the firm. Salomon was finally able to settle with the SEC for a penalty of US$ 290 million. Michael Lewis's 1989 book *Liar's Poker* describes the inner workings of the firm that dominated the game of extra-ordinary profit-making. The firm's top bond traders, calling themselves the *Big Swinging Dicks,* were the inspiration for Tom Wolfe's 1987 book *The Bonfire of the Vanities.*

Buffett's leadership of the bank impressed all, managers, regulators (including Breeden, the SEC head known for his toughness and no-nonsense approach), and politicians alike. He is one of the first investment bankers to apologize at a US Senate hearing: "I would like to start by apologizing for the acts that have brought us here. The Nation has a right to expect its rules and laws will be obeyed. At Salomon, certain of these were broken." He also issued his famous letter in the *New York Times, Wall Street Journal,* and the *Washington Post* where he attacks Salomon's pay scale. He stated that he had no problem with extraordinary pay for extraordinary performance; however, he also stated that Salomon's "share the wealth" system was subsidizing all, even the mediocre, at shareholders' expense. Even though performance in 1991 turned out twice as good as in 1990, 1991 bonuses were below those of 1990. Some people left, leading Buffett to comment that "in the end, we must have people to match our principles, not the reverse."

Buffett then shocked Wall Street by suddenly leaving the Chair and CEO seat to Bob Denham, his tough and tight-lipped lawyer from LA. Buffett was very happy to "get his life back." Salomon Brothers came out of the episode weakened. Denham orchestrated the sale to the Travelers Group in 1996. Buffett's stock in Salomon was worth US$ 81 at the time of the sale to Travelers, up from US$ 38 when he bought it in 1987. The Travelers Group merged with Citicorp in 1998 to form a financial services giant, Citigroup.

Travelers merged Salomon with Smith Barney. The name fully disappeared in 2003. Buffett would later describe his board stint at Salomon as "interesting and worthwhile, but far from fun." He would not do it again, sticking to his passion, investing, and again abiding by his principle, which is to stick to what you know.

Meeting Other Challenges in the Market and at Home

Buffett's new challenge was to adapt his investment choices to the new digital economy, something he had underestimated at the emergence of the digital wave. Being an Omaha boy, it took him quite some time to endorse modern technologies and investments in companies such as Apple and Microsoft.

Buffett relentlessly applies his remarkable talents with great discipline when selecting investments. His choices regarding his own succession as the richest man in the world would abide by his principles as well: "I want to give my kids just enough so that they would feel that they could do anything, but not so much that they would feel like doing nothing." All three children now head foundations endowed by their father's great wealth.

Buffett never divorced from his wife, though she left Omaha in 1977 for California, which she enjoyed much more than Nebraska. There she became a social activist promoting civil rights, abortion rights, and family planning. It is In California that she met Bill and Melinda Gates, whom Buffett would judge to be better at charity work than himself. After his wife passed away in 2004 from oral cancer, Buffett grew closer to Bill and Melinda Gates. In 2006 he pledged to transfer 85% of his wealth to their foundation. He realized, late, that his had opened a new horizon for him and given him a social purpose while sticking to what he knows and likes best.

At the 2021 Annual General Meeting of Berkshire Hathaway shareholders, Charlie Munger, Buffett's 97-year-old long-time partner and Vice-Chair, revealed that Greg Abel, 58, was next in line to succeed Buffett should something happen to him.[2] Abel has been running all of Hathaway's non-insurance investments, and is regarded as highly intelligent and tough. The news came as somewhat of a relief to investors as the fund had been silent on the issue. The future is likely to be different for Berkshire Hathaway as Buffett has pledged to donate most of his class-A shares which then will become class-B common stock. His successor will not be shielded from shareholder pressure the way Buffett and Munger were. Buffett, however, was quick to add that he expected to continue being active in his firm going forward.

2 Anu Aga: Learning to Be an Owner and Trustee

The next profile is offered as a very different path to ownership. It contrasts with Buffett's journey, even if some themes are common, such as the emergence of a set of principles guiding an owner's action, and the mentorship enjoyed along the path to becoming an owner. Anu Aga is an Indian social worker who became a businesswoman and led Thermax, an energy and environment engineering business, as its Chairperson from 1996 to 2004.

I was born and raised in Mumbai. I have two older brothers and my parents regularly reminded me during my youth that my brothers would join the family business (the firm started by our father), while I would have to marry and raise a family. Furthermore, my father never talked much about the business when at home and joining this business was never something I was expected to do.

My father, with a partner, had started a manufacturing firm, National Steel Equipment, which made sterilizers, hospital beds, and hospital equipment. Customers being mostly the government, payments were very much delayed which created risk for the company and tensions for its leaders. My future husband Rohinton, was a good friend of my older brother Jamshed (who decided to move to the US) and strongly recommended that my father hire Rohinton, who had studied at Cambridge University and had worked for multinationals. That is when my future husband joined my father, who then split with his partner. They quickly decided to move away from relying on government orders and decided to make industrial boilers. They collaborated with a Belgian company Wanson and named the new company Wanson India. My younger brother Darayus bought over National Steel and Rohinton and my father took care of Wanson.

I attended St. Xavier's College and did my B.A in Economics and Political Science. The College had a very active social service league (SSL) which held 2-week camps in rural and urban areas. A bunch of us were very active members of SSL and attended camps and helped other local causes. After completing my BA, my choice was clear - being a social worker. For my post graduate degree, I joined the prestigious Tata Institute of Social Sciences (TISS), where I was fortunate to be selected and did extremely well.

The Head of Medical and Psychiatric Social Work at TISS had a profound influence on me. She made us realise that most women were scared of visiting slums, fearing they could be raped, robbed or murdered. Once we confronted those fears and came to terms with them, we would be liberated and felt free to visit any site.

Rohinton and I decided to marry and had two children; a daughter whom we named Meher and a son called Kurush. Business needed to expand, and since we could not afford to buy land in Mumbai, we moved to Pune. My husband took over

Wanson after my father retired. Under his leadership, the company did very well and though we were a small private limited company, he could attract the best of talent.

My husband had a tremendous influence in my life and was my mentor and later my daughter influenced me a lot. My husband made me feel special and competent; he helped me develop my self-confidence, which I consider vital for leadership, at the same essential level as honesty and openness to learning from others.

Rohinton was a heavy smoker and loved to eat all the wrong things which were not good for health. When he was in his late 40s he had a massive heart attack, damaging a large part of his heart. We went to London for his bypass surgery and on the second day, he had a stroke. My brilliant husband could not recognise me and forgot to read and write. With great effort, determination and grit he re-learnt everything, though it took him 20 years to get back to his old self.

When we returned to India, well wishers suggested that I take interest in the company (which by then was renamed Thermax). I joined the Human Resource Division and worked under a very nurturing boss who invested in me. When he decided to leave, he suggested to Rohinton that I should be made to lead HR. I enjoyed working in HR and Thermax was known for its innovative practices, winning many awards.

Both our children studied engineering abroad and joined Thermax as trainee engineers. Meher decided to marry a wonderful boy from Pune named Pheroz who also joined the company. They were sent to turn around a small company we had bought in the UK. With the help of the head of R&D (who joined them in the UK for a year) they turned around the ailing company. I had promised my daughter that when she had her first child, I would be with her for 6 months. Four years later when she was pregnant, I went to the UK and kept my promise. I had decided that when I get back, I would move out of HR and learn about operations. After my stint in the UK, when I was returning to India, Rohinton was delighted to have me back and drove to Mumbai to pick me up. Destiny had other plans and before reaching the airport, he had a massive heart attack and died. Instead of my husband receiving me at the airport, I was greeted with the news of his passing away.

A year before Rohinton's death, our company had gone public. The board decided that I should take over as the Executive Chairperson. I was most reluctant as I felt inadequate to assume this responsibility and was very much grieving for my husband's death. In order to build my inner strength, I decided to join a residential 10 day Buddhist meditation programme, where participants are not allowed to read, write or distract themselves in any way. It was very tough, but I came out of it by accepting death as inevitable. We refer to death as a tragedy, but I realised that what is inevitable for every human being, cannot be termed as tragedy. What is a tragedy is, if the living do not invest in relationships which matter. I also felt it was futile for me to keep comparing myself with my husband and keep feeling inadequate and small. What was expected of me was to give out my best – I realised that an apple tree cannot give oranges, no matter how much you wished for it. I returned to the business world with a lot of self-confidence.

A couple of years after I took over, the company went through a downturn and our shares which were at Rs 420 fell to Rs 36 (the entire Indian economy was going through a rough time). Much against the wishes of my senior executives, I decided to hire a consulting company. With their help we made major changes and got out of business that added to our top line but eroded our bottom line. We also brought in manpower productivity. Asking our employees to leave was one of the toughest decisions for me. Thermax reconstituted the entire board (which was done for the first time in India). The family decided to take non-executive positions on the board. It was difficult for Meher and Pheroz as they were used to running divisions and being on the board. But today, they understand and value this decision. With all these drastic changes, Thermax turned around; and of course the economy also revived.

14 months after my husband's death, our son Kurush died in a car accident, at the age of 25. The pain I felt when my husband had died receded into insignificance as compared to what I felt when Kurush died. But my daily meditation and having accepted that death is inevitable, I was able to come to terms with my son's death.

My relationship with Kurush was very close and occasionally volatile. One day Kurush confronted me by demanding that a large part of our earning be given to the social sector. Soon after this, my son passed away and I was keen on looking for a credible NGO. I was strongly recommended to meet a young girl named Shaheen Mistry who had started an NGO called Akanksha in Mumbai. Akanksha ran centres for underprivileged children for 21/2 hours. Kids came to these centres after attending their municipal schools and were taught English, Math, values and some fun. Shaheen and I got on very well and later Shaheen invited me to be on the board and I brought the centres to Pune. About 14 years ago, Shaheen asked if I would partner her in starting Teach for India (modeled after Teach for America) and I readily agreed. Today TFI is a very successful leadership movement, which also brings quality primary education to all children across 8 cities in India.

About 10 years ago, Meher, Pheroz and I decided that 30% of our dividend from Thermax would go towards the social sector; from this year, we have raised it to 50%. Our family, including my grandchildren meet 3–4 times a year, to review our social investment.

At the age of 61, I decided to step down as the Chair of Thermax and spend more time with the social sector, with my family (especially my 2 grandchildren) and travel. I was still on the Thermax board, but at 75, I retired from there too. I strongly believe in letting go of positions and having a smooth, planned succession. The Board selected Meher to be the Chair and under her leadership for over 25 years, Thermax has done extremely well and is moving towards a green company. Pheroz is on the board and does a great job managing our Family Office. I feel very comfortable leaving Thermax in the hands of Meher, Pheroz, our professional MD and a great board. Am proud to state that besides focusing on growth and profit, Thermax believes in taking good care of all its stakeholders and not just our shareholders. My husband always believed and lived by the words 'profit is not just a set of figures, but of values.'

This is reflected by our following an ethical policy of not taking short cuts. It takes years to build a positive reputation in the market and it takes one wrong decision to tarnish it.

3 Dominique Moorkens: Checking all the Boxes and Sharing the Lessons Gained along the Way with Others

Our next owner shares similar features with the two previous profiles, particularly the importance of the early years in shaping one's identity, as well as a thirst for learning and developing. The story also gets us more into business leadership, which Buffett largely limited to investing and governing (as Chair of Salomon Brothers), and succession, which Buffett, though recently naming his successor at the firm, largely pre-empted by major donations to the Bill & Melinda Gates Foundation, and which for Anu Aga became evident in the figure of her daughter.

Early Years and Early Training

Dominique Moorkens is the youngest in a family of six children, four boys and two girls. Their parents had their children at an early age, Dominique's father being 20 when his first child was born. There is a 12-year difference between their youngest and oldest, including a five-year gap due to World War II. The age difference meant that Dominique barely got to know his older siblings, born before or at the outset of the war. His relationship with older brother Pierre, born two and a half years before him, was always a close and supportive one. Dominique also enjoyed, as the last child, a close and nurturing relationship with his mother, who he describes as a superb Chief Emotional Officer.

His father was constantly busy developing what would become the family business in two- and four-wheel automotive distribution. Dominique nevertheless always felt supported by his father, in both his personal and professional development. His father provided him with invaluable oxygen to build his self-confidence. This also grew his genuine admiration for his father, which never waned.

Dominique's early education outside the home was chaotic. He even describes it as wild at times. His parents were distant, torn, when not tired, by the dual demands of business and family. Dominique hated his school days. Indiscipline and poor learning ability regularly forced him out of schools (five exits in total). However, this did have a silver lining by forcing him to adapt to constantly changing environments and to learn to cope with the disciplinary processes prevailing in the various educational institutions he attended. He remained a rebel throughout these ordeals. All the transitions only confirmed his dislike of school environments. Being an intern felt like living in prison. He admits that he was seen everywhere as a troublemaker. He was forced to redo classes, sometimes even twice. But through all of this he built up a resilience to face unfavorable environments and a desire for autonomy in leading one's own life. Both traits would prove beneficial in his business career.

First Move into Entrepreneurship

Dominique counts his father as one of the five people that fundamentally shaped him. His father was a BMW distributor in Antwerp at a time when the brand was taking off throughout Europe. Being a former racer, his father had spotted the racing talents of Jacky Ickx, who would become one of Belgium's greatest automotive legends. In that environment, Dominique's attention naturally turned to car racing. He quickly developed a deep passion for the sport and finally felt comfortable in a world that he could consider his own. He drove cars as of the age of 16, 2 years ahead of the official age limit. Caught by police, he was obliged to sign a paper confirming that he would not drive again on public roads until he reached 18.

For his first race he disposed of a BMW2002TI, the logical consequence of his father being a BMW dealer and former racer. He provided Dominique with the space and support to grow. The competition was the Tour of Belgium where he registered in the category of road series. A key challenge for his first race was to have adequate security harnesses installed in the car. He asked a friend to be his mechanic and co-pilot. His abbot, a racing car fanatic too, was one of the controllers of the Royal Automobile Club of Belgium. He greatly contributed to preparing Dominique for the race as well. The beginning was auspicious: he finished first in his category. The result confirmed his talent and strengthened his determination. Dominique rapidly developed a name for himself in Belgian racing, particularly in short uphill and closed-circuit categories.

The absence of financial sponsoring by his father forced Dominique to manage and finance his small entrepreneurial venture. His association with the Moorkens BMW dealership allowed him contacts with potential sponsors and taught him the value of a good network. It landed him a sponsorship with Castrol, among others. The experience was superb for further developing Dominique's confidence—which school did not—and for the development of his business skills. It also taught him about risk management. Seeing several of his friends die in races marked him forever.

Driving in the 24 h race at Francorchamps Dominique realized that going full throttle around the circuit was just too risky, even if some did it at their own peril. Dominique realized that he was insufficiently reckless to become a top driver, notwithstanding his talents. Jacky Ickx, whom he describes as mega talented, went full throttle, but did indeed suffer major accidents which he fortunately and miraculously escaped from, even the most serious ones. Dominique considers surviving racing champions as either lucky or wise enough to have stopped before major harm hit them. He considers himself firmly in the latter group. The lesson was not wasted on the manager and future owner.

Thrown into the Business Early with Father's Coaching

Turning 20, Dominique started a tour in his father's automobile distribution company going around the various departments. After 3 years of gaining experience and familiarizing himself with concession work, his father put him in charge of the worst performing unit in the group. Dominique was still living at home. Every evening his father was open, if not eager, to discuss the management challenges Dominique was confronted with. His father taught him empathy toward employees and customers. His father appreciated giving his youngest son not only advice, but also autonomy and space to grow and develop. Father and son also went fishing, sailing, and hunting, which he later realized were simple though meaningful exchanges on the essence of life and death that marked him forever.

Dominique finally had in his father met his best teacher. Confronted with a context radically different from school, Dominique proved coachable. The empathic and real family business context suited him perfectly. Confronted very early in his professional life with a horrendous business climate in the concessions he was asked to manage, he learned to lay off and distance himself from toxic people. He intuitively understood the importance of presenting collaborators with a motivating vision for the concessions that needed to be turned around. All these experiences and challenges proved invaluable, though he admits they represented hard training for a young adult who regularly would have trouble falling asleep, having absorbed too many pressures during the day.

Fatherly support and coaching allowed him to turn around in 2 years the concession that was his first management job. It soon became the most profitable in the dealer network. Dominique learned to rely on the strategic work done by the automotive manufacturers and that the key value add of a concession is the people dimension. A compensation for the challenge of leading the franchise was that he was given a coupé BMW CSL, a car he would never have dared to entrust to his own children the way his father did with him.

This first success led his father to promote him at the age of 27 as head of all dealerships held by the family. In this job, he needed to deal with people one if not two generations older than him. The training provided by his father paid off handsomely. Dominique gained legitimacy with the "older" employees and continued to refine his business leadership competencies and his self-awareness of both his managerial talents and his limits. His discussions also turned to more advanced business topics regarding the family firm.

BMW Drops the Family Firm which Opens an Asian Chapter

In 1973–74 BMW suddenly announced that it would stop the franchise agreement with the Moorkens family. The BMW distributorship represented at the time 80% of the turnover of the group, so the news hits the family like a tsunami. The dream of becoming one of BMW's leading franchises in Europe was crushed. Dominique's father especially took the episode badly, feeling betrayed by BMW management in Munich. The decision forced the family to diversify into different businesses (Piper airplanes, naval shipyards, sports equipment, etc.). Some investments paid off, others less so. It obliged the family to learn how to become a good investor.

The family had built ties with the East, distributing Suzuki bikes. Older brother Léopold decided that it might be opportune to go on a trip to Japan to meet with car manufacturers there. These were gradually building what would become global empires. The trip was remarkably successful, Léopold returning as a Belgian importer of Mitsubishi cars. This opened a new chapter for the family, Japan replacing Germany as the main business partner for the family. This is how the family reinforced its sights to the East.

Collaboration with older brother Léopold was very rich and instructive. Dominique saw how Léopold was a real leader of people. Dominique learned a lot from collaborating under his command on converting all distributorships from BMW to Mitsubishi. Plenty of collaborators preferred to stay with BMW and left the firm. This presented one advantage: the group recovered a start-up mentality. To celebrate this new spirit, the firm decided to join the Tour de France for a majestic 21-leg ride with the runners across France, celebrating endurance, competition, and conquest. It also celebrated the success of the transformation of the distributor network: the volume of cars sold in 1976 equaled the number sold at the time of the break with BMW.

Seeing his older brother lead the Mitsubishi distributorship convinced Dominique that his leadership profile would differ from that of his successful brother and encouraged him to be his own person rather than aspire to be someone he was not. This committed him to being more consensus-oriented, an approach he practiced and refined with Japanese partners Mitsubishi and Suzuki. This strong practice of engagement of colleagues and building commitment would become a trademark of his leadership.

The President of Mitsubishi suggested to Dominique and Léopold that they ought to visit a Korean company that Mitsubishi had signed technological agreements with. The brothers took on the challenge and went to visit Hyundai Motor Company. Distribution agreements soon followed at the end of 1978, opening another Asian chapter of the evolving family business. Coincidentally, Dominique and his wife Lily had three adopted daughters, two from Korea and one from Thailand.

The Death of the Patriarch and the Birth of Alcopa

Dominique's father Albert passed away on August 6, 1979, during the Admiral's Cup in Southampton. He was only 63 years old, but his heart was tired. However, Dominique was prepared as his father had confided that his life was likely to end soon. Each year, on the date of his father passing, the family continues to celebrate their patriarch and remembers deceased family members.

The process proved difficult as their father did not prepare his succession. The two older brothers were fully dedicated to their respective distributor networks. Jean-Albert, the oldest, was facing challenges in the truck import, distribution, and service business. The Spanish truck manufacturer Pegaso faced several problems including plant strikes, sabotage, and ensuing technical difficulties. These reverberated in the dealer network. Léopold was fully absorbed by the growth of the Mitsubishi business. The organization of succession naturally fell in Dominique's lap.

A great number of discussions followed regarding how best to transfer ownership of the business to the next generation. The siblings decided to put all their businesses and dealership into a single holding company, Alcopa, named after the initials of their parents, Albert and Constance, the last two letters referring to the newly formed owner partnership. Each of the siblings owned one sixth of the shares. The siblings decided that the organization of the group fell to their younger brother, as CEO of the newly established holding company. He had earned their trust. The operating principle was shared ownership and decentralized operations. This fitted well with the strong character of the two elder siblings. It also allowed the integration into Alcopa of the office furniture business of their brother Pierre.

The governance would be simple and direct: enjoying the trust of their two sisters, all male siblings would meet every 2 weeks at the family property in Ranst, starting with a luncheon and then proceeding with a formal meeting. Their mother attended the meetings, but never had to interfere. Her mere presence seemed to induce the siblings to find good solutions when problems proved tricky or contentious. Regrettably, Constance died in 2001. All agreed that her silent supervisory and coordinating influence were superb and maintained the unity of the siblings. All remain grateful to this day that she did not pass away earlier, like her husband. They regard her as having nursed Alcopa through early childhood and adolescence, the same way she nursed each of her six children.

Pierre, the third brother, with whom Dominique is close, inherited the entrepreneurial zest of their father and developed an office furniture business. In need of capital, the business was absorbed into Alcopa, diversifying the holding, and proving the centripetal forces among the siblings, largely attributed to their mother.

Dominique enjoyed putting some order into a portfolio that had become unwieldy. Businesses that did not fit were sold off. Times for the family group were good: Mitsubishi had become the center of the group and developed well. Suzuki followed not far behind. Quotas on Japanese car imports allowed good margins. The two-wheeler business developed nicely as well and gained an international footprint in Europe. All brothers contributed to the group, each in their specific way. Their brother-in-law was invited to contribute as well, to the delight of their older sister.

Entry of the G3 and Formalization of the Alcopa Governance

The 1990s instituted major changes which proved challenging: the entry of the third generation (G3) into the business occurred without sufficient preparation, rendering matters difficult for G3 members, for the group, and for the CEO. Dominique was eager to pursue new business opportunities, but discussions proved difficult. Family members started discussing the possibility of an IPO of the group. A few discussions were held with quoted firms to understand the benefits and constraints of this option. Agreement emerged that regardless of the final decision to go public, it probably was a good idea to put the group into shape for a possible IPO. The family thus agreed to the first step, the creation of a formal Board of Directors with independents.

To anchor the family character of the group, Dominique invited all family shareholders for a meeting to discuss where they had come to as a business family and where they now wished to go. A charter was developed describing the family's values, and the relations between family, business, and shareholding. These discussions allowed the formulation of a proper frame for the Board of Directors, appreciated by the four independent directors who were invited to join the board, with the four brothers. The Chair would be one of the independent members. A prominent lawyer, Jean-Pierre de Bandt, known by the family, accepted the invitation to chair the board. Beyond the chair, the board contained an investment banker, a consultant, and the HR head of Belgium's leading telecom. Alcopa became one of the first Belgian family groups with a professional and formal governance structure.

The board immediately provided clearer and stronger governance of the group, and a more open platform to discuss the group's strategic issues. Family tensions reduced, particularly when a G3 member expressed the desire to exit the group. The mediation of the Chair, experienced in such matters, greatly facilitated the exit, which increased the commitment of the remaining shareholders. As group CEO, Dominique enjoyed an excellent relationship with the Chair, who was an accessible and attentive listener. The board's creation yielded other benefits, including greater credibility of the group with family shareholders, with outside stakeholders (banks, automotive manufacturers, etc.), and with employees. All stakeholders felt better off.

The shareholder agreements stipulated the retirement from active management for every family member upon reaching the age of 65. By 2005–06, Léopold was very happy to retire to his property in France where he was desirous to open a new chapter of his life. A sensitive question was the replacement of the brothers as board members. Whereas the brothers favored a replacement by one of their children, Dominique—whose adopted children had other interests and were unlikely to join the business—greatly preferred not to adopt a representation on the board by family branch. Having been approached for a board position for one the large retail businesses of the French Mulliez family, he had seen the benefits, in terms of business strength and family relations, of a single and united business family, with no separation between the branches on the business side. Dominique's observation of the greatly more experienced Mulliez family allowed him to import better practices from this leading retail and distribution family. The provision of micro-liquidity for family shareholders helped the smooth exit of a family shareholder and appeared beneficial for family unity and commitment, which can never be forced.

Creation of the Owners' Board

The succession of Dominique as Alcopa CEO now loomed. This triggered the next round of family discussions, facilitated by outside experts. A new family ownership policy was agreed to, as well as the creation of an ownership board, called the *Family Shareholders Committee* (FSC). The latter entity would be distinct from the *Family Council*, which would be centered on the celebration and governance of family life and well-being, including the development of next generation members. The responsibility of the FSC was to focus on ownership matters, with the aim of having the family speak with a single voice on ownership matters. Its main decisions pertained to the vision and values of the family group, its scope and mission, and finally the nomination of the Board Directors, as well as its supervision.

The family shareholders further agreed that the FSC would contain between three and seven members, with the possibility that not all branches would be represented and that some branches could have several members on the FSC. The FSC and the Board of Directors would be asked to pay attention to preserving and growing the value of the entire family shareholding, and not the part belonging to certain members.

Election of FSC members took several rounds, each member needing a majority of the votes expressed at any round to be elected. This would ensure that each elected member would feel responsible for the entire shareholding and not just to her or his branch. The number of votes by each shareholder was proportional to that member's shareholding, as is traditional in such matters. All shareholders voted, and members from different generations could present themselves.

The outcome of the first election led to the election of two members of the G2– Dominique and his elder brother—and five of the G3. Dominique was elected as well, again demonstrating the trust of his family and of his colleagues on the FSC who asked him to serve as first President of this newly created owners' board (while also CEO of the group). Dominique's brothers now felt comfortable to leave Alcopa's Board.

The attention could now turn to Dominique's succession as CEO. It was a key topic on people's minds, but somehow it was never formally addressed. Dominique had identified one of his nephews as his candidate and had started to groom him. He was the CEO of the automotive distribution division. The family group had also identified an opportunity to extend its distribution activities to Switzerland through the purchase of a bankrupt distribution network. The family and the group welcomed a business opportunity in the same sector, with similar brands, and in a multi-cultural country like Belgium which the family knew well. The board also had a Swiss member who could help. The Board asked the CEO of the automotive distribution division to take the lead in the integration of the Swiss operations under his wing.

Unfortunately, the acquisition, part of the former and bankrupt Erb group, proved to be in worse shape than anticipated and a major competitor in Switzerland—akin to Alcopa's position in Belgium—pulled all the levers to counter the business entry of a foreign distribution group into its markets (which it largely dominated). More concessions needed to be closed or sold and the operation needed to be fully turned around. The entire project also started to take too much of the CEO's attention and time. The complexity of the project had been underestimated by all, including the Board. The project should have benefited from closer and greater supervision, outside counsel, and close and regular review.

Time for CEO Succession

Reviewing the difficult conditions the group found itself in, the FSC then decided to ask Dominique to become the group's Chairman and oversee Alcopa's return to a promising future. Dominique would admit, after leaving the Chair position, that he did not truly like the supervisory role, missing the active entrepreneurship he enjoyed as CEO. However, with the group facing serious challenges, he accepted a role which he viewed as critical to ensuring the group's continuity in challenging post 2007–08 financial crisis times. He assumed the position for a couple of years and was happy to leave the Chairmanship to his nephew, Axel Moorkens.

With a new Chair, the Board then ran a succession process to find Dominique's replacement as Group CEO. The choice fell on an outside CEO from a large French automotive group.

The fit between the French CEO and the family group not improving, the Board decided that it was time to find a replacement. A second non-family CEO was hired, with substantial experience in automotive distribution as COO of a greatly more homogeneous distribution company. However, the Alcopa group having become increasingly diverse and decentralized, the fit proved again far from ideal. The new CEO tended to centralize all decisions, a strength in his former role which now proved a liability. His strength was his substantial experience in automotive distribution.

Two successive failures led the Board and the FSC to accept the idea that it was probably best to return to family leadership at the top of the group. Dominique and the Board converged on an uncommon leadership transition: Axel would leave the Chairmanship of the Board to become co-CEO with his cousin, the former CEO of the automotive division at the time of the Swiss acquisition.

It was most welcome news for the family that the two co-CEO cousins proved wonderfully complementary, jointly providing intuition and rational strategic thinking at the top of the group. Both had close knowledge of the group's operations, enjoyed solid control over their egos, loved the family firm, and had ambition for it, and brought different personalities to the top of the firm. One was closer to people and great in relationships, the other more interested in strategy and economic performance. Both shared a mutual appreciation of their complementary strengths and talents, greatly facilitating their interactions.

The two CEOs started with a review of the portfolio. Poorly fitting and performing businesses were sold and new risks taken. The group in this review took a definite turn away from its high exposure to the carbon economy. It was agreed that in a couple of years the portfolio of the family group would have a different and much greener outlook. A major decision was taken with regard to automotive distribution assets which were to be sold. As to imports, a major partnership was signed with a Spanish family group. G3 leaders proved less emotional than their G2 predecessors and approved the break with the past. G2 members who had led a business which they then considered their child tended to protect these businesses with the zeal displayed by good parents. Dominique found the transition to a less emotional and more rational investment approach healthy. It also grew his confidence about the future of the group under the new leadership.

Consulting trusted friends on the question, Dominique received the advice that the best time to leave the family business always proves too early, and that hanging on risks blocking the necessary renewal of the Board, in people and functioning. Taking the advice to heart he retired from the Chairmanship in 2014. He was succeeded in the Chair by a former manager of the Mulliez group, who again proved an excellent source of new talent compatible with Alcopa's culture.

Enjoying Being an Active Shareholder of a Group Exiting the Carbon Economy

Dominique would admit, though, that the departure, after so many years of active leadership in and of the group, proved emotionally challenging. Being the biggest individual shareholder, he decided that in this new phase he would position himself as an active and engaged investor. He asked for an office in the group's headquarters.

The request was happily and immediately granted. The other family shareholders encouraged his continued involvement, trusting his competence, wisdom, and his positive intentions on behalf of the current leadership and the group's future. He had pledged to himself that he would be disciplined in his new role, keeping his interventions rare and ensuring that they would be well thought through and clearly presented, with proper arguments. He felt a bit like an engaged opera viewer with a seat on the balcony, but one who can also occasionally be seen in the inner halls. Seeing the various executive and supervisory functions perform smoothly, notwithstanding the fundamental challenges that a turbulent and changing world posed to the group, filled him with great pride.

In this new capacity, he saw how remarkably well the group dealt with the COVID crisis. The use of MS Teams greatly increased communications inside the group, and with shareholders as well. The co-shareholding with management teams of the portfolio companies supported and deepened the ownership and commitment culture. It also contributed to meeting the COVID challenges positively.

Having always been clear that his daughters would not have any operational roles in the family group, Dominique started to devote time to share his ownership competences with his daughters. He had always been clear that he had zero private agenda regarding his daughters entering the business. They would not. This had facilitated the exercise of his authority as leader of the family group, and later as Chair of the FSC and then of the Board of Directors.

Reviewing his journey from his early entry into the group to his current position, he realized how much he did learn throughout the various positions he assumed in the group. This review further grew his gratitude for what his parents allowed him to achieve and how much they supported him, giving him the trust and the autonomy he needed to function. Being the youngest, he learned to deal carefully with older siblings, always seeking consensus. His closeness to the group's Japanese partners and their collaborative Kaizen management methods reinforced that direction. The collaborative practice took time and effort, but allowed much better execution once decisions were made on which most converged. Aiming to be a Fair Process Leader was natural for Dominique, and essential to his leadership success.

The most difficult moments for him were moments of conflict, which he truly does not like. He recognizes that this shyness to confront can generate problems on its own. Being Chair coincided with the more difficult and tedious moments of leadership he experienced. He felt that a good Chair needs to synthesize the various options under consideration. This facilitation reduced his ability to express himself and constrained his entrepreneurial talent, which he felt was his value add to the group. He much preferred being CEO or Board member, such positions allowing him greater scope for contributing.

Reviewing his contribution, Dominique is proud to have ensured the growth of the group, including geographically, particularly in countries like the Netherlands and South Africa. His ability to generate trust with the group's partners proved central for the growth of these partnerships. It also helped the family entrust the group's leadership to him.

When not talking to Board members or the group's senior executives, including those leading the group's various businesses, Dominique remains active on the boards of other family groups which he regularly is called to help, particularly with succession and wealth transfer issues. His one anxiety concerns having to start playing golf to fill his days. For the moment, that risk does not loom large on the horizon.

4 Bart Huisken: Remarkable Entrepreneur and Orphan Owner[3]

Dreams Can Come True

Bart always wished to start his own company. Being of Dutch origin, the son of two teachers, he did his MSc studies in electrical engineering at the Technical University of Delft. His final thesis project brought him to the Universitat Politècnica de Catalunya (UPC) in Barcelona. He further complemented this education with summer courses in fiber optics at the KTH Royal Institute of Technology in Stockholm and image recognition courses at Télécom Paris. Bart was as passionate as he was well schooled when graduating in 1993 in electrical engineering and telecom. He quickly received an offer from Ericsson in the Netherlands and soon transferred to Ericsson Australia, where he held various product management jobs.

While at Delft, he ran a student restaurant, which he enjoyed. However, the experience made him realize that his passion for the hospitality sector was limited. Other ventures provided him with further entrepreneurial experience. He finally hit upon an idea that looked ideal to him: manufacturing satellite dishes. But a visit to a Czech supplier proved sobering and disappointing. Time to reassess and best gain an MBA first. That could only help him and provide the necessary business skills which he lacked.

Bart entered INSEAD in January 2000, his profile and background proving ideal for their one-year MBA program. The international business school presented four attractors: the short duration of the program (1 year), a summer recess in the middle for students starting in January (the school had two entry times), the extensive entrepreneurship curriculum the school was known for, and plenty of multi-cultural work in small study groups.

His choice in favor of INSEAD was confirmed on the first day: Bart immediately met two fellow students, Alberto and Cedrik, who shared his dreams of creating a company. They quickly agreed to collaborate on a study of the wireless internet. They would interview 51 companies located in 14 countries and five continents. Sponsorship from Ericsson, Ogilvy, and Siemens was invaluable to cover the expenses of interviewing experts across the globe. They explored how major companies such as Microsoft, Orange, Nokia, and start-ups such as Phone.com or Wapit, saw the wireless internet evolve. Their 67-page report was presented to interviewees and sponsors invited to campus for the occasion. The study generated many insights and references, and a great network of contacts.

Heading for an interview with Telstra, the leading Australian phone carrier in Melbourne, Bart was hit with a major insight taking a taxi from the airport following the exhausting long-haul flight from Europe. The friendly Greek driver excused himself for answering the loud ring on his mobile phone. While doing so, the car took a sudden shift to the right and soon occupied the two lanes. Conscious of the danger, Bart immediately imagined a headset that would allow the driver to safely answer the phone. Voice portals were obvious applications of the wireless internet the team had been researching. A headset would be ideal to interface with the communication services offered by the operators. The careless taxi driver had just provided Bart with a clear vision for the road ahead.

Bart returned from Australia, full of energy and motivation. INSEAD's Venture Competition, sponsored by the consulting firm Roland Berger, provided Bart and the team with an ideal opportunity to test their ideas. The team won first prize in a contest where INSEAD's MBA entrepreneurs squared off with gusto and commitment. The jury was impressed by the industry insights gained by the team and reflected in their business plan. Their mention of a strong advisory board was another plus. The award came with a 20,000 euro check, 4 months of a free office on campus, 20% part-time assistance of a Roland Berger consultant, and mentoring by one of the firm's partners. The latter, Greek and German, were both INSEAD MBAs. This greatly facilitated their collaboration.

Launching the Project and Meeting Ericsson (Again)

Alberto and Cedrik celebrated with Bart, but then soon announced that they were accepting job offers "they could not refuse." Bart received an offer from BCG in Sydney and declined, committed to starting the venture they had prepared over the last few months. Winning the Venture Competition had created a lot of interest in the project. Bart soon welcomed a fellow MBA student to the venture, Satish. He had helped with the preparation of the summer workshop offered to sponsors and interviewees.

Bart and Satish worked tirelessly at refining their business plan, paying particular attention to how headsets could drive ARPU (Average Revenue per Unit) for mobile operators. They continued to research the headset market, analyzing strengths, weaknesses, and the nature of the threats posed by competitors. The value proposition was refined. They finally were satisfied with plans for their first product, Safety Lite. Celebrating the INSEAD building that housed them, they called their venture SouthWing.

Confident about their business proposal, Bart and Satish decided to aim for one of the biggest players in the industry, Swedish telecom giant Ericsson. Bart had worked at Ericsson, in the Netherlands, Sweden, and Australia. Connections in the firm yielded a meeting with the President of New Business Ventures. SouthWing presented their radical innovation in headsets, arguing it greatly increased styling, quality of voice, customer comfort, and ARPU. A host of advanced services would drive increased usage of voice and data services by mobile customers. Beyond comfort, the product would also offer users security and compliance with new laws addressing latent safety issues in this rapidly evolving market. Use of mobile phones was growing exponentially. This came with a quickly rising number of traffic accidents involving mobile phones. A study in the famous *New England Journal of Medicine* estimated that mobile phones increased such a risk by a factor of four.[4]

Ericsson agreed to meet Bart at its headquarters in Stockholm. Bart and Satish hoped to meet their first major milestone and felt their all-nighters were starting to pay off. "We believe in this product and in you both," concluded their Ericsson host, "so much so that we would like to invest 200 000 € for 40% of equity." Bart's heart skipped a beat. The Ericsson support from day one would indeed be a superb endorsement.

On the other hand, the 40% of equity asked by the Swedish firm seemed prohibitive. As founders they had always had a clear vision. This had been an important anchor for both. Their future headset technology could go far beyond "being just a headset." One application that motivated them greatly was that this would help people having difficulties reading and writing gain access to valuable information. They also believed that literacy should not be taken for granted and that everyone ought to be able to experience great learning opportunities.

Relinquishing a 40% control of their company and of their vision in this early stage, with more funding rounds to come, appeared inacceptable to them. They wanted to be entrepreneurs, not employees reporting to corporate. Perhaps they had contacted Ericsson too early and more time would ensure greater traction. Maybe a structure like Ericsson was the wrong business partner. So, they left Sweden telling Ericsson "No, not now, too early." They proposed to meet again in a few months. The exchange left them even more committed to their entrepreneurial vision. They were onto something big if Ericsson was willing to invest 200,000 euros in two founders with a few slides.

Going Alone with Clear Business Principles and Aiming for a Market over US$ 2 Billion

Back in Fontainebleau, they resumed their market research with renewed energies, interviewing mobile phone store employees, owners, and consumers. They held focus groups at INSEAD campus and applied the *Blue Ocean Strategy* (BOS) framework developed by two INSEAD faculty, Chan Kim and Renée Mauborgne, to guide developers like them onto an innovative product and/or service offer. They loved the course, which left them capable to search for blue oceans, and even blue lakes or pools, in the mobile phone market. They identified how SouthWing could make a difference: hands-free functionality and comfort, voice and data services, style, and price. They identified the price points where their products would bring value to customers over the product lifecycle.

Bart and Satish could not cease deliberating on the distinctive purpose of the SouthWing project, its philosophy, and the culture they wished to see in their company. Investors, strategic or not, would need to be compatible with these givens. They were committed to build quality products with real impact that anyone could use, including competitors, offering voice services, quality in design, ergonomics, comfort, safety, and compliance with existing legislation. They also believed in meeting their obligations toward society. They would be "bridge builders, not ferry operators," in reference to the book *Built to Last* by Jim Collins which deeply influenced both founders. In their venture, people would be ends, not means. No discussion. To mobile operators, their key partners, they would offer the chance to increase traffic and generate more revenue through voice and data traffic. Increased time-to-market of new services would be important as well as the distinctiveness of their offer.

The conclusion that they could not meet all these aims on their own gradually dawned on them. Their team, working out of Fontainebleau, had expanded. Bart was CEO, Satish COO. They were complemented by an industrial designer, a market researcher, an office administrator, and the one-day-a-week consultant from Roland Berger. This wasn't enough. They needed an outside view, more seniority, mentoring skills, access to bigger networks, and angel funding. More established people should join the team.

They identified a senior INSEAD faculty member who seemed to bring a lot to the venture: seniority, operations expertise, credibility, the capacity to mentor, and interest in the venture. He had advised them during the Roland Berger competition, so they invited him to join their advisory board. Concerned that such a board would be ornamental, the faculty member quickly replied: "Bart, I am not that cheap. Take me seriously, raise the bar, set up a real board. You need one at your stage of your venture, it will support you and facilitate financing." Bart and Satish immediately agreed and drafted a letter to the faculty member, who became the first member of their newly formed Board of Directors, and thus Chair. The position would allow the faculty member to learn about the roles of real boards when starting a company from scratch. This was a topic he was interested in, and the SouthWing experience would help shape his views and inform his teaching. Equally importantly, he believed in the project, and was pleased to mentor the team, and support the founders in setting up a real board, when most were of the opinion that it was too early to do so.

Bart contacted Hannu Bergholm, whom they had interviewed at the time of their first market research. Hannu had been President of Nokia Consumer Electronics, CEO of the Finnish start-up Wapit, and was now interim CEO of Elcoteq, a US$ 2 billion contact manufacturer. He declined to join the Board of SouthWing, simply not having time for anything else on his calendar. But he admitted being intrigued by the project and expressed willingness to join the Board in 9 months or so, once his Elcoteq interim was completed.

The third candidate for the Board was the partner at Roland Berger who mentored the team as a part of the award. They regularly met and he was engaged in the venture. But he requested, apart from equity, significant cash payments, which was not acceptable to Bart and Satish. There too a later appointment could be envisaged.

While working on the business plan in greater detail, the team came up with a greatly improved version of Safety Lite: Personal Voice Interface (PVI) would be the next generation personal input device for mobile networks. It presented a host of advantages including SMS to voice, instant voice messaging, tasks, reminders, calendars, business group talk, and a lot of other functionalities. PVI was universal and could be used on any device, from mobile phones to PDAs, MP3s, and Portable PCs. They estimated the market to exceed 2 billion euros. The figure made them realize how much work lay ahead.

Where to Locate? How to Sell? How to Manufacture? How to Finance? Meeting Ericsson Again

It was time to find a base that made financial and strategic sense. Many of the team members were inclined to move to Barcelona. Bart had a network there, dating from his days at the engineering school. Barcelona was known for its industrial design capabilities and high-quality engineering. The town was attractive to young professionals and relatively low cost. However, funding was needed for a project of the envisaged magnitude. They drew a funding tree that outlined the amounts needed during each stage of the business development process: 21 M euros! They thought of Ericsson again, which to them seemed like the best first port of call. Ericsson agreed to visit SouthWing on the INSEAD campus.

After listening attentively to the presentation, the Ericsson team congratulated the team on its ambition and positive progress. But they informed them that they were now focused on Ericsson's merger with Sony. They also stated that the project seemed too far along to still be nudged in a direction desirable for Ericsson.

Bart did not sleep well that night, worried about how to fund the venture. In a state of semi-consciousness, he suddenly remembered a flight he had taken back in 1994. On a standby ticket, he had been upgraded to business class and found himself next to the President of CIDEM, the Centre for Innovation and Business Development of Catalunya. Bart remembered how they had great fun sharing thoughts and how the President had invited him to call if ever he needed anything. Now was certainly the time to do so.

The contact was no longer working at CIDEM, but people there immediately encouraged Bart to take the project to the Polytechnic University (UPC), which hosted a program called Trampolín financing early stage technology projects that would generate start-ups in Catalunya.

Barcelona had proven remarkably welcoming to Bart and his venture. Every institution that was approached seemed to help. UPC was no different. One of their managers, Teresa, quickly saw SouthWing's potential. The government agency sponsoring the program called Trampolin Tecnológico was willing to contribute 100,000 € with one caveat: the money could only be transferred against paid invoices, so only once the wheels were already in motion!

Bart wondered how to indeed get these wheels in motion. What if they couldn't even start the engine? The venture was in urgent need of cash. Salaries and bills needed to be paid. Satish could no longer sustain the uncertain lifestyle and accepted a job opportunity in Austria. The team members now needed a salary to support themselves in Barcelona. With no other option, Bart jumped on a plane to Barcelona with 0 Euros left in his pocket. He lived in an apartment a friend lent him. It was anything but fancy, but it was free and functional. He remained convinced that SouthWing was going to turn his life around.

Early Growth Supported by Angel Money

In the end, Bart looked for angel money to meet the challenge of disposing of sufficient capital to get started. Several people, all personal acquaintances of Bart or of employees, put in small amounts of money. This allowed the venture to collect the money from the Catalonian government. The project was ready to finally take off.

By then Bart had regular meetings with the INSEAD Professor and Chair and with Hannu Bergholm who agreed to join the Board. They discussed strategy, the business model (consulting services vs product manufacturer), supply issues, financing options, and partnerships. Bart was very pleased to be thus supported in his leadership role for the venture, which proved demanding given the uncertainty and regular setbacks.

The search for technological expertise resumed in parallel with the search for board members. Intellectual Property (IPR) licensing was going to be a cornerstone of SouthWing's strategy. Bart had identified a partner at Brother & Newton, a renowned antitrust and IP lawyer, author, historian, and speaker, who had dealt with start-ups as well as complex IP cases with SUN and Microsoft. He managed to have Hannu meet with him at Helsinki Airport for a first encounter. Unfortunately, Hannu mistook another passenger, sharing the same first name for Bart. On not finding the "real" Bart, at the airport as agreed, Hannu called Bart and in no uncertain terms said that he was no longer interested.

Bart approached other potential candidates, including a senior professor of entrepreneurship at IESE, the renowned business school in Barcelona. Bart, the Chair, and Hannu had a very pleasant dinner with a senior IESE professor, who convinced the SouthWing Board members of the value of having good local contacts with broad networks. However, he declined joining the venture and wished the venture well.

SouthWing fortunately had more success growing its Technology Advisory Board. Technologists from big tech companies such as Corning, Faraday, Fractus, and Philips were ready to engage with a project they considered innovative and timely. A technology board containing experts from the fields of telecommunications, microelectronics, robust speech recognition, and so on was for Bart essential to map the desired technological trajectory for SouthWing and help secure the project. Bart had even attracted the main inventor of the Bluetooth standard, but a conflict of interest with Ericsson forced him to decline the invitation.

Meeting the VCs and Enjoying First Breakthroughs

The project having taken shape, the most pressing constraint now was financing. Bart looked up several Catalan VCs, but none proved ready to finance SouthWing. Finally, he identified a public funding opportunity through NEOTEC, an initiative emanating from the Spanish Ministry of Science and Innovation. The agency could provide a 300,000 euro loan at a 0% interest rate on condition that Bart find another 280,000 euros of angel and investor money. One of the angel investors he contacted referred him to two venture consultants, Pietro and Martin, who might help Bart find the money needed to complement the 160,000 euros of angel money already promised. The two investors agreed and asked for two seats on the Board. They also proposed to help with OEM licensing, sales, and financing. The first angel financing round was now closed, and the venture could be formally launched. In 2003 Pietro and Martin helped secure a 500,000 euro financing round with a family office related to Martin.

The product was quickly imposing itself in the market. FNAC, the French retailer, was the first to order, soon followed by UK operator 02 and T-Mobile, the German mobile operator. The SouthWing headset was soon featured in 100 retail outlets of T-Mobile. Market data was remarkable for SouthWing: in nearly all weeks, SouthWing outsold its major competitor, Jabra. Weekly T-Mobile sales oscillated between 250 and 450 units.

The confidence of the team grew in proportion to this first market success. But so did the financing requirements of SouthWing, which needed more working capital. An A-round of investors had to be completed by summer 2004. A positive development was that Jean-François Pontal agreed to join the board. Pontal had opened Carrefour in Spain and was the first CEO of Orange after it had been acquired by France Telecom. He liked the personality of Bart, who reminded him of the vision of Hans Snoek, the co-founder of Orange. The early achievements of the venture and a well-functioning Board, whose members had contributed to the early financing, further convinced him to join the project.

The success of SouthWing was by now known in the Barcelona business community. Odyssey, a VC belonging to the founders of a consulting firm to mobile operators which they had just sold for close to one billion euros, expressed interest. The founders had set up a couple of funds with proceeds from the sale. One fund was focused on tech investments. Odyssey founders and analysts liked SouthWing. They found a great fit between the aims of the fund and the purpose of SouthWing. A two million euro investment was quickly agreed. It came with a silver lining.

Though Martin and Pietro had helped the company in financing and sales, Bart was increasingly experiencing difficulties with Martin's and Pietro's managerial behaviors. Odyssey agreed to invest on condition that Martin and Pietro exited the management team. Exit payments were proposed to both, which they accepted. Odyssey demanded two board seats and negotiated the right to nominate a third board seat and veto rights. They also insisted on drag-along rights for any sale above 40 million euros.

Every decision for something or someone is often a decision against something or someone else. Bart had recently received interest from a French listed company eager to invest and possibly buy the company. The deal with Odyssey led Bart to turn the French suitor down, feeling that discussions with Odyssey were too far along. He also did not wish to risk the deal with Odyssey.

The shareholding structure now was as follows: 39% for Bart, 20% for Pietro and Martin's VC, 25% for Odyssey, and 16% for the three initial angel investors (including one employee) and other seed investors. Bart remained Chair and CEO.

2004: VC Puts Pressure on the Venture and Yields Remarkable Results

Eager to contribute to the development of the company, the new investors pushed Bart and his management to speed up product development and increase revenues. They insisted on meeting with the ExCom weekly and imposed several committees on the management. One of their demands concerned HR. They wished to introduce clearer management policies into the firm. They also wished to see greater efficiency in the company, particularly in product development. The development of new mono headsets was accelerated, as was the design of new car kits (for hands- free communication when driving) and stereo headsets. The arrival of the new investors had increased the pace inside the company in a major way. The new investors were also very visible inside the company, particularly in marketing and sales, product development, and HR.

The arrival of Odyssey initially produced great results: the company broke even in 2004, reaching revenue slightly above four million euros, compared with a 2003 revenue slightly above 0.6 million euros. Large orders from T-Mobile Germany and Spain's Telefonica coupled with another large order by Amena, another Spanish mobile brand, contributed to this. The Amena order benefited from their connections with Odyssey.

SouthWing was now clearly focused on mobile operators, which had always been one of its aims. Amena offered its customers a special Christmas offer bundling a SouthWing NeoCar device with a Nokia handset. Amena gained 30,000 customers in this end-of-year promotion. A similar deal was soon offered by Telefonica, consisting of a SouthWing Neo507 headset coupled with a Blackberry 7290 phone.

A new VP Sales was appointed originating from the consulting firm that Odyssey had founded and sold. He brought a more structured approach to sales and marketing. Due to his previous affiliation with Odyssey, he communicated regularly and directly to the Odyssey board members, bypassing the CEO. In addition, the new VP was focused and heavily incentivized on sales growth, not on profitability. This increasingly put pressure on working capital.

The best news came from a review of headsets by *Mobile Magazine* in the UK. The SouthWing SH305 headset came out on top among 50 OEM headsets and universal brands. These included products from competitors such as O2blue, Sony Ericsson, Jabra, Nokia, and Samsung.

The growth continued, with revenue of 9.3 million euros in 2005, doubling the figure in the preceding year. Development had its best run, developing a patent for the PUSH4 ™ button, which offered a direct link to additional operator services such as voice mail service, preferred customer number, operator voice portal, and traffic information services. Another innovation was a revolutionary man-machine interface, called RotaVoice™, which simplified access to multiple devices through a voice menu structure. A unique headset, the SouthWing SA505, with exceptional stereo audio and a unique feature set including PUSH4 ™ and auto answer features, was also planned for release.

2005: Conflicts Emerge, at Board Level First, Then with CEO/Chair

The original board members found their new Odyssey colleagues on the board too intrusive into the organization, causing issues of authority with respect to Bart. They also regularly expressed quite negative comments on Bart's leadership. The repeated a pattern that had occurred with Pietro and Martin and had been negative for the organization's development. The arrival of Odyssey had elegantly solved the latter problem, but they had repeated the pattern. The issue here was more subtle: Odyssey board members knew the industry, had superior marketing competences and connections, and truly wished to help. Their negative views proved surprising, having invested two million euros in the venture. The original board members warned them that the venture would not be worth much without the CEO and that they risked their investment if they continued in this vein. Some of the exchanges became quite heated.

The arrival of the new shareholder had changed the tone in the board and the company. As Board Chair, Bart tried to temper matters but was not effective, being the object of the exchanges. The Odyssey board members wished to see the firm managed differently. Criticizing Bart's leadership and exercising more direct control of operations were two ways the new shareholders steered the company in the direction they desired.

The appointments of a new CFO and a new COO further changed the tone inside the firm. The organization now was increasingly divided into two camps: the one loyal to the CEO, and the other loyal to the new investors and their board members. Committee meetings of the Board with the Executive Committee increasingly veered into management meetings with board members acting as senior executives. Unity at the Board and inside the firm became unglued and "politics" took hold of the management.

Financially, things had never been better. Sales growth was strong, even if fixed costs increased due to increased R&D and to a larger commercial structure. EBITDA had grown to a healthy 12.5% figure. The greatest risk now was operational: organizational complexity had increased considerably, with the multiplicity of products and markets, and a rather complex supply chain.

In late 2005 the Odyssey board members called Bart into their office and officially pressured him to retire from the CEO position. Bart agreed under two conditions: (1) commitment to another capital raise, a B-round; and (2) he would remain in place as Non-Executive Chairman, VP Sales US, and Chief Innovation Officer. Seeing the US as one sales area where the firm could break through in a major way, Bart remained motivated notwithstanding the request for him to step down from the CEO position. If he were to succeed in the US, his position inside the company and with the board would be restored. Another bright spot was that Bart finally earned a real salary, something he had refused to do previously, in a desire to support the venture that was so dear to him. The board agreed to hire a headhunter to help find a new CEO.

Major Problems Mitigated by Two Further Breakthroughs

Revenue growth had again triggered cash needs. The Odyssey investors had used their first fund (Odyssey 1) but had not kept a reserve for supporting their investments in case of urgent needs, a common practice in PE funding. In addition, their own governance rules prohibited them from using their Odyssey 2 fund to support Odyssey 1 projects. They called Bart who was in the US, meeting Cingular (the former AT&T), a key prospect, demanding he come back immediately to discuss the cash position of the company. He flatly refused to return before the Cingular meeting. "Your discussion can wait one week," he told the investors. After his return, the VC investors agreed to a one million euro emergency bridge loan.

It was in this charged context that the new SouthWing SC705 car kit proved to suffer from major software issues. The root cause for this failure was the wrong choice of subcontracting partner, resulting in ineffective cooperation between the two organizations. A display component which proved out of stock also was responsible for the delays. SouthWing procurement learned that the lead-time for reordering was 16 weeks. The issues were largely solved by Bart and his team going to Taiwan for several weeks, and the product went to the market just before Christmas.

However, product uptake by the market was limited, as the market had moved to visor-mounted car kits, a different type of hands-free device. The sanction was immediate: Telefonica, SouthWing's major client, canceled most of its orders due to the limited uptake. The revenue loss for SouthWing was 1.5 million euros. The incident also put a major dent in SouthWing's reputation. The devices had to be sold at a much lower margin, or even at a loss.

Then came good news from the US. Bart's skills had come through again: Cingular confirmed an order for 183,000 headsets, amounting to a single PO of US$ 4 million. Products were clearly doing well in the market and the client account list was impressive, including such operator names as Orange, Amena, O2, T-Mobile, China Mobile, Telcel, Bouygues Telecom, Optimus, SFR, Proximus, and KPN - to which one could now add Cingular and Telefonica. Others on the client list included retailers such as Best Buy, The Phone House, Dixons, and FNAC, and manufacturers such as Alcatel and NEC.

With this record Odyssey investors would now approach VCs for a B-round. Unfortunately, such investors are very limited in Spain, while foreign VCs showed little appetite for investing in the country. Further difficulties were the size of the deal, which was too small for many PE players, and the fact that

Odyssey did not wish to sell. In August 2006 a Spanish investor, Costa Brava, agreed to invest five million euros in SouthWing, for a post-money valuation of 25 million euros.

International members, including the INSEAD professor and the former Nokia President of Consumer Electronics, had by now all left the board. One member had already asked to leave the board for a while. Communication problems had broken down with the Odyssey board members and there seemed little point in them continuing under such conditions. The exit of the international board members allowed one of the original angel investors, having supported the venture all along and in a major way, to be invited to take a board seat. He was unable to join the board earlier, due to his very limited English. With the exit of the international board members, meetings could now be held partially in Spanish.

The board was restructured, each VC (including that of Pietro and Martin) now having one board seat and one observer each. Bart remained on the board, as well as Mark, the new CEO. The shareholding was simplified too, the smaller original investors being bought out by the Costa Brava PE, increasing its shareholding. They earned a multiple around five on their investment. Bart as founder kept his equity in the firm.

A New A Team at the Helm

With the new funding of Costa Brava, prospects became bright again, at least for a while. The new CEO hired a new "A Team," including a VP International, a CTO, and a COO. Only the VP Sales and Bart remained from the previous team. "A Team" compensation was asked, and the Board approved it. The new team quickly presented a new strategic plan built around three pillars: growth, differentiation, and operational excellence. The Board accepted it too, somewhat relieved.

In early 2007 the Board thought they finally had turned the corner. The disappointment was great when Mark, the new CEO, in May 2007 informed the Board that there were cracks in the execution of the new strategic plan. Objectives set forth would not be reached. Worse, Mark asked for more investment into the firm, for a total of five million euros, equal in amount to the new equity issued the previous August to Costa Brava. The announcement of the sudden departure of the CFO compounded the bad news.

The consequences of the arrival of the new "A Team" were now becoming visible. Their arrival led to the exit of the staff that had joined SouthWing early. The new team did not share the values that animated the original team, nor did the new sales force understand the market or the technology as well as the founder and his original team. In addition, the high salaries paid to the new employees added to their distance from the older members. This also increased the monthly burn rate, which now stood at 500,000 euros. The cherry on the cake was the new CFO not watching exchange rates carefully, leading to a one million euro loss on USD/euro exchange rate contracts.

By September 2007, less than 14 months after his arrival, Mark decided to call it quits, due to increasing differences with shareholders. Existing investors refused the call for more investment in view of the drastic reduction in revenue, which had fallen to seven million euros in 2007, after reaching a peak of 13 million euros in 2006. SouthWing had started to lose traction in its markets as of mid-2006. One year later the results showed the losses more clearly.

A New Management Team

In this context, the Board had no choice but to ask Bart to step up again. Still committed to the venture, Bart was even considering returning as CEO, but the investors showed no support for this. A team of three managers, consisting of Bart, the COO, and the CFO, were asked in September 2007 to manage the company until a more permanent solution could be found.

Bart lived the worst day of his life when he had to ask 13 people, representing a quarter of the workforce, to leave the company. Searching for a more permanent solution, Bart was lucky to find a Finnish company willing to merge with SouthWing. The Board refused the terms proposed.

The interim team did a good job redressing the company, sales recovering in Q1 2008. A third CEO was recruited from competitor Jabra, where he was VP Sales of Emerging Markets. He successfully opened new markets in LATAM and Eastern Europe. The current investors proved again supportive of SouthWing and another financing round was initiated at a 12 million euro valuation.

The Endgame

Even if he came from the same sector, the new CEO needed time to learn about SouthWing's operations, strategy, and R&D. The sales rebound of Q1 was not confirmed in Q2. The company then hit a major stumbling block: it missed a critical delivery deadline with Cingular, which was key for its sustainability. The incident proved too much in an industry with little patience for repeatedly missing delivery deadlines. The Board in June 2008 finally agreed to sell the company when it realized that expected sales figures for the year would hardly exceed three million euros, despite promising possibilities in Russia and LATAM.

Bart tried one more move with RIM, the manufacturer of the Blackberry. Multiple meetings and conference calls led to an initial agreement on terms for a sale, and a deal room was set up. The approval of the potential deal by RIM's co-CEO allowed Bart and the Board to hope that SouthWing might be saved after all.

Conditions at RIM unfortunately led the firm to eventually walk away from the deal. The company was experiencing problems with its new phone, aptly called "Storm," intended as a competitor to the iPhone. Litigation against SouthWing in the US, legacy of an aggressive termination of a contract by SouthWing's second CEO, was a further complicating factor. The initial enthusiasm for acquiring a company in Barcelona waned and by October 2008 it was clear that the deal would not materialize.

Bart's other contacts failed for reasons that generally had more to do with the take-over candidates. One small public company agreed to buy SouthWing and even announced it to the stock market. Yet it still needed to raise money for the deal, and the market crash of late 2008 sealed the fate of SouthWing. The Board finally agreed that bankruptcy protection while searching for another buyer during these proceedings was now the only option. This option proved unsuccessful and the company filed for liquidation in 2009.

5 Priscilla de Moustier: Leading More than 1000 Family Shareholders into the Fourth Century of the Family Business's Existence[5]

It is remarkable how life repeats in surprising ways. Having been appointed Chair and Director General of Wendel Participations, the holding controlling the Wendel Group, Priscilla de Moustier never imagined that she would be asked one day to assume a responsibility and take steps for family unity that were taken, in a different context and in earlier times, by her father, Pierre Celier.

Wendel is an exceptional story of sustainability in ownership in a context of incredible turbulence over three centuries, vanquished each time through the leadership and support of a united family shareholding, forever committed to conquering challenges and going forward. These events, as the reader will shortly see, included the French Revolution, the Franco-Prussian War of 1870, two world wars, fights with the French Government, and, finally, a series of crises that also emanated from inside the family firm. Each of these could have terminated the firm; without a controlling and committed family shareholding, the firm undoubtedly would have disappeared.

The Wendel story illustrates the famous urging of Tancredi to his uncle, the Prince of Salina, to abandon his allegiance to the vanishing Kingdom of the Two Sicilys in view of the uprising by Garibaldi and his Italian nationalists: "Unless we ourselves take a hand now, they'll foist a republic on us. If we want things to stay as they are, things will have to change."[6] The next sections illustrate how the Wendel family did just that, managing, at crucial points in its history, to stay united and guide the future direction of the family enterprise. This allowed it to successfully continue its life into a fourth century, not without challenge, nor without change, and still in control. The ownership and business story is long and detailed, as it covers more than three centuries, with unbelievable turmoil over that period. Therefore, we plead for indulgence from our readers. The story attests strongly to the business sustainability that family ownership can bring to a business.

Forging for the King

The Wendel history in iron and steel started in 1704, with the acquisition by Jean-Martin Wendel of an iron forge in Hayange in Lorraine, the French region near the German border. The region offered many relatively small iron ore deposits and a large supply of wood for heating furnaces. Running a forge was one of the rare economic activities allowed by the King to the aristocrats. French kings elevated their forge masters to be noblemen but, in caution, attached their title with their activities. Being of Belgian and German origin ("van Dael"), Jean-Martin Wendel's forges soon supplied iron bullets for the King and rapidly gained prominence. Jean-Martin's son, Charles I, further expanded the forge. He improved the production process by adding coal as a heat source, allowing production to increase without devastating the surrounding forests. Toward the end of Charles's life, his wife, Marguerite d'Hausen, started to manage the forges with the help of her two sons-in-law.

King Louis XV asked Charles's son, Ignace, an artillery officer, to manage several royal forges that were in need of reorganization. He traveled extensively throughout Europe to learn from other forge masters. He sought to "discover" the production process used in England to heat iron ore with pure coal (coke cast iron). He tested this process in his mother's forges before applying it in Le Creusot in Burgundy, where he built a large and exemplary forge for his King, giving the area a prominence known to this day. Limited royal finances prohibited the completion of the great enterprise. Ignace then substituted the royal administration with private companies which he founded with a most qualified British associate met during his travels. He was also a social forerunner, building schools and housing in Le Creusot for the families of the employees of the forges. Le Creusot became famous in France for steel works (eventually known as Creusot-Loire and falling into the hands of the Empain-Schneider family), energy (with Framatome and Siag), and transport (Alstom, Safran-Snecma).

A First Upheaval: The French Revolution

The French Revolution erupted in 1789 and put an end to Ignace's considerable development of Le Creusot. The Wendel family did not escape the turbulence of those revolutionary times. A death sentence was pronounced on one of Ignace's children. Most members of the family, including Ignace, chose exile into Habsburg territory, as many aristocrats did at the time. Ignace spent the last part of his life in Saxony near Weimar, reading the French philosophers with enthusiasm, meeting Goethe, and ceaselessly pursuing new experiments to benefit the iron industry.

Remarkably, Ignace's mother, Marguerite d'Hausen, despite her age, stayed in France to continue to run the family forge. She was alone, her son and sons-in-law having emigrated. She showed tremendous tenacity, energy, and courage on all fronts: in the forge to supervise production and in Paris to demand payment from the government to provide for her workers and their families, until being arrested in 1794. The forges were closed and sold as "state properties."

The new owner of the forges had no experience in iron production. He rapidly went bankrupt, allowing Ignace de Wendel's son, François I de Wendel, a cavalry officer who had returned from his Habsburg exile, to repurchase the forges in 1803, supporting Bonaparte's industrialization and militarization effort. François sold all his belongings and greatly indebted himself. The Napoleonic Wars consumed enormous amounts of ammunition, boosting production. This allowed François, after just a few years, to reimburse all his debts and to even acquire other forges.

The revolutionary upheavals caused the coke cast iron process to be lost. In 1816, the wars having ended, François de Wendel traveled to England to retrieve the lost knowledge. He returned to France with a few English workers who successfully transferred their know-how to the family's forges in Lorraine. François continued to invest in upgrading the production facilities. His political influence was growing too, and he was elected to the French parliament, to represent Lorraine.

Major Actors of French Industrialization during the Nineteenth Century

The emerging industrialization created a wealth of opportunities. Added to protectionism, these new trends contributed significantly to the expansion of the company. When François de Wendel died in 1825, the forges employed 3000 people. In his will, François left the ownership of the forges to his wife, Joséphine de Fischer de Dicourt. She managed them with the help of her son, Charles II de Wendel, and a son-in-law, Théodore de Gargan. Both were graduates from the Ecole Polytechnique, France's foremost engineering school, founded by the young Republic to supply it with skilled engineers.

Activities at the forge continued to see significant social developments: progressive policies were furthered; pension and health insurance systems, as well as a thirteenth month of wages were introduced. Charles de Wendel and Baron de Gargan adopted an "open-door" policy with their employees. Any employee had the opportunity to meet with them.

The construction of railways and iron ships opened huge markets for the forges, while protectionism maintained high prices. New forges were built in the small village of Stiring, and a new important coal colliery was opened there. In addition to providing housing for the firm's employees, the family built schools, a town hall, and churches. Stiring was triumphantly inaugurated by Napoleon III in 1857. The company prospered and in the 1860s the forges employed over 10,000 people.

Creation of a Partnership to Support the Sustainability of the Family Company

At Charles's death in 1870, his mother, Joséphine Fischer de Dicourt, still owned the forges, but had no surviving children ready and able to manage the family business. Her grandchildren would now have to take over the destiny of the forges. To favor family cohesion and ensure the future of the enterprise, she created a partnership company in 1871, called Les Petits Fils de François de Wendel, which owned 100% of the Wendel mines and forges. The articles of association stipulated that the shares could only be owned by descendants of François de Wendel. In-laws at the time were excluded from share ownership but could be involved in the management of the company. The partners active in the business would receive 10% of the company's profits and would be personally liable for all the company's debts.

The first shareholders of this partnership company were François de Wendel's nine surviving grandsons and granddaughters, the children of her sons Charles and his older brother Victor François, and of her oldest daughter Joséphine Marguerite, who had married Théodore de Gargan. The latter three had all passed away in a period of 3 years (1850–1853). Interestingly, the Wendel descendants identify themselves to this day with one these three family branches, namely Gargan (Joséphine Marguerite branch), Curel (Victor-François, whose daughter Pauline married Albert de Curel, a cavalry officer), and Wendel (Ignace branch). Wendel Participations is the current name of the family holding.

Facing Prussian Annexation of Lorraine and the Challenge of Steel

The next leadership generation was represented by Charles's sons, Henri I de Wendel and Robert de Wendel, and their cousin, Théodore II de Gargan. Théodore II de Gargan was in his early 40s, and about 20 years older than his cousins. He had worked in the forges with his uncle Charles and ensured the transition to the next generation. The circumstances would quickly give Henri the opportunity to display his leadership qualities. Having graduated from the École Centrale in Paris, Henri brought his industrial expertise to the company while his brother Robert, a graduate from the new Hautes Études Commerciales business school, handled the commercial side of the business.

The family now faced two major difficulties. On the political side, Lorraine had been annexed to Germany following France's defeat in the disastrous 1870 Franco-Prussian war which ended the Second Empire and created the Third Republic (after first relatively short-lived attempts in 1792 and 1848). On the industrial side, steel was increasingly replacing iron. This technological change proved a major risk as the excessive phosphorus content of iron ore in Lorraine prohibited steel production.

In order not to leave the business in German hands, Henri decided to stay in Lorraine and applied for German nationality. He was even elected to the German parliament as a "protesting representative of Lorraine." He made a point of continuing French as the language used in the forges. He also built houses in France, at Joeuf close to the border, to allow workers to keep their jobs in the company while remaining French and, for the same reasons, built a "château" for his wife and children. Most family members moved to Paris.

Henri spent most of the next decade trying to develop a process to manufacture steel with Lorraine's phosphorus iron ore. During those years, the forges went through economic hardship, exacerbated by the difficult political climate that resulted from the proclamation of the Third French Republic against the wishes of the royalist party. The Wendels were considered foreigners by both Germans and French. Low iron prices, high railway costs for the transportation of iron ore and coal, and the progressive replacement of iron by steel all contributed to the deterioration of the family business. The workforce on one of the Wendels' biggest industrial sites dropped from 6000 to 800.

Despite all these difficulties, the cousins unanimously refused to receive funds from German investors. They did not wish to relinquish their majority ownership and followed Henri's advice:

> *Our business is getting worse and worse, because of technical problems. A German group of investors is offering us more money for our operations than they are currently worth. My opinion is that we have not lost the game; if we sold, we would regret it, and I can hardly envisage selling our company to Germans after our resistance of the past years. Our people also follow us unanimously in such a decision.*

At last, the Thomas process was invented, which allowed the production of steel from phosphorus iron ore. Henri bought the patent in 1879, at a very high cost, further draining the treasury. However, the production of steel was now feasible. It ushered in a new era for the forges and, as of 1883, prosperity returned. New operations and a new town were built on French territory, in Joeuf, in partnership with long-time French rival Schneider at Le Creusot. The family continued its tradition of social progress, building schools, housing, dining halls, churches, and hospitals, turning Joeuf into a "*cité modèle.*"

Surviving World Wars

At the beginning of the twentieth century, a new generation took over the leadership of the business. François II and Humbert (both Henri's sons) and Charles III (Robert's son) become the new managing partners of a business owned by 33 family shareholders. Prosperity continued: the group employed as many as 40,000 workers and had zero debt. Family and employees were, however, longing for the return of "their" beloved Lorraine to France. World War I would achieve this, but with plenty of suffering and destruction.

The eruption of the war led the Wendel family members who were in Germany to seek refuge in France. Wendel's German operations were confiscated while French plants were destroyed. The Versailles Treaty of 1919 returned Lorraine to France. The Wendels were warmly acclaimed upon their return to the region, recognized as a symbol of Lorraine's unwavering resistance to Germany. Operations were restarted and forges rebuilt, using both war indemnities and family reserves.

Charles III, a passionate engineer who had spent 5 years in the US at the beginning of the twentieth century and brought back engineers and plans to build a mill, fell into a depression that unfortunately altered his management abilities. When he refused to leave the business, his cousins had to go to court to force him out. His brother Guy, a war hero, became managing partner for about 10 years, but his passion for gambling would lead him to be excluded from the partnership. Guy remained, however, an active politician as senator for Lorraine. His cousin Maurice replaced him as the third managing partner of the company, together with his brothers François II and Humbert. Only Henri's sons now managed the business.

François II, an engineer from the prestigious École des Mines, managed the coal and iron mines, and the steel operations. He was also a prominent member of the French Parliament and, through his leading role in the Banque de France, shaped French monetary policy. Working closely with François, Humbert ran operations and assumed responsibility for international matters. Maurice took responsibility for the company's social programs, which remained a given for the family.

Economic recovery was unfortunately short-lived: 1930 was an excellent year, immediately followed by the Great Depression. The workforce again fell, from 40,000 to 25,000. Another war between France and Germany was about to erupt.

Following Germany's invasion of France in 1940, the forges and mines were confiscated by German authorities. Some equipment was disassembled and transported to Bohemia. Several members of the Wendel family took a leading role in the war against Germany. Maurice's daughter helped prisoners escape and was arrested by the Germans. His son-in-law, Pierre Celier, joined the resistance while a "Petit Fils de François de Wendel" by marriage, Maréchal Leclerc de Hauteclocque, led the famous Division Leclerc into Paris, Nancy, and Strasbourg. His division took control of Hitler's Eagle Nest in Bavaria, snatching this coveted prize from the American troops.

Facing Nationalisation Following World War II

The end of World War II allowed the Wendels to re-join their beloved Lorraine region once again. Times seemed to have irremediably changed. The atmosphere was by no means as triumphant as in 1918. Buildings had been devastated. The forges were gradually rebuilt, with an initial workforce of 4000 compared with 15,000 before the war. Emmanuel de Mitry (François's son-in-law) took leadership of the company, joined by two younger relatives, Pierre Celier (Maurice's son-in-law) and Henri II (François's son).

The post-war years witnessed the first attempt at the construction of a unified Europe. The first realization was the creation of a single European market for coal and steel. In France, unlike in Germany, this period was unfortunately accompanied by growing interference by the French State, which led Wendel's French coal mines to become nationalized in 1946. The company was now forced to buy their own German coal via a national trade organization. Having decreed the steel sector of national importance the French government then decided to freeze steel prices in support of French industry. In compensation, the family business was offered favorable credit terms on loans by the State. The French steel industry became more and more indebted to the State and therefore overseen and regulated by a government constantly interfering in the firm's decision-making process. This de facto dependency situation severely risked Wendel's survival as an independent economic entity.

Restructuring Lorraine's Iron and Steel Industry

There were, however, positive sides to the difficult situation. The development of the automotive industry after World War II opened huge markets for steel plates. These, in turn, required substantial investments in rolling mill capacity. The Wendel family could, however, no longer contemplate such huge investments alone, already being increasingly indebted to the French Government. The family leaders thus initiated collaboration with other iron and steel firms in Lorraine through a partnership, Sollac, which they largely controlled. The Wendels brought to Sollac their know-how in steel sheets and tin plate production. Sollac's financing was facilitated by the Marshall Plan for European post-war reconstruction.

Production at Sollac started in 1952. The business immediately saw a spectacular development. The group recruited Mr Dherse, an engineer from the elite Ponts-et-Chaussées school, to manage operations. He proved an outstanding pick. Sollac's initial production capacity of 1.2 million tons was progressively raised to 3.5 million tons. Sollac's success was a positive windfall for Lorraine: it boosted its development until the early 1970s, when the steel crisis hit Europe.

The growing size and financial stake of the family business led to a change in the structures of the company. In 1952, all operations were placed in a subsidiary of Les Petits Fils de François de Wendel, Société de Wendel et Compagnie, a limited liability company whose shares were introduced on the Paris Stock Exchange. These were of today's Wendel Participations (the family holding) and of Wendel (the family business).

Meeting Financing Constraints, Competition, and Europe's Steel Crisis

Sollac's tin plate and steel activities enjoyed a remarkable position on world markets. Limited financial resources, however, slowed down investments in certain areas. Considerable time in the 1960s was devoted to lifting this capital constraint. In 1968, Société de Wendel et Compagnie merged with Sidelor and Société Mosellane de Sidérurgie, two of their partners in Sollac. The merger was considered a necessity, despite Sidelor's high level of debt. The new steel group was called Wendel-Sidelor, and upon Henri de Wendel's retirement in 1973, Sacilor was among the largest in the world. The merger did allow substantial productivity improvements. The workforce was gradually reduced from 64,000 to 48,000. Throughout this time, Wendel sought to retain its commitment to progressive social policies. No redundancies were made without alternative job proposals.

A new form of competition emerged from iron and steel mills built near harbors. These mills were supplied with cheaper coal and iron ore imported by sea. The imported ore was also much richer in iron. This led the Sollac partners to build a new iron and steel plant by the sea. Excellent 1970 results and successful discussions with the government, which agreed to support a long-term financing plan provided the plant, Solmer, was located near Marseille, allowed the enormous investment. Sollac partners could thus meet global competition.

In 1975, the Wendel family company, now named CLIF (Compagnie Lorraine Industrielle et Financière), took control, after a major battle, of Marine-Firminy, another holding with stakes in Sacilor's and Sollac's other partners. The move was meant to prevent Usinor, the main steel producer in Northern France and major competitor, from purchasing Marine-Firminy and entering Sollac. The Wendels, by now, controlled all of Lorraine's iron and steel industry, holding the majority of Sacilor and Sollac. Governmental pressure forced them to share Solmer's capital with Usinor.

Notwithstanding all these developments, the economic situation continued to deteriorate for iron and steel, in France as well as in the rest of Europe. The US market tolled the bell by introducing protectionist legislation, heavily limiting steel imports from Europe. European prices plunged. Despite a profitable year in 1974, the emergence of a major crisis in the steel sector was confirmed. The crisis was shaking Europe's industry and state support was envisaged everywhere. In France, prices had been fixed on national markets soon after World War II. As already mentioned earlier, this had led to further indebtedness toward the State and the nationalized banks, the government compensating its price controls with favorable terms on the loans provided by the State. Wendel family representatives met ever more frequently with the government and the Ministry of Finance to negotiate loans and discuss the future of Sacilor, Sollac, and Solmer.

The Wendel Group in 1976

The acquisition of Marine-Firminy added a new "layer" between the family and their iron and steel operations, called Marine-Wendel. CLIF, still owned by family members only, held the majority of the new holding company. Other investors and the public held minority stakes. Marine-Wendel in turn owned the majority of Sacilor and that of many other companies, all downstream steel operations.

In 1976, Marine-Wendel was headed by Pierre Celier, who chaired the Board of Directors. While several family members, including Henri de Wendel, sat on the Board, none had a role in the management of the company. Two senior executives were long-time associates of the family and were considered members of the "extended" family: the General Manager, Jean Droulers, came from another business family, while Jean-Marc Janodet's father had been finance director before him. Both played key roles in managing the family firm through these turbulent times.

Pierre Celier, the only member of the family actively involved in steel operations, was also President of the Supervisory Board of Sacilor. He had replaced Henri de Wendel on his retirement in 1973. Prior to this, Pierre Celier had been a member of the Management Board of Wendel-Sidelor.

A Business in Steel and Upstream and Downstream Activities

Besides Sacilor and forges in Germany (Dilling, which belonged to Marine-Firminy), Marine-Wendel also had stakes in about 50 smaller companies in other activities such as metal transformation and mechanical engineering, metal packaging, cement factories and mines, trading, services (sale of steel products, oil, construction materials, railway carriages), banking, and finance. The profitability of most of these companies was low and the complexity of running Marine-Wendel was high, given the massive scope of the activities in its portfolio. As a result of the Marine-Firminy deal, Marine-Wendel also had a 50% participation in a large metallurgical and engineering company, Creusot-Loire, where it had agreed to a non-management status, to the benefit of the Schneider group.

The Role of Family Shareholders in Crisis Times

Until 1976, the family shareholders had left total power in the hands of their owner-managers, exerting virtually no countervailing power. A few members of the younger generation, who were pursuing successful careers in French industry including the fund business, had expressed some concerns about the management of the family business in the 1960s and the governance of the family group. They questioned the wisdom of continuing substantial and ever-increasing investments in the steel sector in the face of rising competition from developing countries. They considered the sector's prospects as limited at best. For them, the family's unquestioned attachment to the steel industry and to Lorraine would risk the family's eventual downfall, following the fate of the French and European steel industry. Particularly in a context where de facto nationalization threatened the family firm's survival.

It was at about this time that one of the founder's descendants, Ernest-Antoine Seillière, decided to leave a promising career in the French Civil Service to join the company, at the invitation of his uncle and head of the family group, Pierre Celier. Together, they committed to restructuring the up- and downstream activities of the previous family empire. These formed the only hope for saving the family's holding. Having a talented and trusted family member, with diplomatic and government experience, could only be a plus. It also gave Pierre Celier in 1977 the idea of proposing, as an alternative to outright liquidation, a major restructuring program of CLIF.

Staying in Business Together, or Not: That Is the Question

In order for it to be implemented, Henri and Pierre asked that their offer to the family be accepted unanimously by its 350 shareholders. They reasoned that only the full support of the family would make such an operation legitimate and preserve family unity, considered musts for the success of the proposed venture. The essence of their proposal was to dissociate the steel activities from the other activities and to argue with the government that it would be unfair and detrimental to also nationalize the family's non-steel activities. About 50 companies were owned or controlled by Marine-Wendel, the publicly quoted holding company, majority-owned by CLIF. The core steel activities would stay in Marine-Wendel, while non-steel activities would be grouped in a newly created subsidiary, the Compagnie Générale d'Industrie et de Participations (CGIP), to be listed and providing family members with liquidity.

Two new family holdings would replace CLIF. As before, ownership of the holdings would be restricted solely to the descendants of François de Wendel and their spouses, the buying or selling of shares being restricted to family members. The two new family holdings, Sogeval and SLPS, would control Marine-Wendel, and through it, the newly created CGIP, for the shares owned by Marine-Wendel.

The family shareholders were asked to redeem all their CLIF shares. In return, they would receive three equally valued stakes in: a) the newly created family holdings (Sogeval and SLPS); b) Marine-Wendel shares (controlled by Sogeval and SLPS); and c) CGIP shares (which they would own individually and could sell if they wished). Marine-Wendel shares were already traded on the Paris Stock Exchange, and hence could be sold freely, if the proposal was accepted. CGIP shares would soon be introduced on the Paris Exchange.

It was possible that some shareholders would opt for a once-and-for-all "cash out" of the family venture, by requesting publicly quoted stocks only, and by refusing to block one third of their shares in the two closed family holdings. However, all 350 family members eventually accepted the management proposal to continue the family business history, even if attempted with leftovers from the steel venture. The family had owned a steel empire, so leftovers were not uninteresting, consisting of a, for now, hardly profitable collection of trading, service, mechanical engineering, packaging, cement, and financial service companies. But good governance and leadership could turn this collection into something with much greater shine.

As feared and predicted, the state in 1978 nationalized Wendel's main steel operation, Sacilor, transforming the state loans into capital. Pierre Celier succeeded in keeping Marine-Wendel's significant stakes in smaller and more specialized forges (Dilling, Gueugnon) out of the now state-controlled Sacilor.

From "Iron and Steel Baron" to "Shareholder Entrepreneur"

Following the family's acceptance of CGIP's creation, the restructuring of the portfolio of companies could be initiated. After 1 year of a tour in the company's iron and steel operations, Ernest-Antoine Seillière started working in CGIP as of its creation in 1977. He was appointed its General Manager in 1981 and replaced his uncle, Pierre Celier, as President in 1986, the latter becoming Honorary President. He led the business in a way that confirmed his uncle's judgment: his strong character and purposeful energy were revealed to be valuable assets for the family enterprise.

Some activities, such as machine tool manufacturing, were discontinued, considered economically unsustainable in the longer term. Other companies were sold, some rapidly, others after substantial and tedious restructuring. The last forges were sold in 1985–86: Gueugnon was sold to Sacilor after their acquisition of Gueugnon's main steel supplier, as was the family's stake in Dilling, when Sacilor sought to develop its German business. Metal trading and transport activities were sold, having insufficient justification on their own. Through restructuring and a bold policy of acquisitions, a few sectors, like cement operations and metal packaging, started to witness significant developments. CGIP also entered totally new sectors, such as information services (through the Cap Gemini Sogeti software firm) and biology. As a result, in 1996 CGIP was present in a few economic sectors, through partial or full ownership of leading companies in these sectors.

Building Leading Companies: The Packaging Venture

At its creation, CGIP held the majority stake in Carnaud, a French metal packaging manufacturer. Carnaud was one of the "leftovers" of the former steel empire and one of the significant subsidiaries of CGIP. Its 1977 turnover amounted to FF 1.7 billion.

During the 1980s, the company was reinforced through several acquisitions. But the big move took place in early 1989, with the merger of Carnaud and the UK MetalBox Packaging company. This merger formed the second largest European packaging company, CMB Packaging, with combined sales of FF 24 billion. Carnaud and MetalBox's main shareholders, CGIP and MB Caradon, each owned 25.5% of the shares of CMB Packaging.

In April 1993, MB Caradon sold its stake in Carnaud MetalBox. CGIP purchased 7%, raising its stake to 32%. It was was the maximum that CGIP could buy without having to make a full take-over bid, which they could not nor wished to finance. They owned 46% of the voting rights. To secure control of the company, they succeeded in building an alliance with two investors, Paul Desmarais from Canada and Albert Frère from Belgium, who bought another 6%.

In May 1995, Crown-Cork and Seal (CCS), a leading US packaging manufacturer, made an offer to purchase Carnaud MetalBox. The deal created the world's largest packaging company, with a US$ 8.3 billion turnover. In exchange for its 32% share of Carnaud MetalBox, CGIP received 20% of the merged entity. This made CGIP by far CCS's largest shareholder. CCS was listed on the NYSE, where such a shareholding level is uncommon and typically provides full control of the company. Underlining its desire for a deal, CCS agreed to change its 40-year policy of not distributing dividends to satisfy Wendel shareholders. CGIP received the nomination rights for three directorships on the CCS Board, out of 15. Ernest-Antoine Seillière and the family were pleased and the merger was formally sealed in February 1996.

In just a few years, CGIP, through a sequence of strategic moves, had successfully transformed its majority stake in the medium-sized, hardly profitable Carnaud into a controlling stake of the new global leader in metal packaging. The family could now contemplate a new industrial venture in a business that was close to its origins.

However, it soon appeared that Philadelphia, where CCS headquarters were located, would not be the place where the family would feel comfortable as a new immigrant investor in America. CGIP would soon divest its controlling stake. The choice surprised many, yet the reasons were multiple and converging.

The mission of the family group was that of a trusted shareholder, accompanying an industrial transition from a precarious initial condition. CCS did not fit that mission: the business was mature and not in trouble. Its management, used to largely govern the firm, was not really looking for help or even advice from its board or a controlling shareholder. Then there was the issue that the US looked far away from Paris where the family, collectively, had great access to the multiple networks that influenced, as in any country, French economic and political life. The control of a major US listed firm generated little social value for the family. The prospect of selling its CCS stake did not generate high emotions for the family shareholding.

Initiating Major Diversification into Technology

The family was pleased that CGIP made a bold move into a totally new sector, by taking a 27.5% stake in Cap Gemini Sogeti (CGS), the French IT ology services company, created and owned by well-known IT guru Serge Kampf. The leading team at CGIP, and Ernest-Antoine Seillière in particular, felt that a diversification into industries of the future would help secure CGIP and its growth. The traditional industries in which CGIP held important stakes had persistent and sizeable problems. An extension to less vulnerable domains, in which real expansion could be sought, was a natural opportunity to pursue.

CGS had a great leadership team, but felt it needed a reference shareholder beyond its founder. It had enjoyed rapid growth over the past years, in France and abroad, and its future market developments offered strong potential. It seemed a perfect opportunity. Furthermore, there also could be synergies between CGS and other firms in the CGIP and Wendel portfolios. The rules of the game concerning CGIP were clearly specified: while Serge Kampf, founder and majority shareholder, had exclusive competence and responsibility for CGS's management, its strategic thinking and development would be decided jointly.

In 1983, CGIP increased its stake in CGS to 33.5%. Its growth proved spectacular. In 1985, the company was successfully introduced on the Paris Stock Exchange, having more than doubled its turnover in 3 years, from FF 1 billion in 1982 to FF 2.2 billion in 1985. The trend continued, with both strong internal growth and several acquisitions.

By 1991, CGS's turnover reached FF 10 billion, ten times that of 1982. Its continued growth required more capital. Daimler subscribed to a capital increase, and became the prime outside shareholder, with 34% of the shares, and CGIP's shareholding was reduced to 26%. Much synergy was expected with Daimler's IT subsidiary, Debis. An agreement gave Daimler an option to purchase CGIP's shares in 1996, at a fixed price. Conversely, CGIP had a right of first refusal on any shares Daimler wished to sell.

However, the economic recession of 1992–93 caused the growth to stop, profitability plunged, and losses prevailed for 3 years. This contributed to the development of internal competition between the CGS and Debis teams, replacing the expected synergy. Daimler did not exercise its right to purchase CGIP's shares in 1996, in part because of the high price, but also because of

Daimler's decision to now refocus on its automotive activities, moving away from a holding focused on transportation and mobility.

This led to CGIP's decision to IPO the company. Wendel (having absorbed CGIP in the meantime) would eventually sell its last shares in 2006. The implosion of the IT bubble in 2001 hit Cap Gemini's share price considerably, which attained 350 euros at its highest point. It slumped to 15 euros and reached close to 40 euros at the beginning of 2006 when Wendel sold its last shares.

The stable ownership and governance CGIP provided Cap Gemini allowed the company a remarkable period of growth, leading it to become a major player in IT and consulting sectors, particularly after the absorption of Ernst & Young, which it acquired in 2000 for US$ 11 billion. Capgemini Ernst&Young, like many of its rivals, suffered from the traditional culture clash between technical IT (or auditing) people and consultants. The firm finally retook the name Capgemini.

Under Wendel ownership, the company had grown its revenues 45x. Having invested US$ 1290 million over its 24 years of ownership, the investment multiple was much less favorable, partly due to the missed integration with Ernst & Young and largely because growth had been pursued rather than profitability (which should have led it to sell its shares earlier). But the ownership journey was seen as successful and greatly added to Wendel's reputation as an entrepreneurial and competent shareholder with a long-term vision, ready to invest what it takes to grow its portfolio companies and not limiting its intervention due to short- or medium-run constraints of profitability.

Restructuring and Diversifying the Marine-Wendel Portfolio

The strategy of the major family company, Marine-Wendel, followed a similar trend toward new sectors. Initially the holding company of the family's iron and steel activities, Marine-Wendel owned 20% of CGIP at its creation, as the French Government did not agree to a complete separation of the steel and iron assets from the family's other assets.

Marine-Wendel progressively increased its stake in CGIP to obtain a full majority. It also stepped into new industrial sectors, acquiring stakes in medium-sized companies. In 1996, Marine-Wendel owned a 50% stake in Reynolds SA, a manufacturer of pens and writing instruments (with an FF 450 million turnover in 1995). The firm had been sold by the owner's widow who gave priority to Marine-Wendel over American groups, influenced by

Marine-Wendel's family ownership and its medium- to long-term development philosophy. Very favorable terms would lead Wendel to sell this asset in 1999 to the US Newell Rubbermaid group.

In 1993 Marine-Wendel acquired a 75% stake of Stallergènes, a laboratory making allergy treatments through immunotherapy (FF 215 million turnover). In 17 years of ownership, Wendel turned this company into the world leader of allergen immunotherapy, multiplying the revenue ten-fold and earning an investment multiple of 35 (albeit on a small initial investment). It eventually sold the firm to another holding with a strong industrial focus belonging to the Bertarelli family.

In 1995 Marine-Wendel made an investment of 25 million FF for 19% of the capital of Bureau Veritas, the second largest firm in security and compliance services with a turnaround of less than 400 million euros. It is one of the longest held investments of Wendel, and has turned out to be a most successful partnership over the years. Today Burau Veritas has a turnaround of around 5 billion euros and a market capitalization of 11.4 Billion euros, Wendel holding 35.5%. The value of this equity today represents over 50% of the value of Wendel's portfolio. Knowing that the cumulative investment over the years by Wendel in Bureau Veritas was close to 400 million euros, the value multiple on Wendel's investment is massive, contributing to Wendel's continuing reputation as a valuable and reliable development partner for its investee companies.

The family holding also participated in a venture fund, Alpha, founded in 1985, with the support of Wendel and of Lazard, active in the French and German mid-markets, investing in midcaps and allowing public market investors to benefit from such private investments through Marine-Wendel. The fund fitted the mission of the family holding perfectly. Its originator and manager was Nicolas ver Hulst, a cousin who from 1985 onwards had been Seillière's right hand and participated in all the big moves of CGIP and Marine-Wendel. The fund and its management would gradually gain their independence from Marine-Wendel and its management. Though it fitted Wendel's mission well, it would eventually leave the family group in 2000 to form Alpha Associés, which became a leading European PE player.

Ernest-Antoine Seillière: The "Shareholder-Entrepreneur"

Throughout this restructuring period, the mission of CGIP had being steadily refined. In the 1991 Annual Report, Ernest-Antoine Seillière formally revealed

CGIP's philosophy as that of a "shareholder entrepreneur." It fitted Seillière's personality perfectly and he described it in the following terms:

> *CGIP is a holding company. But if, by saying 'holding company', one means a company that holds a portfolio of other firms, in other words, a mere shareholder, then CGIP is more than that. This is why we define it as the 'shareholder entrepreneur'. We are controlling shareholders,* i.e., *we own the majority of our subsidiaries, alone or together with a partner. For instance, we own the majority of Orange-Nassau or Cedest. We have the majority together with a partner on equal terms in CMB Packaging. We are the sole partner of the majority shareholder, as in Bio Participations with Alain Mérieux, in Demachy Worms with MM. Worms et Cie, and we were in Sogeti with Serge Kampf and the managers until Daimler-Benz's arrival this year.*
>
> *It is precisely this position as a controlling shareholder that is the basis for our attitude as entrepreneur regarding our subsidiaries. What is it? It consists of being actively involved in the key domains of the Group's enterprises: strategy, investments, acquisitions, cessions, organisation, choice of the key executives, financial decisions,* etc. *Thanks to a direct contact with the management teams, through our participation in executive committees or boards, we take an active part in the decision-making process. CGIP has a long-term strategy. It is involved in few activities, but for a long time.*

In September 1996, CGIP was the principal shareholder in two publicly quoted companies: Crown-Cork and Seal and Cap Gemini. Besides these, CGIP held stakes in several unlisted companies: BioMérieux Alliance, Wheelabrator-Allevard, Orange-Nassau (a real estate and energy company based in Benelux), and the certification and quality assurance Bureau Veritas. Having stakes in unlisted companies was important to justify CGIP's uniqueness vis-à-vis non-family investors, who could access such unlisted companies by buying CGIP stock.

Valeo: A Late Return to French Industrial Roots

It was with this background that, in September 1996, Ernest-Antoine Seillière invited his two cousins, Louis-Amédée de Moustier and Hubert Leclerc de Hauteclocque, who chaired the two controlling family holdings, Sogeval and SLPS. He wished to discuss the possible sale of the 10% shareholding in CCS and to acquire, with the proceeds of the sale, 20% of the French automobile component maker Valeo.

It had become increasingly clear that the CCS part of the CGIP holdings, which now represented over 50% of its assets, had grown too large. This was due to the consolidation of the packaging sector and divestitures from other sectors, in particular cements (Cedest) and finance. Ernest-Antoine Seillière was increasingly concerned over the negative impact on CGIP's outside investors. If investors were interested in the packaging sector, they should buy directly into Crown-Cork and Seal (CCS); if they were looking for a diversified holding, the increasing weight of CCS would worry them. CCS's success posed a problem for CGIP's valuation in the financial markets.

At the time, the investment community was starting to take bets that Carlo de Benedetti's continued difficulties with Olivetti would force him to contemplate the sale of his 28% stake in Valeo, France's leading automotive equipment manufacturer. Valeo designed and manufactured components and systems for cars and trucks. It had grown through a succession of mergers with, and acquisitions of, smaller suppliers in the French automobile sector. It had grown into a major worldwide competitor of companies such as Bosch, TRW, Delphi, and Nippondenso.

Valeo's range was wide and included clutches, friction material, heating units, radiators, lighting, signals, electrical units, windscreen wipers, security systems, and electronics. Valeo sold two thirds of its production in France, where PSA (Peugeot and Citroën) and Renault were its major clients. But it also had operations in 20 other countries. In addition, Seillière was seduced by the forceful management of Noël Goutard, who he viewed as an entrepreneur who had created a French global competitor in automotive supply. Valeo had achieved competitive production cost levels and realized an FF 29 billion turnover. Net annual profit stood at FF 1.2 billion. The company was continuously pursuing its rationalization program while also making acquisitions and alliances to further its growth and secure its position in a global and very competitive automotive market. Another feature of its development was its shift toward assembling and selling entire systems (e.g., fuel, heating, control) rather than components. The intention here was to capture a large fraction of the automobile's value chain and thus secure its market position. In a context of global consolidation, the two leading French car manufacturers had strongly expressed their fears of Valeo being purchased by American component makers, such as TRW or General Motors' Delphi. In a characteristic move, PSA's CEO, Jacques Calvet, threatened to boycott Valeo's products if this proved to be the case. This caught the attention of the French Government, which was now eager to see a French holding own a controlling stake in Valeo.

The story here is interesting, as CGIP had been a shareholder of Valeo. In 1986, CGIP sold what they considered non-strategic activities to Valeo, receiving a 7% stake in Valeo in return. Not viewing Valeo as a company upon which they could exert a major influence, CGIP progressively reduced its stake and in 1993 completely withdrew from Valeo's capital. As a major shareholder, Ernest-Antoine Seillière had been on the board of Valeo for several years, which grew his appreciation of Noël Goutard's leadership. He was also a member of the PSA board, and enjoyed personal links with Carlo de Benedetti. All these relations greatly facilitated the deal that would ensue.

The chairs of the two family holdings approved Seillière's idea, even though the proposal surprised them. They were also concerned that the automotive sector might not be best to enter at this stage. They would eventually be proven right, but the market was betting on automotive system integrators at that time. Both family shareholders were pleased at the prospect of seeing a major French industrial actor enter the family's portfolio. In the end, they allowed their cousin to pursue the deal if he was truly convinced that it would be good for the family's shareholding.

The Valeo investment would not prove a success and the end was brutal. CGIP reduced its Valeo stake from 20 to 9% in April 2002, putting Valeo in difficulty on the stock market, its share price falling close to 6% on the day of the sale. Valeo needed to scramble to buy back one million shares, to limit the market downfall of its share price. This is not what Valeo needed during a restructuring plan involving the closing of 30 sites and the layoff of 5000 workers. But Seillière, and especially the family shareholders, had grown tired of the poor results delivered by Valeo. The investment is indeed not cited by the Wendel family among its success stories.

The Family Ownership and Governance in 1996

The Wendel family's interests in 1996 were regrouped into two family holdings, Sogeval and SLPS, restricted to family members. These holdings jointly owned 50.1% of Marine-Wendel shares and 65.6% of the voting rights. Marine-Wendel, in turn, owned 51.9% of CGIP where it had 66.6% of the voting rights. The remainder of the shares belonged to market investors, many of which were institutional investors. The US investment fund Templeton Global Investors had, for example, a 6% stake in Marine-Wendel and a 2% stake in CGIP. SBC Warburg held another 2% of CGIP.

Sogeval and SLPS held joint Board of Directors meetings that allowed 18 family members (nine for each board) to be engaged in the business discussions concerning Marine-Wendel and CGIP. Much care was taken to ensure that the three branches of the Wendel family (i.e., the descendants of François de Wendel's three children) were equitably represented on the two boards.

Over 80% of the 450 shareholders typically attended, or were represented at, the annual shareholder meetings of SLPS and Sogeval. These meetings were followed by a cocktail party to which all family members over the age of 15 were invited. Colored badges identified attendees by family branch, a practice which continues to this day.

Family members could always seek financial advice from Mr Lacour, Marine-Wendel's corporate secretary. Lacour also acted as a "stockbroker" for an internal market where family members could buy and sell their SLPS and Sogeval shares. This internal market operated with a price set following a share-based valuation of their Marine-Wendel and CGIP shares, discounted for liquidity. Lacour would act as the broker and find matches between buyers and sellers.

One of Lacour's other activities was the regular update of the family tree, whose updated version was sent to all family members every few years. Major family events were shared among family members through Lacour's office. As a result of these tasks and interactions, Lacour had a very detailed knowledge of the family and a unique view of its history. One of his concerns was with the increasing number of family shareholders: higher than average fertility would lead family shareholders to exceed 2000 by the year 2020. He surely would need a larger office to continue his activities, and his task would probably change in nature as well. In fact, his prediction proved to be an overestimate. In 2022 the family counts about 1270 shareholders.

The two Chairmen of the family holdings, Louis-Amédée de Moustier and Hubert Leclerc de Hauteclocque, represented the family's voices as non-executive Directors on the Boards of CGIP and Marine-Wendel. They had a good sense of family values and expressed their concerns, both financial and non-financial, from a family shareholder's viewpoint. In turn, they would go before the family shareholders to explain and justify important decisions.

Hubert de Hauteclocque and Louis-Amédée de Moustier complemented each other perfectly. They had very different backgrounds and sensitivities: Hubert came from a family of forest-owners and understood the traditional and more conservative landowners. Louis-Amédée had been a highly innovative international financier. He liked to take more provocative stances, for instance that a family firm was only a transitory stage between an entrepreneurial firm and a public company and that the Wendel enterprise, with its three-centuries-old history, was atypical, and that family ownership would sooner or later become diluted.

Trust was a key element in the relationships between the family representatives and the family managers of Marine-Wendel and CGIP. The fact that Pierre Celier and Ernest-Antoine Seillière were both family members was seen as key to ensuring the trust. It also significantly eased communication. For example, both attended family meetings, which a non-family manager could not do. The family had displayed its trust in business decisions, such as when Ernest-Antoine Seillière had proposed to take a substantial stake in Cap Gemini Sogeti. With its industrial past, the family was reluctant to enter services. Eventually, they followed Seillière in its first major diversification effort, on one condition: that he was certain that this was a good business opportunity for the family. Serge Kampf's personality also reassured them: he sincerely looked for a shareholder to accompany his company's growth and share in the value creation, and did not appear to be eager to make a profit on account of their partnership.

Family values did play a considerable role in business discussions. The family refused the management's proposal to take a stake in the French tobacco manufacturer Seita at the time of its privatization. It also refused to buy into a firm that manufactured stockings and women's underwear. Both were seen as profitable business opportunities by CGIP's management, but the family did not consider these sectors as fitting their values of contributing to the welfare of their region, which increasingly was seen as France, and not just Lorraine.

As far as dividends were concerned, the healthy business climate had allowed dividends to increase each year. This also contributed to successful family relations and continued family support.

Marine-Wendel

The Honorary Chairman of the Board of Directors of Marine-Wendel was Pierre Celier, who had been the principal negotiator with the French Government during the steel crisis of the late 1970s that resulted in the creation of CGIP. He had attracted Ernest-Antoine Seillière to the family group and groomed him to be his successor. When Pierre hit the mandatory retirement age of 75, the family named him Honorary Chairman. He would continue to come to the office daily where he enjoyed frequent discussions with Ernest-Antoine, who greatly appreciated the presence of this experienced and wise partner. Pierre Celier had benefited from a similar situation with his predecessor Humbert de Wendel.

Louis-Amédée de Moustier and Hubert Leclerc de Hauteclocque represented the family holdings. Marine-Wendel's other family directors were Henri de Mitry and Guy de Wouters. Following a long career at Shell, Guy de Wouters had been with the family group for ten years, bringing his multinational experience to bear on the international aspects of the group. In particular, he was the Chairman of Orange-Nassau, a subsidiary in natural resources and real estate, and sat on the Board of Crown-Cork and Seal. The last three directors of Marine-Wendel were prominent members of the French business community, without family links: Paul Aussure, François Périgot, and Bruno Roger.

CGIP

On the Board of Directors of CGIP could be found Pierre Celier, again as Honorary Chairman, Ernest-Antoine Seillière as Chairman, Hubert Leclerc de Hauteclocque, Louis-Amédée de Moustier, Guy de Wouters, and Pierre-Louis de la Rochefoucauld, all family members. Jean Droulers, former Chief Executive Officer of the CLIF, the family holding at the time of the iron and steel industry, and creator with Pierre Celier of CGIP, was Honorary Chairman too. Although not a Wendel family member, Jean Droulers came from a business family and shared many values with the Wendel family. The two outsiders on the Board were Alain Mérieux, majority shareholder and CEO of BioMérieux Alliance (Marine Wendel had been a shareholder of the Mérieux firm), and Didier Pineau-Valencienne, a long-time business relation from the iron and steel days, as former CEO of the Schneider Group.

An Air of Wall Street Enters Wendel

With Pierre Celier having retired, it became time to think of a younger partner at the helm of Wendel. Seillière set his sights on Jean-Bernard Lafonta and offered him to be his close associate as general manager of the group. A student of the École Polytechnique and the Corps des Mines, he started his career at Jeumont-Schneider, Wendel's competitor from the north of France. He left the latter to join several ministries, until Bruno Roger invited him to join Lazard in 1993. There he quickly learned investment banking. Michel Pébereau, PDG of BNP, noticed his talents and put him in charge of the bank's strategy in 1996. In 1997 he was put in charge of BNP's capital markets division until, 3 years later, he was named head of the online bank Banque Directe. Due to his brilliance, he was considered to have the necessary background to be a great successor of Ernest-Antoine Seillière, when the latter was approaching retirement age.

Lafonta's first decision was to simplify the internal organization of Wendel. The low valuations of Cap Gemini due to the IT bubble and the less than anticipated results of Valeo had greatly reduced the value share of CGIP into the Marine-Wendel's portfolio. This proved an opportune time for Marine-Wendel to absorb CGIP through a share swap proposed to shareholders. It provided the further benefit of answering repeated questions as to the distinct missions of both structures. The integration was replicated at the ownership level, with Sogeval and SLPS merging into Wendel Participations, Marine-Wendel adopting the name Wendel Investissement, and then Wendel.

In search of greater value add and financial performance, Lafonta would initiate a change in strategy which consisted in shifting Wendel's focus on listed companies, away from non-quoted ones, and aiming for outright control to implement greater value creating strategies. This shift also introduced greater risk and higher leverage into the group. Then the basic law of finance correlates return with risk. The move was a natural for Lafonta whose background lay in investment banking.

Wendel thus, in 2002, took an equal stake, with KKR, one of the US champions of LBO investing, in Legrand, a leading supplier of electrical equipment and solutions. The story adds to the glory of Wendel: a total investment of 659 million euros in Legrand would generate a total investment return of 19% and an investment multiple of 3.9. Over the 11 years of ownership, Legrand revenues increased by 55%. The joint ownership by Wendel and KKR boosted growth, as did the excellent managerial skills of Gilles Schnepp, elected CEO in 2006, having joined Legrand in its finance department in 1989.

A new team was quickly put in place, Bernard Gautier having been hired in 2003 as Director of Development and Participations. Both Lafonta and Gautier were appointed in 2005 as the two members of the Executive Committee, with Lafonta as CEO and Gautier as his Deputy. Lafonta, having modified Wendel's strategy, changed the entire senior team. Arnaud Desclèves was put in charge of Legal Affairs. Philippe Donnet was recruited in 2006 to take charge of Wendel's Asian desk in Singapore.

The results of the Lafonta-Gautier team were excellent in the early years: the share price, which in December 2003 was 45 euros, jumped in four years to 130, an annual gain of 33%. The growth in Wendel's share price doubled that of the French CAC40 index over the same period. Dividends doubled too.

Methods changed as well, including remuneration. Senior managers were now offered, with the approval of the Supervisory Board, options to buy shares in Wendel. The argument presented by Lafonta was to reward Wendel's entrepreneurial leaders for the return they generated for shareholders. The style of the house became that of an activist investor in big firms. Lafonta initiated the practice of hostile bids, which certainly was not the tradition of the house.

The Saint Gobain investment was presented by Lafonta to the family as a great opportunity to change the leadership of a poorly governed firm, and to recover a position of reference shareholder for a French global firm. But the new Wendel methods lacked transparency, leading French market authorities to eventually punish both Lafonta and Wendel for dissimulating their acquisition intentions on Saint Gobain to the market. Wendel being publicly listed, the family was not informed of the name of the intended target before the acquisition.

With a 17% stake, Wendel became the largest shareholder of Saint Gobain, a firm which had been run by its iconic PDG Jean-Louis Beffa. The latter strongly believed that firms should be governed for the firm, and not for the interests of the shareholder at the expense of the firm's interests. The last thing Beffa imagined the year of his retirement year, after presiding over the destinies of the firm for more than 20 years, was to have an aggressive PE investor on his board telling his successor how to run the firm. His answer to the aggressive move by Wendel was to immediately confirm that he would stay on as President to fight the battle with Wendel. Wendel should have realized that given the size of Saint Gobain and Wendel's relatively small stake, Beffa would have the final word, unless Wendel could find investment partners to join it in the attack. This proved fruitless and should have been done before the acquisition. In addition, Beffa called for a capitalization increase that Wendel would be unable to fully follow, diluting its stake further. The battle was lost, and Beffa had the final word. But worse was to come.

Going Down with Wall Street

The 2007–08 financial crisis hit the world and Wendel by surprise. It revealed the risk of LBO strategies and proved nearly fatal to the family group that had just celebrated its 300-yearanniversary in 2004. The share price, which had reached 137 euros in July 2007, ended the year 2008 at 37 euros per share, while reaching a low of 18 euros in March 2009. Moody's did not like its high debt to net asset value as a result of the indebtedness necessitated by the new strategy. Covenant terms for the Saint Gobain acquisition had been agreed before the crisis. When the shares dropped dramatically in value during the crisis, covenant terms were breached. All this led to a serious downgrade of the Wendel stock, now obtaining a junk status rating. The indebtedness due to the combination of the Legrand and Saint Gobain moves left the group exposed like never before in its post-nationalization history. The worldwide depression in the construction market that followed the financial crisis hit Saint Gobain's share price further and compounded Wendel's problems.

Family shareholders, who had approved Lafonta's strategy, now experienced the other side of the bets taken and were in shock. They largely changed their minds on the high leverage methods introduced by Lafonta, which were a complete discontinuity with the past. The more prudent, non-listed strategy previously pursued would not have put the group in the precarious situation they were in.

Lafonta recognized he had lost the engagement of the family shareholders. The very public legal attack from a board member of the family claiming that the Lafonta-Seillière team had defrauded family shareholders with a compensation scheme that would yield 300 million euros of Wendel shares to the group's top managers shocked many family shareholders. Lafonta had collided with family shareholders. He submitted his resignation ahead of the announcement of the 2007 results. It was time for Wendel to return to more conservative paths.

Paradoxically, Lafonta would restart another PE, HLD, emphasizing the Wendel values: entrepreneurial spirit, commitment to their investments without time limits, ambition, trust, and a commitment to ESG. It looked like he had taken away quite a few lessons from his stay at Wendel. Probably to manage Wendel susceptibilities at Wendel, and to avoid looking like a financial player after the crisis, HLD presented itself as an industrial group, and not a financial holding taking participations. However, in 10 years HLD did just that, boasting an excellent performance and becoming recognized as one of the French and European PE stars.

Lafonta would suffer three major setbacks after leaving Wendel, beyond having been responsible for the solvability crisis of the group. First, as noted earlier, his lack of transparency in the Saint Gobain acquisition, with operations organized by swaps with major banks, was sanctioned by French market authorities in 2011 as a breach of required transparency. Both Wendel and Lafonta personally were fined 1.5 million euros. The very attacks in the courts by a family Board member of the Wendel family holding, Sophie Boegner, largely contributed to making the entire affair public, even if she lost all her cases in court. The Wendel Legal Director, Arnaud Desclèves, would also go to court for deceiving and forcing a compensation scheme on employees that put Wendel in a light that the family shareholding would completely disapprove of, pitting management further against both owners and employees. The courts noted that the harm done to employees on the stock option scheme was hardly imposed by the company and that employees were acting on their own responsibility. Desclèves and his fellow Wendel managers would lose their case against Wendel and its leadership in court.

Still, the harm was done, and the story indeed would not end well for the Wendel leadership. Both Lafonta and Seillière, with ten other senior managers of the group, were handed suspended prison terms and a 37,500 euro fine in March 2022, for fiscal evasion on the compensation system devised by Lafonta. Lafonta received the harshest term, 4 years. Seillière was not far behind, receiving 3 years. Both were suspended terms.

Recovering from the Crisis and Rebuilding the Portfolio

In crisis, Wendel needed to quickly appoint someone familiar with the company. Frédéric Lemoine joined Wendel in April 2009 as its new CEO. He knew the company well, having been Deputy CEO and Finance Director of Capgemini, and then Finance Director of Capgemini Ernst&Young. Before that, he had been Deputy Secretary General of the French Presidency under Jacques Chirac (2002–04) and Chairman of Areva, the French nuclear group (2005–2009).

Surprisingly, the transition proved as seamless as it was timely and effective. The Board had chosen the right man to redress Wendel from the abyss it had found itself in. The group was highly indebted, its share price had plummeted, and it was in dire need of cash. Lemoine wasted no time selling the oil and gas assets of its historical Oranje-Nassau subsidiary for 630 million euros in May 2009. This would be followed in June 2010 by selling its 17-year-old stake in the world leader in immunotherapy for allergic respiratory diseases, Stallergènes Greer, to the Ares Life Sciences Group of the Bertarelli family. It realized an investment multiple of 35 and a value add of 300 million euros. One year after Lemoine's arrival the share price had doubled and Wendel had exited the crisis.

To pay off its debt after the painful Saint Gobain experience, Wendel decided to sell its stake in Legrand, acquired jointly with KKR in 2002. As indicated earlier, its multiple on the investment was 3.9. But the opportunity cost would be considerable, as Wendel would have gained substantially more with Legrand's successful IPO in 2006. Relations with Gilles Schnepp, the Legrand CEO, would remain cordial, the latter agreeing to become Wendel's second nominee on the Saint Gobain Board. Lemoine showed his political skills by pacifying relations with Saint Gobain, the two agreeing on a long-term vision and development. Indeed, Saint Gobain aiming for African growth was seen as a useful asset in a new investment priority which was Africa. But Wendel would no longer be able to force its views upon Saint Gobain. This clause, mutually agreed, officially ended the battle, allowing Beffa to retire secure about the positive prospects of a group he led for over two decades.

It was now time for Lemoine to announce a new strategy more focused again on non-quoted firms and turning away from France, because of the high valuations in a very competitive French acquisition market. Wendel would set its sights on America, and Asia, in addition to Africa, opening offices in these regions or growing the Wendel teams already present.

A first investment of 275 million euros in IHS Holding was made in July 2013. IHS was the largest provider of telecommunications infrastructure in the world (by number of towers). It was founded by Sam Darwish in Nigeria in 2001. Wendel would invest a total of US$ 700 million in IHS Holding. The company was functioning well and very profitable, but markets proved chilly on Nigeria and the forex risk IHS represented. Its recent introduction on the NYSE did not go well, the share price going from US$ 17 at launch to less than US$ 6. Wendel also invested in the pan-African group Saham, majority held by its Moroccan founder, Moulay Hafid Elalamy. However, the latter was soon appointed Minister, leaving a leadership vacuum at his group. Wendel would limit damages here and sell its stake at its purchase price.

Europe was not forgotten in this turnaround. Stahl, the global leader in the chemical treatment and solutions of leather, has been in Wendel's portfolio since 2006. In April 2014, it announced that it intended to buy the leather services division of Clariant.

One of the great deals initiated by Lemoine, with Deputy CEO Gautier, in 2015 was the AlliedBarton acquisition, a leader in the US security industry. The ensuing merger in 2018 with Universal Services of America created Allied Universal, the leader in security services in North America. The company's developments attracted a lot of interest. It led Wendel to agree to sell its controlling stake in separate parts, first to the Quebec Pension Fund in 2019, and a year later to a group of investors led by Warburg Pincus and the J. Safra Group. The 5-year ownership led to over ten acquisitions, multiplying revenue by a multiple of three, and producing an investment multiple of 2.5, for an IRR of approximately 28%.

In the 2016 Annual Meeting, Lemoine was able to inform shareholders that the group had realized its investments for the year ahead of its schedule and that it would invest between 2 and 4 billion euros over the 2017–20 period essentially out of France, which now represented only 13% of the value of its portfolio.

The performance of Wendel allowing it to reduce its Saint Gobain debt, the firm was now ready to consider partnerships with other big international investors like the Peugeot and Santo Domingo families, the Singapore CIC sovereign wealth fund, and Rag, the German Foundation created to help in the conversation of German coal mines.

The departure of Seillière in 2013, at the age limit of 75, made Lemoine the leader of the family group. The controlling shareholder engaged discussions regarding the future direction of the group. The result of the deliberations was again surprising: Lemoine announced in September 2017 that he would leave Wendel at the end of the year, having completed the turnaround of the group. He confirmed that it was time for a new governance of the group. Two historical figures of the investment world, Nicholas Ferguson, former President of Permira, and Nicolas ver Hulst, former partner of Ernest-Antoine Seillière and former head of the Alpha fund, joined Wendel's board. Their arrival may not have been foreign to Lemoine's exit from the family group. The market did not approve Lemoine's exit, the share price falling by 6.44% in morning trading and finishing the day at the Paris Exchange at 2.37%.

Lemoine's financial record during his leadership of Wendel had been remarkable. Then the investment climate had been most favorable following the financial crisis. Debt had been reduced from 6 billion euros to 1, the value of assets in the Wendel portfolio grew from just over 1 billion euros to 7.8 billion, and the share price had grown from below 20 euros to over 130. His financial performance could not have been the main issue, but rather the less than full approval by the family of the new mission he had outlined for the future of the redressed group. Some of his views and methods must not have suited the board either. Lemoine believed, based on the group's strong recent performance, that it would be opportune to open the capital to other shareholders and dilute the family's control. This would increase Wendel's scope and investment power. But the family and especially the board of Wendel decided otherwise. Lemoine's exit from Wendel was amicable. He remained Wendel's representative on the Saint Gobain board.

Priscilla Takes the Chair of Wendel Participations in a Major Governance Reset

Priscilla's arrival at the helm of Wendel Participations in June 2019 was part of the renewal of the governance of the Wendel Group that Lemoine and François de Wendel, Seillière's successor as Chair of Wendel's Supervisory Board, had called for. The latter two had been increasingly at odds regarding the future vision and mission of Wendel. François de Wendel had been a very active Chairman over a difficult 10 years rebuilding family cohesion, being active as Chairman of both Wendel and its family holding, Wendel Participations.

Nicolas ver Hulst was chosen to succeed François de Wendel as Chair of the Wendel Supervisory Board. His return took the form of the return of the lost son. Nicolas had left the group in early 2000, when he bought the Alpha fund from Wendel with a partner. Seillière, then in charge of the group, had selected Jean-Bernard Lafonta, who would replicate the strategy of the Alpha fund, but at a much larger scale and—the essential difference—focusing on large, listed firms. The arrival of Nicolas coincided with the arrival of André François-Poncet as non-family successor of Frédéric Lemoine.

The appointment of Priscilla as Chairwoman of the family holding, Wendel Participations, completed the renewal of the leadership of the unique private equity group. The trio was fully aligned on a mission wholly returned to building, over a time horizon, sustainably leading companies. Values would be driving the group more strongly, centered on engagement, excellence, and entrepreneurial spirit. This entails a long-term shareholder charter that guarantees shareholder stability and a long-term partnership that does not hesitate to make financial commitments even during tough times, when justified.[7] An exceptional liquidity provision was introduced for the family by share buy-back. Simultaneously, a capital increase in Wendel Participations was accomplished.

The arrival of the new leadership team at Wendel was quickly noticed. In March 2019, the group announced a share buy-back of its own shares, thanks to a 200 million euro loan from Goldman Sachs. It offered an exit option to shareholders that might wish to leave the group, while increasing family control of Wendel to 39%. End 2019, Wendel announced the acquisition of the Crisis Prevention Institute, the Milwaukee-based leading provider of behavior management and crisis prevention training in the US. In June 2020 Wendel decided to sell its South African asset, Tsebo, confirming that it would concentrate future investments in Europe, particularly France, and in North America. The sale also ended Wendel's diversification in Africa, initiated by Lemoine.

In October 2021, Wendel sold its Cromology asset, a specialist in decorative paint, to Dulux Group for a value of 1.26 billion euros, having reinvested 125 million euros 2 years earlier in a company that would otherwise have had to be written off. The group also announced that it would diversify its portfolio by privileging technology investments into software, health, and other business services. And indeed, in January 2022, Wendel announced a US$

338 million investment into ACAMS, a global certification specialist in the fight against money laundering. The investment confirmed the more value-driven investment strategy announced by the new leadership team, and the move toward software and services. It also nicely complemented the CPI acquisition done 2 years earlier. One piece of negative news was that the share price was hit by the disappointing introduction of IHS at the NYSE. The NYSE was perhaps not the best place to introduce a Nigerian operating company; London might have been a more natural place for the listing. A further diversification was the creation of Wendel Lab, which became Wendel Growth. This new fund represents a 500 million euro commitment by the group into tech and digital by dual investments into funds complemented with direct investments. The portfolio by now had been restructured and simplified. André François-Poncet also clearly committed the group to CSR and ESG practices, rapidly recognized by several awards.

Yet, the history of this now more than 300-year-old group would continue to be written in surprising ways, fitting the statement of the Count of Lampedusa that we evoked regarding the vanishing Kingdom of the Two Sicilys and which states that sustainability is a task requiring constant action. The announcement of the departure ahead of its 2025 term of Wendel CEO, André François-Poncet, in June 2022, surprised many in the financial markets, the share price falling by 9%. When joining the group, François-Poncet had stated that he had joined to manage the group following the departure of Lemoine with the mission of realigning the portfolio according to certain values and strategic principles, and to decline these inside Wendel, in its operations. Indeed, he substantially changed the group's operating processes, particularly in IT, Audit, and ESG, and introduced a more active management of the portfolio, going all the way to pushing for the replacement of management in the portfolio companies. The progress was noted, Wendel obtaining various awards in 2021, including the Grand Prix de la Transparence (all categories) for the quality of its financial and non-financial information to investors and the Agefi award for Diversity in Management Bodies, and the obtention of a 76/100 rating on the Dow Jones Sustainability Indew (World and Europe), placing Wendel far above the 27/100 average rating in its Diversified Financials category.

His task having been accomplished ahead of schedule, François-Poncet felt that it was a good time for Wendel to transition to a new leadership. He confirmed that he would assume the leadership of Wendel until a successor was found, and that he would do this with David Darmon, the Deputy CEO. Darmon had opened the Wendel office in North America and had been responsible for Wendel's investments there. In September 2022, Nicolas ver

Hulst announced that Laurent Mignon, the head of BPCE, France's leading savings bank, would take over no later than January 1, 2023. A new team had taken over the leadership of the more than 300-year-old firm, initiating another leadership cycle and chapter.

Priscilla's Views on Ownership Philosophy and Practice

Wendel is the oldest among Europe's large family investment companies, the largest being Investor, owned by the Wallenberg family. Priscilla, a member of the ninth generation, views ownership foremost as a responsibility and a duty, a legacy to be built and transmitted. She is delighted to see her children active in Wendel's Next Generation group, which she created, stimulated by what she learned from the Wendel International Centre for Family Enterprise, and also through her attendance of the meetings of the Family Business Network International, where she was a Board member.

A responsible shareholder must be aware of the company and of the changing world. She or he will continuously think about the fit between the company's purpose and capabilities, and the needs of an ever-changing environment. Meeting CSR challenges has always been a preoccupation of the family, which organized the first pension system in France in 1850 (later taken over by the state). As of 1836, it increased pay with seniority to alleviate the unfairness of pay based on task alone. In 1857, Charles de Wendel built Stiring-Wendel, a working-class housing estate to accommodate employees. The estate, like Joeuf, had a church, schools, food stores, and cooperatives to provide food at moderate prices. So ESG is the modern version of what is a natural priority for Wendel, which today it rigorously declines in its investment process, and which continues Wendel's long-held commitment to society. The ESG emphasis today has clearly shifted to the environment when in the past the social dimension was the more prominent focus.

The group has been a founding sponsor of the Centre Pompidou-Metz since its creation in 2010. The group was delighted to provide long-term support for a flagship project benefiting Lorraine, the birthplace of the group and its founding families. Wendel was awarded the title of Grand Mécène de la Culture by Minister of Culture Frédéric Mitterrand in 2012. In 2022, Wendel set up its endowment fund, Wendel Cares, with its own Board of Directors, through which the group will finance its philanthropic projects going forward.

Being part of a family business was always present in Priscilla's life, though she admits not having been fully aware of it for quite some time. That only came when, being an INSEAD alumna, she became responsible for the family firm's relations with INSEAD, which had benefited in 1996 from a major gift to create the Wendel Chair for the Large Family Enterprise. This association brought her in contact with the Family Business Network, and particularly with its French chapter, where she has been holding the Vice-Presidency for many years. She was on the Board of FBN International for 6 years and is now an FBN Ambassador.

These experiences made Priscilla greatly more conscious of the distinct reality of family firms, compared to non-family firms. This realization was furthered by some of the nastier challenges issued by some family members to the group's leadership. This made her even more interested in the family holding board than she otherwise would have been. She created and became Chair of the Family Cohesion Committee. Wendel had two family holdings when she joined, soon merged into one, simplifying the ownership structure and allowing a clearer voice for the family shareholding. She joined the Board of Wendel in 2013 and was appointed Executive Chair of the family holding in 2018. She felt well prepared for the responsibilities that fell on her shoulders.

Priscilla grew up in Paris, her father leaving three days each week to Lorraine. Her mother was a private person, passionately attached to Wendel. The 1977 nationalization was a tragedy for her. She entered a period of intense depression and even suffered a brain hemorrhage that paralyzed her for the rest of her life. Priscilla was very close to her father who took her to official functions as her mother shunned social activities. He managed in negotiations with the French Government to keep the upstream and downstream activities out of the nationalization. Raymond Barre, the Prime Minister at the time, had the final vote and accepted her father's position, against the recommendations of his own administration. She remembers this stressful episode very well, being 26 at the time. It was a tragedy for the whole family, as they were close to losing it all to the State.

Her first position after university was selling factories around the world for Creusot-Loire Enterprises, mainly in Russia and Czechoslovakia. Having studied for 1 year in Leningrad, she was eager to work in Russia. She was well schooled for the assignment: a BS in Math at Paris VI, MA in Economics at Sciences Po, and a DESS in Soviet Studies where she was a student of Hélène Carrère d'Encausse, France's eminent specialist on Russia. An exchange program in 1975–76 in the suburbs of Leningrad was indeed a unique learning experience. Lodging conditions were terrible, though this stands as one of the best years of her life. She was fascinated by the Russian and Slavic minds, as they kept reminding her of the different angles and interpretations various actors can espouse on the same reality. This thought helps her in dealing more effectively with family shareholders, which she describes as loyal and demanding. These two aspects, for her, go together.

She feels life has prepared her well for her current governance and ownership responsibilities, though she is mindful of continuously upgrading her knowledge about being a responsible owner, particularly on the governance and ESG fronts. It is paradoxical that she repeated something her father had done exiting the nationalization crisis: providing a liquidity option to family shareholders desirous to exit from the group, even if hopefully only partially. Indeed, imprisoning a shareholder is hardly conducive to obtaining her or his commitment. So, she was happy, as Executive Chair, that the family holding formally agreed to offer this exit option to its shareholders, hoping like her father that few would exercise it and that it would only generate greater commitment among the shareholders, and very few exits, if any.

Priscilla is very proud of the more than 300-year history of her family group. She did not think she would contribute to it as much as she has. She regards the task of extending the economic life of the family group as quite a challenge. Then she is comforted by the entrepreneurial character of the group; meeting challenges and adversity is in the family's DNA. It is also the foundation for the contribution family ownership makes to the investment companies.

Cohesion and consensus among family shareholders is very important. The 2007–08 crisis triggered a financial crisis for Wendel, but doubled up with a severe crisis in the family shareholding. She felt the Saint Gobain operation had been run too secretively and was not reflective of the family values, either in substance or in process. Its hostile nature particularly shocked Priscilla. Saint Gobain also was a large, listed company which was hard for Wendel to influence, particularly with Wendel's limited ownership stake. The investment furthermore unbalanced the portfolio and put the company in immense debt in a credit crisis, setting it on a very risky course which ultimately backfired. At the time of the crisis, Priscilla had to spend 2–3 days a week to keep family members informed and united in what again were very turbulent times. Even more so since a family crisis had to be addressed at the same time as an economic one.

This made Priscilla realize that actions had to now be taken to restore and strengthen the family's *affectio societatis.* So she initiated open workshops for family shareholders who could choose which workshops to join where shareholders were invited to express their needs and wishes. Both horizontal and vertical communication greatly improved as a result of a number of actions, including the mailing to all shareholders of the newsletters and information releases by Wendel, the creation of a family intranet, and the mailing of a weekly family shareholder brief. So-called Traits d'union meetings were organized ranging from thematic dinners, to visits of particular exhibits, and even sporting events. Some of these meetings focused on educating family shareholders how best to read the annual reports emanating from the portfolio companies of Wendel. Others pertained to the education of the Next Gen members. Smaller groups of shareholders were also invited to meet with one or two Wendel Participations board members, with the presence of Priscilla as Director General of the Wendel Participations. Family shareholders are regularly invited to two-day seminars, with some reserved for the Next Gen.

To stimulate the family's entrepreneurship an annual prize for the best family initiative was created. The winner is selected by a jury consisting of family members. The winner is awarded both a *prêt d'honneur*, which is a loan with the promise to reimburse when feasible, as well as coaching for the members active in the start-up. To give the initiative good exposure, the prize is awarded at a second annual meeting of family shareholders—complementing the General Annual Meeting. Shareholders are invited to meet the Executive Directors of Wendel, as well as the CEOs of the portfolio companies.

Priscilla is very proud of having started and supported these actions, which have indeed greatly restored the needed cohesion and spirit among family shareholders. She also makes the board of Wendel Participations work hard and has doubled the frequency of its meetings (now eight per year). The frequency helps build consensus among board members. Priscilla wishes the family holding board to have a clear ownership view that she can bring to the Wendel board meetings, where family board members and competent independent board members have constructive and engaged discussions. There is no split at the Wendel board in roles, family members contributing their views on behalf of the company, as do its independent members.

Lessons have been learned, though, centered on values, and a more systematic and transparent approach to the integration of these values in the processes of the investment company, and, from there and as appropriate, in each of the portfolio companies. Greater transparency has been obtained. Priscilla is also very pleased that the group is now more principled and disciplined, even if the realignment of Wendel along these lines had a cost in terms of share price. It has been hard work, but it is now established, and it makes her confident that it will pay off going forward, for the family shareholding, the group, and for the investment companies.

The balancing of stock market performance, which is tilted to the short run, and long-term value creation will remain a challenge. The key is to understand the gap that may exist between expectations of the Wendel leadership and its holding company, and that of the market. As in every private equity, the biggest challenge is how to repeat the great successes of the past, in a quickly changing world and with a major focus on an ESG lens in line with family values. This, she feels, is the group's current ambition and should focus everyone's mind. Dividends and share price will be, in the longer term, the consequence of what is the key task of the owner, the board, and the management: setting the mission and the direction, and then seeing its implementation in capital allocation decisions, as well as overseeing this allocation.

Notes

1. https://en.wikipedia.org/wiki/Berkshire_Hathaway and https://en.wikipedia.org/wiki/Warren_Buffettt are good sources of a man whose life is by now well known, as is https://www.berkshirehathaway.com.
2. https://www.ft.com/content/bee2a000-75f0-48d6-8027-d2c29c50f1c9.
3. This account is based on the experiences of the founder of this venture and of one of the authors who was one of his main mentors throughout the venture, and also angel investor, and first Chairman of the Board. Like all such accounts, even if based mainly on facts, biases and omissions are acknowledged. The purpose of the account is mainly to underline the challenges of start-ups for founders, shareholders, and directors, and to underline the often-neglected role of boards even at the early stage of such ventures. Some names are disguised to preserve anonymity. The "orphan owner" description refers to a founder not benefiting from ownership experience as is traditional in owning families.
4. Donald A. Redelmeier and Robert J. Tibshirani, "*Association between cellular-telephone calls and motor vehicle collisions,*" *The New England Journal of Medicine,* February 1997.
5. Some of the material in this section has been lifted from the INSEAD Case 09/1999–4784, *The Wendel Family: "Affectio Societatis" (A), The Story of a French Industrial Dynasty (1704–1976,* and *The Wendel Family: "Affectio Societatis" (B), CGIP: The Family as "Shareholder Entrepreneur" (1977–1996),* by Chrstine Blondel and Ludo Van der Heyden, 1999
6. Giuseppi Tomasi di Lampedusa, *Il Gattopardo ("The Leopard"),* Feltrinelli, 1958.
7. https://www.wendelgroup.com/en/about-us/investing-for-the-long-term/.

15

Transitioning to Ownership and Developing as Owner

The third part of the book is devoted to the personal aspects of ownership, which we referred to as "humanware," and which complement the more structural elements, the "hardware," and the relational elements, the "software." The profiles presented in Chap. 13 provide rich stories and context to discuss the critical role played by personality in determining ownership effectiveness.

In this chapter, we first comment on whether ownership is a talent or a competence, or both. We then review the five profiles for the lessons they hold about the role of personality in shaping ownership effectiveness, next to the more structural and relational elements. In commenting on these profiles, we will thus also comment on the latter elements, moving to closure of our treatment of ownership in this treatise.

1 Talents and Competences: The Vital Mix

Ownership life is marked by a number of dualities: sole versus multiple, short run versus long run horizon, ownership, and supervision versus execution, internal versus external, global versus local, minority versus majority. Dualities consist of opposites that are too often seen as substitutes, when they should be seen as complementary. These dualities then pose the risk of becoming divisive, eroding owner as well as corporate performance. Talents and competencies are very much such a complementary duality.[1]

Talent is innate. It is a gift at birth, received from our parents, or from our grandparents, since the former themselves inherited their talents from their

M. Massa et al., *Value Creation for Owners and Directors*,
https://doi.org/10.1007/978-3-031-19726-0_15

parents, etc. The saying "life is unfair" is one outcome of this reality, as so much in our lives is determined at birth, by our parents. The unfairness in the saying refers to the truism that we do not choose our parents. Then we do not choose the family we join upon birth, nor our birth order, nor whether we are boy or girl, first in birth order, or last. And all these aspects matter tremendously, and greatly influence our life histories. The unfairness of choice with regard to what are outcomes of our parents' decisions (influenced, themselves, by their parents' decisions, etc.) makes fair process the key fairness to strive for in life, as the "shares" of personality and traits we are given at birth are distributed very unfairly. What is left then is to pick up these traits and personalities, and do the best we can in utilizing and benefiting from them. Living one's life fairly then becomes the main agenda, and not blaming or referring ceaselessly to the unfair conditions in which one came to join life on this planet. In contrast, competence can be acquired by study, practice, training, and endurance. Competence is a matter of will, talent is a matter of luck. Competence is strenuous work; talent is a gift.

Talent and competence are two complementary and reinforcing aspects of ownership: ownership talents, provided at birth and revealed over time as a function of circumstances, and ownership competencies, acquired and refined with experience, learning, and practice. A table contrasting talents with competencies appears in Fig. 15.1. The owner profiles presented in this chapter show that both talents and competences contribute to successful ownership.

We are blessed: we all have talents. We are most performing when utilizing our talents, and more sustainable. There is a caveat: our talents are limited and idiosyncratic. They are the result of what our parents gave us at birth, and even they did not make any conscious selection of which talents they would

Dimension	Talent	Competence
Time	Unpredictable yet lasting	Predictable but eroding
Emotions	Fun and energizing	Draining and energy consuming
Understanding	Implicit and observable	Explicit and verifiable
Physical	Individually located	Broadly distributed
Spiritual	Surprising and uplifting	Expected and normal

Fig. 15.1 Contrasting talent with competence over the five fundamental energies

endow us with. Then there are the events in life that shape and define us, by revealing in us talents that were latent, but came to the forefront.

One part of our development consists in becoming aware of our talents and learning how to best utilize and benefit from them. Given that our talents are natural, we are less aware of them than those that observe us. That is what coaching, mentoring, and feedback are all about: our coaches, mentors, and close ones help us by revealing the talents we have and which they observed. The realization becomes a pivot in our life, as we then use our talent with greater awareness, and more strategically.

However, talent can also become a trap, precisely because it is reliable, natural, and relatively effortless for us to deploy. Someone who has a visionary talent might always go back to telling a visionary tale, when more precise and analytical statements are expected or called for. Someone who is seductive will use his powers to avoid confrontation with negative outcomes that he or she better take responsibility for.

Talent cannot be developed as it is innate. It can, however, be revealed, often through challenge, and is identified through careful observation. Talents are innate and immediate to recall, without much effort. In a crisis, we instinctively turn to our talents to save ourselves.

Lionel Messi has remarkable dribbling and scoring talents. Steve Curry can shoot hoops in basketball as few people can. Ronaldo and Nadal have remarkable physical talents and stamina that Messi and Federer do not possess. The latter rely on other talents to make a difference. These athletes attest to both the importance and limits of talents: Messi is a great offensive player yet is known not to defend well: most agree that he would be a terrible defender and that asking him to defend greatly reduces his offensive performance. Federer relies on incredible skill—he is all flow—which makes his game incredibly smooth and powerful.

Talent is rarely ubiquitous or 360°. Context matters a lot. For example, Federer is most performing on faster surfaces, like grass or fast synthetic. Federer has eight Wimbledon and six Australian Open titles, all on grass and fast synthetic. Only one of his victories is on the slower clay courts at Roland Garros. Nadal also has 22 Grand Slam titles, 14 of which at Roland Garros, on slower clay. "Only" four of Nadal's titles are at the US Open, three at Wimbledon, and two at the Australian Open. All these are faster surfaces which suit Nadal's game less. There are contexts where talents come out better, or are more needed, than elsewhere; there also are contexts that do not allow us to demonstrate our talents, or where these are not useful. At such moments, we rely on our competences.

So it goes with owners, as the following sections will show. Owners are far from superior in all aspects of the business game; they excel at certain aspects, and then indeed excel incredibly well. To be sustainably successful, they had to complement their talents with other skills, which they learned and acquired along the way, some with much effort or as hard-earned lessons. In team sports, one can compensate for one's limits with the skills of others, not in individual sports. That is why owner founders rarely make their impact alone: there is no Bill Gates without Paul Allen, no Steve Jobs without Steve Wozniak, and no Ernest Solvay without his younger brother Alfred. Human history prefers individual stories over team stories, as they are so much easier to tell. Team efforts are more complex to share and rarely provide us with a clear template or benchmark. All "CEO of the Year" awards suggest a personal, Atlas-like contribution by CEOs and founders, when they rely on contributions of others (investors, board members, executives, …) to succeed.

In a team the talent of one individual is ideally reinforced and complemented by the talent and/or competence of another individual. Very rarely are all team members talented in their team roles. One rare example of an all-talented team is the US Dream Team of 1992. It earned Olympic Gold in basketball by winning all its games by more than 43 points and without their coach ever calling a time out during the entire competition. It was a team filled with stars which coach Daley blended into a high-performing team. Being composed of "galactic" players, the team required few interventions by their coach. It forever stands out in a country where even team sports (such as baseball, basketball, or football) are dominated by individual player statistics.

The first message of this chapter is a recognition that highly successful owners, just like successful athletes, owe their success to talent and character—where perseverance looms large—and also on the many events and people who each contributed, often small, sometimes large, to the ultimate success.

Each of these journeys is idiosyncratic. Yet there are also common principles shared by all and governing these journeys. Owners benefit from mentors that provide advice and expertise on how to do things, from sponsors that provide the resources required to perform and achieve their goals, and from coaches who help them reveal answers they already have in them.

Having underlined the complementary roles of talents and competences, and the diversity of talents and competences needed to succeed, one of the key messages of the preceding chapter is to underline the great diversity of personalities among owners, and how these personalities are intricately woven in the journey and contribute to shape it. To be radical, there is no such thing as a typical owner.

Thus, our first conclusion is that just like athletes, owners need to continuously develop their craft by leveraging their talents and continuously building their competencies and networks. All owners need to be able to relate to other talented and less talented individuals, need to acquire and process information, make decisions, and gain the trust of others around them. Their personalities contribute to how effective owners are in these tasks. It is the point we seek to emphasize in the next section, before turning to reflections on our five owner portraits and journeys.

2 A Rich Diversity of Personalities

Personality refers to a person's pattern of feeling, thinking, and behaving. It is the result of both innate behavioral characteristics—our nature, talents, biases, and also faults—as well as those acquired and nurtured by events on our journey. Personality influences how we act, how we interact with others, how we are perceived, and how effective we ultimately are.

Understanding a person's personality is intended to facilitate our interactions with that person. It also allows us to better understand our impact on others. This is distinct from stereotyping or personalizing, which amounts to putting people in boxes or types, comforting ourselves and our brains so eager for reassurance in the belief that this classification is accurate. Stereotyping or personalization can also be divisive and distancing when it does not do justice to the complexity and diversity that is in each of us. It also supports ingroup/outgroup behaviors.

What is important to recognize in personality testing and querying is that all of us have behavioral patterns we have become used to, that are often unconscious, and are also not easy to change. Learning and understanding these patterns as habits is helpful; judging them immediately as good or bad, is detrimental to building healthy relations with people. Personality typology shows us clearly that individuals in their feeling, thinking, and behaving patterns differ greatly, and that easy conclusions are generally wrong and unfair. The next step is the realization that what is true about others is also true about us, when others look at us. That builds relativity and understanding.

The profiles in the previous chapter show how fundamental personality is in shaping ownership—and of leadership more generally—and how the "human-ware" dimension interacts, positively and negatively, with the other two fundamental dimensions of hardware and software exposited in the first two parts of the book. Napoleon, again, provides an excellent and very clear illustration of how this interaction was generally if not extremely positive when he was a young general, and how his personality entered a vicious cycle of retrenchment and increasing isolation when he aged and became a largely dictatorial Emperor. The transformation is as shocking as it is common in leadership.

One of the simplest leadership classifications is provided by Richard Olivier (Fig. 15.2). The framework is most insightful and combines the basic Freudian "Male vs Female" dimension with the "Static vs Dynamic" Jungian developmental dimension. Jung countered Freud with an assertion that people could develop and change, and indeed were not necessarily fixed in their traits over their lifetime. The combination of both dimensions identifies four fundamental leadership archetypes which Olivier calls Nurturing Mother/Father, Warrior/Amazona, Good King/Queen, and Fairy/Magician. Each identifies a basic facet of leadership which can be summarized, respectively, as developing people, action and execution, judgment and decision making, and innovation and creativity. This is made clear in Fig. 15.2.

Ownership types can be analyzed using the four archetypes identified in Fig. 15.2. The more talents people have the better. The more talent the more they will be able to present enticing visions, develop and support people, make the right decisions, and propose innovative solutions when things turn more difficult. Of course, managing a platoon or a small team is not the same as managing an army or an organization. Complexity calls for training as it demands greater intelligence. Effective leadership is thus always a combination of acquired competences and innate talents.

Napoleon showed quite early that he could command people, but it also ought to be recognized that he had spent years reading the great leaders that

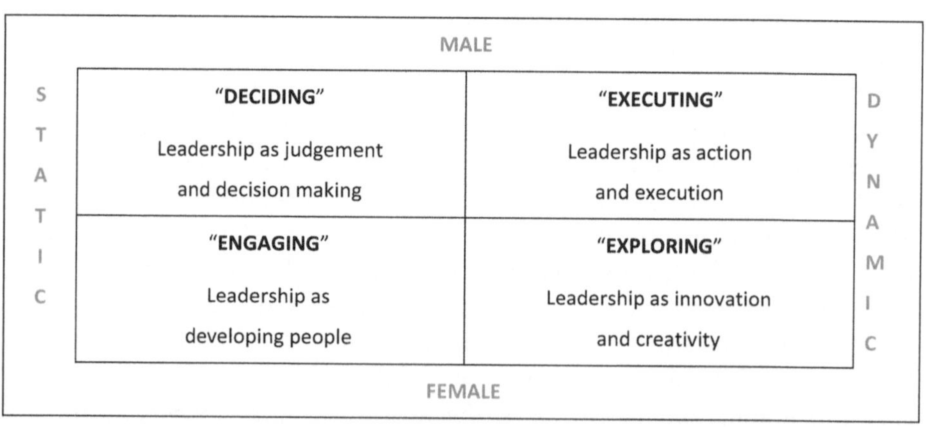

Fig. 15.2 Leadership typology. Source: Inspirational Leadership, by Richard Olivier (Richard Olivier, *Inspirational Leadership,* Nicholas Brealey Publishing, Boston, MA, 2013)

were Alexander, Hannibal, and Julius Caesar. They greatly influenced his military strategies founded on speed and surprise. Napoleon's diplomatic skills were much inferior to his military skills. He conquered an Empire and lacked the diplomacy to keep it. Even when Talleyrand, his Foreign Minister, rightly suggested that he should start focusing on winning the peace. His continental embargo against Britain weakened continental allies whose economies depended on British trade. It caused Russia to defect on its promises and triggered the 1812 "special military operation" intended to bring Russia back to these promises. The result was the opposite: the military operation greatly put an end to Napoleon's hegemony and the Empire started to crumble. Leaders need to develop and can't rely on their talents only, for then their talents turn into weaknesses, possibly leading to their downfall. Napoleon became trapped in his superior military mindset, and increasingly saw the other European countries as countries to be conquered and submitted to his imperial reign. When these resisted, he would send his troops. This would typically work, even though the cost in human lives became increasingly high with time. That was partly because he failed to come to an agreement with powers that he could not dominate, mostly Britain and Russia. That is what eventually set himself up for failure. He missed the diplomatic mindset and talents of a Talleyrand or a Metternich, entrapped as he was by his military thinking and genius which limited his development.

Warren Buffett here presents us with a remarkable counterexample of "sticking to one's knitting": he seemed to show little hesitation to rely on Bill and Melina Gates and their foundation to "do good" leaving big chunks of his fortune to the foundation, which he viewed as so much better at this global charity work than he could ever be or become interested in doing.

So, there are indeed two dimensions that owners ought to keep in mind. First, ownership is a mindset, distinct from being a board member or being an executive. The first point this book has aimed to make throughout is the importance of the ownership mindset, which is not a natural one for most people, and often is given short billing relative to the executive mindset of "getting things done" and the governance mindset, which is about supervising what gets done. That makes the development of a true and distinct ownership mindset so critical for owners, typically requiring several transitions as we have indicated. The second point we make here is a consequence: the development of such a mindset rests on a mix of talents and competences, and it is best if indeed owners have multiple talents and are aware of those they have and of those they miss. The danger comes from only relying on one talent, and one corresponding leadership archetype, and then abusing it. This is what turns talented entrepreneurs into dictators, talented visionaries into manipulators. Missing talents must be compensated by acquired competences, or by delegation to trusted advisors and allies. This is where owner and corporate boards find their justification and their *raison d'être*. They favor the collective and distributed leadership model which FPL supports and advocates. The negative transitions from benevolent owners into dictatorial ones are more likely to occur in the absence of such advisors and allies, or in their complicit silence.

Founders—and angel investors—often start as Fairy Queens or Magicians, then develop into Warrior or Amazona CEO types, and, later in the journey, into Good Kings or Queens, which is the leadership archetype that best characterizes a great Chair. The Nurturing Mother archetype is the owner who inspires and develops others and showers them with love all along the entrepreneurial journey. The examples presented in Chap. 13 provide evidence and validation for these archetypes and for the transitions required to develop into effective and sustainable ownership.

Repeated in the portraits and pictures of owners presented in Chap. 13, the reader will have noticed the critical importance of the personal development that owners need to experience to become great owners. The ownership role is much less studied in the academic and professional literatures than the managerial or executive one.[2] Particularly in relation to her or his value creation responsibilities. A key feature of this development is the determining impact of context and environment, as of early age, which are often critical and are best understood by all those providing the owner and her or his venture with the crucial support needed for sustainability and progress. What characterizes successful owners as well, and this has been said already, yet deserves repetition, are their extremely strong drives and sense of purpose, which keeps fueling them, even at times when the venture turns sour, or is at great risk of doing so. In other words, the energies and strength of owners is often a key part of what makes their firms more sustainable and also longer lasting. In contrast, publicly listed firms here are more prone to discontinuities, including the possibility of being acquired (often by owner-led corporate structures).

The five owner profiles presented in Chap. 13, each in their own way, detail and provide powerful lessons for the diversity of experiences, challenges, and transitions that define the ownership journey. These different profiles bear a common message: ownership is an intensely human experience, one of remarkable achievements, but also of uncommon challenges and defeats, where resilience is built by turning today's defeats into the preparation of future victories. All the relations and interactions—the software—and all the structures—the hardware—that we presented in this book must be governed by and are intended to support competent, talented, and persistent owners:

peopleware—with all its intricacies—remains at the root of performance. One can dispose of powerful hardware and excellent software, but if it does not align with the person owning or in front of the machine, both the hardware and the software are likely to be wasted.

The effectiveness of the peopleware/hardware/software tripod is thus vital for ultimate and sustainable success of each owner. All three legs are necessary to own and direct a successful enterprise. The owner's personal tripod in turn supports the other tripod, consisting of ownership, supervision, and management, which provides the backbone for value creation. This conclusion stands as a stark contrast to Karl Marx, who worried about the abusive and destructive powers of ownership, which are real, but should at least be compared by mentioning the extremely positive role played by owners, which both economics and society often ignore, as well as owners themselves. This book spurs owners and their directors to equip themselves with a sufficient mix of care, confidence, and humility—yet another tripod—that will serve them and their ventures well.

The science of ownership, which we aim to contribute to, is still emerging. In this emergence, we do not need to agree on all aspects, nor to be complete or always precise about the notions we present. But we can agree that our great writers, Smith, Friedman, and Marx, were unjust with the genre, like Friedman by denying its importance or, like Marx by painting a horrid picture of menace and destruction. It is this unfair picture that the stories are intended to counter.

We now turn to detailing the ownership and lessons from each of the individuals profiled in the preceding chapters.

3 Lessons from Warren Buffett

For Warren Buffett, the main lesson is one of unabating focus on developing and attaining financial mastery. Buffett is the pure owner type: what Buffett cares about and focuses on are investing, capital allocation, products, and services he has experience with and cherishes, and on the selection of CEOs and management teams that know how to execute and deliver value to customers. These are fundamental competencies that owners will cultivate to their benefit and that of their corporation. It is one that Buffett has refined into an uncontested art form.

Being fulfilled with the mastery he has gained, Buffett still pursues his craft at the age of 90. He also has managed the succession of the enormous wealth he has generated by transferring major chunks of his wealth to the Gates

Foundation. That transfer was also fueled by his overriding "stick to your knitting" principle. The story is not yet finished, but it is unlikely that there will be a Warren Buffett Junior taking over in his footsteps, whether family member or adopted heir. The Berkshire Hathaway machine is now solidly based on value-investing, having been fine-tuned over the years. It can continue to pursue the journey without the cherished master, at least for a while. One of the characteristics of organizations is indeed to have inertia inside them. The Buffett journey contains many idiosyncratic features, just as in every owner's story. Yet it also abides by general principles that should be of wider interest and applicability.

Summary Lessons for Owners and Directors

- The main lesson from one of the most remarkable individuals in modern capitalism is that he found his passion and talent for business and investing early, never strayed away from it too long, and kept refining his craft to an unequaled level of mastery.
- Buffett shows us that one can become the wealthiest man in the world without seeking that goal, but rather by pursuing what the man liked to do and was superb at it. Buffet never sought great material wealth.
- Buffett so much enjoys investing that he never pays a dividend. His focus and passion are to remain an investor (this could change with his successor at Berkshire Hathaway). What motivates Buffett is to master the investment game. He is an example of the "pure owner" type, focused on capital allocation where, like his mentors, he has developed a series of clear principles guiding his investment choices.
- Warren Buffet does not believe in perfect capital markets. He always stated that he became rich by taking advantage of market mispricing in the short and medium run, markets eventually correcting themselves in the longer term.
- Buffett is a long-term investor, very much trusting management to do the job, after having studied the company, its products, and its management in detail. His stint as Chairman of the Board of Salomon Brothers turned him away from taking on such major board responsibilities again. Many aspects of the case of Buffett are also idiosyncratic, even if some principles can be derived from it, as we tried to do.

4 Lessons from Anu Aga

Anu Aga's remarkable story is one of overcoming personal tragedies that led her having to learn to become an owner and a trustee. It is not something she envisaged to ever do earlier in her life. Both her husband and now her daughter were fundamental to her leadership. Aga presents a remarkable combination of personal drive, self-awareness, confidence, taking and benefiting from plenty of advice and endowed with "the courage to become the person she is."

Summary Lessons for Owners and Directors

- There is much written about the need for "continuous" learning throughout one's life. There is less written of the requirement of an attitude of openness and a lack of fear in showing one's vulnerabilities. Aga has a personality that is open to ask for help and taking considered advice. These traits are often missing in second and subsequent generations of ownership. Chance will play its hands, tragically. Having a centered, mindful attitude is a requirement not just to overcome adversity but to grow and flourish. A warm, loving family, as between Aga and her daughter and grandchildren, and earlier between Aga and her husband and son, is the basis on which different opinions can be freely voiced, discussed, and required action taken. The real tragedies are seen when families fall apart, talking over each other, even destroying each other, instead of deep listening and becoming closer as a unit.

5 Lessons from Dominique Moorkens

The story of Dominique Moorkens might be seen to lie at the other extreme from Warren Buffett: being born into an ownership family, his life's journey might be seen as preparing him for the task. Then it also shares common features. He found passion early on, for motor racing, and enjoyed early managerial training being coached by his father. Finally, though being the youngest of six children including four brothers, he transited to CEO and then Chairman of a very successful Alcopa family group.

These experiences shaped him into becoming a wise owner, now enjoying the coaching of other owners faced with many issues he had to confront himself, sharing the experience and knowledge he accumulated along the way. He also returned to being an active family shareholder, mentoring and nudging the leaders of the succeeding generation in their transition out of the automotive sector.

Summary Lessons for Owners and Directors

- Leadership succession is probably the most important decision to get right in a business and particularly in a family business, where ineffective leadership of the business quickly ripples through the family and the shareholding.
- One of the most meaningful activities is training one's children not just as individuals but also professionally. It reminds us too that a business family is a wonderful locus for business education from an early age. In this case, the training Dominique Moorkens received from his father on entrepreneurship was invaluable. Dominique today extends such teaching to other families, especially on the topic of governance of the family business.
- Entrepreneurs are doers. Governance is typically not their thing. Very often they can be seen as the enemy of governance. The opposite is the case here. This example shows a family organizing its business governance as of the second generation (G2), with a professional board. The family followed this by organizing the ownership governance at the third generation (G3), with the creation of an owner's board. This structure allowed the family business to weather a number of transitions, and ultimately to successfully exit the automotive business altogether, when it became clear that the fundamental business preferences of G3 members were no longer those of the founder, and of the G2.
- Privately owned family businesses can make these sectorial changes because they are committed to continuing doing business together. To do so, changing business contexts render such transitions unavoidable if indeed family ownership is to be sustained. These transitions are facilitated by a clear agreement that the previous mission of the family business is leading the family firm into obsolescence, ceasing to be a great motivational force for the next generation. That is an unmistakable signal that the mission needs a serious update. Such a change of mission is actually harder to achieve by publicly listed firms, unless they are acquired—often late—by another corporate which imposes a change as the new owner. Holdings fall into the purview of this as they act as corporate owners of the firms they hold.
- To keep all family members united, a move from a single operational business to a family holding or PE structure is logical. Such change in "hard-

ware" allows different sensitivities to be expressed in the family. Ownership in a group then becomes easier to sustain than in a single business. As underlined earlier, having an owner's board will greatly facilitate the discussion of business continuity among family shareholders, as they otherwise occur in sub-groups, favoring the formation of cliques, or fall on the corporate board. Non-family directors can provide useful inputs here but are typically less emotionally engaged in such decisions. These discussions concern the mission of the family firm, which is the purview and the responsibility of owners. However, that should not prohibit independent directors from making meaningful contributions, regarding value, prospects and fit, and risk.

- Exits of branches should always be considered, and even anticipated. These are best faced as a time of recommitment. Full commitment indeed requires free choice, without pressure. Exits of family shareholders are the other side of the commitment coin and should not be considered as exceptional, but part of the normal life of ownership. Hence, they should not be avoided or prohibited. Effective ownership is a regular choice of exercising commitment and reviewing it.

6 Lessons from Bart Huisken

Then there is the orphan owner, a figure one rarely speaks about. Bart Huisken, unlike Anu Aga or Dominique Moorkens, had no father or mother, spouse or uncle, exposing him to ownership and, beyond that, training him into the craft. That is one of the many points of this story. Bart has devoted a major part of his life to entrepreneurial start-ups and scale-ups.

His experience at SouthWing, his first major entrepreneurial venture, underlines how difficult walking the ownership road alone really is, and how effective governance and angel investors can facilitate the journey. It also is a story about how things can go astray when new owners come in. Particularly if they heavily lean on their newly acquired power to force their way into the emerging venture … only to bankrupt it. Bart's venture did not fail because it was destined to. It failed because the governance was too weak to preserve it and because new owners were value destroying. Ownership is and remains a risky enterprise, not all necessarily ends well.

Summary Lessons for Owners and Directors

- The remarkable early product and sales success of the company confirms that the company was not destined to fail. The root cause of its failure was not technology, nor product, but ineffective governance and oversight. The major vulnerabilities of the venture were a lack of risk oversight of an excessively rapid early growth phase when the business model was insufficiently mature. The case describes a clear case of *governance risk,* which is the risk when poor or ineffective governance does not allow a firm to cope with the *business risks* that every early venture faces, and that in this case centered principally on the supply chain.
- Governance risk is often structural in start-up firms in that start-up boards do not have the resources that the boards of more established businesses possess. The latter indeed have a clear oversight role and will less likely step over the line separating oversight from management and execution, which is a permanent risk associated with ineffective governance.
- VC investors proved too eager to run the business and impose their own ideas, plans, and people. They also appeared to insufficiently understand the key values the founder/CEO brought to the company, and which were a glue that kept the company together and functioning in its early years. Through its decisions and appointments, the board reduced and eventually removed this glue altogether.
- The decision to exit the international independent board members, who opposed the plans of the Odyssey VC, proved fatal. These members challenged the VC investors to preserve the company from the agendas of these new shareholders which they considered detrimental. Their fiduciary duty as board members forced them to do so. When the disagreement with the majority shareholders persisted, the only outcome was exit. Paradoxically, these board members also had shares they had earned more as angel investors; they also were among the only ones to profit from the venture when they redeemed their shares to the new owners.
- Liberal capitalism permits shareholders to destroy financial value if they do not harm other stakeholders (no harm duty). Such an outcome requires an agreeable board. Its fiduciary duty should have led it to challenge and eventually stop value destroying initiatives or plans by shareholders. Unfortunately, the "business judgment" rule is too easily invoked by board members and shareholders in defense of a charge of value destruction. Excessive board control by majority shareholders reduces the power of

independent members to challenge such shareholders and represents governance risk.

- Excessive power by founders is a risk to the success of their own venture. Emotional commitments and the desire for control often induce founders not to relinquish such powers. This is precisely where collaboration and input from independent directors are invaluable. Most founders underestimate the value of a real board, including at the early stages of the venture. They see it as unnecessary bureaucracy standing in the way of their venture. The other side of this coin is that it signals owners not able to either understand or collaborate with effective boards, which they themselves approve.
- The creation of an owners' board that supervises and evaluates the governance of the "owned" firm exercised by the Board of Directors is particularly helpful to support the exercise of the complementary responsibilities of shareholders from those exercised by the supervisory board. Founders, not having sufficient ownership and board experience, will here be at a disadvantage, leading to the "orphan owner" label used in the title of this section. Founders born in a context familiar with ownership responsibilities and benefiting from ownership and board training, as well as coaching and mentoring, will likely be more successful in their ventures.
- The role played by geography in venture success deserves to be underlined. Barcelona and Spain proved excellent locations for start-up support and early government financing, but ultimately did not prove great for meeting the larger financing needs during the growth phase of the business which followed the successful start-up phase.

7 Lessons from Priscilla de Moustier

Priscilla de Moustier is President of Wendel Participations, the family holding that owns and controls Wendel as reference shareholder. The Wendel Group, more simply referred to as Wendel, is one of Europe's leading publicly listed investment firms, describing itself as a long-term investor operating at the intersection of industry and finance. It is more than three centuries old.

Priscilla's story pleads for sustainable ownership of a firm that, though founded more than 300 years ago, today presents a stable family shareholder basis, a robust balance sheet, and a diversified portfolio of companies across sectors and geographies. Her father saved the firm at a critical moment of its history when the French Government sought to nationalize it. His daughter is now at the helm of the family holding that governs Wendel, which it oversees principally through Board oversight and nominations. It lies at the opposite of Bart Huisken's and Warren Buffett's context: a history of ownership transcending generations, sustaining to this day, and projecting itself forward through entrepreneurial investments, providing them with reference ownership and governance that aim to favor their development.

The history of the Wendel corporation and its family is amazing. They resemble an unabating sequence of challenges and successes. It is only through the recurrent emergence and commitment of family members eager to avoid the ending of the journey at times of crises that the firm has survived to this day. The firm nearly disappeared at the time of the French Revolution, and again during the German occupation of Alsace Lorraine. Men left for German territories, leaving women in charge. Having successfully fought off that ordeal, it had to face off a government all too eager to nationalize it. Here again, the family produced a savior, none less than Priscilla's father. With Priscilla women are back leading the family group, but in a more balanced way, both men and women, family members and independents, governing the group through what again are hectic times, with confidence that crises have been conquered before and eager to transmit this confidence through effective ownership and governance.

Key Lessons for Owners and Directors

- The Wendel family business attests to the sustainability of one family's ownership across centuries and dramatically different contexts. It shows, repeatedly, over the life of the business the difference committed family ownership makes in terms of corporate survival and growth. Quite simply, ownership by financial market investors would have led the Wendel business to fail or disappear at several critical moments in its history.
- At each of these times, the family came together to sustain the business or to save what could be saved. The leadership of family leaders was critical at these times. These leaders fully embraced the task of ensuring continuity, more for emotional reasons and for purpose, than for personal glory. They included women as well as men, in-laws as well as bloodline descendants, family members as well as non-family members.
- At these critical moments, the family was able to change its mission with the majority if not full support of its family shareholders. The emergence of full family support was at times considered highly unlikely if not illusory. At these moments survival of the business benefited from the realization

that the end of the business would result as the end of the (larger) family. These thoughts generated the emotional and spiritual energies needed for survival, though intellectual and rational energies had to be cleverly and effectively woven into the path toward survival.

- The biggest challenges to Wendel did not come from market competitors, but from the geopolitical contexts it found itself in (French Revolution, Franco-Prussian War, followed by two World Wars), from the French political context (nationalization), or from inside the firm (forces proposing to dilute the family ownership in favor of growth that proved too risky).
- When faced with the choice to increase value creation versus diluting family ownership, the family resolutely chose for the preservation of family ownership, even of a smaller firm. The commitment to the Wendel Group by its family shareholders came out of these challenges strengthened. The family's desire for continuity provided the energy and the rationale that convinced the family to continue its active family ownership.
- The history of the Wendel family firm also demonstrates the risk of an entrepreneurial leader ineffectively governed by family shareholders (e.g., Saint Gobain episode). The Wendel history attests the value of active oversight by an owners' board for assuring survival over shorter-term economic gains or profit, and particularly when actions are considered that do not fit the mission set by the owners, or their values, or that violate basic rules of the governance game.
- The Wendel history, particularly as of late, illustrates the complexity of being an entrepreneurial shareholder with a large and diverse shareholder base, even one belonging to the same family. Entrepreneurial leaders will unavoidably take risks, some of which will not materialize positively. In those cases, a united shareholder basis is a necessity for surviving these difficult times in a reasonable way. So is the value of a good governance process that identifies and mitigates these risks ex ante.
- A contrario, divisions among the shareholders at these critical times will by themselves be value destroying by, for example, causing the exit of talented executives, originally attracted to join family groups precisely because of the solidity of shareholder commitment in challenging times. A lack of alignment of shareholders and executives with the governance in place (people, outcomes, or process) generates governance risk.
- The case also illustrates that a statement of mission should not be restricted to objectives and targets but can also reflect the values that owners like to see reflected by their directors and executives, including duty of care and sensitivity to the risk incurred by owners as a result of their commitment

and the selected strategies. Breaches in values are difficult to repair since they destroy the trust of owners in the firm, its leadership and its governance.
- The major themes addressed by this book (mission, values, financing, growth, control, risk, Fair Process Leadership) are all illustrated over the long, rich, and turbulent history of the Wendel business family. One point that the story illustrates vividly is the trade-off between profitability, growth, and sustainability. By and large, the Wendel family has typically privileged sustainability in family ownership when confronting these choices. When they did not, and favored profitability or growth, they nearly went under. By and large, the result is that they are still operating three centuries later. This most uncommon feat was achieved by managing and weathering a great number of transitions.
- Sustaining family cohesion—like the active management of the companies in the Wendel portfolio—is everyday work. High and continued engagement of family members is a superb foundation on which the Wendel management and its board can count.

Notes

1. The competence versus talent dichotomy is well known, though its importance in ownership is underdeveloped. For a treatment with roots in sports, we refer the interested reader to *It's all about character,* by Domnique Monami and Alain Goudsmet, Editions Lannoo, 2007, which we liberally borrow from.
2. The classic on CEOs and management is Henry Mintzberg's doctoral dissertation at MIT, entitled *The manager at work; determining his activities, roles, and programs by structured observation,* Massachusetts Institute of Technology, Doctoral Thesis, 1968.

16

Ownership in the Twenty-First Century: Closing Thoughts

In this concluding chapter we review the main challenges that owners, their directors, and executives will face in this twenty-first century, marked already by two most turbulent decades. Turbulence is both a challenge and an opportunity for value creation.

Our aim is not to extensively review the topics and issues presented in the book, nor to discuss themes that are extensively written about in the news and professional media. We instead try to summarize the main frameworks and concepts that we have presented in the chapters and that are particularly relevant for corporate owners—as well as their directors and their executives—in facing the challenges of what appears as possibly the most radical of centuries. We specifically focus on the competences and talents that corporate owners and their directors must possess for governance to be effectively exercised and for value creation to result.

1 The Great Thinkers on Capitalism and Ownership: Friedman, Smith, and Marx

The remarkable contributions of Milton Friedman have a strong source of bias in favor of free or liberal market capitalism. Relevant for our subject, we note that Friedman supported the notion that capitalism exists in many forms—including owner-led capitalism—and that it thus needs to be qualified: "*I think it is only because capitalism has proved so enormously more efficient than alternative methods that it has survived at all. (...) I'm not sure capitalism is*

M. Massa et al., *Value Creation for Owners and Directors*,
https://doi.org/10.1007/978-3-031-19726-0_16

the right word. There is a sense in which every society is capitalist. The Soviet Union was capitalist, but it was state capitalism. Latin American societies in the past have been capitalist, but it has been oligarchic capitalism. So, what we really need to talk about is not capitalism but free market or competitive capitalism which is the system that we would like to have adopted, not just capitalism."[1]

Friedman's obsessive concern was power, and particularly its concentration: "*The problem in this world is to avoid concentration of power – we must have dispersion of power.*"[2] He was suspicious of government, which ought to have a well-specified role restricted to the upholding of civil law inside the country, with freedom of choice as the core principle, dealing with market externalities like pollution and market concentration due to economies of scale. Being confronted with the choice between big business and big government, Friedman was very clear: he resolutely stated his preference for the former, arguing that big business, unlike big government, did not possess the government's power of coercion and at least was forced to provide sufficient value for inducing consumers to part with their money. Overall, Friedman felt that big business and big government were both dangers for society when not submitted to the constraints of true market competition. Major tragedies such as Dieselgate, the leaded gasoline crisis, and now the climate crisis show how the combined forces of big automotive players with "big oil" did indeed contribute in a major way to the current climate crisis. Owners are not absent from the scene here: Volkswagen was owned by the Piëch and Porsche families, while the responsibility of the Sackler family in the US opioid crisis has been well documented. These would clearly fall under Friedman's "big business" label.

Friedman held as a basic tenet that human greed was positive subject to the conditions of freedom of choice and market competition. Greed would then be directed to delivering value for customers in ways that were efficient. In defending the virtue of the market, Friedman is very much a student of Adam Smith. The latter described the virtue of the free market economy 200 years earlier and was equally afraid of collusion by business: "… *every individual necessarily labours to render the annual revenue of the society as great as he can. He generally, indeed, neither intends to promote the public interest, nor knows how much he is promoting it. By preferring the support of domestic to that of foreign industry, he intends only his own security; and by directing that industry in such a manner as its produce may be of the greatest value, he intends only his own gain, and he is in this, as in many other cases, led by an invisible hand to promote an end which was no part of his intention. Nor is it always the worse for the society that it was no part of it. By pursuing his own interest, he frequently promotes that of the society more effectually than when he really intends to promote it.*"[3]

Adam Smith aligns with Friedman in limiting the role of the government, warning that "*there is no art which one government sooner learns of another, than that of draining money from the pockets of the people.*" Smith and Friedman agree on the need for governments to defend borders, enforce property rights and freedom, punish crime, and provide general education, to provide civic training and counter the narrowness of minds generated by the division of labor.

It should be noted that Smith considered himself primarily a moral philosopher not merely a student of what was later called "economics." The book Smith was most proud of was his *The Theory of Moral Sentiments*, in which he cautions against a narrow outlook. He emphasized the need for empathy along with self-interest. He urged that we put ourselves in other people's shoes, writing, "I not only change circumstances with you, but I change persons and characters." As part of his moral philosophy Smith pointed out that people are not merely inanimate "*different pieces upon a chess–board.*" For Smith it was important to fully understand that "*in the great chess–board of human society, every single piece has a principle of motion of its own.*" It is thus not surprising that Smith expected more from governments than Friedman and other adherents of the Chicago School. Smith's advice included helping young firms in establishing themselves to uphold market competition by facilitating entry.

No discussion of capitalism can ignore Karl Marx, who is the antithesis of Smith and Friedman, even if Marx admits that an initial phase of free market ownership might be good in building a nation's capital stock. In his Manuscripts, Marx expresses his concern that ownership will eventually reduce "*the relation of the worker to work and to the product of his labor and to the non-worker, and the relation of the non-worker to the worker and the product of his labor.*"[4] Marx was concerned that the accumulation of wealth by the owner of the means of production, with little wealth being generated for the multitude of workers, would lead to the alienation of men from the fruits of their own labor, and ultimately from themselves and from their fellow men. Marx tolerates private property if it allows the free development and the free choice of workers. But his views on unavoidable wealth accumulation by property owners leads Marx to conclude that land and other major means of production must belong to the community if the worker is to avoid becoming a slave. It is the latter concern that leads Marx to put severe limits on ownership rights.

These fundamental works, taken together, have cast a great and unfortunate shadow on the nature and virtues of effective ownership, when exercised responsibly. The implicit, if not explicit, conclusion of Smith and Friedman was that companies for whom governance mattered were mostly listed companies with widely dispersed shareholders, all of whom viewed value creation in one, monolithic manner. The market became cast as an archetypical virtual owner. Its fractioned nature largely reduced its power, which was welcomed given these thinkers' major concerns with the excessive powers that owners might exercise, which for Smith and Friedman would impact prices negatively and reduce social welfare. Both in their concern about power align with Marx but conclude very differently. Remarkably, all ignore the roles and responsibilities of owners and their boards respectively, biasing their conclusions.

It is interesting, and rarely mentioned, that Friedman says little about governance or about how it should be exercised, except that both should be governed by *"the laws of the market."* Marx ends very differently, in a collective or national ownership, again stating little about how such ownership should be exercised. The views of Friedman have largely framed the notion of "control of corporations by the market," a view shared by many governance students we encountered, even though it is legally false and misleading. Markets and shareholders do provide feedback to executive management and their boards, but exercise no direct control, as the latter is the responsibility of the Board of Directors.

Concluding Thought #1 *Free market capitalism as conceived by Friedman thinks of ownership in a restricted way, being largely concerned with excessive concentration of power that would limit market dynamics. A stock market with many relatively small owners, having little effective power over the companies "they own," meets such concerns very well. In the realities of corporate law, owners do not literally "own" their corporations, but rather own economic or dividend rights, and the right to appoint board members. Owners have no direct control over their companies, unless they start collaborating and align, as Marx suggests workers do, for a collective ownership of the means of production. But even in the latter case, corporate capitalism holds that the ultimate responsibility for the corporation rests with boards, mandated to act in the best interest of their corporations, and not first in the interest of the so-called owners, even if there is only a single owner.*

2 Views of the Firm: Modern Economic Theory Versus Legal Reality

The most common model in economics to deal with ownership is the *principal-agent model,* commonly attributed to Stephen Ross,[5] Barry Mitnick,[6] and Jensen and Meckling.[7] The model deals with situations where one person (the principal) is responsible for another person's actions (the agent). Personal preferences may drive the agent to pursue actions that deviate from the principal's interests. Examples are when an individual person, having taken out insurance, engages in reckless actions he would not have taken if not covered by the insurance (*moral hazard)*. Another such example is when a sports club employs a star player with a life-long contract, leading the player not to put in the same effort as he did before he signed the contract. Politics is full of such relations where the principal is the people electing a person who will represent them. Economic theory focuses on contracts that the principal could offer to the agent to align interests to the greatest extent. The cost to the principal of misalignment is called an *agency loss.*

The typical economic model of governance fits the theory of shareholder dominance well, the latter being typically cast as the principal. On the agent's side the application is less clear, since the board could be seen as the agent, but so could the executive. In fact, the introduction of a Board of Directors between shareholders and management introduces a double principal-agent relation, which renders the application of the model more complex and ambiguous than economic theory generally admits. Indeed, most economists follow Smith and Friedman: they rarely, if ever, mention boards of directors as distinct from shareholders, as if boards are the agents of the principal, contrary to the tenets of corporate capitalism.

Jensen and Meckling defined the firm as a "*legal fiction which serves as a nexus for contracting relationships and which is also characterized by the existence of divisible residual claims on the assets and cash flows of the organization which can generally be sold without the permission of the other contracting individuals … Viewing the firm as the nexus of a set of contracting relationships among individuals also serves to make clear that the personalization of the firm implied by asking questions such as 'what should be the objective function of the firm', or 'does the firm have a social responsibility' is seriously misleading. The firm is not an individual … In this sense the 'behavior of the firm' is like the behavior of a market, i.e., the outcome of a complex equilibrium process.*" The theoretical premises and deductions of Jensen and Meckling have been broadly accepted following their validation by the economic community. But the application of these theoretical views to real firms should be more thoroughly debated as they violate the legal standing of the firm, which indeed is that of a legal person, represented by the Board of Directors, collectively.

Fifty years after the seminal Jensen and Meckling paper appeared, it is also now well accepted that firms have social impacts, and hence that corporate responsibility matters. The very negative market externalities of the 2007–08 financial crisis, the social impacts of GAFAM firms, and the growing climate crisis have made this abundantly clear. Jensen and Meckling in this sense are misleading, as the firm, in a legal sense, was already—and for a couple of centuries in fact—a reality, and not the fiction that Jensen and Meckling refer to.

Chapter 1 indicated that corporate law has its roots in the Roman Empire. Its modern version is traced to the Joint Stock Companies Act of 1844 and the Limited Liabilities Act 1855, which limited the responsibilities of shareholders to their invested capital. Indeed, stock markets could not function if one traded unlimited liability. Societies wishing their corporations to be responsible placed corporate responsibility collectively on the Board of Directors. The legal view of the firm makes the Directors fiduciaries on behalf of the firm, and not sole agents of the shareholders. The firm has a great number of relationships with other parties, referred to in governance as *stakeholders*. This makes the Board of Directors the nexus of the firm, assuming full responsibility for the firm and its relations with all stakeholders and mediating and governing the contracts Jensen and Meckling refer to. That also makes a corporation very different than the marketplace Jensen and Meckling make it out to be.

Board members thus collectively act as fiduciaries for the firm. One can, by definition, hold only one fiduciary duty at a time. This duty implies being responsible for the firm's relations with its stakeholders, including shareholders who hold the distinctive power of appointing board members, and also exiting them. Corporate ownership in a liberal democracy is built on a subtle duality that distinguishes the benefits of ownership from the exercise of that responsibility, which is vested in the Board of Directors acting of their own free will and judgment, respecting the agreements and constraints these directors freely accepted when they joined the board at the invitation of their shareholders.

There is thus a check and balance in corporate governance in that directors act on behalf and have a fiduciary duty to the corporation, and not only to the shareholder or shareholders who would be tempted to use their corporate ownership for their own benefit, against the interests of the corporation and its other stakeholders. It is not only shareholders who benefit from their association with a corporation; most stakeholders do as well. Hence, the values created by a corporation far exceed the value provided to shareholders. Directors are accountable to all stakeholders and must decide how the values created by the corporation are to be shared among these stakeholders, which include the executives that run the business. Directors are tasked with the fundamental responsibility for the creation, delivery, and capture of value given the owner's statement of the mission to be pursued, and any other governance constraints they might wish to impose on the directors and the firm they "own." Such constraints are typically written down in *shareholder agreements*. What is distinct—and completely changes the nature and mechanics of the governance system in owner-led businesses—is that such owners, as distinct from owners of firms with diffuse ownership, have real power, constrained only by the governance regulations applicable in the country, region, or state in which the business is incorporated.

Shareholders are, as explained in Chap. 2, privileged stakeholders, enjoying *shareholder supremacy* over the Directors, by virtue of their right to appoint and dismiss them.[8] This arrangement is democratic in that it respects both the freedom of shareholders (who secure their investment by appointing directors and are free to buy and sell their shares, while not harming the firm in doing so) and of firms, protected and governed by their directors. Directors are not enchained to owners, are free to resign, and exercise their fiduciary duties in all independence and collectively. The latter is an additional protection for the corporations and for the individual directors.

It is remarkable and always surprising how corporate reality often strays far from this ideal concept, including from the duties and responsibilities as written in the law. The concept is clear: executives must, at any time, be able to know the views of the corporation, which are expressed by the Board of Directors. Shareholders differ in their preferences and their views and cannot be asked to express these, since they typically disagree. One of the great benefits of a Board of Directors is that it clearly anchors the responsibility for the corporation, allowing the corporation to speak with a single voice. Shareholders are too numerous, having different preferences (including for money). This is one of the reasons why one cannot place the responsibility for the corporation with shareholders. In order not to be defrauded, shareholders have another right: a first pick at buying shares when the corporation issues new ones.

Concluding Thought #2 *Free market capitalism is built on a number of dualities. The first is that of shareholder supremacy, which needs to be understood as shareholders being free to set up corporations and to agree with any shareholder agreements they hold as necessary to secure their investments in the corporate venture. The other principle is that the legal responsibility for the firm rests with the directors who act as fiduciaries for the corporation and whose duty is to first serve the corporate interest (and not that of the specific interest of a single shareholder, even when holding a majority of shares, unless the latter's interest is aligned with that of the corporation).*

The dual foundations of free market capitalism lead to a governance indeterminacy where the outcome of a disagreement between owners and their boards cannot be predicted in advance: if either had full control, they would indeed prevail. But given existing arrangements, the actual outcome is the result of an interactive process intended to realign owners with their board. When this is not possible, the board will have resignation as the only option, unless they prefer to be dismissed, leading to the same outcome. As of that point, the owners will seek to appoint a new Board of Directors, who may accept the offer to join the board if conditions appear right to these candidate directors.

3 Owner-Led Capitalism: A Distinct Capitalistic Form

This is where owner-led firms diverge fundamentally from so-called market-led firms. The difference lies with the effective power of shareholders, as explained in Chap. 1: in owner-led firms shareholders have effective power by virtue of their shareholding and are in a position to exercise it. This is not the case when shareholders are too numerous, each with stakes that are too small to be heard.

Power in the latter case requires a convergence of interests among many shareholders, which is rarely the case. Even prolonged periods of poor performance—as in the case of GE following the succession of Jack Welch—did not cause such convergence. In cases of diffused ownership and an ineffective board, the effective power de facto devolves to the executives since shareholders are unable to muster sufficient countervailing power. This is even more the case when the CEO duplicates as Chairman of the Board. Examples of such instances are Jamie Dimon at JP Morgan, and Carlos Ghosn at Nissan.

This structural difference between market-led and owner-led firms is fundamental. When owners have a controlling ownership stake, they have a determining influence over the organization of the governance system. Absent of controlling ownership, the organization of the governance largely falls to the executive. Beyond the responsibility for the governance of the corporation, the fundamental power of owners lies in determining the mission of the corporation, which then becomes the direction along which the other two boards (directors and management) align.

The great privilege of business ownership lies in crafting a mission that challenges a firm to deliver on the mission. A mission statement defines performance in a way that "making money"—a statement that confuses means and ends—does not. It provides the business with an existential and leadership clarity that is the owner's fundamental contribution to performance. A mission statement may state the values and key business principles the firm is committed to. This may include the position the firm will take toward people and the planet, a topic we return to later in this concluding chapter. Finally, a clear mission statement also provides the context for owners to appoint the members of the Board of Directors and serves as a guide for evaluating them at the end of their term.

In contrast, market-led firms leave choices of the mission in the hands of the Board of Directors, if not the executives, with the result that these choices often vary as new directors and executives are appointed, changing the value creation logic. In fact, in such firms it is not the owners that set the mission, but given the observed mission of the company, the owners buy or sell its shares. That is, ownership adapts to mission as opposed to imposing the mission. The share price implications of this may lead to hostile take-overs, activism investment, LBOs, and to the CEO being fired. The resulting effect is that the CEO no longer becomes constrained in the choice of her or his mission for fear of stock market "retribution." That is, shareholders do not monitor by using their voice but by using their "feet" ("voice or exit").

The accountability of directors is also completely different in the two systems: the interaction with shareholders in publicly listed companies is often reduced to the General Assembly Meeting, acting like a parliament for the business and amounting to approving proposals submitted by the Board of Directors, if not the executives. In contrast, accountability in owner-led firms amounts to real face-to-face discussions, centered on the progress regarding the mission. A clear mission statement by owners frames accountability clearly and provides for a three-way discussion involving owners, directors, and executives. Such a setting is more dynamic than a two-party discussion between directors and executives. The latter typically results in either agreement or confrontation. The creation of a formal owners' board, as presented in Chap. 8, will support the search for alignment and facilitate the emergence of consensus. It also favors the exercise of accountability.

We here summarize this key property of owner-led firms, which is fundamental in differentiating owner-led firms from firms with many shareholders.

Concluding Thought #3 *Owner-led capitalism rests on the distinctive opportunity enjoyed by controlling owners to define the longer-term objectives to be pursued by the owned corporation, the key values with which these objectives will be pursued, and specific "rules of the game" that will be followed in the governance of the corporation. These three fundamental choices frame the course of action that is entrusted to the Board of Directors whose duty of loyalty then obliges them to align with them. These choices frame value creation by the firm for the owners as progress in the realization of the mission, given the framework created by the values and rules.*

4 Owner Dilemmas and Trade-offs: Autonomy, Control, and Collaboration

We have introduced the first responsibility of owners as defining the mission of the firm they own, the values that are fundamental to them, and the rules that define the governance of their firm. The next task of owners is to engage Board members who will be charged with the responsibility of delivering on the mission. The talent most cherished in owners, as indicated in the previous chapter, is in seeing opportunities in the world around them and assembling a group of board members excited by the project and committed to delivering on that mission. Great owners will invite their boards to apply their talents to deliver on the accepted mission. The duality of control over the mission and autonomy over how to deliver on the mission is a fundamental tension affecting the relation between owners and boards. Our recipe here is simple: owners can determine the "what" but not the "what and the how," for that will overly restrict the contribution that boards can make to their owners' venture.

The relationship between boards and executives in many ways mirrors that between owners and their directors. Boards will frame the issue and executives will be tasked to address it. Boards will ask questions and executives will address them. The same relationship holds between senior executives and their direct reports, replicated all the way down the line of command, until value is finally delivered to the end customer. Even at this final point of contact between the customer and the company, the company is well served by asking the customer to frame his preferences and allowing the representatives of the firm sufficient autonomy to provide the best value given the customer's expectations. The duality of control and autonomy, as well as the tension it generates, are fundamental in the value creation game. On this topic, Chaps. 11 and 12 made clear that commitment inside a company is generated when its people are given the autonomy to develop options and to make choices on how best to respond to customer requests.

Given people's biases for control, which we discussed in Chap.s. 9 and 10, owners will set the tone for how best to resolve these fundamental tensions, first those between owners and their boards, then down the line of command in the organization. How these tensions are managed is one of the fundamental drivers of value creation inside the firm. Owners will do well to keep in mind that temptations of control should be tempered with the realization that narrow control invariably has a cost in terms of commitment, creativity, and ultimately value delivery.

Concluding Thought #4 *A fundamental tension faced by owners resides in finding the right balance between control and autonomy. The key principle here is that value creation depends on both dimensions, which are complementary. Narrowly framed tasks reduce risk and surprise but will not generate much value; tasks that are defined too broadly provide directors and executives with great opportunities, and may deliver a lot of value to some stakeholders, but will at some point leave owners dissatisfied. It is good for such owners to understand that the responsibility for their dissatisfaction was generated by them, and by directors that did not warn their owners sufficiently of the eventual outcome of a mission too loosely defined. In such matters, there is no best practice; there is only good and bad practice, better and worse practice. Best practice restricts autonomy, typically quite narrowly.*

5 A World in Crisis … Learning to Deal with ESG?

Many believe that the post-COVID world will be different from the world we knew when we entered the global pandemic. Just like the 2007–08 financial crisis forever changed both the worlds of finance and governance, the bet is that COVID-19 will leave its trace—especially if it takes years before the disease is fully conquered, its effects understood, and its lessons learned.

The victory over COVID-19 was a victory of technology and technological bets in a context of global cooperation and competition. The world of Initial Coin Offerings (ICOs) and Initial Exchange Offerings (IEOs), as well as other token business models, has also underlined the impact of technological change on ownership. In this context, the question has been raised as to whether new forms of ownership might not arise in these radical times and provide some new solutions to our problems. These issues are discussed in greater detail in Appendix C, but here we state our conclusion. While the wrapping may look different, the fundamental issues affecting new technologies, and their impact on products and business models, will continue to center around mission, governance, and board practices. Our view is that these will remain the critical issues, rather than the technological ones.

The COVID pandemic has tested owners, their boards, and their corporations in unprecedented ways. Entire sectors—such as the hospitality sector—faced demise, and now a slow and bumpy recovery. Crises come and go, and appear to accelerate in pace in this new century. One effect is clear: these crises leave us begging for *sustainability*.

Our current times have contributed to making the notion of sustainability more salient. Climate change and, more precisely, global warming have raised unprecedented scenarios[9]: humans on Earth are now confirmed to be on a suicide path. The activities and decisions of some are harming and even killing others through climate interactions at the planetary level. Humanity has entered the era of *human-made externalities.* This change is, by itself, a major risk that increasingly hangs over us all. It also calls for major change in the governance of both the environment and our societies. This is the fundamental meaning of ESG. It is likely to become the major theme of our century. It also provides a context for owners and their businesses to contribute in major and novel ways.

Climate change reminds us harshly that markets can malfunction, and particularly so in the context of major externalities. Markets can indeed generate significant and toxic externalities. Regulatory answers, therefore, impose themselves, as even Milton Friedman assumed in his famous article on the obligation of business managers to manage their firms for profitability "within the limits of the law."[10] Even Friedman recognizes that societal interests should, in the case of externalities and other market failures, be dealt with through government intervention, legislation, or regulation. Friedman was highly concerned with government abusing its power and excessively limiting free choice and initiative, but he was never ideologically opposed to government intervention. Now, are the "limits of the law" set and created in the interest of society? What happens when political contribution and lobbying distort the laws in the interest of monopolies and vested interest? This is what Friedman was concerned with: interference of big business pressuring big government to issue laws in its interest.

Friedman's foundational article does not say anything about boards. They are conspicuously absent from the article, which indeed is remarkable given that legally the board "is" the corporation. Friedman was primarily concerned with limiting CEO and executive discretion in allocating funds for activities that do not ultimately contribute to profits. Allowing such discretion comes at the expense of shareholders' interests and will reduce the trust of shareholders in the management. This will reduce management autonomy and investment and reduce growth and value creation. These were Friedman's principal concerns that led him to write the article.

Concluding Thought #5 *ESG, by which we mean the interaction between the Environment (the planet we live on, and also the other living beings that inhabit it, and its basic dynamics), Societies (humanity, in its interacting social, political, and economic dimensions), and Governance, will become a fundamental context for business owners to understand and integrate in our twenty-first century. For* *many business owners, with their local roots, concerns for the well-being of their communities have always been present. ESG concerns for them are nothing new, though the formulation and some of the tools may be. This also explains why entrepreneurial and family firms are among the first businesses to show leadership in this area, and why ESG statements by owner-led firms rarely lead to the concerns that are raised by ESG when it comes to market-led firms, where shareholders have very different views about ESG.*

6 An Earth in Search of Responsible Ownership and Effective Governance

The recasting of the Mission has led to the emergence of new criteria to drive economic activity. The pioneer here is John Elkington, the author of *Cannibals with Forks: The Triple Bottom Line of 21st Century Business.* Elkington argues that businesses must take into account their impact on the planet and on people (and communities) when evaluating their strategies. Elkington stresses that the three objectives of environmental protection, social equity, and economic prosperity are interlinked when a choice regarding strategy is made.[11] He also notes that, should the impacts of economic growth become negative for the planet and its inhabitants, alternative paths ought to be searched for. A positive "**Triple Bottom Line**" (TBL) business strategy is a strategy that has positive impacts on the environment and on people while also making a profit, but this must not come at the expense of people and the planet.

These concerns fit our MGSF framework perfectly, as such considerations can be immediately integrated in the Mission and addressed further in the Goals. A telling example is by Patagonia, a company whose mission it is to "*Build the best product, cause no unnecessary harm, use business to inspire and implement solutions to the environmental crisis.*"[12] It was founded by Yvon Chouinard, a Yosemite rock climber who on a trip to Scotland in 1970 bought some rugged rugby shirts and sold them with great success.

Chouinard's Patagonia mission statement underlines the importance of the fundamental act the business founder makes through the framing of the mission statement. This point was the object of the first chapter of the book and cannot be repeated enough. Patagonia's mission statement makes it clear that its target audience is the climbing community, that it will not do any unnecessary harm, and that it wishes to be a leader in environmental sustainability.[13] Patagonia demonstrates that one can build and grow a profitable business paying attention and being measured by the TBL.[14] It is the promise and commitment of the owner, Yvon Chouinard, a passionate climber of the peaks in the Western USA, for whom business, people, and the environment are interlinked.

This commitment has recently led Chouinard to his most radical decision, which is to give full ownership of the fashion company to a charitable trust, stating "that the earth is now Patagonia's only shareholder."[15] Chouinard's remarkable act superbly exemplifies the distinct possibility offered by private ownership. It is also a true innovation in ownership: no one had yet made the Earth the owner of a company.

Chouinard's business life began in 1957 with his purchase of a coal-fired forge, renamed Chouinard Equipment Ltd. He redirected to making hardened steel pitons for securing vertical climbing ascents of "big walls" like that in Yosemite National Park. The steel pitons were a great success for his firm, soon representing 70% of the firm's income. They also increasingly damaged the cracks in the Yosemite wall. So Chouinard, and his business partner Tom Frost, replaced the steel pitons with aluminum ones, thus also inventing "clean climbing." Notwithstanding destroying, in truly Schumpeterian fashion, his firm's income stream with the new technology, the firm entered a new phase of success. To protect the firm from liability lawsuits, Chouinard and Frost, in 1989, filed for bankruptcy protection.[16] This appeared necessary to protect the firm from lawsuits filed by amateurs who had accidents with the gear, attacking the company for insufficient precautionary instructions and warnings. Most felt that climbing had always been and remained a dangerous sport and that amateurs knew that accidents could happen. It was also true that the equipment was better than it had ever been. Chouinard nevertheless admitted that warnings were insufficient and filed for Chap. 11 precisely to shield the firm from the lawsuits. In a surprising outcome, the firm was bought by its employees and still operates successfully under the name Black Diamond Equipment Ltd.

Novo Nordisk provides another remarkable example. Its mission statement is as follows:

> *Our purpose is to drive change to defeat diabetes and other serious chronic diseases, such as obesity and rare blood and endocrine disorders. We do so by pioneering scientific breakthroughs, expanding access to our medicines, and working to prevent and ultimately cure diabetes.*[17]

The statement makes clear what its battlefield is and that it is committed to winning, which is described as eventually preventing and curing diabetes. Furthermore, as indicated in Chap. 1, a mission statement includes a set of basic principles on how the battle will be fought. The message here too is clear: the basic means for winning the war against diabetes is through scientific breakthroughs and expansion of access to Novo Nordisk's products. The mission statement includes a statement on values that are adhered to by all employees, summarized under the Novo Nordisk Way:

> *The Novo Nordisk Way is a set of guiding principles which underpins every decision we make. It describes who we are, how we work and what we want to achieve, and sets a clear direction for our company and our employees. Ultimately, it's a promise we make to each other - and to the millions of patients all over the world who rely on our products to lead full and healthy lives.*
>
> *In 1923, our Danish founders began a journey to change diabetes. Today, we are thousands of employees across the world with the passion, skills and commitment to drive change to defeat diabetes and other serious chronic diseases.*
>
> - *We aim to lead in all disease areas in which we are active.*
> - *Our key contribution is to discover and develop innovative biological medicines and make them accessible to patients throughout the world.*
> - *Growing our business and delivering competitive financial results is what allows us to help patients live better lives, offer an attractive return to our shareholders and contribute to our communities.*
> - *Our business philosophy is one of balancing financial, social and environmental considerations - we call it 'The Triple Bottom Line'.*
> - *We are open and honest, ambitious and accountable, and treat everyone with respect.*
> - *We offer opportunities for our people to realise their potential.*
> - *We never compromise on quality and business ethics.*
>
> *Every day, we must make difficult choices, always keeping in mind what is best for patients, our employees and our shareholders in the long run.*
>
> *It's our way. It's the Novo Nordisk Way.*[18]

Again, the role of ownership is key: Novo Nordisk is 28.3% owned by Novo Holdings, the remainder being listed on the Danish Stock Exchange. Novo Holdings is fully owned by the Novo Nordisk Foundation, whose ownership mission is to "*provide a stable basis for the commercial and research activities conducted by the companies with the Novo Group (of which Novo Nordisk A/S is the largest, the other being Novozymes, a spinoff of Novo Nordisk) and to support scientific, humanitarian and social purposes.*"[19]

Relying on a dual share structure, the Foundation (through Novo Holdings A/S) controls 76.8% of the votes, ensuring full control of the company. Institutional and private investors thus fully know what they commit to when buying Novo Nordisk shares. The ownership role of the Foundation is thus as fundamental as Chouinard's role in Patagonia. The Foundation is also clear on its role as an "Engaged Owner" interacting with the Board of Directors: "Novo *Nordisk Foundation wishes to be an 'Engaged Owner' in relation to Novo Nordisk and apply engaged ownership objectives and principles which among other things are described in 'Objectives and Principles for engaged ownership in relation to Novo Nordisk A/S and Novozymes A/S, which is available at the Foundation's website. The Foundation supports Novo Nordisk in achieving its vision its vision, ensuring competitive financial results, and adhering to the Charter for Companies in the Novo Group. However, all strategic and operational matters are decided solely by the Board of Directors and Executive Management of Novo Nordisk.*" These statements illustrate the points we made in Chap. 1.

Concluding Thought #6 *Owners have a major governance responsibility with respect to the firms they own. Specifically, they will see to it that the company they own upholds a number of governance principles:*

- ***Governance as an objective****: the Company's owners, its Board of Directors, and its Senior Executives agree that the Company will aim for a clear direction in which to go and a well-defined set of objectives that will shape the governance system and practice.*
- ***GOVERNANCE as value****: the Company's owners, its Board of Directors, and its Senior Executives agree that one of the enduring values of the Company is its commitment to a performing governance system and practice.*
- ***Governance as a rule of the game****: the Company's owners, its Board of Directors, and its Senior Executives have described a set of principles and policies that support the Company's commitment to a performing governance system and practice.*
- ***Governance as roles****: the Company's owners, its Board of Directors, its Senior Executives, and all employees understand their respective roles in upholding a performing governance system and practice.*
- ***Governance as processes****: the Company's owners, its Board of Directors, its Senior Executives, and its employees are exercising their governance responsibilities through a set of well-defined processes (e.g., the General Assembly, the Nomination and Evaluation of Board Members, a set of Committees, a set of training, compliance, and other governance processes, etc.).*
- ***Governance as individual commitments:*** *Owners, Directors, Senior Executives, and all employees are asked to commit to uphold the governance standards and norms that the Company has set for itself.*

7 The Promise of Ownership in the Twenty-First Century

We have, in this final chapter, tried to review the major "macro" issues that owners will have to deal with in this new century. The reader will hopefully conclude that they are new and unprecedented, even if owners have had similar thoughts over the ages.

If ever the task of ownership was important, it is now. If ever ownership allows the swift exercise of responsibility unhampered by the formalities of listing in public markets, it is now. Given that change is accelerating all around us, and in many dimensions, we believe that responsibilities have never been greater and more challenging.

To meet these challenges and their complexity owners will be well advised to surround themselves with ownership boards, comprising ownership partners and future owners so as to bring them up to speed and prepare them for their time as owners, as well as a number of trusted advisors. All will seek to provide owners with a wise echo chamber focused very much on the specification and adaptation of the mission to be provided to the Board of Directors, and on the values and basic rules of the game regarding the governance of their enterprise. Effective governance will thus continue to be an aim and one that will develop into a more established and verifiable competence than it has been so far, partly because it mattered less and partly because the responsibility of ownership and its impacts on society and our environment have only grown. Governance as a mechanism for stakeholders to be accounted for and to be able to weigh in on owner choices is here to stay and grow as well. This leads us to our final Concluding Thought.

Concluding Thought #7 *Looking to the future we conclude the book by venturing to state that companies with clearly defined owners appear to be able to more effectively prepare for the longer term than publicly listed ones. They are also more likely to successfully meet the innovation and value creation challenges that our century poses, as well as the formidable economic and social challenges that lie ahead of us.*

Notes

1. Randall E. Parker (Ed.), *Reflections on the Great Depression,* Cheltenham, UK: Edward Elgar Publishing, 2002.
2. Milton Friedman on Big Business, Big Government. https://www.youtube.com/watch?v=R_T0WF-uCWg.

3. Adam Smith, *An Inquiry into the Nature and Causes of the Wealth of Nations,* London, UK, 1776 (in public domain).
4. Karl Marx, *Economic and Philosophical Manuscripts of 1844,* Moscow: Progress Publishers, 1959.
5. Stephen A. Ross, "The economic theory of agency: The principal's problem, " *American Economic Review 62(2):134–139,* 1973.
6. Barry M. Mitnick, "Fiduciary rationality and public policy: The theory of agency and some consequences," *Proceedings of the Annual Meeting of the American Political Science Association,* 1973.
7. Michael C. Jensen and William H. Meckling, "Theory of the firm: Managerial behavior, agency costs and ownership structure," *Journal of Financial Economics 3(4): 305–360,* 1976.
8. We define shareholder supremacy differently from the notion of shareholder primacy, which is a theory that states that the firm should be run and governed primarily for shareholders. Friedman in his famous *New York Times Magazine* article formulated this as follows: "… in his capacity as a corporate executive, the manager is the agent of the individuals who own the corporation ... and his primary responsibility is to them." Friedman never mentioned boards, nor addressed the point that most shareholders do not agree.
9. https://www.nytimes.com/2021/08/09/climate/climate-change-report-ipcc-un.html.
10. Milton Friedman, "The Social Responsibility of Business is to Increase its Profits," *The New York Times Magazine,* September 13, 1970.
11. John Elkington. *Cannibals with Forks: The Triple Bottom Line of 21st Century Business.* Wiley. 1999.
12. https://www.patagonia.com/static/on/demandware.static/-/Library-Sites-PatagoniaShared/default/dw824fac0f/PDF-US/2017-BCORP-pages_022218.pdf.
13. https://www.patagonia.com/our-footprint/.
14. https://www.ft.com/content/1564e99a-5766-11e8-806a-808d194ffb75.
15. https://www.bbc.com/news/business-62906853.
16. https://www.latimes.com/archives/la-xpm-1989-05-11-we-3605-story.html.
17. https://www.novonordisk.com/careers/working-at-novo-nordisk.html.
18. https://www.novonordisk.com/careers/working-at-novo-nordisk.html.
19. https://www.novonordisk.com/about/corporate-governance/the-novo-nordisk-foundation.html.

Appendix A: Igniting Performance: Drawing on Our Five Energy Batteries

Our perspective here is inspired by high-performance sport teams and builds on the notion of energy.[1] Simply stated, it affirms that great teams are teams that possess and muster greater energies than their opponents. Boards are teams united in a shared commitment to serve and care for an organization. There are good reasons to refer to them as "corporate athletes," having to perform, as individuals and as a team, under pressure and with limited time.[2] Hence, owners, corporate board members, and managers can all benefit from frameworks developed in support of top-level athletes and sport teams. This positive, action-oriented perspective, borrowed from top sports coaching, has been found to be very beneficial by owners, directors, and managers when applied to (owners, supervisory, management) board development and composition.

The foundational insight of this approach is to recognize that good board members bring and generate positive energies to their board work and to their fellow board members, allowing these boards in turn to generate further positive energies in the company and its various organizational units. Bad board members, on the contrary, generate negative energies in themselves and in others, and act like destructive viruses or cancer cells do, sapping life out. The approach is as simple as it is fundamental and powerful. It generates the simple and obvious question after every board meeting: Did the meeting generate positive energies through the board's decisions and exchanges, and will these energies eventually generate further positive energies throughout the organization, and for how long? When board members and meetings are flat, no such energies have a chance to be generated. At best, it will not make a

M. Massa et al., *Value Creation for Owners and Directors*,
https://doi.org/10.1007/978-3-031-19726-0

difference; at worst, decisions were not taken, movement is halted, and competitive position worsened, obsolescence growing consequently.

The framework refers to the five distinct energies that individuals, teams, or organizations have at a given time in their "batteries," and how these energies are grown, depleted, and regenerated. These five energies are depicted in Fig. A.1 and are Information and Competence; Emotions and Relations; Courage to Act; Time and Experience; Purpose and Spirit. Each of these energies emanates from specific talents and competences the individual board members inherit, leverage, deplete, and rebuild.

Each energy also corresponds to complexity, as the continued generation of such positive energies in a board context may indeed be challenging, and typically is. The framework explains why board effectiveness is so difficult. To be truly effective, board members need to generate positive energies in each dimension: indeed, the absence of one energy (e.g., positive emotions or poor insights) may nullify the potential contribution of a director or board, and, worse, may turn it into value destroying territory. We review and comment on each energy in turn, referring without distinction to boards or the directors that compose them.

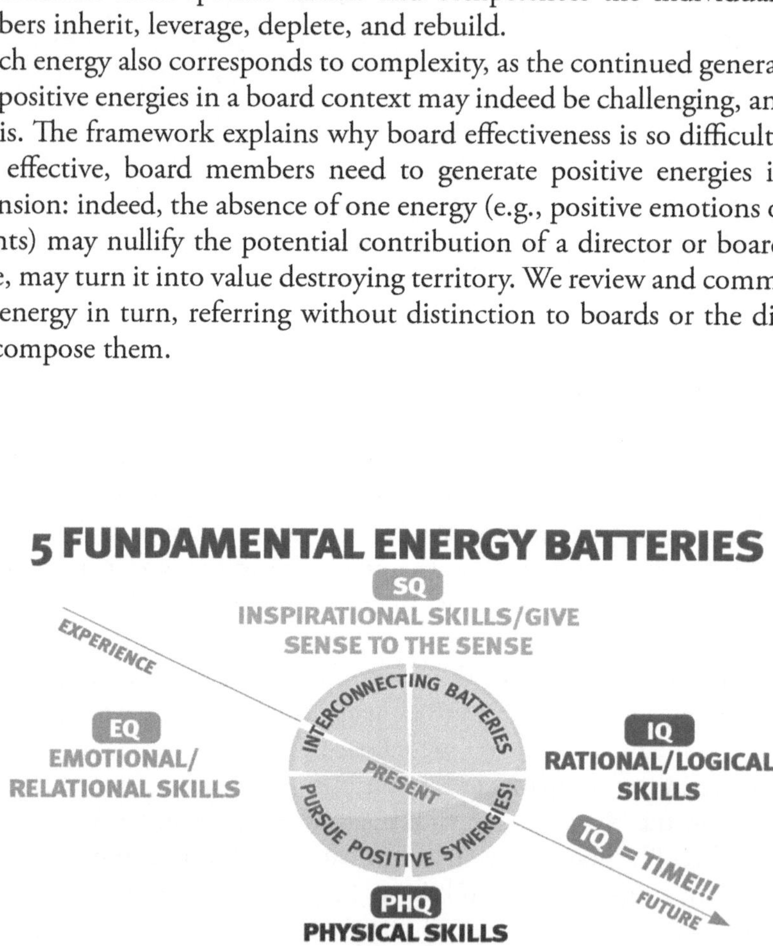

Fig. A.1 The five energy batteries of great board members. Source: Goudsmet and Van der Heyden (2022)

Energy battery	Explanation
# 1 Information and Competence (IQ)	The need for directors to have the appropriate competences and skills, as well as knowledge about the company they serve on the board of. Access to the right and relevant information is required for effective understanding of the issues in front of the board. This is a first requirement for directors eager to bring new and valuable insights to the board which provide the core of their value add. This also very much relies on management's capability to provide the information needed in a format that allows easy understanding by board members. This criterion by itself underlines how crucial collaboration is between board members and managers with high expertise on the matters the board needs to decide on.
# 2 Emotions and Relations (EQ)	Board work is often carried out in a context of stress and tensions, if only due to time. Disagreements are inherent to the role, and board members come at these issues from a distance, certainly relative to executives. Board members need to display emotional stability and keep the right focus in such challenging times to foster and maintain positive working relations, even when facing the possibly biased and emotional statements of their colleagues. Directors ideally are the "sages" in the company. They should also be able to be positive about and see the merit of ideas that they disagree with, but that they can accept as a result of the exchanges with their fellow board members.
# 3 Courage and Action (PHQ)	Evidently, directors need to be more than "yes men," including when they do not know. They must have the courage to state that they wish to know more, and when they do, to dissent and act with resolve and without fearing repercussions. The exercise of their mandate with true independence, without pressure except for that which is self-generated and is performance enhancing, is of vital importance. Board members must have strong and confident profiles, able to align with the views of the group even when they disagree. When unable to do so, they should consider resigning because responsibility is carried collectively, which leaves board members responsible for decisions that they do not agree with.
# 4 Time and Experience (TQ)	Being an effective board member is a competence that is developed with experience. Taking sufficient time to prepare for meetings, being actively engaged in such meetings, and managing follow-up are just some of the requirements of effective directors. This includes understanding where the company and the board came from, what the current situation is that one has come to, and, finally, the ability to envisage the future scenarios that lie ahead, both in terms of opportunities and in terms of threats and risk.
# 5 Purpose and Spirit (SQ)	Serving on a board is a fiduciary responsibility on behalf of a company. This demands the ability to be motivated by a spirit of care and accountability, as well as a good degree of generosity as the role is to serve the company. Great board members strive to inspire and be an exemplar for their fellow board members, for executives, and for all stakeholders.

Challenge # 1: Information and Competence (IQ)

A US Government report on the Deepwater Horizon tragedy pointed to a defective plan for BP's Macondo oil well in the Gulf of Mexico: there was insufficient cement between the 7-inch production casing and the 9 7/8-inch protection casing. These indeed are technical causes underlying the explosion. The governance question is whether the BP board members were aware that such a risk could occur and, if they were, whether appropriate risk mitigation measures were undertaken. Did they—at least collectively, with the help of the management and of course not each of them individually—have the required knowledge and competence to understand the challenges of deep-water drilling? One of the key issues behind the tragedy is whether BP, as the company owning the well and responsible for it, had the competence to evaluate the work of its contractors (Transocean, owner of the rig, and Halliburton, who was responsible for laying the cement) and to assess the risks associated with what was a very complex operation indeed. What is more damning for BP is that both contractors had provided warnings about possible blowout risks, which BP de facto ignored. Finally, the BP people operating the well and Transocean as the rig operator had experienced a great number of safety issues that should have spurred them to be more prudent. But the well had accumulated long delays, and the managers on the rig were under pressure to produce. These questions should have at some point been brought to a discussion at board level, by way of a Risk Committee or an HSE Committee of the board. The failure of BP was indeed largely one of a lack of competent oversight of what were very complex operations.

Many will argue that a board, such as BP's, could, because of its distance from the well, not be held responsible for the accident that eventually triggered the explosion. First, the damage caused was massive, killing people and wildlife, threatening life in the Gulf and the survival of BP, which survived the crisis only through massive asset sales. The board, being the nexus of corporate governance, is the body ultimately responsible for risk oversight and monitoring of the company's most risky projects. So, while the board did not directly cause the accident, it indeed was ultimately responsible for ensuring (through visits, discussions with site managers and experts, suppliers) whether the safety of the rig and its crew was assured to a sufficient degree. It is important to note that BP had suffered major accidents in its North American operations before. If they did not have the knowledge and were not provided with the required information, and even more, if they did not seek the information, there is indeed a breach of corporate governance. It is in that sense that governance is "much to do about very little," or in more plain words, plenty of effort and time to ensure that nothing bad happens. Governance activity is often more justified by the costs foregone than by the costs spent.

Whereas the technical aspects of the Macondo explosion do not look good for BP, what is even more ominous is the very poor safety records of both BP and Transocean before the accident. The pressure from the senior executive team to get the well operating (it was far behind schedule) did indeed contribute to imprudent decision making by BP and the well operator. The visit to the platform by a senior BP executive 2 h before the explosion congratulating the platform's crew for its operations seems to confirm that it was not just the board that was unaware of the safety hazards on the rig.

Such examples consistently evidence individuals who believe themselves to be more intelligent and capable than the situation warrants or who take risks they did not spend time evaluating for possible negative outcomes. The danger in governance typically does not come from people who know they don't know—they seek further evidence—but more from people who think they know when they don't. An awareness of one's fallibility and the need for the right skills (competencies) and accurate data (information) is the first major challenge for board members. Appropriate humility, duty of care, and concern are needed virtues here.

Challenge # 2: Emotions and Relations (EQ)

Maintaining effective working relationships and keeping emotions within bounds such that communication is facilitated is of paramount importance. Looking at VW's Dieselgate, described in Chap. 1, the crisis occurred in the background of severe infighting among the founding families. The Porsche and Piëch families had reached a point where they would no longer discuss issues with appropriate civility. This situation led to ineffective board discussions. Disagreements on the family holding board affected behaviors on the corporate board, and ultimately in the organization itself. It is again the duty of care that directors hold that obliges them to maintain respectful relations with fellow members and executives, and to address these head-on if they are wanting.

The ability to maintain open relations with other board members who hold differing views requires both emotional maturity and the virtue to maintain these relations in difficult contexts to remain true to one's mandate. It is the continued exploration and revisiting of different hypotheses, and from several distinct angles, that allows a good validation of the assumptions one holds on to.

Challenge # 3: Courage and Action (PHQ)

In October 2016 Cyrus Mistry was abruptly fired as Executive Chairman of Tata Sons, the holding company of the Tata Group. Chapter 1 described how the Tata Group had difficulties differentiating its mission from its culture, to the detriment of its failing operating companies. The directors on the board of Tata Sons, instead of focusing on these key issues, seemed to follow Ratan Tata's bidding in summarily disposing—the word execution fits here—of Group Chairman Mistry, with the collaboration of an outside director and Dean of a prestigious US business school, which furthermore had received a major gift from Tata.

The board members did not seem to muster sufficient courage in their meetings to insist on due process. They seemed to be driven by a propensity toward action centered on the removal of Chairman Cyrus Mistry. They seemed to be too rapidly willing to say "yes" to Ratan Tata's proposals as Chairman of the Tata Trusts to remove the successor he had nearly single-handedly chosen a few years earlier. The board members might have mustered the courage to point out that Mistry was increasingly shedding light on the international deal making of his predecessor that events increasingly proved to be economically problematic and increasingly jeopardized the dividends expected by the Tata Trusts for their philanthropic endeavors. Mistry had inherited a group that was not in good shape, save for TCS, its consulting and IT services arm.

The challenges of courage to confront and to act accordingly are faced by boards not just in times of crisis, but at any meeting where "leading" directors may be all too eager to impose their views, intimidating or even just nudging less prestigious directors into silent approval.

More ordinary "physical" aspects of being a director amount to presence at board meetings, availability for discussions with senior managers and board colleagues, as well as the simple implication of where board meetings are being held and being aware of the physical and operational realities of what is being discussed. Geography matters a lot in governance. The location of incorporation of the company and the places where board meetings are held—in hotels, or on the company's premises around the world—matter and influence the outcome of board meetings.

Challenge # 4: Time and Experience (TQ)

Dominic Barton and Mark Wiseman in their article "Where boards Fall Short" write that "Most governance experts would agree that public company directors need to put in more days on the job."[3] They quote experts on the number of days directors should spend on board responsibilities for "large, complex firms," suggesting a range of 24 to 54 days a year. The authors recommend that directors dedicate at least 35 days a year to the job.

This is the challenge directors must confront: to dedicate sufficient time to preparing for board meetings and to carry out one's duties as a director on boards. The implication is that one cannot effectively hold many such positions at the same time. For non-executive directors who also have a regular executive day job, taking on several NED positions will unavoidably have the unfortunate consequence of having too little actual time to fulfill one's board duties. The expectations on the number of directorships have fortunately considerably and positively evolved since the financial crisis.

Challenge # 5: Purpose and Spirit (SQ)

This, in our view, is the most important challenge, often neglected, facing the Board of Directors. Do directors have the spirit of responsibility expected from board members? Do they pursue their mandate with the right purpose?

Author Daniel Pink describes a person's key, inner motivations as being driven by "autonomy, purpose, and mastery." This is an excellent summary of what we call the spiritual challenge facing board directors: Is one as board director truly driven by a purpose to be a good if not great director, by a desire to master the challenge of being a sustainably effective director exercising fiduciary duties on behalf of the company, and does one have the autonomy (the more traditional governance term is independence) to ensure that one's actions match the intention?

Hopefully, this concise description will have informed owners, or members of the nomination committee and their nominees, of the multiple challenges to becoming an effective director, and to nominating one. In the end, the proof is in the eating. One fundamental reason is that—as in all team sports—a great player may not necessarily fit in with and contribute to making a great team. Much depends on the capability of each individual director to add her or his potential value to the group, which in governance comes first and which each member serves. This is where duplication hurts, and differentiation helps a lot. Indeed, the more board members are similar, the less they add value, and the less their absence matters (since the others think the same). "Social loafing" is a well-accepted phenomenon in psychology: the more people pull a rope, the less each one exerts maximal effort. This is where professionalism and a sense of purpose are essential.

Having described the five fundamental challenges that all boards face, we take the opportunity to also list five further challenges that directors face and that will provide them and their owners with a useful checklist.

Five additional challenges for board effectiveness

Challenge	Explanation
# 6 – Governance Culture	Culture in a company concerns the habits of interaction and decision making of its employees, which is particularly dependent on the habits of its managers and board members. One of the key challenges of any company consists in building a governance culture so that each employee considers it part of her or his role to contribute positively to effective governance (e.g., through information sharing including responsible whistle blowing). Such a culture greatly supports effective board work; its absence makes effective board work much more challenging.
# 7 - Performance	The challenge here is for the governance system to perform and to sustainably deliver results, support and induce high performance and avoid value destruction. Again, this challenge arises both within the company—does it have a performance culture—and at the board level—does the board demonstrate a performance culture for its own work?
# 8 - Communication	Many people typically find it hard to understand what the board stands for, does, and expects. This is the first challenge of any board: be clear about its expectations, its decisions, and its achievements. Operationally, communication amounts to privileging of "ask" over "tell", without being afraid to turn to a strong "tell" when appropriate. This "asking" builds an engaged community—as well as an engaged board—"pulling" in people rather than pushing them into compliance with decisions made by others.

Challenge	Explanation
# 9 - Structure	The challenge here is structuring the governance systems for effectiveness and hopefully high performance. The choice of members, the architecture of governance committees, and the deployment of governance inside the company are key structural determinants of a good governance system. What goals, values, rules guide the governance roles and at board level and inside the company, and what individual commitments do people make to the fulfillment of the governance task.
# 10 - Continuous Improvement	This is the challenge of adopting the "Kaizen" spirit of continuous improvement of board work. This spirit reminds us that there is no best practice, only better practice, and that the goal of today is to outdo yesterday. While that practice can be seen in most factories around the world today, the practice is much less diffused up the hierarchy and certainly much rarer at board level. And yet, it is fundamental if a board ever hopes to aim for high performance. Boards insufficiently evaluate themselves, and when they do the exercise is often very formal.

Notes

1. The framework borrowed from high-performance sport teams is the result of a collaboration with Alain Goudsmet, founder of Mentally Fit, an organization that applies models and approaches inspired by high-level sports to energize individuals, teams, and organizations. For more detail, see https://mentallyfit.global/en/about-mentally-fit/ as well as Alain Goudsmet and Ludo Van der Heyden, "The Six Dimensions of Winning Teams," *INSEAD Working Paper,* 2022.
2. Koen Gonnissen and Alain Goudsmet, *The Corporate Athlete: Managing (yourself) under pressure,* B+B Vakmedianet BV, 2010.
3. https://hbr.org/2015/01/where-boards-fall-short.

Appendix B: Napoleon Bonaparte: Lessons in Fair Process Leadership

Fair Process Leadership in the Early Years

Birth and Early Years

Napoleon was a Corsican, born on August 15, 1769, of Tuscan descent through his mother. He received a French education, entering a religious school in Autun at the age of ten, and then the Royal Military College in Brienne. He was 19 when the French Revolution broke out on July 14, 1789. He did not play a big role in those early days. At the time, he was a fervent Corsican nationalist and asked to leave the Army to serve the cause of Pasquale Paoli, who had returned to Corsica from his exile in Britain. Napoleon's brothers chose the side of the French Republic, squaring with Paoli, who favored Corsican independence from France. In the end, Paoli chose the English side, and Corsica found a great ally in England. This led to a full split with the Bonapartes, particularly after the Paoli troops destroyed the Napoleon family home in Ajaccio. This anchored the Bonapartes firmly in the camp of the Revolution, particularly after having to take refuge in Toulon. It also led Bonaparte to re-join his regiment.

The Revolution promised *Liberté, Egalité, Fraternité* (Liberty, Equality, Fraternity) for all, even though *Fraternité* was added to the French motto only in 1848, because of another revolution. The remarkable statement promised fair play in French society, a characteristic that had been absent for too long under the reign of the Bourbon kings. The successors of the Sun King Louis XIV were the formal owners of the Royaume de France. Soldiers then were

M. Massa et al., *Value Creation for Owners and Directors*,
https://doi.org/10.1007/978-3-031-19726-0

told to live and die for the King, as were his subjects. The Revolution changed all that. Soldiers now fought for a Nation that was theirs, united in the pursuit of a single goal: save the Republic (against the Habsburgs) and defend their newly earned *Liberté et Égalité.*[1] The Republic recognized its heroes: wives of fallen soldiers would become Widows of the Nation and their children Pupils of the Nation. The choice faced by the soldiers of the new Republic was simple: fight and contribute to the survival of the Republic or submit to Europe' aristocratic regimes, and to a royal regime they had just freed themselves from. Soldiers enthusiastically chose the Republic, and its armies, led by capable generals like Dumouriez and Kléber, countered Habsburg and Prussian attacks in the North. But the Revolution still needed to find a leader that would ensure them ultimate victory. This is where the arrival of Bonaparte on the scene met the aspirations and captured the imagination of the revolutionary soldiers and of the entire French nation. It was a journey that was remarkable and unimaginable, but relatively short-lived. It barely lasted a generation, Napoleon never had a successor, and the Bourbon kings returned to power for what the French call the Restauration.

The French Revolution created tremendous energies in society and in the army. The Revolution eliminated the distance separating the people from its leaders, the soldiers from their aristocratic officers, who were gradually appointed not by aristocratic lineage but by merit. Bonaparte, as a military mastermind, had quickly understood the psychological and intellectual need for officers to be competent and appointed on the capabilities they demonstrated on the battlefield. He often, after a major battle, spent several days with senior officers to identify and promote the junior officers who had distinguished themselves on the battlefield. This was an innovation, and a major discontinuity with the practices of the preceding royal regime, which was also in place in the European aristocratic armies the French faced. The superior quality of the leadership in the French Army created a major advantage in battle.[2] It introduced fair process in the army.

Emerging Military Leader

Napoleon first distinguished himself at the siege of Toulon in 1793 as a young commander of the artillery. His good relations with the younger brother of revolutionary leader Robespierre and fellow Corsican Salicetti earned him the appointment, which was needed after his unsuccessful stint in Corsica. His brilliant leadership in Toulon was pivotal in chasing the British Royal Navy out of France's main military harbor in the Mediterranean. The victory was greeted with relief by the powers in Paris, who were eager for good news. It also much increased the visibility of the young captain with the revolutionary leadership in Paris.

His defeat of a royalist uprising in Paris in 1795 assured him of the command of the Army of the Interior. The French Republic was again being threatened in the north by Habsburg forces. Napoleon proposed to the Revolutionary Government to also attack the Habsburgs in their Italian possessions. He was appointed head of the newly created Army of Italy and conquered northern Italy in blitzkrieg fashion (1796–1797). All now realized the superior talents of this extremely gifted military commander. A key element of Napoleon's success was a radical new military strategy called "fighting between the lines."

An Innovative Military Strategy Leveraged by FPL Software

One of Napoleon's major innovations was to accelerate the change in military doctrine in the French Army. French Army command had benchmarked on the agile practices of the front troops of the Habsburg armies that often created havoc in disciplined linear French movements. Napoleon went much deeper in this rethinking of military doctrine.

Having all become citizens of the French nation, the army was standardized into a national army, with a modular structure that greatly facilitated combined movements, speed, and agility. The previous organization had divided it into regional regiments (Picardie, Gascogne, Bretagne, Lorraine, etc.), led by local aristocrats. This would not allow fast recombination into collective movements in the way the revolutionary armies eventually managed. Furthermore, the revolutionary regiments were made lighter to favor speed. Regiments were combined into army corps, which could act like small armies. Marshals and Generals were given much greater autonomy over their units, and disposed of all three arms: infantry, cavalry, and artillery. Napoleon, greatly supported by the uniquely talented Berthier in his role of chief of staff, would communicate directly with his Marshals and Generals through an elaborate central staff, continuously writing orders and dispatching them through a cavalry corps of staff officers. Napoleon would remain in control of the reserve and would, depending on circumstances, take control of one of the main army corps.

The result is a military "platform strategy" where the French armies could deploy themselves in any direction and recombine army corps as needed depending on the position of the enemy. The army would typically move through a region as displayed in Fig. B.1, covering an area of approximately 10,000–25,000 km². Each army corps would have advanced units or guides scanning the terrain for the enemy. When an enemy army was noted "in the square," as depicted in Fig. B.1, movements preparing for an engagement

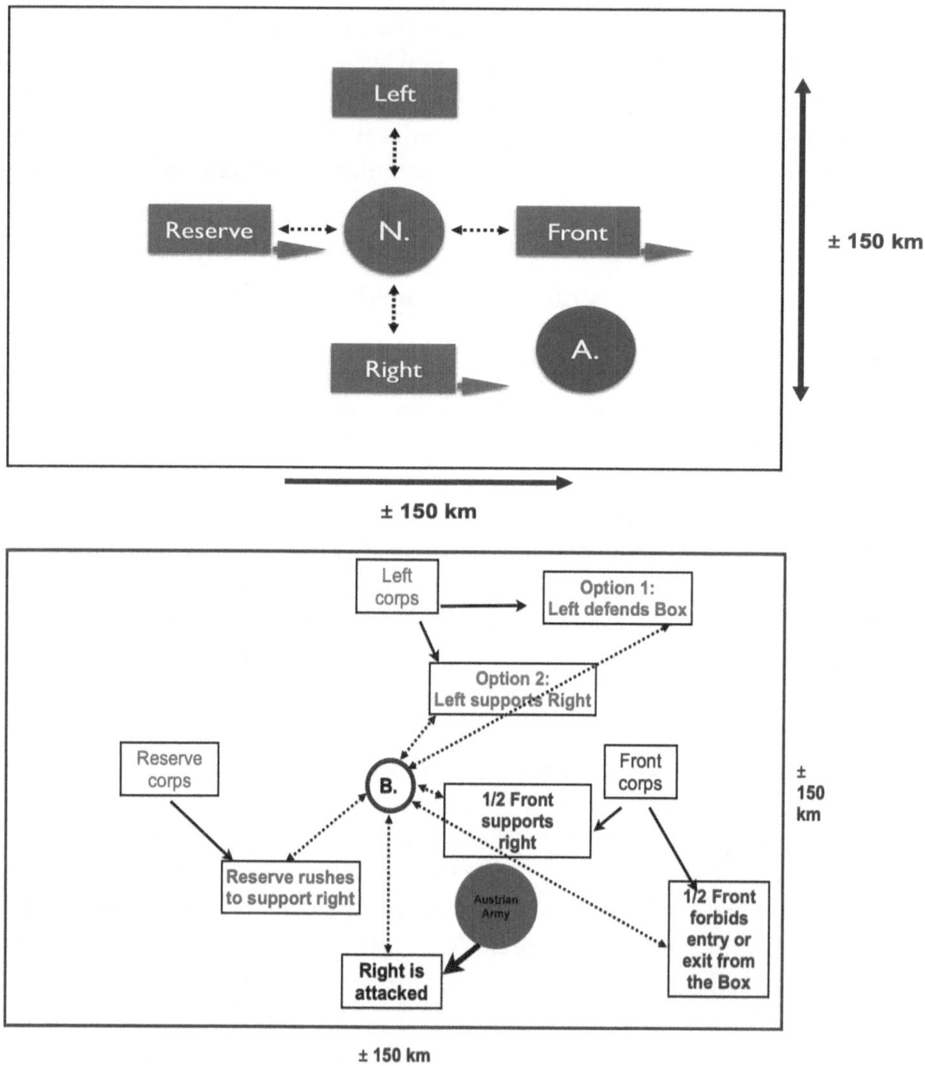

Fig. B.1 Napoleonic strategy of "fighting between the lines" illustrated: Napoleon sets his sights over a large domain, covered by four Army Corps, whose relative positions are determined by the position of the enemy's army. Informed of the presence of an enemy army, Napoleon would order his divisions in motion to fall on the enemy in succession, while other divisions would be sent to the confines of the "virtual" box so as not to allow a trapped enemy to escape from the box, or to be resupplied from outside the box

with the enemy would start. A possible sequence is described in the figure and is now explained.

The image shows four French Army Corps being directed by Napoleon and his staff at the center. The key objective is to engage an Austrian army that was reported to be in the area. Once identified by one of the Army Corps, the latter would be tricked into believing they only faced a single smaller French Army Corps. Feeling stronger, they would engage the French corps in battle, aiming to destroy the smaller opposing force. However, by the end of the day, the French Army Corps would be reinforced by another corps, or half of one, ordered by Napoleon to rush to the battlefield in support of a corps whose odds otherwise would be against survival. The next morning, a third army corps would arrive, or a part of it, having accomplished a forced march during the night (the average speed would be 5 km per hour, which would amount to covering 50 km per night (with pauses), or approximately 100 km for a full day). The Austrians, seeing these successive divisions fall on them over two successive days, would eventually yield, or escape, at which point the French cavalry would be asked to finish the task, or they would fall on another French corps waiting for them.

The tactic was deployed first in the 1796 Italian campaign, where it quickly generated successive victories first over the Piedmont and Sardinia armies, and then over the Habsburg troops defending their Italian possessions. Eventually the Allies opposing the French would start to understand French tactics, especially when informed by French Generals such as Moreau or Bernadotte opposing Napoleon's anti-Republican reign. Wellington applied the Napoleon tactic at Waterloo, in combination with the Prussian army under Blücher. FPL was the software central to the effective utilization of the Emperor's military strategy. Marshalls and Generals were asked to engage their advanced troops scanning for the enemy. Napoleon, at central army headquarters, would, with the information reported by these advanced troops, frame a battle opportunity or a threat to counter. He would then, with Berthier and the Generals, explore alternative options, although gradually he grew so good at it that he would increasingly do so alone. Depending on the context he saw, he would decide on the engagement he sought. Expectations regarding the movements of regiments all had to be clear and coordinated, and regiments would be asked to continuously inform headquarters of their progress and of any new information what would affect the agreed maneuvers. This would be the task done so masterfully by Berthier and his central staff.

Only Napoleon and central staff had the full view of the chosen strategy and its deployment on the entire battlefield. The best commanders—such as Davout and Masséna—and the best troops would typically be given the hardest assignments. Davout, with 35 victories out of as many engagements, comes out as the best overall performer, ahead of Napoleon (who scored 23 victories out of 28 engagements). After engagements, the army corps had to rebuild the now depleted regiments. Victorious officers would be promoted. Generals, who feigned not being able to respond to risky orders, or who outright maneuvered poorly, were insufficiently punished, and this was an FPL miss. This gradually became a problem, also in his family, and with his staff, where dissent, or even foul play, was not severely sanctioned, fostering unhealthy politics. It does appear that Napoleon was a forgiving man loyal to his family and his subordinates, and probably somewhat delusional in thinking he could manage it all. It proved in the end to be one of his personality failures that would end up costing his leadership dearly, militarily or politically.

Napoleon's Obsession with Britain

Betrayed by Paoli who had chosen the English side against the French revolutionary cause, the Napoleonic family had seen their house burned by Paoli's loyalists. This nurtured a hatred against the English that would eventually lead him completely astray. The first error was that it led him to think of going to Egypt to cut British supply lines to India.

The invasion of Egypt was a great military success, but disaster soon struck: the French fleet was defeated in Aboukir Bay by Admiral Nelson, a battle which the English refer to as the Battle of the Nile. The (best French) Army was now stuck in Egypt, which the Austrians took advantage of by reconquering the Italian possessions lost in the first Italian Campaign of 1796. Napoleon tried returning to France via Palestine and Syria but was soon pushed back, first by the Ottomans and their allies, and then by the plague which badly hit soldiers and their morale. Stuck in Egypt, he escaped and left the Army to the command of Kléber, spurred by learning that France's Army of Italy had suffered a number of defeats at the hands of the Second Coalition: the Empires of Austria, Great Britain, Russia, and the Ottomans, joined by the Kingdoms of Naples, Sardinia, Sicily, and Sweden, all aligned in a commitment to stop Napoleon and return the Bourbon kings back to the throne, and stop this revolutionary thinking from spreading through Europe.

Saving France from the Chaos and the Enemies of the Revolution

Napoleon is very lucky and escapes British naval control of the Mediterranean. He even skips the quarantine mandated for soldiers returning from Egypt. He soon takes part in a successful coup against the royalists devised by his brother Lucien, Speaker of the Council of Five Hundreds. Bonaparte is installed as First Consul with two other members, Sieyès and Ducos. He clearly dominates both and now masters the Paris scene. The inglorious episode, known as the coup of Brumaire 18 (November 9, 1799), ends the Revolutionary Period and the reign of terror and anarchy. Yet, it is far from glorious, and he loses the support of some key Republican Generals such as Moreau and Bernadotte. The French people accept it, having grown tired of the Revolution and its successive governments. They long for a savior, law, and order.

Bonaparte is the ideal man. He fills the role perfectly and quickly endows the country with a Constitution (Constitution de l'An VII) that vests large powers in the executive, through the Council of the State (Conseil d'Etat). The latter discusses and writes the laws that are then submitted to a legislative Chamber that approves them. The Senate has no teeth, only verifying the conformity of the new laws with the Constitution. Sieyès, his democratic rival, is appointed President of the Senate. For all practical purposes Napoleon is now firmly in control of the country.

Having taken power and reorganized the institutions to fit his reign, his next major project is again military: retaking Italy, the country lost by neglect and incompetence of the previous leadership to the Austrians during the Egyptian campaign. It should be stated too that the best troops and generals were with Napoleon in Egypt. Nearly defeated at Marengo, two generals, Desaix and Kellermann, combine to turn a near defeat into a complete victory, ending the second Italian Campaign. The battle at Marengo, fought on June 2, 1800, is a French victory but a Napoleonic defeat. This is the reason why the famous painting by David (Fig. 13.2) shows Napoleon crossing the Saint Bernard on his way to Marengo, and not on the battlefield. Here he is contemplating defeat, until at the last minute Desaix returns to the battlefield of his own initiative (having heard the cannon). Together with Kellermann, Desaix saves the day with a vigorous counterattack taking the Austrians by complete surprise. Unfortunately, Desaix dies in the charge. Napoleon loses one of his most capable generals.

In the north, General Moreau defeats the Austrians at Hohenlinden on December 3, 1800. The two victories, Hohenlinden and Marengo, seal the defeat of the Second Coalition. The Austrian Empire signs the Treaty of Lunéville with France on February 9, 1801, leaving the British no choice but to enter similar peace negotiations with the French. Joined by the Dutch and the Spaniards, they sign the Peace Treaty of Amiens on March 25, 1802, which finally recognizes the French Republic, allowing France to end hostilities in Europe, at least for a while. It provides him with an opportunity to turn his energies to reorganizing the French Republic until, nudged by British duplicity, he will get his armies marching again.

Organizing Modern France

In the 2 years that follow the signing of the Amiens Peace Treaty, Napoleon will be an energetic leader and very effective administrator, restoring civil order in French society. Balancing the budget, he establishes the basis for the modern-day French administration through the introduction of several legislative codes and other dispositions. The most famous is the Napoleonic Code (Code Napoléon*)*, a sweeping reform and codification of French civil law. It was originally named the Code Civil des Français, but a second edition, promulgated in 1807, renames it after the Emperor. The fundamental judicial work is done by a committee of four lawyers, supervised by Arch-Chancellor of the Empire and Second Consul, Jean-Jacques-Régis de Cambacérès. Napoleon attended less than half of the committee's sessions, military priorities taking him away from attending the second half of the committee's work. This allowed the committee to conclude the work, intended to secure the rights of citizens. Napoleon had been arguing for features of control rather than of liberation. Napoleon is not considered to have had a major influence in the writing of the civil code. The leading writer was Portalis, a lawyer from Aix-en-Provence. If Napoleon had inspired the Code, he would likely not have become one of its strongest offenders.

Worn out after 10 years of unending internal and external strife, France will be most grateful to Bonaparte (as he was then called) for consolidating the rights won by the people during the Revolution while restoring peace and order, in France and with its enemies. Codification continues with codes of commerce, and civil and criminal procedures, and a rural code is the final one.

Increasing Unfair Process Leadership as Emperor

Unfortunately for Europe and eventually for France, Napoleon remains a soldier at heart, fueled by a growing hatred of the British. He reorganizes Europe increasingly under French rule. The Brits rightly feel shut out of Europe, which they cannot accept. The reorganization of Switzerland under French supervision (Acte de Médiation, 1803) lays the basis of modern Switzerland, with the exception that the country is ordered to supply troops to the imperial army and that it is told to stay out of European affairs. The Brits take Napoleon's interference in Europe's affairs badly, particularly when both countries fail to enact the neutrality commitments agreed to in Amiens. The French do not allow Holland and Italy to become fully independent, while the Brits do not allow the Knights of Malta to become independent of the English either. The latter is used as a reason by Napoleon to resume hostilities. On the opposing side, the rest of Europe joins in the Third Coalition, comprising Austria, Britain, Naples, Russia, and Sweden.

Napoleon is eager to invade England. He assembles an army in Boulogne that will invade Britain using over 1000 ships and barges to cross the channel. His plans are thwarted (again) by Nelson's decisive victory over the combined French and Spanish fleets at Cape Trafalgar. These were meant to pull the English navy out of the channel. The English invasion is finally called off, after 2 years of extensive preparation.

The troops assembled in Boulogne are now urgently needed to defeat the armies of the Third Coalition, as Austrians and Russians are planning to meet in Bavaria to stop Napoleon. This sets the stage for one of Napoleon's most remarkable victories.

Once a General, Always a General: Writing the Most Illustrious Pages of France's Military and World History

The first Battle of the Three Emperors, fought at Austerlitz in 1805, remains crucial reading in all military colleges to this day. It is possibly the greatest battle Napoleon won. To the surprise of all in Europe, the French defeat the main Russian army, reinforced by the reserve troops of the Austrian Emperor, at Austerlitz. The victory rests on superior skill, speed, and modular recombination of army divisions and corps. It is also a perfect illustration of FPL, with all troops informed of the plan that will be executed and with multiple traps being set to lull the Russians into believing the French are afraid of them, which will only confirm them in their arrogance. They do not pay much attention to Austrian warnings stating that the French troops are remarkably fast and surprising in their maneuvers.

The management of the Austerlitz battle is a vivid illustration of FPL in use and of its power. On the Russian side it shows the destruction FPL violations can generate, when the framing of the battle is poor, and officers are forced to execute plans that are insufficiently explored and based on false assumptions. On the French side and in FPL parlance, Napoleon beautifully engaged, explored, and explained his decisions with his Marshals and Generals. He was aware of the needs of the men in his army (physical, emotional, intellectual, spiritually, and also in terms of time). He knew that motivation and commitment of front-line troops were crucial keys to victory, at the same level as the quality of the plan, and particularly when, like at Austerlitz, the plan was risky.

The Austerlitz victory ends the campaign against Russia and Austria, but the Prussians now take up their weapons against the French imperial forces. The Prussian Campaign again demonstrates remarkable maneuvering by the French Army Corps and ends in the decisive victory at Jena-Auerstedt on October 14, 1806. Though Davout, with his single army corps, defeats the main Prussian army at Auerstedt, Napoleon will again take the credit for his victory with his superior army over the rear guard of the Prussian army. Though Davout will be rewarded with the title of Duke of Auerstedt, Napoleon takes most of the credit for this victory, and it goes down in history books as the Battle of Jena, where Napoleon defeats the Prussian rearguard. He thus minimizes the heroic and decisive contributions of Davout, unfairly little known by the French for his multiple heroic contributions.

The victory over the Prussians allowed Napoleon to issue the Decree of Berlin on November 23, which enforces a trade embargo with Britain (Blocus Continental). The aim is, by a combined effort of France, its allies, and its defeated opponents, to deprive Britain of both commerce and essential foodstuffs. The blockade is equivalent to a declaration of war on Britain. It also imposes a large burden on France's allies, which find the alliance suddenly much less beneficial, denting their commitment to their French victors. The ceaseless pursuit of this embargo strategy by Napoleon will end up being one of the main reasons for the fall of the Empire, particularly compared with the counterfactual where a nearly bankrupt England would be allowed to trade with an Empire that it did not have the means to threaten. Napoleon could have obtained terms much more favorable than what continued warfare would bring him, particularly that he never had the means to defeat the British Navy.

The invasions of Portugal first and then Russia will be the most fateful consequences of the Blocus Continental strategy, directly leading to the fall of the Empire. French industrialists are much less negative as the Empire provides them with a nearly monopolistic situation throughout Europe, which they have never even dreamed of. It also will lead the City's merchants to spend their last pounds paying for Wellington's army in Spain. It was their only hope to stop Napoleon and his destructive dreams concerning Britain. The ceaseless pursuit of the Blocus Continental is, from a strategic and diplomatic view, utter madness. The idea is again purely military, indicating that Napoleon's talents at diplomacy far from match his talents on the battlefield, even if the overwhelming defeat at Austerlitz ended the 300-year-old Habsburg reign over Europe. Napoleon's military prowess, formidable administrative skills, and tremendous energies formed the legs of the tripod on which his military and organizational powers rested. His many victories attest that Napoleon had mastered the principles of high performance in the military arena. They show FPL largely at play in his engagement of his Marshals and Generals. However, as his Empire and power grow, this engagement will wane, and so will the FPL with his inner circle.

Napoleon is disappointed when, having defeated the Russians at Austerlitz, they re-enter the fight. Napoleon understands that he has made a mistake in not having been tougher with them after their disastrous defeat at Austerlitz. When they are beaten again at Friedland on July 7, 1807, Tsar Alexander I has no other choice but to accept the Peace of Tilsit, where Napoleon imposes an alliance with Russia against the Brits. But Alexander I already knows that he will renege on this treaty later, when the context will be more favorable for Russia. Napoleon is better at winning battles than at diplomacy, for which he lacks patience and often concludes too hastily.

Imperial Power, Growing Isolation, and Decreasing FPL

In December 1804, Napoleon crowned himself Emperor. He was 35 years old by then and ruled over more than half of Europe. A first warning that things might not last forever was the inconclusive and very bloody battle at Eylau, waged against the Russians in February 1807. This put a first dent into Napoleon's invincibility. Murat, Napoleon's brother-in-law, was heroic in saving the French from defeat with his cavalry. The death toll, however, was enormous. The great victory over the Russians at Friedland in June 1807 restored the image of invincibility to a large extent. It ended the Fourth Coalition and led to the Treaty of Tilsit. Russia is treated with great clemency by Napoleon, who still aims to make the Tsar an ally against Britain. Prussia is largely dismembered, and the Duchy of Warsaw is given to the King of Sachsen, another French ally.

The battles will grow harder and ever bloodier as the opposing armies grow in size, surprises become rarer, and artillery predictably replaces the sweeping and unexpected moves of the army corps. Approximately 750,000 soldiers start the Russian Campaign in June 1812. The French Army takes a new title, *La Grande Armée,* which is an understatement. Its leftovers, just 30,000, will exit the disastrous campaign by crossing the Berezina River into Germany at the end of November 1812; an equal number will die, many of them drowning, trying to cross the river, the others repulsing an attack by Marshal Kutuzov and his troops.

The great successes on the battlefield had brought Napoleon to the pinnacle of his success. But success did not come without issues, largely of the Emperor's own making, such as the forced resignation of Talleyrand, his valuable though conservative foreign minister, who was an aristocrat who considered that his and France's sustainability would benefit from good relations with the Austrians. Until his resignation he had been one of the few dissenting voices Napoleon would listen to. Talleyrand also brought diplomatic competence and talent that eluded the Emperor. As much as the latter was a man of action and conquest, Talleyrand was known for his patience, persistence, and accommodation. He constantly reminded Napoleon that the central requirement was to come to peace terms with the Habsburgs, turned Austrians after the Austerlitz defeat. Following Talleyrand's departure, Napoleon underwent a worrying and visible transformation. In August 1807, he shut down the vociferous and critical Tribunat, the French chamber where laws would be discussed before they were presented for a vote at the legislative assembly. This was surprising as it was a discussion chamber and had virtually no power, only influence.

Increasingly thin-skinned to attacks by the press, Napoleon threatened to close newspapers critical of his leadership. He enforced strict court etiquette, keeping everyone physically at arm's length. He could only be approached with the approval of Duroc, Grand Marshal of the Palace. A letter dated April 4, 1807, to his brother Louis, appointed King of Holland, clearly displayed a disengaging Napoleon: "You govern your nation like a docile, timorous monk ... A king issues orders and does not beg." In FPL parlance, an increasingly authoritarian Napoleon at some point stopped listening, and even engaging, leading to a much-reduced exploration of his ideas, and a much less convincing and detailed narrative for his decisions. With growing attacks from his enemies, ranging from Spain to Prussia and Russia, Napoleon's advisors increasingly favored a more balanced implementation of political, diplomatic, and economic policies, moving away from relying solely on France's superior military capability or military strategies like the commercial blockade of Great Britain. The need was for greater power sharing in a more integrated Europe through diplomacy and political agreements instead of military campaigns that required ever greater resources in men and finances. Napoleon never agreed to such a transition in thinking and goals, forever seeking power through military campaigns that became ever riskier, using his impatience and disdain toward diplomatic approaches as the excuse for turning to war again, which he preferred.

The most damaging blow to FPL was the Emperor's inability to learn and adapt to an increasingly hostile context and a complexity that became unmanageable once the Empire gained size. His never-ending desire to have sole control over the Empire's destiny only worsened matters and led him into a vicious cycle that would engulf him. With armies engaged in battles in Spain and Portugal, in Austria and Russia, he only increased his vulnerabilities, both militarily and administratively. That he did not fathom this seems incomprehensible. As the allies understood that they could engage his armies all over Europe, which would only weaken him, their resolve to finish him militarily grew as well. Napoleon had created his own downfall. He and the French would pay the heavy price.

Bernadotte, one of his illustrious generals, and brother-in-law of his elder brother Joseph, feeling unfairly dealt with, left the imperial team, and accepted the invitation to become Prince of Sweden. He had grown increasingly disappointed by Napoleon's dictatorial style, which he fully disapproved of. Several advisers, fearing for his life, told him that it would indeed be safer to leave France and accept the invitation from the Swedish king who was looking for a successor. When, preparing for the Russian Campaign, Napoleon sought Bernadotte out and asked him to show his true French nature, Bernadotte was not afraid to invoke his new Swedish responsibilities and loyalty, flatly refusing to join the Russian Campaign. He considered the project suicidal and strongly advised Napoleon not to undertake it. Napoleon likely had become deaf at that point when submitted views that were contrary to his own. He simply ignored the superior and informed commonsense advice of his former General and member of the imperial family.[3]

Irritated by increasing dissent, Napoleon had entered a "setup to fail" by disengaging himself from people who could provide him with valuable advice.[4] This lack of openness to negative advice or feedback would only serve to both increase his own biases and eventually erode his decision making abilities and influence. Power, success, and ego increasingly corrupted Napoleon's Fair Process Leadership (FPL).

Napoleon's fateful Russian invasion, leading to the loss of his entire cavalry (a key to the speed and surprise of his maneuvers) and a large part of his armies, cemented his end. The disastrous retreat from Russia in 1812 was the signal that the whole of Europe was waiting to unite in the Seventh Coalition. Although Napoleon fought a brilliant last campaign in France from the end of 1813 to the end of March 1814 against a far superior enemy, the odds were impossible to conquer. The ultimate outcome seemed to be in doubt only in Napoleon's mind. The campaign was heroic and interesting from a military viewpoint. For France, abdication would have yielded much better peace conditions for the country, and also for Napoleon himself.

In April 1814, the Marshals refused to follow his orders to continue to defend France, forcing Napoleon to abdicate (after a failed suicide attempt). Tsar Alexander I obtained the information that Napoleon was sent into exile on the island of Elba in the Mediterranean, not far from his native Corsica. The English already wished him in Saint Helena. Napoleon's first exile was short-lived, due to his boundaryless ambition and the incompetence of the returning Bourbon kings, which increasingly led the army and the French people to desire the return of their Emperor.

Napoleon finally met his fate at Waterloo in 1815. As agreed in their Vienna Conference, the Allies (by now all of Europe had united against France) had committed close to one million troops, while the French Army could at best muster 300,000 at the time. This left little doubt as to the eventual outcome.

The battle at Waterloo, or Mont-Saint-Jean, was the formal end. When analyzed from an FPL viewpoint, it again points to the loss of FPL in the relations between the three French military leaders, Napoleon, Ney, and Grouchy. Each largely fought their own battle when Wellington and Blucher, on the opposing side, engaged each other perfectly. The Belgian Campaign was lost as soon as it started due to poor engagement, faulty framing, insufficient exploration of options, and poor decision making. "Execution" was poor because orders were poorly framed, poorly dispatched, and then poorly executed. Ney's cavalry charges on the unyielding squares without the support of the infantry were suicidal and wasted critical resources. Decision making and communication failed both prior to and during the battle. Grouchy, in charge of the right wing, understood his order as having to "follow" Blucher after his defeat at Quatre Bras, which he literally did. Blucher, executing a semi-circular movement, returned to the Waterloo battlefield, as he had promised Wellington. The order should have been to keep the Prussian General from returning to the battlefield, with whatever means Grouchy had at his disposal.

Blucher's maneuver smartly kept Grouchy behind him and allowed the Prussians a successful junction with Wellington's squares who were suffering badly and about to yield from the repeated French charges. Paradoxically, Wellington and Blucher engaged each other and collaborated in FPL manner, while Bonaparte and his Generals, who had excelled at FPL practice in earlier years, had lost it.

The FPL during this final Belgian Campaign was missing on Napoleon's side, who by now called all the shots while isolated. The results would be remembered forever: for the first time in all these years, the French Army at Waterloo was routed in combat and panicked in its flight from the battlefield. Napoleon and his team had become fully non-FPL. This was at the root of his downfall and that of the Empire. His final lie that Grouchy was joining the battlefield in the hope that this would provide sufficient energy for a final decisive push on the English backfired badly. It greatly contributed to the panic that descended on the French troops when realizing that the cavalrymen that had entered the battlefield were Prussian, and not French. For the first time, terror seized the French ranks, which started fleeing. This left them little chance of surviving the English and Prussian cavalry sent to seal the victory. Napoleon wished to die with his troops but was shuttled away instead.

Summarizing: The Empire Fails Due to the Early and Gradual Loss of FPL at the Top

Figure B.2 summarizes our main argument: the green curve is the FPL intensity exercised in the French command, under Napoleon's leadership, while the red curve depicts the strength of the French as perceived by the enemy, with, for example, conquered lands (asset size) as a proxy for outcome performance.

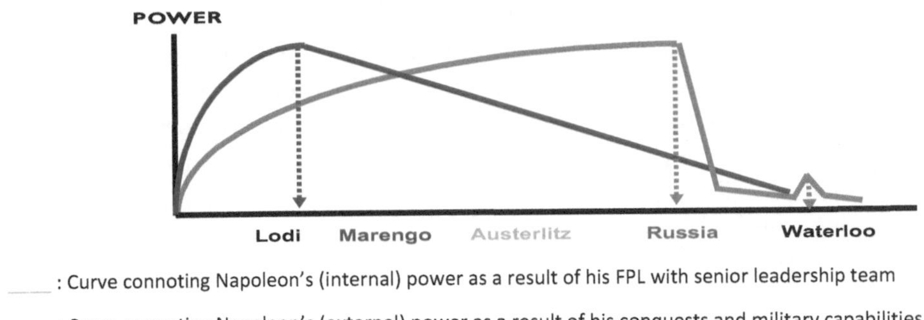

Fig. B.2 The arc of Napoleon's rise and fall as a leader

Of the two curves, the green FPL curve is the one few people and historians consider, for it is known and visible only to insiders, and even then, perhaps only partially. Most historical accounts (as is the case for business) focus on the red curve, concluding too hastily that the turning point in the fate of the French Empire was the Russian campaign, for it destroyed the Grand Army and caused the final vulnerability. Napoleon, in his Memoirs, echoes this when he blames the weather for the tragedy and writes, "I was not defeated by the Russians, but by General Winter." The FPL analysis leads to a starkly different conclusion: FPL started to decline early in his reign and much earlier than most historians have indicated. The latter are biased by the great military victories the French enjoyed, even during the phase of FPL decline. These were the result of a military and leadership capability built much earlier during Napoleon's reign, and before he became Emperor. Russia is only a consequence—and not the fundamental cause—of a leadership that had failed at both military and diplomatic level. Napoleon is solely responsible for his failed leadership, if one omits the failure of his close associates, including at the Council of State, to rein him in.

We provide two further arguments for this radical conclusion which is at odds with historical accounts. The Russian campaign was decided against the advice of nearly everyone whom Napoleon consulted, including Bernadotte, his Marshal who was named Prince of Sweden, in the hope of reconquering Finland, which the Swedes had lost to the Russians, allies of the French. The argument was simple: Russia could not be conquered; it was too big a country, and the Russians might retreat quite far into their territory. Most had not even envisaged the scorched earth tactic that the Russian command would eventually impose on the territories where the French would pass, and on its own people. Napoleon understood part of this logic, but only part of it, aiming at a "special military operation" that would score a quick decisive victory against the Russians, a repeat of Austerlitz or Friedland. Russia would then have to agree to return to its alliance with France.

Napoleon's obsession with Britain was the emotional and spiritual cause of his fall. Instead of co-ercing Russia, his goal should have been to make peace with Britain, which, as a force, could not fundamentally harm the French Empire on the continent. It never had enough troops to do so and this would hence require allies. This realization explains the never-ending sequence of Coalitions against France, all including if not led by Britain. England's great strength was its Navy, which could annoy French aims but not end them. The setbacks of the French Navy in the Antilles eventually contributed to the sale of Louisiana to the American Republic, and the eventual withdrawal of France from that territory. It ended Napoleon's dream of turning the Gulf of Mexico into a French sea. But the British naval superiority was greatly facilitated by Napoleon's poor understanding and leadership of his Admirals.

Napoleon's fatal error was his poor framing of England as the monster to bring to its knees when Napoleon and his regime would prove incapable of doing so. England had been nearly bankrupted by the French wars and their embargo. It would have been happy to settle like it did at the Peace of Amiens. And English merchants wished to trade with the Empire. Instead, Napoleon's obsession with England only turned the entire country into a resolute force devoted to ending his reign. The Continental Blockade applied against English ships and trading with England was particularly harsh on France's Dutch, German, and Scandinavian allies. Russia could not envisage stopping its trade through the Baltics and was only waiting for the moment it could regain the upper hand and free itself of forced agreements with the French. This all only angered Napoleon to the point of irrationality, always returning to his thought that he had defeated them every time on the battlefield, and that he would do so again if necessary. He became obsessed with keeping Russia inside his Continental Regime, when Russia by itself could not endanger French power, unless it offered Russia the chance to do so. British merchants lost the most in the blockade and promised millions in gold coins if the Russians were to renege on French collaborative terms as set out in the Peace of Tilsit. The Russians were easily convinced, both by the millions sent from Britain and by their own interests and pride. The same merchants paid for Wellington's army in Spain, which took many years to reach France from its original position in Portugal.

It is interesting to note that Tsar Alexander I engaged Napoleon's Corsican archenemy, Pozzo di Borgo, desirous to obtain insights into Napoleon's psychology and thinking. Unbelievably, no Russian was ever engaged on the French side in the planning and decisions concerning the Russian Campaign. The French cause of *Liberté, Égalité, et Fraternité* had followers in Russia as well. It should not have been hard to engage a few Russians, disenchanted with the regime of the Tsars or with the murder of Tsar Paul I, who was sympathetic to the French cause. Such sympathizers could only have helped Napoleon better read and understand Alexander's psyche, the Russian mindset, its climate, and the many other challenges the French would face in Russia. This underlines the critical importance of the first FPL step, which starts with *Engaging.*

We close by contrasting the lack of collaboration among the French leadership at Waterloo with the decisive events at the Marengo battle in 1800, which ended the second Italian Campaign against the Habsburg Empire. The famous picture of Bonaparte crossing the Grand Saint Bernard pass on his way to the battle, shown in Fig. B.1, illustrates the point perfectly.

Several features allow us to categorize this picture as "fake news of the gravest kind." As indicated earlier, Marengo is a French victory over the Austrians, but a Napoleonic defeat. Few French know this, as the point is subtle and somewhat miraculous. Indeed, the battle plan devised by First Consul Bonaparte goes terribly wrong: a surprise attack by General Michael von Melas on the main French troops led by Bonaparte's close and loyal associate, General Berthier, seems to announce a decisive defeat. The French center is broken around 2:30 pm. The French's only move is to aim for an orderly retreat.

General Desaix arrives on the battlefield around 17:00, having heard the cannons firing on the Marengo battlefield.[5] Seeing Napoleon desperate, Desaix is said to have replied, "Sir, this battle is lost, but there is time to win another!" One of Napoleon's strengths was to fully transfer authority, without further control or micro-management, when the situation was becoming critical, and he saw no better solution. Desaix takes over at that point and orders his arriving troops immediately into action. The Austrians are maneuvering too slowly and fail to convert their charge into a full victory. The tide turns with a superb cavalry charge led by Kellermann and Murat that takes the Austrian army completely by surprise. The sudden counterattack stops the Austrians, completely disorganizes them, and allows the French infantry to follow and cement a late French win, which is major and decisive.

Unfortunately, Desaix, the hero of the battle, is shot during the charge he leads and dies on the battlefield. Napoleon unceremoniously takes the limelight and credit for the victory, as the painting in Fig. 13.2 implicitly suggests. An informed eye will notice that the painting does not show Napoleon on the battlefield but depicts Napoleon crossing the Grand Saint Bernard to take attention away from the inconvenient fact that his strategy on the battlefield was a failure, which, according to some historians, could have allowed Austrian forces to invade France in 1800. Entirely exuding non-FPL, the painting shows a God-like figure, pointing to the sky, reminding the viewer of the Creation of Adam by Michelangelo. The painting does celebrate Napoleon, the Adam of the new French order in Europe. The painting is one more illustration of Napoleon's superb propaganda machine, started in the first Italian campaign, directed to bring Napoleon to the heights of French society. The latter effort will eventually succeed, but European nations will ultimately have the better end. His fall and that of France with him will be stark and spectacular. That the generals, who knew events on the battlefield, did not insist at least on a Requiem mass at Notre-Dame in Paris to honor Desaix, the fallen comrade, is another remarkable aspect of this story. Yielding to their pleas, Napoleon accepts that his body is brought back from Milan Cathedral to France, but at the last minute, the order comes to leave him at the Saint-Bernard pass, where his body rests to this day.

Napoleon, having been defeated at Marengo, may have needed the illusion of immortality more than his generals. At Marengo, he tasted defeat. Again, like Muiron at the Pont d'Arcole and later Murat at Eylau, another of his comrades saved him. Napoleon must have enjoyed, if not been reassured at, this beautiful depiction of strength and glory by David. But it was a grave misrepresentation of the facts and done at the expense of one of Napoleon's most talented generals, who had sacrificed his life for the benefit of the cause.[6] The move at glorification based on "fake news" is quite cynical and should have been countered by the Marshals and Generals. But they failed to muster the courage to confront Napoleon collectively and early; they must have become accustomed to these grandiose misrepresentations and lost the nerve to do so, nor did they understand the deep need to do so. Some did, and were then framed as enemies of the Empire, and joined the opposing ranks, like Moreau or Bernadotte. This was regrettable as it allowed the increasing power grab and the gradual decline of FPL at the top, which foreshadowed a decline in force and performance of imperial leadership, and, subsequently, of the armies.

The lesson is clear: Napoleon benefited from a remarkable team of Marshals, engaged and motivated by good FPL practice when he was on the rise. As remarkable success was achieved, FPL practice was gradually abandoned, and relatively early on. Napoleon, the Emperor, did not have the humility or the intelligence to consider the merits of FPL. One trusts that modern leaders can learn the lessons associated with his downfall. We can only judge a leader's true and permanent understanding of and commitment to FPL when the latter is at the top and has the power. Washington and his "band of brothers" fared much better and are a stark contrast to the French generals.

Notes

1. *Fraternité* will be added to the French motto in the Revolution of 1848, which ends the monarchy in France.
2. This shift to merit was not as radical in the French navy and contributed to the superiority of the British navy. The lack of Napoleon's competence in naval warfare was another contributing factor behind France's major naval defeats at Aboukir and Trafalgar.

3. Bernadotte followed his advice to Napoleon when appointed Prince of Sweden with the mission to recapture Finland, which had been lost to Russia due to the weakness of the previous King. Bernadotte was very clear with the Swedes: never take on Russia, as it is too powerful and too strong. He captured Norway instead, without any loss of soldiers, which endeared him to the Swedes and ensured the crown would eventually land on his head. He largely applied the great administrative reforms that Napoleon had carried out in France, and turned Sweden into a modern industrial state. One can state that the French Revolution actually succeeded … in Sweden under the leadership of Bernadotte who was a true Republican and never developed the dictatorial behaviors of Napoleon. Following Napoleon's first abdication, the Tsar wished Bernadotte to become King of France. But Talleyrand, already aligned with the Bourbons, killed the project and secured the return of Louis XVIII, the brother of Louis XVI. This set back France for decades, leading the Industrial Revolution to pass to England.
4. Jean-François Manzoni and Jean-Louis Barsoux, *The Set-up-to-Fail Syndrome,* Harvard Business School Press, 2002.
5. There is controversy about whether, as he wrote in his *Bulletins*, it was indeed Napoleon's order that made Desaix return to the battlefield. More likely is the account by which Desaix on his own, hearing the cannons firing at Marengo, took the decision to return to the battlefield.
6. Desaix also conquered Upper Egypt with 1500 grenadiers. He was remarkable and Napoleon intended to name him Minister of War. This also attests that the French victors were never a one-man show, and that in fact Napoleon was able to endure only because of the sacrifice of some of his close associates.

Appendix C: New Ownership Forms

The rise of Initial Coin Offerings (ICOs) and Initial Exchange Offerings (IEOs), as well as other token business models, has raised the question as to whether the twenty-first century might see new forms of ownership. Their recent emergence has resulted over the past few years in both substantial interests and intense scrutiny.

A majority of them have been identified as scams, Ponzi schemes, and so on. This has led to a widespread dismissal of token-based models, grounded in the belief that they constitute a Wild West outside the reach of current laws. In reality, these models are not as ungovernable as stated; however, being entities with two distinct value systems, tokens and traditional securities will present disparities in governance. Existing governance and accountability standards may in fact apply to token business models and, with some adaptation, may actually result in more diligent oversight than is common in the non-token world.

In the US, the very definition of token and investor protection is linked to whether the token can be defined as a *security*. This depends on the Howey Test, articulated in three independent requirements: an investment of money, a common enterprise, and an expectation of profits, predominantly from the efforts of others. This would suggest that a token is a security, while traditional Bitcoin is not.

Regulating security tokens raises corporate governance issues that are distinct from those used for traditional securities. Yet, the issues concerning security tokens are also related to the latter. For example, a publicly traded security has *promoters*—that is, underwriters, a founder, and residual owners. The sales

M. Massa et al., *Value Creation for Owners and Directors*,
https://doi.org/10.1007/978-3-031-19726-0

of tokens, too, are promoted, but this works differently. Relevant questions for regulators may include: Will these people retain a stake in the firm whose security the token is? Will they have decision power? What type of discretion will they have in using the cash that has been raised with the token issue?

The next question is the *return* that the token holders expect to receive. Will this be just an increase in value of the token or also distribution of cash flows (profits) or some usage right? How much will the usage right compensate them for the loss of their voting rights? By how much is the token expected to increase in value?

Related to the return, are there any duties of the promoter? Does the promoter have any duty to induce such an increase in value? And is such an increase in value is linked to the increase in value of the underlying firm? If not, will it be a duty of the promoter to engage in *speculations* (e.g., buying back tokens) to increase their value?

We can then turn to the *duty of care* of the promoter in terms of investing the proceeds that have been raised with the token issuance. What are the constraints imposed on the promoter to expend the funds from proceeds of the token issuance? This is a key source of friction. On the one hand, laying out how the funds should be used in a binding and very detailed contract may be constraining for the promoter if the circumstances change and conflict with the principle of "best business judgment" that regulates enterprise business. On the other hand, the lack of a proper system of checks and balances due to the scarce voting and supervisory power of the token holders may make it almost impossible to even assess whether the funds have been spent as opposed to being held in cash or used to buy back tokens.

The final key question is about the degree of disclosure of the profit-making of the enterprise and how such disclosure will be regulated and enforced by the Securities Act. Which people, other than the promoter, will control the company, and what are the governance tools for the token holders?

All these issues suggest that the general protection afforded to the investors does not differ from the statutory regulation (Securities Act) already existing for securities as well as the more flexible Law of Tort ("fiduciary duty"). Both will apply and can be used to protect token holders.

Shareholder Value Versus Firm Value

Consider the role of boards and some key questions they face. How might they guarantee that companies issuing tokens do not engage in Ponzi schemes by, for example, distributing fundraising proceeds to some token holders and/or founders? Also, how can they ensure that cash is in fact invested? What is the degree of disclosure in the market beyond some almost-unintelligible GitHub?

The requirements for boards should at least formally be the same as those of board members in normal companies. In many countries, existing corporate governance mechanisms incentivize boards to act in the interest of the firm (according to their "best business judgment"). This implies maximizing shareholder value only when aligned with firm value. Of course, the key question is whether token value coincides with firm value or with shareholder value. In cases where the token is anything other than equity, the business has two distinct value systems. Operations such as token issuance or token repurchase should be enacted by maintaining fairness among the investors.

If the board determines that shareholder value can be unlocked through the issuance of a new token, it can do this even if this puts downward pressure on the price of the token, as this will raise cash required for investment. Similarly, the board may authorize the repurchase of tokens in order to increase the firm value—and, therefore, indirectly, shareholder value.

For example, Ripple was revealed to have purchased some US$ 46 million worth of XRP tokens in the third quarter of 2020. Ripple claimed that it had done this in order to support "healthy markets" and that the buybacks could continue to support the brand's new Line of Credit initiative. The fact that the clients are paid in tokens to use their product and that the very same clients publicly state that they immediately dump the token for cash places a negative selling pressure on the token that Ripple can offset by itself buying back tokens. Of course, the ability of the clients to offload their tokens allows Ripple to capture market share and communicate customer relationships. This maximizes firm value.

In this case, as with standard companies, the buyback of equity does not need to be facilitated by retained earnings, as it is by itself instrumental in gaining market share and therefore increasing profits.

Token Holders and their Rights

So far, these issues are not different from those in normal companies except for the ability of the token holders to enforce their right. This is the major issue with tokens. While in a normal company the shareholders can protect themselves by holding voting rights, this is very highly restricted in the case of tokens where the voting rights are often null or replaced by usage rights. In such cases, protection will not go through the ordinary apparatus of assembly of shareholders and the board elected by them.

These questions must be addressed by the regulatory authorities and require clear intervention that replaces the role traditionally played by boards and shareholders. In fact, in the absence of the latter, the only other alternative is more flexible and effective supervision by regulatory authorities. Rules around token governance, issuances, buybacks, and disclosures would need to be implemented. This would in fact make blockchain-based financing much more regulated than traditional stock exchanges.

Alternatively, a new set of "analysts," more skilled in checking the engineering-related intricacies of the GitHubs, should arise. These would play a role similar to the rating agencies and should cater to a set of "enforcers" that will act as the short-sellers. Indeed, the ultimate regulation that will survive will be the action of the short-sellers—the best enforcer of governance even in traditional markets.

Concluding Thought *New forms of ownership, driven by technology and culture, require a new set of tactical practices and regulatory responses, but will not lead to a replacement of the fundamental concerns around governance, missions, and board practices. These challenges remain, although the wrapping may look different.*

As we were writing these lines, the cryptocurrency exchange FTX filed for bankruptcy after a run by customers on their deposits left the company owning them US$ 8 billion.[1] The lawyer representing FTX stated at a hearing in federal court in Delaware that substantial amounts of assets either had been stolen or gone missing. This proved another case of a talented entrepreneur, Sam Bankman-Fried, operating without the necessary transparency, without a board, and without due regulatory supervision. When will corporate America take governance as seriously as it does technology?

Note

1. https://www.nytimes.com/2022/11/22/business/ftx-bankruptcy-sam-bankman-fried.html.

Index[1]

[1] Note: Page numbers followed by 'n' refer to notes.

M. Massa et al., *Value Creation for Owners and Directors*,
https://doi.org/10.1007/978-3-031-19726-0